About the Cover

The design shown on the cover of this book was created by a special kind of photography. The artist-photographer calls the pictures "pendulum pictures." He used a pencil-type flashlight as his pendulum and suspended it by a string from the ceiling of a darkened room. Time exposures of the moving "pendulum" made with various color filters resulted in many beautiful patterns. The curves of these patterns are expressible in complicated mathematical equations such as this one:

$$F[(l^{-\frac{1}{2}}g^{\frac{1}{2}}\tau),(ml^{-\frac{2}{3}}g^{\frac{1}{2}}\mu^{-1}),\theta] = 0$$

Book One
MODERN ALGEBRA
STRUCTURE AND METHOD

REVISED EDITION

Mary P. Dolciani

William Wooton

Editorial Advisers

Andrew M. Gleason

Albert E. Meder, Jr.

Houghton Mifflin Company • Boston
New York • Atlanta • Geneva, Illinois • Dallas • Palo Alto

ABOUT THE AUTHORS

Mary P. Dolciani, Professor and Chairman, Department of Mathematics, Hunter College of the City University of New York. Dr. Dolciani has been a member of the School Mathematics Study Group (SMSG) and a director and teacher in numerous National Science Foundation and New York State Education Department institutes for mathematics teachers.

William Wooton, Associate Professor of Mathematics, Los Angeles Pierce College. Mr. Wooton has been a teacher at the junior and senior high school levels. He has also been a member of the SMSG writing team and a team member of the National Council of Teachers of Mathematics summer writing projects.

EDITORIAL ADVISERS

Andrew M. Gleason, Professor of Mathematics, Harvard University. Professor Gleason is prominently associated with curriculum changes in mathematics. He was Chairman of the Advisory Board for SMSG as well as co-chairman of the Cambridge Conference which wrote the influential report, *Goals for School Mathematics*.

Albert E. Meder, Jr., Dean and Vice Provost and Professor of Mathematics, Emeritus, Rutgers University, The State University of New Jersey. Dr. Meder was Executive Director of the Commission on Mathematics of the College Entrance Examination Board, and has been an advisory member of SMSG.

1975 IMPRESSION

COPYRIGHT © 1973, 1970 BY HOUGHTON MIFFLIN COMPANY
STUDENT'S EDITION   ISBN: 0–395–14507–4
TEACHER'S EDITION   ISBN: 0–395–14370–5

CONTENTS

7 Special Products and Factoring 248

8 Operations with Fractions 294

12 Rational and Irrational Numbers   452

13 Quadratic Equations and Inequalities   494

LIST OF SYMBOLS

		PAGE			PAGE
$=$	is equal to	1, 20	$\vert\;\vert$	absolute value	79
$\neq$	is not equal to	2, 21	$\geq$	is greater than or equal to	80
$\overline{YF}$	line segment Y, F	10	$\leq$	is less than or equal to	80
$<$	is less than	12	$\Re$	{the real numbers}	113
$>$	is greater than	12	$\cap$	intersection of sets	169
{ }	set	16	$\cup$	union of sets	169
$\in$	is an element of	16	$\%$	percent	303
$\notin$	is not an element of	16	$\sqrt{a}$	the positive square root of a	461
$\emptyset$	empty set	18			
$\ldots$	continue unendingly	21	$\pm$	positive or negative	461
	or and so on through	22		*or* plus or minus	498
$\doteq$	is approximately equal to	35	$\overrightarrow{AB}$	ray AB	528
$\therefore$	therefore	44	$\angle A$	angle A	528
$\overset{?}{=}$	Is this statement true?	74	$m\angle A$	measure of angle A	530
$\sqrt{}$	Yes, it is.	74	$\overrightarrow{AB}$	vector AB	557

PICTURE CREDITS

. . . earthrise photographed from the Lunar Module

Numbers and Sets

Where is science taking us? In the direction of our dreams.
Mathematics, the language of science, is the language of dreamers
who plan to achieve their dreams.

The trips that astronauts take to the moon would be impossible
without science and mathematics and, most importantly, without
electronic computers to carry out the necessary calculations
rapidly and accurately.

The algebra that you will learn in this course is one of the
essential foundations for the theories on which space travel is
based.

NUMBERS AND NUMERALS

1-1 Naming Numbers; Equality and Inequality

In algebra, numbers and the ways to name them play a very
great part. You already know many ways of naming certain numbers.
For example, the number of dots in Figure 1–1 can be named by the
Arabic numeral "4" or by the Roman numeral "IV". The
English word "four," the Spanish word "cuatro" (pronounced kwah-tro), and the Swahili word "nne" (pronounced en-nay) also name that number. In Morse code,
····— represents four. Each of the expressions

Figure 1–1

$$3 + 1, \quad 8 \div 2, \quad 9 - 5$$

designates four. Names, or symbols, for numbers are called **numerical
expressions** or **numerals**. The number named by a numerical expression
is called the **value** of the expression. Thus, 4 is the value of "3 + 1,"
of "8 ÷ 2," and of "9 − 5."

To show that the numerical expressions "3 + 1" and "4" have the
same value, you use the important symbol =, which stands for the
word **"equals"** or for the words **"is equal to."** Thus, you write the
statement

$$3 + 1 = 4$$

and you say, "Three plus one equals four." Any statement of equality is called an **equation**. Do you agree that the following equations are true statements?

$$8 \div 2 = 9 - 5; \quad 3 + 1 = 8 \div 2.$$

The statement

$$3 \times 1 = 4$$

is false because "3×1" names the number three, not four. One way to change this statement into a true one is to use the symbol $\neq$, read **"is not equal to"** or **"does not equal."** Thus, a true statement is

$$3 \times 1 \neq 4.$$

Any statement asserting that two numerical expressions do not have the same value is called an **inequality**. Which of the following inequalities is true? (See the footnote* on page 4 for the answer.)

$$10 - 1 \neq 3 \times 3$$
$$6 \div 1 \neq 1 \div 6$$

Oral Exercises

Tell whether or not each statement is true. Give a reason for your answer.

SAMPLE 1. $5 + 3 = 2 \times 4$

Solution: True, because "$5 + 3$" and "2×4" both name the number 8.

SAMPLE 2. $3 \times 12 \neq 12 \div 3$

Solution: True, because "3×12" names 36, but "$12 \div 3$" names 4.

1. $3 \times 4 = 4 + 4 + 4$
2. $8 \times 6 = 6 \times 8$
3. $2 + 8 \neq 8 + 2$
4. $0 \times 1 = 0$
5. $5 \times 0 \neq 5$
6. $7 + 0 \neq 7$
7. $16 \div 4 = 4 \div 16$
8. $37 - 7 = 3 \times 5 \times 2$

9. $8 \times 0 = 0 \times 6$
10. $2 - 0 \neq 2 + 0$
11. $1 \times 9 = \frac{1}{3} \times 27$
12. $4 \div 1 = \frac{4}{1}$
13. $2 + 3 + 6 = 12 - 1$
14. $17 - 3 - 3 \neq 17 - 6$
15. $\frac{50}{2} \neq 5 \times 1 \times 5$
16. $3 - 1 = 1 - 3$

Written Exercises

In Exercises 1–12, copy each sentence and replace the __?__ with one of the symbols $=$ or $\neq$ to make a true statement.

A

1. 8×24 __?__ 48×4

2. $56 \div 7$ __?__ 4×2

3. 8×0 __?__ $8 + 0$

4. $6 \div 3$ __?__ $\frac{3}{6}$

5. $\frac{1}{2} + \frac{5}{10}$ __?__ 1

6. $\frac{1}{3} + \frac{9}{3}$ __?__ $\frac{10}{3}$

7. $0 + 0$ __?__ 0×0

8. $\frac{1}{5} \times 6$ __?__ $\frac{5}{6}$

9. $1 + 1\frac{2}{4}$ __?__ $2\frac{1}{2}$

10. $\frac{3}{7} - \frac{2}{7}$ __?__ $3 \times \frac{1}{21}$

11. $0.7 + 0.2$ __?__ 3×0.3

12. $0.45 - 0.25$ __?__ $2 \div 10$

In Exercises 13–34, copy each sentence and make it a true statement by replacing each __?__ with a numeral. In any sentence containing more than one __?__, the same replacement should be used for each __?__.

SAMPLE. $63 \neq 7 \times$ __?__

Solution: $63 \neq 7 \times 4$. **Answer.**

    (In place of "4" you may use any numeral that does not name 9.)

13. $7 + 2 = 2 +$ __?__

14. $8 \times 5 =$ __?__ $\times 8$

15. $14 -$ __?__ $\neq 10$

16. __?__ $+ 57 \neq 57$

17. $15 +$ __?__ $= 5 \times 3$

18. $6 \times$ __?__ $= 3 + 3$

19. __?__ $\div 9 = 0$

20. __?__ $\div 5 \neq 1$

21. $7 \div$ __?__ $= 1$

22. $1 \times$ __?__ $= 1$

23. $4 \div$ __?__ $= \frac{1}{2}$

24. __?__ $\times \frac{1}{3} \neq 2$

B

25. $7 + 12 +$ __?__ $= 42 - 9$

26. $33 + 16 +$ __?__ $= 94 - 21$

27. $3\frac{1}{2} -$ __?__ $= 2\frac{1}{4} + \frac{3}{4}$

28. $\frac{15}{6} - \frac{3}{2} =$ __?__ $\times 3$

29. $0.24 \div 0.6 = 1 -$ __?__

30. $4.5 \div 0.9 = 1 \div$ __?__

31. __?__ $\times$ __?__ $= 1$

32. __?__ $\div$ __?__ $= 1$

33. __?__ $+$ __?__ $=$ __?__

34. __?__ $-$ __?__ $=$ __?__

1–2   Punctuation Marks in Algebra

  Suppose that you were asked to copy the following string of words in the given order, but to put in punctuation marks and capital letters to produce a grammatically correct and meaningful sentence:

bill shouted joe is missing

You might write

Bill shouted, "Joe is missing!"

Or you might write

"Bill," shouted Joe, "is missing!"

Each of these sentences is meaningful and correct in grammar. The differences in punctuation, however, produce a world of difference in meaning. Without punctuation marks, the given string of words could be interpreted in more than one way.

In everyday language and in mathematics, expressions that can be interpreted in more than one way are called *ambiguous* (am-**big**-you-us). Here is an ambiguous numerical expression:

2 × 5 + 6

Does it mean, "The sum of twice five and six, that is, 16"? Or does it mean, "Twice the sum of five and six, that is, 22"? To make the meaning of this expression clear, you may use **parentheses** (pa-ren-the-sees) as punctuation marks. When you write

(2 × 5) + 6,

you name the number 16. When you write

2 × (5 + 6),

you name 22.

A pair of parentheses is called a **symbol of inclusion** or a **grouping symbol** because it is used to enclose, or include, an expression for a particular number. In the expression "2 × (5 + 6)," the parentheses group the numerals "5" and "6" together with the symbol +, and thus show that the *sum* of 5 and 6 is to be multiplied by 2.

In writing "2 × (5 + 6)," you usually omit the symbol × and write simply

2(5 + 6).

Similarly, the product 2 × 11 may be expressed in any of the forms

2(11),   (2)11,   or   (2)(11).

Brackets and braces are also used as grouping symbols:

Parentheses	Brackets	Braces
2(5 + 6)	2[5 + 6]	2{5 + 6}

---

*The first inequality at the center of page 2 is false; the second is true.

The horizontal bar in a fraction symbol often acts as a grouping symbol, as well as a division sign. For example, in the expression below, the bar groups the "17" and "3"; it also groups the "8" and "1." The bar tells you that the number (17 − 3) is to be divided by the number (8 − 1).

$$\frac{17 - 3}{8 - 1} = \frac{14}{7} = 2.$$

Notice that each of the expressions "$\frac{17 - 3}{8 - 1}$," "$\frac{14}{7}$," and "2" names the number two. But the last numeral, "2", is a *simpler name* for two than the other expressions. Whenever you replace a numerical expression by the simplest or most common numeral for the number named, you say that you have **simplified the expression**.

The statement

$$\frac{17 - 3}{8 - 1} = \frac{14}{7}$$

suggests that substituting "14" for "17 − 3" and "7" for "8 − 1" in the fraction "$\frac{17 - 3}{8 - 1}$" does not change the value of the fraction. Whenever you simplify a numerical expression, you use the following:

Substitution Principle

Changing the numeral by which a number is named in an expression does not change the value of the expression.

In the expression "4[70 − (8 × 7)]," you see a pair of parentheses inside a pair of brackets. Using different grouping symbols (such as pairs of parentheses and brackets) helps you to keep track of the mates in each pair. To simplify an expression which shows one grouping inside of another grouping, you first simplify the numeral in the inner-most grouping symbol and then work toward the outermost grouping symbol until all symbols of inclusion have been removed. Thus:

$$4[70 - (8 \times 7)] = 4[70 - 56]$$
$$= 4[14]$$
$$= 56$$

Fractions may also involve more than one grouping. For example,

$$4 + \frac{3 + (15 \div 5)}{7 - 1} = 4 + \frac{3 + 3}{6} = 4 + \frac{6}{6} = 4 + 1 = 5.$$

Oral Exercises

In Exercises 1–12, simplify the given expression.

SAMPLE 1. $(10 \div 2) + 7$

Solution: $(10 \div 2) + 7 = 5 + 7 = 12$

1. $2 \times (3 + 4)$

3. $\dfrac{8 + 1}{3}$

5. $4 \div (2 - 1)$

2. $2 + (3 \times 4)$

4. $\dfrac{12}{7 - 3}$

6. $4 - (2 \div 1)$

7. $\dfrac{6 \div 2}{3}$

9. $3 \times 4 \times 0$

11. $(12 \div 3)(6 \times \frac{1}{2})$

8. $\dfrac{18}{4 \div 2}$

10. $(12 \times 8) \div (2 + 0)$

12. $(4 \times 3) \div (4 + 2)$

In Exercises 13–20, tell whether or not the given statement is true. Give a reason for your answer.

SAMPLE 2. $3 + 4 \neq 2(3 + 1)$

Solution: True, because $3 + 4 = 7, 2(3 + 1) = 2 \times 4 = 8,$ and $7 \neq 8.$

13. $8 - 2 = 12 \div (1 + 1)$

14. $6 - 3 = 12 \div (5 - 2)$

15. $5[3 + 1 - 2] = \dfrac{4 + 16}{2}$

16. $\dfrac{15 - 5}{2 \times 10} = \dfrac{6 \times 2}{8 - 2}$

17. $(6 + 8) \div 2 \neq 100 \div 10$

18. $4 - (9 \div 3) \neq 2$

19. $(8 \times 2) \div 4 = 5 - 1$

20. $9 \times (1 \div 3) = (9 \times 1) \div 3$

Written Exercises

Simplify each of the following expressions.

A

1. $(40 + 7) - 18$

2. $93 - (6 + 22)$

3. $0 \times [3 - (1 \times 2)]$

4. $4 \times [0 + (3 \div 1)]$

5. $(21 \times 3) + 2$

6. $22 + (16 \times 2)$

7. $\dfrac{8 \times 4}{5 - 1} + 3$

8. $7 - \dfrac{6 \times 18}{22 + 5}$

9. $[7 \times (8 + 4)] \div 70$

10. $144 \div [3 \times (8 + 4)]$

11. $(12 \times 4) \div (3 \times 2)$

12. $[8 - (15 \div 3)] \times 8$

Make a true statement by replacing each __?__ with one of the symbols = or ≠.

13. $\dfrac{100 - 64}{10 - 8}$ __?__ $10 + 8$

14. $\dfrac{100 + 64}{10 + 8}$ __?__ $10 - 8$

15. $\dfrac{15 \times 3}{8 + 1}$ __?__ $40 \div 8$

16. $\dfrac{7 + 28}{7 \times 5}$ __?__ $(27 \div 3) - 8$

17. $6 \times \{4 + 7\}$ __?__ $\{5 \times 5\} \times 5$

18. $28 \div (8 - 4)$ __?__ $(10 \div 5) \div 2$

19. $2 \times [3 \times (4 + 1)]$ __?__ $(6 \times 6) - 6$

20. $3 \times [24 \div (5 + 3)]$ __?__ $36 - (6 \times 6)$

B **21.** $2 \times [2 \times (3 \times 4)]$ __?__ $64 \div [32 \div (2 \div 1)]$

22. $4 \times [3 \times (5 - 2)]$ __?__ $96 \div [32 \div (5 - 3)]$

23. $(5 + 7) \times (3 + 8)$ __?__ $8 + [(17 \times 3) + 5]$

24. $3 \times [(5 + 1) \times (6 \div 2)]$ __?__ $[18 + (144 \div 8)] + 3$

25. $\dfrac{[8 \times 6] \div 12}{4 - [6 \div 2]} + 1$ __?__ $27 - \dfrac{40 + 4}{8 - 6}$

26. $\dfrac{(6 \times 8) - 8}{(36 \div 2) + 2} + 2$ __?__ $1 + \dfrac{30 - 3}{1 + 4}$

27. $\dfrac{(4 \times 3) + 22}{8 + (27 \div 3)} - \dfrac{8 - 4}{2 + 2}$ __?__ $\dfrac{(7 \times 6) + 6}{30 - (2 \times 3)} - 1$

28. $\dfrac{\{[(2 \times 2) \times 2] + (2 \times 2)\} + 40}{\{[(3 \times 3) \times 3] - (3 \times 3)\} - 5}$ __?__ $\dfrac{[2 \times (3 \times 3)] + (2 \times 3)}{[3 \times (2 \times 2)] - (2 \times 3)}$

C **29.** $2 \left\{ \dfrac{[5 - (2 \times 2)] + (8 \times 3)}{[(24 \div 6) + 4] - 3} \right\}$ __?__ $[2 + 5 - (30 \div 6)] \times \dfrac{12 - 2}{5 - 3}$

30. $\dfrac{90 - [(13 \times 18) \div 3]}{[7 + (6 \times 4)] - 19}$ __?__ $\{[(18 \times 3) \div 9] - 5\} \times \dfrac{18 \div 2}{3 \times 3}$

31. $\dfrac{1}{2} \times \dfrac{\{[17 + (9 \div 3)] - 5\} \times 2}{(16 \times 2) - (3 \times 3)}$ __?__ $\dfrac{(8 \times 12) \div 3}{(8 \times 8) \div 8} - \dfrac{18 - 2}{2 \times 4}$

32. $\dfrac{1}{4} \times \dfrac{16 + [(48 \div 3) - (4 \times 4)]}{[29 - (11 \times 2)] - (3 \times 2)}$ __?__ $\dfrac{6 + [(8 \times 2) - 4]}{[(6 \div 3) \times 3] + 3} \times \dfrac{16 - (3 \times 5)}{14 - (3 \times 4)}$

NUMBERS AND POINTS

1–3 The Number Line

In arithmetic, you learned a good deal about how to use numbers like 0, 1, $\frac{2}{3}$, $\sqrt{3}$, and $4\frac{1}{2}$. Figure 1–2 shows how you picture such numbers as points on a line.

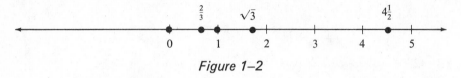

Figure 1–2

To construct such a **number line** (*number scale*), choose a starting point (**origin**) on a line and label it "0." At some convenient distance on one side of the origin, select a second point and mark it "1." The side containing the point paired with the number 1 is called the **positive side** of the line, and the direction from the origin to the point labeled "1" is called the **positive direction** on the number line. (On a horizontal number line, the side to the right of the origin is usually chosen to be the positive side of the line.)

Using the distance between the points labeled "0" and "1" as the *unit length* on the line, you can pair each point on the positive side of the line with the number which measures the distance along the line from the origin to the point. You call the numbers paired with points on the *positive* side of the line **positive numbers**. Thus, 1, $\frac{2}{3}$, $\sqrt{3}$, and $4\frac{1}{2}$ are all positive numbers.

On the number line, the point paired with a number is called the **graph** of that number. The number paired with a point is called the **coordinate** (ko-**or**-din-et) of that point.

EXAMPLE 1. State the coordinate of each of the points *A, B,* and *C* on the given number line.

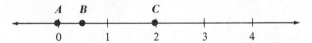

Solution: $A: 0$; $B: \frac{1}{2}$; $C: 2$. **Answer.**

EXAMPLE 2. Draw a number line and on it show the graphs of $\frac{3}{4}$ and 2.5.

Solution: The graph of each number is marked by a heavy dot on the number line below.

Do points to the left of the origin on the number line shown in Figure 1–2 have coordinates? To assign coordinates to those points, you introduce **negative numbers**. In Figure 1–3, the coordinate of R is $^-3$ (read "negative three") because R is 3 units **to the left** of the origin. Similarly, the coordinate of S is $^-1$ ("negative one"), and the coordinate of T is $^-\frac{1}{2}$ ("negative one-half"). Notice that a negative number is named by a numeral with a negative (minus) sign $^-$ written above and to the left of an ordinary number symbol.

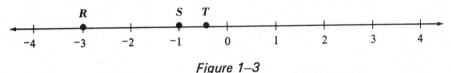

Figure 1–3

Can you guess what we call the side of the number line that contains the points with negative coordinates? It is the **negative side** of the line. The direction from the origin to any point on the negative side of the line is called the **negative direction** on the line.

Any number which is either a positive number, a negative number, or 0 is known as a **real number**. In working with a number line, you take the following facts for granted.

1. There is exactly one point on the number line paired with any real number.
2. There is exactly one real number paired with any given point on the number line.

Sometimes to emphasize that a number like 1 is a *positive* number, we call it "positive 1" and denote it by the symbol "$^+1$". Similarly, we may call 2 "positive 2" and denote it by "$^+2$", and so on. Notice that the small signs $^+$ and $^-$ in the symbols "$^+1$" and "$^-1$" indicate the directions of the corresponding points from the origin on a number line. They do *not* indicate addition and subtraction.

Because positive and negative numbers suggest opposite directions, they are sometimes called **directed numbers**. They are very useful in describing measurements that involve *direction* as well as *size*. Here are a few examples:

1. Let 10 refer to a *profit* of $10. Then $^-10$ refers to a *loss* of $10.
2. Let $3\frac{1}{2}$ refer to $3\frac{1}{2}$ miles *east*. Then $^-3\frac{1}{2}$ refers to $3\frac{1}{2}$ miles *west*.
3. Let 5 refer to 5 seconds *after* launch time of a rocket. Then $^-5$ refers to 5 seconds *before* launch time.

Oral Exercises

In Exercises 1–24, identify the points that are the graphs of the given numbers or state the coordinates of the given points. Refer to the number line below.

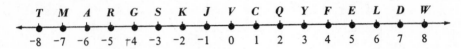

SAMPLE.   **a.** K **b.** $3\frac{1}{2}$

Solution: **a.** The coordinate of K is $^-2$.

   b. The graph of $3\frac{1}{2}$ is the point halfway from Y to F, or the midpoint of $\overline{YF}$ ($\overline{YF}$ is read "line segment Y, F"). **Answer.**

1. W	**5.** $^-6$	**9.** $2\frac{1}{2}$	**13.** $^-3\frac{1}{2}$	**17.** $^-2\frac{1}{4}$
2. A	**6.** 0	**10.** $1\frac{1}{2}$	**14.** $^-4.5$	**18.** $^-6\frac{1}{3}$
3. 1	**7.** V	**11.** $\frac{1}{4}$	**15.** $\frac{30}{10}$	**19.** $^-7.25$
4. $^-5$	**8.** L	**12.** $\frac{4}{3}$	**16.** $^-\frac{4}{8}$	**20.** 5.75

21. The midpoint of $\overline{AR}$ **23.** The midpoint of $\overline{RY}$

22. The midpoint of $\overline{KJ}$ **24.** The midpoint of $\overline{KF}$

Express each of the following measurements by means of a real number. Take the directions *above, north, east, up,* and *right* as positive.

25.   **a.** Four degrees below zero   **b.** Five degrees above zero

26.   **a.** A gain of 15 pounds   **b.** A loss of 12 pounds

27.   **a.** A deposit of $50   **b.** A withdrawal of $35

28.   **a.** An altitude of 2000 feet above sea level

   b. An ocean depth of 500 feet below sea level

29.   **a.** Latitude of 45° south   **b.** Latitude of 20° north

30.   **a.** Longitude of 15° west   **b.** Longitude of 34° east

31.   **a.** Six steps to the right   **b.** Four steps to the left

32.   **a.** One step down   **b.** Two steps up

Written Exercises

Draw a horizontal number line and on it show the graphs of the given numbers.

A   **1.** 4   **3.** $^-5$ **5.** $^-1.5$ **7.** $^-4\frac{1}{3}$

   2. 2   **4.** $^-3$ **6.** $^-2.5$ **8.** $^-5\frac{1}{4}$

In Exercises 9–14, state the coordinate of the point at which you would arrive on a number line if you were to start at the origin and:

9. Move five units in the positive direction, then three more units in that direction.

10. Move four units in the negative direction, then seven more units in that direction.

11. Move six units in the positive direction, then six units in the negative direction.

12. Move three units in the negative direction, then three units in the positive direction.

13. Move five units in the negative direction, then two units in the positive direction.

14. Move eight units in the positive direction, then nine units in the negative direction.

In Exercises 15–30, name the coordinate of the point described. Refer to the number line below.

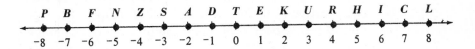

SAMPLE. The point that is one-fourth of the distance from A to R.

Solution: The length of $\overline{AR}$ is 6 units. Let us call the desired point X. Then X is $\frac{1}{4} \times 6 = \frac{3}{2}$, or $1\frac{1}{2}$, units from A toward R. As shown in the diagram below, its coordinate is $^-\frac{1}{2}$.

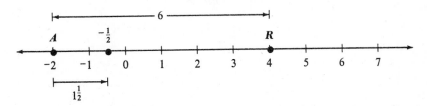

15. The midpoint of $\overline{DK}$ **16.** The midpoint of $\overline{SR}$

17. The point 5 units to the right of N

18. The point 3 units to the left of I

19. The point $2\frac{1}{2}$ units to the right of E

20. The point $3\frac{1}{2}$ units to the left of U

21. The point 1.5 units to the left of K

22. The point 5.5 units to the right of B

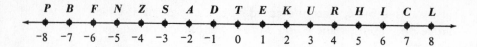

	P	B	F	N	Z	S	A	D	T	E	K	U	R	H	I	C	L
	-8	-7	-6	-5	-4	-3	-2	-1	0	1	2	3	4	5	6	7	8

B 23. The point one-fourth of the way from *B* to *E*

24. The point one-third of the way from *N* to *E*

25. The point one-sixth of the distance from *S* to *I*

26. The point one-fifth of the distance from *A* to *L*

27. The point two-thirds of the distance from *C* to *A*

28. The point three-fourths of the distance from *H* to *S*

C 29. The point between *D* and *H* that is twice as far from *H* as it is from *D*

30. The point to the right of *U* that is half as far from *U* as it is from *I*

1–4   Comparing Numbers

The true statement "⁻3 ≠ 2" is pictured on the horizontal number line in Figure 1–4 by the fact that the graphs of ⁻3 and 2 are different points. The positive direction in this figure is toward the right, and the graph of ⁻3 lies *to the left* of the graph of 2. Thus, in moving *from* the graph of ⁻3 *to* the graph of 2, you go in the positive direction on the line.

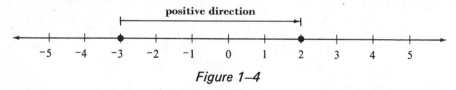

Figure 1–4

Because numbers increase as you move in the positive direction, you say that

⁻3 is less than 2,

and you use the *directed inequality symbol* < (read "**is less than**") to write

$$^{-}3 < 2.$$

The *directed inequality symbol* > stands for the words "**is greater than.**" When you write

$$2 > {}^{-}3,$$

you say that

2 is greater than ⁻3.

On the number line in Figure 1–4, this means that the graph of 2 lies *to the right* of the graph of ⁻3. Therefore, a move *from* **the graph of 2** *to* **the graph of** ⁻3 is in the negative direction on the line (Figure 1–5).

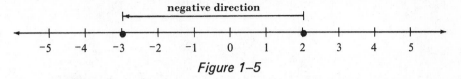

Figure 1–5

Do you see that the inequalities "⁻3 < 2" and "2 > ⁻3" give the same information?

You can avoid confusing the symbols > and < by thinking of them as arrowheads whose small ends point (in a true statement) toward the numeral naming the smaller number.

The statement "2 is *between* ⁻5 and 3" is true because ⁻5 is less than 2 *and* 2 is less than 3 (Figure 1–6). You can express this latter statement in symbols by writing

$$⁻5 < 2 \quad \textit{and} \quad 2 < 3.$$

However, a more compact way to state this fact is

$$⁻5 < 2 < 3,$$

(read "⁻5 is less than 2, which is less than 3").

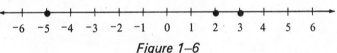

Figure 1–6

The relationship among ⁻5, 2, and 3 can also be stated:

$$3 > 2 > ⁻5$$

(read "3 is greater than 2, which is greater than ⁻5").

EXAMPLE. **Write each statement in compact form and then tell whether the statement is true or is false.**

  a. ⁻5 < ⁻2 and ⁻2 < 4.   **b.** ⁻5 < 3 and 3 < 1.

Solution: **a.** ⁻5 < ⁻2 < 4; true.   **b.** ⁻5 < 3 < 1; false.

A statement, such as

$$⁻5 < ⁻2 \quad \textbf{and} \quad ⁻2 < 4$$

or

$$⁻5 < 3 \quad \textbf{and} \quad 3 < 1,$$

which is formed by joining two statements by the word *and* is called a **conjunction** (con-**junk**-shun) of statements. For a conjunction to be true, *both* of the joined statements must be true. Thus, "⁻5 < 3 and 3 < 1" is false because "3 < 1" is false.

Oral Exercises

Tell whether or not the statement in each of the following exercises is true. Give a reason for your answer.

SAMPLE 1. $7 + 4 < 5 \times 3$

Solution: True, because $7 + 4 = 11$, $5 \times 3 = 15$, and $11 < 15$.

SAMPLE 2. ⁻1 < 4 < 3.

Solution: False, because the given statement is a conjunction in which one part, "⁻1 < 4," is true, but the other part, "4 < 3," is false.

1. $\dfrac{5 + 1}{2} < 4 - 1$

2. $\dfrac{30 - 18}{6} > 5 - 3$

3. $\dfrac{10 + 3}{2} > \, ^{-}1$

4. $\dfrac{12 + 21}{3} < 4 + 21$

5. $49 \times 61 < 61 \times 49$

6. $57 \times 13 > 12 \times 57$

7. $7 \times 8 > 50 + 8$

8. $^{-}9 \times 0 > 0$

9. $\frac{3}{5} + \frac{2}{5} < \frac{2}{5} + \frac{3}{5}$

10. $^{-}5 + 4 < 4 + \, ^{-}5$

11. $4 < 8 < 12$

12. $7 > 5 > 9$

13. $^{-}2 < \, ^{-}1 < 3$

14. $^{-}2 < \, ^{-}3 < 0$

15. $^{-}5 > \, ^{-}7 > \, ^{-}1$

16. $^{-}6 > \, ^{-}10 > \, ^{-}25$

Written Exercises

In Exercises 1–20, copy each sentence and replace the __?__ with one of the symbols =, <, or > to make a true statement.

SAMPLE 1. ⁻5 __?__ ⁻6   *Solution:* ⁻5 > ⁻6. **Answer.**

A

1. $4 \underline{} 7$

2. $0 \underline{} 0$

3. $\frac{15}{3} \underline{} 3 + 1$

4. $12 \times 0 \underline{} 12 + 0$

5. $^{-}1 \underline{} 1$

6. $5 \underline{} \, ^{-}5$

7. $\dfrac{8 - 3}{5 - 2} \underline{} 1 + 0.6$

8. $^{-}2 \underline{} \dfrac{24 - 6}{9}$

9. $6 \div 3 \underline{} 12 \div 6$

10. $72 \times 1 \underline{} 73$

11. $^-3$ _?_ $^-3 \times 0$

12. $^-2$ _?_ $^-2 \times 1$

13. $\frac{1}{2}$ _?_ $\frac{1}{3} + \frac{0}{2}$

14. $0.75 + 0.25$ _?_ $\frac{3}{4} + \frac{1}{4}$

15. 1.2431 _?_ 1.2432

16. $^-1.2431$ _?_ $^-1.2432$

17. $\frac{1}{5} \div 4$ _?_ $\frac{4}{5}$

18. $\frac{1}{5} \times 4$ _?_ $\frac{5}{4}$

19. $0.9 \div 3$ _?_ $0.1 + 0.4$

20. $0.7 - 0.3$ _?_ 0.2×2

In Exercises 21–52, copy each sentence and make it a true statement by replacing each _?_ with a numeral. In any sentence containing more than one _?_, the same replacement should be used for each _?_.

SAMPLE 2. $25 \times 3 > 70 +$ _?_

Solution: $25 \times 3 > 70 + 1$. (In place of "1," you may write the numeral for any number less than 5.) **Answer.**

21. $26 +$ _?_ $= 2 \times 13$

22. $6 + 2 = 2 +$ _?_

23. _?_ $\div 5 = 0$

24. $124 +$ _?_ $= 124$

25. $13 -$ _?_ > 0

26. _?_ $\times 4 > 0$

27. _?_ $\div 2 = 1$

28. $5 \div$ _?_ $= 5$

29. $16 - 6 <$ _?_ $\times 2$

30. $9 \times 4 < 4 \times$ _?_

31. $0 \times$ _?_ $> ^-3$

32. $1 \times$ _?_ $> ^-1$

33. $\frac{3}{4} \times \frac{8}{15} =$ _?_ $\times \frac{3}{4}$

34. $6 \div$ _?_ $= \frac{1}{2}$

35. $9 \div$ _?_ > 2

36. _?_ $\times \frac{1}{2} < 3$

B 37. $\dfrac{48 +\ ?}{12} = 4 + 1$

38. $\dfrac{42 -\ ?}{6} = 7 - 2$

39. $5 - 1 <$ _?_ $< 5 + 1$

40. $4 + 1 >$ _?_ $> 4 - 1$

41. _?_ $\times$ _?_ $= 1$

42. _?_ $\div$ _?_ $= 1$

43. $\dfrac{56 + 16}{14} <$ _?_ $< \dfrac{56 + 18}{14}$

44. $\dfrac{32 - 5}{8} >$ _?_ $> \dfrac{32 - 7}{8}$

45. $\frac{2}{5} <$ _?_ $< \frac{3}{5}$

46. $\frac{5}{7} >$ _?_ $> \frac{3}{7}$

47. $3.2 - 2.2 <$ _?_ $< 3.4 - 2.2$

48. $7.5 + 3.1 >$ _?_ $> 7.3 + 3.1$

C 49. $3.14159 <$ _?_ < 3.15159

50. $\sqrt{7} >$ _?_ $> \sqrt{6}$

51. _?_ $\times$ _?_ $<$ _?_

52. _?_ $\times$ _?_ $>$ _?_

SETS OF NUMBERS

1–5 Specifying Sets

You are accustomed to talking about all sorts of collections, or sets, of objects. Your favorite baseball team, your newest pair of shoes, and all the real numbers are familiar examples of collections of objects. In mathematics, such a collection of objects is called a *set*. Each object in a set is called a **member** or **element** of the set.

For example, all the teachers in your school form a set, and your algebra teacher is a member, or element, belonging to that set. However, objects such as the letter *r*, the school custodian, and the number 9, are not elements in the set of all your teachers. Thus, a set is any collection of objects so well described that you can always tell whether or not an object belongs to the set.

Suppose that a set is composed of five real numbers. Use a capital letter, say *F*, to name or refer to the set. You have no way of telling whether the number 3 is or is not an element of *F* until the five real numbers are specified. If you specify the set by listing the objects forming the set within braces $\{\ \}$, then you may have

$$F = \{0, 3, {}^-7, 8, {}^-14\}$$

This says, "*F* is the set of numbers 0, 3, $^-7$, 8, $^-14$." You can easily see that the number 3 is a member of this set and that the number 4 is not. We use a special symbol, $\in$, to mean "**is an element of,**" and $\notin$ to mean "**is not an element of.**" Thus, $3 \in F$ and $4 \notin F$.

Specifying a set by listing its elements in braces gives you a **roster**, or **list**, of the set. The objects named in the listing, {our moon, the Alamo, Alaska, Albert Einstein}, form a set. Note that the elements of a set need have no relation with one another other than being grouped together. Furthermore, the order of listing the elements is unimportant. What is important is that each element be named in the listing and **no element is listed more than once.**

Often it is inconvenient or impossible to specify a set by roster. For example, you cannot list the names of all members of the **set of real numbers**. So you simply write

{**the real numbers**}

(read "**the set whose members are the real numbers**" or "**the set of the real numbers**"). Thus, you have specified the set by writing within braces a *description*, or *rule*, that identifies the members of the set.

Here are three other sets specified by rule:

{the states of the U.S.A.}

{the positive real numbers}   {the negative real numbers}

EXAMPLE 1.   Specify the following set by roster: {the days of the week whose names begin with T}

Solution: {Tuesday, Thursday}.   Answer.

EXAMPLE 2.   Specify by rule: {Washington, John Adams, Jefferson}

Solution: {the first three Presidents of the U.S.A.}.   Answer.

You can also specify a set of numbers by graphing the numbers on a number line. The set of points corresponding to a set of numbers is called the **graph** of the set. For example,

Set   *Graph*

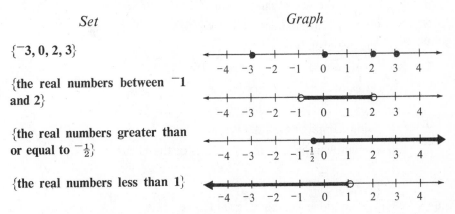

{⁻3, 0, 2, 3}

{the real numbers between ⁻1 and 2}

{the real numbers greater than or equal to ⁻$\frac{1}{2}$}

{the real numbers less than 1}

A heavy shading is used to show that all points on the indicated portion of the line belong to the graph. Open dots or portions of the line not shaded show points not belonging to the graph. A heavy arrowhead implies that the graph continues without end in the indicated direction.

To specify a set, you can identify its elements by:

1. a roster, listing the names of the elements,
   or

2. a rule, describing the elements,
   or (if the elements are real numbers)

3. a graph, locating the elements as points on a number line.

Can a set have no members at all? Think about the set of those positive numbers that are less than 0. This set certainly has no members because every positive number is greater than 0. We call the set with no members the **empty set** or the **null set**, and we denote it by the symbol ∅. Note that there is only one empty set. Thus,

$$\emptyset = \{\text{the positive numbers less than 0}\},$$

and

$$\emptyset = \{\text{the New England states west of the Mississippi River}\}.$$

Oral Exercises

Specify each nonempty set by a roster.

SAMPLE 1. {Hindu-Arabic numerals on the face of a clock}

Solution: {1, 2, 3, 4, 5, 6, 7, 8, 9, 10, 11, 12}. **Answer.**

1. {the days of the week whose names begin with S}
2. {the months whose names begin with M}
3. {the positive even integers less than 7}
4. {the negative odd integers greater than 8}
5. {the states of the U.S.A. bordering on the Pacific Ocean}
6. {the two most recently admitted states in the U.S.A.}
7. {the living persons now 1000 years old}
8. {the women who have been Presidents of the U.S.A.}

Specify each set by rule.

SAMPLE 2. {London; Washington, D.C.}

Solution: {the capital cities of England and the U.S.A.}. **Answer.**

9. {red, white, blue}
10. {Vermont, Virginia}
11. {November, December}
12. {January, February}
13. {2, 4, 6, 8, 10}
14. {⁻11, ⁻9, ⁻7, ⁻5, ⁻3, ⁻1}

Tell which statements are true and which are false.

15. x ∈ {the first three letters in the English alphabet}
16. y ∈ {the last three letters in the English alphabet}
17. 3 ∉ {0, 2, 4, 6}
18. 5 ∉ {1, 3, 5, 7}
19. ⁻1 ∈ {the real numbers greater than ⁻2}
20. ⁻3 ∈ {the real numbers less than 4}

Specify the graph of each set in Exercises 21–28 by referring to the number line below.

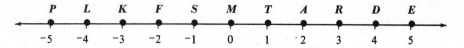

SAMPLE 3. {the real numbers between 1 and 4, including 1}.

Solution: {Point T and all the points between T and D}. **Answer.**

21.   {⁻3, ⁻1, 0, 3}   **22.**   {⁻5, ⁻2, 3, 4}

23.   {the real numbers greater than 1}

24.   {the real numbers less than 2}

25.   {the real numbers between ⁻1 and 2}

26.   {the real numbers between ⁻1 and 2, including ⁻1 and 2}

27.   {the real numbers between ⁻3 and 0, including 0}

28.   {the real numbers between ⁻1 and 5, including ⁻1}

Written Exercises

Specify each nonempty set by roster.

A

1.   {the living ex-Presidents of the U.S.A.}

2.   {the Governor and U.S. Senators of your state}

3.   {the first five months of the year}

4.   {the last six months of the year}

5.   {the authors of this textbook}

6.   {the years between 1850 and 1860}

Specify each set by rule.

7.   {Washington, California, Florida, Maine}

8.   {Lake Superior, Lake Michigan, Lake Huron, Lake Erie, Lake Ontario}

9.   {Houston, Dallas}

10.   {New York, Chicago, Los Angeles}

11.   ∅

12.   {30, 31, 32, 33, 34, 35, 36, 37, 38, 39}

Graph the given set of numbers.

13.   {⁻4, 6, 1}   **15.**   {0}   **17.**   {$\frac{1}{2}$, $\frac{3}{2}$, $\frac{5}{2}$}

14.   {⁻1, 1, 2, ⁻2}   **16.**   ∅   **18.**   {3, 5, 7, 11}

19.   {the real numbers between ⁻2 and 1}
20.   {the real numbers between ⁻3 and 2}
21.   {the real numbers greater than ⁻2}
22.   {the real numbers less than ⁻1}
23.   {the positive real numbers less than 4}
24.   {the negative real numbers greater than ⁻3}
25.   {the negative real numbers less than or equal to ⁻2}
26.   {the positive real numbers greater than or equal to 1}
27.   {the real numbers less than $\frac{3}{2}$ and greater than ⁻4}
28.   {the real numbers greater than ⁻1$\frac{1}{2}$ and less than 5}

B   **29.**   {the positive and negative real numbers}
     30.   {the real numbers that are neither positive nor negative}

Copy each sentence and make it a true statement by replacing each __?__ with a numeral or with one of the symbols ∈ or ∉.

31. $\dfrac{8 \times \underline{\ ?\ }}{4} \in \{8\}$

32. $5 \times \underline{\ ?\ } \notin$ {the positive and negative numbers}

33. $\dfrac{27 - 3}{6} \ \underline{\ ?\ }$ {the nonnegative numbers}

34. $5(16 - 6) \ \underline{\ ?\ }$ {the nonpositive numbers}

35. $\{[(3 \times 5) + 7] - (3 \times 5)\} \ \underline{\ ?\ }$ {the numbers greater than or equal to 2}

(Notice that the braces on the left side of the sentence in Exercise 35 form a grouping symbol and do not mean "the set whose members are.")

36. $[(7 \times 5) - \{75 \div (5 \times 5)\}] \ \underline{\ ?\ }$ {the numbers less than ⁻1}

37. $[(4 \cdot 15) - (18 \div 9)] - (2 \cdot 29) \in$ {the numbers between ⁻3 and __?__}

38. $[5(3 + 6) - 7(2 + 4)] - (48 \div \underline{\ ?\ }) \notin$ {the positive numbers}

1–6   Comparing Sets

What can you say about the sets $\{⁻1, 0, 6\}$ and $\{0, 6, ⁻1\}$? They have the same members!   Do the symbols "$\{⁻1, 0, 6\}$" and "$\{0, 6, ⁻1\}$" name different sets?   No; they both name the set whose members are ⁻1, 0, and 6.   Therefore, you write

$$\{⁻1, 0, 6\} = \{0, 6, ⁻1\}$$

and say, "The set whose members are negative one, zero, and six equals (or is equal to) the set whose members are zero, six, and negative one."

On the other hand, $\{^-1, 0, 6\}$ and $\{^-1, 0, 2\}$ do *not* have the same members. Hence, you write

$$\{^-1, 0, 6\} \neq \{^-1, 0, 2\}$$

and say, "The set whose members are negative one, zero, and six **does not equal** (or **is not equal to**) the set whose members are negative one, zero, and two."

Although the sets $\{^-1, 0, 6\}$ and $\{^-1, 0, 2\}$ are not equal, there is an important relationship between them. Figure 1–7 shows a pairing which assigns to each member of each set *one and only one* member of the other set. Such a pairing of the elements of two sets is called a **one-to-one correspondence**. The number line is a one-to-one correspondence between the set of real numbers and the set of the points on a line (section 1–3).

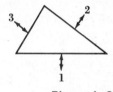

$\{^-1, 0, 6\}$

$\{^-1, 0, 2\}$

Figure 1–7

Whenever you "count" the members of a given set, you set up a one-to-one correspondence between the given set and a set of numbers. For example, in counting the sides of a triangle (Figure 1–8), you pair the members of the set of sides with the members of $\{1, 2, 3\}$.

Figure 1–8

The set of numbers used in counting is called the set of **counting numbers** or **natural numbers**; we name it N. Can you list all the members of N? No. If you start to list all the elements of

$$N = \{1, 2, 3, 4, 5, \ldots\},$$

you will never come to the end of the list. The three dots after the "5" are read "and so on," and indicate that the pattern shown in the list continues without end. We say that N is an **infinite set** because the process of counting its members would *never* come to an end. We say that it is specified above by an *incomplete roster*. The set N may also be specified by the graph

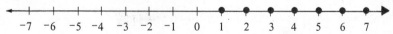

where the heavy arrowhead implies that the graph continues without end.

Here are some other infinite sets, each specified by rule and by incomplete roster and graph.

$W = \{\text{the whole numbers}\} = \{0, 1, 2, 3, 4, 5, 6, \ldots\}$

$J = \{$the integers$\} = \{0, 1, ^-1, 2, ^-2, 3, ^-3, \ldots\}$
$\qquad\qquad\qquad = \{\ldots, ^-3, ^-2, ^-1, 0, 1, 2, 3, \ldots\}$

$E \cdot = \{$the even integers$\} = \{0, 2, ^-2, 4, ^-4, 6, ^-6, \ldots\}$
$\qquad\qquad\qquad\qquad = \{\ldots, ^-6, ^-4, ^-2, 0, 2, 4, 6, \ldots\}$

$D = \{$the positive odd integers$\} = \{1, 3, 5, 7, 9, \ldots\}$

Notice that when you specify an infinite set by incomplete roster, *you must list enough elements to show the pattern in the list.*

The **set of real numbers** is another infinite set. It cannot be represented by roster. Its graph is the entire number line:

Is the set of the sides of a triangle an infinite set? It is not, because the process of counting the sides ends with the number 3. If there is a counting number which is the number of members in a set, or if the set is the empty set, then the set is a **finite set.** Thus, the sides of a triangle form a finite set. Each of the following sets is also finite:

$A = \{2, 4, 6, 8, 10\}$
$B = \{$the negative numbers greater than 0$\}$
$C = \{$the whole numbers named by two-digit decimal numerals$\}$.

You can also specify C by writing

$$C = \{10, 11, 12, 13, \ldots, 99\}.$$

The three dots between "13" and "99" are read "and so on through" and mean that the missing numerals follow the pattern indicated by the first four items in the list.

Oral Exercises

State which of the following sets are finite and which are infinite.

1. $\{$the men who have orbited the moon$\}$
2. $\{$the men who have landed on Mars$\}$

3. {the integers between 0 and 1}
4. {the grains of sand on the beaches of Hawaii}
5. {the words in your mathematics textbook}
6. {the line segments that are 3 inches long}
7. {the odd integers greater than 6}
8. {the positive even integers less than 23}
9. {the negative real numbers greater than $^-1$}
10. {the odd integers less than 8}

In Exercises 11–18, find a set named in Column II equal to each set named in Column I.

Column I

11. {$^-4, ^-1, ^-3, ^-2$}
12. $\emptyset$
13. {1}
14. {0}
15. {1, 3, 5, 7, 9, . . .}
16. {$^-2, ^-4, ^-6, ^-8, ^-10, . . .$}
17. {1, 3}
18. {$^-2, 0$}

Column II

a. {the positive odd integers}
b. {the smallest natural number}
c. {the negative even integers}
d. {the even integers between $\frac{5}{2}$ and $\frac{7}{2}$}
e. {the even integers between $^-3$ and 1}
f. {the integers that differ from 1 by at least 1}
g. {the negative integers between $^-5$ and $\frac{4}{3}$}
h. {the number whose sum with 5 is 5}
i. {the positive odd integers less than π}

Written Exercises

Give a (complete or incomplete) roster for each set, and state whether or not the set is finite.

1. {the natural numbers less than 7}
2. {the whole numbers between 7 and 19}
3. {the whole numbers greater than 12}
4. {the even integers less than $^-2$}
5. {the odd integers between 7 and 39, inclusive (that is, including 7 and 39)}
6. {the even integers between $^-4$ and 4, inclusive}

7. {the even integers between 3 and 4}

8. {the odd integers between ⁻2 and ⁻3}

In Exercises 9–14, specify each set by rule.

SAMPLE.   {1, 3, 5, 7, . . . , 21}

Solution: {the odd integers between 0 and 22} or {the odd integers between 1 and 21, inclusive}.   **Answer.**

Specify each set by rule.

9. {21, 22, 23, 24, . . . , 29}

10. {0, ⁻1, ⁻2, . . . , ⁻12}

11. {1, 7, 5, 3, 9}

12. {⁻5, ⁻3, ⁻1, ⁻2, ⁻4}

13. {0, 5, 10, 15, . . .}

14. {2, 4, 6, 8, . . .}

Draw the graph of each set.

15. {the positive integers less than $5\frac{3}{4}$}

16. {the natural numbers less than 7 but greater than 5}

17. {the integers between 3 and 7, inclusive}

18. {the negative integers greater than or equal to ⁻4}

Let A = {1, 3, 5, 7} and B = {2, 3, 5, 7}.   Specify each of the following sets.

B **19.** {the integers belonging to A and also to B}

20. {the integers belonging to A, to B, or to both A and B}

21. {the integers in A but not in B}

22. {the integers in B but not in A}

C **23.** {the positive integers that are neither in A nor in B}

24. {the positive integers not in both A and B}

In Exercises 25 and 26, show that there is a one-to-one correspondence between the two sets specified.

25. {the natural numbers} and {the even natural numbers}

26. {the integers} and {the odd integers}

● CHAPTER SUMMARY ●

Inventory of Structure and Method

1. Names, or symbols, for numbers are called **numerical expressions** or **numerals**. Numerical expressions that name the same number are said to have the same **value** and to be **equal**. A statement which asserts that two numerical expressions are **equal** is called an **equation**. A statement asserting that two numerical expressions do not have the same value is called an **inequality**.

2. **Symbols** of **inclusion**, or **grouping symbols**, are used to make clear the meaning of *ambiguous* numerical expressions. The **Substitution Principle** is used in **simplifying** numerical expressions.

3. On the number line the **point** paired with a number is called the **graph** of that number. The number paired with a point is called the **coordinate** of the point. *Positive* and *negative* numbers are sometimes called **directed numbers**, since, on the number line, their graphs are in opposite directions from the **origin**.

4. The **directed inequality symbol** $<$ is read "is less than." The **directed inequality symbol** $>$ is read "is greater than." To say that $3 > {}^{-}1$ means that the graph of 3 lies *to the right* of the graph of ${}^{-}1$ on a horizontal number line with the positive direction toward the right.

5. A statement which is formed by joining two statements by the word *and* is called a **conjunction** of statements.

6. To specify a **set**, identify its **members**, or **elements**, by **roster**, **rule**, or **graph**. The set with no members is called the **empty set** or the **null set**.

7. Two sets are **equal** when they have the same members. Given two sets, a pairing which assigns to each member of each set *one and only one* member of the other set is called a **one-to-one correspondence**. A set is an **infinite set** if the process of counting its members would never end. If the number of members in a set can be named by a **counting number**, or if the set is the empty set, the set is a **finite** set.

Vocabulary and Spelling

Review the meaning of each term by reference to the page listed.

numerical expression (*p. 1*)

numeral (*p. 1*)

value (*p. 1*)

equals (*p. 1 and p. 20*)

statement (*p. 1*)

equation (*p. 2*)

does not equal (*p. 2 and p. 21*)

inequality (*p. 2*)

ambiguous (*p. 4*)

parentheses (*p. 4*)

symbol of inclusion (*p. 4*)

grouping symbol (*p. 4*)

brackets (*p. 4*)   is less than (*p. 12*)
braces (*p. 4*)   is greater than (*p. 12*)
simplified expression (*p. 5*)   between (*p. 13*)
Substitution Principle (*p. 5*)   conjunction (*p. 14*)
number line (*p. 8*)   member of a set (*p. 16*)
origin (*p. 8*)   element of a set (*p. 16*)
positive direction (*p. 8*)   roster (*p. 16*)
positive number (*p. 8*)   empty set (*p. 18*)
graph (*p. 8*)   null set (*p. 18*)
coordinate (*p. 8*)   one-to-one correspondence (*p. 21*)
negative number (*p. 9*)   counting numbers (*p. 21*)
negative direction (*p. 9*)   natural numbers (*p. 21*)
real number (*p. 9*)   infinite set (*p. 21*)
directed number (*p. 9*)   finite set (*p. 22*)

Chapter Test

1–1   **1.** Replace each __?__ with one of the symbols $=$ or $\neq$ to make a true statement.

     a. $0 + 2$ __?__ 0×2 **b.** $0.37 - 0.02$ __?__ 5×0.07

   2. Replace each __?__ with a numeral which makes the statement true.

     a. $6 +$ __?__ $= 3 \times 3$ **b.** __?__ $+ 29 \neq 29$

1–2   **3.** Simplify: $[6 - (18 \div 3)] + (4 \times 3)$

1–3   **4.** Draw a number line, and on it show the graphs of the given points.

     a. 2

     b. The point 5 units to the right of 2.

     c. The point 3 units to the left of the origin.

     d. The point halfway between ⁻1 and 3.

1–4   **5.** Replace each __?__ with one of the symbols $=$, $>$, or $<$ to make a true statement.

     a. $^-4$ __?__ $^-4 \times 0$ **b.** $\frac{16}{4}$ __?__ 3 **c.** $\dfrac{9-3}{4-2}$ __?__ $9-3$

1–5   **6.** Specify the given set by roster:

        {months of the year whose names begin with A}

   7. Specify the given set by rule:

        {Washington, Oregon, California}

8. Graph the given set:

{even counting numbers less than ten}

1–6 **9.** Tell whether the two given sets are equal.

    a. {1, 2, 3} and {3, 1, 2}

    b. {0, 1, 2, 3, 4, 5} and {counting numbers less than 5}

10. Tell whether the following sets are finite or infinite.

    a. {even integers less than 7}

    b. {people living on the earth}

Chapter Review

1–1 **Naming Numbers; Equality and Inequality**   *Pages 1–3*

  1. A name for a number is called a __?__.

  2. The number named by a numerical expression is called the __?__ of the expression.

  3. The symbol which stands for the word "equals" is __?__.

  4. The statement "5 ÷ 2 ≠ 3" is called a(n) __?__.

1–2 **Punctuation Marks in Algebra**   *Pages 3–7*

  5. Parentheses, __?__, and __?__ are called symbols of inclusion or __?__ symbols.

  6. Simplify: $5[(24 \div 8) - 2]$

  7. The __?__ Principle is as follows: Changing the numeral by which a number is named in an expression does not change the __?__ of the expression.

1–3 **The Number Line**   *Pages 8–12*

  8. The starting point on a number line is called the __?__. It is labeled __?__.

  9. The distance between points labeled "0" and "1" is the __?__ length on the number line.

10. The direction from the origin to the point labeled "1" is called the __?__ direction on the number line.

11. On the number line, the point paired with a number is the __?__ of that number.

12. The number paired with a point on a number line is the __?__ of that point.

13. On the usual horizontal number line, the graphs of __?__ numbers lie to the left of the origin.

1–4 Comparing Numbers   *Pages 12–15*

14. 8 > 5 is read, "8 is __?__ than 5," which means that the graph of 8 is to the __?__ of the graph of 5 on the usual horizontal number line.

15. "Six is less than eight" may be written in symbols as __?__.

16. 4 < 5 < 9 is read, "4 is less than __?__ and __?__ is less than __?__.

17. A statement formed by joining two statements by the word *and* is called a __?__.

18. In a true conjunction, __?__ of the joined statements are true.

1–5 Specifying Sets   *Pages 16–20*

19. Any collection of objects is a __?__.

20. Each object in a set is a(n) __?__ of the set.

21. The symbol __?__ means "is an element of."

22. When you identify a set by listing its elements within braces, you are making a __?__.

23. When you identify a set by describing its elements within braces, you are giving a __?__.

24. When you locate the elements of a set of numbers on a number line, you are making a __?__ of the set.

25. The set with no members is the __?__ set or the __?__ set.

26. ∅ is the symbol for the __?__ set.

1–6 Comparing Sets   *Pages 20–24*

27. Two sets which have exactly the same members are __?__ sets.

28. Given two sets, a pairing which assigns to each member of each set *one and only one* member of the other set is called a __?__ correspondence.

29. The set of numbers used in counting is the set of __?__ numbers.

30. The process of counting the members of a(n) __?__ set would never come to an end.

31. If there is a counting number which is the number of elements in a set, the set is a(n) __?__ set.

32. Is the empty set a finite set or an infinite set?

Why We Call It "Algebra"

It all seems to have started at the court of Caliph al-Mamun, who was ruler of Baghdad from 809 to 833. Al-Mamun was a scholar, interested in all branches of knowledge. He included in his court many learned men. Among these, the greatest mathematician and astronomer was a man called Muhammad ibn Musa al-Khwarazmi, whose name meant "Mohammed, son of Moses, the Khwarazmite." This man is best known for having written a mathematical treatise with the title "hisab al-jabr wa'l muqabalah." Years later, the Moors took this work into Spain. There, during the twelfth century, it was translated into Latin, the common language of European scholars, and its ideas were carried to Italy and many other countries. Along the way, the word "al-jabr" was changed into the word "algebra," the form in which we use it today.

The title of al-Khwarazmi's treatise, "hisab al-jabr wa'l muqabalah," means "the science of reduction and comparison." Because the word "al-jabr" referred to the reduction of parts to a whole, it also took on a meaning that seems a far cry from its mathematical one. An "algebrista" was a "restorer," a man who reset broken bones!

One of the greatest Arab mathematicians of the century following al-Khwarazmi was al-Karkhi, who wrote a treatise to which he gave the title "al-Fakhri." He called it this in honor of his patron, the vizier Abu Galib, whose familiar name was "Fakhr al-Mulik." If this had been the work chosen for translation, who knows? You might today be studying "alfakhri" instead of "algebra."

This picture represents scholars at Baghdad using astronomical instruments. They found algebra helpful in their work.

. . . a unique photograph of organ pipes taken from above

The Language of Algebra

To study algebra successfully you need to learn its language. This language has many special symbols and terms. Some of the basic ones appear in this chapter. Take time to be sure you fully understand them.

VARIABLES AND MATHEMATICAL EXPRESSIONS

2–1 Variables

On each of the cards pictured in Figure 2–1, you see a numeral printed in red. Suppose that you begin with Card 1 and take the following steps:

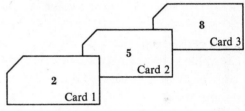

Figure 2–1

1. Read the red numeral on the card.

2. Multiply the number whose name you read in Step 1 by 7.

3. On a sheet of paper, write the simplest numeral for the product obtained in Step 2.

4. If you have worked with all the cards, then write the word "**STOP**" on your paper; otherwise, return to Step 1 and work with the next card.

These four steps describe a computation to be carried out, and they form a program. A **program** is any list of steps used to carry out a particular job.

The table at the top of page 32 shows what happens when you go through the program formed by the four steps given above.

Step	Card 1	Card 2	Card 3
1.	2	5	8
2.	7×2	7×5	7×8
3.	14	35	56
4.	Go to Step 1 for Card 2.	Go to Step 1 for Card 3.	STOP

Look at the numerical expressions written for Step 2 in the program:

$$7 \times 2, \qquad 7 \times 5, \qquad 7 \times 8$$

Each of them fits a pattern that you can show by writing

$$7 \times n$$

In this pattern, the letter n may stand for "**2**," for "**5**," or for "**8**"; n is called a *variable*. A **variable** is a symbol which may represent any of the members of a specified set, called the **domain** or **replacement set** of the variable. Thus, the domain of n in this example is $\{2, 5, 8\}$. An individual member of the replacement set, such as 2, 5, or 8, is called a **value** of the variable.

A variable with just one value is called a **constant**. For instance, the symbol "7" is a constant because it represents the single number *seven*.

An expression, such as "$7 \times n$," which contains a variable is called a **variable expression** or an **open expression**. A variable expression or a numerical expression (page 1) is sometimes called a **mathematical expression**.

To read "$7 \times n$," you say "seven times n" or "seven multiplied by n," or "the product of seven and n." Of course, in referring to "$7 \times n$" as a "product," you mean that when n is replaced by the name of a number, the resulting expression names a *product of numbers*. For example, if you write "2" in place of n, you have the expression "7×2," which names the product of 7 and 2, that is, 14.

When you write a product that contains a variable, you usually omit the multiplication sign, $\times$. Thus, "$7 \times n$" is written "$7n$". But notice that in the expressions "7×2" and "$7(2)$" you do not omit the multiplication symbol, for "72" names seventy-two, not 7 times 2.

Furthermore, in any expression involving "$7n$," the "7" and "n" are considered to be grouped. For example "$7n + 5$" means "$(7 \times n) + 5$." Similarly, "$ab \div 7n$" means "$(a \times b) \div (7 \times n)$."

Given a particular value for the variable in an open expression, the process of replacing the variable by the numeral for the given value and simplifying the result is known as **evaluating the expression** or **finding its value**.

EXAMPLE. If the value of a is 4 and the value of d is 1, find the value of

$$\frac{4a + 11d}{a - d}.$$

Solution: 1. Replace the letter a by "4" and d by "1," and insert the necessary multiplication and grouping symbols.

$$\frac{4a + 11d}{a - d}$$

$$\frac{(4 \times 4) + (11 \times 1)}{4 - 1}$$

2. Simplify the expression obtained in Step 1.

$$\frac{16 + 11}{3} = \frac{27}{3} = 9. \quad \textbf{Answer.}$$

A mathematical expression using numerals or variables or both to indicate a product or a quotient is called a **term**. The expression "$3n$" is a term, and so are "8," "$5xy$," and "$\dfrac{x}{a - b}$." In the expression "$3ab + 3(a - b) - \dfrac{b - 2a}{5}$," there are three terms: "$3ab$," "$3(a - b)$," and "$\dfrac{b - 2a}{5}$." "$a + b$" has two terms, but "$(a + b)$" is a single term.

Oral Exercises

In each of Exercises 1–16, the given expression indicates one or more operations to be performed. For each expression, describe the operation(s).

SAMPLE 1. $2 + 5c$ *Solution 1:*   Multiply 5 and c, and then add the product to 2. **Answer.**

                             Solution 2:   Add to 2 the product of 5 and c. **Answer.**

SAMPLE 2. $\dfrac{a}{b} - 6$ *Solution:*   From the quotient of a by b subtract 6. **Answer.**

1. $2a$	**5.** $\dfrac{b}{2}$	**9.** $\dfrac{c}{a} + b$	**13.** $4(a + 2)$
2. $4b$	**6.** $\dfrac{c}{3}$	**10.** $bc - a$	**14.** $5(b - 2)$
3. $c - 1$	**7.** $\dfrac{15}{c}$	**11.** $\dfrac{6}{bc}$	**15.** $\dfrac{a + c}{b}$
4. $5 - a$	**8.** $\dfrac{24}{b}$	**12.** $\dfrac{2}{ab}$	**16.** $\dfrac{b}{c - a}$

17–32. If in Exercises 1–16 the values of a, b, and c are 1, 2, and 3, respectively, what is the value of each of the given expressions?

Written Exercises

In each of the following exercises, state the number of terms in the given expression. Then evaluate the expression, given that the value of *a* is 1, *b* is 2, *c* is 3, *x* is 12, *y* is 0, and *z* is $\frac{1}{2}$.

SAMPLE. $\dfrac{ax - 2}{b + c}$ *Solution:* There is one term in the expression.

$$\frac{(1 \times 12) - 2}{2 + 3} = \frac{12 - 2}{5} = \frac{10}{5} = 2.$$

Answer.

A

1. bc
2. cx
3. $x - bc$
4. $b - cy$
5. $xz - bc$
6. $ac - yz$

7. $b(x - c)$
8. $c(a - y)$
9. $(bb)(cc)$
10. $(zz)(bb)$
11. $bc(x - y)$
12. $bz(x - c)$

13. $abcxy$
14. $abcxz$
15. $(x - 2c)(2c - b)$
16. $(c - 2y)(bc - a)$
17. $\dfrac{x - 2c}{b}$
18. $\dfrac{bx - c}{2c + a}$

B

19. $b(c - a) + \dfrac{x}{bc}$
20. $5(b + c) - \dfrac{bx}{c}$
21. $\dfrac{4(bcc - xz)}{b}$

22. $\dfrac{6(bbc - 2zc)}{2x + c}$
23. $\dfrac{16cz - 2x}{a - 3xy} + \dfrac{x - 2b}{bz}$
24. $\dfrac{x(2c - b)}{b(c - b)} - \dfrac{x(bz + 1)}{2c + b}$

Problems

Evaluate each of the following expressions which are taken from practical situations. In each problem assign the indicated values to the variables.

A

1. Distance traveled at constant rate *r* in time *t*:   *rt*
   Let *r* be 280 (miles per hour) and *t* be 18 (hours). Distance is then in miles.

2. Area of a rectangle of width *w* and length *l*:   *lw*
   Let *l* be 84 (feet) and *w* be 27 (feet). Area is then in square feet.

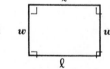

3. Perimeter of a rectangle: $2l + 2w$
   Let *l* be 210 (feet) and *w* be 162 (feet). Perimeter is then in feet.

4. Amount (in dollars) of an investment of *P* dollars at simple interest:
   $P + Prt$
   Let *P* be 2500 (dollars), *r* be 4% (per year), and *t* be 10 (years).

5. Perimeter of a triangle: $a + b + c$
Let a be 6 (inches), b be 8 (inches), and c be 10 (inches). Perimeter
is then in inches.

6. Area of a right triangle: $\frac{1}{2}ab$
Let a be 12 (inches) and b be 16 (inches). Area is then in square inches.

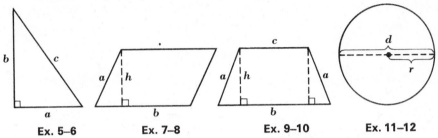

Ex. 5–6   Ex. 7–8   Ex. 9–10   Ex. 11–12

7. Area of a parallelogram: bh
Let b be 12.5 (centimeters) and h be 7.5 (centimeters). Area is then in
square centimeters.

8. Perimeter of a parallelogram: $2(a + b)$
Let a be 5.5 (meters) and b be 25.2 (meters). Perimeter is then in meters.

9. Perimeter of an isosceles trapezoid: $2a + b + c$
Let a be 54 (yards), b be 98 (yards), and c be 48 (yards). Perimeter is
then in yards.

10. Area of a trapezoid: $\frac{1}{2}h(b + c)$
Let h be 25 (yards), b be 50 (yards), and c be 25 (yards). Area is then
in square yards.

11. Area of a circle: $(\pi r)r$
Let r be 14 (inches). $\pi \doteq \frac{22}{7}$ ($\doteq$ means **"is approximately equal to"**).
Area is then in square inches.

12. Circumference of a circle: πd
Let d be $3\frac{1}{2}$ (feet). $\pi \doteq \frac{22}{7}$.
Circumference is then in feet.

B **13.** Perimeter of a Norman window: $2(r + h) + \pi r$
Let r be 2.00 (feet), h be 6.00 (feet). $\pi \doteq 3.14$.
Perimeter is then in feet.

14. Perimeter of the adjoining figure: πr
Let r be 3.75 (feet). $\pi \doteq 3.14$.
Perimeter is then in feet.

15. Volume of a rectangular solid: lwh
Let l be 12.5 (inches), w be 5.5
(inches), and h be 7.5 (inches).
Volume is then in cubic inches.

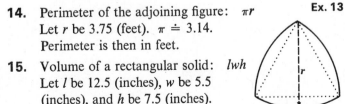
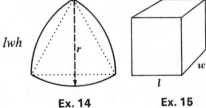

Ex. 13

Ex. 14   Ex. 15

16. Surface area of a rectangular solid: $2(lw + wh + lh)$
Let l be 10 (inches), w be 6 (inches), and h be 8 (inches). Surface area is then in square inches.

17. Cutting speed of a tool on a lathe: $\dfrac{\pi dn}{12}$
Let d be 1.80 (inches) and n be 200 (rpm, that is, revolutions per minute). $\pi \doteq 3.14$. Speed is then in feet per minute.

18. Velocity of a satellite orbiting the earth at the equator: $\dfrac{2\pi(3960 + h)}{P}$
Let h be 22,300 miles and P be 24 hours. The velocity is then in miles per hour. $\pi \doteq 3.14$.

19. A value that is $\frac{4}{5}$ of the way from l to r: $l + \frac{4}{5}(r - l)$
Let l be 3502 and r be 3522.

20. Temperature (in degrees) on Kelvin (absolute) scale: $\frac{5}{9}(F - 32) + 273$
Let F be 77 (degrees Fahrenheit).

C **21.** Focal length of a thin lens: $\dfrac{rs}{(n - 1)(r + s)}$
Let r be 11.6 (centimeters), s be 9.4 (centimeters), and n be 1.6 (index of refraction).

22. Total resistance of three resistances in parallel: $\dfrac{rst}{st + rt + rs}$
Let r be 19 (ohms), s be 90 (ohms), and t be 318 (ohms).

2–2 Factors, Coefficients, and Exponents

When two or more numbers are multiplied, each of the numbers is called a **factor** of the product. Thus, 5 and 7 are factors of 35; two other factors are 1 and 35.

In such an expression as $\frac{1}{4}yz$, each factor is the **coefficient** (ko-e-**fish**-ent) of the product of the other factors. Thus, in the product $\frac{1}{4}yz$, $\frac{1}{4}$ is the coefficient of yz, $\frac{1}{4}y$ is the coefficient of z, and $\frac{1}{4}z$ is the coefficient of y. Also, yz is the coefficient of $\frac{1}{4}$. Usually, you refer to the numerical part of a term as its (numerical) coefficient. For example, the coefficient of $25yz$ is 25. Also, the coefficient of x is 1, since $x = 1 \cdot x$.

In writing a product, a raised dot $\cdot$ is often used as a symbol of multiplication. Thus,

$$8 \cdot 9 = 8 \times 9$$

and

$$7 \cdot 7 = 7 \times 7.$$

Do you know another way to denote the product $7 \cdot 7$? You can write "7^2," and say "the *square* of 7" or "the *second power* of 7." Here is how the powers of 7 are defined:

First power: $\quad 7^1 = 7$

Second power: $\quad 7^2 = 7 \cdot 7$ (also read "seven squared" or "seven-square")

Third power: $\quad 7^3 = 7^2 \cdot 7 = (7 \cdot 7) \cdot 7$ (also read "the cube of seven" "seven cubed" or "seven-cube")

Fourth power: $\quad 7^4 = 7^3 \cdot 7 = [(7 \cdot 7) \cdot 7] \cdot 7$ (also read "seven to the fourth" or "seven-fourth")

and so on.

In general, if x denotes any real number and n denotes any positive integer, then

$$x^n = \underbrace{x \cdot x \cdot \cdots \cdot x}_{n \text{ factors}}$$

You call x^n the **nth power** of x. In x^n, the number represented by the small raised symbol n is called an **exponent** (**ek**-spo-nent). The exponent tells the number of times the **base** x occurs as a factor in the product. Thus:

$$\text{Exponent} \longrightarrow x^n = \text{the } n\text{th power of } x \longleftarrow \text{Base}$$

In writing a power such as "x^3" in the form "$x \cdot x \cdot x$," you say that you have written the power in **factored form** or **expanded form**. The expression "x^3" is called the **exponential** (ek-spo-**nen**-shal) **form**.

EXAMPLE 1.   **If the value of m is 5, find the value of:**

         a. m^3 **b.** $3m$

Solution: **In each case, replace m by 5 and simplify the resulting expression.**

         a. $m^3 = (m \cdot m) \cdot m$ **b.** $3m = 3 \cdot m$

                 $= (5 \cdot 5) \cdot 5$ $= 3 \cdot 5$

                 $= 25 \cdot 5$ $= 15.$ **Answer.**

                 $= 125.$ **Answer.**

As Example 1 shows, the expressions "m^3" and "$3m$" may have very different values for a given value of m. In "m^3," 3 is an exponent and shows that m is a factor three times. In "$3m$," 3 is the coefficient and thus is itself a factor.

In an expression such as "$5y^2$," 2 is the exponent of the base y. On the other hand, "$(5y)^2$" stands for "$5y \cdot 5y$"; in this case, the parentheses show that the base is $5y$. Consider the following examples:

$$4 \cdot 3^2 = 4(3 \cdot 3) = 36, \quad \text{but } (4 \cdot 3)^2 = (4 \cdot 3)(4 \cdot 3) = 144$$
$$yz^3 = y(z \cdot z \cdot z), \quad \text{but } (yz)^3 = (yz)(yz)(yz)$$
$$6 + x^2 = 6 + (x \cdot x), \quad \text{but } (6 + x)^2 = (6 + x)(6 + x)$$

Oral Exercises

Read each expression as a product and state its (numerical) coefficient.

SAMPLE 1. $8(x - 3)$ *Solution:* 8 times the difference $x - 3$; coefficient 8

SAMPLE 2. $\frac{2}{5}y$ *Solution:* $\frac{2}{5}$ times y; coefficient $\frac{2}{5}$

1. $3y$	**4.** $\frac{2}{3}t$	**7.** xy	**10.** $4(z - 8)$
2. $5a$	**5.** $0.3y$	**8.** $2yz$	**11.** $\frac{7}{3}a$
3. $\frac{1}{2}r$	**6.** $1.2c$	**9.** $3(y + 2)$	**12.** $\frac{4}{9}z$

For each term, state the coefficient, the base, and the exponent. Then read the term with the power in factored form.

SAMPLE 3. $6x^2$ *Solution:* Coefficient 6, base x, exponent 2; factored form $6 \cdot x \cdot x$ (read "six times x times x")

13. $2y^4$	**15.** $(xy)^2$	**17.** $(a + b)^3$
14. $3z^3$	**16.** $2(xy)^2$	**18.** $3(x - y)^3$

Evaluate each expression for the given value of the variable.

19. l^2; l: 7	**23.** $(2x)^2$; x: 3
20. $2l$; l: 7	**24.** $2x^2$; x: 3
21. z^3; z: 2	**25.** $(x - 4)^2$; x: 8
22. $3z$; z: 2	**26.** $x^2 - 4$; x: 8

State the exponential form of the given expression.

SAMPLE 4. $3 \cdot y \cdot y \cdot x \cdot x \cdot x$ *Solution:* $3y^2x^3$

27. $x \cdot x$	**31.** $3 \cdot c \cdot c \cdot d \cdot d$
28. $y \cdot y \cdot y$	**32.** $12 \cdot a \cdot a \cdot b \cdot b \cdot b \cdot c$
29. $x \cdot x \cdot y$	**33.** $(a + 1)(a + 1)$
30. $a \cdot b \cdot b \cdot b$	**34.** $3(x - 2)(x - 2)(y - 3)$

Written Exercises

Write each expression in exponential form.

[A]
1. $x \cdot x \cdot x$
2. $b \cdot b \cdot b \cdot b$
3. z squared
4. y cubed
5. $10 \cdot x \cdot y \cdot y$
6. $11 \cdot c \cdot c \cdot c \cdot d \cdot d$
7. $23u \cdot u \cdot u(w + 3)$
8. $(x - 2)(x - 2)(x - 2)$

9. $(r + s)(r + s)(r + t)$
10. $3 \cdot y \cdot y \cdot (x + 1)(x + 1)$
11. The cube of $x + 8$
12. The fourth power of $z - 3$
13. The product of 5 and the cube of $y + z$
14. The sum of 7 and the square of x
15. The fourth power of the sum of a and b
16. The fifth power of the square of $x + 1$

Evaluate each expression for the given value of the variable.

17. y^2; 6
18. z^2; 11
19. $2x^3$; 3
20. $7y^3$; 2

21. $2x^2$; $\frac{1}{3}$
22. $3a^4$; $\frac{1}{2}$
23. $(3x)^2$; 2
24. $(4p)^2$; 3

25. $(6m)^3$; $\frac{1}{2}$
26. $(12n)^4$; $\frac{1}{12}$
27. $(z + 2)^2(z - 1)$; 3
28. $2(t + 1)(t + 1)^2$; 4

In Exercises 29–36, if the values of x, y, and z are 2, 3, and 5, respectively, evaluate the given expression.

[B]
29. $\dfrac{x^2 + y}{z}$

30. $\dfrac{z^2 - y}{x}$

31. $\dfrac{y^2 + 3x}{z}$

32. $\dfrac{2z + 4x}{y^2}$

33. $(\frac{1}{5}z)^2 + (2y)^2$

34. $(3x)^3 - (2y)^3$

35. $\dfrac{y^3 - 27}{xy}$

36. $\dfrac{x^4 + y^2}{z^2}$

Problems

Evaluate each of the following expressions, replacing the variables as indicated.

[A]
1. Volume of a square prism: lw^2
Let l be 6 (feet) and w be 3 (feet). Volume is then in cubic feet.

2. Surface area of a square prism: $2w^2 + 4lw$
Let l be 4 (yards) and w be 2 (yards).
Surface area is then in square yards.

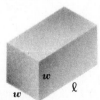

Ex. 1–2

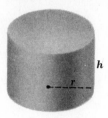

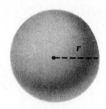

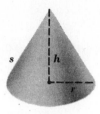

Ex. 3–4   Ex. 5–6   Ex. 7–8

3. Surface area of a right circular cylinder: $2\pi r(r + h)$
Let r be 14 (inches) and h be 15 (inches). $\pi \doteq \frac{22}{7}$. Surface area is then in square inches.

4. Volume of a right circular cylinder: $\pi r^2 h$
Let r be 2 (meters) and h be $3\frac{1}{2}$ (meters). $\pi \doteq \frac{22}{7}$. Volume is then in cubic meters.

5. Surface area of a sphere: $4\pi r^2$
Let r be 7 (centimeters). $\pi \doteq \frac{22}{7}$. Surface area is then in square centimeters.

6. Volume of a sphere: $\frac{4}{3}\pi r^3$
Let r be 21 (feet). $\pi \doteq \frac{22}{7}$. Volume is then in cubic feet.

B **7.** Volume of a right circular cone: $\frac{1}{3}\pi r^2 h$
Let r be 6 (inches) and h be 20 (inches). $\pi \doteq 3.14$. Volume is then in cubic inches.

8. Surface area of a right circular cone: $\pi r(s + r)$
Let r be 3 (feet) and s be 10 (feet). $\pi \doteq 3.14$. Surface area is then in square feet.

9. Area of a ring: $\pi(R^2 - r^2)$
Let R be 12 (feet) and r be 5 (feet). $\pi \doteq 3.14$. Area is then in square feet.

Ex. 9

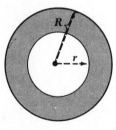

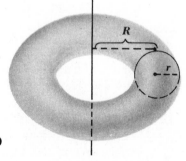

Ex. 10

10. Volume of a torus: $2\pi^2 r^2 R$
Let r be 4 (inches) and R be 12 (inches). $\pi \doteq 3.14$. Volume is then in cubic inches.

11. Power in an electrical circuit: I^2R

Let I be 8 (amperes) and R be 0.2 (ohms). Power is then in watts.

12. Illumination on a surface: $\dfrac{I}{s^2}$

Let I be 28 (candles) and s be 2 (feet). Illumination is then in foot-candles (or lumens per square foot).

[C] **13.** Kinetic energy of a moving body: $\dfrac{Wv^2}{2g}$

Let W be 30,000 (pounds) and v be 44 (feet per second). $g \doteq 32$ (feet per second). Energy is then in foot-pounds.

14. Height of a body thrown vertically upward with velocity k: $kt - \dfrac{gt^2}{2}$

Let k be 48 (feet per second) and t be 10.2 (seconds). $g \doteq 32$ (feet per second per second). Height is then in feet.

15. Length of a pendulum: $\dfrac{gP^2}{4\pi^2}$

Let P be 2 (seconds). $g \doteq 32.2$ (feet per second per second). $\pi \doteq 3.14$. Length is then in feet.

16. Inductance of circuit: $\dfrac{1}{4\pi^2 f^2 C}$

Let f be 1000 (cycles per second) and C be 0.0000004 farads. $\pi \doteq 3.14$. Inductance is then in henries.

2–3 Order of Operations

Can you decide what the expression

$$6 \times 11 - 2^3$$

means? You might insert grouping symbols to make it mean

$$(6 \times 11) - 2^3, \quad \text{or else} \quad 6 \times (11 - 2^3), \quad \text{or even} \quad 6 \times (11 - 2)^3.$$

To avoid questions about the meaning of an expression in which grouping symbols have been omitted, mathematicians have agreed on the following steps to simplify such expressions. However, it is best to use enough grouping symbols to avoid ambiguity.

1. Simplify the names of powers.
2. Then simplify the names of products and quotients in order from left to right.
3. Then simplify the names of sums and differences in order from left to right.

Using the rules at the foot of page 41, you find that $6 \times 11 - 2^3 = (6 \times 11) - 2^3 = 66 - 8 = 58$.

When grouping symbols are used, you apply these rules within each grouping symbol.

You recall from section 1–2 that when there are grouping symbols, you simplify the expression within each pair of grouping symbols, beginning with the innermost pair.

EXAMPLE 1. $392 \div (12 - 4) \cdot 3 = 392 \div 8 \cdot 3$
$$= (392 \div 8) \cdot 3 = 49 \cdot 3 = 147$$

EXAMPLE 2. $[(3 \times 5)5 + 1]2 - 6 = [15 \cdot 5 + 1]2 - 6$
$$= [76]2 - 6 = 146$$

EXAMPLE 3. If the value of x is 2 and the value of y is 1, find the value of $5x^3 - 4x^2y + 3y^2 - 6y^4$.

Solution:

In the given expression, replace x with "2" and y with "1," insert necessary multiplication signs, and simplify the resulting numerical expression.

$$
\begin{aligned}
&5x^3 \quad - 4x^2y \quad + 3y^2 \quad - 6y^4 \\
&= 5 \cdot 2^3 - 4 \cdot 2^2 \cdot 1 + 3 \cdot 1^2 - 6 \cdot 1^4 \\
&= 5 \cdot 8 \quad - 4 \cdot 4 \cdot 1 \quad + 3 \cdot 1 \quad - 6 \cdot 1 \\
&= 40 \quad\quad - 16 \quad\quad + 3 \quad\quad - 6 \\
&= \quad\quad\quad 24 \quad\quad\quad + 3 \quad\quad - 6 \\
&= \quad\quad\quad\quad\quad 27 \quad\quad\quad\quad - 6 \\
&= 21. \quad \text{Answer.}
\end{aligned}
$$

Oral Exercises

Simplify each expression.

1. $10 - 7 - 2$
2. $38 - 0 - 6$
3. $72 \div 6 \div 2$
4. $45 \div 3 \div 3$
5. $7 - 8 \cdot 0$
6. $6 \cdot 1 + 9$
7. $12 \div 1 \times 2$
8. $12 \times 2 \div 1$
9. $32 \div 4 \times 2$
10. $32 \div 2 \times 4$
11. $18 - 2^3 + 3 \times 4$
12. $18 \div 9 + 3^2$
13. $0 \div 2^2 \div 2$
14. $4 \times 39 \times 0 + 1$
15. $6 \div 2 + 1 \times 4$
16. $10 \div 5 - 2^2 \div 2$
17. $4 \cdot 9 - 4 \cdot 1$
18. $12 \cdot 8 + 12 \cdot 2$

Written Exercises

Simplify each expression.

A 1. $(8 + 4 + 3) \div 3 - 2$

2. $(8 + 4 + 5) \div (3 - 2)$

3. $3(11 + 5) \div 4 + 6$

4. $19 + 7(2 + 8) - 49$

5. $7 + 4 - (3 - 1)$

6. $7 + 4 - 3 + 1$

7. $2 \cdot 3^2 - 5 \cdot 3 - 1$

8. $7 \cdot 2 - 2^2 + 3^2$

9. $\dfrac{2^5 \div 8 + 3}{4 + 3}$

10. $\dfrac{5 \cdot 3 + 5 \cdot 2^2}{9 - 2}$

11. $\dfrac{3^3}{2^3 - 2^2 - 1}$

12. $\dfrac{17 \cdot 5 - 3 \cdot 5}{3^2 + 1}$

13. $(5^2 - 5)(5^2 + 5)$

14. $\dfrac{7^2 - 3^2}{7 - 3}$

B 15. $7(8 - 5) \div 3 - 1$

16. $4(9 + 2) - 21 \div 7$

17. $12 \times 6 \div 3 \times 2 \div 48$

18. $18 \div 2 \times 3 - 5 - 20$

19. $2^6 \div 2^2 \div 2^3 \div 2$

20. $3^4 - 3^2 \div 3^2 - 3$

21. $\dfrac{29 - 5(3 - 2)}{2 - 1 + 7}$

22. $\dfrac{6(2 + 4) - 1}{2 \cdot 3 + 1}$

23. $(24 - 3 + 9 \div 3) \div (8 \times \tfrac{1}{2})$

24. $9(7 - 3) - 30 \div (6 - 1)$

In Exercises 25–38, given that the values of x, y, and z are 2, 4, and 3, evaluate the given expression.

25. $y^2 - 3y + 2$

26. $2x^2 - x - 1$

27. $z^2 - 3z - 2$

28. $3z^2 + 2z - 10$

29. $3x^3 + 2x^2 - x - 5$

30. $y^3 - 3y^2 + 7y - 10$

31. $y^2 - z^2 + x^2$

32. $z^2 - 2x^2 + 3y^2$

33. $xy + z - x^3$

34. $2yz - x + z^3$

35. $\dfrac{z^2 + 2z + 1}{y^2}$

36. $\dfrac{3x^2 + 5x + 3}{(z + 2)^2}$

37. $\dfrac{2y^2 - 3y + 16}{y^2 - x^2}$

38. $\dfrac{4z^2 - 10z + 15}{y^2 - z^2}$

Evaluate each expression for the given values of the variables.

C 39. $\dfrac{3(u - 2)^2 + 6v}{u + (v - 2)^2}$; u: 4, v: 5

40. $\dfrac{2[r + 2(s + r)^2]}{r^2 + 2rs + 5s^2}$; r: 8, s: 2

41. $\dfrac{5(m - 2n)(m^2 + n^2)}{5m^2 - 2mn + n^2}$; m: 6, n: 3

42. $\dfrac{k(l + 3n)^2(l + k)}{2l^2 - 4k^2 + n^2 - 6}$; k: 3, l: 5, n: 4

OPEN SENTENCES

2–4 Variables and Open Sentences

A remark that is true about some members of a set may be false about the other members of the set. For example, if $S = \{0, 1, 2, 3\}$, the sentence

$$x \in S \quad \text{and} \quad x + 4 = 6$$

is true when x is replaced by "2" but false when the replacement is "1" or any other numeral that does not name two.

An equation, such as "$x + 4 = 6$," or an inequality, such as "$y - 1 > 5$," which contains one or more variables is called an **open sentence.** An open sentence is a pattern for the different statements — some true, some false — which you obtain by replacing each variable by the names for the different values of the variable. Consider the equation

$$3r + 8 = 20$$

If the replacement set of r is $\{0, 4\}$, you can find the values of r, if any, which make the given equation a true statement as follows:

$3 + 8 = 20$	$3 + 8 = 20$
$3 \cdot 0 + 8 = 20$	$3 \cdot 4 + 8 = 20$
$0 + 8 = 20$	$12 + 8 = 20$
$8 = 20$, which is false	$20 = 20$, which is true

The set that consists of the members of the domain of the variable for which an open sentence is true is called the **truth set** or the **solution set** of the open sentence *over that domain.* Thus, the solution set of "$3r + 8 = 20$" over $\{0, 4\}$ is $\{4\}$.

Each member of the solution set is said to **satisfy** and to be a **solution** of the open sentence. A solution of an *equation* is also known as a **root** of the equation; thus, 4 is a solution, or root, of "$3r + 8 = 20$." To **solve** an open sentence *over a given domain* means to determine its solution set, or truth set, in that domain. The solution set of an open sentence may be specified by roster, by rule, or by graph. The graph of the solution set is called the **graph of the open sentence.**

EXAMPLE 1. If $z \in \{\text{the integers}\}$, specify the solution set of $z - 2 = 3$ by roster and by graph.

Solution: Ask yourself: "From what integer do I subtract 2 to obtain a difference of 3?" The one and only such integer is 5.

∴ (read "**therefore**") the solution set is $\{5\}$. **Answer.**

EXAMPLE 2. Solve $^-1 < x + 3 < 6$ if $x \in \{0, 1, 2, 3\}$, and draw the graph of the sentence.

Solution: Replace x in turn by "0," "1," "2," and "3."

$^-1 < x + 3 < 6$

$^-1 < 0 + 3 < 6$, or $^-1 < 3 < 6$; true.

$^-1 < 1 + 3 < 6$, or $^-1 < 4 < 6$; true.

$^-1 < 2 + 3 < 6$, or $^-1 < 5 < 6$; true.

$^-1 < 3 + 3 < 6$, or $^-1 < 6 < 6$; false.

$\therefore$ the solution set is $\{0, 1, 2\}$.
     Answer.

Oral Exercises

In Exercises 1–12, replace the variable by the name of each element of the given replacement set, and then:

a. Tell whether each resulting statement is true or false.

b. Give the solution set of the open sentence over that replacement set.

SAMPLE 1. $2x - 1 < x + 3; x \in \{3, 4\}$

Solution: **a.** $2 \cdot 3 - 1 < 3 + 3$; that is, $5 < 6$; **true.**

$2 \cdot 4 - 1 < 4 + 3$; that is, $7 < 7$; false.

b. $\therefore$ over $\{3, 4\}$, the solution set is $\{3\}$. **Answer.**

1. $t + 2 = 4; t \in \{1, 2\}$

2. $z - 3 = 5; z \in \{7, 8\}$

3. $2y + 3 = 7; y \in \{0, 2\}$

4. $3n - 1 = 8; n \in \{3, 4\}$

5. $2t + 1 < 11; t \in \{4, 5\}$

6. $3x + 1 > 8; x \in \{3, 4\}$

7. $4x < x + 2; x \in \{0, 1\}$

8. $d + 3 = 3 + d; d \in \{1, 3\}$

9. $\frac{x}{2} \neq x - 2; x \in \{4, 8\}$

10. $2x \neq 4x - 2; x \in \{\frac{1}{2}, 1\}$

11. $3(y + 1) = 3y + 3; y \in \{2, 4, 6\}$

12. $2(x + 2) = 8; x \in \{0, 2, 4\}$

Solve each open sentence over the given set.

SAMPLE 2. $x + 1 > x$; {the whole numbers}

Solution: Since the sum of x and 1 is one greater than x for *every* whole number x, the solution set of $x + 1 > x$ over {the whole numbers} is {the whole numbers}. **Answer.**

13. $x - 1 < x; x \in \{\text{the whole numbers}\}$

14. $x + 2 > x; x \in \{\text{the whole numbers}\}$

15. $t + 4 = 3; t \in \{\text{the whole numbers}\}$

16. $x + 1 = 7$; $x \in$ {the whole numbers}

17. $x + \frac{1}{2} = 1$; $x \in$ {the positive numbers}

18. $y - \frac{1}{2} = 1$; $y \in$ {the positive numbers}

19. $x + 1 < 2$; $x \in$ {the nonnegative integers}

20. $z + 2 = 2$; $z \in$ {the nonnegative integers}

Written Exercises

In Exercises 1–12, substitute members of the given replacement set in the open sentence, tell whether the resulting statements are true, and specify each solution set by roster.

A

1. $x + 3 = 7$; $\{3, 4, 5\}$

2. $x + 2 = 3$; $\{0, 1, 2\}$

3. $y > 4$; $\{3, 4, 5\}$

4. $z < 2$; $\{0, 1, 2\}$

5. $x \neq 4$; $\{2, 3, 4\}$

6. $y \neq 0$; $\{0, 1, 2\}$

7. $2x = 6$; $\{1, 2, 3\}$

8. $3y = 12$; $\{3, 4, 5\}$

9. $2z < 8$; $\{1, 2, 3\}$

10. $3x > 8$; $\{3, 4, 5\}$

11. $x^2 < 9$; $\{1, 2, 3\}$

12. $y^2 > 2$; $\{0, 1, 2\}$

Solve each sentence over the given set. Specify the solution set of each equation in roster form. Graph the solution set of each inequality.

SAMPLE 1. $2x + 1 = 5$; {the positive numbers}

Solution: By inspection, 4 is the only arithmetic number whose sum with 1 is 5. This means that $2x$ must represent 4. The one and only positive number replacement for x for which $2x = 4$ is 2. $\{2\}$. **Answer.**

SAMPLE 2. $3x < 6$; {the nonnegative numbers}

Solution: Since if $3x$ is to be less than 6, x must be less than 2, you have:

Answer.

13. $y + 3 = 9$ {the whole numbers}

14. $z - 2 = 10$ {the whole numbers}

15. $4t = 12$ {the whole numbers}

16. $7r = 28$ {the whole numbers}

17. $2 = \dfrac{y}{3}$ {the whole numbers}

18. $8 = \frac{1}{2}n$ {the whole numbers}

19. $2x + 1 = 11$ {the positive numbers}

20. $3y + 2 = 11$ {the positive numbers}

21. $11 = 6x - 1$ {the real numbers}

22. $14 = 8z - 2$ {the real numbers}

23. $x + 1 < 7$ {the positive integers}

24. $y + 2 < 10$ {the positive integers}

25. $2x < 13$ {the whole numbers}

26. $5x < 11$ {the whole numbers}

27. $x + 1 > 2$ {the nonnegative numbers}

28. $t + 3 > 5$ {the nonnegative numbers}

29. $10 < 5l$ {the positive numbers}

30. $21 < 7l$ {the positive numbers}

31. $x + 3 = 3 + x$ {the real numbers}

32. $2x = x + x$ {the real numbers}

33. $x^2 < 4$ {the nonnegative numbers}

34. $y^2 > 9$ {the nonnegative numbers}

35. $2x = x + 2$ {the integers}   **36.** $3x = 6 + x$ {the integers}

In Exercises 37–50, substitute the members of the given replacement sets in the open sentence, and tell whether the resulting statements are true or false.

SAMPLE 3. $3l + m = 4;\ l \in \{1, 2\},\ m \in \{0, 1\}$

Solution: $3(1) + 0 = 4$; false $3(2) + 0 = 4$; false

              $3(1) + 1 = 4$; true $3(2) + 1 = 4$; false

$\boxed{B}$ **37.** $r + s = 7$ $r \in \{3, 4\},\ s \in \{3, 4\}$

38. $p - q = 5$ $p \in \{9, 10\},\ q \in \{4, 5\}$

39. $x + 2y = 11$ $x \in \{5, 6\},\ y \in \{3, 4\}$

40. $2w + 3z = 12$ $w \in \{1, 2\},\ z \in \{3, 4\}$

41. $x < 2y$ $x \in \{3, 4\},\ y \in \{1, 2\}$

42. $3x > y + 2$ $x \in \{2, 3\},\ y \in \{4, 5\}$

43. $x + yz = x(y + z)$ $x \in \{1\},\ y \in \{2\},\ z \in \{0, 1\}$

44. $l + mn = lm + n$ $l \in \{0\},\ m \in \{1\},\ n \in \{2, 3\}$

$\boxed{C}$ **45.** $3x - 2y = 9$ $x \in \{5, 6, 7\},\ y \in \{3, 4, 5\}$

46. $2m + 4n = 20$ $m \in \{3, 4, 5\},\ n \in \{2, 3, 4\}$

47. $3x + 2y > 26$ $x \in \{4, 5, 6\},\ y \in \{4, 5, 6\}$

48. $2x < 4z + 2$ $x \in \{4, 5, 6\},\ z \in \{0, 1, 2\}$

49. $x + 3y \neq 2x + y$ $x \in \{0, 1, 2\},\ y \in \{0, 2, 4\}$

50. $2t - r \neq 3t - 2r$ $t \in \{1, 2, 3\},\ r \in \{1, 2, 3\}$

2–5 Variables and Quantifiers

How many real numbers satisfy the equation

$$y + 9 = 9 + y?$$

If you replace y with "1," you obtain the true statement

$$1 + 9 = 9 + 1.$$

In fact, whatever numeral you use in place of y in the given sentence, you will obtain a true statement. To assert this fact, you may write:

For all real numbers y, $y + 9 = 9 + y$.

Other forms of this statement are:

For each real number y, $y + 9 = 9 + y$.

For every real number y, $y + 9 = 9 + y$.

For any real number y, $y + 9 = 9 + y$.

If y is any real number, then $y + 9 = 9 + y$.

Now consider the assertion

For each positive integer x, $x + 1 > 7$.

This statement is surely false, because when you replace x with "2" you obtain the false statement

$$2 + 1 > 7.$$

On the other hand, if you replace x with "8," then you convert the open sentence "$x + 1 > 7$" into the true statement

$$8 + 1 > 7.$$

Because there is a positive integer x for which "$x + 1 > 7$" is a true statement, you can make the following true assertion:

There is a positive integer x such that $x + 1 > 7$.

Of course, there are many positive integers for which "$x + 1 > 7$" is a true statement. But, the existence of *at least one* is enough to guarantee the truth of the given assertion. Other ways to state this fact are:

There exists a positive integer x such that $x + 1 > 7$.

For at least one positive integer x, $x + 1 > 7$.

For some positive integer x, $x + 1 > 7$.

Such key words as *all, each, every, any, there is, there exists, there are, there exist, some,* and *at least one* involve the idea of "how many" or of "quantity." For this reason you call such an expression a **quantifier** when it is used in combination with a variable in an open sentence.

EXAMPLE. Use a quantifier to change each open sentence into a true statement.

a. $2n - 5 = 11$ b. $x \neq x + 1$

Solution: Assume that the domain of each variable is the set of real numbers.

a. There exists a real number n such that $2n - 5 = 11$.

b. For all real numbers x, $x \neq x + 1$.

Oral Exercises

Tell which of the following statements are true and which are false.

1. There exist positive integers.
2. Some numbers are even integers.
3. Some equations have real numbers as roots.
4. Every equation has at least one positive root.
5. All girls have blond hair.
6. Every square has four sides.
7. Each real number is greater than zero.
8. Some negative numbers are less than one.
9. Any positive integer is greater than zero.
10. At least one number satisfies the equation $x^3 = 0$.
11. There is a real number y such that $y^2 > 0$.
12. For all real numbers s, $s + s = 2s$.
13. For each real number k, $k^2 \neq k$.
14. For some real number b, $b = 2b$.
15. If x is any real number, then $3 \times x = x + 3$.
16. If w is any real number, then $w > 0$.

Written Exercises

Show that each of the following statements is true by finding the value of the variable for which the statement is true.

1. For some natural number t, $2t = 6$.
2. There is a real number s such that $s \div 4 \neq 3$.
3. There exists an integer y such that $3y - 1 > 5$.
4. At least one positive number satisfies the equation "$x^2 = 1$."

Show that each of the following statements is false by finding a value of the variable for which the statement is false.

5. For every integer x, $x + 2 = 3$.
6. All real numbers y are greater than 0.
7. Any whole number m is less than $2m$.
8. The square of each natural number k is greater than k.

Show that each of the following statements is true by finding the value of b for which it is true.

SAMPLE. For each whole number a, there is a whole number b that exceeds a by 5.

Solution: Let $b = a + 5$. **Answer.**

9. For each real number a, there is a real number b that is 5 times as great as a.
10. For each real number a, there is a real number b that is half as great as a.

2–6 Applying Mathematical Expressions and Sentences

Mathematical expressions and sentences are often applied in real life situations to describe numerical relationships.

For example, the expression

$$x + 3x$$

can represent the sum of the weights of a boy and his father if the boy weighs x pounds and his father weighs three times as much, that is, $3x$ pounds.

The equation

$$x + 3x = 200$$

describes mathematically the situation in which the sum of the weights of the boy and the man is 200 pounds.

The same mathematical expression or sentence may represent the numerical facts in more than one situation. For instance, the equation "$x + 3x = 200$" also describes the following sentence in symbols.

A certain number when added to 3 times itself yields a sum of 200.

Still another situation represented by the same equation is the following one.

A rope, 200 feet long, is cut into two pieces of different lengths.

The longer piece is 3 times as long as the shorter one.

Can you think of an interpretation of the following inequality?

$$2y > y + 7.$$

Below are two ways of interpreting this inequality.

Twice a given number is greater than 7 more than the number.

Here y represents the given number.

Carlos is twice as old as his sister, Maria. In fact, Carlos is more than 7 years older than Maria.

Here y represents Maria's age in years, and $2y$ represents Carlos' age in years.

Oral Exercises

In Exercises 1–8, let n represent a certain number. Then express the number described in each exercise in terms of n.

1. It is 5 more than n.

2. It is 2 less than n.

3. It is 1 less than twice n.

4. It is 3 more than half of n.

5. Its sum with n is 40.

6. Subtracted from n, it gives a difference of 1.

7. The product of it and n is 24.

8. The quotient of it by n is 3.

9. If y is an integer, what are the next two greater integers?

10. If e is an even integer, what are the next two greater even integers?

11. How much do s six-cent stamps cost?

12. How many calories are there in m glasses of milk, each containing 170 calories?

13. The sum of two numbers is 34. If one number is represented by x, represent the other number in terms of x.

14. From a number y, another number is subtracted to yield a difference of 7. Represent the other number in terms of y.

15. If Al is a years old now, how old will he be next year? 2 years from now? 20 years from now?

16. If Gail is b years old now, how old was she last year? 5 years ago? 10 years ago?

17. Mrs. Sharron helped three more than twice as many customers on Monday than Mrs. Gans did. If Mrs. Gans helped b customers, how many customers did Mrs. Sharron help?

18. The distance across a baseball diamond from first base to third base is 1.4 times the distance from home plate to third base. If the distance from home plate to third base is t feet, what is the distance from first to third base?

19. A salesman sold r cassette recorders during his first week on a new job. If he increased his sales by 15 recorders during each of the next two weeks, how many did he sell during his third week on the job?

20. On his third weekly examination, Pete earned a grade of 90. If his weekly grades had increased at the rate of p points per week, what was his grade on the first examination?

Written Exercises

In Exercises 1–10, explain why the numerical relationship described in words can be represented by the given open sentence.

SAMPLE 1. $x - 4 = 28$
Mrs. Reiner, who is 28 years old, is 4 years younger than her husband.

Solution: Let x represent Mr. Reiner's age in years.
Then $x - 4$ represents Mrs. Reiner's age in years.
Since Mrs. Reiner is 28 years old, $x - 4 = 28$.

SAMPLE 2. $w + (w + 8) + w + (w + 8) < 152$
A rectangle whose perimeter is less than 152 centimeters is 8 centimeters longer than it is wide.

Solution: Let w represent the width in centimeters (cm.) of the rectangle. Then $w + 8$ represents the length in cm. of the rectangle. Since the perimeter is the sum of the lengths of the four sides of the rectangle, and the perimeter is less than 152 centimeters,

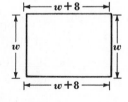

$$w + (w + 8) + w + (w + 8) < 152.$$

A **1.** $k + 8 = 53$
After depositing \$8, Rick had \$53 in his savings-bank account.

2. $24{,}500 = t + 6000$
The population of Bertown is 6000 less today than it was ten years ago when 24,500 people lived there.

3. $g + (g + 1) = 19$
In a certain class of 19 students, the number of boys exceeds the number of girls by 1.

4. $2y + 1 = 15$
Fifteen-year-old Fred is 1 year more than twice as old as his brother, Jody.

5. $s + s + (s - 8) = 35$
In an isosceles triangle whose perimeter is 35 inches, the base is 8 inches shorter than each of the two congruent sides.

6. $z + (z - 2) + (z + 3) = 22$
The sum of three numbers is 22. The second of the numbers is two less than the first, and the third is three more than the first.

7. $t + 2 = 2(t - 7)$
Two years from now, Marge will be twice as old as she was 7 years ago.

8. $39(t + 75) = 48t$
In a certain office, a keypunch operator earns seventy-five cents more per hour than a typist. In 39 hours, the keypunch operator earns as much as a typist does in 48 hours.

9. $10d + 5(d + 11) > 250$
A newsboy has more than \$2.50 in dimes and nickels. He has 11 more nickels than dimes.

10. $6s + 10(s + 15) < 300$
Mr. Hoyer spent less than \$3.00 to buy some six-cent and some ten-cent postage stamps. He bought 15 more ten-cent stamps than six-cent ones.

● CHAPTER SUMMARY ●

Inventory of Structure and Method

1. A **variable** is a symbol which may represent any of the members of a specified set, called the **domain** or **replacement set**. A variable with just one value is called a **constant**. An expression containing a variable is called an **open expression**. **Evaluating an expression** is the process of replacing the variable in an open expression with the numeral for the given value and simplifying the result. A **term** is a mathematical expression using numerals or variables or both to indicate a product or a quotient.

2. When two or more numbers are multiplied, each is called a **factor** of the product. In a term containing numerical and variable factors, the numerical part of the term is called the **numerical coefficient**. The expression $x \cdot x$ can be written in **exponential form** as x^2, where the **exponent** ^{2} indicates the number of times the **base** x occurs as a factor in the product.

3. To eliminate ambiguity about the meaning of an expression in which grouping symbols have been omitted, follow the rules for the **order of operations**:
   a. Simplify the names of powers.
   b. Simplify the names of products and quotients in order from left to right.
   c. Simplify the names of sums and differences in order from left to right.

4. An **open sentence** is a sentence that contains one or more variables. The set consisting of the members of the domain of the variable for which an open sentence is true is called the **truth set** or the **solution set** of the open sentence over a given domain. Each member of this set is known as a **solution**. A solution of an equation is also called a **root**.

5. A **quantifier** is a word denoting the idea of "how many" used in combination with a variable in an open sentence.

6. Mathematical expressions and sentences can be applied to real life situations to describe numerical relationships.

Vocabulary and Spelling

Review the meaning of each term by reference to the page listed.

program (*p. 31*)
variable (*p. 32*)
replacement set (domain) (*p. 32*)
value of a variable (*p. 32*)
constant (*p. 32*)
variable (open) expression (*p. 32*)
mathematical expression (*p. 32*)
evaluate an expression (*p. 32*)
value of an expression (*p. 32*)
term (*p. 32*)
factor (*p. 36*)
coefficient (*p. 36*)

exponent (*p. 37*)
base (*p. 37*)
factored (expanded) form of a power (*p. 37*)
exponential form (*p. 37*)
open sentence (*p. 44*)
truth (solution) set (*p. 44*)
solution (*p. 44*)
root· (*p. 44*)
graph of an open sentence (*p. 44*)
quantifier (*p. 49*)

Chapter Test

2–1 Evaluate the following expressions if x has the value 4 and y has the value $\frac{1}{4}$.

1. $3x$ **2.** $4y + x$ **3.** $3(x - 6y) + xy$ **4.** $(x + y)(x - y)$

2–2 Give the set of factors of each of the expressions.

5. t **6.** $3ab$ **7.** $\dfrac{xy}{2}$

Give the missing coefficients, as indicated.

8. $7xyz = (?)yz$ **9.** $\dfrac{pq}{8} = (?)pq$

Evaluate the following expressions if a, b, and c have the values 1, 2, and 3.

10. ab^2c **11.** $\dfrac{c^2}{ab}$ **12.** $2a^2b + c^3$

2–3 Simplify each of the expressions.

13. $28 \div 7 \times 2^2$ **15.** $14 \div 2 + 2 - 1$

14. $5(6 + 2) \div 4$ **16.** $\dfrac{7 \cdot 3 + 7 \cdot 2^2}{9 - 2}$

2–4 The replacement set for x is $\{2, 4, 6, 8\}$. Which of the elements make each of the following open sentences true?

17. $x - 2 = 2$ **18.** $x - 2 > 2$

From $\{1, 2, 3, 4 \ldots, 10\}$ determine the solution set of each sentence.

19. $3x + 4 = 10$ **20.** $3x + 4 > 10$

2–5 Tell which of the following statements are true and which are false.

21. For all real numbers r, $r^3 \neq r$.

22. For some real numbers t, $t = \frac{1}{2}t$.

23. If y is any real number, then $y - 2 = y \div 2$.

2–6 **24.** Write an algebraic expression for the profit realized on the sale of 12 portable radios if the cost to the dealer for each radio is c, and the selling price for each radio to the customer is s.

25. Write an open sentence stating that the length of a hallway is 2 feet more than four times its width.

Chapter Review

2–1   Variables

Pages 31–36

1. A __?__ is a symbol which may represent any of the members of a specified set.

Evaluate the expression if w has the value 2, x has the value 3, y has the value 4, z has the value 5.

2. $\dfrac{wx - y}{wz + y}$

3. $5yz \div (wy - x)$

2–2   Factors, Coefficients, and Exponents

Pages 36–41

Evaluate the expression if a has the value 0, b has the value 1, c has the value 2, and d has the value 3.

4. $\dfrac{b^2 - a}{d^2 - c}$

5. $[d^3 - (b + c)] \div (c^3 + a)$

2–3   Order of Operations

Pages 41–43

Simplify each expression following the rules for the order of operations.

6. $10 - 2 \cdot 3$

7. $12 + 2 - (3 + 1)$

2–4   Variables and Open Sentences

Pages 44–47

Solve each sentence over the given set.

8. $3x + 1 = 10$; {the positive integers}
9. $24 > 4x$; {the nonnegative numbers}
10. $y + y = 2y$; {the real numbers}

2–5   Variables and Quantifiers

Pages 48–50

Indicate whether the following statements are true or false.

11. All negative numbers are greater than zero.
12. There exists a real number y such that $y^2 = y$.

2–6   Applying Mathematical Expressions and Sentences

Pages 50–53

In Exercises 13–16, translate from words to mathematical symbols.

13. The difference between $7c$ and 7
14. One-half the sum of x and y
15. x^2 increased by 4
16. 8 more than b

Who Uses Mathematics?

One of the newest fields offering career opportunities to both men and women is the one connected with large-scale electronic computers such as the one shown above. There is scarcely an industry or a branch of government that does not make use of a computer. Perhaps your school has had one installed or is connected by a terminal to a computer many miles away.

If you look in the Help Wanted section of any large-city newspaper, you will find that companies are looking for persons who understand computer engineering, computer programming, data processing, program analyzing, data systems, and so on. An interesting project would be to make a collection of such ads.

Perhaps you would like to investigate the field of computers as you look forward to a career. Taking all the mathematics courses you can will be excellent preparation. Some of the Extras for Experts in this book will introduce you to flow charts — a tool of the programmer.

Using Open Sentences in Flow Charts

Below is a diagram of the program described on pages 31–32. To picture the steps in the program, the diagram uses boxes with directions of what to do written in them. The order in which to carry out these directions is shown by arrows. Such a diagram is called a **flow chart** or a **flow diagram**. Flow charts are often used in analyzing lengthy computations to be carried out by an electronic computer like the one pictured on page 57.

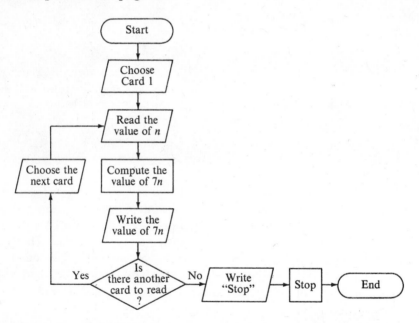

Notice that the shape of each box shows the kind of operation described in the box. Flow charts in this book will use boxes of the four different shapes to indicate four different kinds of operation.

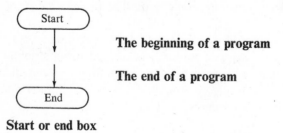

The beginning of a program

The end of a program

Start or end box

Input-output box

In this box, you describe a step to begin or to complete an *input* operation (reading) or an *output* operation (writing). Variables or expressions whose values are to be read or written may be named in the box. Input or output word messages may also be stated in the box. Such messages are shown in quotation marks.

In this box, you describe computations to be carried out, or you assign a value to a variable.

Computation or assignment box

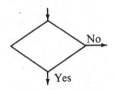

In this box, you ask a question to be answered "Yes" or "No." The box has two exits, labeled to show how the program continues, depending on the answer to the question.

Decision box

EXAMPLE. Given the flow chart at the right, what value will be written by the program if the values read for *a*, *b*, and *c* are 2, 5, and 3?

Solution:

The values of *a*, *b*, and *c* are 2, 5, and 3.

$$\therefore b^2 - 4ac = 5^2 - 4 \cdot 2 \cdot 3$$
$$= 25 - 24$$
$$= 1.$$

Since $b^2 - 4ac = 1$ and $1 > 0$, the answer to the question "Is $b^2 - 4ac$ less than 0?" is "No." Therefore, the "No" path is followed in the flow chart, and the value of $b^2 - 4ac$ is written, that is, 1.   **Answer.**

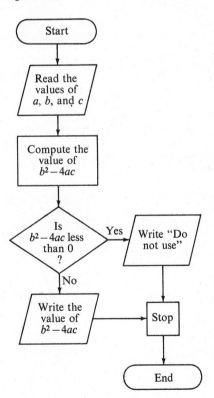

Often the question asked in a decision box is written as an open sentence. When an open sentence is used in a decision box, the exits from the box may be labeled T (for True) and F (for False). For instance, in the Example on page 59, the decision box shown as

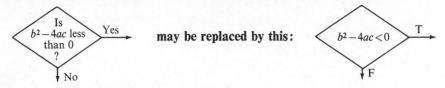

Exercises

In a flow chart what kind(s) of operations are described in boxes of the shapes shown in Exercises 1–4?

1.   **2.**   **3.**   **4.**

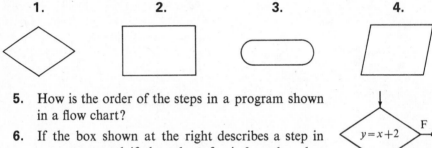

5.   How is the order of the steps in a program shown in a flow chart?

6.   If the box shown at the right describes a step in a program and if the value of x is 3, under what condition will the T path be taken in the program? the F path?

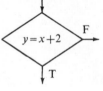

Exercises 7 and 8 refer to the flow chart at the right.

7.   What will be written if the value of a is -3 and the value of b is 4?

8.   What will be written if the values of a and b are both 6?

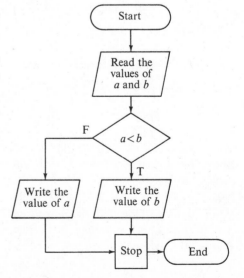

The Shorthand of Algebra

The time was the sixteenth century. France and Spain were at war. As in every war, both sides sent their messages in code to hide their plans from the enemy.

But the Spanish secrets could not be kept. Whenever the French captured a Spanish messenger, they read the message accurately. How could this be? Who was breaking the code?

It was a French lawyer François Viète (Fron-swah Vee-**yet**) [or Vieta (Vee-ay-**tah**)], whose hobby was algebra. Code-breaking was nothing to him but solving equations.

The French king owed Vieta a debt of gratitude. So do generations of algebra students.

François Viète (1540–1603)

For Vieta not only broke the Spanish code; he simplified the whole subject of algebra. Before his time, there was practically no use of signs and symbols; everything was done in words. Vieta introduced the use of letters (he used vowels for variables and consonants for constants). Also, he used signs of operation — to show whether to add, subtract, multiply, or divide.

Many other people also contributed signs and symbols to the shorthand of algebra. Thomas Harriot (1560–1621) was caught up in the spirit of vigor and creativity which pervaded England during the reign of Elizabeth I. His career began with studies at Oxford, and soon after, he served as Sir Walter Raleigh's tutor in mathematics. To Harriot we owe two of the most useful mathematical notations, the symbols $>$ and $<$. The use of the sign $=$ for equality, though introduced by another mathematician, Robert Recorde (1510?–1558), is partly due to Harriot, since he helped persuade other mathematicians of the day to adopt this notation.

1. 14.ᵶℯ.─┼─.15.ϙ.════71.ϙ.

2. 20.ᵶℯ.──────.18.ϙ.═══.102.ϙ.

3. 26.ᵶ.─┼─10ᵶℯ══9.ᵶ.──10ᵶℯ─┼─213.ϙ.

4. 19.ᵶℯ─┼─192.ϙ.═══10ᵶ.─┼─108ϙ──19ᵶℯ

5. 18.ᵶℯ─┼─24.ϙ.══8.ᵶ.─┼─2.ᵶℯ.

6. 34ᵶ.────12ᵶℯ══40ᵶℯ─┼─480ϙ──9.ᵶ.

Lines from Robert Recorde's Whetstone of Witte (*London, 1557*) *showing his equality signs.*

... the IBM Building in Seattle, Washington,
designed by Minoru Yamasaki and Associates

Addition and Multiplication
of Real Numbers

You will now learn about some of the basic assumptions on which algebra is built. You will begin to understand what is meant by the *structure* of algebra.

IDENTIFYING AXIOMS

3–1 Axioms of Closure and Equality

When you add two whole numbers, is the sum *always* a whole number? To try every example would be an endless task. After checking a large number of varied examples,

$$138 + 51 = 189, \qquad 174 + 236 = 410, \qquad \text{and so on,}$$

you would probably *assume* that the answer is, "Yes, the sum of two whole numbers is always a whole number."

Is this true also for multiplication? Again you try many examples:

$$5 \times 37 = 185, \qquad 23 \times 48 = 1104, \qquad \text{and so on.}$$

Again you will, no doubt, assume that the product of two whole numbers is always a whole number.

Any set S is said to be **closed under an operation** performed on its elements, provided that each result of the operation is an element of S. Thus, the set of whole numbers is closed under both addition and multiplication. In general, calculations with real numbers are based on the often unstated assumption that the set of real numbers is closed under addition and multiplication.

In mathematics, assumptions (statements accepted as true without proof) are called **axioms** or **postulates**. The **axioms of closure** follow.

Axiom of Closure for Addition

For all real numbers a and b, the sum $a + b$ is a unique (one and only one) real number.

Axiom of Closure for Multiplication

For all real numbers a and b, the product ab is a unique real number.

Notice that closure under any operation depends on *both* the particular *operation* and the *set* of numbers used. For example, the set of odd numbers is closed under multiplication. But it is *not* closed under addition because there are odd numbers whose sum is not odd, for instance, $3 + 5 = 8$. On the other hand, under division the set of whole numbers is not closed, but the set of positive real numbers is.

Can a finite set be closed under an operation? Looking at the addition and multiplication tables at the right, you can see that $\{0, 1\}$ is closed under multiplication, but *not* under addition (since $2 \notin \{0, 1\}$).

+	0	1
0	0	1
1	1	2

×	0	1
0	0	0
1	0	1

The way that we have agreed to use the equals symbol $=$ (section 1–1) gives equality the following properties.

Axioms of Equality

For all real numbers a, b, and c:

Reflexive Property $a = a$

Symmetric Property   If $a = b$, then $b = a$.

Transitive Property   If $a = b$ and $b = c$, then $a = c$.

EXAMPLE 1. Name the property of equality which is illustrated.

    a. If $5 + 4 = 9$, then $9 = 5 + 4$.

    b. If $1 + 6 = 7$ and $7 = 5 + 2$, then $1 + 6 = 5 + 2$

Solution: **a.** The symmetric property

                b. The transitive property

EXAMPLE 2. Which property of equality asserts that

    a. every equation is reversible?

    b. every real number is equal to itself?

    c. if each of two given numbers equals a third number, then the given numbers are equal?

Solution: **a.** The symmetric property

                b. The reflexive property

                c. The symmetric and transitive properties

Oral Exercises

Which of the following sets are closed under the given operation? Why?

SAMPLE 1. $\{0, 2, 4, 6, \ldots\}$, multiplication

Solution: Closed, because the product of two even whole numbers is an even whole number.

SAMPLE 2. $\{1, 2, 3, 4, \ldots\}$, finding the average of two numbers. (Recall that the average of two numbers is one-half their sum.)

Solution: Not closed, because $\dfrac{1 + 2}{2} = \dfrac{3}{2}$, and $\dfrac{3}{2}$ is not a counting number.

1. $\{0, 1, 2\}$, addition
2. $\{1, 3, 5\}$, multiplication
3. $\{1\}$, multiplication

4. $\{0\}$, addition
5. $\{0, 3\}$, subtraction
6. $\{1, 2\}$, division

7. $\{1, 3, 5, 7, \ldots\}$, multiplication
8. $\{0, 2, 4, 6, \ldots\}$, addition
9. $\{$the natural numbers$\}$, division
10. $\{3, 6, 9, 12, \ldots\}$, addition
11. $\{$the powers of 2$\}$, multiplication
12. $\{1, \frac{1}{2}, 2, \frac{1}{4}, 4, \frac{1}{8}, 8, \ldots\}$, division
13. $\{$the positive even integers$\}$, multiplication by 3
14. $\{$the positive even integers$\}$, finding the average of two numbers

Name the closure axiom or the property of equality illustrated by each of the following true statements.

15. If $15 - 3 = 12$, then $12 = 15 - 3$.
16. $7 \cdot 3$ is a real number.
17. $8 + (^-9)$ is a real number.
18. Given that $2 = 8 - 6$; therefore, $8 - 6 = 2$.
19. For all real numbers x and y, $x + y = x + y$.
20. If r denotes a real number and $r + 2 = 0$, then $0 = r + 2$.
21. Given that $x + 4 = 13$ and that $13 = 9 + 4$; therefore, $x + 4 = 9 + 4$.
22. Given that $7y = 35$ and that $35 = 7 \cdot 5$; therefore, $7y = 7 \cdot 5$.
23. Given that $2(1 + 0) = 2$ and that $2 = 2 + 0$; therefore, $2(1 + 0) = 2 + 0$.
24. Given that $\frac{3}{5} \div \frac{2}{7} = \frac{3}{5} \times \frac{7}{2}$ and that $\frac{3}{5} \times \frac{7}{2} = \frac{21}{10}$; therefore, $\frac{3}{5} \div \frac{2}{7} = \frac{21}{10}$.

Written Exercises

Which of the following sets are closed under each of the operations of addition, multiplication, subtraction, and division (excluding division by zero)? When the set is not closed, give an example which shows this.

SAMPLE.   {the real numbers between 0 and 1}

Solution: Addition — not closed, as $\frac{7}{8} + \frac{3}{8} = \frac{10}{8}$, which is not in the set.
Subtraction — not closed, as $\frac{1}{4} - \frac{1}{4} = 0$, which is not in the set.
Division — not closed, as $\frac{1}{2} \div \frac{1}{4} = 2$, which is not in the set.
Multiplication — closed.

A
1. {1}
2. {2}
3. {0}
4. {$\frac{1}{2}$}

5. {0, 1}
6. {1, 2}
7. {1, $\frac{1}{2}$, 2}

8. {0, 5, 10, 15, . . .}
9. {the natural numbers}
10. {the whole numbers}

B
11. {the real numbers greater than 1}
12. {1, $\frac{1}{3}$, $\frac{1}{9}$, $\frac{1}{27}$, $\frac{1}{81}$, . . .}
13. {the positive real numbers}
14. {the positive real numbers that are not whole numbers}

3–2   Commutative and Associative Axioms

In arithmetic you assume that when you add two numbers, you get the same sum no matter what order you use in adding them. Thus,

$$8 + 2 = 2 + 8 \quad \text{and} \quad 10 + 3 = 3 + 10.$$

This assumption is called the **commutative** (kuh-**myū**-tuh-tiv) **axiom of addition**.

Commutative Axiom of Addition

For all real numbers a and b, $a + b = b + a$.

Similarly, $8 \times 2 = 2 \times 8$ and $10 \times 3 = 3 \times 10$. When you multiply numbers, you obtain the same product regardless of the order of the factors.

Commutative Axiom of Multiplication

For all real numbers a and b, $ab = ba$.

You say that addition and multiplication of real numbers are *commutative operations*. Notice that subtraction and division are *not* commutative operations. For example, $8 - 2 \neq 2 - 8$ and $8 \div 2 \neq 2 \div 8$.

Addition and multiplication of real numbers are **binary operations** because you find a sum or a product by working with *two* numbers at a time. Therefore, to find the sum

$$93 + 7 + 78$$

you must decide how to begin. You may decide to add 93 and 7 first, obtaining 100, and then add 78 to the result, getting 178. But if you add 7 and 78, and then add that sum, 85, to 93, you also get 178. Thus,

$$(93 + 7) + 78 = 93 + (7 + 78).$$

This example suggests that the way that you group, or *associate*, real numbers in a sum of three (or more) numbers makes no difference in the result. We say that addition in the set of real numbers is an *associative* (a-**so**-she-aý-tiv) *operation* or that addition satisfies the **associative axiom**.

Associative Axiom of Addition

For all real numbers a, b, and c, $(a + b) + c = a + (b + c)$.

Similarly, products of real numbers do not depend on the way you group the factors. For example,

$$(5 \cdot 2) \cdot 6 = 5 \cdot (2 \cdot 6) \quad \text{and} \quad (14 \cdot \tfrac{1}{3}) \cdot 9 = 14 \cdot (\tfrac{1}{3} \cdot 9).$$

Associative Axiom of Multiplication

For all real numbers a, b, and c, $(ab)c = a(bc)$.

Are subtraction and division associative operations? The following examples show that they are *not!*

EXAMPLE 1. $(24 - 12) - 3 = 12 - 3 = 9;$

$24 - (12 - 3) = 24 - 9 = 15$

$\therefore (24 - 12) - 3 \neq 24 - (12 - 3).$

EXAMPLE 2. $(24 \div 12) \div 3 = 2 \div 3 = \frac{2}{3}$;

$24 \div (12 \div 3) = 24 \div 4 = 6$

$\therefore (24 \div 12) \div 3 \neq (24 \div 12) \div 3.$

Wise use of the associative and commutative axioms of addition and multiplication can often make computations easier.

EXAMPLE 3. $17 + 2\frac{1}{3} + 63 + 7\frac{2}{3} = (17 + 63) + (2\frac{1}{3} + 7\frac{2}{3})$

$= 80 \qquad + 10$

$= 90$

EXAMPLE 4. $\frac{7}{9} \times 4 \times 27 \times 25 = (\frac{7}{9} \times 27)(4 \times 25)$

$= 21 \times 100$

$= 2100$

Oral Exercises

Name the axiom illustrated by each of the following true sentences. Assume that the replacement set of each variable is the set of real numbers.

SAMPLE. $4 + (^-3 + 5) = (^-3 + 5) + 4$

Solution: Commutative axiom of addition

1. $7 + 9 = 9 + 7$
2. $(12 + 4) + 6 = 12 + (4 + 6)$
3. $8 \cdot (9 \cdot 0) = (8 \cdot 9) \cdot 0$
4. $\frac{1}{2} \cdot 10 = 10 \cdot \frac{1}{2}$

5. For each r, $3(2r) = (3 \cdot 2)r$.
6. For each t, $t \times 7 = 7 \times t$.
7. $^-6 \cdot (8 + 1) = (8 + 1) \cdot ^-6$
8. $^-3 + 0 = 0 + ^-3$

9. For each y, $3 + (5 + y) = 8 + y$.
10. For each w, $2(3w) = 6w$.
11. $\frac{3}{5} \times (10 \times 4) = (\frac{3}{5} \times 10) \times 4$
12. $12.94 + (2.06 + 79) = (12.94 + 2.06) + 79$
13. For each m and each k, $7m + (2m + 5k) = (7m + 2m) + 5k$.
14. For each r and each s, $(r + 5)s = s(r + 5)$.
15. $(^-9 \times 7\frac{1}{2}) \times 2 = {}^-9 \times (7\frac{1}{2} \times 2)$
16. $\frac{2}{11} \times (\frac{11}{2} \times 5) = (\frac{2}{11} \times \frac{11}{2}) \times 5$
17. For each x and each y, $3 \times (6x) \times y = 18xy$.
18. For each c and d, $[5 + (c + d)] + 4(c + d) = 5 + [(c + d) + 4(c + d)]$.
19. $39 + (84 + 11) = 39 + (11 + 84)$
20. $2 \times (93 \times 50) = 2 \times (50 \times 93)$

Name the property that justifies each lettered step in these chains of equalities. A check (✓) shows that the step is justified by the substitution principle (section 1–2). In writing each chain, the transitive property of equality is also used.

21. $57 + (19 + 33) = 57 + (33 + 19)$ (a)
$= (57 + 33) + 19$ (b)
$= 90 + 19$ (✓)
$= 109$ (✓)

22. $4 \times (67 \times 25) = 4 \times (25 \times 67)$ (a)
$= (4 \times 25) \times 67$ (b)
$= 100 \times 67$ (✓)
$= 6700$ (✓)

23. For each real number g:
$8 \times (g \times 3) = 8 \times (3 \times g)$ (a)
$= (8 \times 3) \times g$ (b)
$= 24g$ (✓)

24. For each real number u:
$8 + (u + 3) = 8 + (3 + u)$ (a)
$= (8 + 3) + u$ (b)
$= 11 + u$ (✓)

25. For all real numbers t and v:
$(t + 2) + (3 + v) = [(t + 2) + 3] + v$ (a)
$= [t + (2 + 3)] + v$ (b)
$= (t + 5) + v$ (✓)
$= (5 + t) + v$ (c)
$= 5 + (t + v)$ (d)

26. For all real numbers p and q:
$(\tfrac{1}{2}p)(6q) = [(\tfrac{1}{2}p)6]q$ (a)
$= [(p \cdot \tfrac{1}{2})6]q$ (b)
$= [p(\tfrac{1}{2} \cdot 6)]q$ (c)
$= (p \cdot 3)q$ (✓)
$= (3p)q$ (d)
$= 3(pq)$ (e)

Written Exercises

In each of Exercises 1–10, simplify the expression.

A **1.** $396 + 134 + 6 + 4$ **4.** $2 \times 16 \times 19 \times 5$
2. $530 + 28 + 70 + 32$ **5.** $\tfrac{1}{2} \cdot 21 \cdot 10 \cdot \tfrac{1}{7}$
3. $25 \times 17 \times 2 \times 4$ **6.** $\tfrac{1}{3} \cdot \tfrac{5}{11} \cdot 44 \cdot 12$

7. $6\frac{1}{2} + 2\frac{1}{3} + 1\frac{1}{2} + \frac{2}{3}$ **9.** $\frac{7}{5} \cdot \frac{4}{3} \cdot \frac{5}{7} \cdot 18$

8. $99\frac{3}{5} + 1\frac{3}{7} + \frac{2}{5} + 8\frac{4}{7}$ **10.** $2 + 31 + 8 + 17\frac{1}{2} + 9 + 2\frac{1}{2}$

Given that the replacement set of the variable in each of the following sentences is the set of real numbers, specify the solution set of the sentence.

SAMPLE. $(5 + z) + 6 = 6 + (5 + z)$

Solution: The commutative axiom of addition guarantees that the equation is true for every real value of z.

∴ the solution set is the set of all real numbers.   **Answer.**

B **11.** $4 \cdot 5a = 20a$ **14.** $9d \cdot 7 = 63 \cdot 2$

12. $2 + (b + 4) = b + 6$ **15.** $4 + (x + 2) < (x + 4) + 2$

13. $(1 + n) + 5 = 5 + (6 + 1)$ **16.** $3 \cdot 4m > 4 \cdot 3m$

In each exercise an operation $*$ is defined over the set of natural numbers. In each case:

a. Find $2 * 5$.

b. Determine whether or not the set of natural numbers is closed under $*$.

c. State whether or not $*$ is (1) commutative, (2) associative.

C **17.** $a * b = a + (b + 1)$ **19.** $a * b = a - b$

18. $a * b = 2a + b$ **20.** $a * b = ab^2$

ADDING REAL NUMBERS

3–3 Addition on the Number Line

On the number line, you can illustrate some of the axioms and other facts about sums of real numbers by representing numbers by *displacements* (changes of position) on the line. A displacement in the positive direction represents a positive number, and a displacement in the negative direction represents a negative number.

For instance, to picture adding 3 and **4** on the number line in Figure 3–1, start at the origin and move 3 units to the right. The short black arrow in the diagram shows this displacement and repre-

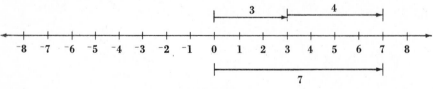

Figure 3–1

sents the number 3. Then, starting at the graph of 3, move **4** units to the right (the red arrow). Together, the two displacements amount to a displacement of 7 units to the right from the origin. Thus, the diagram pictures the fact that

$$3 + 4 = 7.$$

Figure 3–2 pictures the sum

$$4 + 3 = 7.$$

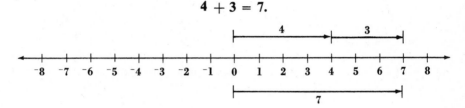

Figure 3–2

Together, Figures 3–1 and 3–2 illustrate the fact that

$$3 + 4 = 4 + 3.$$

Do you know what the sum of ⁻4 and 3 is? Figure 3–3 shows a way to determine it. Notice that ⁻4 has been represented by a displacement from the origin of 4 units to the left. When you follow this displace-

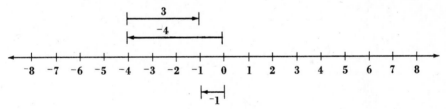

Figure 3–3

ment by a move of 3 units to the right, the net effect is a displacement from the origin of **1** unit to the **left** (heavy black arrow). Thus, the diagram suggests that

$$⁻4 + 3 = ⁻1.$$

A slightly different way to picture this fact is simply to show the displacement of 3 units, starting at the graph of ⁻4 and ending at the graph of ⁻1 (Figure 3–4).

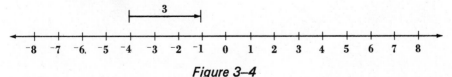

Figure 3–4

To add ⁻4 to 3, start at 3 and move 4 units to the left, again arriving at the graph of ⁻1 (Figure 3–5).

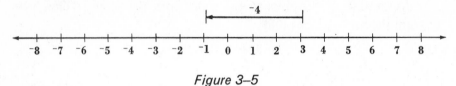

Figure 3–5

Thus, $3 + {}^-4 = {}^-1$, the same as $^-4 + 3$, illustrating again the commutative axiom.

EXAMPLE. State the addition fact suggested by each diagram.

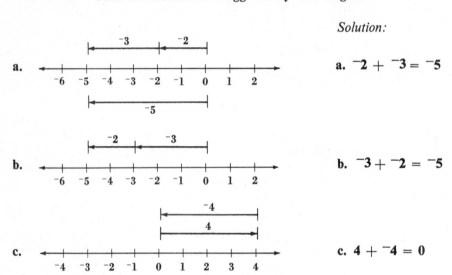

Solution:

a. $^-2 + {}^-3 = {}^-5$

b. $^-3 + {}^-2 = {}^-5$

c. $4 + {}^-4 = 0$

On the number line, you can find the sum of any two real numbers by following either one of the following rules.

> **To add two real numbers:**
>
> 1. Start at the origin and draw an arrow representing the first number. Then, from the head of that arrow, draw an arrow representing the second number. The arrow from the origin to the head of the second arrow represents the sum of the two numbers; or
>
> 2. Start at the graph of the first number, and draw an arrow representing the second number. The head of this arrow points to the graph of the sum of the two numbers.

Can you visualize ⁻4 + 0 on the number line? Interpreting "add 0" to mean "take no displacement," you can see that

$$^-4 + 0 = {}^-4 \quad \text{and} \quad 0 + {}^-4 = {}^-4.$$

These equations illustrate the special role that zero plays for addition in the set of real numbers: When 0 is added to any given number, the sum is identical with the given number. We call 0 the **identity element for addition** and accept the following statement as true.

Additive Axiom of Zero

The set of real numbers contains a unique element 0 having the property that for every real number *a*,

$$a + 0 = a \quad \text{and} \quad 0 + a = a.$$

Oral Exercises

Give an addition statement pictured by each diagram.

1.

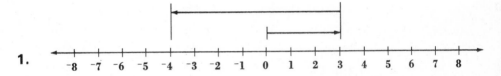

2.

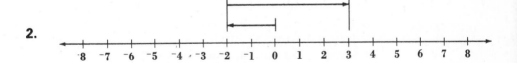

3.

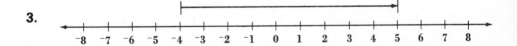

4.

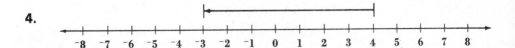

Simplify each expression. Think of displacements along the number line.

5. $^-9 + 0$	**11.** $8 + ^-5$	**17.** $46 + ^-46$
6. $0 + ^-2$	**12.** $^-2 + 1$	**18.** $6 + ^-16$
7. $^-1 + 1$	**13.** $^-9 + 4$	**19.** $^-7\frac{1}{2} + 0$
8. $3 + ^-3$	**14.** $^-6 + ^-8$	**20.** $0 + ^-\frac{2}{3}$
9. $^-7 + ^-2$	**15.** $^-43 + ^-7$	**21.** $^-5\frac{1}{2} + \frac{1}{2}$
10. $^-2 + ^-7$	**16.** $^-1 + ^-99$	**22.** $^-1\frac{1}{4} + 2\frac{1}{4}$

23. $(^-2 + ^-1) + 3$ **24.** $^-3 + (^-3 + 5)$

Written Exercises

In Exercises 1–14:

a. Simplify each expression using the number line if necessary.

b. Use the associative axiom of addition to regroup the terms in the given expression, and then simplify the resulting expression.

1. $(^-4 + 3) + ^-7$		**8.** $^-0.12 + (^-0.28 + 0.08)$
2. $(6 + ^-42) + ^-8$		**9.** $(\frac{7}{2} + ^-\frac{1}{2}) + 0$
3. $(12 + ^-24) + 6$		**10.** $(^-\frac{3}{5} + ^-\frac{7}{5}) + 2$
4. $(^-15 + ^-17) + 27$		**11.** $(^-2 + 5) + ^-3\frac{2}{3}$
5. $38 + (^-8 + 30)$		**12.** $(^-6 + 6) + ^-7\frac{3}{4}$
6. $48 + (8 + ^-22)$		**13.** $[(^-2 + 3) + ^-5] + ^-8$
7. $^-2.3 + (1.3 + 1.6)$		**14.** $[2 + (^-12 + ^-8)] + ^-22$

Solve each of the following equations given that the replacement set of the variable is the set of real numbers. Use the number line as needed.

SAMPLE 1. $^-4 + x = 2$

Solution: To arrive at 2 from $^-4$, you take a displacement of 6 units to the right.

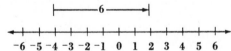

Check: $^-4 + 6 \overset{?}{=} 2$ ($\overset{?}{=}$ means "Is this statement true?")
                    $2 = 2 \checkmark$ ($\checkmark$ means "Yes, it is.")

            $\therefore$ the solution set is $\{6\}$. **Answer.**

15. $y + ^-3 = ^-5$	**18.** $t + ^-2 = ^-5$	**21.** $0 = ^-7 + b$
16. $6 + x = ^-1$	**19.** $a + ^-9 = ^-9$	**22.** $12 = ^-4 + c$
17. $^-8 + z = ^-6$	**20.** $s + 6 = 0$	**23.** $t + 8 = 20$

24. $r + {}^-4 = {}^-3$

25. $w + 24 = 0$

26. ${}^-30 + x = {}^-30$

27. $x + 5 = {}^-1$

28. $4 + y = {}^-4$

29. $n + n = 0$

30. $m + m = 8$

31. If $A = \{{}^-1, 0, 1\}$, find the set of all sums of pairs of elements of A. Be sure to include the sum of each element with itself. Is A closed under addition? Justify your answer.

Problems

a. First write the answer to each of the following questions as a sum of real numbers.

b. Find the sum.

c. Answer the question.

SAMPLE. An elevator starts at the ground floor and goes up to the 7th floor. It then goes down 5 floors and up 3 floors. At what floor is the elevator then located?

9th floor
8th floor
7th floor
6th floor
5th floor
4th floor
3rd floor
2nd floor
1st floor

Solution: **a.** $7 + {}^-5 + 3$ **b.** 5

c. The elevator is at the 5th floor. **Answer.**

A **1.** A ship sails directly north from a point A for 42 miles and then sails directly south for 57 miles. Where is the ship then located with reference to point A?

2. A saleswoman drives from her office on a turnpike 90 miles west to see a customer. She then drives 110 miles east to see a second customer. Where is she then located with respect to her office?

3. The pilot of a jet traveling at 27,000 feet above sea level is ordered by ground control to descend 8000 feet. Later, the pilot is ordered to climb 3500 feet to a new altitude. At what altitude will the jet then be flying?

4. A submarine dives to a level 730 feet below the surface of the ocean. Later it climbs 200 feet and then dives another 80 feet. What is then the depth of the submarine?

5. Lois bought four objects for \$2.15, \$3.05, \$3.40, and \$2.85. She later sold them for \$2.25, \$2.85, \$3.15, and \$2.75, respectively. What was the net financial result of the transactions?

6. A stock selling for $30 per share rose 2 dollars per share each of two days and then fell $1.75 per share for each of three days. What was the selling price per share of the stock after these events?

7. Mrs. Allen owned 650 shares of stock in the McNiff Corporation. On Monday she sold 75 shares, on Tuesday she sold 50 shares, on Wednesday she purchased 350 shares, and on Thursday sold 125 shares. How many shares of the stock did she then own?

8. On a revolving charge account, Mrs. Dallins purchased $27.50 worth of clothing, and $120.60 worth of furniture. She then made two monthly payments of $32.00 each. If the interest charges for the period of two months were $3.25, what did Mrs. Dallins then owe the account?

9. Mr. Gordon's normal blood pressure was 142. During a particularly trying period his blood pressure rose 17 points, fell 22 points, and then rose 8 points. How did his blood pressure then compare with his normal blood pressure?

10. During and after the passage of a cold front, the temperature at Pokesville fell 45°, rose 8°, fell 3°, rose 12°, and then rose 5°. How did the temperature then compare to the temperature prior to the passage of the cold front?

3–4 The Opposite of a Real Number

Figure 3–6 suggests a useful way to pair points on the number line. The paired points are at the same distance from the origin, but on opposite sides of the origin. Notice that Figure 3–6 shows the origin paired with itself.

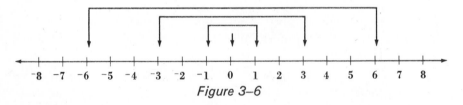

Figure 3–6

This pairing of points suggests that we also pair the coordinates of the points; for example, $^-1$ with 1, $^-3$ with 3, $^-6$ with 6, 0 with 0, and so on. You can check that adding two such paired numbers on the number line gives 0. For example, as shown in Figure 3–7

$$^-6 + 6 = 0.$$

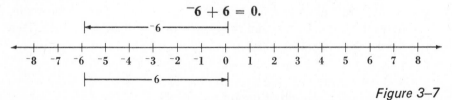

Figure 3–7

Each number in such a pair is called the **opposite** or the **additive inverse** or the **negative** of the other number. The symbol

$$-a \quad \text{(note the lowered position of the minus sign)}$$

denotes **the opposite of a** or **the additive inverse of a** or **the negative of a.** For example:

$$-6 = {}^-6, \text{ read "the opposite of six equals negative six";}$$
$$-({}^-5) = 5, \text{ read "the opposite of negative five equals five";}$$
$$-0 = 0, \text{ read "the opposite of zero equals zero."}$$

The following axiom is a formal way of saying that every real number has a unique opposite and that the sum of a number and its opposite is always zero.

Axiom of Opposites

For every real number a there is a unique real number $-a$, such that

$$a + (-a) = 0 \quad \text{and} \quad (-a) + a = 0.$$

The equation "$-6 = {}^-6$" indicates that the numerals "-6" and "${}^-6$" name the same number. This means that you can always use the numeral "-6" (lowered minus sign) in place of the numeral "${}^-6$" (raised minus sign). It also means that you can read "-6" either as "negative 6" or as "the opposite of 6." *Throughout the rest of this book, lowered minus signs will be used in the numerals for negative numbers.*

Caution! Be careful about reading *variable* expressions like $-a$. This should be read "the opposite of a" or "the additive inverse of a" or "the negative *of a*." Never call it "negative a," because $-a$ may denote either a negative number, a positive number, or zero.

By looking at the number line in Figure 3–6, you can see that the following statements are true:

1. If a is a positive number, then $-a$ is a negative number; if a is a negative number, then $-a$ is a positive number; if a is 0, then $-a$ is 0.
2. The opposite of $-a$ is a; that is, $-(-a) = a$.

EXAMPLE 1. Simplify: **a.** $-(-3)$ **b.** -0 **c.** $-(3+4)$

Solution: **a.** 3   **b.** 0   **c.** -7 **Answer.**

EXAMPLE 2. $-(-3)+(-5)=3+(-5)=-2$

Oral Exercises

Name the opposite (additive inverse) of each of the following real numbers.

SAMPLE. -14 *Solution:* 14

1. 3	**4.** -7	**7.** $-1\frac{2}{5}$	**10.** $-(3+17)$
2. 1	**5.** $\frac{1}{2}$	**8.** $-3\frac{1}{6}$	**11.** $8+(-4)$
3. -2	**6.** $\frac{1}{3}$	**9.** 1	**12.** -0

13. $5+(-4)$ **15.** $-8+(-4)$

14. $(-3)+(-6)$ **16.** $12+(-12)$

In each of Exercises 17–22, simplify the expression.

17. $11+[7+(-7)]$ **20.** $[9+(-1)]+1$

18. $(-17+17)+(-2)$ **21.** $(8+a)+(-a)$

19. $(-8+2)+(-2)$ **22.** $a+[(-a)+1]$

23. If x denotes a negative number, then $-x$ denotes a __?__ number.

24. If x denotes a positive number, then $-x$ denotes a __?__ number.

Simplify.

25. $-(-8)$ **27.** $-[-(-9)]$ **29.** $6+[-(-1)]$

26. $-(-15)$ **28.** $-[-(-0)]$ **30.** $-(-2)+2$

Written Exercises

Simplify each of the following expressions.

SAMPLE 1. $-(-5)+8$

Solution: Since $-(-5)=5$, $-(-5)+8=5+8=13$. **Answer.**

1. $-(-4)+6$ **4.** $7+[-(-4)]$ **7.** $-(-\frac{1}{2})+\frac{1}{2}$

2. $-(-8)+3$ **5.** $-(6+8)$ **8.** $-\frac{1}{3}+[-(-\frac{1}{3})]$

3. $-8+[-(-3)]$ **6.** $-(-3+10)$ **9.** $-(2.1+5.2)$

10. $-[6.75 + (-0.75)]$

11. $-[-2 + (-1)]$

12. $-[8 + (-6)]$

13. $-(-2 + 3) + (-1)$

14. $[4 + (-7)] + [-(-2)]$

15. $2\frac{1}{2} + (-3\frac{1}{2}) + \frac{1}{2}$

16. $-4\frac{2}{3} + (-\frac{1}{3}) + 2\frac{2}{3}$

In each of Exercises 17–34, replace the variable in turn by the name of each member of $\{-2, -1, 0, 1\}$, and then:

a. Tell whether each resulting statement is true or false.

b. Give the solution set of the open sentences over that replacement set.

SAMPLE 2. $-x < 0$

Solution: $-(-2) < 0$; that is, $2 < 0$; false
$-(-1) < 0$; that is, $1 < 0$; false
$-0 < 0$; that is, $0 < 0$; false
$-1 < 0$; **true**

$\therefore$ over $\{-2, -1, 0, 1\}$, the solution set is $\{1\}$.   **Answer.**

B   **17.** $-x = 2$

18. $-1 = -t$

19. $-y = 0$

20. $-s = 1$

21. $-4 = -a$

22. $-b = -2$

23. $c + (-2) = 1$

24. $d + 1 = -1$

25. $-z > 1$

26. $-x < 1$

27. $-m < -2$

28. $-y > -1$

29. $1 + [-(-x)] = -1$

30. $-(-r) + 3 = 0$

31. $-1 < -y < 2$

32. $-2 < -x < 0$

33. $0 > -m > -3$

34. $2 > -q > -2$

Given the values $\frac{5}{2}$ for x, $-\frac{1}{2}$ for y, 0.25 for z, and 1.75 for w, evaluate each expression.

C   **35.** $x + (-y) + z$

36. $-x + y + (-z)$

37. $-[x + y + (-z)]$

38. $-[-y + z + (-w)]$

39. $x + [-(w + z)]$

40. $(x + y) + [-(w + z)]$

3–5   Absolute Value

In any pair of nonzero opposites, like 5 and -5, one number is a positive number, while the other is a negative number. You call the positive number of any pair of opposite real numbers the **absolute value** of each of the numbers. Thus, 5 is the absolute value of 5; 5 is also the absolute value of -5.

The absolute value of a number is denoted by writing a name of the number between a pair of vertical bars $|\ \ |$. For example,

$$|5| = 5 \quad \text{and} \quad |-5| = 5.$$

The **absolute value of** 0 is defined to be 0 itself: $|0| = 0$.

In terms of displacement on the number line, the absolute value of a number is the length of the arrow representing the number, without regard to the direction of the arrow (Figure 3–8). You can also think of the absolute value of a number as the *distance* between the origin and the graph of the number.

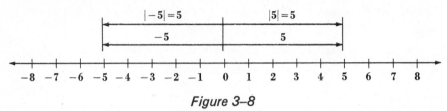

Figure 3–8

EXAMPLE 1. **Draw the graph of $|a| = 3$ if $a \in$ {the real numbers}.**

Solution: **The graph of $|a| = 3$ consists of the two points which are 3 units from the origin, that is, the points with coordinates -3 and 3.**

EXAMPLE 2. **Draw the graph of $|x| < 2$ if $x \in$ {the real numbers}.**

Solution: **The graph of $|x| < 2$ consists of all the points which are less than 2 units from the origin in either direction.**

Another inequality with this graph is $-2 < x < 2$.

The following example uses the inequality symbol $\geq$, which stands for "is greater than or equal to." Can you guess what the symbol $\leq$ means? $\leq$ stands for "is less than or equal to."

EXAMPLE 3. **Draw the graph of the set of all real numbers y such that $|y| \geq 1$.**

Solution: **The graph of $|y| \geq 1$ consists of all the points which are *at least* 1 unit from the origin on either side of the origin.**

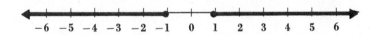

Oral Exercises

State the absolute value of each number.

1. 9	**3.** -6	**5.** $-\frac{1}{2}$	**7.** 18.6
2. 7	**4.** -10	**6.** $-\frac{4}{3}$	**8.** -27.3

Evaluate each expression.

9. $3 + |3|$ **11.** $-3 + |-3|$ **13.** $-(|-3| + |2|)$

10. $3 + |-3|$ **12.** $-|3| + |-3|$ **14.** $-(-|2| + |-2|)$

Tell whether the given statement is true or false. Give a reason for your answer.

SAMPLE 1. $|-3| > 3$

Solution: False, because $|-3| = 3$, and "$3 > 3$" is a false statement.

15. $|0| = 0$ **21.** $|-5| \leq |1 + (-6)|$

16. $|-25| \geq -25$ **22.** $|2 + (-1)| \geq |0|$

17. $|33| \leq |-33|$ **23.** $|5| + |-2| > 5 + (-2)$

18. $|-\frac{1}{2}| \leq |\frac{3}{4}|$ **24.** $|-3| + |-2| = |3| + |2|$

19. $|5 + (-1)| < |5 + 1|$ **25.** $-|2| = |-2|$

20. $|3 + (-2)| > |3 + (-3)|$ **26.** $-|-3| = -3$

27. The absolute value of every real number is greater than zero.

28. Some real numbers do not have absolute values.

29. The absolute value of any real number equals the absolute value of the opposite of the real number.

30. There is a real number which equals the absolute value of its opposite.

Written Exercises

Determine the value of each expression.

SAMPLE 1. $2|3| + (-|2|)$

Solution: $2|3| + (-|2|) = 2(3) + \{-(2)\} = 6 + (-2) = 4.$ **Answer.**

1. $6|-5|$ **5.** $|5 + (-2)| \div 3$ **9.** $2|-5| + |3|$

2. $-|3|$ **6.** $|-5 + 8| - 3$ **10.** $3|-2| + |-6|$

3. $2|-5| + |2|$ **7.** $-|-8 + 10|$ **11.** $-[3|2|] + [-|2|]$

4. $3|7| + |-7|$ **8.** $-|15 + (-9)|$ **12.** $-[4|-3|+(-6)]$

Solve each equation over the set of real numbers.

SAMPLE 2. $|x| + 1 = 5$

Solution: Since the sum of 4 and 1 is 5, $|x|$ must be equal to 4. That is, $|x| = 4$. The only two real numbers whose absolute value is 4 are -4 and 4.

         $\therefore$ the solution set is $\{-4, 4\}$.   **Answer.**

13. $|x| = 2$ **15.** $|y| + 3 = 8$ **17.** $|t| + (-2) = 3$

14. $|y| = 7$ **16.** $|z| + 5 = 20$ **18.** $|x| + (-4) = 10$

Graph the solution set of each open sentence over the set of real numbers.

B 19. $|x| < 3$ 22. $|s| \leq 4$ 25. $|y| \leq 0$

20. $|y| > 2$ 23. $|-a| = 5$ 26. $|w| > 0$

21. $|t| \geq 4$ 24. $|-b| = 1$

C 27. A teacher wrote the following statement on the chalkboard.

If a is a real number, then

$$|a| = a \quad \text{if } a \geq 0;$$
$$|a| = -a \quad \text{if } a < 0.$$

Explain why the statement is true or why it is false.

28. For what real values of y is it true that $|y| < -y$?

3–6 Rules for Addition

Numerical work often suggests general properties of real numbers. Consider the following example.

EXAMPLE 1. **Show on the number line that**

a. $-(3 + 5) = -8$ and

b. $-3 + (-5) = -8$; and, therefore, that

c. $-(3 + 5) = -3 + (-5)$.

Solution: **a. Add 3 and 5, and then find the opposite of this sum, -8.**

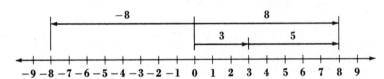

b. Add the opposite of 3 and the opposite of 5; that is, add -5 and -3. The sum is -8.

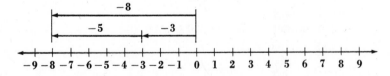

c. By part a, $-(3 + 5) = -8$.

By part b, $-3 + (-5) = -8$, so that by the symmetric property of equality, $-8 = -3 + (-5)$.

Therefore, by the transitive property of equality

$$-(3 + 5) = -3 + (-5).$$

You can use the method of Example 1 to show that the equations below are also true:

$$-[3 + (-5)] = -3 + 5, \quad -(-3 + 5) = 3 + (-5),$$
$$-[-3 + (-5)] = 3 + 5.$$

All these examples suggest the following general statement.

Property of the Opposite of a Sum

The opposite of a sum of real numbers is the sum of the opposites of the numbers; that is, for all real numbers a and b,

$$-(a + b) = (-a) + (-b).$$

You will find the property of the opposite of a sum very useful in making such substitutions for negative numbers as these:

$$-9 = -(6 + 3) = -6 + (-3), \quad -4\tfrac{1}{2} = -(4 + \tfrac{1}{2}) = -4 + (-\tfrac{1}{2}).$$

Also, by using this property along with the familiar addition facts for positive numbers and the axioms that you have learned, you can compute sums of any real numbers without having to think of the number line.

EXAMPLE 2. Simplify: $-8 + (-5)$

Solution:

$-8 + (-5) = -(8 + 5)$	**Property of the opposite of a sum**
$= -13$	**Substitution principle**
$\therefore -8 + (-5) = -13.$	**Transitive property of equality**

EXAMPLE 3. Simplify: $14 + (-6)$

Solution:

$$14 + (-6) = (8 + 6) + (-6)$$
$$= 8 + [6 + (-6)]$$
$$= 8 + 0$$
$$= 8$$
$$\therefore 14 + (-6) = 8.$$

EXAMPLE 4. Simplify: $-9 + 3$

Solution:

$$-9 + 3 = -(6 + 3) + 3$$
$$= [(-6) + (-3)] + 3$$
$$= -6 + [(-3) + 3]$$
$$= -6 + 0$$
$$= -6$$
$$\therefore -9 + 3 = -6.$$

See if you can supply the property to justify each step in Examples 3 and 4.

After computing many sums by using either the number line or the methods of Examples 2 through 4 above, you would probably figure out the short-cut method given in the following rules.

Rules for Addition

1. If a and b are each positive numbers or zero, then $a + b = |a| + |b|$.

    EXAMPLE. $6 + 8 = 14$

2. If a and b are each negative numbers, then $a + b = -(|a| + |b|)$.

    EXAMPLE. $(-6) + (-8) = -(6 + 8) = -14$

3. If a is a positive number and b is a negative number and $|a| \geq |b|$, then $a + b = |a| - |b|$.

    EXAMPLE. $14 + (-6) = 14 - 6 = 8$

4. If a is a positive number or zero and b is a negative number and $|b| \geq |a|$, then $a + b = -(|b| - |a|)$.

    EXAMPLE. $8 + (-14) = -(14 - 8) = -6$

EXAMPLE 5. Simplify: $6 + (-11) + 13 + (-5)$

Solution 1:

Step 1	Step 2	Step 3	
$6 + (-11) = -5;$	$-5 + 13 = 8;$	$8 + (-5) = 3$	**Answer.**

Solution 2:

	Step 1	Step 2	Step 3	
	6	-11	19	
	$\underline{13}$	$\underline{-\ 5}$	$\underline{-16}$	
	19	-16	3	**Answer.**

EXAMPLE 6. Add:

		Solution:	Step 1	Step 2	Step 3	
	-214		-214	132	-456	
	132		-142	211	$\underline{\ 343}$	
	211		$\underline{-100}$	$\underline{343}$	-113	**Answer.**
	-142		-456			
	$\underline{-100}$					

Oral Exercises

Give two expressions for the opposite or additive inverse of each of the following.

SAMPLE 1. $-8 + 12$ *Solution:* $8 + (-12)$, or -4

1. $-9 + (-2)$	**3.** $7 + (-7)$	**5.** $8 + (-1) + (-2)$
2. $-10 + 6$	**4.** $9 + (-5)$	**6.** $-3 + (-4) + 7$

Add.

7. 7
   $\underline{5}$

8. -3
   $\underline{-4}$

9. -7
   $\underline{5}$

10. 8
   $\underline{-11}$

11. -12
    $\underline{-10}$

12. -2
   $\underline{8}$

13. -15
    $\underline{7}$

14. -12
    $\underline{-5}$

15. $-\frac{1}{2}$
   $\underline{\frac{3}{2}}$

16. $\frac{2}{3}$
   $\underline{-\frac{8}{3}}$

Replace each __?__ by one of the words *always*, *sometimes*, *never* to convert the given sentence into a true statement having the widest application.

SAMPLE 2. The sum of two positive numbers is __?__ a positive number.

Solution: The sum of two positive numbers is always a positive number.
          Answer.

17. The sum of two negative numbers is __?__ a negative number.

18. The sum of a positive number and zero is __?__ a negative number.

19. The sum of a positive number and a negative number is __?__ a positive number.

20. The sum of two positive numbers is __?__ zero.

21. The sum of a positive number and a negative number is __?__ zero.

22. The sum of zero and a negative number is __?__ a negative number.

State whether each expression names a positive number, a negative number, or zero. Then simplify the expression.

23. $-3 + (-5)$	**29.** $-1 + (-4) + 4$
24. $-7 + 15$	**30.** $6 + (-1) + 1$
25. $18 + (-18)$	**31.** $3 + (-5) + 6$
26. $20 + (-30)$	**32.** $(-4) + 2 + 5$
27. $8 + 4 + (-4)$	**33.** $(-8) + x + (-2) + (-x)$
28. $-3 + 7 + (-7)$	**34.** $3 + (-y) + 5 + y$

Written Exercises

Simplify each expression for a sum.

A
	1.	2.	3.	4.	5.	6.
	8	−8	$2\frac{1}{2}$	4.3	123	412
	3	−2	$3\frac{1}{4}$	−2.6	−148	−213
	−5	6	$-\frac{3}{4}$	−8.1	215	−309
	2	5	−4	10.0	−300	156

7. $-8 + 7 + (-9) + 5$

8. $-12 + (-5) + 8 + 20$

9. $28 + (-17) + (-48) + 30$

10. $(-62) + (-18) + 40 + 3$

11. $122 + (-47) + (-83) + 28$

12. $-210 + (-80) + 250 + 65$

13. $-[25 + (-3)] + [-(-2 + 5)]$

14. $[-3 + (-5)] + [-(3 + 5)]$

15. $6.5 + (-2.3) + 0 + (-5.4) + (-7.2) + 15.1$

16. $-0.7 + 1.38 + (-4.4) + (-12.9) + 2$

17. $\frac{1}{2} + 3\frac{1}{2} + (-2\frac{1}{2}) + 4\frac{1}{2} + 2\frac{1}{3} + (-\frac{1}{3}) + (-1\frac{2}{3}) + 4\frac{2}{3}$

18. $\frac{4}{5} + 3\frac{2}{5} + (-2\frac{1}{5}) + 0 + (-7)$

Replace each __?__ with a numeral to make a true statement.

B
19. $\underline{} + 5 = 2$

20. $11 + \underline{} = 7$

21. $5 + \underline{} = -5$

22. $\underline{} + (-6) = 3$

23. $-2 + \underline{} = -5$

24. $-3 + \underline{} = 7$

25. $\frac{2}{5} + \underline{} = -1$

26. $\underline{} + \frac{3}{4} = -\frac{1}{4}$

In each of Exercises 27–30, write a chain of equations leading to the stated equation. Justify each step.

SAMPLE. $(a + b) + [(-a) + (-b)] = 0$

Solution: $(a + b) + [(-a) + (-b)]$

$= [a + (-a)] + [b + (-b)]$ Commutative and associative axioms of addition

$= 0 + 0$ Axiom of opposites

$= 0$ Additive axiom of zero

$\therefore (a + b) + [(-a) + (-b)] = 0.*$ Transitive property of equality

C
27. $(-5) + [(-s) + (s + 5)] = 0$

28. $-[(-a) + b] + b = a$

29. $(a + b) + [-(a + b + c)] = -c$

30. $t + [-(t + r)] = -r$

---

* This statement means that the sum of $a + b$ and $(-a) + (-b)$ is zero. But the one and only number whose sum with $a + b$ is zero is the opposite of $a + b$, that is, $-(a + b)$. Hence, $-(a + b) = (-a) + (-b)$, that is, the property of the opposite of a sum (page 83).

Problems

A 1. The Appleton Arms apartments has two levels of garage below the ground level. Starting at the lowest garage level, an elevator went to the fourth floor. From there it rose 2 floors and then dropped 4 floors. Where was the elevator then located?

2. Julie was on a diet. Her weight over a 4-week period fell 12 pounds, rose $7\frac{1}{2}$ pounds, fell 8 pounds, and rose $3\frac{1}{2}$ pounds. How did her weight then compare with her weight at the start of her diet?

3. "Whirlwind" McCoy, the left halfback on a football team, made the following yardage on successive carries of the ball: 12, -3, 5, -11, 2, -3. What was his net yardage on these six plays?

4. The ferryboat that constituted the only connection between Argyle Island and the mainland made 3 round trips. It carried 83 persons to the island on its first trip and returned 114 to the mainland. It then delivered 109 and returned 121, delivered 114 and returned 98. How did the population of the island then compare with the population before the first trip?

5. During 4 days, Mercy Hospital received 12 new patients and discharged 9, received 14 and discharged 21, received 5 and discharged 12, and received 11 and discharged 10. How did the number of patients in the hospital then compare with the number at the start of the 4-day period?

6. Miss Thompkins had a balance of $121.50 in her checking account. During the next week, she wrote checks for $47.20, $18.55, and $32.40. On Friday, she made a deposit of $52.00. What was her balance after making the deposit?

7. A helicopter was flying in Death Valley at an altitude of 47 feet below sea level. If it climbed 125 feet and then dropped 117 feet, at what altitude was it then flying?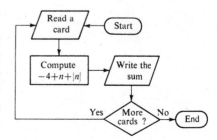

8. The Shakespeare Book Company had 7200 copies of a novel in its warehouse. During a one-week period, it shipped out 3140 books and received 2700 return copies. What was then the number of copies of this book in the warehouse?

EXTRA PROBLEM

The following values of n are shown on successive cards: 1, 0, 3, -5, 6. Given the flow chart at the right, what numbers will be written by the program? (*Note:* It is not always necessary to have a "Stop" box in a flow chart.)

MULTIPLYING REAL NUMBERS

3–7   The Distributive Axiom

Paul works Friday evenings and Saturdays at a local branch of the public library and is paid $1.60 an hour. He works 3 hours on Friday and 7 hours on Saturday. Since he works $3 + 7$ hours, his weekly earnings in dollars are

$$1.60(3 + 7) = 1.60 \times 10 = 16.00.$$

His weekly earnings are also the sum of his Friday earnings and his Saturday earnings:

$$(1.60 \times 3) + (1.60 \times 7) = 4.80 + 11.20 = 16.00.$$

Either way you compute them, his weekly earnings are the same; that is,

$$1.60(3 + 7) = (1.60 \times 3) + (1.60 \times 7).$$

Note that 1.60, the coefficient (multiplier) of the sum $3 + 7$, is *distributed* as a multiplier of each term of $3 + 7$. This example illustrates a fact that we will use in working with real numbers: multiplication is *distributive* (dis-**trib**-u-tiv) with respect to addition.

Distributive Axiom of Multiplication with Respect to Addition

For all real numbers a, b, and c,

$$a(b + c) = ab + ac \qquad \text{and} \qquad (b + c)a = ba + ca.$$

By applying the symmetric property of equality, you can also state the distributive axiom in the following form.

For all real numbers a, b, and c:

$$ab + ac = a(b + c) \qquad \text{and} \qquad ba + ca = (b + c)a.$$

The following examples show some uses of the distributive axiom.

EXAMPLE 1.   a. $36(\frac{1}{2} + \frac{1}{9}) = 36 \times \frac{1}{2} + 36 \times \frac{1}{9} = 18 + 4 = 22$

            b. $7(5\frac{2}{7}) = 7(5 + \frac{2}{7}) = 7 \times 5 + 7 \times \frac{2}{7} = 35 + 2 = 37$

            c. $\frac{1}{8} \cdot 23 + \frac{1}{8} \cdot 9 = \frac{1}{8}(23 + 9) = \frac{1}{8} \cdot 32 = 4$

EXAMPLE 2. **Show that for every real number** x,

$$4x + 3x = 7x.$$

Solution: $\quad 4x + 3x = (4 + 3)x$ **Distributive axiom**

$\qquad\qquad\quad = 7x$ **Substitution principle**

$\therefore\ 4x + 3x = 7x$ **Transitive property of equality**

Because properties of real numbers guarantee that for *all* values of the variable, each of the expressions

$$4x + 3x \quad \text{and} \quad 7x$$

represents the same number as the other expression, we call them **equivalent expressions.** When you replace a given expression by an equivalent expression with as few terms as possible, you say that you have **simplified** the given expression.

EXAMPLE 3. **Simplify:** $7y^2 + 6 + (-5)y^2$

Solution: $7y^2 + 6 + (-5)y^2 = 7y^2 + (-5)y^2 + 6$

$$= [7 + (-5)]y^2 + 6$$

$$= 2y^2 + 6$$

$\therefore\ 7y^2 + 6 + (-5)y^2 = 2y^2 + 6.$ **Answer.**

Terms such as "$7y^2$" and "$(-5)y^2$" are called *similar terms* or *like terms.* Two terms are **similar** if they are exactly alike or if they differ only in their numerical coefficients. Examples 2 and 3 show how the distributive axiom enables you to replace a sum of similar terms by a single term. Notice that an expression like "$2y^2 + 6$" in which the terms are unlike cannot be replaced by a single term.

Oral Exercises

Name the property that justifies each step.

1. $32 \times 5\frac{1}{2} = 32(5 + \frac{1}{2})$
$= 32 \cdot 5 + 32 \cdot \frac{1}{2}$
$= 160 + 16$
$= 176$

2. $45(\frac{3}{5} + \frac{2}{9}) = 45 \cdot \frac{3}{5} + 45 \cdot \frac{2}{9}$
$= 27 + 10$
$= 37$

3. $896(101) = 896(100 + 1)$
$= 896 \cdot 100 + 896 \cdot 1$
$= 89{,}600 + 896$
$= 90{,}496$

4. $\frac{1}{3}(15 + 36) = \frac{1}{3} \cdot 15 + \frac{1}{3} \cdot 36$
$= 5 + 12$
$= 17$

5. For all real numbers x, y, and z:
$$(x + y)z = z(x + y)$$
$$= zx + zy$$
$$= xz + yz$$

6. For each real number n,
$$3n + (7 + 5n)$$
$$= 3n + (5n + 7)$$
$$= (3n + 5n) + 7$$
$$= (3 + 5)n + 7$$
$$= 8n + 7$$

In each of Exercises 7–30, give an equivalent expression in which no two terms are similar.

SAMPLE. $7r + 5 + 2r + (-6)$ *Solution:* $9r + (-1)$. **Answer.**

7. $4x + 8x$
8. $7a + 10a$
9. $15c + (-5)c$

10. $8m + (-2)m$
11. $(-3)D + (-5)D$
12. $(-1)L + (-6)L$

13. $2m + 18m + 1$
14. $4t + 3 + 9t$
15. $5q + 6q + 2p$

16. $3p + 17q + 8p$
17. $2x + 5x + (-1)x$
18. $7v + (-6)v + (-2)v$
19. $2(a + 3) + 5a$
20. $1 + 4(b + 3)$
21. $3s + 5(2s + 7)$
22. $7r + 3(2 + 8r)$

23. $(-8)m + 6(5 + 3m)$
24. $9a + 12a + (-3)b + (-1)b$
25. $(7x^2 + 5x) + (3x^2 + 2x)$
26. $(9y^2 + 6y) + (2y^2 + 4y)$
27. $(5n + 4n^2) + (2n^2 + 7n)$
28. $(12u^3 + 8u^2) + (9u^3 + 2u^2)$

Written Exercises

Simplify each expression.

SAMPLE 1. $156x + 32y + 14x + (-7)y$

Solution: $156x + 32y + 14x + (-7)y = (156 + 14)x + [32 + (-7)y]$
$$= 170x + 25y. \textbf{ Answer.}$$

A

1. $31x + 16x$
2. $45y + 32y$
3. $100b + (-18)b$
4. $(-16)c + 37c$
5. $12z + 3z + 37z$
6. $15t + (-2)t + (-8)t$
7. $15a^2 + 14 + 9a^2$
8. $17d^3 + 9 + 73d^3$

9. $2m + 3k + 5m + 6k$
10. $4g + 2h + 9h + 45g$
11. $12m + 19 + (-8)m + 5$
12. $16e + 38 + 13e + (-17)$
13. $2s + 5r + 3s + (-1)r$
14. $6s + (-7)t + 12s + 9t$
15. $5c + 7d + (-1)c + 2d + 3c$
16. $4y + 3y + 5 + 28 + (-11)$

17. $12 + 19h^2 + 15h + (-6) + (-3)h$
18. $23 + 5w^2 + 8w + (-2)w + (-8)$
19. $4ab + 7a + 5ab + (-2)a$
20. $7xy + 3x + (-2)xy + 8x$

SAMPLE 2. $3(2k + 5m) + 9(7m + 4k)$

Solution: 1. Apply the distributive axiom.

$$3(2k + 5m) + 9(7m + 4k) = 6k + 15m + 63m + 36k$$

2. Simplify the resulting expression.

$$6k + 15m + 63m + 36k = (6 + 36)k + (15 + 63)m$$
$$= 42k + 78m$$
$$\therefore 3(2k + 5m) + 9(7m + 4k) = 42k + 78m. \quad \textbf{Answer.}$$

B **21.** $5(x + y) + 12(x + y) + 3x$ **25.** $3(x^2 + x) + 6(2x^2 + 4)$

22. $2(a + b) + 7(a + b) + 3b$ **26.** $12(4y + 5y^2) + 2(7 + 8y^2)$

23. $6(a + 2) + 9(3 + a)$ **27.** $3(a + 2b + 4) + 5(2a + 3)$

24. $4(r + 3) + 13(r + 5)$ **28.** $4(r + 3s + 6) + 7(s + 2)$

29. $2(3x^2 + 5x + 9) + 9(8x^2 + 2x)$

30. $5(2t^2 + 3t + 4) + 6(7t^2 + 5t)$

31. Five times the sum of a and b, increased by twice the sum of $2a$ and $3b$.

32. Twice the sum of 5 and the square of x, increased by three times the sum of $6x^2$ and 11.

33. Ten more than the sum of negative seven, y, and the square of y.

34. The product of eight and the cube of d, increased by the sum of nine and negative six times the cube of d.

C **35.** $3[7y + 4(5 + 2y)] + (-16)$ **36.** $21 + 2[3z + 5(3z + 8)]$

37. $8(2p + q) + 13[2p + 3(4q + 2p + 6)]$

38. $9[2(4x + 3y + 4) + 7(x + 14)] + 8(5x + 3y)$

Determine the value of each numerical expression. Whenever you can, use properties of numbers to simplify the calculation.

39. $98 \times 54 + 2 \times 54$ **44.** $\frac{1}{2} \cdot 83 + 99\frac{1}{2} \cdot 83$

40. $66 \times 23 + 34 \times 23$ **45.** 628×1001

41. $50(\frac{4}{5} + \frac{1}{2})$ **46.** $40 \times 7\frac{3}{10}$

42. $827 \cdot 11 + 827 \cdot 9$ **47.** $2 \times 37 + 5 \times 37 + 3 \times 37$

43. $3\frac{1}{2} \cdot 9 + 3\frac{1}{2} \cdot 1$ **48.** $7 \times 59 + 1 \times 59 + 2 \times 59$

EXTRA PROBLEM

Draw a flow chart of a program to compute and write the area of the shaded region bounded by the rectangles shown in the diagram. The values of a, b, and c are to be read from a card. Assume that more than one card is to be read and processed.

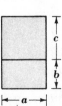

3–8   Rules for Multiplication

Can you guess why 1 is called the *identity element for multiplication?* The following equations suggest the reason:

$$6 \times 1 = 6 \quad \text{and} \quad 1 \times 6 = 6.$$

One is the **identity element for multiplication** because whenever you multiply a given real number and 1, the product is the given real number.

Multiplicative* Axiom of One

The set of real numbers has a unique element 1 having the property that for every real number a,

$$a \cdot 1 = a \quad \text{and} \quad 1 \cdot a = a.$$

The equations

$$6 \times 0 = 0 \quad \text{and} \quad 0 \times 6 = 0$$

illustrate the *multiplicative property of zero:* when one of the factors of a product is 0, the product itself is 0.

Multiplicative Property of Zero

For each real number a,

$$a \cdot 0 = 0 \quad \text{and} \quad 0 \cdot a = 0.$$

Would you guess that $a(-1) = -a$? You might be led to this guess by noticing that

$$2 \times (-1) = -1 + (-1) = -2$$
$$3 \times (-1) = -1 + (-1) + (-1) = -3, \text{ and so on.}$$

To verify that $a(-1)$ is the opposite of a for every real number a, you must show that the sum of $a(-1)$ and a is zero:

$$
\begin{aligned}
a(-1) + a &= a(-1) + a(1) & &\text{Multiplicative axiom of one} \\
&= a[(-1) + 1] & &\text{Distributive axiom} \\
&= a(0) & &\text{Axiom of opposites} \\
&= 0 & &\text{Multiplicative property of zero}
\end{aligned}
$$

Thus, multiplying any real number by -1 produces the opposite of the number.

---

* Pronounced: mul-ti-plik-a-tiv.

Multiplicative Property of −1

For all real numbers a,

$$a(-1) = -a \qquad \text{and} \qquad (-1)a = -a.$$

A special case of this property occurs when the value of a is -1; you have $(-1)(-1) = 1$.

You can use the multiplicative property of -1 together with the multiplication facts for positive numbers to compute the product of any two real numbers. For example:

1. $3 \cdot 4 = 12$
2. $(-3) \cdot 4 = (-1 \cdot 3)4 = -1(3 \cdot 4) = -1(12) = -12$
3. $3(-4) = 3[4(-1)] = (3 \cdot 4)(-1) = 12(-1) = -12$
4. $(-3)(-4) = (-1 \cdot 3)(-1 \cdot 4) = [-1(-1)](3 \cdot 4) = 1 \cdot 12 = 12$

Similarly, for all real numbers a and b:

$$(-a)b = (-1 \cdot a)b = -1(ab) = -ab$$
$$a(-b) = a[b(-1)] = (ab)(-1) = -ab$$
$$(-a)(-b) = (-1 \cdot a)(-1 \cdot b) = [-1(-1)](ab) = 1(ab) = ab$$

Property of Opposites in Products

For all real numbers a and b,

$$(-a)b = -ab, \qquad a(-b) = -ab, \qquad (-a)(-b) = ab.$$

Practice in computing products will lead you to discover the following rules.

Rules for Multiplication

1. The product of a positive and negative number is a negative number.
2. The product of two positive numbers or of two negative numbers is a positive number.
3. The absolute value of the product of two real numbers is the product of the absolute values of the numbers:

$$|ab| = |a| \times |b|$$

Of course, by pairing the negative numbers in a product, you can extend these rules to any number of factors.

A product of nonzero real numbers of which an even number are negative is a positive number. A product of nonzero real numbers of which an odd number are negative is a negative number.

The absolute value of the product of real numbers is the product of the absolute values of the numbers.

EXAMPLE 1. State whether the given expression names a positive number, a negative number, or zero. Then simplify the expression.

a. $-7(-2)(-5)$ b. $3^2 \cdot (-2)^3 \cdot 0$

c. $3^2 \cdot (-2)^3 \cdot (-1)^5$

Solution: a. A negative number; -70 b. 0

c. A positive number; $3^2 \cdot (-2)^3 \cdot (-1)^5 =$ $9 \cdot (-8)(-1) = 9 \cdot 8 = 72$. **Answer.**

EXAMPLE 2. Simplify each expression.

a. $(-4x)(-6x)$ b. $3y + (-4y)$

Solution: a. $(-4x)(-6x) = [-4(-6)]x \cdot x = 24x^2$

b. $3y + (-4y) = 3y + (-4)y = [3 + (-4)]y =$ $(-1)y = -y$. **Answer.**

Oral Exercises

Simplify each of the following expressions.

SAMPLE 1. $(-7)(5)$ *Solution:* -35

SAMPLE 2. $(-1)^4$ *Solution:* $(-1)^4 = (-1)(-1)(-1)(-1) = 1$.

1. $(-7)(3)$	9. $14 \cdot 0 \cdot 17$	17. $(-3)^3$
2. $(6)(-4)$	10. $-6 \cdot -3 \cdot 0$	18. $(-2)^4$
3. $(-3)(-6)$	11. $(3a)(-2a)$	19. $2(-3)^2$
4. $(-8)(-2)$	12. $(-2)(-a)(a)$	20. $-1(-5)^3$
5. $(-1)(4)(-3)$	13. $(-a^2)(b^2)(a)$	21. $|(-4)^3|$
6. $(2)(-5)(-1)$	14. $(-x)(-y^2)(-xy)$	22. $|(-6)^2|$
7. $(-1)(-2)(-3)$	15. $-3(5 + 4)$	23. $-x(xy)^2(0)$
8. $(-2)(-4)(-5)$	16. $-2(6 - 8)$	24. $(-7t)^2(0)(-6)$

SAMPLE 3. $6a + (-7a)$

Solution: $6a + (-7a) = 6a + (-7)a = [6 + (-7)]a = (-1)a = -a.$
Answer.

25. $4t + (-3t)$ **27.** $-9y^3 + 8y^3$ **29.** $-4kt + (-8kt)$

26. $6u + (-6)u$ **28.** $-7x^2 + 8x^2$ **30.** $-3ms + (-2ms)$

Show that the given expressions are equivalent by stating the reason that justifies each step in the given chain of equations.

SAMPLE 4. $a[b + (-c)]$ and $ab + (-ac)$

<table>
<tr><td align="center">*Steps:*</td><td align="center">*Solution:*</td></tr>
<tr><td>$a[b + (-c)] = ab + a(-c)$</td><td>Distributive axiom</td></tr>
<tr><td>$= ab + a[c(-1)]$</td><td>Multiplicative property of -1</td></tr>
<tr><td>$= ab + (ac)(-1)$</td><td>Associative axiom of multiplication</td></tr>
<tr><td>$= ab + (-ac)$</td><td>Multiplicative property of -1</td></tr>
<tr><td>$\therefore a[b + (-c)] = ab + (-ac).$</td><td>Transitive property of equality</td></tr>
</table>

31. $-(-c)$ and c
$$-(-c) = (-1)(-c)$$
$$= (-1)[(-1)c]$$
$$= [(-1)(-1)]c$$
$$= 1 \cdot c$$
$$= c$$
$$\therefore -(-c) = c.$$

32. $-(a + b)$ and $-a + (-b)$
$$-(a + b) = (-1)(a + b)$$
$$= (-1)a + (-1)b$$
$$= -a + (-b)$$
$$\therefore -(a + b) = -a + (-b).$$

Written Exercises

Evaluate each of the following expressions in two ways.

SAMPLE. $(-4)[5 + (-3)]$

Solution: 1. Simplify the sum $[5 + (-3)]$ and then multiply it by -4:
$$(-4)[5 + (-3)] = -4(2) = -8$$

2. Apply the distributive axiom to $(-4)[5 + (-3)]$ and then simplify the resulting expression:
$$(-4)[5 + (-3)] = (-4)(5) + (-4)(-3)$$
$$= -20 + 12 = -8. \quad \textbf{Answer.}$$

A

1. $(-3)(7 + 5)$ **5.** $0[-6 + (-15)]$

2. $(-2)[(-1) + (-8)]$ **6.** $12[3 + (-3)]$

3. $[15 + (-6)](-1)$ **7.** $5 \cdot 1 + 5(-11)$

4. $[-4 + 18](-2)$ **8.** $-6 \cdot 13 + (-6) \cdot 1$

9. $-7(-4) + (-7)$

10. $15 + 15(-21)$

11. $23(99) + 23(-99)$

12. $(-11)(-4) + (-4)(11)$

13. $-5 + 5(-69)$

14. $-99(7) + (-7)$

15. $-(-8 + 25)$

16. $-[-6 + (-19)]$

17. $(-12)(\frac{5}{6} + \frac{2}{3})$

18. $42(-\frac{2}{7} + \frac{16}{21})$

19. $0.7 - [2.8 + (-0.4)]$

20. $-0.5 - [-0.3 + (-5.6)]$

Simplify each expression.

21. $2x + 3y + (-x)$

22. $3a + 3c + (-2a)$

23. $4m + (-2n) + m + (-3n)$

24. $2z + (-5w) + (-3z) + w$

25. $-4t + 3 + 6t + (-7)$

26. $-7p + 14 + 3p + (-21)$

27. $3xy + (-2yz) + 7yz + (-6xy)$

28. $5rs + 2rt + (-8rs) + 10rt$

29. $-x + 2 + 3x + (-4) + (-6x)$

30. $3 + (-y) + 3y + (-7) + 2y$

31. $10t^2 + (-4t) + 7t + (-8t^2)$

32. $z^3 + (-5z^2) + 3z^2 + (-3z^3)$

33. $2.3x + 5y + (-1.7x) + (-4.6y)$

34. $-0.2m + 3.1n + (-2.1n) + (-1.3)m$

35. $-xyz + \frac{1}{2}xy + \frac{3}{4}xyz + \frac{3}{2}xy + (-xyz)$

36. $2u^2v + (-3uv^2) + 6u^2v + (-2uv^2)$

B 37. $2(u + 2v) + (-3)(2u + v)$

38. $6[r + (-s)] + 5(3r + s)$

39. $-2(3a + b) + 7[a + (-b)]$

40. $-3(6m + n) + (-2)(n + 10m)$

41. $-4(-y + 2z) + (-3)[y + (-5z)]$

42. $-6[r + (-3s)] + (-5)(3s + r)$

43. $2[-3(x + 4y) + (-y)] + 8x$

44. $3[2(-3z + w) + (-z)] + (-6w)$

45. $-2 + (-3)[2(-1 + x) + (-2x)]$

46. $3y + (-2)[3(-y + 1) + y]$

Let the value of a be -1, the value of b be 0.2, the value of c be -2, the value of x be -0.2, and the value of y be 0. Evaluate each expression.

47. $a(b + x)$

48. $c(a + b)$

49. $3a + 4c$

50. $4a + (-2c)$

51. $-a + (5b + c)^2$

52. $-bc + (b + x)^2$

53. $0.3c[-(x^2 + a^2)]$

54. $-2.1a + b(a + c)$

C **55.** $x(b + c)^2$

56. $c^2(a + c)^2$

57. $[a + (-c)][b + (-x)]$

58. $(c^2 + a^2)(b^2 + x^2)$

59. $64x^2[bc^2 + (-1)]$

60. $-36b^2[cx^2 + (-a)]$

3–9   The Reciprocal of a Real Number

Numbers, like $\frac{3}{4}$ and $\frac{4}{3}$, whose product is 1 are called **reciprocals** or **multiplicative inverses** of each other. For example:

1. -2 and $-\frac{1}{2}$ are reciprocals of each other because $-2(-\frac{1}{2}) = 1$.

2. 0.1 is the reciprocal of 10 and 10 is the reciprocal of 0.1 because $0.1 \times 10 = 1$.

3. -1 is its own reciprocal because $(-1)(-1) = 1$.

4. 0 has no reciprocal because the product of 0 and any real number is 0, *not* 1.

The symbol $\dfrac{1}{a}$ denotes the reciprocal, or multiplicative inverse, of a. For example:

"$\dfrac{1}{\frac{3}{4}} = \dfrac{4}{3}$" means "the reciprocal of three-fourths equals four-thirds."

"$\dfrac{1}{-2} = -\dfrac{1}{2}$" means "the reciprocal of negative two equals negative one-half."

That *every real number except 0 has a reciprocal* is a basic assumption.

Axiom of Reciprocals

For every real number a except zero, there is a unique real number $\dfrac{1}{a}$, such that $a \cdot \dfrac{1}{a} = 1$ and $\dfrac{1}{a} \cdot a = 1$.

EXAMPLE 1.   Simplify $(-a)\left(-\dfrac{1}{a}\right)$ for $a \neq 0$.

Solution: By the multiplicative property of -1 (page 93),

$$-a = (-1)a \quad \text{and} \quad -\frac{1}{a} = (-1)\frac{1}{a}.$$

$$\therefore (-a)\left(-\frac{1}{a}\right) = (-1)a \cdot (-1)\frac{1}{a}$$

$$= \underbrace{(-1)(-1)}_{1} \cdot \underbrace{a \cdot \frac{1}{a}}_{1}$$

$$= \qquad 1 \qquad \quad 1$$

$$= 1.$$

$$\therefore (-a)\left(-\frac{1}{a}\right) = 1.$$

Do you see that the result of Example 1 means that $-a$ and $-\dfrac{1}{a}$ are reciprocals of each other? Thus,

$$\frac{1}{-a} = -\frac{1}{a}$$

for every nonzero real number a.

EXAMPLE 2.   Simplify each expression:

        a. $(7 \cdot 2)(\frac{1}{7} \cdot \frac{1}{2})$ **b.** $(a \cdot b)\left(\dfrac{1}{a} \cdot \dfrac{1}{b}\right)$, $a \neq 0, b \neq 0$

Solution: **a.** $(7 \cdot 2)(\frac{1}{7} \cdot \frac{1}{2}) = (7 \cdot \frac{1}{7})(2 \cdot \frac{1}{2}) = 1 \cdot 1 = 1$

        b. $(ab)\left(\dfrac{1}{a} \cdot \dfrac{1}{b}\right) = \left(a \cdot \dfrac{1}{a}\right)\left(b \cdot \dfrac{1}{b}\right) = 1 \cdot 1 = 1$

Example 2 suggests the following fact about the reciprocal of a product that corresponds to the property of the opposite of a sum.

Property of the Reciprocal of a Product

The reciprocal of a product of real numbers, each different from zero, is the product of the reciprocals of the numbers; that is, for all real numbers a and b such that $a \neq 0$ and $b \neq 0$,

$$\frac{1}{ab} = \frac{1}{a} \cdot \frac{1}{b}.$$

Oral Exercises

State the reciprocal, or multiplicative inverse, of each number.

1. 1

4. $\frac{1}{9}$

7. $-\frac{1}{12}$

10. $\frac{d}{5}, d \neq 0$

2. -1

5. -3

8. $-\frac{2}{7}$

11. $\frac{3}{c}, c \neq 0$

3. 6

6. $\frac{5}{3}$

9. $\frac{a}{2}, a \neq 0$

12. $-\frac{1}{r}, r \neq 0$

In each of Exercises 13–16, find the value of x.

13. $\frac{1}{x} = -4$

14. $\frac{1}{x} = -\frac{1}{5}$

15. $\frac{1}{x} = -1$

16. $\frac{1}{x} = -\frac{7}{3}$

Show that the given expressions are equivalent by stating the reason that justifies each step in the given chain of equations.

SAMPLE. $56 \cdot \frac{1}{8}$ and 7

Steps:	*Solution:*
$56 \cdot \frac{1}{8} = (7 \cdot 8)\frac{1}{8}$	Substitution principle
$= 7(8 \cdot \frac{1}{8})$	Associative axiom of multiplication
$= 7 \cdot 1$	Axiom of reciprocals
$= 7$	Multiplicative axiom of 1
$\therefore 56 \cdot \frac{1}{8} = 7.$	Transitive property of equality

17. $(-35)\frac{1}{7}$ and -5

$(-35)\frac{1}{7} = [(-1)35]\frac{1}{7}$
$= (-1)(35 \cdot \frac{1}{7})$
$= (-1)[(5 \cdot 7)\frac{1}{7}]$
$= (-1)[5(7 \cdot \frac{1}{7})]$
$= (-1)(5 \cdot 1)$
$= (-1) \cdot 5$
$= -5$
$\therefore (-35)\frac{1}{7} = -5.$

18. $26(-\frac{1}{2})$ and -13

$26(-\frac{1}{2}) = 26[\frac{1}{2}(-1)]$
$= (26 \cdot \frac{1}{2})(-1)$
$= [(13 \cdot 2)\frac{1}{2}](-1)$
$= [13(2 \cdot \frac{1}{2})](-1)$
$= (13 \cdot 1)(-1)$
$= 13(-1)$
$= -13$
$\therefore 26(-\frac{1}{2}) = -13.$

19. $(-56)(-\frac{1}{8})$ and 7

$(-56)(-\frac{1}{8})$
$= [(-1) \cdot 56][(-1)\frac{1}{8}]$
$= [(-1)(-1)](56 \cdot \frac{1}{8})$
$= 1(56 \cdot \frac{1}{8})$
$= 56 \cdot \frac{1}{8}$
$= 7$ (See the Sample above)
$\therefore (-56)(-\frac{1}{8}) = 7.$

20. $26x^4 \cdot (-\frac{1}{2})$ and $-13x^4$

$26x^4 \cdot (-\frac{1}{2})$
$= -\frac{1}{2}(26x^4)$
$= (-\frac{1}{2} \cdot 26)x^4$
$= [26(-\frac{1}{2})]x^4$
$= (-13)x^4$ (See Ex. 18 above)
$= -13x^4$
$\therefore 26x^4 \cdot (-\frac{1}{2}) = -13x^4.$

In Exercises 21 and 22, replace the __?__ by a variable so as to obtain a true statement.

21. For all real numbers a and all nonzero real numbers b, $(ab)\dfrac{1}{b} = $ __?__.

22. For all real numbers y and all nonzero real numbers x, $\left(-\dfrac{1}{x}\right)(-xy) = $

__?__.

Written Exercises

Simplify each expression.

SAMPLE 1. $-28xy(-\frac{1}{4})$

Solution: $-28xy(-\frac{1}{4}) = [-28(-\frac{1}{4})]xy = [(-1)(-1)](28 \cdot \frac{1}{4})xy$
$$= 1 \cdot 7 \cdot xy = 7xy. \quad \textbf{Answer.}$$

SAMPLE 2. $\frac{1}{3}[24r + (-6s)]$

Solution: $\frac{1}{3}[24r + (-6s)] = \frac{1}{3}(24r) + \frac{1}{3}(-6s)$
$$= (\frac{1}{3} \cdot 24)r + [\frac{1}{3}(-6)]s$$
$$= 8r + (-2)s = 8r + (-2s). \quad \textbf{Answer.}$$

$\boxed{\text{A}}$

1. $\frac{1}{9}(63)$

2. $\frac{1}{12}(72)$

3. $51(-\frac{1}{3})$

4. $(-\frac{1}{2})(-22)$

5. $72(-\frac{1}{4})(-\frac{1}{6})$

6. $\frac{1}{3}(-90)(-\frac{1}{5})$

7. $\dfrac{1}{-7} \cdot 42 \cdot \frac{1}{2}$

8. $(-36)(\frac{1}{12})\left(\dfrac{1}{-3}\right)$

9. $5ab(-\frac{1}{5})$

10. $8xy(-\frac{1}{8})$

11. $(-12b^2)(-\frac{1}{4})$

12. $(-50c^3)(\frac{1}{10})$

13. $-\frac{1}{9}(27k^3)$

14. $-\frac{1}{15}(-150z^8)$

15. $\dfrac{1}{x}(5xy), \; x \neq 0$

16. $(4ab)\dfrac{1}{a}, \; a \neq 0$

17. $\dfrac{1}{r^3}(10r^3)(-\frac{1}{2}), \; r \neq 0$

18. $-\frac{1}{8}(48s^2)\dfrac{1}{s^2}, \; s \neq 0$

19. $\frac{1}{2}(10x + 8)$

20. $\frac{1}{3}(12y + 21)$

21. $-\frac{1}{5}(-25c + 70d)$

22. $[8r + (-12s)](-\frac{1}{4})$

23. $[-54mk + (-6k)](-\frac{1}{6})$

24. $-\frac{1}{9}(36uv + 81u)$

25. $\frac{1}{7}(-7a^2 + 7b^2)$

26. $\frac{1}{8}[8x^3 + (-8)y^3]$

$\boxed{\text{B}}$

27. $\frac{1}{2}(4a + 6b) + \frac{1}{3}(-9a + 3b)$

28. $\frac{1}{5}(-5g + 10h) + \frac{1}{2}[2g + (-8h)]$

29. $6[\frac{1}{2}s + (-\frac{1}{3})t] + (-\frac{1}{7})[7s + (-14t)]$

30. $-3[\frac{1}{3}c + (-\frac{1}{3}d)] + \frac{1}{4}[8c + (-12d)]$

31. $-\frac{1}{6}[24a^2 + (-6)] + (-\frac{1}{4})(16a^2 + 4)$

32. $\frac{1}{5}(-20s^2 + 5) + (-4)(\frac{1}{2}s^2 + \frac{1}{4})$

33. $-3[\frac{1}{2}(4a + 1) + (-\frac{1}{2})] + 7a$

34. $5d + (-\frac{1}{2})[8 + 40(-\frac{1}{5} + \frac{1}{4}d)]$

● CHAPTER SUMMARY ●

Inventory of Structure and Method

The following statements are true for all real values of each variable except as noted in items 15, 16, and 17.

1. Axioms of Equality

Reflexive property	$a = a$
Symmetric property	If $a = b$, then $b = a$.
Transitive property	If $a = b$ and $b = c$, then $a = c$.

2. Axioms of Closure The sum $a + b$ is a unique real number. The product ab is a unique real number.

3. Commutative Axioms $a + b = b + a$ $ab = ba$

4. Associative Axioms $(a + b) + c = a + (b + c)$ $(ab)c = a(bc)$

5. $a + b + c = (a + b) + c$, $a + b + c + d = (a + b + c) + d$, and so on. $abc = (ab)c$, $abcd = (abc)d$, and so on.

6. Additive Axiom of 0 There is a unique real number 0 such that
$$a + 0 = a \quad \text{and} \quad 0 + a = a.$$

7. Axiom of Opposites For every a, there is a unique real number $-a$ such that
$$a + (-a) = 0 \quad \text{and} \quad (-a) + a = 0.$$

8. $-(-a) = a$

9. Property of the Opposite of a Sum $-(a + b) = (-a) + (-b)$

10. Distributive Axiom $a(b + c) = ab + ac$

Also: $(b + c)a = ba + ca$, $ab + ac = a(b + c)$, $ba + ca = (b + c)a$.

11. Multiplicative Axiom of 1 There is a unique real number 1 such that $a \cdot 1 = a$ and $1 \cdot a = a$.

12. Multiplicative Property of 0 $\quad a \cdot 0 = 0 \quad$ and $\quad 0 \cdot a = 0$

13. Multiplicative Property of -1 $\quad a(-1) = -a \quad$ and $\quad (-1)a = -a.$

14. Property of Opposites in Products $\quad (-a)b = -ab, \quad a(-b) = -ab,$
$(-a)(-b) = ab$

15. Axiom of Reciprocals $\quad$ For every a different from 0, there is a unique real number $\dfrac{1}{a}$ such that
$$a \cdot \frac{1}{a} = 1 \text{ and } \frac{1}{a} \cdot a = 1.$$

16. $\dfrac{1}{\dfrac{1}{a}} = a$ and $\dfrac{1}{-a} = -\dfrac{1}{a} \quad (a \neq 0)$

17. Property of the Reciprocal of a Product $\quad \dfrac{1}{ab} = \dfrac{1}{a} \cdot \dfrac{1}{b} \quad (a \neq 0 \text{ and } b \neq 0)$

Vocabulary and Spelling

Review the meaning of each term by reference to the page listed.

assumption (*p. 63*)
axiom (*p. 63*)
postulate (*p. 63*)
unique (*p. 63*)
closure (*p. 63*)
commutative operations (*p. 67*)
binary operations (*p. 67*)
associative operation (*p. 67*)
displacement (*p. 70*)
identity element (*p. 73 and p. 92*)

opposite (*p. 76*)
additive inverse (*p. 77*)
absolute value (*p. 79*)
distributive (*p. 88*)
equivalent (*p. 89*)
simplified (*p. 89*)
similar (*p. 89*)
reciprocal (*p. 97*)
multiplicative inverse (*p. 97*)

Chapter Test

3–1 Name the closure axiom illustrated by each of these examples.

1. $2 \cdot 11$ is a real number. $\qquad$ **2.** $9 + (^-1)$ is a real number.

Which property of equality justifies each of these statements?

3. If $10 \div 2 = 5$, then $5 = 10 \div 2$.

4. If $x = y$ and $y = 15$, then $x = 15$.

3–2   Name the axioms which allow us to make each of the following statements.

    5. $(2 \times 3) \times 6 = 2 \times (3 \times 6)$

    6. $1.2 + 2.1 = 2.1 + 1.2$

3–3   **7.** Draw a number line to picture the sum $4 + {}^-3$.

Simplify each expression.

    8. $6 + 0$ **9.** $0 + {}^-8\frac{3}{4}$ **10.** ${}^-7 + {}^-16$

3–4   Simplify.

    11. $-(17 + 3)$ **12.** $-[14 - (-2)]$ **13.** $\frac{1}{4} - (-\frac{3}{4})$

    14. Given x a member of the set $\{0, 1\}$. Is $-x > 1$?

3–5   State the absolute value of each number.

    15. 27 **16.** -27

    17. The graph of $|x| \geq 2$ consists of all points which are at least __?__ units from the __?__.

3–6   Simplify.

    18. $7.1 + 2.9 + (10.0)$

    19. $3\frac{1}{2} + (-5\frac{1}{2})$

3–7   **20.** Multiplication is __?__ with respect to addition.

Simplify.

    21. $4y + 15y$

    22. $2x + 3y + (-x) + 10y$

3–8   **23.** The __?__ element for multiplication is 1.

    24. Whenever you multiply a given real number and 1, the __?__ is the given real number.

Complete.

    25. $(-1)(-1) = $ __?__   **27.** $(-3)(5) = $ __?__

    26. $(-4y)(-9y) = $ __?__   **28.** $3r + (-11r) = $ __?__

3–9   **29.** The __?__ of 2 is $\frac{1}{2}$.

    30. __?__ is the reciprocal of -5.

Chapter Review

3–1   Axioms of Closure and Equality   *Pages 63–66*

1.   "If $x = y$, then $y = x$" illustrates the __?__ property of __?__.
2.   Any set of numbers is said to be closed under an operation on its members if each result of the operation is a __?__ of the set.
3.   If $x = y$ and $y = 192$, then $x =$ __?__.

3–2   Commutative and Associative Axioms   *Pages 66–70*

4.   For all real numbers a and b, $a + b = b +$ __?__.
5. $(96 + {}^-7) + 42 = 96 + (\underline{\;?\;})$
6. $(2 \cdot {}^-3) \cdot 4 = 2 \cdot (\underline{\;?\;} \cdot 4)$

3–3   Addition on the Number Line   *Pages 70–76*

7.   The diagram pictures the addition fact $4 +$ __?__ $= {}^-1$.

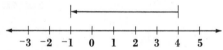

8.   Simplify the expression $2 + ({}^-2 + 4)$.

3–4   The Opposite of a Real Number   *Pages 76–79*

Simplify.

9. $-(-4 - 3)$ 10. $[-14 - (6 + 2)]$
11.   What is the additive inverse of $-\frac{1}{4}$?

3–5   Absolute Value   *Pages 79–82*

12.   Simplify: $|-5|$; $\;-5 + 1$; $\;-(5 + 1)$
13.   What is the absolute value of $-\frac{1}{4}$; of $\frac{1}{4}$?

3–6   Rules for Addition   *Pages 82–87*

Find the sum.

14. $42 + (-41) + 60$ 15. $\frac{1}{3} + (-\frac{2}{3}) + \frac{4}{3}$

3–7   The Distributive Axiom   *Pages 88–91*

Simplify.

16. $l + (-6)l + (-1)l$ 18. $6(x + 2y) + 3(3x + 6y)$
17. $2x + (-4y) + (-x) + y$ 19. $6 \times 42 + 9 \times 42$

3–8 Rules for Multiplication   *Pages 91–97*

Simplify.

20. 20×0 **22.** $-1 \cdot a$

21. 21×1 **23.** $(-1)(-a)$

3–9 The Reciprocal of a Real Number   *Pages 97–101*

Find the reciprocal of:

24. $-a$ **26.** $4 \cdot 2 \cdot 6$

25. 4 **27.** ab, if $a \neq 0, b \neq 0$

EXTRA FOR EXPERTS

More about Flow Charts

Before reading this Extra you may wish to review pages 58–60.

Consider the following program to compute the squares of the integers from 1 to 99, inclusive.

1. Let n be a variable whose *initial* (first) value is 1.
2. Compute the value of n^2, and let the result be the value of s.
3. Print the values of n and s on one line of the output sheet.
4. If the value of n is 99, stop (your work is done). Otherwise, go to step 5.
5. Add 1 to the value of n, and then go back to step 2.

Notice that the first time you go through steps 2, 3, and 4 in the program, the value of n is 1.

But when you execute step 5, the value of n is increased to 2. Next, the program tells you to go through steps 2, 3, and 4 again, but this time with 2 as the value of n.

After step 5 is executed a second time, the value of n is 3.

You continue repeating steps 2, 3, 4, and 5 until finally you reach step 4 with 99 as the value of n, and you stop.

The result of the program is to compute and print the squares of the integers 1 through 99.

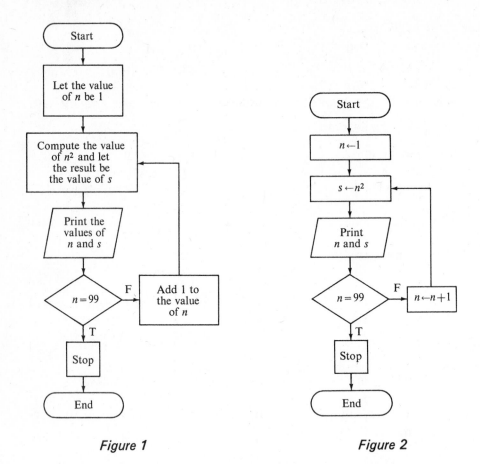

Figure 1   Figure 2

Figure 1 shows a flow chart of the program on the preceding page. The same flow chart is shown in Figure 2. However, in the assignment boxes of Figure 2, left-pointing arrows are used to show assigned values. Thus, in the new flow chart,

"$n \leftarrow 1$"   stands for "Let the value of n be 1."

"$s \leftarrow n^2$"   stands for "Compute the value of n^2 and let the result be the value of s."

"$n \leftarrow n + 1$"   stands for "Add 1 to the value of n."

Note also that in the output box in Figure 2, the instruction "Print n and s" means "Print *the values of n and s.*"

EXAMPLE. Answer the following questions for the program whose flow chart is given.

a. What are the first two values printed?

b. How many values of k are printed?

c. What is the last value of $5k - 3$ that is printed?

Solution:

a. The first two values printed are the initial value of k and the initial value of $5k - 3$; that is, 1 and $5 \times 1 - 3$, or 1 and 2.

b. 100

c. $5 \times 100 - 3$, or 497.   **Answer.**

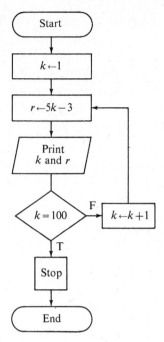

Exercises

In Exercises 1–4, the program pictured at the right below is to be executed. In each exercise, display the output of the program for the given values of R and T.

1. $R \leftarrow 3,\ T \leftarrow 6$

2. $R \leftarrow 15,\ T \leftarrow 2$

3. $R \leftarrow 650,\ T \leftarrow \frac{1}{2}$

4. $R \leftarrow 1200,\ T \leftarrow \frac{1}{3}$

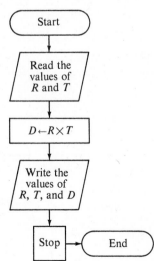

Exercises 5–8 refer to the flow chart at the right.

5. What is the value of n when the end of the program is reached?

6. How many values of $a + nd$ are computed by the program?

7. What are the first two values of $a + nd$ if the values of a and d are 5 and 3?

8. What are the first two values of $a + nd$ if the values of a and d are 0 and 7?

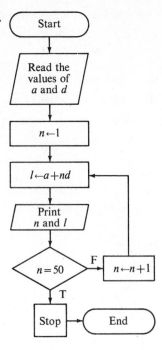

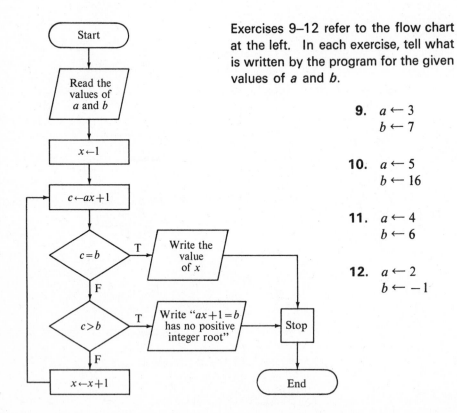

Exercises 9–12 refer to the flow chart at the left. In each exercise, tell what is written by the program for the given values of a and b.

9. $a \leftarrow 3$
$b \leftarrow 7$

10. $a \leftarrow 5$
$b \leftarrow 16$

11. $a \leftarrow 4$
$b \leftarrow 6$

12. $a \leftarrow 2$
$b \leftarrow -1$

In Exercises 13–18, name the variable whose value will be written by the program shown in the flow chart at the right for the given values of *a, b,* and *c.*

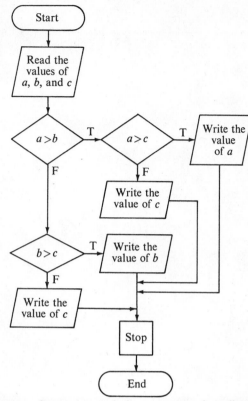

13. $a \leftarrow -2$
    $b \leftarrow 3$
    $c \leftarrow 5$

14. $a \leftarrow 6$
    $b \leftarrow -5$
    $c \leftarrow 6$

15. $a \leftarrow 3$
    $b \leftarrow 7$
    $c \leftarrow -1$

16. $a \leftarrow 0$
    $b \leftarrow -3$
    $c \leftarrow -2$

17. $b < a < c$

18. $a > b; \ c < b$

In each of Exercises 19–24, draw a flow chart of the program described in the exercise. Assume that the program is to be executed by a device that can at least read and remember data, add, subtract, multiply, divide, compute powers, compare numbers, and write messages.

19. Read the values of a and b; then compute and write the value of $(a + b)^5$, and stop.

20. Read the values of r and h; then compute and write the value of $\frac{1}{3}\pi r^2 h$, and stop. In the program take the value of π to be 3.1416.

21. Compute and print the values of $n^4 - 1$ for each of the integer values of n from 0 through 15.

22. Compute and write the values of $x^2 + 3$ for values of x from 0 to 1 inclusive, at intervals of 0.05.

23. Suppose that A and B are given as the degree measures of two angles of a triangle. Read the values of A and B, and then write the value of the degree measure of the third angle of the triangle. In case the input data cannot be the measure of two angles of a triangle, write the message "No such triangle."
    Hint: The sum of the degree measures of the angles of a triangle is 180. Therefore, the input data cannot fit a triangle unless $A + B < 180$.

24. Read the values of R, S, and T, and then write the least of these values.

CHAPTER

. . . a launching of a Titan III rocket

Solving Equations and Problems

In this chapter you will study how to solve an equation by transforming it into a simpler equivalent equation. You will then be able to solve a number of interesting problems.

TRANSFORMING EQUATIONS

4–1 Transforming Equations by Addition

Mathematical ideas are often discovered by thinking about things in everyday life. Consider the following situation.

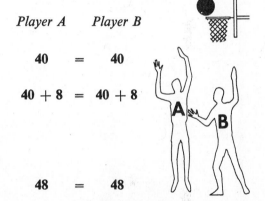

In a game, two basketball players have scored the same number of points, say 40.

Player A   *Player B*

$$40 \;=\; 40$$

Each man scores 8 more points.

$$40 + 8 \;=\; 40 + 8$$

Although the scores change, the total number of points scored by Player A equals the total scored by Player B.

$$48 \;=\; 48$$

These thoughts suggest the **addition property of equality**: *if the same number is added to equal numbers, the sums are equal.* A more formal way to state this property is given below.

Addition Property of Equality

If a, b, and c are any real numbers such that $a = b$, then

$$a + c = b + c \qquad \text{and} \qquad c + a = c + b.$$

The addition property of equality follows from facts you already know. The reasoning leading from the given assumption (the *hypothesis*) "a, b, and c are real numbers and $a = b$" to the *conclusion* "$a + c = b + c$ and $c + a = c + b$" is shown in the following sequence of true statements. Notice that the truth of each statement except the first (the given assumption) is guaranteed by one of the properties that you have already learned.

1. *a*, *b*, and *c* are real numbers; $a = b$.   **Given**

2. $a + c$ is a real number and   **Axiom of closure for addition**
   $c + a$ is a real number.

3. $\therefore \ a + c = b + c$ and   **Substitution principle (substituting**
   $c + a = c + b$.   ***b* for *a* in $a + c$ and in $c + a$)**

This kind of logical reasoning from known facts and given assumptions to conclusions is called a **direct proof**. Assertions that are proved are called **theorems**. Thus, the addition property just proved is a theorem.

Theorems about real numbers are often discovered in numerical calculations. For instance, look at the following calculation:

$$(8 + 9) + (-9) = 8 + [9 + (-9)]$$
$$= 8 + 0$$
$$= 8$$
$$\therefore (8 + 9) + (-9) = 8.$$

The calculation suggests a useful idea: *to "undo" the addition of a given number to another number, add the opposite of the given number to the sum.* This idea is stated in the following theorem.

For all real numbers *a* and *b*, $(a + b) + (-b) = a$.

You can use this theorem along with the addition property of equality to solve equations. To explain the method, it helps to know that in an equation or an inequality the expressions joined by the equals sign or inequality symbol are called the **members** of the equation or inequality. For example, in the equation

$$x + 9 = -1$$

left member   right member

the left member is "$x + 9$" and the right member is "-1."

Now study the following sequence of equations:

(1) $x + 9 = -1$
(2) $x + 9 + (-9) = -1 + (-9)$
(3) $\therefore$ $x = -10$

To obtain the third equation, you add -9 to each member of the first equation (Step 2) and simplify the expressions that result (Step 3). On the other hand, if you add 9 to each member of the third equation, you obtain the first equation:

$$x = -10$$
$$x + 9 = -10 + 9$$
$$\therefore x + 9 = -1$$

Thus, the addition property of equality implies that any root of one of these equations must also satisfy the other equation. Therefore, the equations have the same solution set, namely $\{-10\}$.

Equations having the same solution set over a given set are called **equivalent equations** over that set. To solve an equation, you usually try to change, or **transform**, it into an equivalent equation whose solution set can be found by inspection. The properties of real numbers ensure that:

Each of the following transformations always produces an equivalent equation:

Transformation by Substitution: Substituting for either member of a given equation an expression equivalent to that member.

Transformation by Addition: Adding the same real number to each member of a given equation.

In the following examples and throughout the rest of this book, we use the script letter $\mathcal{R}$ to denote the set of real numbers. Thus,

$$\mathcal{R} = \{\text{the real numbers}\}.$$

EXAMPLE 1. Solve $y + (-3) = -19$ over $\mathcal{R}$.

Solution:

$$y + (-3) = -19$$
$$y + (-3) + 3 = -19 + 3$$
$$y = -16$$

Since $y + (-3)$ shows -3 added to y, you add 3 (the opposite of -3) to the sum to obtain y.

Check:

$$y + (-3) = -19$$
$$-16 + (-3) \overset{?}{=} -19$$
$$-19 = -19 \checkmark$$

$\therefore$ the solution set is $\{-16\}$.   **Answer.**

Because you may make a numerical mistake in transforming an equation, you should check your work by substituting each root of the transformed equation in the original equation, as shown in Example 1 above.

EXAMPLE 2. **Solve** $17 = 11 + 2a$ over $\mathcal{R}$.

Solution:

$$-11 + 17 = -11 + 11 + 2a$$
$$6 = 2a$$

By inspection, the one and only root of $6 = 2a$ is 3.

Check:

$$17 = 11 + 2a$$
$$17 \stackrel{?}{=} 11 + 2 \cdot 3$$
$$17 \stackrel{?}{=} 11 + 6$$
$$17 = 17 \checkmark$$

$\therefore$ **the solution set is $\{3\}$. Answer.**

Oral Exercises

Simplify each expression.

1. $(7 + 3) + (-3)$
2. $(8 + 2) + (-2)$
3. $[6 + (-1)] + 1$
4. $[9 + (-10)] + 10$

5. $[z + (-4)] + 4$
6. $(5 + k) + (-5)$
7. $(-7 + 2x) + 7$
8. $[1 + (-b)] + b$

Tell the number that must be added to each member of the first equation to obtain the second equation. Then, name the root of the first equation.

9. $x + 3 = 9; x = 6$
10. $y + 2 = 10; y = 8$
11. $t + (-4) = 17; t = 21$
12. $s + (-1) = 34; s = 35$
13. $7 + z = -3; z = -10$
14. $8 + a = -1; a = -9$
15. $-3 + r = 5; r = 8$
16. $-2 + v = 0; v = 2$

17. $2b + (-3) = -1; 2b = 2$
18. $2c + (-5) = -1; 2c = 4$
19. $4 + 6x = 10; 6x = 6$
20. $7 + 3w = 7; 3w = 0$
21. $12 = x + (-3); 15 = x$
22. $1 = 1 + u; 0 = u$
23. $0 = -\frac{1}{2} + t; \frac{1}{2} = t$
24. $-6 = -5 + k; -1 = k$

The following proofs are valid for all real numbers a, b, and c. Justify each step.

SAMPLE. To prove: If $a + c = b + c$, then $a = b$.

Steps	*Reasons*
1. a, b, and c are real numbers, and $a + c = b + c$.	Given
2. $-c$ is a real number.	Axiom of opposites
3. $(a + c) + (-c) = (b + c) + (-c)$	Addition property of equality
4. $a + [c + (-c)] = b + [c + (-c)]$	Associative axiom of addition
5. $a + 0 = b + 0$	Axiom of opposites
6. $\therefore a = b$.	Additive axiom of zero

25. To prove: If $a = b$, then $ac = bc$ and $ca = cb$.

1. a, b, and c are real numbers; $a = b$.
2. ac is a real number and ca is a real number.
3. $ac = bc$ and $ca = cb$.

26. To prove: If $a = b$ and $c = b$, then $a = c$.

1. a, b, and c are real numbers; $a = b$ and $c = b$.
2. $b = c$
3. $\therefore a = c$.

27. To prove: $(a + b) + (-b) = a$

1. a and b are real numbers.
2. $a + b$ is a real number.
3. $-b$ is a real number.
4. $(a + b) + (-b)$
$\qquad = a + [b + (-b)]$
5. $\qquad = a + 0$
6. $\qquad = a$
7. $\therefore (a + b) + (-b) = a$.

28. To prove:
$a + b + [(-a) + (-b)] = 0$

1. a and b are real numbers.
2. $-a$ and $-b$ are real numbers.
3. $a + b$ and $-a + (-b)$ are real numbers.
4. $a + b + [-a + (-b)]$
$\qquad = [a + (-a)]$
$\qquad\qquad + [b + (-b)]$
5. $\qquad = 0 + 0$
6. $\qquad = 0$
7. $\therefore a + b + [-a + (-b)]$
$\qquad\qquad = 0$.

Written Exercises

Use transformation by addition to solve each equation over $\mathcal{R}$.

A

1. $x + (-32) = 5$
2. $w + (-17) = 7$
3. $-14 + A = 58$
4. $-32 + B = 76$
5. $75 + k = 75$
6. $42 = m + 42$

7. $r + 30 = 80$
8. $s + 29 = 35$
9. $c + 17 = 0$
10. $d + 31 = 0$
11. $200 = 150 + n$
12. $172 = 2 + d$

13. $f + (-2.1) = 4.3$
14. $g + (0.6) = 1.6$
15. $-\frac{3}{5} + M = \frac{13}{5}$
16. $-\frac{2}{7} + N = \frac{9}{7}$
17. $\frac{3}{4} = L + \frac{1}{4}$
18. $\frac{7}{10} = H + \frac{7}{10}$

B 19. $-d + 7 = 28$

20. $-k + 5 = 21$

21. $-36 = 12t + (-36)$

22. $\frac{3}{4} = 0.75 + 6s$

23. $-w + (-1) = 4$

24. $-t + 3 = 10$

25. $-3 + 2P = -5$

26. $-1 + (-3)Q = 5$

27. $(x + 1) + (-6) = 4$

28. $(y + 2) + (-8) = 3$

29. $7 + (3 + m) = -12$

30. $14 + (n + 6) = -2$

31. $-1 + [x + (-2)] = 7$

32. $-5 + [y + (-1)] = -4$

33. $(2a + 3) + (-2) = 0$

34. $(3a + 1) + 4 = 5$

C 35. $|x| + (-1) = 4$

36. $|y| + (-2) = -1$

37. $-3 + |t| = 0$

38. $-6 + |w| = -4$

4–2 Subtracting Real Numbers

If you buy a ten-cent news-paper and give the newsdealer a quarter, he may count your change as he says:

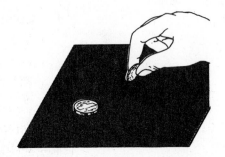

"10, 15 (handing you a nickel),
25 (handing you a dime)."

The dealer does a subtraction ($25 - 10 = 15$) by adding ($10 + 15 = 25$). Another way to say this is: the same number satisfies both of the equations

$$25 - 10 = x \quad \text{and} \quad 10 + x = 25.$$

Guided by the newsdealer's thinking, we define the **difference** $a - b$ between any two real numbers a and b to be the number whose sum with b is a; that is, *$a - b$ is the real number satisfying the equation $b + x = a$.*

Using only this definition, you compute a difference such as $a - b$ by asking yourself, "What number added to b gives a?" The following example shows how to use the number line to do subtraction problems this way.

EXAMPLE 1. Simplify $3 - (-2)$.

Solution: On the diagram below, to move from the graph of -2 to the graph of 3 requires a displacement of 5 units to the right.

$$\therefore 3 - (-2) = 5. \quad \textbf{Answer.}$$

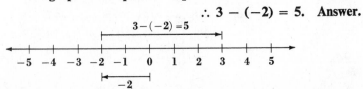

You can find a simple expression for $a - b$ by transforming the equation "$b + x = a$" by addition:

$$b + x = a$$
$$x + b = a$$
$$x + b + (-b) = a + (-b)$$
$$x + 0 = a + (-b)$$
$$\therefore x = a + (-b)$$

The last equation evidently has just one root, $a + (-b)$. Checking this root in the original equation, you have:

$$b + x = a$$
$$b + a + (-b) \overset{?}{=} a$$
$$b + (-b) + a \overset{?}{=} a$$
$$0 + a \overset{?}{=} a$$
$$a = a \checkmark$$

Since the one and only root of "$b + x = a$" is $a + (-b)$, the following theorem has been proved.

Rule for Subtraction

For all real numbers a and b,

$$a - b = a + (-b).$$

To perform a subtraction, replace the number you are subtracting by its opposite, and add.

Since every real number has a unique opposite (section 3–4), if you know b, then you know $-b$. Also, since $a + (-b)$ denotes a sum of real numbers, it represents a real number. Therefore, the rule for subtraction shows that $\Re$ is closed under subtraction.

Using this rule, you can always replace a difference by a sum:

Difference		Sum	Value	Check
$3 - 2$	$=$	$3 + (-2) = 1$		$2 + 1 = 3$
$3 - (-2)$	$=$	$3 + 2$	$= 5$	$-2 + 5 = 3$
$-3 - 2$	$=$	$-3 + (-2)$	$= -5$	$2 + (-5) = -3$
$-3 - (-2)$	$=$	$-3 + 2$	$= -1$	$-2 + (-1) = -3$

EXAMPLE 2. **Simplify** $5 - 12 - 4 + 3$**.**

Solution 1.

Step 1	Step 2	Step 3
$5 - 12 = -7$	$-7 - 4 = -11$	$-11 + 3 = -8$. **Answer.**

Solution 2.

Step 1	Step 2	Step 3
$5 + 3 = 8$	$-12 + (-4) = -16$	$8 + (-16) = -8$. **Answer.**

Expressions for sums such as

$$5 + (-x) \quad \text{and} \quad 3 + (-2x)$$

are usually written as differences:

$$5 - x \quad \text{and} \quad 3 - 2x$$

EXAMPLE 3. **Simplify** $5 - x + 3 - 2x + 7x$**.**

Solution:
$$5 - x + 3 - 2x + 7x = 5 + 3 + (-x - 2x + 7x)$$
$$= 8 + 4x. \quad \textbf{Answer.}$$

EXAMPLE 4. **Solve over** $\mathfrak{R}$**:** **a.** $x - 3 = -18$ **b.** $y + 7 = 31$**.**

Solution:

a.
$$x - 3 = -18$$
$$x - 3 + 3 = -18 + 3$$
$$x = -15$$

b.
$$y + 7 = 31$$
$$y + 7 - 7 = 31 - 7$$
$$y = 24$$

Check:

$$-15 - 3 \overset{?}{=} -18$$
$$-18 = -18 \; \checkmark$$

$$24 + 7 \overset{?}{=} 31$$
$$31 = 31 \; \checkmark$$

∴ **the solution set is** $\{-15\}$**.**
Answer.

∴ **the solution set is** $\{24\}$**.**
Answer.

Because you can describe the method used in Example 4(b) as *subtracting* 7 from each member of the equation (rather than adding -7 to each member), you may call the method **transformation by subtraction.** Of course, transformation by subtraction is just a special kind of transformation by addition.

Oral Exercises

From the first number named subtract the second. In each case, describe your method.

SAMPLE. $\quad \begin{array}{r} -5 \\ -3 \\ \hline \end{array}$ $\quad$ *Solution:* To subtract -3 from -5, add the opposite of -3 to -5. $-5 + 3 = -2$. **Answer.**

1. 18 $\underline{7}$	**5.** 6 $\underline{-3}$	**9.** -27 $\underline{-18}$	**13.** -23 $\underline{-23}$
2. 23 $\underline{15}$	**6.** 15 $\underline{-12}$	**10.** -50 $\underline{-42}$	**14.** 0 $\underline{6}$
3. 8 $\underline{12}$	**7.** -20 $\underline{3}$	**11.** -7 $\underline{-26}$	**15.** $x + 3$ $\underline{x}$
4. 9 $\underline{15}$	**8.** -35 $\underline{20}$	**12.** -11 $\underline{-19}$	**16.** $x + (-2)$ $\underline{x + 3}$

Simplify each difference. Assume that each variable denotes a real number.

17. $32 - 8$

18. $27 - 10$

19. $6 - 9$

20. $8 - 14$

21. $0 - 2\frac{1}{2}$

22. $0 - 3\frac{3}{4}$

23. $2 - 1.6$

24. $5 - 3.8$

25. $2 - 5.3$

26. $7 - 8.1$

27. $\frac{1}{2} - \frac{3}{2}$

28. $\frac{1}{4} - \frac{9}{4}$

29. $-7 - 0$

30. $3.2 - 0$

31. $4 - (-5)$

32. $7 - (-8)$

33. $-2 - (-3)$

34. $-1 - (-8)$

35. $-3 - 5$

36. $-7 - 2$

37. $(y + 5) - (y + 3)$

38. $(z + 2) - (z + 5)$

39. $k - (k + 1)$

40. $t - (t - 3)$

Tell the number that must be subtracted from each member of the first equation to obtain the second equation.

41. $x + 6 = 10; \ x = 4$

42. $y + 7 = 2; \ y = -5$

43. $2t + 8 = 6; \ 2t = -2$

44. $3z + 1 = -4; \ 3z = -11$

45. $6k + 9 = -5; \ 6k = -14$

46. $-3n + 8 = 10; \ -3n = 2$

Supply the reason for each lettered statement in each proof. A check ($\checkmark$) shows that the step involves substitution using an addition or subtraction fact for positive numbers. The replacement set for all variables is $\Re$.

47. To prove: If $x + 5 = 8$, then $x = 3$.

$x + 5 = 8$	Given
$(x + 5) + (-5) = 8 + (-5)$	a. $\underline{\ ?\ }$
$x + [5 + (-5)] = 8 + (-5)$	b. $\underline{\ ?\ }$
$x + \quad 0 \quad = 8 + (-5)$	c. $\underline{\ ?\ }$
$x = 8 + (-5)$	d. $\underline{\ ?\ }$
$x = 8 - 5$	e. $\underline{\ ?\ }$
$x = 3$	$(\checkmark)$

48. To prove: If $y - 5 = 7$, then $y = 12$.

$$
\begin{array}{ll}
y - 5 = 7 & \text{Given} \\
y + (-5) = 7 & \text{a.} \ \underline{\ ?\ } \\
[y + (-5)] + 5 = 7 + 5 & \text{b.} \ \underline{\ ?\ } \\
y + [(-5) + 5] = 7 + 5 & \text{c.} \ \underline{\ ?\ } \\
y + [(-5) + 5] = 12 & (\checkmark) \\
y + \quad 0 \quad = 12 & \text{d.} \ \underline{\ ?\ } \\
y = 12 & \text{e.} \ \underline{\ ?\ }
\end{array}
$$

The following proofs are valid for all real numbers a, b, and c. Justify each step.

SAMPLE. To prove: $a(b - c) = ab - ac$

Steps	Reasons
a, b, and c are real numbers.	Given
$a(b - c) = a[b + (-c)]$	Rule for subtraction
$= a(b) + a(-c)$	Distributive axiom
$= ab + [-(ac)]$	Property of opposites in a product
$= ab - ac$	Rule for subtraction
$\therefore a(b - c) = ab - ac.$	Transitive property of equality

This exercise shows that multiplication of real numbers is distributive with respect to subtraction.

49. To prove: $-(a - b) = b - a$.
a and b are real numbers.

$$
\begin{aligned}
-(a - b) \\
= (-1)[a + (-b)] \\
= (-1)a + (-1)(-b) \\
= -a + b \\
= b + (-a) \\
\therefore -(a - b) = b - a.
\end{aligned}
$$

50. To prove: $-(-a - b) = a + b$.
a and b are real numbers.

$$
\begin{aligned}
-(-a - b) \\
= (-1)[-a + (-b)] \\
= (-1)(-a) + (-1)(-b) \\
= a + b \\
\therefore -(-a - b) = a + b.
\end{aligned}
$$

Written Exercises

Rewrite each of the following differences as a sum and then simplify. In a column arrangement, assume that the number being subtracted is named by the lower numeral.

SAMPLE 1.   23
        27
        —

Solution: $23 + (-27) = -4$

Check: $-4 + 27 = 23 \ \checkmark$

SAMPLE 2. $(x + 3) - (x - 5)$

Solution: $(x + 3) - (x - 5) = (x + 3) + \{-[x + (-5)]\}$
$$= x + 3 + (-x) + 5 = 8. \quad \textbf{Answer.}$$

Check: $(x - 5) + 8 = x - 5 + 8 = x + 3 \checkmark$

A

1. 15
    23
    ___

2. 27
    19
    ___

3. -53
    42
    ___

4. -47
    38
    ___

5. -16
    -24
    ___

6. -31
    -14
    ___

7. 3
    $-2\frac{1}{2}$
    ___

8. 5
    $-7\frac{1}{3}$
    ___

9. $x + 8$
    $x + 10$
    ___

10. $y + (-3)$
    $y + (-7)$
    ___

11. $x + 2.3$
    $x + 1.7$
    ___

12. $z + 5.6$
    $z + (-2.1)$
    ___

13. $4 + (-3) - 7$

14. $0 - (-\frac{8}{7}) + (-\frac{8}{7})$

15. $(217 + 185) - (182 - 27)$

16. $-(413 - 212) + (-182 + 450)$

17. $(x + 7) - (-3 + x)$

18. $(7 - t) - (-3 - t)$

Solve each equation over $\Re$.

19. $t + 34 = 123$

20. $s + 59 = 211$

21. $-13 = x + 28$

22. $-34 = y + 57$

23. $2t + 5 = 5$

24. $7 + 3g = 7$

25. $Q + \frac{1}{2} = -2\frac{1}{2}$

26. $S + \frac{2}{3} = 4\frac{2}{3}$

B

27. $22 - m = 15$

28. $17 - d = -8$

29. $(n + 7) + 4 = 10$

30. $(3 + c) + 6 = -1$

Write each phrase using algebraic symbols, and simplify.

31. -3 decreased by 8

32. -7 decreased by -3

33. x less $(x - 5)$

34. y less $(7 + y)$

35. Subtract $3\pi + 2$ from $3\pi - 2$.

36. From $5 - 6\pi$ subtract $8 - 6\pi$.

37. Decrease the sum of -8 and 17 by -6.

38. Decrease -18 by the sum of -34 and 12.

C

39. Prove that if $y + 2 = 11$; then $y = 9$.

40. Prove that if $x + 8 = 12$, then $x = 4$.

41. Prove that if $x - 3 = 2$, then $x = 5$.

42. Prove that if $z - 6 = 0$, then $z = 6$.

Which of the following sets are closed under subtraction? Explain.

43. {natural numbers}

44. {integers}

45. {even integers}

46. {odd integers}

Problems

Using real numbers, solve each problem.

A

1. How much greater is the altitude of Death Valley, California, 282 feet below sea level, than the altitude of the Dead Sea, 1,296 feet below sea level?

2. Find the difference in the altitudes of the Qattara Depression in Egypt, 436 feet below sea level, and the top of Mount McKinley in Alaska, 20,320 feet above sea level.

3. An astronaut entered his space capsule 1 hr. 40 min. before launching time. How long had he been in the capsule 2 hr. 32 min. after launching?

4. Assuming that the Greek mathematician Pythagoras was born in 532 B.C. and died before his birthday in 497 B.C., how old was he when he died?

5. Assuming that the Roman statesman Seneca was born in the year 4 B.C., and died after his birthday in 65 A.D., how old was he when he died? (Assume no year 0.)

6. Jean owed $3.45 to Susan. After paying Susan the money she owed, Jean had $2.17 left. How much money had Jean before she paid Susan?

7. What is the difference between the melting and boiling points of chlorine, if it boils at 34.6° below 0° centigrade and melts at 101.6° below 0° centigrade?

8. Mercury melts at 38.87° below 0° centigrade and boils at 356.9° above 0° centigrade. What is the difference of these temperatures?

9. Mr. Hooker drove a golf ball from a point 180 yards to the east of a hole to a point 47 yards to the west of the hole. How far did the ball travel?

10. Mrs. Adams rode the subway from a point 53 blocks south of Main Street to a point 41 blocks north of Main Street. How many blocks did she travel?

EXTRA PROBLEM

Draw a flow chart of a program to read the value of x from a card and to determine whether x is greater than or equal to zero or whether it is negative. In case $x \geq 0$, the value of $1 + x$ is to be computed and printed. Otherwise, the value of $1 - x$ is to be computed and printed. Assume that more than one card is to be read. What is printed by the program if the value of x is 3? −2? 0?

4–3 Transforming Equations by Multiplication

The **multiplication property of equality** means that when equal numbers are multiplied by the same number, the products are equal. For example, since

$$7 = 5 + 2$$
$$7 \cdot 3 = (5 + 2)3 \quad \text{and} \quad 3 \cdot 7 = 3(5 + 2).$$

Multiplication Property of Equality

If a, b, and c are any real numbers such that $a = b$, then

$$ac = bc \quad \text{and} \quad ca = cb.*$$

This property guarantees that:

The following transformation always produces an equivalent equation.

Transformation by Multiplication: Multiplying each member of a given equation by the same *nonzero* real number.

EXAMPLE 1. Solve $8m = 72$ over $\mathcal{R}$.

Solution:
$$8m = 72$$
$$\tfrac{1}{8} \cdot (8m) = \tfrac{1}{8} \cdot 72$$
$$m = 9$$

$\left\{ \begin{array}{l} \text{Since } 8m \text{ shows } m \text{ multiplied by} \\ 8, \text{ you multiply the product by } \tfrac{1}{8} \\ \text{(the reciprocal of 8) to obtain } m. \end{array} \right.$

Check:
$$8(9) \overset{?}{=} 72$$
$$72 = 72 \checkmark \quad \therefore \text{ the solution set is } \{9\}. \quad \textbf{Answer.}$$

When you write "m" in place of "$\tfrac{1}{8}(8m)$" and "9" in place of "$\tfrac{1}{8} \cdot 72$" or "$\tfrac{1}{8}(8 \cdot 9)$," you use a very helpful idea: *to "undo" the multiplication of a number by a given number, multiply the product by the reciprocal of the given number.* In general:

For all real numbers a and all nonzero real numbers b,
$$\frac{1}{b}(ba) = a.$$

*See Exercise 25, page 115.

In the following examples, and in fact, from here on in this book, you can assume, unless otherwise stated, that *open sentences are to be solved over* ℛ, *the set of real numbers.*

EXAMPLE 2. $\frac{1}{3}t = -5$

Solution: $\frac{1}{3}t = -5$

$3 \cdot \frac{1}{3}t = 3 \cdot -5$

$t = -15$

Check: $\frac{1}{3}(-15) \overset{?}{=} -5$

$-5 = -5 \checkmark$

∴ the solution set is {−15}. **Answer.**

EXAMPLE 3. $-5d = 120$

Solution: $-5d = 120$

$-1(-5d) = -1(120)$

$5d = -120$

$\frac{1}{5} \cdot 5d = \frac{1}{5}(-120)$

$d = -24$

Check: $-5(-24) \overset{?}{=} 120$

$120 = 120 \checkmark$

∴ **the solution set is** {−24}. **Answer.**

Do you know why you do not use zero as a multiplier in transforming an equation? Consider the equation "$\frac{1}{3}t = -5$" whose solution set is {−15}. If you multiplied by 0, the equation "$0 \cdot \frac{1}{3}t = 0(-5)$" would be satisfied by any value of t; its solution set would be ℛ. Thus, the original equation "$\frac{1}{3}t = -5$," and the transformed equation "$0 \cdot \frac{1}{3}t = 0(-5)$" would have different solution sets; they would not be equivalent equations (see page 113). Therefore, *multiplication by zero* cannot be used because it does not produce an equivalent equation.

Oral Exercises

Simplify each expression.

1. $\frac{1}{6}(6 \cdot 5)$

2. $\frac{1}{4}(4 \cdot 3)$

3. $-\frac{1}{2}(-2 \cdot 7)$

4. $-\frac{1}{13}[-13 \cdot (-1)]$

5. $\frac{1}{9}(9y)$

6. $-\frac{1}{3}(-3x)$

7. $(7t)\frac{1}{7}$

8. $(-8q)(-\frac{1}{8})$

Tell the number by which each member of the first equation must be multiplied to obtain the second equation.

9. $\frac{1}{2}x = 17$; $x = 34$

10. $\frac{1}{3}y = -2$; $y = -6$

11. $\frac{1}{5}k = -4$; $k = -20$

12. $\frac{1}{8}t = 0$; $t = 0$

13. $7u = 28$; $u = 4$

14. $-3v = 18$; $v = -6$

15. $-12 = -4v$; $3 = v$

16. $-1 = -\frac{1}{9}g$; $9 = g$

17. $\frac{2}{3}y = 10$; $y = 15$

18. $\frac{4}{5}q = -\frac{1}{5}$; $q = -\frac{1}{4}$

Written Exercises

Solve each equation over $\Re$.

A
1. $\frac{1}{8}q = 17$
2. $\frac{1}{11}t = 12$
3. $\frac{1}{9}y = -15$
4. $\frac{1}{6}x = -32$
5. $3x = 96$
6. $4x = -128$

7. $13t = -52$
8. $-14k = 84$
9. $5 = -\frac{1}{13}p$
10. $-8 = -\frac{1}{5}b$
11. $\frac{1}{11}m = -3.7$
12. $-\frac{1}{7}h = -2.5$

13. $\frac{1}{2} - d = \frac{7}{2}$
14. $\frac{1}{3}w = \frac{5}{3}$
15. $-\frac{12}{5} = \frac{1}{5}M$
16. $\frac{3}{7} = -\frac{1}{7}K$
17. $0.8 = 0.8h$
18. $-1.7 = 1.7q$

B
19. $\frac{1}{3}p = 4\frac{1}{3}$
20. $\frac{1}{2}u = 5\frac{1}{2}$
21. $\frac{1}{7}k = -3\frac{2}{7}$
22. $-\frac{1}{8}x = 1\frac{5}{8}$

23. $0 = -4.3c$
24. $-1 = 7.75a$
25. $\frac{1}{2}x + 5 = 20$

26. $\frac{1}{5}g - 6 = 4$
27. $15 = 4z + 11$
28. $2 = -7x + 2$

C
29. $4 - \frac{1}{3}y = -7$
30. $-1 - \frac{1}{5}t = 2$

31. $\frac{1}{5}|a| + 1 = -1$
32. $-2 + \frac{1}{3}|b| = +5$

4–4 Dividing Real Numbers

Why is the statement "$24 \div 6 = 4$" true? You know that $24 \div 6 = 4$ because $6 \times 4 = 24$, and you call $24 \div 6$, or 4, the *quotient* of 24 by 6. In general, the **quotient** $a \div b$ of any real number a by any *nonzero* real number b is the number whose product with b is a; that is, $a \div b$ is the real number satisfying the equation $bx = a$.

The quotient $a \div b$ can also be represented by a fraction:

$$a \div b = \frac{a}{b}.$$

When you studied fractions, you learned facts like these:

$$\frac{7}{2} = 7 \times \frac{1}{2}; \qquad \frac{3}{5} = 3 \times \frac{1}{5}; \qquad \frac{8}{4} = 8 \times \frac{1}{4}.$$

These statements suggest how to use reciprocals to express any quotient as a product.

Rule for Division

For all real numbers a and all nonzero real numbers b,

$$a \div b = a \times \frac{1}{b}.$$

To perform a division, replace the divisor by its reciprocal, and multiply.

You can show that this rule is correct by transforming the equation "$bx = a$" by multiplication:

$$bx = a$$

$$\frac{1}{b} \cdot bx = \frac{1}{b} \cdot a \qquad (b \neq 0)$$

$$1 \cdot x = a \cdot \frac{1}{b}$$

$$\therefore \; x = a \cdot \frac{1}{b}$$

The last equation has just one root, $a \cdot \dfrac{1}{b}$. Checking this root in the original equation, you have:

$$bx = a$$

$$b\left(a \cdot \frac{1}{b} \right) \overset{?}{=} a$$

$$a\left(b \cdot \frac{1}{b} \right) \overset{?}{=} a$$

$$a \cdot 1 \overset{?}{=} a$$

$$a = a \checkmark$$

Since the one and only root of "$bx = a$" is $a \cdot \dfrac{1}{b}$, it follows that

$$a \div b = a \cdot \frac{1}{b}, \qquad \text{or} \qquad \frac{a}{b} = a \cdot \frac{1}{b}.$$

Since every nonzero real number has a unique reciprocal, if you know b ($b \neq 0$), then you know $\dfrac{1}{b}$. Since $a \cdot \dfrac{1}{b}$ denotes a product of real numbers, it represents a real number. Therefore, this theorem implies that *the set of real numbers is closed under division,* **excluding division by zero.**

Using this theorem, you can replace any quotient by a product.

Quotient	Product	Value	Check
$24 \div 6$ or $\frac{24}{6}$	$24 \times \frac{1}{6}$	4	$6 \times 4 = 24$
$24 \div (-6)$ or $\dfrac{24}{-6}$	$24 \times -\frac{1}{6}$	-4	$-6 \times (-4) = 24$

Quotient	Product	Value	Check
$-24 \div 6$ or $\dfrac{-24}{6}$	$-24 \times \frac{1}{6}$	-4	$6 \times (-4) = -24$
$-24 \div (-6)$ or $\dfrac{-24}{-6}$	$-24 \times -\frac{1}{6}$	4	$-6 \times (4) = -24$

Why must division by zero be excluded in the set of real numbers? For any number a, $\dfrac{a}{0} = c$ would mean that $a = 0 \times c$. If $a \neq 0$, *no* value of c can make the last equation a true statement, since $0 \times c = 0$ for each value of c. But if $a = 0$, *every* value of c makes the equation a true statement. Therefore, a "quotient" $\dfrac{a}{0}$ either would have *no* value or would have an *infinite set* of values. Therefore, *division by zero has no meaning in the set of real numbers.*

You cannot divide zero by zero. But can you divide zero by any other number? Consider these examples:

$$\tfrac{0}{9} = 0 \cdot \tfrac{1}{9} = 0$$
$$0 \div (-8) = 0 \cdot -\tfrac{1}{8} = 0$$

For $a \neq 0$, $0 \div a = 0 \cdot \dfrac{1}{a} = 0$. Thus, *the quotient of zero divided by any nonzero number is zero.*

EXAMPLE. Solve each equation: a. $4x = -56$ b. $-15 = -\dfrac{x}{3}$

Solution:

a. $4x = -56$

$$\frac{4x}{4} = \frac{-56}{4}$$

$$x = -14$$

Check: $4(-14) \stackrel{?}{=} -56$

$-56 = -56$ ✓

∴ the solution set is $\{-14\}$. **Answer.**

b. $-15 = -\dfrac{x}{3}$

$$-3 \cdot (-15) = -3 \cdot \left(\frac{x}{-3}\right)$$

$$45 = x$$

Check: $-15 \stackrel{?}{=} -\frac{45}{3}$

$-15 = -15$ ✓

∴ the solution set is $\{45\}$.

Answer.

Because you can describe the method used in part (a) of the preceding example as dividing each member of the equation by 4 (rather than multiplying each member by $\frac{1}{4}$), you may call the method **transformation by division**. Of course, transformation by division is just a special case of transformation by multiplication.

Oral Exercises

Simplify each expression.

SAMPLE 1. $\dfrac{-50}{10}$ **SAMPLE 2.** $\dfrac{14a}{-2}$

Solution: $\dfrac{-50}{10} = -5.$ **Answer.**   *Solution:* $\dfrac{14a}{-2} = -7a.$ **Answer.**

1. $\dfrac{15}{3}$ **6.** $\dfrac{9}{9}$ **11.** $-8 \div 8$ **16.** $a \div (-1)$

2. $\dfrac{24}{8}$ **7.** $\dfrac{-39}{-3}$ **12.** $\dfrac{-17}{1}$ **17.** $\dfrac{10t}{-2}$

3. $\dfrac{24}{-8}$ **8.** $0 \div 7$ **13.** $\dfrac{18}{-1}$ **18.** $\dfrac{-30s}{-6}$

4. $\dfrac{-18}{6}$ **9.** $\dfrac{0}{-4}$ **14.** $\dfrac{5}{20}$ **19.** $a \div a,\ a \neq 0$

5. $\dfrac{-21}{-7}$ **10.** $\dfrac{-6}{-6}$ **15.** $\dfrac{a}{1}$ **20.** $\dfrac{a}{-a},\ a \neq 0$

Read each quotient as a product. Then state the value of the quotient.

SAMPLE 3. $14 \div (-\tfrac{1}{2})$

Solution: $14 \div (-\tfrac{1}{2}) = 14 \times (-2) = -28.$ **Answer.**

21. $7 \div (\tfrac{1}{6})$ **24.** $-84 \div 12$ **27.** $-9 \div \dfrac{1}{z},\ z \neq 0$

22. $-1 \div (-\tfrac{1}{8})$ **25.** $5x \div \tfrac{1}{3}$ **28.** $6a \div (2a),\ a \neq 0$

23. $-30 \div (-10)$ **26.** $-8b \div (-\tfrac{1}{5})$

Tell the number by which each member of the first equation must be divided to obtain the second equation.

29. $7x = 28;\ x = 4$ **32.** $-10y = 50;\ y = -5$

30. $8z = 8;\ z = 1$ **33.** $15b = -30;\ b = -2$

31. $-3t = 27;\ t = -9$ **34.** $-12c = -48;\ c = 4$

Solve each equation.

35. $6k = -36$ **37.** $-4t = -16$ **39.** $-3 = -3s$

36. $-5r = 15$ **38.** $-5q = 0$ **40.** $-22 = 11v$

Determine which of the following sets are closed under division, excluding division by zero.

41. $\{1\}$ **43.** {the positive numbers}   **45.** $\{\tfrac{1}{2}, 1, 2\}$

42. $\{-1, 0, 1\}$ **44.** {the negative numbers}   **46.** $\{-1\}$

Replace the __?__ by one of the words *positive, negative, zero,* to produce a true statement.

47. The quotient of a positive number by a negative number is always __?__.

48. The quotient of a negative number by a negative number is always __?__.

49. The quotient of zero by any negative number is always __?__.

50. In a quotient, the divisor can never be __?__.

Written Exercises

State the value of each quotient.

1. $125 \div (-25)$ **7.** $-1.44 \div (1.2)$ **13.** $-6.96 \div (24)$

2. $-96 \div 16$ **8.** $-0.09 \div 0.3$ **14.** $16.8 \div (-12)$

3. $-18 \div (-\frac{1}{9})$ **9.** $-0.49 \div 7$ **15.** $0 \div (-\frac{3}{8})$

4. $0 \div (-15)$ **10.** $-16 \div (-\frac{1}{8})$ **16.** $\dfrac{0}{1.89}$

5. $0 \div 49$ **11.** $\dfrac{5}{-\frac{1}{4}}$ **17.** $-7x \div \frac{1}{3}$

6. $-17 \div (-\frac{1}{3})$ **12.** $\dfrac{8}{-\frac{1}{2}}$ **18.** $8z \div (-\frac{1}{11})$

Solve each equation.

19. $18y = 360$ **22.** $234 = -78s$ **25.** $1.5q = -2.25$

20. $33x = 165$ **23.** $-63a = 378$ **26.** $-1.3p = -1.69$

21. $-270 = -20t$ **24.** $21x = -252$

Find the average of the numbers in each set given in Exercises 27–30. (The **average** is the quotient of the sum of the numbers by the number of the numbers.)

27. $\{-9, 14, -33, 22, -44\}$ **29.** $\{-67, -25, -8, 8, 25, 67\}$

28. $\{-91, -39, 45, 80\}$ **30.** $\{-42, 0, -19, 42, -56\}$

If the value of x is -2, y is -1, z is 3, and w is 6, evaluate each expression.

B **31.** $\dfrac{3xy}{w}$ **34.** $\dfrac{4w}{x^2 z}$ **37.** $\dfrac{w+z}{y^2}$ **40.** $\dfrac{w+2y}{x^2}$

32. $\dfrac{w}{xz}$ **35.** $\dfrac{wz}{xy^2}$ **38.** $\dfrac{w^2}{z^2 - 3y}$ **41.** $\dfrac{y^2 - 4x}{w+z}$

33. $\dfrac{xz^2}{w}$ **36.** $\dfrac{wy}{xz}$ **39.** $\dfrac{z-x}{z+x}$ **42.** $\dfrac{w-z}{y^2 - x}$

43. $\dfrac{(z+1)^2 - w}{x - 4y}$ **45.** $\dfrac{x^2 + 2xy + y^2}{(w - z)^2}$ **47.** $\dfrac{x^2 + y^2 + z^2}{y - 2z}$

44. $\left(\dfrac{w}{z}\right)^2 - \left(\dfrac{x}{y}\right)^2$ **46.** $\dfrac{x^2 + 2(w + y)}{z^2 - w + y}$ **48.** $\dfrac{(x + y + z)^4}{w^2 + y^2}$

Give the reason justifying each step in the following proofs.

C

49. *To prove:* If a, b, and c are any real numbers such that $a = b$ and $c \neq 0$, then $\dfrac{a}{c} = \dfrac{b}{c}$.

1. a, b, and c are real numbers; $a = b$; $c \neq 0$.

2. $\dfrac{1}{c}$ is a real number.

3. $a \cdot \dfrac{1}{c} = b \cdot \dfrac{1}{c}$

4. $\dfrac{a}{c} = \dfrac{b}{c}$

50. *To prove:* If a, b, and c are any real numbers such that $c \neq 0$ and $\dfrac{a}{c} = \dfrac{b}{c}$, then $a = b$.

1. a, b, and c are real numbers; $c \neq 0$; $\dfrac{a}{c} = \dfrac{b}{c}$.

2. $\dfrac{a}{c} \cdot c = \dfrac{b}{c} \cdot c$

3. $\left(a \cdot \dfrac{1}{c}\right) c = \left(b \cdot \dfrac{1}{c}\right) c$

4. $a\left(\dfrac{1}{c} \cdot c\right) = b\left(\dfrac{1}{c} \cdot c\right)$

5. $a \cdot 1 = b \cdot 1$

6. $a = b$

4–5 Using Several Transformations

You know that $9 + 4 - 4 = 9$ and $9 - 4 + 4 = 9$. In general,
$$a + b - b = a \quad \text{and} \quad a - b + b = a.$$

Because the operations of adding and subtracting the same number are "opposite" in effect, you can "undo" the result of one of these operations by "doing" the opposite operation. We call addition of a given number and subtraction of the same number *inverse operations*. Can you explain why multiplication and division are inverse operations?

The following example shows that in solving an equation, you *undo* the *operations* used in building the equation, but in *reverse order*.

Building an Equation		*Solving the Equation*	
$t = 4$	**Given**	$4t - t + 5 = 17$	**Given**
$3 \cdot t = 3 \cdot 4$	**Multiply by 3**	$3t + 5 = 17$	**Substitute**
$3t = 12$			**$3t$ for $4t - t$**
$3t + 5 = 12 + 5$	**Add 5**	$3t + 5 - 5 = 17 - 5$	**Subtract 5**
$3t + 5 = 17$		$3t = 12$	
		$\dfrac{3t}{3} = \dfrac{12}{3}$	**Divide by 3**
$4t - t + 5 = 17$	**Substitute** **$4t - t$ for $3t$**	$t = 4$	

The following steps are usually helpful in transforming an equation into an equivalent equation that can be solved by inspection.

1. Simplify each member of the equation.

2. If there are indicated additions or subtractions, use the inverse operations to undo them.

3. If there are indicated multiplications or divisions involving the variable, use the inverse operations to undo them.

4. If you can now solve the transformed equation by inspection, check its root in the given equation.

EXAMPLE 1. Solve $12x - 3 - 2x = 23 + 19$

Solution:

1. Copy the equation; simplify each member.

$$\underbrace{12x - 3 - 2x}_{} = \underbrace{23 + 19}_{}$$
$$10x - 3 \qquad = 42$$

2. Add 3 to each member.

$$10x - 3 + 3 = 42 + 3$$
$$10x = 45$$

3. Divide each member by 10.

$$\frac{10x}{10} = \frac{45}{10}$$
$$x = 4.5$$

Check: $12(4.5) - 3 - 2(4.5) \overset{?}{=} 23 + 19$
$$54.0 - 3 - 9.0 \overset{?}{=} 42$$
$$42 = 42 \checkmark$$

$\therefore$ the solution set is $\{4.5\}$.   **Answer.**

EXAMPLE 2. Solve $38 = 2 - 3(y - 5)$

Solution:

1. Copy the equation; use the distributive axiom and simplify the right member.

$$38 = 2 - 3(y - 5)$$
$$38 = 2 - 3y + 15$$
$$38 = 17 - 3y$$

2. Subtract 17 from each member.

$$38 - 17 = 17 - 3y - 17$$
$$21 = -3y$$

3. Divide each member by -3.

$$\frac{21}{-3} = \frac{-3y}{-3}$$
$$-7 = y$$

Check is left to you.

Written Exercises

Solve each equation.

A

1. $3x + 2 = 17$

2. $5z - 3 = 17$

3. $\dfrac{y}{2} - 3 = 6$

4. $\dfrac{z}{3} + 5 = -1$

5. $7x - 5x = -18$

6. $11t - 8t = -3$

7. $-2 = 3z - z$

8. $-8 = 5a - 3a$

9. $3w + 1 - 2w = 3$

10. $4t - 3 - 3t = -5$

11. $2 = 6x - 3 - x$

12. $-7 = 2y - 3 - 3y$

13. $b - \frac{1}{2}b - 4 = 0$

14. $\frac{7}{6}c - c - 6 = 0$

15. $5.5r - r = 90$

16. $8.4s - s = 14.8$

17. $99 - 4p - 6p = -1$

18. $-36 - b - 4b = 64$

19. $2x - 1 + x + 1 = 27$

20. $-2 + p + 2p + 2 = -12$

21. $7 = 6g - 5g - 1$

22. $0 = 7m + 4 - 3m$

23. $0 = -y - 3y - 16$

24. $0 = 35 - 5x - 2x$

25. $18k - 6k - 14k = 6$

26. $11h - 5h + 16 = 4$

27. $2h - 3h + 4 - h = 10$

28. $5y + 10 - 3y - y = -7$

29. $x + (x + 1) + (x + 2) = 9$

30. $(y - 2) + (y - 1) + y = -3$

B

31. $19n - 11 - 12n - 5 = 5$

32. $-7h - 17 - 6 + 4h = 17$

33. $-2t + 3(2 + t) = -10$

34. $2(a + 5) - a = -7$

35. $2(x + 3) - 6x - 4 = 8$

36. $4z + 3(z + 7) = -14$

37. $-5(1 + w) + 4w = 8$

38. $-3(2 - y) + 2y = 7$

39. $5a - (1 - a) + 4 = 9$

40. $-7 - (-3 - 2g) - 10 = 0$

41. $1.5k - (k + 2.4) = 17.4$

42. $3s - (0.5s + 7.2) = 32.8$

C

43. $5(m + 2) - 4(m + 1) - 3 = 0$

44. $3(8n - 2) - 3(1 - n) + 8 = 8$

45. $74 - 2[(35 + 2x) - 3] = -6$

46. $2a - [(3a + 4) - 5] - a = 5$

47. $-2[z + 3(5 - z)] - 5(z - 7) = 0$

48. $6[x - 2(2x + 3) + 1] + 3(5 + 6x) + x = 0$

49. $7(|x| - 2) - 3|x| - 16 = 2$

50. $2|t| - (|t| - 1) = 7$

USING EQUATIONS

4–6 Using Equations to Solve Problems

In a "word problem" you are told how certain numbers are related to one another. If you can translate these numerical relationships into an equation, then you can solve the problem by solving the equation.

EXAMPLE 1. The length of the service module containing the engines of the Apollo 11 spacecraft was 4 feet shorter than twice the length of the command module housing the crew. Also, the lunar module was 1 foot longer than the command module. If the overall length of Apollo 11 was 45 feet, how long was the command module?

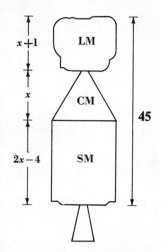

Solution:

1 ▶ The first step in solving this problem is to select a symbol to represent the number you wish to find: the number of feet in the length of the command module.

Let x represent this number. You know that the length of the service module was 4 feet less than 2 times the length of the command module, so $2x - 4$ represents the length of the service module. Also, the lunar module (LM) was 1 foot longer than the command module, so that the LM was $x + 1$ feet long. The replacement set for x must be the set of positive real numbers because x represents a nonzero length.

2 ▶ The second step is to write an open sentence. You do this by setting one expression for the length of Apollo 11 equal to another.

length of command module	added to	length of service module	added to	length of lunar module	equals	length of Apollo 11
x	$+$	$2x - 4$	$+$	$x + 1$	$=$	45

3 ▶ The third step is to solve the open sentence.

$$x + 2x - 4 + x + 1 = 45$$
$$4x - 3 = 45$$
$$4x - 3 + 3 = 45 + 3$$
$$4x = 48$$

∴ the one and only root of the equation is 12. Hence, the only possible length of the command module is 12 feet.

$$\frac{4x}{4} = \frac{48}{4}$$
$$x = 12$$

(Cont. on p. 134)

4▶ **The fourth step is to check your results with the words of the problem.**

Length of command module	12
Length of service module (4 feet less than 2 times 12 feet)	20
Length of lunar module (1 foot more than 12 feet)	13
Length of Apollo	$\overline{45}$ ✓

The steps taken to solve the preceding problem suggest the following plan that usually helps you to solve any problem.

Plan for Solving a Word Problem

After carefully reading the problem, decide what numbers are asked for. Then take these steps:

1. Choose a variable with an appropriate replacement set, and use the variable in representing each described number.
2. Write an open sentence by using facts given in the problem.
3. Find the solution set of the open sentence.
4. Check your results with the words of the problem.

Oral Exercises

Translate each sentence into an equation.

SAMPLE 1. When negative eight is subtracted from twice a certain number, the difference is 11.

Solution: Let n represent the number. Then:
$2n$ represents twice the number.
$\therefore 2n - (-8) = 11$. **Answer.**

SAMPLE 2. In an isosceles triangle whose perimeter is 44 centimeters, the base is 2 centimeters longer than each of the congruent sides which are each x centimeters long.

Solution: Each congruent side is x cm. long.
$\therefore$ the base is $(x + 2)$ cm. long.
Since the perimeter is 44 cm.,
$x + x + (x + 2) = 44$. **Answer.**

1. One number is three times another number and their sum is -16.
2. One number is 6 more than another number and their sum is 2.

3. Seven less than one-half a number is 5.

4. Twelve more than twice a number is 8.

5. Multiply a number by 4, then multiply this product by 5, and you get 80.

6. Multiply a number by 6, then multiply this product by $\frac{1}{6}$, and you get -7.

7. Add 4 to a number, then subtract 5 from the sum, and you get 43.

8. Subtract 5 from a number, then subtract 6 from the difference, and you get 0.

9. Double a number, add 1 to the product, and you get 29.

10. Add 1 to a number, then double the sum, and you get 56.

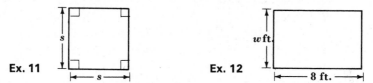

Ex. 11   Ex. 12

11. The perimeter of a square, s inches on a side, is 76 inches.

12. The area of a rectangle 8 feet long and w feet wide is 40 square feet.

13. The $15 that Mrs. Stevens gives to charity each week is one-twelfth of her weekly take-home pay of p dollars.

14. At a restaurant, Mrs. Rojas spent $10.40, which was one-fifth of the d dollars that she had in her purse.

15. Fran has $207 in her bank account, which is three times as much as her brother's savings of b dollars.

16. Sally has t dimes worth a total of $5.60.

17. In s slices of bread, each containing 65 calories, there are 585 calories.

18. Maura, who is y years old now, was 12 years old 5 years ago.

19. A football team that played 85 games lost x games, won five times as many as it lost, and finished only 1 game in a tie.

20. A soccer field has a perimeter of 380 yards, a width of y yards, and a length that is 40 yards more than its width.

Problems

Whenever a sketch will help you to solve a problem, draw one.

A **1.** The area of a rectangle 6 yards wide is 78 square yards. Find the length of the rectangle.

2. The perimeter of a square is 124 meters. How long is each side of the square?

3. In a certain school $\frac{1}{3}$ of the students are boys. Find the number of students in the school if 436 of them are boys.

4. Linnie weighs one-third as much as her father. If Linnie weighs 73 pounds, how much does her father weigh?

5. An airplane's altimeter reads 2,546 feet. What is the airplane's altitude if this reading is 3.5 feet less than the true reading?

6. In checking a patient's pulse rate at 6:00 A.M., Nurse Perlman found that the rate was 7 beats less per minute than the rate recorded at 8:00 P.M. the previous night. If Miss Perlman found the pulse rate to be 72 beats per minute, what was the rate recorded the previous night?

7. On Sunday morning, a copy of the *Times* costs 30 cents more than a copy of the *News*. Mr. Donnelly, who buys both papers, spends 70 cents for the Sunday editions. How much does a copy of each paper cost on Sunday?

8. Together, a house and lot cost $40,000. The house cost seven times as much as the lot. How much did the lot cost? the house?

9. In an election for town clerk, 584 people voted for one or the other of the two candidates. The winner received 122 votes more than her opponent. How many people voted for the winner?

10. Professor Landers took 55 minutes to drive from her home to the University and back. The return drive took 7 minutes less than the trip to the University. How long did it take her each way?

11. Tom rides the school bus part way and walks the remainder. He walks 3 minutes longer than he rides. If it takes Tom 17 minutes to arrive at school, how long does he spend on the bus?

12. John spent 7 hours on the lake. If he sailed his boat for two more hours than he fished, how long did he sail?

13. Water is a compound made up of 8 parts by weight of oxygen and 1 part by weight of hydrogen. How many grams of hydrogen are there in 225 grams of water?

14. On a 600-mile trip, Mrs. Seda traveled by automobile and airplane. If she traveled seven times farther by airplane than by automobile, how far did she travel by automobile?

15. Mr. Brown will need 186 ft. of fence to enclose his rectangular yard. If the length of his yard is 9 feet more than the width, what are the dimensions of his yard?

16. The width of a rectangle is 7 centimeters less than the length. If the perimeter is 410 centimeters, what are the dimensions of the rectangle?

17. The sum of twice a number and 27 is 51. Find the number.

18. The sum of three times a number and 11 is -13. Find the number.

19. Four times a number diminished by 27 is 45. Find the number.

20. Find a number such that 93 less than twice the number is 59.

B **21.** One number is 22 less than a second number. If the greater number is subtracted from twice the lesser number, the difference is 16. Find the lesser number.

22. The difference of two numbers is 17. If twice the greater number is subtracted from 5 times the lesser number, the difference is 2. Find the greater number.

23. A 98 foot length of TV cable is cut so that one piece is 10 feet shorter than twice the length of the other piece. Find the length of the shorter piece.

24. The entertainment portion of a 30-minute TV program lasted 4 minutes longer than 4 times the portion devoted to advertising. How many minutes of the program were devoted to advertising?

25. In solving a maze problem, Barb took 13 fewer moves than twice the number of moves Ann took. If together they made 23 moves, who made more moves, and by how many moves did they differ?

26. One of the longer sides of Mr. Shima's lot borders on a straight river. He needs 420 feet of fence to fence the three sides not on the river. If the length of the lot is 60 feet less than 2 times its width, what are the dimensions of the lot?

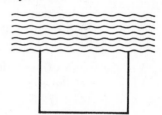

27. Sally and Jim went blueberry picking. Sally picked 3 fewer pints than twice as many as Jim did. If together they picked 21 pints of berries, how many pints did Sally pick?

28. The entire freshman class of City High went on a skiing trip. The girls numbered six more than twice the number of boys. If there are 291 students in the freshman class, how many are boys and how many are girls?

29. Ken had 8 coins in his pocket. If he had 2 fewer dimes than nickels, and one more penny than nickels, how much money did Ken have?

30. Susan had 20 coins. If she had 1 fewer pennies than dimes, and 3 fewer nickels than dimes, how much money did Susan have?

31. Tracy has 6 times as many dimes as nickels and 3 times as many pennies as nickels. If she has $17, how many coins of each kind has she?

32. Mrs. Richards bought 4 times as many six-cent stamps as ten-cent stamps, and 3 times as many four-cent stamps as ten-cent ones. If she paid $6.90 for all the stamps that she bought, how many stamps of each denomination did she buy?

33. In a day, Machine X produces twice as many plastic bowls as Machine Y. Machine Z produces 50 more bowls than Machine Y. If the total production is 6,170 bowls, how many bowls does each produce?

34. Information in numerical units called "bytes" is stored in the memory of an electronic computer. The storage capacity of Computer II is twice that of Computer I, while Computer III has a capacity four times as great as that of Computer II. If the total storage capacity of the three machines is 88,000 bytes, find the capacity of each computer.

C 35. The back of a sweater contains 6 fewer stitches than the front. Together the back and the front of the sweater contain 96 stitches more than each sleeve, each sleeve having half as many stitches as the front. How many stitches does the front of the sweater contain?

36. A pattern can be used to make either a sleeveless or a long-sleeved dress. When made with long sleeves, $\frac{3}{4}$ yard more material is required than if it is made sleeveless. Two sleeveless dresses would require $1\frac{1}{2}$ more yards of material than one long-sleeved dress. How much material is needed to make the dress in the sleeveless pattern?

37. The record low temperature at the U. S. installation at Antarctica is 5.5° warmer than the record low at the Russian station. The average of the two record low temperatures is minus 118.65 degrees F. What is the official U. S. record low?

38. The length of one side of a triangular lot is 11 feet less than twice the length of the second side. The third side is 7 feet longer than the first side. Find the length of each side of the lot. Its perimeter is 235 feet.

39. Wilma is 5 years older than Sue, and Sue is 3 years older than Phyllis. The sum of their ages is 32. How old is Wilma?

40. There is a two-year age difference between each child in the Smith family and the next older child. If there are four children in the family and the sum of their ages is 44, how old is the oldest?

EXTRA PROBLEM

The coefficients a, b, and c in the equation "$ax + b = c$" are given on a card. Draw a flow chart of a program to determine whether $a = 0$ or not. In case $a = 0$, the program should print the message, "Not a linear equation." Otherwise, the program should compute and print the root of the equation. Assume that cards for several equations are to be processed.

4–7 Equations Having the Variable in Both Members

In the equation

$$2p = 63 - 5p$$

the variable appears in both members. Are you allowed to add "$5p$" to each member?

For every real number p, "$5p$" denotes a product of real numbers, and, therefore, it represents a real number. Because you are permitted to add the same real number to each member of the equation, you are also allowed to add "$5p$" to each member without changing the solution set of the equation. Thus, you may solve the equation as follows:

$$2p = 63 - 5p$$
$$2p + 5p = 63 - 5p + 5p$$
$$7p = 63$$
$$\frac{7p}{7} = \frac{63}{7}$$
$$p = 9$$

Check:
$$2p = 63 - 5p$$
$$2 \cdot 9 \overset{?}{=} 63 - 5 \cdot 9$$
$$18 \overset{?}{=} 63 - 45$$
$$18 = 18 \checkmark$$

$\therefore$ the solution set is $\{9\}$.   **Answer.**

Must every equation have a real root? The next Example shows that the answer is "No!"

EXAMPLE 1.   Solve $1 - (2x + 8) = (x + 9) - 3x$

Solution:
$$1 - (2x + 8) = (x + 9) - 3x$$
$$1 - 2x - 8 = -2x + 9$$
$$-2x - 7 = -2x + 9$$
$$-2x - 7 + 2x = -2x + 9 + 2x$$
$$-7 = 9$$

Since the given equation is equivalent to the false statement "$-7 = 9$," the *equation has no root.*

$\therefore$ the solution set is $\emptyset$.   **Answer.**

Example 2 involves an equation that is satisfied by every real number.

EXAMPLE 2.   Solve: $\frac{3}{5}(5 - 10n) - 2 = 1 - 6n$

Solution:
$$\frac{3}{5}(5 - 10n) - 2 = 1 - 6n$$
$$\frac{3}{5} \cdot 5 - \frac{3}{5} \cdot 10n - 2 = 1 - 6n$$
$$3 - 6n - 2 = 1 - 6n$$
$$1 - 6n = 1 - 6n$$
$$1 - 6n + 6n = 1 - 6n + 6n$$
$$1 = 1$$

Since the given equation is equivalent to the true statement "$1 = 1$," the equation is satisfied by every real number.

$\therefore$ the solution set is $\Re$.   **Answer.**

Any equation which is a true statement for every numerical replacement of the variable(s) in the equation is called an **identity**. Thus, "$\frac{2}{5}(5 - 10n) - 2 = 1 - 6n$" is an identity.

In many fields of applied mathematics, equations called **formulas** represent the numerical relationships between physical measurements. You may recall, for example, such formulas as:

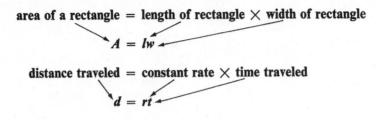

area of a rectangle = length of rectangle × width of rectangle

$$A = lw$$

distance traveled = constant rate × time traveled

$$d = rt$$

and

simple interest = principal × rate of interest × time

$$I = Prt$$

In applying formulas, you often have to find equivalent equations in which a particular variable is expressed in terms of other variables.

EXAMPLE 3. Solve $A = P + Prt$ for r.

Solution:

$$A = P + Prt$$
$$A - P = P + Prt - P$$
$$A - P = Prt$$
$$\frac{A - P}{Pt} = \frac{Prt}{Pt}$$
$$\frac{A - P}{Pt} = r$$

or $\quad r = \dfrac{A - P}{Pt}$, $(P \neq 0, t \neq 0)$.   **Answer.**

Notice that the result in Example 3 is given in the form of an equation rather than as a statement of a solution set. This is customary in working with formulas. Also, because Pt was used as a divisor, neither P nor t can equal 0.

Oral Exercises

Tell how to transform the equation into an equivalent one in which one member is a variable and the other member is a constant. Then state the transformed equation.

SAMPLE. $2x + 15 = 7x$

Solution: **1.** Subtract $2x$ from each member of the given equation.

2. Divide each member of the resulting equation by 5.

$$2x + 15 = 7x$$
$$2x + 15 - 2x = 7x - 2x$$
$$15 = 5x$$
$$\frac{15}{5} = \frac{5x}{5}$$
$$\therefore 3 = x. \quad \textbf{Answer.}$$

1. $6a = 8 + 5a$	**7.** $5m - 10 = 7m$	**13.** $c = -8c$
2. $9u = 8u - 3$	**8.** $2z = 3z - 1$	**14.** $3b = 5b$
3. $g = 10 - g$	**9.** $8n = 5n - 9$	**15.** $1.4q = 0.4q - 3$
4. $3p = 16 - p$	**10.** $5w - 6 = 11w$	**16.** $-0.2s = 1.8s - 10$
5. $d = 14 + 2d$	**11.** $-3v = 3v + 1$	**17.** $2x + x^2 = x^2 + 6$
6. $4k = 1 + 5k$	**12.** $6t - 14 = -t$	**18.** $w^2 + 5w = w^2$

Solve each equation for x, y, or z.

19. $x - a = b$	**21.** $y + c = 2c$	**23.** $-z = a - 2z$
20. $y + c = a$	**22.** $z - k = 3k$	**24.** $b - x = 3x$

Written Exercises

Solve each equation in one variable. If the equation is an identity, state this fact. If the equation contains more than one variable, solve for the variable in red.

A

1. $8q = 35 + 3q$	**7.** $28 - 2m = 2m$	**13.** $4a = 2a - 12$
2. $11a = 8a + 42$	**8.** $9n - 70 = 2n$	**14.** $5w = w - 64$
3. $7b = 54 - 2b$	**9.** $168 - 12p = 0$	**15.** $2x - 45 = -x$
4. $9x = 84 - 5x$	**10.** $0 = 196 - 7s$	**16.** $-r = 93 - 4r$
5. $21y = 16y - 30$	**11.** $195 + 18z = 15z$	**17.** $4t + 6 = 2t$
6. $31t = 25t - 48$	**12.** $182 + 53c = 40c$	**18.** $-5z - 8 = -3z$

19. $22 - x = 7x - 2$	**26.** $17 - 4h = 14 - h$
20. $12m - 5 = 2 - 5m$	**27.** $3x + 7 - x = 5x - 1$
21. $8 + 2z = z + 15$	**28.** $2y - 3 + 5y = y + 15$
22. $27 + 5r = 9 + 3r$	**29.** $P = 1 + 2w$
23. $3z - 5 = z + 11$	**30.** $A = \pi + 2h$
24. $-2w + 7 = 5w - 21$	**31.** $12w - 8t = 4u$
25. $4b + 33 = 9b + 5$	**32.** $24a - 3y = 5y$

33. $2x + 3y = 1$

34. $5x - 2y = 1$

35. $M = \dfrac{x + y + z}{3}$

36. $P = l + 2w + 2h$

B **37.** $-3(2t - 5) = 3(t - 1)$

38 $4(6 - z) = -2(3z + 1)$

39. $-3r + 2(r + 1) = 7$

40. $-2n + 3(2n - 1) = 29$

41. $T = 2\pi rh + 2\pi r^2,\ r \neq 0$

42. $T = mg - mf,\ m \neq 0$

43. $a = S(1 - r),\ S \neq 0$

44. $S = \dfrac{n}{2}(a + l),\ n \neq 0$

45. $2(5x + 1) + 16 = 4 + 3(x - 7)$

46. $6(y - 3) + 5 = 23 + 2(y - 2)$

47. $5(2z - 4) + 6 = -2(7 - 5z)$

48. $5x + (x + 15) - 3(2x + 4) = 3$

49. $10t + (5t - 4) = 9t + (6t + 2)$

50. $4(4y + 6) + 8 = -12 - 16(1 - y)$

51. $2.5z + 0.3(480 - z) = 3.2$

52. $0.5x - 0.25(7 - 4x) = 0.1x - 0.7(4 + x)$

C **53.** $4(x - a) + 4a = 7(b + 3) - 21$

54. $-3(c + y) + 3c = 6(c - 2) + 12$

55. $-2[x - 3(2 - x)] - 4 = 3(x + 1) - 6$

56. $8[3 + 2(2y + 3)] = -2[16 - (y + 7)]$

57. $5[z - 2(3z - 6)] = 3(24 - 9z)$

58. $2[4t + 7 - 3(2t + 3)] = 8(3t - 4) - 7(2t - 3)$

59. $3[2(2r + 3) - (r + 1) - (r + 2)] = 0$

60. $2[3(y - 4) - 2(5y + 1)] = 3(y - 2) - 4(2y + 1)$

61. $7[2x + 2(3 - 2x) + 1] = 4 + 5(2 - 3x) - x$

62. $-3[2(y - 5) - y] = 2[3y - 5(-3 + y)] + y$

Problems

Solve each of the following problems. Draw a sketch, if needed.

SAMPLE. Jim is exactly 7 years older than his sister, Myra. Next year, he will be twice as old as Myra will be. How old is Jim?

Solution:

1▶ Let $y =$ Myra's age in years now. (The symbol $=$ here is used to mean "represent.")

The facts in the problem are arranged in the chart below.

	Myra	Jim
Age now	y	$y + 7$
Age next year (1 yr. hence)	$y + 1$	$y + 7 + 1 = y + 8$

2 ▶ Next year:

$\underbrace{\text{Jim's age}}$	$\underbrace{\text{will be}}$	$\underbrace{\text{twice Myra's age}}$
$y + 8$	$=$	$2(y + 1)$

3 ▶ $\qquad y + 8 \;=\; 2y + 2$

$\qquad\qquad\qquad 6 = y$

4 ▶ If Myra is 6 years old, Jim is $6 + 7$, or 13, years old. Will Jim be twice as old as Myra next year? That is:

$$13 + 1 \overset{?}{=} 2(6 + 1)$$
$$14 \overset{?}{=} 2(7)$$
$$14 = 14 \checkmark$$

∴ Jim is 13 years old. **Answer.**

A 1. Find a number which equals its opposite increased by 8.

2. Find a number which equals its opposite decreased by 12.

3. Multiplying a certain number by 2 yields the same result as adding 15 to 3 times the number. Find the number.

4. Five times a certain number is twelve more than twice the number. What is the number?

5. Fritz asked: "Can you tell me the number I am thinking of? When I multiply it by 3 and then add 5, I get the same answer as when I multiply it by 5 and then subtract 3."

6. Gerry challenged: "Tell me my number. When I add 1 to it and then multiply the sum by 2, I get the same result as when I subtract 7 from my number."

7. Sandra has five coins of the same kind. Two twenty-cent stamps and one of the coins have the same total value as all five coins put together. What kind of coin does Sandra have?

8. Beth has 4 steel balls of the same size and shape. She found that when she put three of the balls in one pan of a beam balance and put the fourth ball together with an 8-ounce weight in the other pan, the pans balanced each other. How much does each ball weigh?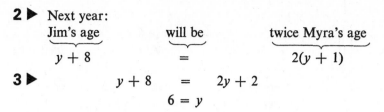

9. Neil weighs 25 pounds more than Ed, while Mike weighs 125 pounds less than twice as much as Ed. If Mike and Neil have the same weight, how much does each of the three men weigh?

10. Joan is three times as old as June, while Jane is 6 years older than June. If Joan and Jane are twins, how old is each of the three girls?

11. Charles is twice as old as Faye. He is also exactly 15 years older than Faye was last year. How old are Charles and Faye?

12. On her diet, Mrs. Klein has been losing 1 pound a week for the last year. Her husband weighs 110 pounds more than she does now. If his weight is twice what her weight was six weeks ago, how much does Mrs. Klein weigh now?

13. The sum of two numbers is 17. Six times the smaller number is two less than twice the greater. What are the numbers?

14. The difference between two numbers is 8. Five times the smaller number is 4 more than three times the greater. What are the numbers?

15. The sum of two numbers is 15. Four times the smaller number is 60 less than twice the greater number. Find the numbers.

16. Express 11 as a sum of two addends, such that the larger addend is four times the sum of 9 and the smaller addend.

17. One house is four times as old as another. Eighteen years from now it will be twice as old. How old are the houses?

18. Mrs. Harvath is three times as old as her daughter, Sue. Ten years from now she will be twice as old as Sue. How old are Mrs. Harvath and Sue?

19. In a game of tic-tac-toe, Judy made one move more than Sue, or two fewer than twice as many as Sue. How many moves did each of the girls make?

20. A molecule of sucrose contains 8 more oxygen atoms than a molecule of silver nitrate, or 1 fewer than 4 times as many as a molecule of silver nitrate. How many oxygen atoms does a molecule of each of these compounds contain?

21. Karl, who is 18 years old, has a great-grandfather, aged 78 years. How many years ago was Karl's great-grandfather 7 times as old as Karl?

22. A father aged 37 has a son aged 4. In how many years will the father be 4 times as old as his son?

23. The length of one rectangle is 3 feet more than the length of another rectangle. The width of the first rectangle is 5 feet. The width of the second is 2 feet. If the area of the first rectangle is 120 square feet greater than the area of the second, find the length of each rectangle.

24. The perimeter of a rectangle is 24 meters. Three times the length is 9 meters less than 6 times the width. Find the dimensions of the rectangle.

25. The perimeter of an isosceles triangle is 28 centimeters. Five times the length of the base is 4 centimeters more than 7 times the length of each of the congruent sides. How long is each side of the triangle?

26. The length of one rectangle is 4 inches greater than the width of a second rectangle. The width of the first rectangle is 6 inches and the length of the second rectangle is 9 inches. The area of the second rectangle is 3 square inches less than the area of the first rectangle. Find the dimensions of the first rectangle.

27. An apple has 29 more calories than a peach and 13 fewer calories than a banana. If 3 apples have 43 fewer calories than 2 bananas and 2 peaches, how many calories does an apple have?

28. A cup of coffee contains 20 more milligrams of caffeine than a cup of tea and 85 more milligrams of caffeine than the average cola drink. If one cup of tea and four cola drinks contain the same amount of caffeine as one cup of coffee, how many milligrams of caffeine are there in one cup of coffee?

B **29.** One year the folk-rock group The Gypsy Traders made two 45 r.p.m. records and one $33\frac{1}{3}$ r.p.m. record. During that year one of the 45's sold 50,000 more records than the other 45 and 30,000 more than 14 times as many records as the $33\frac{1}{3}$. If the best-selling 45 sold 745,000 more records than the $33\frac{1}{3}$, how many of each recording were sold?

30. If the Washington Monument were 85 feet taller, it would be just as tall as the Gateway Arch in St. Louis. If the height of the Washington Monument is 240 feet more than one-half the height of the Gateway Arch, how tall is each of these structures?

31. The Suez Canal, which is about 104 miles long, was opened 45 years before the Panama Canal (length, about 51 miles). Up to 1959, the Suez Canal had been operating twice as long as the Panama Canal. In what year was the Suez Canal opened? the Panama Canal?

32. In tennis, the length of a doubles court and a singles court are the same, but the width of a doubles court is 9 feet greater than that of a singles court. The length of a singles court is 6 feet greater than twice the width of a doubles court, and the width of a singles court is 1 foot greater than one-third the length of a doubles court. What are the dimensions of a singles court?

33. George Washington was born 11 years before Thomas Jefferson. In 1770 Washington's age was 3 years more than 7 times the age of Jefferson in 1748. How old was each man in 1750?

34. On a rendezvous mission, a spacecraft traveling in a circular orbit makes a forward burn in order to transfer into the orbit in which a second spacecraft is traveling. The apogee (highest point) of the first orbit is 5 miles higher than the perigee (lowest point). The apogee of the second orbit is 18 miles higher than the apogee of the first orbit, and the perigee of the second orbit is 19 miles higher than the perigee of the first orbit. Six times the number of miles in the apogee of the first orbit is 100 miles more than five times the number of miles in the perigee of the second orbit. Find the apogee of the first orbit.

35. "Tom is 2 times older than I am," Dick said to Mary. "On the other hand, I am 4 years younger than Harry while Tom is 8 years older than Harry. How old are Harry, Tom, and I?"

36. At one time, 4 pounds of onions cost the same as 2 pounds of string beans. At the same time, 1 pound of string beans cost 3 times as much as a pound of potatoes, while 1 pound of onions cost 4 cents less than 2 pounds of potatoes. What was the cost of 1 pound of each vegetable?

EXTRA PROBLEM

The coefficients a, b, c, and d in the equation "$ax + b = cx + d$" are given on a card. Draw a flow chart of a program to compute and print the unique root (if any) of the equation. (*Hint:* the equation has a unique root if $a - c \neq 0$; it has no root if $a - c = 0$ and $d - b \neq 0$; it has all real numbers as roots if $a - c = 0$ and $d - b = 0$.)

4–8 Equations and Functions

You can use an equation such as "$y = 2x - 1$" to assign to each number in the domain of the variable x another number, the value of y. For example, if $x \in \{3, 4, 5\}$, then "$y = 2x - 1$" makes the assignments, or pairings, shown below:

$$x \quad : \quad 3 \qquad\qquad 4 \qquad\qquad 5$$
$$\downarrow \qquad\quad \downarrow \qquad\qquad \downarrow \qquad\qquad \downarrow$$
$$y = 2x - 1 : 2 \cdot 3 - 1 = 5 \quad 2 \cdot 4 - 1 = 7 \quad 2 \cdot 5 - 1 = 9$$

Do you see that the given equation pairs each member of $\{3, 4, 5\}$ with a single member of $\{5, 7, 9\}$? This example illustrates the mathematical idea of a *function*.

A **function** consists of two sets D and R together with a rule that assigns to each element of D exactly one element of R. The set D is called the **domain** of the function, and R is called the **range** of the function. Thus, in the preceding example the domain of the function is $\{3, 4, 5\}$ and the range is $\{5, 7, 9\}$.

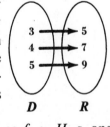

Functions are often named by single letters such as f, g, H, s, and so on. The arrow notation

$$f: x \rightarrow 2x - 1$$

is read "the function f that pairs x with $2x - 1$." Of course, to specify the function completely, you must also identify the domain D of the function. The numbers assigned by the rule then form the range.

EXAMPLE 1.   Specify in roster form the range of

$$g: x \to x^2 + 1 \quad \text{if} \quad D = \{-1, 0, 1, 2\}.$$

Solution: In "$x^2 + 1$," replace x with the name of each member of D to find the members of the range, R.

x	$x^2 + 1$
-1	$(-1)^2 + 1 = 2$
0	$0^2 + 1 = 1$
1	$1^2 + 1 = 2$
2	$2^2 + 1 = 5$

$$\therefore R = \{1, 2, 5\}. \quad \text{Answer.}$$

Notice that the function g assigns to both -1 and 1 the number 2. However, in specifying the range of g you name 2 only once. (Recall page 16.)

Members of the range are called the **values** of the function. For instance, in Example 1, the values of g are 1, 2, and 5.

To state that

$$g: x \to x^2 + 1$$

assigns to the number 2 the number 5, you use the equation

$$g(2) = 5,$$

which may be read: "g at **two** equals five," or "g of **two** equals five," or "the value of g at **two** equals five." Notice that $g(2)$ does *not* name the product of g and 2! It names the *number* that g assigns to 2.

EXAMPLE 2.   Given

$$H: t \to t^3 \text{ with } D = \{0, 1, 2\},$$

find: a. $H(0)$ b. $H(1)$ c. $H(2)$

Solution: You can first write the equation

$$H(t) = t^3.$$

Then: $$H(0) = 0^3 = 0$$
$$H(1) = 1^3 = 1$$
$$H(2) = 2^3 = 8$$

$$\therefore H(0) = 0, \ H(1) = 1, \ H(2) = 8. \quad \text{Answer.}$$

The variable used in defining a function does not matter. For instance,

$$m: z \rightarrow z^3 \text{ with } D = \{0, 1, 2\}$$

is the same function as H in Example 2. Both H and m pair each member of $\{0, 1, 2\}$ with its cube.

At first, the only functions studied were ones whose values could be given by a single equation or formula, like the functions in Examples 1 and 2. Nowadays, functions that cannot be defined so simply are also important. For instance, the function that assigns the number 1 to each positive number, 0 to 0, and -1 to each negative number is very useful. You can define it in symbols this way:

$$s: s(x) = \begin{cases} 1 \text{ if } x > 0 \\ 0 \text{ if } x = 0 \\ -1 \text{ if } x < 0, \ x \in \mathfrak{R} \end{cases}$$

To read these symbols, you say: "The function s with domain $\mathfrak{R}$ such that s at x equals one if x is greater than zero, zero if x equals 0, and negative one if x is less than zero."

Oral Exercises

Give the meaning of each of the following. Assume that the domain of each function is $\mathfrak{R}$.

SAMPLE 1. $g: z \rightarrow 3z + 6$

Solution: The function g that pairs z with $3z + 6$.

1. $f: x \rightarrow 2x$
2. $h: t \rightarrow t^2$
3. $g: z \rightarrow 2z - 1$
4. $k: n \rightarrow 5n^2 + 2$
5. $f: a \rightarrow 3a^2 + 2$
6. $f: x \rightarrow 3$.

State the range of the specified function.

SAMPLE 2. $f: x \rightarrow 3x, \ D = \{1, 2, 3\}$ *Solution:* $R = \{3, 6, 9\}$

7. $g: y \rightarrow y + 2, \ D = \{0, 1, 2\}$
8. $h: z \rightarrow z - 1, \ D = \{3, 4, 5\}$
9. $f: n \rightarrow 2n + 1, \ D = \{-1, 2, 3\}$
10. $l: t \rightarrow 2t - 1, \ D = \{1, 2, -3\}$
11. $f: x \rightarrow 2x^2, \ D = \{0, 1, 2\}$
12. $g: s \rightarrow \dfrac{s}{4}, \ D = \{1, -4, -8\}$

Let $f(x) = 2x + 3$. State the given value of f.

SAMPLE 3. $f(-2)$ *Solution:* $f(-2) = 2(-2) + 3 = -1$

13. $f(0)$
14. $f(1)$
15. $f(-3)$
16. $f(-4)$

Given $k: x \rightarrow x^2 - 1$, state the number in the range of k paired with the given number in the domain.

17. 1 **18.** 2 **19.** -3 **20.** 0

Exercises 21–24 refer to the function $A: x \rightarrow |x|$ with $D = \Re$.

21. The value of A at 2 is __?__.
22. $A(-3) =$ __?__.
23. The value of A at __?__ is 0.
24. The value of A at both __?__ and __?__ is 1.
25. At each number in its domain any function has __?__ (one, more than one, fewer than one) value.

Written Exercises

Use arrow notation to represent the function whose values are given by the expression shown. Assume that the domain is $\Re$.

SAMPLE. $g: 3t^2 + 1$

Solution: $g: t \rightarrow 3t^2 + 1$. **Answer.**

1. $f; 4x - 3$ **3.** $h; x(x + 1)$ **5.** $g; x(x^2 + x + 1)$
2. $g; 3m^2 + 2m + 1$ **4.** $s; \frac{1}{2}(t^2 + 1)$ **6.** $f; (s + 1)^2 + 2s$

Specify in roster form the range of the given function.

7. $f: x \rightarrow 2x + 5, \ D = \{0, -1, 2\}$
8. $g: z \rightarrow 4z - 3, \ D = \{-1, 2, 3\}$
9. $h: y \rightarrow y^2 - 5, \ D = \{3, -4, -5\}$
10. $f: t \rightarrow 2t^2 + 1, \ D = \{0, -1, -2\}$
11. $l: n \rightarrow \dfrac{n + 3}{2}, \ D = \{1, 3, 5\}$
12. $s: x \rightarrow \dfrac{3}{x + 1}, \ D = \{2, 5, 8\}$
13. $g: x \rightarrow x(x + 2), \ D = \{0, 5, -10\}$
14. $h: z \rightarrow (z + 1)(z + 2), \ D = \{0, -5, 10\}$
15. $f: x \rightarrow x^2 - 2x + 3, \ D = \{8, -9, -10\}$
16. $s: t \rightarrow 2t^2 - t + 1, \ D = \{5, -6, -7\}$

Given $f: f(x) = (x + 1)^2$, find:

17. $f(1)$ **18.** $f(3)$ **19.** $f(-5)$ **20.** $f(-4)$

Given $g: t \rightarrow (t - 2)^2$, find:

21. $g(2)$ **22.** $g(4)$ **23.** $g(-1)$ **24.** $g(-4)$

Given $h: z \rightarrow (z^2 + 1)^2$, find:

B   **25.** $h(1)$ **26.** $h(3)$ **27.** $h(3) - h(1)$ **28.** $h(3) + h(1)$

Given $f: y \rightarrow (y^2 - 2)^2$, find:

29. $f(3)$ **30.** $f(4)$ **31.** $f(4) - f(3)$ **32.** $f(4) + f(3)$

Given $f: x \rightarrow (x + 1)^2 + 1$ and $g: z \rightarrow z^2 + 1$, find:

33. $f(3)$ **34.** $g(3)$ **35.** $f(3) - g(3)$ **36.** $f(3) + g(3)$

Given $f: x \rightarrow 3x + 2$ and $h: y \rightarrow \dfrac{y - 2}{3}$, find:

C   **37.** $f[h(3)]$ *Hint:*   First find $h(3)$.
   38. $h[f(3)]$ **39.** $f[h(5)]$ **40.** $h[f(5)]$

In each of Exercises 41–44, state the values at $-1, 0$, and $\frac{1}{2}$ of the function whose values are given by the indicated formulas. Assume that $D = \mathcal{R}$ for each function.

41. $F(x) = \begin{cases} 3 \text{ if } x \geq 0 \\ -3 \text{ if } x < 0 \end{cases}$ **43.** $f(a) = \begin{cases} a \text{ if } a \leq 0 \\ 2a \text{ if } a > 0 \end{cases}$

42. $T(c) = \begin{cases} 1 \text{ if } c \text{ is an integer} \\ 0 \text{ if } c \text{ is not an integer} \end{cases}$ **44.** $f(x) = \begin{cases} x \text{ if } x \geq 0 \\ -x \text{ if } x < 0 \end{cases}$

● CHAPTER SUMMARY ●

Inventory of Structure and Method

1. **A theorem** is a statement which has been proved through logical reasoning from known facts and given assumptions.

2. In the following two theorems, a, b, and c represent any three real numbers.
   Addition property of equality: If $a = b$, then $a + c = b + c$.
   Multiplication property of equality: If $a = b$, then $ac = bc$.

3. **Rule for subtraction:** $a - b = a + (-b)$.

4. **Rule for division:** $a \div b = a \cdot \dfrac{1}{b}$.

5. To solve an equation you **transform** it into an **equivalent equation** by undoing each indicated operation with the appropriate **inverse operation** (addition — subtraction; multiplication by a nonzero number — division by a nonzero number) until you derive an equation which shows the solu-

tion set. To **check** the tentative value, you **substitute** it for the variable in the **original equation** and see whether or not it satisfies the equation by evaluating each member separately.

6. Suggested steps in solving an equation as outlined in item 5:
    (a) Simplify each member.
    (b) Undo any indicated additions or subtractions.
    (c) Undo any indicated multiplications or divisions involving the variable.
    (d) Check the tentative answer in the original equation.

7. In solving word problems, first read the problem carefully and decide what numbers are asked for. Then:

    1 — Choose a variable with an appropriate replacement set and use the variable in representing each described number.

    2 — Form an open sentence by using facts given in the problem.

    3 — Find the solution set of the open sentence.

    4 — Check your answer with the words of the problem.

8. A **function** consists of two sets D and R together with a rule that assigns to each element of D exactly one element of R. The set D is called the **domain** of the function, and R is called the **range** of the function. Members of R are the **values** of the function.

Vocabulary and Spelling

Review the meaning of each term by reference to the page listed.

hypothesis (*p. 111*)
conclusion (*p. 111*)
direct proof (*p. 112*)
theorem (*p. 112*)
members of an equation (inequality) (*p. 112*)
equivalent equations (*p. 113*)
transformation (*p. 113*)
difference (*p. 116*)

quotient (*p. 125*)
inverse operation (*p. 130*)
identity (*p. 140*)
formula (*p. 140*)
function (*p. 146*)
domain (*p. 146*)
range (*p. 146*)
values of a function (*p. 147*)

Chapter Test

4–1 Solve:

    1. $t - 17 = 22$ **3.** $-\frac{4}{7} + y = \frac{10}{7}$

    2. $x - 0.03 = 0.3$ **4.** $|p| - 2 = 4$

4–2 Solve:

    5. $-27 = q + 21$ **7.** $(c + 8) + 3 = 14$

    6. $n + \frac{3}{5} = 4$ **8.** $Z + 0.07 = 0.008$

4–3 Solve:

9. $-13r = 91$

10. $\frac{1}{3}h = \frac{7}{3}$

11. $\frac{1}{6} = 3k$

12. $\frac{3}{2}q = 72$

4–4 Solve:

13. $-12 = -4x$

14. $\frac{3}{4}x = \frac{9}{8}$

15. $17t = -408$

16. $14x = -7$

4–5 Solve:

17. $4t - 2 + 3t + 8 = -15$

18. $-3r + 2(4r + 11) = -3$

19. $-1.8r + 5.7 + 3.3r = 1.2$

20. $\frac{5}{4}k - 3(\frac{1}{4}k + 6) = 12$

4–6 21. A Ritewell pen and pencil set costs $3.39, the pen costing $0.69 more than the pencil. Find the cost of each.

22. During the summer Pam's older sister, Jill, earned $46 less than twice the amount Pam earned. If their total earnings amounted to $818, how much did each earn?

4–7 23. $2(3h - 5) + 12 = 5(2h + 3) + 9h$

24. The width of a rectangle is 4 inches less than twice the width of a smaller rectangle. The larger rectangle is 15 inches long; the smaller is 16 inches long. If the area of the larger rectangle is 108 square inches more than the area of the smaller, find the width of the larger rectangle.

4–8 25. Specify in roster form the range of the given function.
$f: x \to (x - 1)^2$, $D = \{-1, 0, 1, 2\}$.

26. Given $g: x \to \dfrac{1}{1 + x}$, find:

a. $g(-2)$ b. $g(0)$ c. $g(2)$

Chapter Review

4–1 Transforming Equations by Addition   *Pages 111–116*

1. The properties of equality are called __?__ because they can be proved.

2. The expressions joined by the equals sign or inequality symbol are the __?__ of the equation or inequality.

3. Equivalent equations have the same __?__ set.

4. Adding the same real number to each member of an equation is called __?__ by addition.

5. Solve $0 = t - 8$.   6. Solve $r - 7 = 7$.

4–2 **Subtracting Real Numbers** *Pages 116–122*

7. To subtract real numbers, replace the __?__ by its opposite, and then __?__.

8. Subtracting a real number is the __?__ operation of adding it.

9. Solve $x + 3 = -7$. **10.** Solve $\frac{13}{5} = y + \frac{3}{5}$.

4–3 **Transforming Equations by Multiplication** *Pages 123–125*

11. To find x, __?__ each member of the equation $\frac{1}{3}x = 10$ by __?__.

12. To undo the multiplication of a number by a given number, multiply the product by the __?__ of the given number.

13. In transforming an equation by multiplication you may not multiply each member by __?__.

14. Solve $\frac{5}{9}x = \frac{10}{63}$. **15.** Solve $\frac{7}{3}x = \frac{14}{9}$.

4–4 **Dividing Real Numbers** *Pages 125–130*

16. The inverse operation of __?__ is division.

17. To divide real numbers replace the __?__ by its reciprocal, and multiply.

18. Dividing both members of an equation by __?__ does not result in an equivalent equation.

19. Solve $36r = -288$. **20.** Solve $6.4s = 1.6$.

4–5 **Using Several Transformations** *Pages 130–132*

21. Before considering multiplications and divisions, undo indicated __?__ and __?__.

22. Solve $7t - 3t = 7 - 3$. **23.** Solve $2 + r = \frac{7}{3}$.

24. The sum of a number n and 5 times that number may be represented by $n +$ __?__, or __?__.

25. Four times a number decreased by eight-tenths the number gives 32. Find the original number.

26. $5.2a + 3 + 1.8a = -25$ **27.** $3(2b + 3) - 4b = -3$

4–6 **Using Equations to Solve Problems** *Pages 133–138*

28. Uncle John is 3 years younger than four times his nephew Paul's age. Their ages total 57. Find the age of each.

29. In a telephone survey 649 people voiced their opinions on a tax proposal. If those in favor of the tax outnumbered those against it by 127, how many people supported the tax proposal?

30. The perimeter of a rectangle is 32 inches. The length of the rectangle is one inch longer than the width. Find the dimensions of the rectangle.

4–7   Equations Having the Variable in Both Members

Pages 138–146

31. When an equation has the variable in each member, transform it into an equation containing the variable in only __?__ member.

32. Solve $\frac{3}{2}(6r - 7) = 4r - 4(\frac{1}{2}r + \frac{7}{2})$.

33. Solve $F = \frac{9}{5}C + 32$ for C.

34. A father aged 39 years has a son aged 14. In how many years will the age of the son be one-half that of his father?

4–8   Equations and Functions

Pages 146–150

35. In a function exactly one element of the __?__ can be assigned to each element of the __?__.

36. In the function $f: x \rightarrow x + 1$ each element of the domain is one __?__ than the corresponding element of the range paired with it.

37. Given: $h: y \rightarrow |y|$, find

    a. $h(-3)$ **b.** $h(-1)$ **c.** $h(1)$ **d.** $h(3)$

38. Specify in roster form the range of the given function.

$$g: y \rightarrow \frac{y}{1 - y}, \quad D = \{-4, -2, 0, 2, 4\}$$

EXTRA PROBLEMS

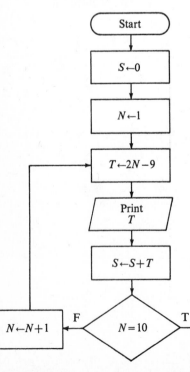

1. The flow chart at the left assigns the initial value 0 to S and the initial value 1 to N. Then, it computes $2N - 9$ (initially $2 \cdot 1 - 9$ or -7) and assigns this value to T and prints it. Next it adds the "current" values of S and T and makes the sum the "new" value of S (when the "current" values of S and T are 0 and -7, the "new" value of S is $0 + (-7)$, or -7). If $N = 10$, then it prints the value of S and stops; otherwise, it increases the value of N by 1 and repeats the cycle. **a.** What are the ten values of T printed by the program? **b.** What value of S is printed by the program?

2. Draw a flow chart of a program to compute and print the sum of the values of $N(N - 1)$ for $N = -3, -2, -1, 0, 1, 2, \ldots, 15$.

Cumulative Review: Chapters 1–4

Make a true statement by replacing each __?__ with one of the symbols
=, > or <.

1. $(3 \times 2) \div (5 - 4)$ __?__ $[(5 + 4) + 3] \div 2$

2. $(5 \times 4) - (3 \times 2)$ __?__ $[(6 + 5) - 4] \times 3$

3. $\dfrac{10 - 6}{8}$ __?__ -1

4. -5 __?__ $-2\frac{1}{2}$ __?__ $-\frac{1}{2}$

For each of the following sets, indicate whether it is finite or infinite.
If the set is given by a roster, specify it by a rule; if it is given by a rule,
specify the set by a roster.

5. {the states in U.S.A. whose names begin with the letter A.}

6. {3, 6, 9, 12, 15, . . .}   **7.** {a, b, c, . . . , x, y, z}

8. {the positive integers less than 10}

Draw the graph of each set described below.

9. {the numbers less than or equal to 4}

10. {the numbers between -5 and -1, inclusive}

Given the sets: $P = \{1, 2, 4, 8, 16\}$ and $Q = \{2, 4, 6, 8, 10\}$, find the set
specified as follows:

11. {the elements in P or Q, or in both}

12. {the elements that are in both P and Q}

If the values of a, b, c, and d are $\frac{1}{2}$, 3, 6, and 8, respectively, evaluate each
expression.

13. $3(d - 2b) + 4a(c + 1)$

14. $\dfrac{b^2 - ad}{b^3 - ac}$

Simplify each expression.

15. $3 \cdot 2^2 - 18 \div 3 + 1$ **16.** $(4^3 - 2^3) \div 7 + 3$

If the replacement set for n is $U = \{0, \frac{1}{2}, 3, 5\}$, find the subset of U
whose elements make each of the following sentences true.

17. $4n \geq 2$ **19.** $n(n + 1) = n^2 + n$

18. $3(n - 1) = 6$ **20.** $\frac{1}{2}n < 1$

Write an algebraic expression for each of the following.

21. The larger of two numbers when their sum is 20 and the smaller is y.

22. One-fourth of the difference between a and b.

23. The third side of a triangle whose perimeter is 18, and whose second side is twice the first, s.

In each case, state the axiom or property which makes the conclusion true.

24. If $5p = r$, then $r = 5p$.   **26.** If $p = q$ and $q = 7$, then $p = 7$.

25. $2(y - 3) = (y - 3)2$ **27.** $2(y - 3) = 2y - 6$.

State whether or not each of the given sets is closed under the indicated operation.

28. $\{10, 8, 6, 4, 2, 0\}$, subtraction

29. $\{0, 4, 8, 12, 16, \ldots\}$, multiplication by 6

Simplify the following expressions.

30. $-[(-4) + (-3)] - 7$ **31.** $5(b + 2) - 3b + (-4)$

32. $(4x + 3y) + [2x + (-3)y]$

33. $7s + (-9) + 3t + (-4)s + (-2)t + 5$

34. $\frac{2}{3}[18p + (-12)q]$

35. $\frac{2}{5}[(-10)a + 15b] + \frac{3}{4}[16a + (-4)b]$

Solve each equation.

36. $12y + 15 = 9y - 6$ **38.** $2(7t - 1) + 3 = 5(2t - 3)$

37. $0.6x - 7 - 1.4x = 1.2x + 13$ **39.** $8(6z + 18) = 21(4z - 10) - 1$

Solve each problem.

40. The sum of two numbers is 25. Four times the smaller is 2 more than three times the larger. Find the numbers.

41. Bruce bought a shirt and a tie for his father's birthday. If the shirt cost $2.80 more than the tie and Bruce spent a total of $10.70, how much did the shirt cost?

42. Mrs. Evans is sixteen times as old as her daughter, but in 8 years she will be only four times as old as her daughter. How old is each now?

Specify in roster form the range of the given function; $D = \{-1, 0, 1\}$.

43. $f: x \rightarrow x + 1$ **44.** $g: x \rightarrow x^2 - 1$ **45.** $h: t \rightarrow 3b + 4$

Given $f: x \rightarrow 2x^2 - 3x$, find:

46. $f(1)$ **47.** $f(-1)$ **48.** $f(0)$ **49.** $f(-3)$

Who Uses Mathematics?

Engineers who design and build the bridges that cross our rivers and harbors study a great deal of mathematics in preparation for their careers. Shown are two views of Delaware Memorial Bridge near Wilmington, Delaware — actually two bridges, parallel and 250 feet apart.

Just for Fun

Copy the adjoining diagram on squared paper, and then solve this cross number puzzle as you would a crossword puzzle.

Across

1. The greatest multiple of 9 less than 10^4.
5. 143 is one-half of this number.
9. One more than the square of 13.
10. $15^2 - 2^4 - 2^2 - 1$
11. The area in square feet of a square whose perimeter is 112 feet.
14. Two dozen.
15. Number of yards in one mile.
16. The sum of a number and its opposite.
17. Number of feet per second equal to 60 m.p.h.
19. $-5 \times 5(-1)$
21. The product of a number and its reciprocal.
22. $\frac{1}{151}$ of 151^2
25. The degree measure of the complement of a 70° angle.
26. 0.064×10^5
27. $7 \times 10^2 + 5 \times 10 + 8$
29. A square whose digits add up to 13.
30. The reciprocal of 0.001
31. The cube of five.

Down

2. $[([(914 \times 2) \div 2] \times 2)] \div 2$
3. A prime number.
4. Number of degrees in a right angle.
5. Root of $\frac{1}{2}x - 5 = 6$.
6. $2^3 \times 10^2$
7. The square of -8.
8. Number of cubic inches in one cubic foot.
12. $x^2 + 4x + 22$ if the value of x is 90.
13. Number of days in leap year.
15. Baker's dozen.
18. If you buy plums at 3 for 10¢ and sell them at 5 for 20¢, how many must you sell to make a profit of $1?
20. The number of feet in a land mile.
22. The year Columbus discovered America.
23. 75% of 140
24. 19 is $\frac{1}{9}$ of this number.
26. $1 + 10 \times 4^3$
28. $6(7 + 2) - 15 \div 5 - 1$

EXTRA FOR EXPERTS

A Shortcut for Finding Averages

The **arithmetic average,** or **mean,** of a set of n numbers is their sum divided by n. Sometimes you can reduce the labor of computing it by using positive and negative numbers as follows:

> 1. Assume an average; that is, make a guess.
>
> 2. Find the difference (or *deviation*) between each number and your guess.
>
> 3. Find the average of these differences (the *average deviation*).
>
> 4. Add the average deviation to the assumed average (your guess), and you have the correct average.

EXAMPLE.   Excluding the ends, the linemen on the State University football team weighed as follows: 227 lb., 194 lb., 200 lb., 189 lb., 230 lb. Find the average weight.

Solution:

1. Assume an average of 200 pounds.	Assumed Average: 200 lb.
2. Subtract the assumed average from each weight to get the deviations.	

Weight	Deviation
227	27
194	-6
200	0
189	-11
230	30

3. Divide the sum of the deviations by the number of cases to find the average deviation.	Sum of deviations: 40 Average deviation: $\frac{40}{5} = 8$
4. Add the average deviation to the assumed average to find the true average.	True average $= 200 + 8$ $= 208$ lb. Answer.

The better your guess, the smaller the average deviation, but what you guess really doesn't matter. Suppose that you had assumed 210 pounds as the average in the preceding Example:

Weight	Deviation
227	17
194	−16
200	−10
189	−21
230	20

Average deviation: $\dfrac{-10}{5} = -2$

True average $= 210 - 2$

$= 208$ lb.   **Answer.**

Sum of deviations: −10

To see why this method works, suppose that M represents the **true average** of numbers represented by a, b, c, d, e, and f and assume an average m. The deviations are $a - m, b - m, c - m, d - m, e - m$, and $f - m$, where m is the assumed average.

Sum of deviations $= a + b + c + d + e + f - 6m$

Average deviation $= \dfrac{a + b + c + d + e + f}{6} + \dfrac{-6m}{6}$

∴ Average deviation $=$ M $-$ m

or $M = m +$ average deviation.

Of course, the same method would have worked for 7, 8, or any number of members, as well as for 6.

Exercises

Do each problem by assuming an average and finding the deviations from it.

1. Find the average of the following tuition charges: $2200, $1980, $2050, $1880, $2100, and $1930.

2. Weather balloons released on successive days reached these altitudes (in meters): 7650, 8630, 5600, 9550, 8550, 7550, 8520. Find the average altitude reached by these balloons.

3. In test dives, a diving bell reached these depths: −5200 ft., −5600 ft., −5900 ft., −6100 ft., −6500 ft. Find the average depth.

4. Find the average of the following weights: 17.4 g., 16.6 g., 16.7 g., 17.9 g., 15.9 g., 17.3 g., and 17.5 g.

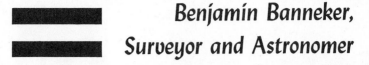

Benjamin Banneker, Surveyor and Astronomer

Born in Maryland, Benjamin Banneker (**Ban**-eck-er) attended a private school near Baltimore, which was open to both black and white students. While there, he developed a keen interest in science and mathematics. In 1753, at the age of 22, he constructed from wooden materials what is said to have been the first clock made entirely in America.

Later, he became friendly with George Ellicott, a Quaker who had moved into the neighborhood to establish a flour mill. Impressed with the young man's intelligence and mechanical skill, Ellicott began to lend Banneker books on mathematics and astronomy. Banneker not only mastered the material in the books quickly but discovered errors in the calculations they contained. In 1789 he demonstrated his proficiency in astronomy by predicting a solar eclipse with a great degree of accuracy.

Banneker continued his interest in astronomy and in 1791 published his first almanac. This attracted the attention of many prominent men. Among these was James McHenry, later Secretary of War in the cabinet of President John Adams, who pointed out that Banneker's work "was begun and finished without the least information or assistance from any person, or from any other books." A manuscript copy was sent to Thomas Jefferson, then Secretary of State in President Washington's cabinet, and drew his warm praise.

What was probably Banneker's most distinguished honor was his appointment to serve on the commission to define the boundary line and lay out the streets of the District of Columbia. His friend George Ellicott was also a member of this commission. After completing this work, Banneker returned to his home in Maryland, where he continued his astronomical investigations and resumed publication of his almanacs.

Like all almanacs, Banneker's included a variety of information and comments besides those relating to astronomy and the weather. For example, in 1793 he was so disturbed by the disastrous European wars that he proposed in his almanac for that year the establishment of a Secretary of Peace as a cabinet official.

Benjamin Banneker (1731–1806)

. . . a work of art inspired by musical structure, using geometric patterns to express rhythm and counterpoint

Solving Inequalities;
More Problems

Earlier you have learned about transformations that produce an equivalent equation. There also are transformations which are useful in the solution of inequalities, as you will discover in this chapter.

SOLVING INEQUALITIES

5–1 Axioms of Order

How many of the following statements are true?

$$-5 < 2; \quad -5 = 2; \quad 2 < -5.$$

Of course, only the first one is true. In comparing real numbers, you make the following basic assumption.

Axiom of Comparison

For all real numbers a and b, one and only one of the following statements is true:

$$a < b, \quad a = b, \quad b < a.$$

Now suppose that you have a horizontal number line with positive direction toward the right. Suppose also that you know two facts about the graphs of three numbers a, b, and c (Figure 5–1):

1. The graph of a is left of the graph of b (that is, $a < b$).

2. The graph of b is left of the graph of c (that is, $b < c$).

Question: Where is the graph of a relative to the graph of c?

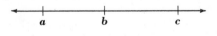

Figure 5–1

Figure 5–1 suggests the answer: The graph of a is left of the graph of c (that is, $a < c$). This sort of thinking makes the following assumption reasonable.

Transitive Axiom of Order

For all real numbers a, b, and c:

1. If $a < b$ and $b < c$, then $a < c$; similarly,
2. If $a > b$ and $b > c$, then $a > c$.

Next look at Figures 5–2 and 5–3. On the number lines shown in those figures, the graph of -5 is left of the graph of 2. In each figure, if you move 4 units from the graph of -5 and also 4 units *in the same direction* from the graph of 2, you arrive at points *in the same order* on the line as the graphs of -5 and 2. Thus, Figures 5–2 and 5–3 picture the following statements:

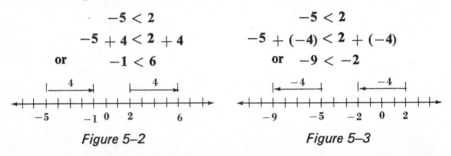

$-5 < 2$	$-5 < 2$
$-5 + 4 < 2 + 4$	$-5 + (-4) < 2 + (-4)$
or $\quad -1 < 6$	or $\quad -9 < -2$

Figure 5–2   Figure 5–3

These statements suggest the next assumption to make.

Addition Axiom of Order

For all real numbers a, b, and c:

1. If $a < b$, then $a + c < b + c$; similarly:
2. If $a > b$, then $a + c > b + c$.

What happens when each member of the inequality "$-5 < 2$" is multiplied by a nonzero real number?

Case 1. **Multiply by 2.**

$$-5 < 2$$

Question: $-5 \cdot 2 \underline{\quad ? \quad} 2 \cdot 2$

That is: $-10 \underline{\quad ? \quad} 4$

Answer: $-10 < 4$

$$\therefore -5 \cdot 2 < 2 \cdot 2.$$

Case 2. **Multiply by -2.**

$$-5 < 2$$

Question: $-5(-2) \underline{\quad ? \quad} 2(-2)$

That is: $10 \underline{\quad ? \quad} -4$

Answer: $10 > -4$

$$\therefore -5(-2) > 2(-2).$$

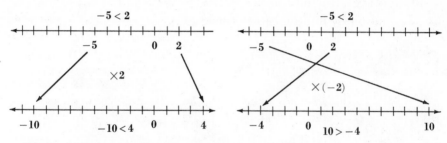

The two cases suggest that *multiplying each member of an inequality* by

(1) a positive number preserves the *direction, order,* or *sense* of the inequality;

(2) a negative number reverses the direction of the inequality.

These results illustrate our next axiom.

Multiplication Axiom of Order

For all real numbers a, b, and c:

1. If $a < b$ and $c > 0$, then $ac < bc$; similarly, if $a > b$ and $c > 0$, then $ac > bc$.
2. If $a < b$ and $c < 0$, then $ac > bc$; similarly, if $a > b$ and $c < 0$, then $ac < bc$.

When you multiply any inequality by a nonzero real number, you *must take into account the direction associated with the multiplier.* Can you guess what happens when the multiplier is zero?

Given: $-5 < 2$

Question: $-5 \cdot 0 \underline{} 2 \cdot 0.$ *That is:* $0 \underline{} 0$

Answer: $0 = 0.$ $\therefore -5 \cdot 0 = 2 \cdot 0.$

Because of the multiplicative property of zero, *multiplying each member of any inequality by* 0 *produces the identity* "$0 = 0$."

The axioms that have been stated guarantee that the following transformations of a given inequality always produce an **equivalent inequality,** that is, one with the same solution set. As was noted in the development of transformations that produce equivalent equations, transformation by subtraction is a special kind of transformation by addition (page 118) and transformation by division is a special case of transformation by multiplication (page 127).

> **Transformations That Produce an Equivalent Inequality**
>
> 1. Substituting for either member of the inequality an expression equivalent to that member.
> 2. Adding to (or subtracting from) each member the same real number.
> 3. Multiplying (or dividing) each member by the same positive number.
> 4. Multiplying (or dividing) each member by the same negative number and reversing the direction of the inequality.

EXAMPLE. Solve $7z - 2 \leq 3(z + 3) + 1$ over $\mathcal{R}$, and graph its solution set.

Solution:

1. Copy the inequality. $\qquad\qquad 7z - 2 \leq 3(z + 3) + 1$

2. Use the distributive axiom $\qquad 7z - 2 \leq 3z + 9 + 1$
   to simplify the right member. $\quad 7z - 2 \leq 3z + 10$

3. Add 2 to each member. $\qquad\quad 7z - 2 + 2 \leq 3z + 10 + 2$
   $$7z \leq 3z + 12$$

4. Subtract $3z$ from each member. $\quad 7z - 3z \leq 3z + 12 - 3z$
   $$4z \leq 12$$

5. Divide each member by 4. $\qquad\qquad \dfrac{4z}{4} \leq \dfrac{12}{4}$

$$z \leq 3$$

∴ the solution set is {all real numbers less than or equal to 3}. **Answer.**

6. Draw the graph of the solution set.

Oral Exercises

Tell how to transform the first inequality in order to obtain the second one. Then specify the solution set of the given inequality over $\mathcal{R}$.

SAMPLE 1. $-\dfrac{x}{2} < 2$; $x > -4$

Solution: Multiply each member by -2 and reverse the direction of the inequality.

∴ the solution set is {all real numbers greater than -4}. **Answer.**

1. $y - 3 < -1$; $y < 2$

2. $t + 2 \geq 0$; $t \geq -2$

3. $2k \leq 16$; $k \leq 8$

4. $3n > -18$; $n > -6$

5. $-5 < \dfrac{x}{2}$; $-10 < x$

6. $1 > \dfrac{p}{3}$; $3 > p$

7. $-12v \geq 48$; $v \leq -4$

8. $-\dfrac{q}{5} \leq -6$; $q \geq 30$

9. $-6 < m - 4$; $-2 < m$

10. $-10 > n - 7$; $-3 > n$

11. $5a + 1 \leq -4$; $a \leq -1$

12. $-7 + 3k \geq 2$; $k \geq 3$

13. $6 \leq -8 + 7s$; $2 \leq s$

14. $t \geq t$; $0 \geq 0$

15. $b \leq b - 2$; $0 \leq -2$

16. $1 - z \geq 4$; $z \leq -3$

In each of Exercises 17–22, tell how to transform the given inequality into an equivalent inequality in which one member is a variable and the other member is a numeral for a specific number. State the transformed inequality.

SAMPLE 2. $-7 + c \geq -7$

Solution: Add 7 to each member; $c \geq 0$. **Answer.**

17. $r + 9 \geq -2$

18. $-5 \geq t - 1$

19. $-v < 3$

20. $-2u > 0$

21. $-6 > \dfrac{d}{3}$

22. $-7 < q - 4$

Written Exercises

Solve each inequality. In each of Exercises 1–22, show also the graph of the solution set.

1. $x - 40 < -100$

2. $y + 25 > 30$

3. $14z \geq -98$

4. $15t > 225$

5. $2z - 3 > 9$

6. $5t + 2 \leq 7$

7. $1 + \dfrac{x}{5} \leq -1$

8. $2 + \dfrac{z}{3} < -2$

9. $-2n + 6 > -4$

10. $-13t + 1 \geq -38$

11. $1 - \dfrac{y}{3} < 1$

12. $2 - \dfrac{n}{4} \geq 2$

13. $-3y + 7 + 5y \leq 1$

14. $4x + 3 - 2x < -1$

15. $2(a - 1) < 8$

16. $3(b + 5) > 9$

17. $\frac{3}{4}x - \frac{1}{2} \geq \frac{1}{4}$

18. $\dfrac{3}{2}u + \dfrac{1}{6} \leq \dfrac{7}{6}$

19. $2z - 1 \leq 3 - 2z$

20. $-3s + 6 > s - 30$

21. $16 - 8n \leq n - 20$

22. $21 - 15x < -8x - 7$

B 23. $4(t - 2) > 5(t - 3)$ 25. $5(4x + 3) - 7(3x - 4) \leq 10$

24. $3(y + 12) \geq 6(y - 4)$ 26. $2(6n - 8) - 9(n + 4) > 2n$

27. $6(z - 5) \leq 15 + 5(7 - 2z)$

28. $3(2r + 3) - (3r + 2) > 12$

29. $-2(t - 5) - 1 \leq 5t + 7(1 - t)$

30. $3(y - 4) - (6y + 2) \geq 5 - 3y$

31. $4(s + 1) - 2(s + 3) \geq 2(s - 1)$

32. $5(g - 4) - (g + 2) \leq 4(g - 4) - 6$

Transform each inequality into an equivalent inequality in which one member is the variable in red.

C 33. $4(3x - a) < 6x + 7a$ 35. $9(t + 4c) \leq 8(t - c)$

34. $3(y - 6b) > 2(6b - y)$ 36. $d - 3(2z - 3d) \geq 2(3z - d)$

5–2 Intersection and Union of Sets

Most of the work in this book deals with sets whose members are real numbers. Therefore, we say that the set of all real numbers, $\mathcal{R}$, is the *universe* of the discussion. In general, the **universe,** or **universal set**, of a discussion is the overall set that includes all the elements in all of the sets under consideration.

Figure 5–4 uses a diagram* to picture a universe U and a set A whose elements all belong to U. In the figure, the region inside and on the rectangle represents U, while the region inside and on the circle represents A. Because every member of A is also a member of U, A is called a **subset** of U. In symbols, you write

Figure 5–4

$$A \subset U,$$

and you say "A is a subset of U."

EXAMPLE 1. Let $U = \{0, 2, 5\}$. Specify in roster form all subsets of U that have exactly two members.

Solution: $\{0, 2\}, \{0, 5\}$, and $\{2, 5\}$. **Answer.**

Is $\{0, 2, 5\}$ a subset of $\{0, 2, 5\}$? Since every member of $\{0, 2, 5\}$ is, indeed, a member of $\{0, 2, 5\}$, the statement "$\{0, 2, 5\} \subset \{0, 2, 5\}$" is certainly true. In fact, *every set is a subset of itself.*

*Diagrams that picture set relationships are called Venn diagrams in honor of the English mathematician John Venn (1834–1923).

Is the empty set Ø a subset of $\{0, 2, 5\}$? Yes! In working with sets, it is useful to agree that Ø *is a subset of every set.*

Figure 5–5 pictures relationships among the sets:

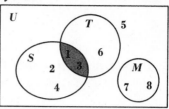

$U = \{1, 2, 3, 4, 5, 6, 7, 8\}$

$S = \{1, 2, 3, 4\}$

$T = \{1, 3, 6\}$

$M = \{7, 8\}$

Figure 5–5

Notice that the names of the set members are shown in red on the diagram.

Can you describe the set represented by shading in Figure 5–5? It is $\{1, 3\}$ and consists of the elements that $\{1, 2, 3, 4\}$ and $\{1, 3, 6\}$ have in common. You call $\{1, 3\}$ the *intersection* of $\{1, 2, 3, 4\}$ and $\{1, 3, 6\}$, and write

$$\{1, 2, 3, 4\} \cap \{1, 3, 6\} = \{1, 3\},$$

read "the intersection of $\{1, 2, 3, 4\}$ and $\{1, 3, 6\}$ equals $\{1, 3\}$."

In general, for any two sets S and T, the set consisting of the elements belonging to *both* S and T is called the **intersection** of S and T, denoted by $S \cap T$.

In a Venn diagram, $S \cap T$ is pictured by the overlap of the regions representing S and T. Look at Figure 5–5 again. Do the regions representing T and M overlap?

They do *not*, because $T = \{1, 3, 6\}$ and $M = \{7, 8\}$ do not have any common members. Sets, such as T and M, which have no elements in common are called **disjoint sets**. Do you see that $T \cap M = \emptyset$?

The shaded region in Figure 5–6 represents the set consisting of all the elements which belong to *at least one* of the following sets: $S = \{1, 2, 3, 4, 5\}$ and $T = \{1, 3, 5, 7, 9\}$. This set contains all the elements of S together with all the elements of T. You call it the *union* of the two sets and write

$$\{1, 2, 3, 4, 5\} \cup \{1, 3, 5, 7, 9\} = \{1, 2, 3, 4, 5, 7, 9\},$$

read "the union of $\{1, 2, 3, 4, 5\}$ and $\{1, 3, 5, 7, 9\}$ equals $\{1, 2, 3, 4, 5, 7, 9\}$."

In general, for any two sets S and T, the set consisting of all the elements belonging to *at least one* of the sets S and T is called the **union** of S and T, denoted by $S \cup T$.

Figure 5–6

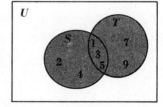

$S \cup T = \{1, 2, 3, 4, 5, 7, 9\}$

EXAMPLE 2. If $A = \{1, 2, 3, 4, 5\}$, $A \cap B = \{1, 3\}$, and $A \cup B = \{1, 2, 3, 4, 5, 6, 7\}$, draw a Venn diagram showing A and B. Identify B by roster.

Solution:

1. **Draw a diagram. Mark it to show the elements of $A \cap B$.**

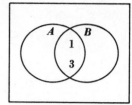

2. **Mark it to show the remaining elements of A.**

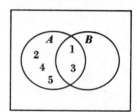

3. **Indicate, as members of B (but not A), the elements of $A \cup B$ not shown in Steps 1 and 2.**

$\therefore B = \{1, 3, 6, 7\}$.   **Answer.**

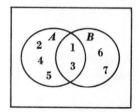

Oral Exercises

Tell which statements are true and which are false. Justify your answer.

1. $\{2, 4, 7\} \subset \{8, 7, 6, 5, 4, 3, 2, 1\}$ 2. $\{0, 2\} \subset \{1, 2, 3, 4\}$
3. $\{\text{Alaska}\} \subset \{\text{the states of the U. S. A.}\}$
4. $\{\text{all high school students}\} \subset \{\text{all students of mathematics}\}$
5. $\{1, 2, 3\} \cap \{1, 4, 5\} \neq \{1\}$ 6. $\{1, 2, 3\} \cap \emptyset = \emptyset$
7. $\emptyset \subset \mathcal{R}$
8. $\{1, 2, 3\}$ and $\{-2, 0, 2\}$ are disjoint sets.
9. $\{0, 2, 4\} \cup \{2, 3, 4\} = \{0, 2, 3, 4\}$
10. $\{0, 2, 4\} \cap \{2, 3, 4\} = \{2, 4\}$

Refer to the adjoining diagram and specify each of the following sets by roster.

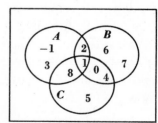

11. $A \cap B$ 15. $(A \cap B) \cap C$
12. $A \cup B$ 16. $A \cup (B \cup C)$
13. $B \cup C$ 17. $(A \cap B) \cup C$
14. $B \cap C$ 18. $A \cap (B \cup C)$

Written Exercises

Let $U = \{-5, 0, 10\}$. Specify by roster all of the subsets of U that have:

A

1. one element
2. three elements
3. no element
4. at least 2 elements

Specify the intersection and union of the given sets. If the given sets are disjoint, state that fact.

5. $\{-1, -3, 5, 7\}$; $\{-3, 4, 5\}$
6. $\{-2, -4, -6, -8\}$; $\{-6, -7, -8\}$
7. $\{-3, 0, 3, 4\}$; $\{-3, 4\}$
8. $\{0, 6\}$; $\{-6, -3, 0, 3, 6\}$
9. $\{0, 2, 4\}$; $\{1, 3, 5\}$
10. $\{-10, -5, 0\}$; $\{5, 10\}$
11. {the even natural numbers}; $\{1, 2, 3\}$
12. {the even natural numbers}; {the odd natural numbers}
13. {the positive numbers}; {the negative numbers}
14. $\mathcal{R}$; $\emptyset$

In Exercises 15–26, let A be the first set given and B, the second. Graph: **a.** A; **b.** B; **c.** $A \cap B$; **d.** $A \cup B$. In case a required set is the empty set, state that fact and omit the graph.

SAMPLE. $A = \{$natural numbers less than 7$\}$;

$B = \{$natural numbers between $3\frac{1}{2}$ and $9\frac{1}{2}\}$.

Solution:

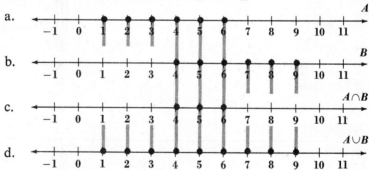

15. {natural numbers less than or equal to 4};
    {2, 6, and the natural numbers between 2 and 6}

16. {the whole numbers less than or equal to 3};
    {7, and the natural numbers less than 7}

17. {natural numbers less than 6};
    {even whole numbers less than 11}

18. {odd whole numbers less than 10};
    {natural numbers less than 5}

19. {negative integers greater than -5};
{-2, 2, and the integers between -2 and 2}

20. {-3, and the integers between -3 and 1};
{nonnegative integers less than 4}

 21. {the real numbers between -1 and 1};
{the positive real numbers}

22. {the real numbers between -2 and 2};
{the negative real numbers}

23. {4, and the real numbers greater than 4};
{the real numbers less than or equal to 6}

24. {the real numbers greater than or equal to -1};
{2 and the real numbers less than 2}

25. {the real numbers less than -2};
{the real numbers less than -3}

26. {the real numbers greater than 0};
{the real numbers greater than 2}

For each of Exercises 27–30, copy the Venn diagram at the right. On your copy, shade the region representing the set named.

27. $A \cup C$ **29.** $(A \cap B) \cap C$

28. $A \cap C$ **30.** $(A \cup B) \cup C$

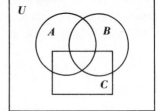

C **31.** $A \cup (B \cap C)$ **33.** $(A \cup B) \cap (A \cup C)$

32. $A \cap (B \cup C)$ **34.** $(A \cap B) \cup (A \cap C)$

In Exercises 35–38, let R, S, and T be subsets of $U = \{1, 2, 3, 4, 5, 6\}$. Specify S by roster in each exercise.

35. $R = \{1, 3, 5\}$, $R \cap S = \{3\}$, and $R \cup S = \{1, 3, 5, 6\}$

36. $R = \{2, 4, 6\}$, $R \cap S = \{2, 6\}$, and $R \cup S = \{1, 2, 3, 4, 6\}$

37. $R = \{3, 5\}$, $S \cap T = \{3\}$, $S \cup T = \{1, 2, 3, 4, 5, 6\}$,
$R \cup T = \{1, 2, 3, 4, 5\}$

38. $R \cap R = \emptyset$, $T \cup R = \{6\}$, $S \cup T = U$, $S \cap T = \emptyset$

5–3 Combining Inequalities

Often you are interested in variables whose values must satisfy *two* inequalities *at the same time*. For example, the solution set of

$$-2 < x < 5$$

consists of those values of x for which *both* of the inequalities in the conjunction (page 14)

$$-2 < x \quad \text{and} \quad x < 5$$

are true.

Similarly, to solve the open sentence

$$-3 < y + 2 \le 6$$

you must find the values of y for which the conjunction of inequalities

$$-3 < y + 2 \quad \text{and} \quad y + 2 \le 6$$

is true. Transforming each of these inequalities by subtracting 2 from each member, you find:

$$-3 < y + 2 \qquad \text{and} \qquad y + 2 \le 6$$
$$-3 - 2 < y + 2 - 2 \qquad | \qquad y + 2 - 2 \le 6 - 2$$
$$-5 < y \qquad\qquad \text{and} \qquad\qquad y \le 4$$

Thus, "$-3 < y + 2 \le 6$" is equivalent to

$$-5 < y \le 4.$$

Its solution set is {4, and all the real numbers between -5 and 4}. The graph is shown in Figure 5–7.

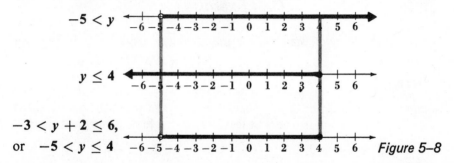

Figure 5–7

Now look at Figure 5–8. In that diagram, you can see that the graph of "$-3 < y + 2 \le 6$" consists of the points that belong to *both* the graph of "$-5 < y$" *and* the graph of "$y \le 4$." In fact, the graph of "$-3 < y + 2 \le 6$" is the intersection of the other two graphs! Similarly, the solution set of "$-3 < y + 2 \le 6$" is the intersection of the solution sets of "$-5 < y$" and "$y \le 4$."

$-5 < y$

$y \le 4$

$-3 < y + 2 \le 6,$
or $-5 < y \le 4$ *Figure 5–8*

Can you identify the *union* of the solution sets of "$-5 < y$" and "$y \leq 4$"? Since every real number satisfies *at least one* of these inequalities, the union of their solution sets is $\Re$, the set of all real numbers. Thus, for every real number y,

$$-5 < y \text{ or } y \leq 4$$

is true. A sentence formed by joining two sentences by the word *or* is called a **disjunction** (dis-**junk**-shun). For a disjunction to be true, *at least one* of the joined sentences must be a true statement.

EXAMPLE. Solve the open sentence and draw its graph:

$$2t + 3 > 7 \quad \text{or} \quad 2t + 3 < -7$$

Solution: Copy the joined inequalities and transform them as follows:

$2t + 3 > 7$	or	$2t + 3 < -7$
$2t + 3 - 3 > 7 - 3$		$2t + 3 - 3 < -7 - 3$
$2t > 4$		$2t < -10$
$\dfrac{2t}{2} > \dfrac{4}{2}$		$\dfrac{2t}{2} < \dfrac{-10}{2}$
$t > 2$	or	$t < -5$

$\therefore$ the solution set is {all real numbers that are greater than 2 or less than -5}. **Answer.**

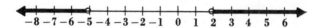

In dealing with two inequalities, it is essential to decide whether you want the set of numbers satisfying *both* of them or the set satisfying *at least one* of them. For example, the set satisfying *both* of the inequalities "$x \leq 3$" and "$x > 3$" is the *empty set*, whereas the set of numbers satisfying *at least one* of them is the set of *real numbers!*

Oral Exercises

Tell whether the given statement is true or false. Give a reason for your answer.

SAMPLE. $3 < 5$ or $0 < 2$

Solution: True. Both "$3 < 5$" and "$0 < 2$" are true statements, and a disjunction is true if at least one of the joined statements is true.

1. $6 < 5$ or $-1 > 0$ **2.** $6 < 5$ and $-1 > 0$

3. $-4 \leq -3$ and $0 = 1 - 1$ **5.** $1 > 2$ or $1 = 2$

4. $-4 \leq -3$ or $0 = 1 - 1$ **6.** $7 > 8$ and $-5 < -1$

In Exercises 7–12, match each graph with one of the open sentences given in **a–g**.

7.

a. $x < -2$ or $x \geq 1$

8.

b. $x \geq -2$ and $x \leq 1$

c. $x > -1$ or $x > 3$

9.

d. $x \leq 2$ and $x > 0$

10.

e. $x \leq -1$ or $x \geq 1$

f. $x \leq 2$ or $x > 0$

11.

g. $-3 < x$ and $x \leq 2$

12.

Written Exercises

Solve each open sentence over $\Re$ and graph each solution set that is not $\emptyset$.

A
1. $-2 \leq x + 3 < 4$ **8.** $3 + x \leq -4$ or $3 + x \geq 4$

2. $1 \leq y + 7 < 6$ **9.** $2r - 1 \leq -1$ or $2r - 1 \geq 1$

3. $-5 \leq -2 + a \leq 0$ **10.** $6m - 3 > 9$ or $6m - 3 < -9$

4. $-4 < -1 + b < 3$ **11.** $2 \geq -3 - 5p \geq -18$

5. $2 < 3t + 2 < 14$ **12.** $5 > 4 - 3u > -13$

6. $-15 \leq 4b - 5 \leq -9$ **13.** $3 - 6c < -15$ or $3 - 6c \geq 15$

7. $y + 2 > 5$ or $y + 2 < -5$ **14.** $7 - 2w > 3$ or $7 - 2w \leq -3$

B
15. $z - 2 > -1$ and $z + 5 \leq 9$

16. $1 + g \leq -3$ and $-2 + g \geq -8$

17. $v + 2 \geq -6$ or $v - 3 < 2$ **19.** $7 + 3q < 1$ or $-12 < q - 1$

18. $5 - y < 2$ or $4 + y > 7$ **20.** $4 < -d + 4$ or $3d - 8 \leq d$

21. $9 - 2m > 11$ and $5m < 2m + 9$

22. $13x \leq 7x - 12$ and $1 - 4x > 13$

23. $3z + 4 \geq z + 10$ or $3z - 3 \geq 2z - 9$

24. $8 - 2k > 2k$ or $5k - 1 < 2k + 14$

C
25. $2r - 1 \leq 2r + 8 \leq 2r + 4$ **27.** $x - 1 < 2x + 3 < x + 4$

26. $3 + 4k < 4k + 7 < 1 + 4k$ **28.** $7 - 3y \geq 6 - 4y \geq 4 - 3y$

5–4   **Absolute Value in Open Sentences (Optional)**

Equations and inequalities involving absolute value (section 3–5) occur in many parts of mathematics.

EXAMPLE 1.   Solve $|6m - 3| = 9$.

Solution: $|6m - 3| = 9$ is equivalent to the *disjunction:*

$$6m - 3 = -9 \qquad \text{or} \qquad 6m - 3 = 9$$
$$6m - 3 + 3 = -9 + 3 \qquad\qquad 6m - 3 + 3 = 9 + 3$$
$$6m = -6 \qquad\qquad 6m = 12$$
$$\frac{6m}{6} = \frac{-6}{6} \qquad\qquad \frac{6m}{6} = \frac{12}{6}$$
$$m = -1 \qquad \text{or} \qquad m = 2$$

∴ the solution set is $\{-1, 2\}$.   **Answer.**

EXAMPLE 2.   Solve $|6m - 3| < 9$.

Solution: $|6m - 3| < 9$ is equivalent to the *conjunction:*

$$-9 < 6m - 3 < 9$$
$$-9 + 3 < 6m - 3 + 3 < 9 + 3$$
$$-6 < 6m < 12$$
$$\frac{-6}{6} < \frac{6m}{6} < \frac{12}{6}$$
$$-1 < m < 2$$

∴ the solution set is {**all real numbers between −1 and 2**}.

Answer.

EXAMPLE 3.   Solve $|6m - 3| > 9$.

Solution: $|6m - 3| > 9$ is equivalent to the *disjunction:*

$$6m - 3 < -9 \qquad \text{or} \qquad 6m - 3 > 9$$

Completing the solution is left to you. You should find that:

the solution set is {**all real numbers that are less than −1 or greater than 2**}.   **Answer.**

Oral Exercises

State a conjunction or a disjunction of open sentences that is equivalent to the given open sentence.

1. $|x - 2| = 4$
2. $|y + 3| = 7$
3. $|a| \geq 3$
4. $|m| < 2$
5. $|t - 6| < 5$
6. $|8 + b| > 0$

7. $|2 - y| \leq 1$
8. $|3 - z| \geq 4$
9. $|1 - 3t| = 2$
10. $|1 - 2m| = 9$
11. $|2v - 9| \leq 1$
12. $|3l - 7| < 9$

13. $|3 - 3x| \geq 0$
14. $|5 - 2y| < 0$
15. $|7 - 2p| < 7$
16. $|12 - 3d| \geq 12$
17. $3|r| + 2 = 8$
18. $3 + 2|a| > -1$

Written Exercises

[A] **1–18.** Solve each of the open sentences in Exercises 1–18 in the preceding set of Oral Exercises, and draw its graph.

Specify and graph the solution set of each open sentence.

[B] **19.** $|1 - (2 - a)| = 5$
20. $|8 - (r - 1)| = 6$
21. $|1 + 2(y - 1)| < 3$
22. $|5 - 3(2 - z)| \geq 0$

23. $4 - 3(2 - |s|) \geq 7$
24. $-6 + 4(1 - 3|y|) \leq 20$
25. $5(1 + |c - 3|) - 9 \leq -4$
26. $4(2 + |1 - m|) + 10 \geq 18$

[C] **27.** $|2d + 1| = d - 4$
28. $|3r + 2| = r + 5$

29. $|3 - 5t| \geq 1 + 3t$
30. $|2w + 6| < 4w - 1$

SOLVING PROBLEMS

5–5 Problems about Integers

On page 22, you saw that the set of integers is the infinite set

$$J = \{\ldots, -3, -2, -1, 0, 1, 2, 3, \ldots\}.$$

If you count by ones from any given integer, then you obtain **consecutive integers.** For example, 6, 7, 8, 9 are four consecutive integers; so are -1, 0, 1, 2. In general, if n is any integer, then $n + 1$, $n + 2$, and $n + 3$ are the next three consecutive integers in increasing order. Similarly, $n - 1$, $n - 2$, $n - 3$, are the preceding three consecutive integers in decreasing order.

EXAMPLE 1. Find three consecutive integers whose sum is 54.

Solution:

1▶ Let n = the first integer.

Then $n + 1$ = the second integer and $n + 2$ = the third integer.

2▶ The sum of the integers is 54.

$$n + (n + 1) + (n + 2) = 54.$$

3▶
$$3n + 3 = 54$$
$$3n + 3 - 3 = 54 - 3$$
$$3n = 51$$
$$\frac{3n}{3} = \frac{51}{3}$$
$$n = 17$$

$\therefore n + 1 = 18$ and $n + 2 = 19.$

4▶ *Check:* Is the sum of 17, 18, and 19 equal to 54?

$$17 + 18 + 19 \overset{?}{=} 54$$
$$54 = 54 \checkmark$$

$\therefore$ the three consecutive integers are 17, 18, and 19. **Answer.**

We call 21 a *multiple* of 3 because $21 = 3 \times 7$. In general, the product of any real number and an *integer* is called a **multiple** of the real number.

Do you know what the multiples of 2 are? They are the *even integers:*

$$\ldots, -6, -4, -2, 0, 2, 4, 6 \ldots$$

If you count by *twos* from an even integer, you obtain **consecutive even integers.** For instance, 6, 6 + 2 or 8, and 8 + 2 or 10, are three consecutive even integers. The integers that are not even are the odd integers:

$$\ldots, -5, -3, -1, 1, 3, 5, \ldots$$

Counting by two from an odd integer yields **consecutive odd integers.** Thus, if a is even, then $a + 2$ is the next greater even integer and $a - 2$ is the preceding smaller even integer. In case a is odd, then $a - 2$, a, and $a + 2$ are three consecutive odd integers in increasing order.

In the next example, an inequality is used to solve a problem about consecutive even integers.

EXAMPLE 2. **Find all sets of four consecutive positive even integers such that the greatest integer in the set is greater than twice the least integer in the set.**

Solution:

1▶ **Let x = the least of the positive even integers in the set; then the next three consecutive even integers are:**

$$x + 2, \ x + 4, \text{ and } x + 6.$$

2▶ **The greatest integer is greater than twice the least integer**

$x + 6$	$>$	$2x$

3▶

$x + 6 - x$	$>$	$2x - x$
6	$>$	x

Since the least even integer must be less than 6 and must be positive, the only choices for the least integer are 2 and 4.

∴ the only possible sets are $A = \{2, 4, 6, 8\}$ and $B = \{4, 6, 8, 10\}$.

4▶ *Check:* **In each set, is the greatest integer greater than twice the least?**
In A: $8 \ \underline{\ ? \ } \ 2 \cdot 2; \ 8 > 4.$ ✓
In B: $10 \ \underline{\ ? \ } \ 2 \cdot 4; \ 10 > 8.$ ✓

∴ the required sets are $\{2, 4, 6, 8\}$ and $\{4, 6, 8, 10\}$. **Answer.**

Oral Exercises

1. Represent 2, 4, 6, and 8 in terms of n, if $n = 1$.

2. Let p represent 21. Represent the numbers 23, 24, and 26 in terms of p.

3. Represent 17, 16, 15, in that order, letting $n = 17$.

4. Let b represent any even integer. What is the next even integer? the preceding even integer?

5. Let c represent any odd integer. What is the next odd integer? the preceding odd integer?

6. Represent 12, 14, 15 in terms of x, letting $x = 13$.

7. Let y be the last integer in the list 3, 5, 7, and 9. Express the other numbers in terms of y.

8. Let x represent an odd integer. Is $x + 1$ an odd integer or an even integer? $x + 2$? $x - 1$?

9. Let n represent any integer. Is $2n$ an even integer or an odd integer? Is $2n + 1$ an even integer or an odd integer?

10. If $2n$ is an even integer, what is the next odd integer? the next even integer? the preceding even integer?

11. If $x + 3$ is any integer, what is the next smaller integer?

12. If $x - 2$ is an odd integer, what is the next larger odd integer?

13. Let m be a multiple of 7. What are the next two multiples of 7? the preceding multiple?

14. Let r be a multiple of 5. What are the next two multiples of 5? the preceding multiple of 5?

Written Exercises

A 1. The sum of two consecutive integers is 45. Find the numbers.

2. The sum of two consecutive odd integers is 36. Find the numbers.

3. Find three consecutive integers whose sum is -33.

4. Find three consecutive odd integers whose sum is 87.

5. Find four consecutive integers whose sum is -102.

6. Find four consecutive even integers whose sum is 76.

7. Find three consecutive integers, if the sum of the first and third is 146.

8. Find four consecutive integers if the sum of the second and fourth is 58.

9. The four Lincoln children are 2 years apart in age. If the sum of their ages is 40, how old is each child?

10. The measures of adjacent sides of a rectangle are consecutive integers. If the perimeter of the rectangle is 22 inches, find the length and the width of the rectangle.

11. Find the two least consecutive odd integers whose sum is greater than 16.

12. Find the two greatest consecutive even integers whose sum is less than 60.

13. The larger of two consecutive even integers is six less than twice the smaller. Find the numbers.

14. The smaller of two consecutive integers is one more than twice the larger. Find the numbers.

B 15. Find four consecutive integers such that four times the second diminished by twice the fourth is 10.

16. Find four consecutive odd integers such that the third is the sum of the fourth and twice the second.

17. Four times the smaller of two consecutive even integers is less than three times the larger. What are the largest possible values for the integers?

18. Three consecutive integers are such that their sum is more than 20 decreased by twice the second integer. What are the smallest possible values for the integers?

19. The smaller of two consecutive integers is less than 4 more than half the larger. Find the largest possible values for the integers.

20. Three consecutive integers are such that the sum of the second and third is greater than half the first diminished by 6. What are the smallest possible values for the integers?

C **21.** Find four consecutive multiples of 5 such that twice the sum of the two greatest integers exceeds three times the least by 15.

22. The ages in years of three brothers are consecutive multiples of 3. Four years ago the sum of their ages was 42 years. Find their present ages.

23. Find all sets of three consecutive multiples of 4 whose sum is between −84 and −36.

24. Find the three greatest consecutive multiples of 7 such that the middle one is greater than their sum decreased by 50.

EXTRA PROBLEM

The coefficients a, b, and c in the inequality "$ax + b > c$" are given on a card. Draw a flow chart of a program to solve the inequality. Assume that $a \neq 0$ and that cards for several inequalities are to be processed.

5–6 Problems about Angles

Think of the figure composed of two rays p and q drawn from a point O. Then think of the ray q as having turned or rotated about O, starting at p and going to its indicated position. As shown in Figure 5–9, the rotation may be clockwise or counterclockwise.

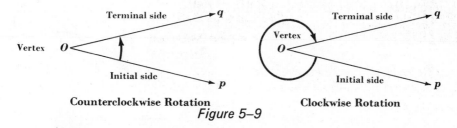

Counterclockwise Rotation   Clockwise Rotation

Figure 5–9

The figure composed of two rays drawn from a point, together with the rotation that sends one ray into the other is called a **directed angle**. Counterclockwise rotation yields a **positive directed angle**; clockwise rotation yields a **negative directed angle**. Ray p is the *initial side* of the angle and ray q is the *terminal side*. The point O is the *vertex* of the angle.

A common unit of measure of an angle is a *degree*, written as 1°. A **degree** is $\frac{1}{360}$ of a complete rotation of a ray about a point. The directed angles whose measures are 1°, 30° (read "30 degrees"), 90°, 180°, −45°, −180°, and −360° are shown in Figure 5–10.

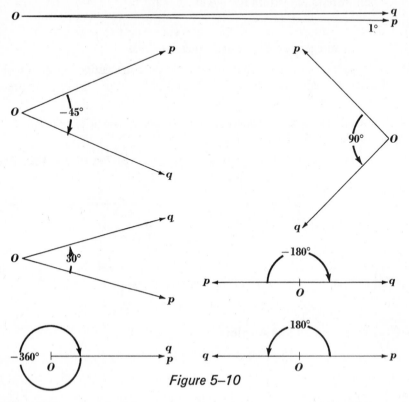

Figure 5–10

Two angles are **complementary angles** if the sum of their degree measures is 90. Each is the *complement* of the other. If an angle measures *n* degrees, its complement measures (90 − *n*) degrees (Figure 5–11).

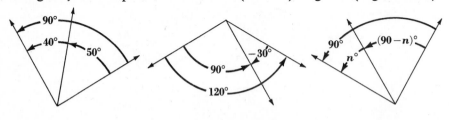

Complementary Angles

Figure 5–11

Two angles are **supplementary angles** if the sum of their degree measures is 180. Each is the *supplement* of the other. If an angle measures *n* degrees, its supplement measures (180 − *n*) degrees (Figure 5–12).

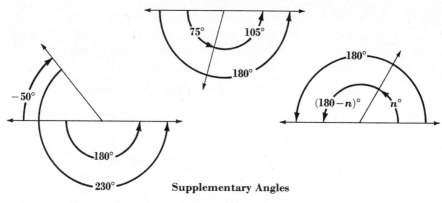

Supplementary Angles

Figure 5–12

EXAMPLE 1. What is the measure of an angle whose supplement measures 32° more than twice its complement?

Solution:

1 ▶   Let x = measure of the angle in degrees.

Then $90 - x$ = measure of its complement in degrees,

and $180 - x$ = measure of its supplement in degrees.

2 ▶ Write an open sentence.

The measure of the supplement	is	twice the measure of the complement	plus	32
$(180 - x)$	$=$	$2(90 - x)$	$+$	32

Steps 3 and 4 are left for you.

The three line segments that compose a triangle intersect by pairs and so form three angles. If you tear off the corners from any paper triangle and fit them together as shown in Figure 5–13, you will notice

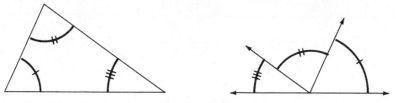

Figure 5–13

that the three angles fit together to form a straight angle. This suggests a property of all triangles which is proved in geometry.

The sum of the degree measures of the angles of any triangle is 180.

EXAMPLE 2. The measure of one angle in a triangle is twice the measure of a second angle, and the third angle has a measure equal to 5° more than twice the measure of the first angle. Find the measures of the angles in the triangle.

Solution:

1▶ Since the second angle has the least measure,

let m = measure of second angle in degrees.

Then $2m$ = measure of first angle in degrees,

and $4m + 5$ = measure of third angle in degrees.

2▶ Write an open sentence.

Sum of measures of angles   equals   180

$$\underbrace{m + 2m + 4m + 5} \qquad = \qquad 180$$

Steps 3 and 4 are left for you.

Oral Exercises

State the degree measure of the angle that is the complement of the angle with given measure.

SAMPLE. $10°$ *Solution:* $90 - 10 = 80$; $80°$. **Answer.**

1. $50°$	**5.** $40°$	**9.** x degrees	**13.** $-100°$
2. $30°$	**6.** $70°$	**10.** $3n$ degrees	**14.** $-90°$
3. $5°$	**7.** $-10°$	**11.** $-y$ degrees	**15.** $(x + 1)°$
4. $82°$	**8.** $-30°$	**12.** $-4y$ degrees	**16.** $(n - 2)°$

State the degree measure of the angle that is the supplement of the angle with given measure.

17. $100°$	**21.** z degrees	**25.** $\frac{1}{2}°$	**29.** $-n°$
18. $170°$	**22.** $3t$ degrees	**26.** $0.25°$	**30.** $-3n°$
19. $20°$	**23.** $-20°$	**27.** $(x - 1)°$	**31.** $-(x + 2)°$
20. $50°$	**24.** $-90°$	**28.** $(2n + 1)°$	**32.** $-(10n - 2)°$

Written Exercises

In each exercise, the measures of two angles of a triangle are given. Find the degree measure of the third angle.

SAMPLE 1. $40°$, $102°$

Solution: Let x = the degree measure of the third angle.

Then: $x + 40 + 102 = 180$ $x = 180 - 142 = 38$

∴ the degree measure of the third angle is 38. **Answer.**

A

1. 30°, 100°
2. 10°, 80°
3. 30°, 60°
4. 60°, 60°

5. 110°, 50°
6. 17°, 5°
7. $n°$, $3n°$
8. $\dfrac{n°}{2}$, $\dfrac{3n°}{4}$

9. $x°$, $y°$
10. $t°$, 80°
11. $x°$, $(2x - 10)°$
12. $3n°$, $(n - 30)°$

In Exercises 13–18, find the degree measure of $a + b$ if the measures of angles a and b are as given.

SAMPLE 2. a measures $\frac{1}{6}$ of a complete rotation clockwise.
b measures $\frac{1}{3}$ of a complete rotation counterclockwise.

Solution: Since one complete rotation in a clockwise direction is equivalent to $-360°$ and one complete revolution in a counterclockwise direction is equivalent to 360°, the degree measure of $a + b$ is given by $\frac{1}{6}(-360) + \frac{1}{3}(360) = -60 + 120 = 60$.

∴ the degree measure of $a + b$ is 60. **Answer.**

13. a measures $\frac{1}{2}$ of a complete rotation counterclockwise.
    b measures $\frac{1}{4}$ of a complete rotation counterclockwise.

14. a measures $\frac{2}{3}$ of a complete rotation counterclockwise.
    b measures $1\frac{1}{2}$ of a complete rotation counterclockwise.

15. a measures $\frac{1}{6}$ of a complete rotation counterclockwise.
    b measures $\frac{2}{3}$ of a complete rotation clockwise.

16. a measures $\frac{2}{5}$ of a complete rotation clockwise.
    b measures $\frac{1}{4}$ of a complete rotation clockwise.

17. a measures $\frac{5}{6}$ of a complete rotation clockwise.
    b measures 120°.

18. a measures $-84°$.
    b measures $\frac{3}{4}$ of a complete rotation counterclockwise.

Exercises 19 and 20 refer to the Law of Reflection: $i = r$.

19.

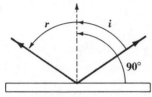

$i = (3x - 5)°$
$r = (75 - x)°$
Find x.

20.

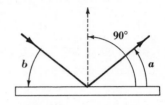

$a = (3z)°$
$b = (5z - 26)°$
Find z.

Exercises 21–26 refer to the science of navigation in which a compass direction is expressed as a bearing. The bearing of a line of motion is the angle it makes with the north line, measured clockwise from north, through a point at which the observations are made. Find each bearing.

21.
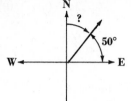

22.
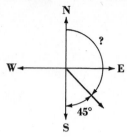

23.
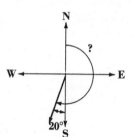

24.
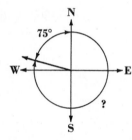

25.
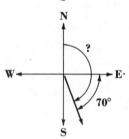

26.
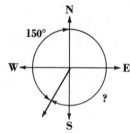

Problems

SAMPLE. An angle is 20° greater in measure than its complement. What is the degree measure of its complement?

Solution:

1▶ Let x = the degree measure of the complement.

Then $x + 20$ = the degree measure of the angle.

2▶ The sum of the degree measures of the angles is 90.

$$x + x + 20 = 90$$

3▶ $\qquad\qquad 2x + 20 = 90, \; 2x = 70, \; x = 35$

4▶ The degree measure of the complement is 35. The angle, therefore, measures $35 + 20 = 55$. Does $35 + 55 = 90$? Yes. ✓

∴ the degree measure of the complement is 35. **Answer.**

A 1. An angle is 40° greater in measure than its supplement. What is the degree measure of its supplement?

2. Find the measure of an angle that has a measure 17° less than that of its complement.

3. Find the measure of an angle that measures 30° less than twice its complement.

4. Find the measures of two supplementary angles if one measures 10° more than twice the other.

5. Find the measure of an angle whose supplement measures 6° more than 4 times its complement.

6. Find the measure of an angle for which the sum of the measures of its complement and supplement is 194°.

7. One angle of a triangle measures twice a second angle, and the third angle measures 12° less than the sum of the measures of the other two. Find the measure of each angle.

8. The three angles in an equilateral triangle have equal measures. What is the measure of each?

9. The degree measures of the angles of a triangle are consecutive even integers. What are the degree measures of the angles?

10. The degree measures of two angles of a triangle are consecutive odd integers. The third angle measures 1° more than the smallest angle of the triangle. What are the degree measures of the angles?

11. In any isosceles triangle, two angles have equal measure. If the third angle in an isosceles triangle measures 12° more than the sum of the measures of the two angles of equal measure, find the measure of each angle in the triangle.

12. In a triangle having two angles of equal measure, the third angle measures 45° less than the measure of one of the angles having equal measure. Find the measure of each angle in the triangle.

13. One angle of a triangle measures 14° more than a second angle, and the third angle measures 32° more than the measure of the complement of the second angle. Find the measure of each angle in the triangle.

14. One angle of a triangle measures 6 degrees more than a second angle. The third angle measures 18 degrees less than twice the sum of their measures. Find the measures of each angle in the triangle.

15. The degree measure of $\angle A$ is twice the degree measure of $\angle B$ and one less than the degree measure of $\angle C$. If the sum of the degree measures of the three angles is at least 61, which is the least possible degree measure of $\angle A$?

16. The degree measure of $\angle P$ is five times the degree measure of $\angle Q$. If $\angle P$ measures at least 240° more than $\angle Q$, what is the least possible degree measure of $\angle P$?

5–7   Uniform-Motion Problems

An object that moves without changing its speed is said to be in **uniform motion.** In solving problems about uniform motion, diagrams and charts often help you to organize the given facts. The basic formula in such problems is:

$$\text{distance} = \text{rate} \times \text{time}$$

$$d \quad = \quad r \quad \cdot \quad t$$

EXAMPLE 1.   (Motion in Opposite Directions)   A submarine left a surface ship and cruised due south at a constant rate of 28 knots (nautical miles per hour). If the surface ship started off at the same time on a course due north at a constant rate of 22 knots, in how many hours will the ships be 125 nautical miles apart?

Solution:

1▶ Let t = the number of hours traveled.

2▶ Make a sketch   The submarine's rate is 28 knots.
       illustrating the   The surface ship's rate is 22 knots.
       given facts.   Distance apart is 125 nautical miles.
                       Each travels the same number of hours.

Arrange the facts in a chart.

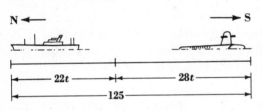

	r	t	d
Submarine	28	t	$28t$
Surface ship	22	t	$22t$

$$\underbrace{\text{Submarine's distance}}_{28t} \;+\; \underbrace{\text{Surface ship's distance}}_{22t} \;=\; \underbrace{\text{Total distance}}_{125}$$

3▶
$$28t + 22t = 125$$
$$50t = 125$$
$$t = 2\tfrac{1}{2}$$

4▶ To check the $2\tfrac{1}{2}$ hour time, you have to answer the question, "How far did each ship travel?"

Submarine traveled	$28 \cdot 2\tfrac{1}{2} =$	70 miles
Surface ship traveled	$22 \cdot 2\tfrac{1}{2} =$	55 miles
The sum of their distances	$\overset{?}{=}$	125 miles

$$125 = 125 \checkmark$$

∴ the ships will be 125 nautical miles apart in $2\tfrac{1}{2}$ hours.   **Answer.**

EXAMPLE 2. (Motion in the Same Direction) Mr. Jones left Elmsville at 8:00 A.M. one morning and drove to Bond City at a constant rate of 50 miles per hour (mph). At 10:00 A.M. the same day, Sgt. Holliday of the Highway Patrol left Elmsville. Following the same route, he arrived in Bond City at the same time as Mr. Jones. If both men arrived in Bond City at 3:00 P.M., at what constant rate had Sgt. Holliday traveled?

Solution:

1 ▶ Let r = the rate of Sgt. Holliday in mph.

2 ▶ Make a sketch showing the given facts.

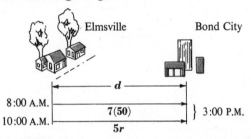

Make a chart of the facts in the given problem.

	r	t	d
Mr. Jones	50	7	350
Sgt. Holliday	r	5	$5r$

$$\underbrace{\text{Distance of Mr. Jones}}_{350} = \underbrace{\text{Distance of Sgt. Holliday}}_{5r}$$

Steps 3 and 4 are left to you.

EXAMPLE 3. (Round trip) To pick up a rare serum needed to treat a very sick child, Major Evans flew from Tinden Air Force Base to Capital City and back. He maintained a constant speed of 480 miles per hour to the city, and 600 miles per hour back to the base. If the actual flying time for the round trip was $1\frac{1}{4}$ hours, how long did the flight to Capital City take? How far is Tinden Air Force Base from Capital City?

(The solution is given on the next page.)

Solution:

1▶ Let t = the number of hours in flying time from TAFB to Capital City. Then $\frac{5}{4} - t$ = the number of hours in flying time from Capital City to TAFB.

2▶ The given facts are these: (a) The total time is $1\frac{1}{4}$ or $\frac{5}{4}$ hours. (b) The rate in one direction is 480 mph. (c) The rate in the opposite direction is 600 mph. (d) The number of miles covered in each direction is the same.

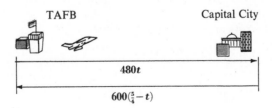

	r	t	d
To Capital City	480	t	$480t$
To TAFB	600	$\frac{5}{4} - t$	$600(\frac{5}{4} - t)$

$$\underbrace{\textbf{Distance to Capital City}} \quad \downarrow \quad \underbrace{\textbf{Distance to TAFB}}$$

$$480\, t \quad = \quad 600(\tfrac{5}{4} - t)$$

Steps 3 and 4 are left to you. Remember that when you have found a value for t, you must use this value to obtain an answer to the problem's second question, which is about a *distance*.

Problems

Make a drawing and a chart for each problem. Then form an open sentence, solve it, check your result in the words of the problem, and, finally, answer the question asked in the problem.

[A] **1.** The steamship Empress Anne sailing due west at 32 knots passed the freighter Oregon which was sailing due east at 24 knots. In how many hours after the meeting will the ships be 448 nautical miles apart?

2. Majestic Airlines flight 324, flying due north at a groundspeed of 460 miles per hour, passed Omega Airlines flight 117 flying due south at a groundspeed of 530 miles per hour. In how many hours after passing each other will these two planes be 1980 miles apart?

3. Tim and a friend left a campsite on a trip down the river in a canoe, maintaining a constant speed of 4 miles per hour. 4 hours later, Tim's father set out after them in a motorboat carrying the camping supplies. The motorboat traveled at a rate of 12 miles per hour. How long after he started did Tim's father overtake the boys?

4. A motorist traveling 55 miles per hour is being pursued by a highway patrol car traveling 65 miles per hour. If the patrol car is 4 miles behind the motorist, how long will it take the patrol car to overtake the motorist?

5. It takes a passenger train 2 hours less time than it takes a freight train to make the trip from Central City to Clear Creek. If the passenger train averages 60 miles per hour on the trip while the freight train averages 40 miles per hour, how far is it from Central City to Clear Creek?

6. A freight train leaves Eastburg at 6:00 A.M. traveling toward Bechton at 42 miles per hour. At 8:00 A.M., a passenger train leaves Eastburg on a parallel track traveling toward Bechton at 70 miles per hour. If the trains arrive at Bechton at the same time, how far is it from Eastburg to Bechton?

7. Marie rode her bicycle from her home to the bicycle shop in town and then walked back home. If she averaged 6 miles per hour riding and 3 miles per hour walking, how far is it from her home to the bicycle shop if her traveling time totaled 1 hour?

8. A ski lift carries a skier up a slope at the rate of 120 feet per minute and he returns from the top to the bottom on a path parallel to the lift at an average rate of 2640 feet per minute. How long is the lift if the round trip traveling time is 20 minutes?

9. An airplane on a search mission flies due east from an airport, turns and flies due west back to the airport. The plane cruises at 200 miles per hour when flying east, and 250 miles per hour when flying west. What is the farthest point from the airport the plane can reach if it can remain in the air for 9 hours?

10. On the West River, Larry paddles a canoe at the rate of 6 miles per hour downstream and 2 miles per hour upstream. If he makes a trip down the river and then back to his departure point in $1\frac{1}{2}$ hours, and if the river is flowing at the rate of 2 mph, how far down the river does he go?

11. A steamship radios the Coast Guard that an ill passenger must be flown to a hospital as soon as possible. If the steamship is 180 nautical miles from the Coast Guard station and sailing directly towards it at the time a helicopter is dispatched from the station, and if the rate of the helicopter is 90 knots while the rate of the ship is 30 knots, how long will it take the helicopter to reach the ship?

12. Two ships are sailing toward each other and are 120 nautical miles apart. If the rate of one ship is 4 knots greater than the rate of the other, and if they meet in 3 hours, find the rate of each ship.

13. Two cars bound for Buffalo on the New York State Thruway leave a service area at the same time. Their average speeds differ by 10 miles an hour. Six hours later the slower car reached an exchange that the faster car had reached an hour earlier. Find the average speed of each car.

14. At midnight, two river steamers are 100 miles apart. They pass Natchez at 5 A.M. headed in opposite directions. If the northbound boat steams at an average speed of 8 miles per hour, find the speed of the southbound boat.

B 15. After an airplane had been flying for 2 hours, a change in wind increased the plane's ground speed by 30 miles per hour. If the entire trip of 570 miles took $3\frac{1}{2}$ hours, how far did the plane go the first two hours?

16. Mr. Ferris can drive from Mountain View to Tuxford at 45 miles per hour in time to meet an appointment. If he takes 30 minutes out of the trip to eat, however, he must drive at 60 miles per hour to make the appointment. How far is it from Mountain View to Tuxford?

17. A private plane had been flying for 2 hours when it encountered head winds which reduced its average speed by 20 miles an hour. If it took the plane 5 hours to travel 640 miles, find its average speed before encountering head winds.

18. Some members of the Rocky Mountain Outing Club hiked to an overnight campsite at the rate of 3 miles per hour. The following morning they returned on horseback over the same route at 10 miles per hour. The total time spent in going and returning was $6\frac{1}{2}$ hours. Find the distance to the campsite.

C 19. It ordinarily takes a bus 20 minutes to travel the 12 miles from the City Hall of Central City to the airport. However, during the rush hours from 4:00 P.M. to 6:00 P.M., the bus will travel only 10 miles in the same length of time. If busses leave City Hall on the hour and every 15 minutes thereafter, and if it takes a person 20 minutes from the time he leaves a bus to get on an airplane, what is the last bus Mr. Samuels can take from City Hall to make a plane leaving at 5:50 P.M.?

20. An aircraft landing at Capital City between the hours of 5:00 P.M. and 7:00 P.M. must expect to "hold" (fly in circles to await a landing clearance) for an average time of 20 minutes. Amalgamated Airlines flight 227 from Los Angeles arrives at Capital City airport 1 hour late due to headwinds which reduced its groundspeed from 500 to 400 miles per hour. If the flight leaves Los Angeles on schedule at 12:50 P.M. Capital City time, when can it expect to land at Capital City?

5–8 Mixture and Other Problems

A merchant often mixes goods of two or more kinds in order to sell a blend at a given price. Similarly, a chemist often mixes solutions of different strengths of a chemical to obtain a solution of desired strength. All such problems are solved in the same way. The sum of the values or weights of the original ingredients must equal the value or weight of the final mixture.

EXAMPLE 1. **The registration fee at a convention of the National Council of Teachers of Mathematics was $5.00 for members and $9.00 for nonmembers. If receipts at the convention were $4450, and 850 persons were in attendance, how many members were registered?**

Solution:

1 ▶ Let n = number of members present.

Then $850 - n$ = number of nonmembers present.

2 ▶

	Number	Fee in dollars	Receipts
Members registered	n	5	$5n$
Nonmembers registered	$850 - n$	9	$9(850 - n)$
Total registered	850	–	4450

$$\underbrace{\text{Receipts from members}}_{5n} + \underbrace{\text{Receipts from nonmembers}}_{9(850 - n)} = \underbrace{\text{Total Receipts}}_{4450}$$

Steps 3 and 4 are left for you.

Does every problem have a solution? Consider the following:

EXAMPLE 2. **Find two consecutive integers whose sum is 46.**

Solution:

1 ▶ Let x = the first integer.

Then $x + 1$ = the second integer.

2 ▶ The sum of the integers is 46.

$$\underbrace{x + (x + 1)}\qquad = 46$$

3 ▶ $2x + 1 = 46$

$2x = 45$

$x = 22\frac{1}{2}$

$x + 1 = 23\frac{1}{2}$

4 ▶ The numbers obtained, $22\frac{1}{2}$ and $23\frac{1}{2}$, are not *integers*. Therefore, they do not satisfy the problem's requirements. What is the trouble? The

> trouble is that the facts of the problem do not fit with one another; they are inconsistent. **In any pair of consecutive integers, one is an even integer and the other is odd. Therefore, their sum is odd and cannot be 46!**

In reading a problem, you should be on the lookout for inconsistent facts. You should also be alert to recognize problems in which not enough facts are given for you to obtain a definite answer. Most of the problems in the following set can be solved. But some of them fail to have solutions either because their facts are inconsistent or because they give too few facts.

Oral Exercises

State the variable expression(s) to complete the sentence correctly.

1. The value of $x + 3$ twenty-cent stamps is __?__ cents or __?__ dollars.

2. The value of $9 - t$ six-cent stamps is __?__ cents or __?__ dollars.

3. If cherries sell at 45 cents a pound, then $2n$ pounds cost __?__ cents or __?__ dollars.

4. If one ticket costs three dollars, then $2x + 1$ tickets cost __?__ dollars.

5. The value of x nickels and $15 - x$ dimes is __?__ cents.

6. If a soda costs a quarter and a candy bar costs a dime, then the value of y sodas and $y + 5$ candy bars is __?__ cents.

7. If 9 grams of water contain 1 gram of hydrogen and 8 grams of oxygen, then w grams of water contain __?__ grams of hydrogen and __?__ grams of oxygen.

8. If a silver coin contains 900 parts of silver to 100 parts of copper, then $\dfrac{x}{10}$ silver coins contain __?__ parts of silver to __?__ parts of copper.

Problems

1. Joe has an equal number of dimes and quarters. If he has $2.10 in all, how many coins of each type does he have?

2. Mr. Cirillo bought some six-cent and ten-cent stamps. He bought 25 stamps in all, and paid $1.70 for them. How many stamps of each kind did he buy?

3. Airline fares for a flight from Century City to Glendale are $30 for first class and $25 for tourist class. If a flight carried 52 passengers for a total fare of $1360, how many first class passengers were on the flight?

4. The Leesburg Little Theatre holds 110 persons. Adult admissions are $1.50, and children can attend for 80¢. If the theatre is full, and total receipts for admissions are $158, how many adults are present?

5. How many pounds of candy worth 90¢ per pound must be added to 10 pounds of a candy worth 60¢ per pound to form a mixture worth 80¢ per pound?

6. How many pounds of coffee worth 50¢ per pound must be added to 15 pounds of coffee worth 80¢ a pound to form a mixture worth 60¢ a pound?

7. Each question in Part I of an algebra test was worth 4 points and each question in Part II was worth 6 points. Kevin answered 18 questions correctly and had a point total of 86. How many questions did he answer correctly in each part of the test?

8. For a kindergarten party, Mrs. Tully bought 4 more bags of jelly beans selling at 35 cents a bag than of lemon drops selling at 45 cents a bag. She spent 3 dollars for the candy. How many bags of jelly beans did she buy?

9. A woman buys 23 more 6-cent stamps than she does 10-cent stamps. How many of each kind of stamp does she buy, if the total cost of the stamps is $4.38?

10. A boy has 12 more quarters than dimes in his savings bank. How many of each kind of coin has he if this bank contains $12.45?

11. Find the least two consecutive positive integers whose difference is 6.

12. The degree measures of the angles of a triangle are consecutive odd integers. What are the degree measures of the angles?

13. Nancy is four times as old as her sister, Fran. Three years ago, the sum of their ages was 4 years. How old was Fran 3 years ago?

14. In going to a medical meeting, Dr. Lloyd made a trip of 500 miles. She traveled by train for $1\frac{1}{2}$ hours and by automobile for the rest of the trip. The average speed of the train was 15 miles per hour more than that of the automobile. Find the average speed of the automobile.

B 15. Mary bought 3 times as many 10-cent stamps as she did 6-cent stamps and 6 more 6-cent stamps than she did 30-cent special delivery stamps. How many of each kind of stamp did she buy if her total expenditure for stamps was $7.44?

16. Roger's savings bank contains 3 fewer quarters than dimes, and 2 more than 3 times as many nickels as dimes. If Roger's bank contains $1.85, how many of each kind of coin does it contain?

17. A drive-in cashier took $20 in bills to the bank to get change. She asked for twice as many dimes as nickels and three times as many quarters as nickels. Was the bank teller able to grant her request?

18. Jack and Jill, together, have 19 paperback books. If Jack lost 3 of his books, but Jill doubled her supply, the two of them, together, would have 40 books. How many does each have now?

19. A gourmet-foods shop sells almonds for $2.10 a pound, pecans for $1.90 a pound, and peanuts for $1.10 a pound. The manager makes a mixture of these nuts to sell for $1.50 a pound. She uses one-half as many pounds of almonds as pecans. How much of each does she use?

20. A tea merchant prepares a blend of 30 pounds of tea to sell for $1.95 per pound. For the blend, he uses two types of tea, one selling at $2.15 per pound, the other at $2.05 per pound. How much of each type should he use for the blend?

21. For two weeks Ruth put all nickels, dimes, and quarters she collected from her paper route into a coin bank. She found that she had twice as many quarters as dimes and $4.65 in all. How many coins of each type did she collect?

22. Romeo spent $3.15 for 16 valentines, getting a mixture of 15-cent, 20-cent, and 25-cent valentines. The number of 20-cent valentines was one more than twice the number of 15-cent ones. How many 25-cent valentines did he purchase?

23. Ellen worked at The China Box on Saturdays packing dishes for shipment. She received 5 cents for each piece she packed successfully and was fined 12 cents for each piece she broke. If she handled 187 pieces and was paid $8.16, how many pieces did she break?

24. An enthusiastic alumnus agreed to contribute $2 for each $5 his college raised above $10,000 in its annual fund drive. If $23,000 was raised in the drive, how much did this alumnus then contribute?

C 25. Find the least two positive integers whose sum is an even integer and whose difference is an odd integer.

26. Find two even integers whose product is a positive integer and whose sum is zero.

27. How much coffee worth $0.84 a pound should be mixed with coffee worth $1.02 a pound to produce a mixture worth $0.96 a pound?

28. Eighteen-carat gold contains 18 parts by weight of gold and 6 parts of other metals. Fourteen-carat gold contains 14 parts of gold and 10 parts of other metals. How much eighteen-carat gold must be mixed with fourteen-carat gold to obtain an alloy containing 17 parts of gold and 7 parts of other metals?

EXTRA PROBLEMS

1. Draw a flow chart of a program to compute and print the different ways of making a dollar's worth of change in nickels and dimes. (*Hint:* If *d* dimes and *n* nickels are used, then $n = \frac{1}{5}(100 - 10d)$ where $d \in \{0, 1, 2, \ldots, 10\}$.)

2. Redraw the flow chart for Extra Problem 1 if quarters as well as nickels and dimes may be used to make the change for one dollar.

● CHAPTER SUMMARY ●

Inventory of Structure and Method

1. **Axiom of Comparison:** For all real numbers *a* and *b*, one and only one of the following statements is true: $a < b$, $a = b$, $b < a$.

2. **Transitive Axiom of Order:** For all real numbers *a*, *b*, and *c*, (1) if $a < b$ and $b < c$, then $a < c$, and (2) if $a > b$ and $b > c$, then $a > c$.

3. **Addition Axiom of Order:** For all real numbers *a*, *b*, and *c*, (1) if $a < b$, then $a + c < b + c$ and (2) if $a > b$, then $a + c > b + c$.

4. **Multiplication Axiom of Order:** For all real numbers *a*, *b*, and *c*, (1) if $a < b$ and $c > 0$, then $ac < bc$; similarly, if $a > b$ and $c > 0$, then $ac > bc$. Also, (2) if $a < b$ and $c < 0$, then $ac > bc$; similarly, if $a > b$ and $c < 0$, then $ac < bc$.

5. Set relationships can be pictured by means of Venn diagrams. The relationships include **subset, union,** and **intersection. Disjoint sets** have no elements in common.

6. Inequalities may be combined by **conjunctions** or **disjunctions.**

7. Both equations and inequalities are useful in solving a variety of problems.

Vocabulary and Spelling

Review the meaning of each term by reference to the page listed.

comparison (*p. 163*)
transitive (*p. 164*)
equivalent inequality (*p. 165*)
universe (*p. 168*)
universal set (*p. 168*)
region (*p. 168*)
subset (*p. 168*)
intersection (*p. 169*)
union (*p. 169*)

disjunction (*p. 174*)
consecutive integers (*p. 177*)
multiple (*p. 178*)
rotation (*p. 181*)
counterclockwise (*p. 181*)
directed angle (*p. 181*)
initial side (*p. 181*)
terminal side (*p. 181*)
degree (*p. 182*)

complementary angles (*p. 182*)
complement (*p. 182*)
supplementary angles (*p. 182*)

supplement (*p. 182*)
uniform motion (*p. 188*)

Chapter Test

5–1 **1.** Solve and then graph the solution set: $7 - 5x > 30$.

5–2 **2.** Given $A = \{2, 4, 6, 8, 10\}$ and $B = \{1, 3, 5, 7, 9\}$.   State
(1) $A \cap B$; (2) $A \cup B$.

5–3 **3.** Solve this open sentence and draw its graph: $y + 1 > 3$ *or*
$6y + 5 < 2$.

5–4 (Optional)   **4.** Solve $|2x - 5| = 7$ **5.** Solve $|2x - 5| > 7$

5–5 **6.** Find 3 consecutive integers whose sum is 96.

5–6 **7.** Two angles of a triangle measure 50° and 60°. Find the degree-measure of the third angle of the triangle.

8. An angle measures 5 times its complement. What is the degree-measure of the angle?

5–7 **9.** At 8 A.M. two planes leave St. Louis. One flies west at 350 miles per hour. The other flies east at 400 miles per hour. At what time will they be 1500 miles apart?

5–8 10. Admission to the skating rink is $1.25 for adults and 75¢ for students. On a day where 430 persons bought admission tickets the total receipts were $387.50. How many students bought tickets?

Chapter Review

5–1 Axioms of Order   *Pages 163–168*

1. Of the three statements $5 < 8$, $5 = 8$, $8 < 5$, only
$\dfrac{\text{?}}{\text{(one, two)}}$ can be true.

2. If $-7 > -9$ and $-9 > -10$, then -7 __?__ -10.

3. If $10 > 3$, then $10 + 3$ __?__ $3 + 3$.

4. If $2 < 8$ and $6 > 0$, then $2 \cdot 6$ __?__ $8 \cdot 6$.

5. Solve $c - 20 < 2$.

5–2 Intersection and Union of Sets   *Pages 168–172*

    6. $\emptyset$ is a subset of __?__ set.

    7. $\{5, 6, 7\} \cap \{5, 1\} = $ __?__   **8.** $\{5, 6, 7\} \cup \{5, 1\} = $ __?__

5–3 Combining Inequalities   *Pages 172–175*

    9. Solve the open sentence: $x + 4 > 6$ *and* $x - 1 < 2$

    10. Solve the open sentence: $x - 2 > 5$ *or* $x - 2 < 5$

5–4 Absolute Value in Open Sentences (Optional) *Pages 176–177*

    11. Solve $|x - 2| > 5$.

5–5 Problems about Integers   *Pages 177–181*

    12. The first of 3 consecutive integers is n. Represent the other two.

    13. If i is a multiple of 3, name the next two multiples of 3.

    14. The sum of 3 consecutive even integers is 9 times half the smallest. Find the integers.

5–6 Problems about Angles   *Pages 181–187*

    15. The sum of two complementary angles is ___°.

    16. Find the degree measure of two complementary angles if the measure of one angle is 40° greater than the measure of the other.

5–7 Uniform-Motion Problems   *Pages 188–192*

    17. John, who walks 3 miles an hour, started on a hike 2 hours before his friend Bill. If Bill walked 4 miles an hour, how many miles did he walk to catch up with John?

5–8 Mixture and Other Problems   *Pages 193–196*

    18. A bank teller was asked to cash a check for $120 so as to give equal numbers of $5 bills and $10 bills. How many of each bill did she count out?

EXTRA FOR EXPERTS

Algebraic Fallacies

   Seemingly valid methods of working with algebraic statements may lead to illogical results because they conceal violations of the properties of numbers. Test your ability to detect improper procedures by trying to find the errors in the arguments on the next page.

Exercises

Justify the valid steps in each series of transformations, and explain the error in each invalid step.

1. To "prove" that $1 = 0$, let a and b be two integers such that

$$a = b + 1.$$

Then: $(a - b)a = (a - b)(b + 1)$

$$a^2 - ab = ab + a - b^2 - b$$

$$a^2 - ab - a = ab + a - a - b^2 - b$$

$$a(a - b - 1) = b(a - b - 1)$$

$$a = b$$

$$b + 1 = b$$

$$\therefore 1 = 0.$$

(*Hint:* Substitute $a = b + 1$ in $a - b - 1$.)

2. To "prove" that $1 = 8$, let $y = 3$; then:

$$\frac{y + 9}{y - 1} - 6 = \frac{15 - 5y}{y - 8}$$

$$\frac{15 - 5y}{y - 1} = \frac{15 - 5y}{y - 8}$$

$$\frac{1}{y - 1} = \frac{1}{y - 8}$$

$$y - 1 = y - 8$$

$$-1 = -8$$

$$\therefore 1 = 8.$$

(*Hint:* What is the value of $15 - 5y$ if $y = 3$?)

3. To "prove" that $0 > 3$, let a be any number such that

$$a > 3.$$

Then: $\qquad 3a > 3(3)$

$$3a - a^2 > 9 - a^2$$

$$a(3 - a) > (3 - a)(3 + a)$$

$$a > 3 + a$$

$$\therefore 0 > 3.$$

4. To "prove" that $1 > 1$, let

$$c > 1$$

and $\qquad c = d.$ Then:

$$c - 1 = d - 1$$

$$c - 1 = -1(1 - d)$$

$$(c - 1)^2 = (-1)^2(1 - d)^2$$

$$(c - 1)^2 = (1 - d)^2$$

$$c - 1 = 1 - d$$

$$\therefore c - 1 = 1 - c.$$

$$2c = 2$$

$$c = 1$$

$$\therefore 1 > 1.$$

(*Hint:* $5^2 = 25$ and $(-5)^2 = 25$, but $5 \neq -5$.)

Having examined these fallacies, you should be aware of the disastrous consequences of dividing by zero, of multiplying an inequality by a negative number without changing the order of the inequality, and of assuming that numbers whose squares are equal must equal each other.

Who Uses Mathematics?

The science of chemistry is fascinating to many students. To become a chemist requires a good knowledge of mathematics, at least through the calculus. The first chemist, pictured at the left, does research work on polymers at temperatures varying from $-423°F$. to $1000°F$. The other photograph shows the machine which helped a team of scientists to "build" the first man-made enzyme. It helped them find the right arrangement out of 19^{124} possibilities.

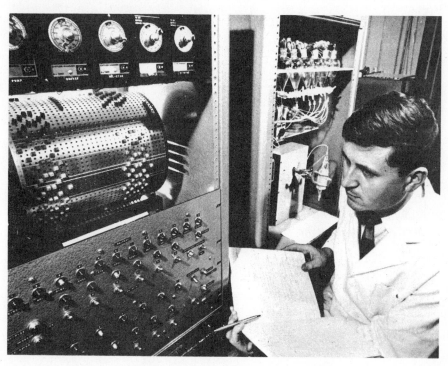

Just for Fun

If you practice a bit, you will be able to mystify your family and friends with your seemingly magical knowledge of numbers.

Tell a friend that you can give his age (or any other whole number he might choose) if he will follow a few instructions. Ask him to do the following silently, as you give him directions. If he will then give you the result, you can tell him his age (or the number he chose).

You say	You think (or write)	He thinks (*if his age is 13*)
Multiply your age by 3.	$3a$	$13 \times 3 = 39$
Add 10 to the result.	$3a + 10$	$39 + 10 = 49$
Subtract twice your age.	$3a + 10 - 2a = a + 10$	$13 \times 2 = 26$ $49 - 26 = 23$
Subtract 6.	$a + 10 - 6 = a + 4$	$23 - 6 = 17$
Tell me the answer.	$a + 4 = 17$ $13 + 4 = 17$ $a = 13$	17
You are 13.		How did you guess it?

Try this with your own age before you try it on anyone else. After a while, you can vary your directions provided you keep track of the steps, using a variable to stand for the number that you want to find. Remember, if your directions say to multiply the number by 5, for example, you must multiply *all your terms* by 5. Or, if the directions say to divide by 3, you must divide *all your terms* by 3.

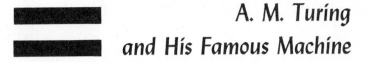

A. M. Turing
and His Famous Machine

As a boy, the distinguished English mathematician and scientist Alan Mathison Turing (**Tour**-ing) was at times the despair of his teachers because his home-made experiments upset the routine of the school. But his capability and earnestness eventually won him the high regard of his associates.

In 1931 he entered King's College, Cambridge, as a mathematical scholar. In 1935 he was elected a Fellow of King's for his dissertation on the "Central Limit Theorem" of probability. About that time, he began work in mathematical logic and initiated the investigation leading to his best-known results, those on computable numbers and the "universal machine," now often referred to as the "Turing machine." His scientific work was interrupted for six years (1939–1945) by his duties for the British Foreign Office, during World War II. For this work he was awarded the O.B.E. (Order of the British Empire).

At the end of the war, he turned his attention to the new automatic computing machines, which were actually realizations of the "universal machine" which he had described as an abstraction in a paper written in 1937. In that paper he had proved the existence of a "universal machine" which could be made to do the work of any particular machine if a tape with suitable "instructions" were inserted into it. He worked for a while on problems closely related to computers and then returned to mathematical analysis. During the last years of his life, he worked on the chemical theory of morphogenesis (the growth and form of living things).

Alan Mathison Turing (1912–1954)

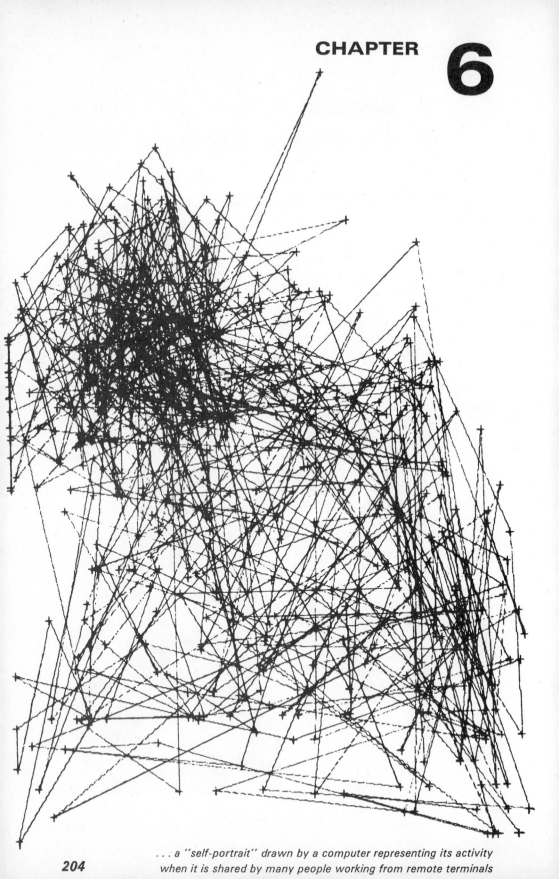

... a "self-portrait" drawn by a computer representing its activity
when it is shared by many people working from remote terminals

Working with Polynomials

Adam is so much FUN!! (handwritten)

You are now ready to learn how to perform operations with expressions called polynomials. You will then use these new techniques in the solution of problems more complicated than those you have solved up to now.

ADDITION AND SUBTRACTION OF POLYNOMIALS

6–1 Adding Polynomials

Each of the terms 8, y, $5x^2$, and $-3ab$ is called a *monomial* (mo-**no**-me-ul). A **monomial** is a term which is either a numeral (8), or a variable (y), or an indicated product of a numeral and one or more variables ($5x^2$ or $-3ab$). (Compare this definition of *monomial* with the definition of *term* on page 33.)

An indicated sum of monomials is called a **polynomial** (pol'e-**no**-me-ul). (The prefix "poly" means many.) A polynomial such as

$$7x^4 + 3x^3 + (-5x^2) + 2x + (-5)$$

is usually written as

$$7x^4 + 3x^3 - 5x^2 + 2x - 5.$$

$2x^2 + 3$ is a polynomial of **two** terms, which is called

a **binomial** (by-**no**-me-ul) since "bi" means two;

$x^2 - 2xy + y^2$ is a polynomial of **three** terms, which is called

a **trinomial** (try-**no**-me-ul) since "tri" means three.

A monomial is considered to be a polynomial of one term.

The **degree of a monomial in a variable** is the number of times that the variable occurs as a factor in the monomial. For example,

$$3x^2y^5z$$

is of degree **2** in x, **5** in y, and **1** in z. The **degree of a monomial** is the sum of the degrees in each of its variables. Thus, the degree of $3x^2y^5z$ is **8**, because $2 + 5 + 1 = 8$. If a monomial other than 0 contains no variables, **its degree is zero.** The monomial 0 has **no degree.**

A polynomial having no two terms *similar* (page 89) is said to be **simplified** (page 89) or to be in **simple form.** The **degree of a polynomial** in simple form is the same as the greatest of the degrees of its terms. The degrees of the terms of

$$15x^4 - 7x^3y^2 + 2xy + 4$$

are, in order, **4, 5, 2,** and **0.** Thus, the degree of this polynomial is **5.** Since $3x^4 + 8x^2 + y - 3x^4$ contains the similar terms $3x^4$ and $-3x^4$, it can be simplified to $8x^2 + y$; therefore, its degree is **2,** not 4.

To add two polynomials such as

$$6r^2s + 11 \quad \text{and} \quad 3r^2s - 5r + 3,$$

you write the sum

$$(6r^2s + 11) + (3r^2s - 5r + 3)$$

and then simplify it by adding the similar terms:

$$(6r^2s + 11) + (3r^2s - 5r + 3) = (6 + 3)r^2s - 5r + (11 + 3)$$
$$= 9r^2s - 5r + 14$$

> To add two polynomials, write the sum and add the similar terms.

You may also do the addition vertically:

$$
\begin{array}{l}
6r^2s \qquad\ + 11 \\
3r^2s - 5r + \ \ 3 \\
\hline
9r^2s - 5r + 14
\end{array}
$$

You can check the addition of polynomials by assigning a numerical value to each variable and evaluating the expressions. For example:

Check: **Let 2 be the value of *r* and 3 be the value of *s*.**

$$
\begin{array}{l}
6r^2s \qquad\ + 11 \rightarrow 6 \cdot 4 \cdot 3 \qquad\qquad + 11 = \ \ 83 \\
3r^2s - 5r + \ \ 3 \rightarrow 3 \cdot 4 \cdot 3 - (5 \cdot 2) + \ \ 3 = \ \ 29 \\
\hline
9r^2s - 5r + 14 \rightarrow 9 \cdot 4 \cdot 3 - (5 \cdot 2) + 14 \stackrel{?}{=} 112 \\
\qquad\qquad\qquad\qquad\qquad\qquad\qquad\quad 112 = 112 \ \checkmark
\end{array}
$$

Though you choose small numbers for checking, why should you not select 1 or 0?

In working with polynomials, it is convenient to arrange the terms in order of either decreasing degree or increasing degree in a particular variable.

In order of decreasing degree in m: $m^3 + 6m^2 + 12m + 6$

In order of increasing degree in y: $16 - 8y^2 + y^4$

In order of decreasing degree in r: $32r^5 + 7r^4s - 2r^2s^2 - 18s^3$

Oral Exercises

Simplify each expression for a sum. State the degree of each simplified expression.

1. $3x + 2$
$ 4x + 6$

2. $2y + 5$
$ 3y - 4$

3. $x^2 + 2$
$ x^2 - 2$

4. $a - b^2$
$ a + b^2$

5. $2x + y + 3z$
$ x - y + z$

6. $3a^2 + 2a - 1$
$ a^2 + a + 1$

7. $z^3 + 2z^2 - z$
$ z^2 + z + 2$

8. $b^3 - 2b^2 + b$
$ b^2 + 3b - 1$

9. $2z - x + y$
$ -3z \quad\; - y$
$ z + x$

10. $-n^3 + n^2 - 7$
$ n^3 - n^2 + 5$
$ -n^3 + n^2 - 2$

11. $(3y + 7) + (-2y + 2)$

12. $(5t - 6) + (t + 7)$

13. $(5a - b) + (2b - 4a)$

14. $(-2c + d) + (c - 3d)$

15. $(2x^2 + 3x - 1) + (x^2 - x + 2)$

16. $(3y^2 + 2y - 5) + (-4y^2 - 3y + 2)$

17. $(2z - z^2 + 5) + (z^2 - 3z + 1)$

18. $(3 - 2t^2 + t) + (t^2 - t - 3)$

19. $(n + m + 2) + (3n + 2m) + (m - 2)$

20. $(r - 2s + 3) + (2r + s) + (s + 4)$

Read each polynomial, giving the terms in order of decreasing degree in a variable.

SAMPLE. $4 + 2x^2 + x^4 + 3x^3$ *Solution:* $x^4 + 3x^3 + 2x^2 + 4$

21. $2y^2 + 1 + 3y$

22. $7z^2 + 3 + 8z$

23. $6 + 2x^2 + 3x$

24. $8 + 3t^2 + 11t$

25. $3n + n^2 - 2$

26. $5p - 2 + 3p^2$

27. $-8u + 2 - u^2 + u^3$

28. $-5 + 2v^3 - v^2 + 4v$

29. $x^2 + 3y^2 + 2xy$

30. $m^3 + 2m^2n + 2n^2 + 3mn^2$

Written Exercises

Simplify each expression for a sum.

A
1. $4m - 2n$
   $3m + 3n$

2. $-3t + s$
   $2t + 4s$

3. $2x - 5y$
   $-3x - 2y$

4. $3z - 2u$
   $-8z + 7u$

5. $3x^2 - 2x$
   $-x^2 + 3x$

6. $5y^2 - 2xy$
   $10y^2 + 18xy$

7. $21rs - 13s$
   $-15rs - 7s$

8. $83u^2 - 17v^2$
   $-15u^2 + 26v^2$

9. $7.2y - 3.1x$
   $-0.6y + 8.3x$

10. $-4.2w + 0.7v$
    $3.9w - 1.2v$

11. $\frac{3}{7}t - \frac{4}{13}s$
    $-\frac{4}{7}t + \frac{7}{13}s$

12. $z^3 - t^3$
    $\frac{1}{5}z^3 + \frac{2}{3}t^3$

13. $x^2 - 3x + 2$
    $3x^2 - 5$
    $ 4x + 8$

14. $x^2 + 8$
    $ 3z + 15$
    $-6x^2 - 2z - 7$

15. $3x^3 - 4x^2 + 7x$
    $ 2x^2 - 6x + 7$

16. $-3y^4 + 3x^3 - 5x^2 + x + 3$
    $ - 4x^3 + 2x^2 - x - 3$

Check each of the following sums. When values are given for the variables, use them. When a sum is incorrect, write the correct sum.

17. $7x - 2$
    $2x + 5$
    $9x + 3$
    Let $x = 3$.

18. $2z - 15$
    $-7z + 8$
    $-9z - 7$
    Let $z = 2$.

19. $2t + 5$
    $t - 7$
    $-4t + 8$
    $-t + 6$
    Let $t = 2$.

20. $3x + y - 2$
    $5x - 2y$
    $ 2y + 6$
    $8x + y + 8$
    Let $x = 2, y = 3$.

21. $2m^2 + 3n$
    $ 6n - 5$
    $-m^2 - n - 6$
    $m^2 + 8n - 11$
    Let $m = 5, n = 3$.

22. $z^2 - 3z + 2$
    $-z^2 + z - 5$
    $2z^2 + 5z + 2$
    $2z^2 + 9z - 1$
    Let $z = 2$.

Simplify each expression for a sum.

23. $(n + 3) + (2n + 5)$

24. $(2m - 7) + (3m + 7)$

25. $(\frac{1}{2}z - \frac{3}{2}) + (\frac{1}{4}z + \frac{1}{2})$

26. $(\frac{2}{3}t + 8) + (-\frac{7}{3}t - \frac{7}{2})$

27. $(3.1x^2 + 0.1) + (1.2x^2 - 2.3)$

28. $(-8.1y^2 - 2.2) + (3.8y^2 + 5.1)$

29. $(3z^3 - z^2) + (z^3 - 4z)$

30. $(5n^4 + 3n^2) + (n^3 - 3n^2)$

B
31. $(4x^3 - 2x^2 + 3x + 1) + (x^3 + 3x^2 - 5x - 1)$

32. $(-2z^3 + z^2 + 5z - 2) + (3z^3 - z^2 - 5z + 2)$

33. $(a^4 - 3a^2 + 2a - 1) + (2a^4 - a^3 + a^2 - 2a - 2)$
34. $(2b^5 + b^4 - 2b + 3) + (2b^4 + 3b^3 - b^2 + 2b - 2)$
35. $(-4t^6 + 2t^4 - 3t^3 + 2t^2 - 1) + (7t^6 + t^5 - 2t^4 + 3t^3 - 2t^2 + t - 1)$
36. $(6 + 3z^3 + 2z^5 - z^6) + (3z^6 - 5z^5 + 2z^4 - 2z^2 - 6)$

6–2 Subtracting Polynomials

To subtract one polynomial (the *subtrahend*) **from another** (the minuend), you use the same procedure as in subtracting real numbers (page 117). That is, you add the *opposite* of each term of the subtrahend. For example, $(12z + 3) - (2z - 4) = 12z + 3 + (-2z) + 4 = 10z + 7.$

EXAMPLE 1. $(17r^2 - 5r + 2) - (9r^2 + r - 5)$

Solution 1:

$(17r^2 - 5r + 2) - (9r^2 + r - 5)$
$= 17r^2 - 5r + 2 - 9r^2 - r + 5$
$= 8r^2 - 6r + 7$

Solution 2:

$$17r^2 - 5r + 2$$
$$9r^2 + \ r - 5$$
$$\overline{8r^2 - 6r + 7}$$

In general:

> To subtract one polynomial from another, add the opposite of each term of the polynomial you are subtracting (the subtrahend).

Grouping symbols (recall page 4) may appear in an equation to indicate addition or subtraction of a polynomial.

EXAMPLE 2. Solve:

$$y^2 + 2y + (y - 5 + 3y) = 3y - (-7 + 3y - y^2)$$

Solution: $y^2 + 2y + (y - 5 + 3y) = 3y - (-7 + 3y - y^2)$

Rewrite without parentheses $\rightarrow$ $y^2 + 2y + y - 5 + 3y = 3y + 7 - 3y + y^2$

Add similar terms $\rightarrow$ $y^2 + 6y - 5 = 0 + 7 + y^2$

Subtract y^2 **from each member** $\rightarrow$ $6y - 5 = 7$

Add 5 to each member $\rightarrow$ $6y = 12$

Divide each member by 6 $\rightarrow$ $y = 2$

Check: $2^2 + 2 \cdot 2 + (2 - 5 + 3 \cdot 2) \overset{?}{=} 3 \cdot 2 - (-7 + 3 \cdot 2 - 2^2)$

$4 + 4 + (2 - 5 + 6) \overset{?}{=} 6 - (-7 + 6 - 4)$

$8 + (3) \overset{?}{=} 6 - (-5)$

$11 = 11 \checkmark$

∴ **the solution set is {2}.   Answer.**

Note: In the solution use was made of the fact that adding the same polynomial to each member of an open sentence produces an equivalent sentence.

Oral Exercises

Subtract the lower polynomial from the one above it.

1. $3x + 5y$
  $\underline{x + 2y}$

2. $4a + 3b$
  $\underline{2a + 3b}$

3. $7m + 2n$
  $\underline{5m + 4n}$

4. $3u + 2v$
  $\underline{5u + 2v}$

5. $2r - s$
  $\underline{r + 2s}$

6. $-3y + 7z$
  $\underline{2y - z}$

7. $3x + y - 2z$
  $\underline{x - 4z}$

8. $6r - 5s - t$
  $\underline{7r + s - t}$

Simplify each expression.

SAMPLE. $(8x + 3) - (5x - 2)$ *Solution:* $8x + 3 - 5x + 2 = 3x + 5$

9. $3x - (x - 1)$

10. $(3y + 2) - 3y$

11. $(a + b) - (a + b)$

12. $(c - d) - (c + d)$

13. $(r - s) - (r - s)$

14. $(u + v) - (u - v)$

15. $(3x + 2y) - (x + 3y)$

16. $(m - 2n) - (2m - n)$

17. $(x^2 + 2x - 1) - (x^2 - 2x + 1)$

18. $(2z^2 + 3z - 4) - (z^2 - 5)$

Written Exercises

Subtract. Check by evaluation, using 2 for x, 3 for y, 4 for a, 5 for b.

A

1. $4a + 4$
  $\underline{2a + 1}$

2. $2b + 3$
  $\underline{b + 2}$

3. $4y + 3$
  $\underline{2y - 5}$

4. $x - 3$
  $\underline{2x + 2}$

5. $4x - 5y$
  $\underline{-3x - 2y}$

6. $7a + b$
  $\underline{-a - 2b}$

7. $x^2 - 3x + 1$
  $\underline{x^2 - 2x - 2}$

8. $2y^2 - 3y + 1$
  $\underline{-y^2 + y + 2}$

9. $2a^2 - 3a + 5$
  $\underline{a^2 - 2}$

10. $2b^2 + 5b - 5$
  $\underline{3b^2 - 4b}$

11. $ax + by$
  $\underline{-2ax + by}$

12. $xy - ab$
  $\underline{xy - 3ab}$

Simplify.

13. $(3r + 2s) - (r + s)$ **15.** $(-5u + v) - (-4u - v)$

14. $(2p + 3q) - (2p - q)$ **16.** $(-2x - 5) - (-x + 7)$

17. $(z^2 - 3z + 2) - (-z^2 - 2z + 2)$

18. $(t^3 - 2t^2 + 3) - (2t^3 + 3t^2 - 2t)$

19. $(2x^4 - 3x^2 + 1) - (x^4 - 2x^2 - x + 2)$

20. $(3y^4 + 2y^3 - 3y) - (2y^4 + 2y^3 - 4y - 2)$

Solve each equation.

21. $2x - (3x + 2) = 5$ **23.** $(4t - 2) - t = -20$

22. $-3y - (7 - 5y) = 15$ **24.** $(4 - 3r) - 2r = -21$

25. $(2s - 5) - (3s + 2) = 5 - 3s$

26. $(2y + 3) - (4 - 2y) = -10 + y$

27. $(-3k + 4) - (k - 6) = -3k - 11$

28. $(5z - 3) - (z - 8) = 2z - 7$

29. $(4 - 2x) - (x - 5) = (x + 2) - (3 - x)$

30. $(-2 - 3a) - (4 - a) = (3 - a) - (5 - a)$

31. $(p^2 - 2p + 1) - (2p^2 + 3p + 5) = 2 - 3p - p^2$

32. $(2s^2 - 5s - 2) - (s^2 - s + 8) = s^2 + 2s - 28$

33. $(4 - 6z + 3z^2) - (14 + z - z^2) = 4z^2 + z + 70$

34. $(-3 - 7x - 5x^2) - (8 + x - x^2) = 49 - 4x - 4x^2$

B **35.** $2t - [3 - (t + 2)] = 29$

36. $4n - [n - (6 + 2n)] = 44$

37. $-2x - [3x - (14 - x)] = -42 + x$

38. $-7y - [8 - (y + 24)] = -2y - 22$

39. $-[3x - (5 - 2x) + 3] = -49 - 2x$

40. $-[17 - (3z - 5) + 6z] = 2z + 18$

When $f(x)$ and $g(x)$ (recall page 147) are as given, simplify $f(x) - g(x)$.

SAMPLE. $f(x) = 3x^2 + 2x - 1; \; g(x) = 2 + 3x - x^2$

Solution: $f(x) - g(x) = 3x^2 + 2x - 1 - (2 + 3x - x^2)$
$$= 3x^2 + 2x - 1 - 2 - 3x + x^2$$
$$= 4x^2 - x - 3. \quad \textbf{Answer.}$$

41. $f(x) = 5x^2 - 3x + 1; \; g(x) = -3x^2 + x - 5$

42. $f(x) = 7 - 3x - 15x^2; \; g(x) = 6 + 2x - 11x^2$

$\boxed{C}$ **43.** $f(x) = 3 - [x + (x - 1)]$; $g(x) = x - (2 - x^2)$
44. $f(x) = x - [3 - (x + 2)]$; $g(x) = (3 - x) - (x + 1)$
45. $f(x) = x^2 - [2 - (x + 1)]$; $g(x) = x^2 - [3 - (2 - 3x)]$
46. $f(x) = 3x - [2x^2 - (x + 1)]$; $g(x) = 7 - [5x^2 - (x + 7)]$

MULTIPLICATION OF POLYNOMIALS

6–3 The Product of Powers

You will recall (page 37) that b^4 (read "b to the fourth" or "b-fourth") stands for $b \cdot b \cdot b \cdot b$. Therefore:

$$b^4 \cdot b^2 = \underbrace{\overbrace{(b \cdot b \cdot b \cdot b)}^{\text{4 factors}} \cdot \overbrace{(b \cdot b)}^{\text{2 factors}}}_{\text{6 factors}} = b^6 = b^{4+2}$$

Thus, in multiplying these two *powers of the same base*, you could have found the exponent by retaining the base and adding the exponents of the factors. In general, for positive integral exponents m and n:

$$b^m \cdot b^n = \underbrace{(\underbrace{b \cdot b \cdots b}_{m \text{ factors}})(\underbrace{b \cdot b \cdots b}_{n \text{ factors}})}_{m+n \text{ factors}} = b^{m+n}$$

This result is usually stated as follows:

Rule of Exponents for Multiplication

For all positive integers m and n; $b^m \cdot b^n = b^{m+n}$

To multiply monomials, you may use this rule of exponents together with the commutative and associative axioms of multiplication to determine the numerical factor and the variable factors of the product. Thus:

$$(6x^2y)(-5x^5y^4) = (6 \cdot -5)(x^2 \cdot x^5)(y \cdot y^4) = -30x^{2+5}y^{1+4} = -30x^7y^5$$

Note that this rule of exponents applies only when the bases of the powers are the *same*. You cannot use it, for example, to simplify the product x^8y^9 because the bases of the powers x^8 and y^9 are *different*. Thus, the product x^8y^9 cannot be simplified.

Oral Exercises

Simplify each expression.

SAMPLE. $(-2x)(3x^2)$ *Solution:* $-6x^3$

1. $(x)(x)(x)$ 2. $(y)(y)(y)$ 3. $(a)(a^2)$ 4. $(c^2)(c^2)$

5. $(3x)(4z)$ 9. $(-2ab)(-2a^2)$ 13. $(-xy)(y)(xy^2)$

6. $(2m)(7n)$ 10. $(-3p^2)(-pq)$ 14. $z^4(2yz)(3y^2)$

7. $(-2y)(y^2)$ 11. $(-5r^2s)(rs^2)$ 15. $7t(-s^2t)(2s^3)$

8. $z^2(-3z^3)$ 12. $(2x^2y)(3xy)$ 16. $-6u(u^3v)(-v^2)$

17. $x \cdot x^n$ 18. $y^n(y^2)$ 19. $(z^m)(z^n)$ 20. $(t^n)(t^{2n})$

Written Exercises

Simplify each expression.

A

1. $(2yz)(3y^2)$ 4. $(pq^3)(-5p^4q^2)$ 7. $(-2y)(-2y)(-2y)$

2. $(5ab)(4a^2)$ 5. $(-2x)(x^2y)(y)$ 8. $(-4z)(4z)(4z)$

3. $(-2m^2n)(mn^3)$ 6. $(-3z)(4zt)(t^3)$ 9. $(-3a^2b)(-2ab)(5b^4)$

10. $(-5k^2m)(-3km^2)(k^2m^4)$ 17. $(-3a^2b^2c)(-3a^2b^2c)(-3a^2b^2c)$

11. $(0.2x)(5x^2y)(-xyz^3)$ 18. $(\frac{1}{2}xy^2z^3)(\frac{1}{2}xy^2z^3)(\frac{1}{2}xy^2z^3)$

12. $(0.3z^2)(12z^4r)(5zr^5)$ 19. $(x^n)(x)$

13. $(\frac{1}{3}m^2n)(\frac{1}{5}mn^5)$ 20. $(y^n)(y^n)$

14. $(-\frac{1}{4}s^3t^2)(\frac{1}{2}s^2t)$ 21. $(2z^{n+1})(z)$

15. $-\frac{1}{5}u(u^5v^5)(-5uv^3)$ 22. $(3t^{n-2})(-2t^{3-n})$

16. $\frac{2}{3}t^2(rs^2t)(6r^2s)$

SAMPLE. $(3p)(pr)(p^2t) - (2p^2)(p^2rt)$

Solution: $(3p)(pr)(p^2t) - (2p^2)(p^2rt) = 3p^4rt - 2p^4rt = p^4rt.$ **Answer.**

B

23. $(-2r)(r^2)(-r^3) + (3r^2)(r^4)$

24. $(-2x)(xy^2)(-5xz^2) + (-x^2)(2xy)(4yz^2)$

25. $(5h^2)(-3hk^2)(k^2) - (-3h)(2h^2k)(k^3)$

26. $(a^3bc)(-2b^2c)(3c^2) + (-a^2b^2c^2)(2a)(-3bc^2)$

27. $(5mn^2)(-3m^3n)(p^2) + (8mp)(3np)(m^3n^2)$

28. $(u^2vw)(-uv^2w)(-uvw^2) + (4u^2v^2w^2)(2u^2v^2w^2)$

C

29. $y^4(3y + 2) + 2y^2(y^3 - 2y^2)$ 31. $x^m(x^n + 1) + x^{m+n}$

30. $t^3(t - t^2) - 2t^2(t^3 + t^2)$ 32. $y^n(y^2 + 2) - y^{n+1}(y + 2)$

6–4 The Power of a Product

Consider $3x^3$ and $(3x)^3$; they are not equal unless x has the value 0. You have:

$$3x^3 = 3 \cdot x \cdot x \cdot x$$
$$(3x)^3 = 3x \cdot 3x \cdot 3x = 27x^3$$

In general, for every positive integral exponent m, you can see that:

$$\overbrace{(ab)^m = (ab)(ab) \cdots (ab)}^{(ab) \text{ is a factor } m \text{ times}}$$

$$\therefore (ab)^m = \underbrace{(a \cdot a \cdot \cdots \cdot a)}_{m \text{ factors}}\underbrace{(b \cdot b \cdot \cdots \cdot b)}_{m \text{ factors}} = a^m b^m$$

This result may be summarized as follows:

Rule of Exponents for a Power of a Product

For every positive integer m: $(ab)^m = a^m b^m$

For example:

$$(-2z)^4 = (-2)^4 z^4 = 16z^4 \quad \textbf{and} \quad (5pq)^2 = 5^2 p^2 q^2 = 25p^2 q^2$$

Of course, the base of a power may itself be a power:

$$(b^2)^3 = b^2 \cdot b^2 \cdot b^2 = b^{2+2+2} = b^6 = b^{2 \cdot 3}$$

In general,

$$\overbrace{(b^m)^n = (b^m)(b^m) \cdots (b^m)}^{b^m \text{ is a factor } n \text{ times}}$$

$$\therefore (b^m)^n = \overbrace{b^{m+m+\cdots+m}}^{n \text{ terms}} = b^{mn}$$

This result gives you the following:

Rule of Exponents for a Power of a Power

For all positive integers m and n: $(b^m)^n = b^{mn}$

You use both of these rules in the following illustration:

$$(-6s^6 t^4)^3 = (-6)^3 (s^6)^3 (t^4)^3 = -216s^{18} t^{12}.$$

Oral Exercises

Simplify each expression.

1. $(3a)^2$ **5.** $(x^2)^2$ **9.** $(c^2d^3)^3$ **13.** $-(x^2)^2$

2. $(4b)^2$ **6.** $(y^2)^3$ **10.** $(ab^2c)^4$ **14.** $-(-xy)^3$

3. $(-3c)^3$ **7.** $(\frac{1}{2}yz)^2$ **11.** $(-2ab^2)^3$ **15.** $x(xy)^2$

4. $(-4d)^2$ **8.** $(-\frac{1}{3}ab)^2$ **12.** $(-4t^2x)^1$ **16.** $s^2(s^2t)^2$

17. $(x^n)^2$ **18.** $(y^2)^m$ **19.** $(y^m)^n$ **20.** $(x^my^n)^3$

State the square of each monomial.

21. $-0.2x^2$ **22.** $0.3y^2z$ **23.** $8u^2v^2$ **24.** $-10a^3b^2$

Written Exercises

Simplify each expression.

A

1. $(2a)^4$ **5.** $3z(2z)^2$ **9.** $(x^2y)^2(xy^2)^3$

2. $(3z)^3$ **6.** $4b(3b)^3$ **10.** $(c^3d)^3(cd^2)^2$

3. $(-4t^2)^2$ **7.** $-2s(st)^2$ **11.** $(-\frac{1}{2}a^2b)^2(4ab^3)^2$

4. $(-2n^3)^2$ **8.** $-3p(p^2q)^3$ **12.** $(-\frac{1}{3}mn)^3(9mn^2)^2$

13. $(-rs)^2(2r^2s)^3(0.5s)$ **16.** $(-2x^2y)^3(\frac{1}{4}xy)^2(-2y^2)^2$

14. $(yz^2)^2(-4y^2)^3(0.25z^2)$ **17.** $(xz)^n(x^2z)$

15. $(c^4k)^2(-3k)^3(\frac{1}{3}c^2)^2$ **18.** $(a^nb^m)^2(a^2b)$

SAMPLE. $(3x^2y)^2 + (3x^2y^2)(2x)^2$

Solution: $(3x^2y)^2 + (3x^2y^2)(2x)^2 = 9x^4y^2 + (3x^2y^2)(4x^2)$

$$= 9x^4y^2 + 12x^4y^2 = 21x^4y^2. \textbf{ Answer.}$$

B

19. $(2ab^2)^3 + (2ab^2)^2(6ab^2)$

20. $(3u)(u^2v)^3 + (2u)^2(-u^5v^3)$

21. $(-2r^3)^2(rs^2t) - (-r^2)^2(rst)(-r^2s)$

22. $(-6y^2z^3)^2(2yz) - (3yz^2)^3(-12y^2z)$

23. $(\frac{1}{3}m^2n)^4(-9mn^2)^2 - (3mn)^2(\frac{1}{9}m^2n^2)(m^3n^2)^2$

24. $(\frac{2}{3}pq^2)^3(-9p^2q)^2 - (-pq^2)^2(2pq)^3(5p^2q)$

C

25. $-3x^2y(y - 2) + 2xy^2(x - 3)$

26. $5ab^2(ab - b^2) - 2a^2(b^3 + b)$

27. $x^n(x^2 - 2x) + x^2(x^n + x^{n-1})$

28. $z^m(2z + 3) - z(z^m + 2z^{m-1})$

6–5   Multiplying a Polynomial by a Monomial

The distributive axiom, together with the rules of exponents for multiplication, enables you to multiply any polynomial by a monomial. For example:

$$3a(4a^2 + 2) = 3a(4a^2) + 3a(2) = 12a^3 + 6a$$

This result is illustrated in the figure:

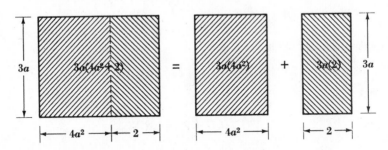

The largest rectangle can be separated into the other two.   Its area is equal to the sum of the areas of the other two rectangles.

You may multiply either horizontally or vertically, as shown here.

$$-6x^3(4x^2 - 2x + 1) = -24x^5 + 12x^4 - 6x^3$$

$$\begin{array}{r} 4x^2 - 2x + 1 \\ -6x^3 \\ \hline -24x^5 + 12x^4 - 6x^3 \end{array}$$

In general:

> To multiply a polynomial by a monomial, use the distributive axiom: multiply each term of the polynomial by the monomial, and then add the products.

Oral Exercises

In each exercise, apply the distributive axiom and state the result.

SAMPLE. $-4x^2(x + 2) = -4x^3 - 8x^2$

1. $2(x - 3)$
2. $y(y + 4)$
3. $-z(2 - z)$
4. $-k(2k + 5)$
5. $4(a - b)$
6. $2(c + d)$
7. $x^2(x - 2)$
8. $y^3(y^2 + y)$

9. $-3z^2(2z^2 - 5z)$

10. $-2t(3t^5 + 5t^3)$

11. $-1(3x^2 - x^3)$

12. $-1(7n^2 + 3)$

13. $-3xy(x^2 - y^2)$

14. $-2ab(-a^2 - b^2)$

15. $x^n(x + 1)$

16. $y^n(y - 2)$

17. $3p - 4t$
$\underline{-p}$

18. $2u - 6v$
$\underline{\frac{1}{2}u}$

19. $2z^2 - 4z + 2$
$\underline{4z}$

20. $5x^2 - 2x + 1$
$\underline{-3x}$

Written Exercises

In each exercise, apply the distributive axiom.

A

1. $3(a^2 + 2ab + 2b^2)$

2. $5(2z^2 - 2z + 6)$

3. $-4(3 - 2x - 3x^2)$

4. $-2(y^2 - 4y + 7)$

5. $2x^2(x + xy - 3y^2)$

6. $-4t^3(3r + 2rt - 4t^2)$

7. $3x^2y(4 + 2y - xy^2)$

8. $6n^2t(4nt - 3nt^2 + 4t^3)$

9. $(6p^2 - 4pq + 3q^2)(-2pq)$

10. $(4k^2 + 3kn + 2n^2)(-5k)$

11. $3xz^2(7 + 5x - 3z + 2x^3z)$

12. $5r^2s(3 - 2r + 7s - 5rs^2)$

13. $-6p^3r(3p - 4pr + 7r^2 - 2p^2r^2)$

14. $-8c^3d^2(c^2 + d^2 - 4c - 5d)$

Solve each equation over $\Re$. (Recall page 113.)

15. $3n + 2(n - 5) = 35$

16. $2z + 5(6 - z) = 3$

17. $-7u + 5(2u - 3) = -39$

18. $-9t + 3(t - 4) = 42$

19. $2(x + 5) - 3(x - 4) = 7$

20. $5(2p - 3) - 2(5 - p) = -7$

21. $-7(y - 3) + 5(3y - 5) = 44$

22. $-10(3 - 4n) - 7(5n + 3) = -51$

B

23. $5p - 7(3 - p) = 6 + 2(p + 5)$

24. $6k - 5(3k + 2) = 5(k - 1) - 8$

25. $\frac{1}{2}(6z + 4) - \frac{2}{3}(9 - 3z) = 2(z + 1) + 3$

26. $\frac{1}{4}(3z + 8) + \frac{3}{4}(z - 4) = \frac{1}{2}(z + 4) - 2$

27. $2 - 5[3t + 2(6 - t)] = -7(t - 4)$

28. $7 + 3[-s - 3(s + 5)] = 5(7 - 2s) + 5$

C

29. $2x + x[3 - (x + 1)] = x(2 - x) + 12$

30. $7z - 4[3 + z(5 - z)] = 2z(6 + 2z) + 8$

Problems

Write a polynomial that represents the number described.

SAMPLE.   The area of a rectangle that is 20 feet longer than it is wide.

Solution: Let w = number of feet in the width.

Then $w + 20$ = number of feet in the length.

Area = $w(w + 20) = w^2 + 20w$ (square feet). **Answer.**

A   1.   The area of a rectangle that is 5 inches longer than it is wide.

2.   The area of a rectangle whose width is 7 inches shorter than its length.

3.   The area of a triangle in which the length of the altitude is 3 feet less than the length of the base.

4.   The area of a triangle in which the length of the base is 5 feet greater than the length of its altitude.

5.   The total distance traveled by an automobile that travels at an average speed of 40 miles per hour for 2 hours and then increases its speed so that its average speed during the next hour is x miles per hour more.

6.   The total distance traveled by an automobile that travels at an average speed of s miles per hour for 2 hours and then increases its speed so that its average speed during the next hour is 10 miles per hour more.

7.   The total distance traveled if I travel for 3 hours at $(40 + x)$ miles per hour and then for 4 hours at $(100 + x)$ miles per hour.

8.   The total distance you travel in flying 2 hours at $(300 + x)$ miles per hour and then 4 hours at $1\frac{1}{2}$ times that rate.

B   9.   A plane traveled for 2 hours at an average airspeed (speed relative to the air) of v miles per hour with an average tail wind of 20 miles per hour. Then the plane traveled against a wind averaging 5 miles an hour for 2 more hours. Write a polynomial in simple form for the total land distance covered.

10.   A man can row x miles per hour in still water. He rowed down a river with a current of 4 miles per hour for half an hour and then up a creek against a current of 2 miles an hour for half an hour. Write a polynomial in simple form for the total distance he rowed.

11.   The dimensions of a rectangular playground are 40 feet by 24 feet. The walk around it is of uniform width. The playground and walk have a combined area of 2240 square feet. Write a polynomial in simple form for the total area.

12.   A picture is 15 inches wide and 20 inches long. It is enclosed in a frame of uniform width. The area of the frame is $\frac{2}{3}$ that of the picture. Write a polynomial in simple form to express the total area.

6-6 Multiplying Two Polynomials

To express the product $(3y + 2)(6y + 1)$ as a polynomial, first treat $(6y + 1)$ as a number to be multiplied by the binomial $3y + 2$ and apply the distributive axiom. Then apply the distributive axiom to each of the products you have obtained. Finally, simplify the resulting polynomial.

$(3y + 2)(6y + 1)$
$= (3y)(6y + 1) \qquad + 2(6y + 1)$
$= (3y)(6y) + (3y)(1) + 2(6y) + 2(1)$
$= 18y^2 \qquad + 3y \qquad + 12y \quad + 2$
$= 18y^2 \qquad + \qquad 15y \qquad + 2$

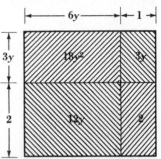

The figure illustrates this product.

> To multiply one polynomial by another, use the distributive axiom: multiply each term of one polynomial by each term of the other, and then add the products.

Usually it is convenient to set up the multiplication of polynomials in vertical form, and to work from left to right, thus:

$$
\begin{array}{r}
6y + 1 \\
3y + 2 \\
\hline
18y^2 + 3y \\
12y + 2 \\
\hline
18y^2 + 15y + 2
\end{array}
$$

This is $3y(6y + 1) \longrightarrow 18y^2 + 3y$
This is $2(6y + 1) \longrightarrow 12y + 2$
This is $(3y + 2)(6y + 1) \rightarrow 18y^2 + 15y + 2$

To check the accuracy of your multiplication, you can evaluate the factors and their product, using any numbers except 0 and 1.

Written Exercises

Express each product as a polynomial in simple form.

1. $(a + 1)(a + 2)$
2. $(c + 3)(c + 4)$
3. $(x - 2)(x + 2)$
4. $(y + 1)(y - 1)$
5. $(z - 3)(z + 6)$

6. $(p - 2)(p - 2)$
7. $(2a + 1)(a + 2)$
8. $(b + 4)(3b + 1)$
9. $(2n + 3)(n - 5)$
10. $(3n - 1)(n + 2)$

11. $(3x - 3)(x - 5)$
12. $(7y - 2)(y - 3)$
13. $(2r + 3)(3r + 2)$
14. $(5t - 2)(3t + 1)$
15. $(6d + 5)(3d - 2)$

16. $(7a - 6)(2a - 5)$
17. $(2x - y)(x + y)$
18. $(3z - u)(2z + 3u)$
19. $(2x + 7z)(2x - 7z)$
20. $(3y + 2v)(3y + 2v)$
21. $(2x - 3t)(2x - 3t)$
22. $(4a + b)(4a + b)$

23. $(0.2z + 1)(1.4z - 2)$
24. $(2.1n + 6)(10n - 0.3)$
25. $(x^2 - y)(x^2 + y)$
26. $(2x^2 + 4)(x^2 - 3)$
27. $(a^2 - b^2)(a^2 - b^2)$
28. $(p^2 + q^2)(p^2 + q^2)$

B 29. $(x + 1)(x^2 + 3x - 2)$
30. $(z + 2)(z^2 - 3z + 5)$
31. $(2x - 1)(x^2 + 3x + 5)$

32. $(a - 2)(3a^2 + 5a - 1)$
33. $(x - y)(x^2 + xy + y^2)$
34. $(r + s)(r^2 + ry + s^2)$

35. $(x + 1)(2x - 3) + (x + 1)(3x - 1)$
36. $(y + 2)(y - 2) + (2y + 1)(2y + 1)$
37. $(2a + b)(3a - b) - (a - b)(2a - 3b)$
38. $(3c - d)(2c + 3d) - (4c + d)(2c - d)$

C 39. $(x^2 + 2x - 1)(x^2 - x + 3)$
40. $(2y^2 + y - 2)(y^2 + 3y + 5)$
41. $(2r - s + t)(r + 2s - t)$
42. $(a + 2b + 3c)(2a - b + 2c)$
43. $(t - 1)(t^4 + t^3 + t^2 + t + 1)$
44. $(k + 1)(k^4 - k^3 + k^2 - k + 1)$

Use the properties of real numbers to prove that each of the following is true for all real numbers a, b, c, and d.

45. $(a + b)(c + d) = ac + bc + ad + bd$
46. $(a - b)(c - d) = ac - bc - ad + bd$
47. $(a + b)(a - b) = a^2 - b^2$
48. $(a + b)(a + b) = a^2 + 2ab + b^2$

6–7 Problems about Areas

The solution of problems concerned with areas requires the ability to multiply polynomials. In analyzing such problems, you will find sketches especially helpful.

EXAMPLE. The length of a page in a book is 2 inches greater than the width of the page. A book designer finds that if the length is increased by 2 inches and the width by 1 inch, the area of the page is increased by 19 square inches. What are the dimensions of the original page?

Solution:

1 ▶ Let w = number of inches in width of the page.

Then $w + 2$ = number of inches in length of the page.

2 ▶

| area of enlarged page | − | area of original page | = | amount of increase in area |

$$(w + 1)(w + 4) \overset{?}{-} w(w + 2) \overset{?}{=} 19$$

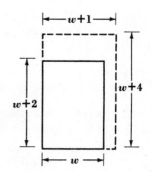

3 ▶ Solve the equation.

$$(w + 1)(w + 4) - w(w + 2) = 19$$
$$w^2 + 5w + 4 - w^2 - 2w = 19$$
$$3w + 4 = 19$$
$$3w = 15$$
$$w = 5$$
$$w + 2 = 7$$

4 ▶ *Check:* (1) Is the length 2 inches greater than the width? $5 + 2 = 7$. Yes.

(2) Does the area increase by 19 square inches if the length is increased by 2 inches and the width by 1 inch?

Area of original page $+ 19$ = area of enlarged page

$$5 \times 7 + 19 \overset{?}{=} 6 \times 9$$
$$35 + 19 \overset{?}{=} 54$$
$$54 = 54 \checkmark$$

Width of original page: 5 inches
Length of original page: 7 inches } **Answer.**

Problems

A **1.** The rectangular base of a radio receiver is twice as long as it is wide. A design engineer finds that in order to fit the receiver into the space available on a space vehicle, he must reduce the length by 3 inches and the width by 1 inch. If this change reduces the area of the base by 27 square inches, what were the original dimensions of the receiver?

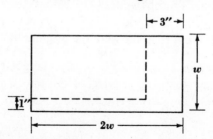

2. The McKay gangplow will plow a strip 3 times as long as it is wide in a given time. The Durley gangplow is 2 feet wider than the McKay plow and will plow 68 square feet more in the same length of time. If the Durley plow can be pulled 4 feet farther than the McKay plow in the given time period, how wide is each plow?

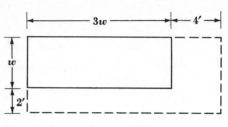

For each problem, make a sketch and solve.

3. A rectangular television picture tube is 3 inches longer than it is wide. If the length and width of the tube are each increased by 2 inches, the picture area is increased by 54 square inches. What are the dimensions of the original tube?

4. A rectangular swimming pool is 5 feet longer than it is wide. If a concrete walk 2 feet wide is placed around the pool, the area covered by the pool and the walk is 156 square feet greater than the area covered by the pool alone. What are the dimensions of the pool?

5. A rectangular picture is 2 inches longer than it is wide. When a frame 3 inches wide is placed around the picture, the area covered by the picture and frame is 168 square inches greater than the area covered by the picture alone. What are the dimensions of the picture?

6. The area occupied by an unframed rectangular picture is 64 square inches less than the area occupied by the picture mounted in a frame 2 inches wide. What are the dimensions of the picture if it is 4 inches longer than it is wide?

7. A manufacturer makes two sizes of cookie pans, each having the same area. One is square and the other is rectangular in shape. If the length of the rectangular pan is 4 inches greater and the width 3 inches shorter than the length of one side of the square pan, what are the dimensions of each pan?

8. Mrs. Carter decided to make a rectangular desk top from a plywood door that was stored in her basement. The door was 2 feet longer than twice its width. To get the desired size desk top she cut 3 feet off its length and $\frac{1}{2}$ foot off its width. If the plywood she cut off had a total area of $9\frac{1}{2}$ square feet, what were the original dimensions of the door?

B **9.** Mr. Balter wanted to make a plywood rectangular table top that would be 3 feet longer than it was wide. He found that by making the top 1 foot narrower and 2 feet shorter than planned, he could save $2.60

on the plywood. If the plywood he was using cost 20 cents per square foot, what were Mr. Balter's original dimensions for his table top?

10. Steve's first aquarium had a rectangular base that was 8 inches longer than it was wide. He replaced this with a larger aquarium that was 2 inches wider and 4 inches longer than the first one. He found that if he filled each to a depth of 10 inches, it required 840 cubic inches more water to fill the new aquarium than the old. What were the dimensions of the base of the original aquarium?

11. A cross section of a circular concrete pipe has a wall 2 inches thick, and a cross-sectional area of $138\frac{2}{7}$ square inches. Find the inner diameter of the pipe. Use $\frac{22}{7}$ for π.

 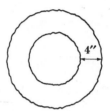

Ex. 11   Ex. 12 (see also picture on p. 248)

12. When the radius of a circular ripple in a pond increases by 4 inches, the area it encloses increases by 352 square inches. What is the radius of the ripple after the increase? Use $\frac{22}{7}$ for π.

6-8 Powers of Polynomials

The area of a square is found by using the formula $A = s^2$, the area of a circle by using $A = \pi r^2$, and the volume of a cube by using $V = s^3$.

The figure shows a cube in which each edge s is given as $(3y - 2)$. The base of this cube, then has an area of

$(3y - 2)^2$, **read "the square of $3y - 2$."**

The volume is

$(3y - 2)^3$, **read "the cube of $3y - 2$."**

$s = 3y - 2$

In each of these expressions, the exponent shows how many times the polynomial is to be used as a factor. To find the product of these factors expressed as a sum of monomials, you **expand the expression**. To expand the expression $(3y - 2)^2$, you express $(3y - 2)(3y - 2)$ as a polynomial in simple form. To expand $(3y - 2)^3$, you express $(3y - 2)(3y - 2)(3y - 2)$ as a polynomial in simple form.

$(3y - 2)^2:$

$3y - 2$

$3y - 2$

$9y^2 - 6y$

$\quad\quad - 6y + 4$

$9y^2 - 12y + 4 = (3y - 2)^2$

$(3y - 2)^3:$

$9y^2 - 12y + 4$

$3y - 2$

$27y^3 - 36y^2 + 12y$

$\quad\quad - 18y^2 + 24y - 8$

$27y^3 - 54y^2 + 36y - 8 = (3y - 2)^3$

Written Exercises

Expand each power. Check your results by numerical evaluation.

A

1. $(x + 1)^2$
2. $(y + 2)^2$
3. $(a - 3)^2$

4. $(b - 4)^2$
5. $(a + b)^2$
6. $(a - b)^2$

7. $(2x - z)^2$
8. $(2 - 3y)^2$
9. $(a + b)^3$

10. $(a - b)^3$
11. $(2x + z)^3$
12. $(3x - 2y)^3$

13. $2x(x + 5)^2$
14. $-3y(y - 2)^2$

15. $(x - y)(x + y)^2$
16. $(a + 2b)(a - 3b)^2$

17. $4x^2 + (x + 2)^2$
18. $3z^2 - (z - 2)^2$

19. $(x + \tfrac{1}{2})^2$
20. $(y - \tfrac{1}{3})^2$
21. $(a - 0.3)^2$
22. $(b + 1.2)^2$

B

23. $(x + y + z)^2$
24. $(x - y + z)^2$
25. $(x + y - z)^2$

26. $(x - y - z)^2$
27. $(x + y)^4$
28. $(x - y)^4$

29. $(x - y)^2(x + y)^2$
30. $(3x^2 - 2x + 5)^2$

C

31. $[(a + b)^2 - (a - b)^2]^2$
32. $[(a + b)^2 + 3(a + b) - 8ab]^2$
33. $(c + d)^3 - (c - d)^3$

34. $(p - q)^3 + (p + q)^3$
35. $(x^n + 3)^3$
36. $(2 - y^n)^3$

Problems

For each problem, make a sketch where helpful, and solve.

A

1. The length of a side of one square is 3 inches greater than the length of a side of a second square. If the area of the first square exceeds the area of the second by 51 square inches, find the lengths of the sides of each square.

2. After a square picture is framed with a two-inch border, the picture and frame occupy 96 square inches more of wall space than did the picture alone. Find the dimensions of the picture.

3. The squares of two consecutive integers differ by 27. Find the integers.

4. The squares of two consecutive even integers differ by 52. Find the integers.

5. The difference of the squares of two consecutive odd integers is 40. Find the integers.

6. The squares of two consecutive integers differ by 95. Find the integers.

7. The product of two consecutive integers exceeds the square of the lesser integer by 15. Find the integers.

8. The product of two consecutive odd integers is 30 less than the square of the greater integer. Find the integers.

B 9. A square window is framed by two rectangular wooden shutters. Each shutter is as long as one side of the window and its width is 18 inches less than its length. If the area covered by one of the shutters is 594 square inches less than the area covered by the window, find the dimensions of one shutter.

Ex. 9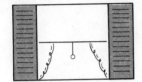

Ex. 11

10. A body falling under the influence of gravity falls approximately $16t^2$ feet in t seconds. At the end of what second after starting would a body have fallen 256 feet?

11. A one-inch thick circular metal casting has a circular hole in the center with radius 2 inches less than the outer radius of the casting. If the casting is made of a metal weighing $\frac{7}{18}$ pounds per cubic inch, and the casting weighs $14\frac{2}{3}$ pounds, find the interior and exterior radius of the casting. (Use $\pi \doteq \frac{22}{7}$.)

12. A concrete walk around a circular fishpond is 3 feet wide. At \$2 per square foot, the total cost of the walk came to \$433. Find the area of the surface of the pond. (Use $\pi \doteq 3.14$.)

DIVISION OF POLYNOMIALS

6–9   The Quotient of Powers

Recall (page 125) that dividing by a number is the same as multiplying by the reciprocal of the number. Thus, you know that

$$\frac{xy}{cd} = xy \cdot \frac{1}{cd}.$$

You also know (page 98) that

$$\frac{1}{cd} = \frac{1}{c} \cdot \frac{1}{d}.$$

Putting these facts together, you can reason as follows:

$$\frac{xy}{cd} = xy\left(\frac{1}{c} \cdot \frac{1}{d}\right) \qquad \text{Substitution principle}$$

$$= \left(x \cdot \frac{1}{c}\right)\left(y \cdot \frac{1}{d}\right) \qquad \text{Commutative and associative axioms of multiplication}$$

$$= \frac{x}{c} \cdot \frac{y}{d} \qquad \text{Rule for division}$$

This gives the following theorem:

Property of Quotients

For all real numbers x and y, and nonzero real numbers c and d:

$$\frac{xy}{cd} = \frac{x}{c} \cdot \frac{y}{d}.$$

In particular, if $c = 1$, you have

$$\frac{xy}{d} = x \cdot \frac{y}{d};$$

and if $x = 1$, you have

$$\frac{y}{cd} = \frac{1}{c} \cdot \frac{y}{d}.$$

For example:

$$\frac{36 \cdot 35}{6 \cdot 7} = \frac{36}{6} \cdot \frac{35}{7} = 6 \cdot 5 = 30$$

$$\frac{11 \cdot 21}{7} = 11 \cdot \frac{21}{7} = 11 \cdot 3 = 33$$

$$\frac{27}{2 \cdot 9} = \frac{1}{2} \cdot \frac{27}{9} = \frac{1}{2} \cdot 3 = \frac{3}{2}$$

This property of quotients is helpful in simplifying quotients of powers. For example:

$$\frac{a^7}{a^3} = \frac{a^4 \cdot a^3}{a^3} = a^4 \cdot \frac{a^3}{a^3} = a^4 \cdot 1$$

$$\therefore \frac{a^7}{a^3} = a^4 = a^{7-3}.$$

Notice that you could have found the exponent in the quotient by retaining the base and subtracting the exponent in the denominator from the exponent in the numerator. Thus, whenever $m > n$, you may write $\left(\text{since } \dfrac{b^n}{b^n} = 1\right)$:

$$\frac{b^m}{b^n} = \frac{b^{m-n} \cdot b^n}{b^n} = b^{m-n} \cdot \frac{b^n}{b^n} = b^{m-n}$$

On the other hand:

$$\frac{a^5}{a^9} = \frac{a^5}{a^4 \cdot a^5} = \frac{1}{a^4} \cdot \frac{a^5}{a^5} = \frac{1}{a^4} \cdot 1$$

$$\therefore \frac{a^5}{a^9} = \frac{1}{a^4} = \frac{1}{a^{9-5}}.$$

Thus, whenever $m < n$, you may write:

$$\frac{b^m}{b^n} = \frac{b^m}{b^{n-m} \cdot b^m} = \frac{1}{b^{n-m}} \cdot \frac{b^m}{b^m} = \frac{1}{b^{n-m}}$$

These are two important rules:

Rules of Exponents for Division

For all positive integers m and n and nonzero real numbers b:

If $m > n$, then $\dfrac{b^m}{b^n} = b^{m-n}$.

If $m < n$, then $\dfrac{b^m}{b^n} = \dfrac{1}{b^{n-m}}$.

When dividing monomials, you use these rules together with the property of quotients obtained above. Thus:

$$\frac{12u^5v^3}{-2uv^2} = \frac{12}{-2} \cdot \frac{u^5}{u} \cdot \frac{v^3}{v^2} = -6 \cdot u^{5-1} \cdot v^{3-2} = -6u^4v$$

$$\frac{-5x^7y^5}{-30x^2y^8} = \frac{-5}{-30} \cdot \frac{x^7}{x^2} \cdot \frac{y^5}{y^8} = \frac{1}{6} \cdot x^{7-2} \cdot \frac{1}{y^{8-5}} = \frac{x^5}{6y^3}$$

Oral Exercises

Simplify each expression. In each case, assume that no divisor is equal to 0.

1. $\dfrac{3y}{y}$

2. $\dfrac{6z}{z}$

3. $\dfrac{y^5}{y^2}$

4. $\dfrac{x^6}{x^3}$

5. $\dfrac{c^7}{-c^3}$

6. $\dfrac{-d^8}{d^6}$

7. $\dfrac{-20a^2}{-5a}$

8. $\dfrac{22b^5}{-11b}$

9. $\dfrac{4x^2y}{2xy}$

10. $\dfrac{-18r^2s^2}{-9r^2s}$

11. $\dfrac{3a}{6a^2}$

12. $\dfrac{5t}{35t^3}$

13. $\dfrac{-4x^2y}{-4x^3y^2}$

14. $\dfrac{32a^2b^2}{16a^3b^3}$

15. $\dfrac{(3rs)^2}{9r^3}$

16. $\dfrac{(2cd)^3}{-4cd^2}$

17. $\dfrac{-(4xy)^2}{(-2xy)^3}$

18. $\dfrac{-27p^6q^3}{(3p^2q)^3}$

19. $\dfrac{x^n}{x^2}$

20. $\dfrac{x^3}{x^n}$

21. $\dfrac{y^m}{y^n}$

22. $\dfrac{z^{2m}}{z^m}$

Written Exercises

Simplify each expression, assuming that no divisor is equal to 0.

A

1. $\dfrac{t^{10}}{t^3}$

2. $\dfrac{s^{12}}{s^3}$

3. $\dfrac{3n^8}{n^8}$

4. $\dfrac{12m^7}{4m^6}$

5. $\dfrac{24x^5y^4}{-6x^3y^3}$

6. $\dfrac{-32t^7s^8}{4t^7s^3}$

7. $\dfrac{-14m^3n^2}{-28m^3n}$

8. $\dfrac{-10a^{10}b^5}{-2a^{12}b^5}$

9. $\dfrac{64p^5q^7}{8p^{10}q^{10}}$

10. $\dfrac{-7x^8y^6}{56x^6y^8}$

11. $\dfrac{48r^{12}s^{10}}{16r^{24}s^{10}}$

12. $\dfrac{14t^{11}s^5}{-42t^{12}s^4}$

13. $\dfrac{(3xy)^2}{6xy^3}$

14. $\dfrac{16a^5b^2}{(2ab)^3}$

15. $\dfrac{(4m^5n^2)^2}{-(2m^2n^2)^3}$

16. $\dfrac{-(3c^3d^2)^3}{6(c^2d^3)^3}$

17. $\dfrac{(-3)^3(x^2)^3(y^2)^2}{(-9)^2(x^3)^3(y^3)^3}$

18. $\dfrac{(-4)^2(a^3)^2(b^4)^2}{(-2)^3(a^3)^3(b^2)^4}$

SAMPLE. $\dfrac{x^2y^3}{x^2y} + \dfrac{6xy^5}{-3xy^3}$

Solution: $\dfrac{x^2y^3}{x^2y} + \dfrac{6xy^5}{-3xy^3} = \dfrac{x^2}{x^2} \cdot \dfrac{y}{y} \cdot y^2 + \dfrac{6}{-3} \cdot \dfrac{x}{x} \cdot \dfrac{y^3}{y^3} \cdot y^2$

$= (1) \cdot (1) \cdot y^2 + (-2) \cdot (1) \cdot (1) \cdot y^2$

$= y^2 + (-2)y^2 = -y^2.$ **Answer.**

B 19. $\dfrac{3t^2}{t} + \dfrac{8t^4}{2t^3}$

23. $\dfrac{24x^5y^3}{-3xy} + \dfrac{8x^4y^6}{2y^4}$

20. $\dfrac{70k^5}{10k^2} - \dfrac{36k^4}{6k}$

24. $\dfrac{38p^3q^5}{19pq^2} - \dfrac{15p^4q^4}{-3p^2q}$

21. $\dfrac{21c^2d}{3d} - \dfrac{18c^3d^2}{6cd^2}$

25. $\dfrac{3c^2d + 9c^2d}{4c} - 2cd$

22. $\dfrac{45a^3b^2}{9ab} - \dfrac{52a^2b^5}{4b^4}$

26. $8x^2y + \dfrac{8x^4y^2 - 12x^4y^2}{x^2y}$

27. $\dfrac{3a^3b^2 + 15a^3b^2}{2ab^2} + \dfrac{4a^6b^3 - 10a^6b^3}{2a^4b^3}$

28. $\dfrac{4rs^3 + 16rs^3}{4s^2} - \dfrac{3r^3s^5 + 11r^3s^5}{2r^2s^4}$

29. $\dfrac{14m^5n^4 - 8m^5n^4}{6mn^2} - \dfrac{8m^6n^2 + m^6n^2}{3m^2}$

30. $\dfrac{-11c^5d^4 + 5c^5d^4}{2c^2d^2} - \dfrac{3c^6d^3 + 5c^6d^3}{4c^3d}$

6–10 Zero and Negative Exponents (Optional)

In the rules of exponents for division on page 227, $m \neq n$. However, if you were to apply those rules to evaluate $\dfrac{b^m}{b^m}$, you would obtain two expressions:

$$\frac{b^m}{b^m} = b^{m-m} \cdot 1 = b^0 \qquad \text{and} \qquad \frac{b^m}{b^m} = \frac{1}{b^{m-m}} = \frac{1}{b^0}.$$

Of course, $\dfrac{b^m}{b^m} = 1$, and so it appears that b^0 ought to be 1.

From these considerations, you make this definition of b^0 (read "b exponent zero"):

b^0 **is 1 for every nonzero real number b.**

We shall not use the expression 0^0.

If you are to apply the rule $\dfrac{b^m}{b^n} = b^{m-n}$ when $m < n$, that is, when $m - n$ represents a negative number, you must give meaning to powers with negative exponents. Suppose you apply the rule as follows:

$$\frac{b^5}{b^2} = b^{5-2} = b^3 \qquad \frac{b^2}{b^5} = b^{2-5} = b^{-3}.$$

Since $\dfrac{b^5}{b^2}$ and $\dfrac{b^2}{b^5}$ are reciprocals, b^3 and b^{-3} should be reciprocals:

that is, it should be true that $b^3 = \dfrac{1}{b^{-3}}$ and $b^{-3} = \dfrac{1}{b^3}$.

In general, you define powers with negative exponents as follows:

$$b^n = \frac{1}{b^{-n}} \quad \text{and} \quad b^{-n} = \frac{1}{b^n} \quad (b \neq 0).$$

The rules of exponents may now be extended to include negative exponents. For example,

$$a^3 \cdot a^{-2} = a^{3+(-2)} = a^1 = a.$$

EXAMPLES: 1. $\ a^3 \cdot b^{-2} = a^3 \cdot \dfrac{1}{b^2} = \dfrac{a^3}{b^2}$

2. $\ \dfrac{x^5}{y^{-3}} = x^5 \cdot \dfrac{1}{y^{-3}} = x^5 y^3$

3. $\ \dfrac{x^0 y^{-2}}{z^2} = x^0 \cdot y^{-2} \cdot \dfrac{1}{z^2} = 1 \cdot \dfrac{1}{y^2} \cdot \dfrac{1}{z^2} = \dfrac{1}{y^2 z^2}$

4. $\ \dfrac{12 \times 10^8}{3 \times 10^{11}} = 4 \times 10^{-3} = 0.004$

Oral Exercises

Give an equivalent expression involving no zero or negative exponent. Assume that 0 is not a member of the replacement set of any of the variables.

1. 3^0

2. $(-4)^0$

3. 2^{-2}

4. $(-3)^{-2}$

5. uv^{-1}

6. $t^{-2}s$

7. $2a^{-2}$

8. $-3b^{-3}$

9. $\dfrac{2x}{y^{-3}}$

10. $\dfrac{5c^{-2}}{d}$

11. $\dfrac{a^{-1}}{b^{-1}}$

12. $(\tfrac{1}{2})^{-1}$

13. $\dfrac{x^0 y^{-1}}{z^{-1}}$

14. $\dfrac{(-2)^0 r^{-2}}{s^{-3}}$

15. $(x^{-1}y)^{-2}$

16. $(p^2 q^{-3})^{-1}$

Written Exercises

Write an equivalent expression using only positive exponents. Assume that 0 is not a member of the replacement set of any of the variables.

A 1. xy^{-3}

4. $\dfrac{t}{s^{-2}}$

7. $(2z)^0$

10. $(x^2y^{-3})^{-2}$

2. $a^{-2}b$

5. $\dfrac{x^0z^{-2}}{u^{-2}}$

8. $(x^2z)^0$

11. $\left(\dfrac{2}{z}\right)^{-1}$

3. $\dfrac{r^{-2}}{s}$

6. $\dfrac{(-2)^0y^{-4}}{z^{-3}}$

9. $(r^{-2}s)^{-3}$

12. $\left(\dfrac{x^2y}{2}\right)^{-1}$

Express each fraction as a product of powers.

SAMPLE 1. $\dfrac{x^{-3}}{y^2}$ *Solution:* $\dfrac{x^{-3}}{y^2} = x^{-3}y^{-2}$. **Answer.**

13. $\dfrac{a^2}{b^2}$

15. $\dfrac{x^{-4}}{y^{-3}}$

17. $\dfrac{a^{-3}b^2}{cd^{-4}}$

14. $\dfrac{t^3}{s^4}$

16. $\dfrac{m^2}{n^{-4}}$

18. $\dfrac{pq^{-3}}{m^2n}$

State a polynomial in simple form equivalent to each expression.

SAMPLE 2. $\dfrac{2x}{x^{-3}} + 3^0x^4$

Solution: $\dfrac{2x}{x^{-3}} + 3^0x^4 = 2x^4 + x^4 = 3x^4$. **Answer.**

19. $3y^2 + \dfrac{1}{y^{-2}}$

23. $\dfrac{1}{(xy)^{-3}} + \dfrac{4x^3y}{y^{-2}}$

20. $4t^3 + \dfrac{2t^2}{t^{-1}}$

24. $\dfrac{-2}{(rs^2)^{-1}} + \dfrac{5rs}{s^{-1}}$

21. $n^0m^3 - \dfrac{m^5}{m^2}$

25. $\dfrac{3xz^{-1}}{z^{-1}} - \dfrac{5x^{-2}z}{x^{-3}z}$

22. $\dfrac{x^{-3}}{x^{-7}} + \dfrac{4x^2}{x^{-2}}$

26. $\dfrac{-4a^3}{-2a^{-2}b^{-3}} - \dfrac{7ab}{a^{-4}b^{-2}}$

B 27. $\dfrac{8 \times 10^7}{4 \times 10^{-2}}$

30. $(\tfrac{4}{7})^2 - (\tfrac{7}{4})^{-2}$

28. $\dfrac{1.6 \times 10^{-3}}{0.4 \times 10^{-6}}$

31. $(x + 2y)^0 + \dfrac{1}{(x - y)^{-1}}$

29. $(\tfrac{3}{5})^{-2} + (\tfrac{4}{3})^2$

32. $(a + 2)^2 - \dfrac{1}{(a - 3)^{-1}}$

6–11   Dividing a Polynomial by a Monomial

One way to simplify the expression $(84 + 28) \div 7$ is to use the distributive axiom:

$$\frac{84 + 28}{7} = \frac{1}{7}(84 + 28) = \frac{1}{7}(84) + \frac{1}{7}(28) = 12 + 4 = 16$$

Similarly, you may simplify the algebraic expression $(ax + ay) \div a$:

$$\frac{ax + ay}{a} = \frac{1}{a}(ax + ay)$$

$$= \frac{1}{a}(ax) + \frac{1}{a}(ay)$$

$$= \left(\frac{1}{a} \cdot a\right)x + \left(\frac{1}{a} \cdot a\right)y$$

$$= 1x + 1y = x + y$$

The effect of this procedure is that of *dividing* each term of the polynomial $ax + ay$ by the monomial a.

EXAMPLE 1. $\dfrac{16x^4 + 12x^3 - 8x^2}{4x^2}$

Solution: $\dfrac{16x^4 + 12x^3 - 8x^2}{4x^2}$

$$= \frac{16x^4}{4x^2} + \frac{12x^3}{4x^2} - \frac{8x^2}{4x^2}$$

$$= 4x^2 + 3x - 2$$

EXAMPLE 2. $\dfrac{bt^2 + t - b}{bt}$

Solution: $\dfrac{bt^2 + t - b}{bt}$

$$= \frac{bt^2}{bt} + \frac{t}{bt} - \frac{b}{bt}$$

$$= t + \frac{1}{b} - \frac{1}{t}$$

Note that $16x^4 + 12x^3 - 8x^2$ is evenly divisible by $4x^2$, but $bt^2 + t - b$ is not evenly divisible by bt. We say that one polynomial is **evenly divisible** or simply **divisible** by another polynomial if the quotient is also a polynomial.

To divide a polynomial by a monomial, divide each term of the polynomial by the monomial, and then add the quotients.

Oral Exercises

Express each quotient as a sum.

1. $\dfrac{2x + 4}{2}$ **4.** $\dfrac{18t^2 - 6}{6}$ **7.** $\dfrac{2x - 5}{2}$ **10.** $\dfrac{4b^2 + 6}{2b}$

2. $\dfrac{5y - 10}{5}$ **5.** $\dfrac{3x^2 + 6x}{3x}$ **8.** $\dfrac{7 - 4r^2}{4}$ **11.** $\dfrac{2z^2 + 4z + 6}{2}$

3. $\dfrac{6n + 9}{3}$ **6.** $\dfrac{27s + 18s^3}{9s}$ **9.** $\dfrac{10 - 8a^2}{2a}$ **12.** $\dfrac{3m^2 + 6m + 9}{3}$

Written Exercises

Simplify each expression by performing the indicated division.

A **1.** $\dfrac{6a + 12}{3}$ **5.** $\dfrac{11z^2 + 22z}{11z}$ **9.** $\dfrac{3t + 5}{t}$ **13.** $\dfrac{3m - n}{2n}$

2. $\dfrac{8t + 16}{4}$ **6.** $\dfrac{14k^2 - 12k}{2k}$ **10.** $\dfrac{8x + 6}{x}$ **14.** $\dfrac{6k - 3r}{2k}$

3. $\dfrac{18 - 9z}{9}$ **7.** $\dfrac{8p^3 - 2p^2}{2p^2}$ **11.** $\dfrac{12k + 3}{6k}$ **15.** $\dfrac{8x + 4y}{2xy}$

4. $\dfrac{24 - 15k}{5}$ **8.** $\dfrac{11g^2 + 33g^3}{11g^2}$ **12.** $\dfrac{14 - 3t}{3t}$ **16.** $\dfrac{3a - 6b}{3ab}$

17. $\dfrac{16x^2 - 12x + 8}{-4}$ **20.** $\dfrac{40pq^2 + 30p^2q - 20p^2q^2}{10pq}$

18. $\dfrac{27z^2 + 18z - 36}{-9}$ **21.** $\dfrac{8z^5 - 32z^4 + 16z^3}{-8z^4}$

19. $\dfrac{3x^2y + 6xy^2 - 9x^2y^2}{3xy}$ **22.** $\dfrac{28u^7 - 16u^5 + 20u^3}{-4u^5}$

B **23.** $\dfrac{14x^2 - 18x}{2x} + \dfrac{15x^2 - 25x}{5x}$

24. $\dfrac{25y^3 - 15y^2 + 30y}{-5y} + \dfrac{8y^5 - 3y^3}{y^3}$

25. $\dfrac{35k^2t - 28kt + 7kt^2}{7kt} - \dfrac{15k^2t^2 - 21k^2t}{3k^2t}$

26. $\dfrac{40cd^2 - 32c^2d + 24c^2d^2}{-8cd} + \dfrac{4c^3d - 12c^2d^2}{3c^2d}$

27. $\dfrac{21x^4y^2 - 14x^3y}{-7x^2y} + \dfrac{16x^5y^3 + 8x^4y^2}{4x^3y^2} + \dfrac{x^4y^4 - x^5y^4}{-x^3y^3}$

28. $\dfrac{-4a^3b + 8ab^2}{-2ab} - \dfrac{12a^4b^3 + 9a^2b^4}{3a^2b^3} + \dfrac{2a^3b^3 - 4ab^4}{2ab^3}$

C **29.** If $\dfrac{x + y}{y} = 2.6$, find $\dfrac{x}{y}$. **30.** If $\dfrac{2a + 4b}{2b} = 3.9$, find $\dfrac{a}{b}$.

Solve each equation over $\Re$.

31. $\dfrac{6x^2 - 4x}{2x} = 3x - 5$ **33.** $\dfrac{18n - 9n^2}{3n} = \dfrac{n^3 + 2n^2}{n^2}$

32. $\dfrac{8y^2 + 6y}{2y} = y + 3$ **34.** $\dfrac{14z - 21z^2}{7z} = \dfrac{2z^3 + 4z^2}{2z^2}$

6–12 Dividing a Polynomial by a Polynomial

The adjoining example shows the use of the division algorithm in arithmetic. Can you recognize these facts?

1. The method uses repeated subtraction. First 20(15), then 2(15) is subtracted from 334.

2. The distributive axiom helps shorten the number of steps. Without it you would have to subtract 15 from 334 twenty-two times. The division ends when the remainder is either zero or a number less than the divisor.

3. The check is a transformation of the division equation,

$$334 - (22)(15) = 4,$$

to

$$334 = (22)(15) + 4.$$

In general form, these statements are:

Dividend − Quotient × Divisor = Remainder

Dividend = Quotient × Divisor + Remainder

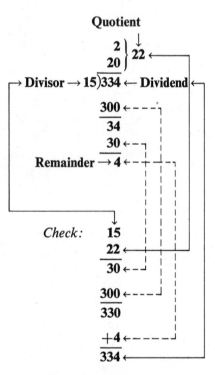

Divide 334 by 15.

As a check on your computational accuracy, you may wish to find:

$$
\begin{array}{r}
22 \\
15 \\
\hline
110 \\
22 \\
\hline
330 \\
\end{array}
\begin{array}{r}
330 \\
4 \\
\hline
334 \\
\end{array}
$$

Each of these equations is equivalent to a third,

$$\frac{\text{Dividend}}{\text{Divisor}} = \text{Quotient} + \frac{\text{Remainder}}{\text{Divisor}},$$

which for the example shown is $\frac{334}{15} = 22\frac{4}{15}$.

It is this last form which gives the **complete quotient**, $22\frac{4}{15}$. For contrast, 22 is sometimes called the "partial quotient."

When dividing polynomials, you write the terms of the divisor and the dividend in order of decreasing degree in a chosen variable.

EXAMPLE 1. $y + 3\overline{)2y^2 + 10y + 12}$

Solution:

$$2y^2 \div y = 2y$$

$$\leftarrow \text{Subtract } 2y(y + 3)$$

$$4y \div y = 4$$

$$\leftarrow \text{Subtract } 4(y + 3)$$

Check: $(2y + 4)(y + 3) + 0 = 2y^2 + 10y + 12$

In Example 2, the steps in the division are shown compactly. This example also shows how to insert missing terms in a dividend, using 0 as a coefficient.

EXAMPLE 2. $x^2 + x - 3\overline{)x^3 - 3}$

Solution:

$$
\begin{array}{r}
x - 1 \\
x^2 + x - 3\overline{)x^3 + 0x^2 + 0x - 3} \\
\underline{x^3 + x^2 - 3x} \\
-x^2 + 3x - 3 \\
\underline{-x^2 - x + 3} \\
4x - 6
\end{array}
$$

Check: $(x^2 + x - 3)(x - 1) + (4x - 6) = x^3 - 3$

When does the division algorithm end? It ends when *the remainder is zero* or *the degree of the remainder in the chosen variable is less than that of the divisor.*

Written Exercises

Corresponding to each quotient, write an equation of the form

$$\frac{\text{Dividend}}{\text{Divisor}} = \text{Quotient} + \frac{\text{Remainder}}{\text{Divisor}}$$

and check your results.

A 1. $\dfrac{y^2 + 3y + 2}{y + 1}$

7. $\dfrac{x^2 + 2x + 3}{x + 1}$

13. $\dfrac{2x^2 + 3x - 2}{2x - 1}$

2. $\dfrac{n^2 + 6n + 5}{n + 1}$

8. $\dfrac{t^2 - 2t + 2}{t - 2}$

14. $\dfrac{3y^2 + y - 2}{3y - 2}$

3. $\dfrac{x^2 - 5x + 6}{x - 2}$

9. $\dfrac{-28 - 3x + x^2}{x - 7}$

15. $\dfrac{6p^2 - 3p + 2}{2p - 3}$

4. $\dfrac{z^2 + 3z - 4}{z + 4}$

10. $\dfrac{-24 - 5r + r^2}{r + 3}$

16. $\dfrac{8d^2 - 3d + 2}{2d - 1}$

5. $\dfrac{a^2 - 9a + 20}{a - 4}$

11. $\dfrac{m^2 - 4}{m + 2}$

17. $\dfrac{x^3 - 8y^3}{x - 2y}$

6. $\dfrac{b^2 + 8b - 20}{b - 2}$

12. $\dfrac{q^2 - 36}{q - 6}$

18. $\dfrac{8a^3 + 27b^3}{2a + 3b}$

SAMPLE. $\dfrac{16a^2 + 46ab + 10b^2}{2a + 5b}$

Solution:

$$
\begin{array}{r}
8a \ + \ 3b \\
2a + 5b\overline{)16a^2 + 46ab + 10b^2} \\
\underline{16a^2 + 40ab} \\
6ab + 10b^2 \\
\underline{6ab + 15b^2} \\
-\ 5b^2
\end{array}
$$

$$\frac{16a^2 + 46ab + 10b^2}{2a + 5b} = (8a + 3b) - \frac{5b^2}{2a + 5b} \cdot \qquad \textbf{Answer.}$$

19. $\dfrac{8t^2 + 2ts - 15s^2}{4t - 5s}$

21. $\dfrac{64n^3 - 125m^3}{4n - 5m}$

20. $\dfrac{18k^2 - 3rk - 10r^2}{6k - 5r}$

22. $\dfrac{x^4 - 16y^4}{x - 2y}$

B 23. $x + 4\overline{)x^3 + 2x^2 - 5x + 12}$

24. $y - 3\overline{)2y^3 - 9y^2 - 8y - 3}$

25. $2r + 3\overline{)6r^3 + r^2 - 2r + 17}$

26. $3k - 2\overline{)12k^3 - 17k^2 + 21k - 8}$

27. $x^2 + 2x - 3\overline{)x^4 + 7x^3 + 9x^2 - 11x - 6}$

28. $z^2 - 2z + 2\overline{)2z^4 - z^3 - 8z^2 + 18z - 12}$

29. $x^2 - 1\overline{)x^8 - 1}$

30. $y^2 - 2\overline{)y^{10} + 20}$

31. One factor of $x^3 - 6x^2 + 11x - 12$ is $x - 4$. Find the other factor.

32. One factor of $x^6 + 1$ is $x^2 + 1$. Find the other factor.

33. Is $3x + 2$ a factor of $3x^3 - 4x^2 - x + 4$? Justify your answer.

34. Is $2y + 3$ a factor of $12y^3 + 18y^2 - 10y - 15$? Justify your answer.

C 35. Find the number c for which $x + 3$ is a factor of $3x^2 + 2x + c$.
Hint: The remainder when $3x^2 + 2x + c$ is divided by $x + 3$ must be 0.

36. Find the number c for which $3y - 5$ is a factor of $6y^2 + 11y + c$.

● CHAPTER SUMMARY ●

Inventory of Structure and Method

1. To **add** polynomials, write the sum and add the similar terms.
   To **subtract** one polynomial from another, add to the minuend the opposite of each term of the subtrahend.
   You can **check** your work with polynomials by substituting a particular value (except 0 and 1) for each variable and evaluating each expression.

2. To **multiply two powers with the same base,** use the rule: For all positive integers m and n, $b^m \cdot b^n = b^{m+n}$.
   To **multiply monomials,** multiply the numerical factors and the variable factors, applying the preceding rule together with the commutative and associative axioms of multiplication.

3. When the base of a power is a product, the rule $(ab)^m = a^m b^m$ applies for every positive integer m.
   When the base is itself a power, then for all positive integers m and n, $(b^m)^n = b^{mn}$.

4. To **multiply a polynomial by a monomial,** apply the distributive axiom, multiplying each term of the polynomial by the monomial and then adding the products.
   To **multiply a polynomial by a polynomial,** use the distributive axiom to multiply one polynomial by each term of the other, and then add the products.

5. **Expand a power** of a polynomial by using the polynomial as a factor as many times as shown by the exponent and by performing the indicated multiplications.

6. **To divide two powers with the same base,** use the rules: For positive integers m and n and nonzero real numbers b, if $m > n$, $\dfrac{b^m}{b^n} = b^{m-n}$, and if $m < n$, $\dfrac{b^m}{b^n} = \dfrac{1}{b^{n-m}}$.

The **Property of Quotients** is: For all real numbers x and y, and nonzero real numbers c and d: $\dfrac{xy}{cd} = \dfrac{x}{c} \cdot \dfrac{y}{d}$

To **divide monomials,** divide the numerical factors and the variable factors, applying the preceding property together with the rules of exponents.

7. To **divide a polynomial by a monomial,** divide each term of the polynomial by the monomial, and then add the quotients.

To **divide a polynomial by a polynomial,** arrange the terms of the divisor and the dividend in order of decreasing degree in one variable, and then proceed as in arithmetic division. The process stops when the remainder is 0, or when its degree is *less* than that of the divisor. In general:

$$\text{Complete Quotient} = \frac{\text{Dividend}}{\text{Divisor}} = \text{Quotient} + \frac{\text{Remainder}}{\text{Divisor}}$$

8. (Optional) By definition, for any nonzero real number b, $b^0 = 1$, $b^{-n} = \dfrac{1}{b^n}$, and $b^n = \dfrac{1}{b^{-n}}$.

Vocabulary and Spelling

Review the meaning of each term by reference to the page listed.

Chapter Test

6–1   Simplify each expression for a sum. Check your work by using the value 2 for the variable.

   1. $(17y + 100) + (21y - 30)$ **2.** $5x^2 + 3x - 7$
   $\underline{-7x^2 + 2x - 8}$

6–2   Subtract the lower polynomial from the one above it, and check your work by using the values 2, 3, and 5 for *a*, *b*, and *c*.

   3. $4a - 2b + c$ **4.** $a^2 - ab + b^2$
   $\underline{a - 3b + 2c}$ $\underline{2a^2 - ab - b^2}$

Solve each equation over $\mathcal{R}$.

   5. $7x - (3 - x) = 29$ **6.** $3t - [4 + (t - 2)] = 0$

Simplify each expression for a product.

6–3   **7.** $(-3x^2y^3z)(-x^4z^2)$ **8.** $(2a^3b^2)(-3a^2)(-b)^3$
6–4   **9.** $(-3r^2t^3s)^3$ **10.** $(-2k)^3(kr^2)^2$
6–5   **11.** $-3s(5s - 6)$ **12.** $2x^2(x^2 - 3x - 2)$
6–6   **13.** $(t - 4)(t + 1)$ **14.** $(3x + 5y)(4x - y)$

6–7   **15.**   A rectangular picture is 3 inches longer than it is wide. It has a frame 2 inches wide whose area is 92 square inches. Find the dimensions of the picture.

6–8   **16.**   One number is 4 greater than another, and the difference of their squares is 64. Find the numbers.

6–9   **17.**   Simplify: $\dfrac{-16x^3y^2z}{4x^2yz^3}$

6–10·   **(Optional)**   Write each expression using positive exponents only.

   18. $\dfrac{t^0s^{-2}}{k}$ **19.** $\dfrac{(-3)^0x^4y^{-1}}{x^{-1}yz^{-2}}$

Simplify each expression for a quotient.

6–11   **20.** $\dfrac{26t^3 + 8t}{2t}$ **21.** $\dfrac{-8x^3 + 12x^2 - 16x}{4x}$

6–12   **22.** $\dfrac{6x^2 - 7x - 3}{2x - 3}$ **23.** $\dfrac{x^3 - 5x^2 + 10x - 12}{x - 3}$

Chapter Review

6–1   Adding Polynomials   *Pages 205–209*

1. A term that is either a numeral, or a variable, or an indicated product of a numeral and one or more variables is called a __?__.
2. The polynomial $2a + 3b - 2$ is also called a __?__.
3. The degree of $3x^2y + 2xy - 3x^2$ is __?__.
4. To check the results of adding polynomials, you assign values to the variables involved and __?__ the expressions involved.
5. $(3p^2 - 2p + 1) + (4p - p^2 + 2) = $ __?__.
6. Using the values 2 and 3 for x and y, check the truth of the sentence

$$(3x^2 - 2xy + y^2) + (x^2 - xy - y^2) = 4x^2 - 3xy.$$

6–2   Subtracting Polynomials   *Pages 209–212*

7. To subtract the polynomial $7x - 2y + z$ from a given polynomial, you add __?__ to the given polynomial.
8. $(3x - 2y + z) - (x - 2y - z) = $ __?__.
9. Using the values 2 and 3 for the variables a and b, check the truth of the sentence

$$(3a + b - 5) - (4a + 2b - 11) = -a - b + 6.$$

10. Solve $(2n - n^2 + 3) - (6 - n^2 - 4n) = 17$ over $\mathfrak{R}$.

Subtract the lower polynomial from the one above it, and check your work by using the values 2, 3, and 5 for $m, n,$ and p.

11. $2m - n$
$3n - p$

12. $m^2 - 2n^2 + p^2$
$-m^2 + n^2 + p^2$

6–3   The Product of Powers   *Pages 212–213*

13. The exponent of the product of two powers of the same base is the __?__ of the exponents of the two powers.
14. The power 7^5 has base __?__ and exponent __?__.
15. $x^4 \cdot x = $ __?__
16. $(2z^3)(-3z^4) = $ __?__
17. $2xy^2(-3x^2y)(-x^3y) = $ __?__
18. $3a(-2a^3b)(a^{10}b^7) = $ __?__

6–4 **The Power of a Product** *Pages 214–215*

19. For every positive integer m, $(ab)^m = $ _?_ .

20. For all positive integers m and n, $(a^m)^n = $ _?_ .

21. $(3xy)^3 = $ _?_   **23.** $-2a^3b(3ab^2)^3 = $ _?_

22. $(-7p^3z^2)^2 = $ _?_   **24.** $(-m^2n)^3(-2mn)^2 = $ _?_

6–5 **Multiplying a Polynomial by a Monomial** *Pages 216–218*

25. To multiply a binomial by a monomial, you use the _?_ axiom.

26. $x(x + 3) = $ _?_   **27.** $-3y(2y^2 - 5y + 2) = $ _?_

28. $4xz(-2x^2 + 3xz + z^2) = $ _?_

Solve over $\Re$.

29. $3(x - 2) + 4(x + 6) = 3(x + 14) - 2$

30. $6z - 2(z - 3) = z - 18$

6–6 **Multiplying Two Polynomials** *Pages 219–220*

31. $(a + b)(x + y) = a(\underline{\ ?\ }) + b(\underline{\ ?\ })$

32. $(x + 1)(x + 3) = $ _?_   **33.** $(2x - y)(x + 3y) = $ _?_

34. Use the values 2 and 3 for p and q to check the truth of the sentence $(p - 2q)(2p + q) = 2p^2 - 3pq - 2q^2$.

Multiply the upper polynomial by the lower one.

35. $3x - 2y$
$\underline{x + 6y}$

36. $3a^2 - 2a + 5$
$\underline{3a - 1}$

6–7 **Problems about Areas** *Pages 220–223*

37. If x represents the width of a rectangle that is 4 inches longer than it is wide, then the length of the rectangle is represented by _?_ and its area by _?_.

38. Mr. Fleming's rectangular pasture is 20 yards longer than it is wide. He did not have enough fence to surround the whole pasture, and so he fenced in a smaller rectangle. If his fence lacked 10 yards of covering the length and 5 yards of covering the width, and if 1400 square yards were un-fenced, what were the dimensions of the pas-ture?

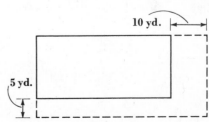

6–8   Powers of Polynomials   *Pages 223–225*

39. $(x + 2)^2 = \underline{\quad ? \quad}$
40. $(2y - 1)^3 = \underline{\quad ? \quad}$
41. $(x^2 + 2x - 1)^2 = \underline{\quad ? \quad}$
42. If the length of a side of one square is 1 inch shorter than the length of a side of another square, and if their areas differ by 17 square inches, find the dimensions of each square.

6–9   The Quotient of Powers   *Pages 225–229*

43. For positive integers m and n and nonzero real number b, if $m > n$, then $\dfrac{b^m}{b^n} = \underline{\quad ? \quad}$, but if $m < n$, then $\dfrac{b^m}{b^n} = \underline{\quad ? \quad}$.

44. $\dfrac{-15x^3z}{-3xz^2} = \underline{\quad ? \quad}$ 45. $\dfrac{7a^3b^5}{14a^7b} = \underline{\quad ? \quad}$ 46. $\dfrac{(-x^2y)^2}{x^2y} = \underline{\quad ? \quad}$

6–10   Zero and Negative Exponents (Optional)   *Pages 229–231*

47. $(-6)^0 = \underline{\quad ? \quad}$ 49. $2z^{-4} = \underline{\quad ? \quad}$

48. $\dfrac{3}{y^{-2}} = \underline{\quad ? \quad}$ 50. $\dfrac{xy^{-2}z}{x^{-2}z} = \underline{\quad ? \quad}$

6–11   Dividing a Polynomial by a Monomial   *Pages 232–234*

51. $\dfrac{32x - 18}{6} = \underline{\quad ? \quad} - \underline{\quad ? \quad}$

52. $\dfrac{15y^2 - 2}{-3y^2} = \underline{\quad ? \quad} + \underline{\quad ? \quad}$

53. $\dfrac{12x^2y - 8xy^2 + 4xy}{-4xy} = \underline{\quad ? \quad}$

54. $\dfrac{27a^3b^2 - 18a^2b^2 - 7ab^2}{9a^2b^2} = \underline{\quad ? \quad}$

6–12   Dividing a Polynomial by a Polynomial   *Pages 234–237*

55. $\dfrac{y^2 + 2y - 3}{y + 3} = \underline{\quad ? \quad}$ 57. $\dfrac{z^3 - 8z - 3}{z - 3} = \underline{\quad ? \quad}$

56. $\dfrac{3x^2 + 5x - 1}{3x - 1} = \underline{\quad ? \quad}$ 58. $\dfrac{4a^3 + ab^2 + b^3}{2a + b} = \underline{\quad ? \quad}$

Who Uses Mathematics?

The communications industries play an enormous role in today's world. When man first stepped onto the moon, some 600 million people around the globe saw pictures and heard the voices of the astronauts transmitted through 240,000 miles of space. Probably few stop to think of the complex mathematics required for this marvelous technology.

Our most common method of communication, the telephone, requires thousands of engineers and technicians. How vital a part they have in society can be imagined from the statistics: over 200,000,000 telephones in use throughout the world, with about half of them in North America.

No doubt you have heard of teletype machines, which automatically type out messages sent from miles away. In the photograph the men are studying a map of the United States showing teletype lines.

EXTRA FOR EXPERTS

Divisibility of Integers

Knowing whether one integer is an integral multiple of (is divisible by) another helps in factoring, reducing fractions, and checking computations. An analysis of the general form of the decimal numeral of an integer will enable you to develop criteria of divisibility.

$$N = a_n 10^n + a_{n-1} 10^{n-1} + \cdots + a_3 10^3 + a_2 10^2 + a_1 10 + a_0$$

Here, the a's represent the values of the digits in the numeral, and the powers of ten correspond to place values. If you were discussing 8,037,291, then $a_6 = 8$, $a_5 = 0$, $a_4 = 3, \ldots, a_1 = 9$, $a_0 = 1$.

Many of these criteria are based on the following property of integers:

If $N = p + q$, and q is a multiple of r, then N is divisible by r if and only if p is a multiple of r.

You may be acquainted with some of these criteria of divisibility.

Divisor	Test
2	Is the last digit 0, 2, 4, 6, or 8?
3	Is the sum of the digits divisible by 3?
4	Is the integer named by the last two digits divisible by 4?
5	Is the last digit 0 or 5?
7	From the right, group the digits by threes, and mark these groups alternately *positive* and *negative;* then total the signed groups. Is this sum divisible by 7?
9	Is the sum of the digits divisible by 9?
10	Is the last digit 0?
11	Mark the digits alternately *positive* and *negative* from the right; then total the signed digits. Is this sum divisible by 11?
13	Compute the sum as in the test for 7. Is this sum divisible by 13?

EXAMPLE 1. Is $386,749 \div 11$ an integer?

Solution: $9 - 4 + 7 - 6 + 8 - 3 = 11; 11 \div 11 = 1.$

∴ $386,749 \div 11$ is an integer. **Answer.**

EXAMPLE 2. Is $296,348,026 \div 13$ an integer?

Solution: $026 - 348 + 296 = -26; -26 \div 13 = -2.$

∴ $296,348,026 \div 13$ is an integer. **Answer.**

EXAMPLE 3. Prove the divisibility test for 3 and for 9.

Solution: Use the commutative property, and reverse the order of the terms in the general form of the integer N.

$$N = a_0 + 10a_1 + 10^2a_2 + 10^3a_3 + \cdots + 10^{n-1}a_{n-1} + 10^na_n$$
$$N = a_0 + (1 + 9)a_1 + (1 + 99)a_2 + \cdots + (1 + \underbrace{99 \cdots 9})a_n$$
$$\qquad\qquad\qquad\qquad\qquad\qquad\qquad\qquad\qquad\qquad n \text{ nines}$$

$$N = (a_0 + a_1 + \cdots + a_n) + (9a_1 + 99a_2 + \cdots + 99 \cdots 9a_n)$$
$$N = \underbrace{(a_0 + a_1 + \cdots + a_n)}_{?} + \underbrace{9(a_1 + 11a_2 + \cdots + 11 \cdots 1a_n)}_{\text{multiple of 9 (and 3)}}$$

$\therefore$ N is divisible by 3 if and only if $a_0 + a_1 + \cdots + a_n$ is divisible by 3.
N is divisible by 9 if and only if $a_0 + a_1 + \cdots + a_n$ is divisible by 9.

EXAMPLE 4. Prove the divisibility test for 4.

Solution:
$$N = a_0 + 10a_1 + (2 \cdot 5)^2a_2 + (2 \cdot 5)^3a_3 + \cdots + (2 \cdot 5)^na_n$$
$$N = a_0 + 10a_1 + 4 \cdot 25a_2 + 8 \cdot 125a_3 + \cdots + 2^n \cdot 5^na_n$$
$$N = \underbrace{(a_0 + 10a_1)}_{?} + \underbrace{4(25a_2 + 250a_3 + \cdots + 2^{n-2} \cdot 5^na_n)}_{\text{multiple of 4}}$$

$\therefore$ N is divisible by 4 if and only if $10a_1 + a_0$ is divisible by 4.

Exercises

1. Test for integral quotients.
   a. $5208 \div 3$ **c.** $5208 \div 5$ **e.** $147,809 \div 7$ **g.** $367,892 \div 11$
   b. $5208 \div 4$ **d.** $5208 \div 9$ **f.** $9819 \div 9$ **h.** $147,810 \div 13$

2. Prove the rules for divisibility:
   a. by 2   **b.** by 5   **c.** by 7   **d.** by 11   **e.** by 13

3. Explain why a number divisible by two different prime numbers is divisible by their product. Use this fact to devise a test for divisibility by 6.

4. Devise a rule to test for divisibility by 12, and test $1346 \div 12$.

5. Devise a rule to test for divisibility by 25, and test $67,475 \div 25$.

6. In this problem, the number N is expressed in its general form.
   a. Show that N is divisible by 4 if $2a_1 + a_0$ is divisible by 4.
   b. Show that N is divisible by 8 if $4a_2 + 2a_1 + a_0$ is divisible by 8.

Just for Fun

Do you know that you can multiply some numbers by 9 just by using your fingers and thumbs?

Suppose that you wish to multiply 8 by 9. Spread your hands on the table, fingers outstretched. Bend the eighth finger from the left. Now you have your product, seven fingers to the left of the bent finger, two fingers to its right, or 72:

$$9 \times 8$$

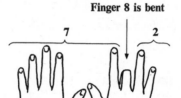

You can multiply by 9 any number from 1 to 10 in this way. Try the other one-digit numbers.

You can also multiply some two-digit numbers by 9 using your fingers. To multiply 46 by 9, you proceed as follows. Start with the 6 of the 46; that is, begin by bending the sixth finger. Now, count off the 4 of 46 by putting the first four fingers together, as shown in the figure below. Your fingers are now in three groups — four together at the far left, one alone just to the left of the bent finger, and four to the right of the bent finger. The product is 414.

$$9 \times 46$$

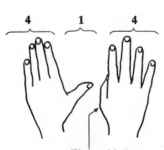

Finger 6 is bent

Why does this method work for such numbers as 35, 58, and 79, but fail for such numbers as 53, 85, and 97?

Lise Meitner
and Nuclear Fission

Lise Meitner (**Lee**-za **Mite**-ner) was born in Vienna, Austria. Her interest in atomic physics began in 1902 when she read of the discovery of radium by Pierre and Marie Curie. In 1906 she was one of the first women to graduate with a doctorate from the University of Vienna, and in 1908 she moved to Berlin, where she studied under Max Planck and began her 30-year collaboration with Otto Hahn. By 1917 she and Dr. Hahn were named joint directors of the Kaiser Wilhelm Institute of Berlin, and Dr. Meitner became head of the Institute's physics department.

The great tragedy of the life of this talented woman was that she was forced, by the rising tide of antisemitism, to leave Germany in 1938 just after making the significant discovery that one of the products of bombarding uranium with neutrons was U^{239}. She found refuge in Sweden and continued her research at the Nobel Institute for Physics in Stockholm. Meanwhile, Dr. Hahn and Dr. Fritz Strassman continued the work in Germany and sent her their findings. From these she developed the explanation of what happened to the uranium nucleus and calculated that the bombarding of one uranium nucleus with a neutron releases an energy of 200 million electron volts. That is 20 million times the explosive energy of an equivalent amount of TNT. She and her nephew, Dr. Otto Robert Frisch, published these results in the British Journal *Nature* in January, 1939, naming the process "nuclear fission."

Dr. Meitner made Stockholm her home for the next 20 years, becoming a Swedish citizen, and working at the Nobel Institute and at the Atomic Energy Laboratory. About ten years before her death in 1968, she retired to England, to be near her nephews and nieces.

In 1966 Dr. Meitner shared the Atomic Energy Commission's $50,000 Enrico Fermi Award with Dr. Hahn and Dr. Fritz Strassman. She always regretted that because of the time of the discovery, the first major use made of atomic energy was in the development of the atomic bomb.

Lise Meitner (1878–1968)

*. . . circular water ripples created by drops of
water and caught by high-speed photography*

Special Products and Factoring

In your earlier courses in mathematics have you been aware of *patterns* that help to make your work easier? In this chapter you will discover several patterns that are helpful in working with polynomials.

THE DISTRIBUTIVE AXIOM IN FACTORING

7–1 Factoring in Algebra

It is often necessary to know whether a number can be expressed as a product of two or more *factors* (recall page 36). Because

$$18 = 2 \times 9 \quad \text{and} \quad 18 = 3 \times 6,$$

2 and 9, and 3 and 6 are factors of 18. Of course, $18 = \frac{1}{2} \times 36$, so that $\frac{1}{2}$ and 36 might also be called factors of 18. However, if no restrictions are placed on the kind of numbers you allow as factors, every nonzero real number is a factor of every real number. For example, 5 could be a factor of 18, since

$$18 = 5 \times \tfrac{18}{5}.$$

Therefore, you usually specify a particular set of numbers to be used as factors.

Finding numbers belonging to a given set of numbers and having their product equal to a given number is called **factoring the number over the given set**. In later work, *integers will be factored over the set of integers, unless another set is specified.*

However, for some purposes, an important subset of the integers is chosen as a set of possible factors, namely, the set of *prime numbers*. A **prime number** is an integer *greater than one*, having no **positive integral factor** other than itself and one. The first prime numbers are

$$2, 3, 5, 7, 11, 13, 17, 19, 23, \ldots.$$

To factor 18 over the set of primes, you write

$$18 = 2 \cdot 3 \cdot 3 = 2 \cdot 3^2.$$

The **prime factors** of 18 are 2 and 3, with 3 occurring twice.

To express a positive integer as a product of primes, you continue factoring until each factor cannot be factored further. For example:

$$
\begin{aligned}
196 &= 7 \cdot 28 \qquad\qquad\text{or}\qquad 196 &= 2 \cdot 98 \\
&= 7 \cdot 7 \cdot 4 & &= 2 \cdot 2 \cdot 49 \\
&= 7 \cdot 7 \cdot 2 \cdot 2 & &= 2 \cdot 2 \cdot 7 \cdot 7 \\
&= 7^2 \cdot 2^2 & &= 2^2 \cdot 7^2
\end{aligned}
$$

In the second method (shown at the right above), you look systematically for the smallest prime factor of the non-prime factor at each stage. That is, you first try 2, and try it again and again until it no longer can be used. Then you try 3, then 5. then 7, and so on until all the factors shown are prime numbers.

It can be proved that the prime factorization of a positive integer is *unique*, except for the order in which the factors may be written. If 1 were considered as a prime factor, the factorization would not be unique, because any number of factors 1 could be written:

$$196 = 2^2 \cdot 7^2 \cdot 1 = 2^2 \cdot 7^2 \cdot 1^2 = 2^2 \cdot 7^2 \cdot 1^3 \cdots$$

Once you know the prime factors of an integer, it is easy to list all its positive integral factors. The (positive integral) factors of 196, for example, are 1 and all possible products of one or both of the primes 2 and 7, each with an exponent less than or equal to its exponent in 196. These factors are

$$1, \quad 2, \quad 2^2, \qquad 7, \quad 2 \cdot 7, \quad 2^2 \cdot 7, \qquad 7^2, \quad 2 \cdot 7^2, \quad 2^2 \cdot 7^2$$

or

$$1, \quad 2, \quad 4, \qquad 7, \quad 14, \quad 28, \qquad 49, \quad 98, \quad 196$$

By factoring integers into products of primes, you can determine the greatest integral factor of both of two integers. To find the **greatest common factor** of 196 and 1260, notice that

$$196 = 2^2 \cdot 7^2 \qquad \text{and} \qquad 1260 = 2^2 \cdot 3^2 \cdot 5 \cdot 7.$$

Thus, the *prime* factors common to 196 and 1260 are 2 and 7. The greatest power of 2 common to 196 and 1260 is 2^2, and the greatest common power of 7 is 7. The greatest common factor is, therefore $2^2 \cdot 7$, or 28.

In algebra you often need to express a polynomial as a product of **polynomial factors**. Expressing a given polynomial in this way is called **polynomial factoring**. For example, each term of the polynomial $5x + 5y$ contains 5 as a factor. Therefore, by the distributive axiom

$$5x + 5y = 5(x + y).$$

Both 5 and $x + y$ are factors of $5x + 5y$.

When factoring polynomials whose numerical coefficients are integers, you look for factors that are either integers or polynomials with integral coefficients. For example, some of the factors of $6x^2y$ are 1, 2, 3, 6, $2x^2$, and $3xy$. You see that $2x^3$ is not a factor of $6x^2y$, since there is no polynomial by which you can multiply $2x^3$ to obtain $6x^2y$. (Recall that $\dfrac{3y}{x}$ is not a monomial.)

Oral Exercises

Express each integer as a product of primes.

1. 6	**3.** 4	**5.** 9	**7.** 12	**9.** 30
2. 15	**4.** 8	**6.** 27	**8.** 18	**10.** 50

Tell why each statement is true or why it is false.

SAMPLE 1.   6 is a prime factor of 12.

Solution: False; although 6 is a factor of 12 because $12 = 6 \cdot 2$, 6 is not prime.

SAMPLE 2.   7 is a factor of 21 over the set of integers.

Solution: True, because $21 = 7 \cdot 3$.

11. 3 is a prime factor of 39.   **15.** 7 is not a prime factor of 49.

12. 5 is a prime factor of 14.   **16.** 6 is a factor of 66.

13. 8 is a prime factor of 16.   **17.** 5 is not a factor of 82.

14. 3 is not a prime factor of 22.   **18.** 2 is a factor of 0.

Name the monomial with the greatest numerical coefficient and the greatest degree in each variable that is a factor of both monomials in each pair.

SAMPLE 3. $9a^3b$; $12a^2b$

Solution: $3a^2b$

19. 16; $24x$ **23.** $20r^3s^2$; $100rs^3$

20. 12; $18y^2$ **24.** $28k^5t$; $35k^2t^2$

21. $5xz^2$; $7x^2z^3$ **25.** $7r^5s^2$; $15t^3$

22. $30a^3b^2$; $45a^2b$ **26.** $16x^5y$; $64x^2y^5$

Written Exercises

Factor each integer over the set of primes.

A	**1.** 34	**3.** 63	**5.** 144	**7.** 19
	2. 52	**4.** 95	**6.** 242	**8.** 1024

Find all the positive integral factors of each number.

9. 15   **11.** 24   **13.** 30   **15.** 444

10. 19   **12.** 25   **14.** 108   **16.** 1000

Find the greatest common factor of each pair of integers.

17. 24; 60   **19.** 315; 350   **21.** 693; 882

18. 45; 105   **20.** 252; 288   **22.** 1925; 2100

Find the monomial with the greatest numerical coefficient and the greatest degree in each variable that is a factor of both monomials in each pair.

23. $154a^2b$; $132ab^4$ **25.** $126x^2yz^3$; $105x^3yz^2$ **27.** $176r^2s^3$; $208s^2t^3$

24. $78x^3y^2$; $52x^2y^4$ **26.** $108a^3b^2c$; $144a^2bc^3$ **28.** $132m^4n^3$; $156n^2p^3$

Give the second factor for each monomial.

29. $6a^2b = 6a(\underline{\ ?\ })$ **31.** $-15x^3y^2 = (-5x^2y^2)(\underline{\ ?\ })$

30. $24r^2s = (12rs)(\underline{\ ?\ })$ **32.** $-32p^3q^4 = (16p^3q^2)(\underline{\ ?\ })$

33. $42u^3v^2w = (-6u^2vw)(\underline{\ ?\ })$

34. $51x^4y^2z^3 = (-17x^3y^2z^2)(\underline{\ ?\ })$

35. $72r^3s^5t^2 = (18r^3s^4t^2)(\underline{\ ?\ })$

36. $102a^3b^2c = (-17a^3b)(\underline{\ ?\ })$

For each pair of monomials, find the highest power of the first monomial that is a factor of the second monomial.

SAMPLE. $3c$; $27c^2d$

Solution: $(3c)^1 = 3c$, and $27c^2d = (3c)(9cd)$

$(3c)^2 = 9c^2$, and $27c^2d = (9c^2)(3d)$

$(3c)^3 = 27c^3$, but c^3 is *not* a factor of c^2.

∴ the highest power is $(3c)^2$. **Answer.**

B	**37.** z; $8z^4t$	**41.** $5xy$; $75x^3y^2$
	38. x^2; $7x^5n$	**42.** $3m^2n$; $54m^7n^4$
	39. $2t$; $24t^3v^2$	**43.** $4a^3b^2$; $128a^{15}b^9$
	40. $3n$; $81n^4p^2$	**44.** $6cd^2$; $108c^2d^8$

7-2 Identifying Monomial Factors

Because each term in $6xy + 9x$ has $\mathbf{3x}$ as a factor, you can use the distributive axiom to write

$$6xy + 9x = 3x(2y + 3).$$

Since $3x$ is a monomial, you say that $3x$ is a *monomial factor* of the polynomial $6xy + 9x$. When you factor a polynomial, you first see whether each term has the same monomial as a factor. A monomial is a **monomial factor** of a polynomial if it is a factor of *every* term of the polynomial.

Notice that 3 and x are also monomial factors of $6xy + 9x$. You should be sure to continue factoring until you find the *greatest monomial factor*. The **greatest monomial factor** of a polynomial is the monomial factor having the greatest numerical coefficient and the greatest degree.

Examine this chart, observing how each polynomial is factored.

Given Polynomial	Factors		Factored Expression
$2a^2 + 5a$	a	$2a + 5$	$a(2a + 5)$
$7t^2 + 28t$	$7t$	$t + 4$	$7t(t + 4)$
$5x^4 - 15x^3 + 35x^2$	$5x^2$	$x^2 - 3x + 7$	$5x^2(x^2 - 3x + 7)$
$12c^3d^2 + 36c^2d$	$12c^2d$	$cd + 3$	$12c^2d(cd + 3)$

The associative and commutative axioms for addition, together with the distributive axiom, may enable you to factor a polynomial by *grouping terms:*

$$ax + by + ay + bx = (ax + bx) + (ay + by)$$
$$= (a + b)x + (a + b)y$$
$$= (a + b)(x + y)$$

In the last step, $(a + b)$ is treated as a single term in applying the distributive axiom.

Here is another polynomial that can be factored readily when you group the terms appropriately:

$$2ax - 3by - 6ay + bx = (2ax - 6ay) + (bx - 3by)$$
$$= 2a(x - 3y) + b(x - 3y)$$
$$= (2a + b)(x - 3y)$$

Of course, there may be more than one convenient way to group terms:

$$2ax - 3by - 6ay + bx = (2ax + bx) + (-6ay - 3by)$$
$$= x(2a + b) + (-3y)(2a + b)$$
$$= [x + (-3y)](2a + b)$$
$$= (x - 3y)(2a + b)$$

Because multiplication is commutative, this result is the same as the preceding one.

Oral Exercises

Give the greatest monomial factor of each polynomial.

SAMPLE. $12x^3 + 15x$ *Solution:* $3x$

1. $4x + 2$
2. $3x - 6$
3. $ab^2 + a$
4. $x^2y^2 + x$

5. $4x^2 - 6y^2$
6. $9z^2 + 12t^3$
7. $3x - 5z$
8. $5t + 4s$

9. $8x^2 + 4x$
10. $10y - 25y^2$
11. $9x^2y^2 - 36xy$
12. $15ab + 30a^2b^2$

13. $4x^2 - 8x + 2$
14. $5 - 10z - 25z^2$
15. $3x^3 + 6x^2 - 5x$

16. $6x^3 - 9x^2 + 3x$
17. $15y^6 + 10y^4 - 5y^2$
18. $12a^4b^4 - 9a^3b^3 + 6a^2b^2$

Written Exercises

Write in factored form. Check by multiplying your factors.

SAMPLE 1. $15t^3 - 5t$ *Solution:* $15t^3 - 5t = 5t(3t^2 - 1)$

1. $4x^2 - 8$
2. $6 + 9y$
3. $4a^2 + 5a$
4. $6b^2 + 7b$

5. $10z^3 - 5z^2$
6. $12n^2 + 24n^3$
7. $6a^2b + 3ab^2$
8. $7rs^3 - 14r^2s$

9. $3p^2 + 3p - 9$
10. $4 - 6q + 10q^2$
11. $5n^2 - 15n + 20$
12. $6 - 3p + 18p^2$

13. $a^3x^3 + a^2x^2 - ax$
14. $b^4y^2 + b^3y^3 - b^2y^4$
15. $4b^2y^2 - 8b^2y + 24b^2$
16. $35k^2 - 42k^2t + 14k^2t^2$

17. $15x^2y - 30xy + 35xy^2$
18. $-18u^3v^2 + 12u^2v^2 - 6uv^2$
19. $9x^5y^2 - 6x^4y^3 + 3x^3y^4$
20. $-12x^3y^3 + 18x^2y^4 + 27xy^5$

Write each expression in factored form, and check.

SAMPLE 2. $y^2(y + 3) + 2(y + 3)$

Solution: $y^2(y + 3) + 2(y + 3) = (y^2 + 2)(y + 3)$

B 21. $n(n - 1) + 3(n - 1)$

22. $x(2x + 3) + 2(2x + 3)$

23. $(3a - b)b + (3a - b)a$

24. $(c + 3d)(2c) + (c + 3d)(3d)$

25. $t^2(y + 5) - 5(y + 5)$

26. $k^2(t + 1) + 2k(t + 1)$

27. $n^2(2n + 1) + (2n + 1)$

28. $2m^2(3m + 1) + (3m + 1)$

29. $a^2(a - b) + b(a - b)$

30. $2n(n^2 + 1) + 3(n^2 + 1)$

31. $5c(a^3 + b) - (a^3 + b)$

32. $m(m + 2n) - n(m + 2n)$

SAMPLE 3. $x^2 + x + xy + y$

Solution: $x^2 + x + xy + y = x(x + 1) + y(x + 1)$
$$= (x + y)(x + 1).$$

C 33. $n^2 + 2n + np + 2p$

34. $a^2 - 3a + ay - 3y$

35. $k^2 + 3k + 2k + 6$

36. $3ab - b^2 + 3a^2 - ab$

37. $2x^2 + 3x + 6 + 4x$

38. $2x^2 - 4x + xz - 2z$

39. $6y^2 - 3y + 2py - p$

40. $n^3 - n^2 - nq + q$

41. $n^2m + 2nm + 2n + n^2$

42. $4x + 8x^3 + 1 + 2x^2$

Problems

Write an expression in factored form for the area A of the shaded region shown.

SAMPLE.

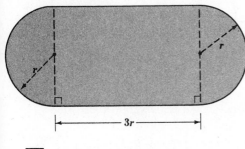

Solution:

$A =$ Area of rectangle $+$ area of circle.

$\quad = (3r)(2r) \qquad\qquad + \pi r^2$

$\quad = 6r^2 \qquad\qquad\qquad + \pi r^2$

$\quad = (6 + \pi)r^2.$ **Answer.**

A 1.

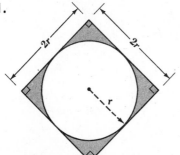

2.

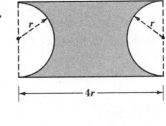

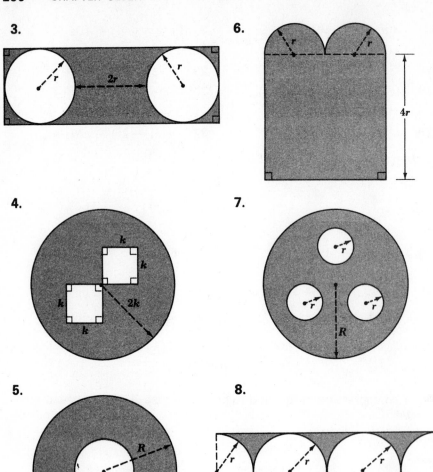

3.

6.

4.

7.

5.

8.

BINOMIALS

7–3 Multiplying the Sum and Difference of Two Numbers

Certain products occur so often that you should recognize them at sight. Study each of the three examples below:

$$
\begin{array}{r}
y + 2 \\
y - 2 \\
\hline
y^2 + 2y \\
 - 2y - 4 \\
\hline
y^2 - 4
\end{array}
\qquad
\begin{array}{r}
3a - 2b \\
3a + 2b \\
\hline
9a^2 - 6ab \\
 6ab - 4b^2 \\
\hline
9a^2 - 4b^2
\end{array}
\qquad
\begin{array}{r}
a + b \\
a - b \\
\hline
a^2 + ab \\
 - ab - b^2 \\
\hline
a^2 - b^2
\end{array}
$$

These examples illustrate this rule:

The product of the sum and difference of two numbers is the square of the first number minus the square of the second number; that is,

$$(a + b)(a - b) = a^2 - b^2.$$

Figure 7–1 shows that the area represented by the product $(a + b)(a - b)$ is the same as the area represented by $a^2 - b^2$.

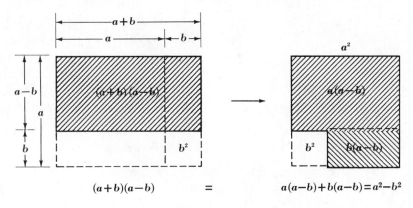

$(a+b)(a-b)$ $\qquad$ = $\qquad$ $a(a-b)+b(a-b)=a^2-b^2$

Figure 7–1

Oral Exercises

Square each monomial.

SAMPLE 1. $-8t^2$ *Solution:* $64t^4$

1. $2a$	**3.** $-5c$	**5.** $3p^2$	**7.** $6st$	**9.** $-5s^2t$
2. $3b$	**4.** $-7x$	**6.** $5y^3$	**8.** $-3ab$	**10.** $7r^2v^2$

Express each product as a polynomial.

SAMPLE 2. $(x - 1)(x + 1)$ *Solution:* $x^2 - 1$

11. $(y + 2)(y - 2)$	**15.** $(t + 6)(t - 6)$	**19.** $(y^2 - 5)(y^2 + 5)$
12. $(z + 3)(z - 3)$	**16.** $(n - 8)(n + 8)$	**20.** $(z^3 + 9)(z^3 - 9)$
13. $(x - y)(x + y)$	**17.** $(2a - 1)(2a + 1)$	**21.** $(3r + \frac{1}{2})(3r - \frac{1}{2})$
14. $(p - q)(p + q)$	**18.** $(3b - 1)(3b + 1)$	**22.** $(5k + \frac{2}{3})(5k - \frac{2}{3})$

23. 19×21 or $(20 - 1)(20 + 1)$ **25.** 35×45

24. 32×28 or $(30 + 2)(30 - 2)$ **26.** 47×53

Written Exercises

Multiply:

a. by using the form $(a + b)(a - b)$; **b.** by using the distributive axiom.

SAMPLE. $(58)(62)$

Solution: **a.** $(58)(62) = (60 - 2)(60 + 2) = 3600 - 4 = 3596$

b. $(58)(62) = 50(62) + 8(62) = 3100 + 496 = 3596$

Ordinary multiplication, which uses the distributive axiom, can also be used for part b.

A								
	1. $(8)(12)$	**4.** $(31)(29)$	**7.** $(41)(39)$	**10.** $(22)(38)$
	2. $(7)(13)$	**5.** $(15)(25)$	**8.** $(49)(51)$	**11.** $(88)(92)$
	3. $(17)(23)$	**6.** $(25)(35)$	**9.** $(34)(46)$	**12.** $(75)(85)$

B				
	13. $(95)(105)$	**15.** $(6\frac{1}{3})(5\frac{2}{3})$	**17.** $(1020)(980)$	**19.** $(0.7)(1.3)$
	14. $(505)(495)$	**16.** $(7\frac{1}{2})(6\frac{1}{2})$	**18.** $(1200)(800)$	**20.** $(1.8)(2.2)$

7–4 Factoring the Difference of Two Squares

By the symmetric property of equality, the relation $(a + b)(a - b) = a^2 - b^2$ is reversible:

$$a^2 - b^2 = (a + b)(a - b).$$

You use this to factor an expression consisting of the difference of two squares:

$$x^2 - 9 = (x + 3)(x - 3)$$
$$16y^2 - x^2 = (4y + x)(4y - x)$$
$$25c^2 - 49d^2 = (5c + 7d)(5c - 7d)$$
$$-u^2v^2 + x^2y^2 = x^2y^2 - u^2v^2 = (xy + uv)(xy - uv)$$

If, as in $49x^2y^4$, the degree in *each* variable is even and the numerical coefficient is the square of an integer, then the monomial is a square;

$$49x^2y^4 = (7xy^2)^2.$$

Sometimes it is difficult to tell at sight whether or not a numerical coefficient is a square. However, Table 3 in the Appendix enables you to tell whether or not each integer from 1 to 10,000 is the square of an integer.

Oral Exercises

Tell whether or not the given binomial is the difference of two squares. If it is, give its factors.

1. $y^2 - 4$ **6.** $9 - t^2$ **11.** $-9x^2 + 36$ **16.** $4t^2 - 9s^2$

2. $t^2 + 1$ **7.** $1 - n^2$ **12.** $16z^2 - 49$ **17.** $a^2b^2 - c^2d^2$

3. $z^2 - u^2$ **8.** $6a^2 - 5c^2$ **13.** $4k^2 - 64$ **18.** $4p^2q^2 - 1$

4. $k^2 - m^2$ **9.** $7t^2 - r^2$ **14.** $100 + 25m^2$ **19.** $18 - 11c^2d^2$

5. $49 + p^2$ **10.** $-25 + d^2$ **15.** $16r^2 - 25y^2$ **20.** $81a^2b^2 - 49$

Written Exercises

Factor and check by multiplication. Use Appendix Table 3 as needed.

A **1.** $t^2 - 9$ **9.** $81t^2 - 100s^2$ **17.** $4r^2 - 64$

2. $k^2 - 4$ **10.** $121a^2 - 144b^2$ **18.** $9p^2 - 81$

3. $4m^2 - 1$ **11.** $a^2b^4 - c^2$ **19.** $x^2 - 169$

4. $9r^2 - 1$ **12.** $d^2 - f^2g^4$ **20.** $144 - n^2$

5. $t^2 - u^2$ **13.** $4y^2 - 1$ **21.** $225a^2 - b^2$

6. $x^2 - 16y^2$ **14.** $16t^2 - 9$ **22.** $4x^2 - 625$

7. $25v^2 - 49$ **15.** $25x^2 - 36y^2$

8. $64 - 25r^2$ **16.** $49m^2 - 64$

SAMPLE. $4ax^{2n} - 36a$. Assume that $n \in \{\text{the positive integers}\}$.

Solution: $4ax^{2n} - 36a = 4a(x^{2n} - 9) = 4a(x^n - 3)(x^n + 3)$

B **23.** $3t^2 - 27$ **29.** $147z^2 - 75$ **35.** $x^{2n} - 9$

24. $5p^2 - 80t^2$ **30.** $112 - 63q^2$ **36.** $-t^{2n} + 25$

25. $x^4 - 25x^2$ **31.** $t^4 - k^4$ **37.** $k^2 - a^{2n}$

26. $y^6 - 36y^4$ **32.** $r^4 - 1$ **38.** $z^{4n} - k^2$

27. $-b^2 + c^2$ **33.** $-n^{2n} + 1$ **39.** $l^6 - w^4h^2$

28. $-m + m^7$ **34.** $-x^{2y} + x^2$ **40.** $x^{2k} - x^2$

C **41.** $x^{4n} - y^{4n}$ **44.** $y^2 - (y - 2)^2$

42. $81a^{4n} - 1$ **45.** $(x + 1)^2 - (x - 1)^2$

43. $(x + 3)^2 - x^2$ **46.** $9(x - 1)^2 - 25(x + 1)^2$

47. Show that the difference between the squares, **a.** of two consecutive integers equals the sum of the integers; **b.** of two consecutive odd integers equals twice the sum of the integers.

QUADRATIC TRINOMIALS

7–5 Squaring a Binomial

The binomial $a + b$ is squared at the right by the usual method of multiplication. Notice how each term in the product is obtained.

$$\begin{array}{r} a + b \\ a + b \\ \hline a^2 + ab \\ ab + b^2 \\ \hline a^2 + 2ab + b^2 \end{array}$$

1. **Square the first term in the binomial.**
2. **Double the product of the two terms.**
3. **Square the second term in the binomial.**

Now examine the square of a binomial difference. The binomial $a - b$ is squared by multiplication at the right. Again, notice how each term is obtained.

$$\begin{array}{r} a - b \\ a - b \\ \hline a^2 - ab \\ - ab + b^2 \\ \hline a^2 - 2ab + b^2 \end{array}$$

1. **Square the first term in the binomial.**
2. **Double the product of the two terms.**
3. **Square the second term in the binomial.**

Whenever you square a binomial, the product is a **trinomial square,** whose terms show this pattern:

$$(a + b)^2 = a^2 + 2ab + b^2.$$
$$(a - b)^2 = a^2 - 2ab + b^2.$$

Each side of the large square in Figure 7–2 is $(a + b)$ units in length. You can consider this square as being made up of four regions, as shown. The total area can be expressed as a square of a binomial, $(a + b)^2$, or as a trinomial square, $a^2 + 2ab + b^2$.

Figure 7–2

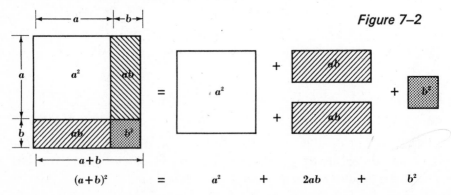

$$(a+b)^2 \qquad = \qquad a^2 \qquad + \qquad 2ab \qquad + \qquad b^2$$

Knowing these relationships, you can write the square of a binomial without performing long multiplication.

EXAMPLES:
1. $(c + 1)^2 = c^2 + 2c + 1$
2. $(d - 1)^2 = d^2 - 2d + 1$
3. $(2x + 5)^2 = 4x^2 + 20x + 25$
4. $(6z^2 - w^3)^2 = 36z^4 - 12z^2w^3 + w^6$
5. $(-r^2s + t^3)^2 = (t^3 - r^2s)^2 = t^6 - 2t^3r^2s + r^4s^2$

Oral Exercises

State each power as a trinomial.

1. $(r + s)^2$
2. $(u - v)^2$
3. $(x + 1)^2$
4. $(y - 2)^2$
5. $(z - 3)^2$
6. $(t + 4)^2$
7. $(k + 5)^2$
8. $(n - 6)^2$

Written Exercises

Write each power as a trinomial.

A
1. $(p + 7)^2$
2. $(q - 8)^2$
3. $(2x - 1)^2$
4. $(3y + 1)^2$
5. $(4t + 3)^2$
6. $(3s - 2)^2$
7. $(6r + 5)^2$
8. $(7k - 3)^2$
9. $(2x - 3y)^2$
10. $(5z + 2u)^2$
11. $(xy - 1)^2$
12. $(2 + rs)^2$
13. $(x^2 + 2)^2$
14. $(y^2 - 5)^2$
15. $(2p^2 - 5q^2)^2$
16. $(u^2v^2 + 7)^2$

B
17. $(x - \frac{2}{3})^2$
18. $(y + \frac{5}{2})^2$
19. $(\frac{1}{2} - m)^2$
20. $(\frac{3}{4} + x)^2$
21. $(n - 0.3)^2$
22. $(p + 2.4)^2$
23. $(0.6x + 1.5)^2$
24. $(1.1y - 3.2)^2$
25. $(\frac{3}{4}y + \frac{4}{3})^2$
26. $(\frac{1}{2}x - \frac{8}{5})^2$
27. $(-x^3 - y^2z)^2$
28. $(-m^2n^2 + p^4)^2$

29. Show that $(a + b + c)^2 = a^2 + b^2 + c^2 + 2ab + 2ac + 2bc$ by considering the figure at the left below.

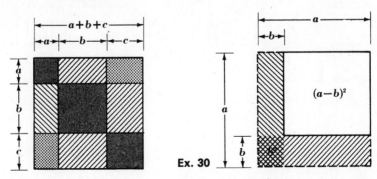

Ex. 29   Ex. 30

30. Show that $(a - b)^2 = a^2 - 2ab + b^2$ by considering the figure at the right above.

31. Show that

$$(a + b)^2 - (a - b)^2 = 4ab$$

by considering the figure at the left below.

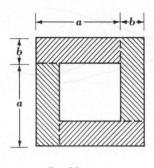

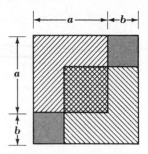

Ex. 31   Ex. 32

32. Show that

$$(a + b)^2 + (a - b)^2 = 2(a^2 + b^2)$$

by considering the figure at the right above.

C **33.** Use the figure at the left below to show that when n has the value 9,

$$1 + 2 + 3 + \cdots + n = \frac{n(n + 1)}{2}.$$

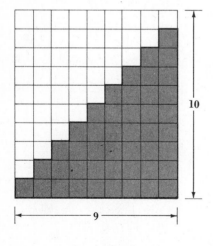

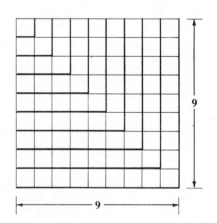

Ex. 33   Ex. 34

34. Use the figure at the right above to show that when n has the value 9,

$$1 + 3 + 5 + \cdots + (2n - 1) = n^2.$$

7–6   Factoring a Trinomial Square

To factor a trinomial square, you reverse the equations you use in squaring a binomial. Thus:

$$a^2 + 2ab + b^2 = (a + b)^2$$
$$a^2 - 2ab + b^2 = (a - b)^2$$

Before you use one of these equations as a rule for factoring, you must be sure that the expression to be factored is a trinomial square. Arrange the terms of the trinomial with exponents in descending order, and then examine each term to see how it may have been obtained. Consider

$$y^2 + 10y + 25.$$

Is the first term a square? Yes, y^2 is the square of y. Is the third term a square? Yes, 25 is 5^2. Is the middle term (neglecting the sign) double the product of 5 and y? Yes, $10y = 2(y)(5)$. Therefore, this trinomial is a square. Since all its terms are **positive**, it is the square of a **sum**; thus,

$$y^2 + 10y + 25 = (y + 5)^2.$$

EXAMPLE.   Factor $81r^2 - 198rs + 121s^2$.

Solution: $81r^2 -\quad 198rs\quad + 121s^2$

$\qquad = (9r)^2 - 2(9r)(11s) + (11s)^2$

$\qquad$ Thus, $81r^2 - 198rs + 121s^2 = (9r - 11s)^2$.   **Answer.**

Check: $(9r - 11s)^2 = 81r^2 - 198rs + 121s^2$ ✓

Oral Exercises

Is each trinomial the square of a binomial? Justify your answer.

1. $x^2 + x + 1$

2. $y^2 - 2y + 1$

3. $z^2 + 4z + 4$

4. $t^2 - 4t - 4$

5. $k^2 + 6k + 9$

6. $r^2 - 8r + 16$

7. $4x^2 + 4x + 1$

8. $9t^2 - 6t + 1$

9. $25p^2 + 10p - 1$

10. $x^2 - 20x + 100$

11. $4n^2 + 4nt + t^2$

12. $a^2 - 2ab + b$

13. $9k^2 + 12kt + 4t^2$ **15.** $n^2p^2 - 2np + 1$ **17.** $a^2b^2 - 14ab + 49$

14. $z^2 - 12zu + 36u^2$ **16.** $r^2s^2 + 2rs + 1$ **18.** $c^2d^2 - 16cd - 64$

19. $25m^2 - 60mn + 36n^2$ **22.** $x^2y^2 + 2xyz + z^2$

20. $36m^2 + 60mn + 25n^2$ **23.** $(x + y)^2 + 2(x + y) + 1$

21. $x^2 - 2xyz + y^2z^2$ **24.** $(r - s)^2 - 2(r - s) + 1$

Written Exercises

Factor and check.

A **1.** $n^2 - 2n + 1$ **13.** $1 - 4t + 4t^2$

2. $m^2 + 2m + 1$ **14.** $25 + 10k + k^2$

3. $k^2 - 6k + 9$ **15.** $64y^2 - 16yz + z^2$

4. $t^2 - 8t + 16$ **16.** $81k^2 + 18kt + t^2$

5. $r^2 + 10r + 25$ **17.** $9 + 12p + 4p^2$

6. $s^2 + 12s + 36$ **18.** $36 - 60q + 25q^2$

7. $4p^2 - 4p + 1$ **19.** $4x^2y^2 - 12xyz + 9z^2$

8. $9q^2 + 6q + 1$ **20.** $16t^2 + 24tuv + 9u^2v^2$

9. $16c^2 + 8c + 1$ **21.** $x^4 + 2x^2 + 1$

10. $25d^2 - 10d + 1$ **22.** $y^4 + 10y^2 + 25$

11. $4x^2 - 4xy + y^2$ **23.** $25y^4 - 10y^2x + x^2$

12. $9u^2 + 6uv + v^2$ **24.** $z^2 + 18zab + 81a^2b^2$

SAMPLE. $18y^2 - 12y + 2$

Solution: $18y^2 - 12y + 2 = 2(9y^2 - 6y + 1) = 2(3y - 1)^2$

B **25.** $7x^3 + 14x^2 + 7x$ **29.** $24x + 24x^2 + 6x^3$

26. $20ay^2 - 60ay + 45a$ **30.** $3z + 42z^2 + 147z^3$

27. $x^3 + 25x - 10x^2$ **31.** $4y^4 - 8y^2x^2 + 4x^4$

28. $4p^2q + pq^2 + 4p^3$ **32.** $6a^4 - 12a^2b^2 + 6b^4$

C **33.** $x^2 + 2x + 1 - y^2$ **35.** $a^2 - b^2 + 2b - 1$

34. $t^2 - 4t + 4 - s^2$ **36.** $4p^2 - q^2 - 6q - 9$

Find k so that each trinomial will be a square.

37. $y^2 - 6y + k$ **39.** $kx^2 - 12x + 9$

38. $b^2 + kb + 25$ **40.** $y^2 - 2ky + 81$

7–7 Multiplying Binomials at Sight

To learn to write the product of two binomials of the form $(ax + b)(cx + d)$ at sight, study these examples which apply the distributive axiom.

EXAMPLE 1. $(2y + 3)(7y - 5)$　　**EXAMPLE 2.** $(ax + b)(cx + d)$

Solution:

$$
\begin{array}{r}
7y \;-\; 5 \\
\times \\
2y \;+\; 3 \\
\hline
14y^2 - 10y \\
21y - 15 \\
\hline
14y^2 + 11y - 15
\end{array}
$$

Solution:

$$
\begin{array}{r}
cx \;+\; d \\
\times \\
ax \;+\; b \\
\hline
acx^2 + adx \\
bcx + bd \\
\hline
acx^2 + (ad + bc)x + bd
\end{array}
$$

> To write the terms in the trinomial product of two binomials, $(ax + b)(cx + d)$, at sight:
>
> 1. Multiply the first terms of the binomials.
> 2. Multiply the first term of each binomial by the last term of the other, and add these products.
> 3. Multiply the last terms of the binomials.

Each term of a trinomial like $14y^2 + 11y - 15$ has a special name. The first, $14y^2$, is the *quadratic term* in the variable y: the second, $11y$, is the *linear term* in the variable y; and the third, -15, is the *constant term*. A **quadratic term** is a term of degree two in the variable. A **linear term** is a term of degree one in the variable. A **constant term** is a numerical term with no variable factor. The trinomial is itself called a **quadratic polynomial** because the term of the highest degree in it is a quadratic term.

Oral Exercises

State the quadratic, linear, and constant terms, and read the product as a trinomial.

SAMPLE. $(x + 3)(x - 1)$　　*Solution:* Quadratic term, x^2; linear term, $2x$; constant term, -3; $x^2 + 2x - 3$.

1. $(y + 1)(y + 2)$　　**3.** $(b - 4)(b - 1)$　　**5.** $(r + 5)(r + 2)$

2. $(a + 3)(a + 2)$　　**4.** $(x - 3)(x - 4)$　　**6.** $(s + 8)(s + 1)$

7. $(t - 6)(t - 3)$	**11.** $(d - 4)(d + 1)$	**15.** $(2 - t)(3 - t)$
8. $(n - 10)(n - 2)$	**12.** $(k + 4)(k - 2)$	**16.** $(5 + x)(6 - x)$
9. $(a + 2)(a - 1)$	**13.** $(z - 4)(z + 3)$	**17.*** $(y + 2a)(y + a)$
10. $(b + 1)(b - 2)$	**14.** $(g + 5)(g - 1)$	**18.*** $(y - 3a)(y + 2a)$

Written Exercises

Write each product as a trinomial.

A **1.** $(n + 6)(n + 3)$ **5.** $(2x + 1)(x + 2)$ **9.** $(3x - 2)(2x - 3)$

2. $(t - 5)(t - 2)$ **6.** $(z + 3)(2z + 5)$ **10.** $(5y + 2)(2y + 5)$

3. $(x + 10)(x - 5)$ **7.** $(3t - 1)(t + 4)$ **11.** $(3r - 5)(2r + 1)$

4. $(y - 9)(y + 3)$ **8.** $(p - 3)(4p + 3)$ **12.** $(5s + 2)(2s - 1)$

13. $(3 - x)(2 + x)$ **19.** $(-z - 1)(-2z - 3)$

14. $(5 - z)(4 + z)$ **20.** $(-r - 2)(-2r - 5)$

15. $(1 - 2s)(3 + 4s)$ **21.** $x(x + 2)(x - 1)$

16. $(2 + 5t)(3 - 2t)$ **22.** $z(3z + 2)(z - 1)$

17. $(x - 2)(-x + 3)$ **23.** $2y(3y - 1)(y + 5)$

18. $(-y + 5)(y - 2)$ **24.** $5k^2(k + 2)(2k - 1)$

Solve each equation and check.

25. $(x - 3)(x + 2) = (x - 6)(x - 1)$

26. $(x + 1)(x - 1) = (x + 5)(x - 2)$

27. $(4x + 3)(x + 3) = (2x + 5)(2x + 2)$

28. $(4x + 3)(x - 2) = (2x - 1)(2x - 3)$

Write each product as a trinomial.

B **29.** $(x + \frac{2}{3})(x - \frac{1}{3})$ **33.** $(a + 0.2)(a - 3.1)$

30. $(z - \frac{2}{7})(z - \frac{3}{7})$ **34.** $(b - 2.3)(b + 5.1)$

31. $(y + \frac{4}{5})(y - \frac{2}{5})$ **35.** $(2.1z + 0.2)(3z - 1.7)$

32. $(\frac{3}{7}x + 1)(\frac{2}{7}x - 1)$ **36.** $(4.2y - 3.1)(2.3y + 1.6)$

Solve and check.

C **37.** $(3x + 1)(x - 1) = (2x - 3)(x + 5) + (x - 2)(x + 2)$

38. $(2x - 5)(3x + 1) = (2x + 3)(x - 4) + (2x - 1)^2 - 4$

39. $(2x + 3)(x + 4) = (x - 6)(x + 2) + (x + 3)^2 - 21$

40. $(3x - 5)(2x + 7) - 7 = (2x - 1)^2 + (x - 3)(2x + 1) + 5$

*Take y to be the variable here.

7–8 Factoring the Product of Binomial Sums or Differences

We shall now need to consider expressing an integer as a product of two integers. For example,

$$30 = 1 \cdot 30 \qquad = 2 \cdot 15 \qquad = 3 \cdot 10 \qquad = 5 \cdot 6 \qquad (1)$$
$$= (-1)(-30) = (-2)(-15) = (-3)(-10) = (-5)(-6) \qquad (2)$$

Notice that 30 may be expressed in several ways, either as a product of *two positive* integers (line 1 above) or as a product of *two negative* integers (line 2). In the work in this section you will need to consider such pairs of factors of positive integers.

To factor the trinomial $z^2 + 6z + 8$, you should notice that

$$(z + r)(z + s) = z^2 + (r + s)z + rs$$
$$\updownarrow \qquad \updownarrow \; \updownarrow \quad \updownarrow$$

and compare the two:
$$z^2 + \quad 6 \quad z + 8$$

Do you see that they would be exactly alike if

$$rs = 8 \qquad \text{and} \qquad r + s = 6?$$

With these clues, you can find the two integers r and s and then write $z^2 + 6z + 8$ as a product of factors $(z + r)(z + s)$.

Observe first that the product, rs, of the desired integers is positive in this case, indicating that r and s are *both positive* or *both negative*. Observe next that their sum, $r + s$, is positive. Therefore, r and s cannot both be negative, and so in this case r and s must both be positive. There are two ways to express 8 as the product of two positive integers:

$$8 = 1 \cdot 8 \qquad \text{and} \qquad 8 = 2 \cdot 4$$
$$\uparrow \; \uparrow \qquad\qquad\qquad\qquad \uparrow \; \uparrow$$
$$r \; s \qquad\qquad\qquad\qquad\quad r \; s$$
$$\downarrow \; \searrow \qquad\qquad\qquad\qquad \downarrow \; \searrow$$
$$r + s = 1 + 8 = 9 \qquad\qquad r + s = 2 + 4 = 6 \checkmark$$

The second set of factors satisfies both clues, and so you conclude that

$$z^2 + 6z + 8 = (z + 2)(z + 4).$$

You can check this by multiplying the factors.

Of course, if you see the right pair of factors at the outset, there is no need to write the remaining possibilities.

EXAMPLE. Factor $y^2 - 9y + 18$.

Solution: $y^2 - 9y + 18 = (y\qquad)(y\qquad)$ $\Big\{$ Since $r + s$ is negative here,

$\qquad\qquad\qquad\quad = (y -\quad)(y -\quad)$ $\Big\{$ both r and s are negative.

$\qquad\qquad\qquad\quad = (y - 3)(y - 6)$. Answer.

Check: $\qquad (y - 3)(y - 6) = y^2 - 9y + 18 \checkmark$

Each of the quadratic polynomials you have factored has a *positive constant term*. Then because $z^2 + 6z + 8$ has a *positive linear term*, it is factored as a product of two binomial sums, $(z + 2)(z + 4)$. On the other hand, $y^2 - 9y + 18$ has a *negative linear term*, and so it is factored as a product of two binomial differences, $(y - 3)(y - 6)$.

Not every quadratic trinomial can be written as a product of binomials having integral coefficients. To factor $x^2 + 2x + 6$, you would have to find positive integers r and s such that

$$rs = 6 \quad \text{and} \quad r + s = 2.$$

The two ways of writing 6 as a product of positive integers are:

$$6 = 1 \cdot 6 \qquad \text{and} \qquad 6 = 2 \cdot 3$$
$$\uparrow \quad \uparrow \qquad\qquad\qquad \uparrow \quad \uparrow$$
$$r \quad s \qquad\qquad\qquad\quad r \quad s$$
$$r + s = 7 \qquad\qquad\quad r + s = 5.$$

In each case, $r + s \neq 2$; therefore, $x^2 + 2x + 6$ cannot be factored over the set of polynomials with integral coefficients. Such a polynomial is said to be *irreducible over this set of polynomials*. A polynomial which cannot be factored into polynomials of lower degree belonging to a designated set is said to be **irreducible** over that set of polynomials.

An irreducible polynomial whose greatest monomial factor is 1 is called a **prime polynomial**. Thus, $2x + 11$ is a prime polynomial. However, $8x + 44 = 4(2x + 11)$, and so $8x + 44$ is irreducible but not prime.

Oral Exercises

For each trinomial, tell which two factors of the constant term have a sum equal to the coefficient of the linear term.

1. $x^2 + 3x + 2$ 3. $z^2 + 5z + 4$ 5. $a^2 - 3a + 2$

2. $y^2 + 5y + 6$ 4. $n^2 + 7n + 12$ 6. $b^2 - 6b + 8$

7. $r^2 - 9r + 20$ **11.** $x^2 + 13x + 30$ **15.** $t^2 + 12t + 32$

8. $s^2 - 11s + 24$ **12.** $y^2 - 17y + 30$ **16.** $n^2 - 15n + 50$

9. $t^2 - 9t + 8$ **13.** $u^2 - 11u + 18$ **17.** $s^2 - 14s + 33$

10. $k^2 + 12k + 20$ **14.** $n^2 + 14n + 24$ **18.** $p^2 + 13p + 12$

Written Exercises

Factor each trinomial and check by multiplication.

A   **1.** $n^2 + 8n + 7$ **7.** $a^2 - 9a + 8$ **13.** $14 + 9k + k^2$

  2. $t^2 + 7t + 6$ **8.** $b^2 - 7b + 12$ **14.** $21 + 10d + d^2$

  3. $y^2 + 5y + 4$ **9.** $x^2 + 7x + 10$ **15.** $42 - 13u + u^2$

  4. $y^2 + 9y + 8$ **10.** $x^2 + 11x + 18$ **16.** $48 - 14v + v^2$

  5. $k^2 - 7k + 6$ **11.** $n^2 - 15n + 26$ **17.** $x^2 + 8xy + 7y^2$

  6. $r^2 - 6r + 8$ **12.** $p^2 - 23p + 60$ **18.** $r^2 + 8rs + 15s^2$

19. $m^2 - 11mn + 28n^2$ **22.** $x^2 - 21xy + 20y^2$

20. $p^2 + 14pq + 24q^2$ **23.** $a^2 - 26ab + 48b^2$

21. $r^2 - 23rt + 76t^2$ **24.** $m^2 - 29mn + 120n^2$

Determine all integral values for k for which the trinomial can be factored over the set of binomials with integral coefficients. In Exercises 29–32, list positive values only.

SAMPLE. $x^2 + kx + 15$

Solution: 15 can be factored into a product of two integers as follows:

$$1 \cdot 15, \quad 3 \cdot 5, \quad (-1)(-15), \quad (-3)(-5).$$

The corresponding values of k are 16, 8, -16, -8.   **Answer.**

B   **25.** $y^2 + ky + 10$ **28.** $y^2 + ky + 4$ **31.** $y^2 + 6y + k$

  26. $z^2 + kz + 12$ **29.** $z^2 + 3z + k$ **32.** $z^2 + 7z + k$

  27. $x^2 + kx + 20$ **30.** $x^2 + 5x + k$

Factor each expression.

C   **33.** $(x + y)^2 - 4(x + y) + 3$ **35.** $(x - 3)^2 + 6(x - 3) + 8$

  34. $(a + b)^2 + 5(a + b) + 6$ **36.** $(5 - y)^2 - 3(5 - y) + 2$

Show that each polynomial is prime over the set of polynomials with integral coefficients.

37. $x^2 + 3x + 5$ **38.** $y^2 - 2y + 2$ **39.** $x^2 + 1$

7-9   Factoring the Product of a Binomial Sum and a Binomial Difference

In the preceding section you factored trinomials in which the constant term was positive. You will now learn how to factor trinomials in which the constant term is negative.

When a negative integer is written as a product of two integers, one factor must be a positive integer and the other, a negative integer. For example,

$$-30 = (-1)(30) = (-2)(15) = (-3)(10) = (-5)(6)$$
$$= (1)(-30) = (2)(-15) = (3)(-10) = (5)(-6)$$

To factor $a^2 + 3a - 10$, you proceed as before to look for r and s such that

$$a^2 + 3a - 10 = (a + r)(a + s) = a^2 + (r + s)a + rs.$$

Your clues are

$$rs = -10 \quad \text{and} \quad r + s = 3.$$

Here, the product, rs, is negative, indicating that one integer, say r, must be positive, while the other, s, must be negative. But, $r + s$ is *positive*, which means that r, the positive member of the pair, must have the greater absolute value. On the basis of these conclusions, consider:

$$10(-1) \qquad \text{and} \qquad 5(-2)$$
$$\uparrow \ \uparrow \qquad\qquad\qquad \uparrow \ \uparrow$$
$$r \ \ s \qquad\qquad\qquad\quad r \ \ s$$
$$r + s = 9 \qquad\qquad r + s = 3 \ \checkmark$$
$$\therefore a^2 + 3a - 10 = (a + 5)(a - 2).$$

On the other hand, in factoring $a^2 - 3a - 10$, you would search for two integers of opposite direction, but with a *negative* sum. Therefore, the negative integer would have to have the greater absolute value. This trinomial is factored:

$$a^2 - 3a - 10 = (a - 5)(a + 2).$$

Written Exercises

Factor each trinomial and check by multiplication.

A

1. $a^2 + a - 6$	**9.** $z^2 - 4z - 21$	**17.** $a^2 - 2ab - 8b^2$
2. $b^2 + 5b - 6$	**10.** $t^2 + 5t - 14$	**18.** $c^2 + 3cd - 10d^2$
3. $x^2 - 2x - 3$	**11.** $x^2 + x - 56$	**19.** $p^2 - 5pq - 24q^2$
4. $y^2 - 4y - 5$	**12.** $y^2 - 2y - 63$	**20.** $u^2 + 6uv - 55v^2$
5. $c^2 - 3c - 10$	**13.** $a^2 + a - 20$	**21.** $r^2 - 10rs - 24s^2$
6. $k^2 + k - 12$	**14.** $c^2 - c - 42$	**22.** $m^2 + 16mn - 36n^2$
7. $u^2 + 7u - 18$	**15.** $x^2 - 4x - 60$	**23.** $x^2 - 9xy - 36y^2$
8. $v^2 - 3v - 18$	**16.** $z^2 + 5z - 50$	**24.** $s^2 - 5st - 24t^2$

Determine all integral values of k for which the given trinomial can be factored over the set of binomials with integral coefficients.

B

25. $x^2 + kx - 10$	**27.** $z^2 + kz - 12$	**29.** $r^2 + kr - 24$
26. $y^2 + ky - 8$	**28.** $t^2 + kt - 15$	**30.** $p^2 + kp - 36$

Find the two negative integers k of least absolute value for which each trinomial can be factored.

31. $x^2 + x + k$	**33.** $z^2 - 3z + k$	**35.** $v^2 + 2v + k$
32. $y^2 - 2y + k$	**34.** $u^2 + u + k$	**36.** $t^2 + 3t + k$

Factor each expression.

C

37. $(s + t)^2 - 5(s + t) - 66$	**39.** $(y - 2)^2 + 4(y - 2) - 45$
38. $(x + y)^2 + 3(x + y) - 70$	**40.** $(3 - z)^2 - 2(3 - z) - 35$

7–10 General Method of Factoring Quadratic Trinomials

To factor a quadratic trinomial product whose quadratic term has a coefficient other than 1, you can use inspection and trial, as in the following.

EXAMPLE. Factor $15x^2 - 31x + 10$.

Solution:

First clue: The constant term is positive, and the linear term is negative. $\therefore$ both binomial factors are *differences*.

Second clue: The product of the linear terms of the binomial factors is $15x^2$, and the product of the constant terms of the binomial factors is 10.

(cont. on p. 272)

The possible pairs of factors of $15x^2$ are

$$x \text{ and } 15x, \qquad 3x \text{ and } 5x.$$

The possible pairs of factors of 10 are

$$-1 \text{ and } -10, \qquad -2 \text{ and } -5.$$

∴ the possibilities to consider are as follows:

Possible Factors	Corresponding Linear Terms
$(x - 1)(15x - 10)$	$-10x - 15x = -25x$
$(x - 10)(15x - 1)$	$-x - 150x = -151x$
$(x - 2)(15x - 5)$	$-5x - 30x = -35x$
$(x - 5)(15x - 2)$	$-2x - 75x = -77x$
$(3x - 1)(5x - 10)$	$-30x - 5x = -35x$
$(3x - 10)(5x - 1)$	$-3x - 50x = -53x$
$(3x - 2)(5x - 5)$	$-15x - 10x = -25x$
$(3x - 5)(5x - 2)$	$-6x - 25x = -31x$ ✓

Third clue: The linear term of the trinomial is $-31x$. Only the last possibility satisfies all three clues.

$$\therefore 15x^2 - 31x + 10 = (3x - 5)(5x - 2). \quad \textbf{Answer.}$$

Check: $(3x - 5)(5x - 2) = 15x^2 - 31x + 10$ ✓

As you gain experience, you will find that often you will not need to write down all the possibilities before discovering the factors.

EXAMPLE 2.   Factor $6x^2 - 7x - 3$.

Solution: $\begin{aligned} 6x^2 - 7x - 3 &= (\quad - \quad)(\quad + \quad) \\ &= (\quad - 3)(\quad + 1) \\ &= (2x - 3)(3x + 1). \quad \textbf{Answer.} \end{aligned}$

Check: $(2x - 3)(3x + 1) = 6x^2 - 7x - 3$ ✓

Written Exercises

Factor each trinomial and check.

A
1. $2x^2 + 3x + 1$
2. $2z^2 + 5z + 3$
3. $3t^2 + 7t + 2$
4. $3k^2 + 8k + 5$
5. $5r^2 - 7r + 2$
6. $6s^2 - 11s + 3$

7. $3y^2 + 7y - 6$
8. $6x^2 - 13x - 5$
9. $4t^2 - 11t - 3$
10. $4k^2 + 4k - 15$
11. $5n^2 - 3n - 2$
12. $7x^2 + 9x + 2$

13. $7x^2 - 10x + 3$
14. $2y^2 - 9y - 5$
15. $5k^2 - 2k - 7$
16. $8r^2 + 2r - 3$
17. $2y^2 + xy - 6x^2$
18. $3b^2 - 17ab - 6a^2$

B **19.** $12x^2 + 11x - 15$ **23.** $6u^2 - u - 12$

 20. $8y^2 - 27y - 20$ **24.** $24v^2 + 5v - 36$

 21. $6t^2 + 25t + 14$ **25.** $10y^2 + 11yz - 18z^2$

 22. $18z^2 - 19z - 12$ **26.** $6a^2 - 47ab - 63b^2$

C **27.** $8(x + y)^2 + 14(x + y) - 15$ **29.** $24(x - 1)^2 - 14(x - 1) - 3$

 28. $10(a - b)^2 - 11(a - b) - 6$ **30.** $14(2 - x)^2 - 15(2 - x) - 11$

7–11   Combining Several Types of Factoring

In factoring a polynomial, first look for the greatest monomial factor. Sometimes a monomial factor conceals:

The difference of two squares	*A trinomial square*	*A trinomial product*
$8y^3 - 18y$	$-t^2 + 8t - 16$	$bz^3 - 6bz^2 + 5bz$
$= 2y(4y^2 - 9)$	$= -1(t^2 - 8t + 16)$	$= bz(z^2 - 6z + 5)$
$= 2y(2y - 3)(2y + 3)$	$= -1(t - 4)^2$	$= bz(z - 5)(z - 1)$

To factor a polynomial product:

1. Find the greatest monomial factor, and then consider the remaining polynomial factor.

2. If a factor is a binomial, is it the difference of two squares? You can factor such a binomial.

3. If a factor is a trinomial, is it a square? You can factor a trinomial square.

4. If a factor is a trinomial that is not a square, assume that it is the product of two binomials, and search for them. Of course, you cannot factor a prime trinomial. But never decide that an expression is prime until you have tried all the ways you know of factoring it.

5. If a factor is neither a binomial nor a trinomial, can you show a common polynomial factor by grouping? If you can, try to factor each of the resulting factors as in Steps 2, 3, and 4.

6. Write *all* the factors, including any monomial factor. The monomial factor may be a product, but all other factors should be prime; the *factoring should be complete*.

7. As a check, always multiply the factors to see that the product is the original expression; the *factoring should be correct*.

Oral Exercises

In Written Exercises 1–24, state the common monomial factor if any.

Written Exercises

Factor if possible. Check by multiplication.

[A]
1. $4x^2 - 4$
2. $3z^2 - 12$
3. $2y^2 + 6y + 4$
4. $3t^2 - 6t + 3$
5. $7x^2 + 13x - 2$
6. $5y^2 + 13y + 6$
7. $-3a^3 - 3ab^2$
8. $2cx^2 + 2c$

9. $ar^2 - 3ar - 4a$
10. $16b^2z^2 + 8bz + 1$
11. $6t^2 - 11t + 5$
12. $7k^2 + 21k - 28$
13. $50r^2 - 20r + 2$
14. $p^3 + 5p^2 + 4p$
15. $3y^2 - 2y - 5$
16. $12c^2 - 24c - 15$

17. $144y^2 - 49x^4$
18. $169a^4 - 36b^2$
19. $-15 + n + 6n^2$
20. $-5 - 28k + 12k^2$
21. $-4s - s^2 + 21$
22. $2t - 48 + t^2$
23. $28x^2 + 87x + 54$
24. $6y^2 - 28y - 480$

[B]
25. $6a^3b - 26a^2b^2 - 20ab^3$
26. $30c^2 + 4cd - 2d^2$
27. $42m^2n - 24mn^2 - 18n^3$
28. $12a^2 - 2ab - 24b^2$
29. $6s^4 - 19s^3 + 10s^2$
30. $2p^3 + 11p^2q + 12pq^2$

31. $z^4 - r^4$
32. $t^4 - 2t^2 + 1$
33. $z^4 - 10z + 9$
34. $n^4 - 17n + 16$
35. $-42a - 27az - 3az^2$
36. $-16a^2b - 10a^2br - a^2br^2$

37. $u^2(u - 3) - 10u(u - 3) - 24(u - 3)$
38. $n^2(n + 2) + 2n(n + 2) - 15(n + 2)$
39. $2x^2(x + 5) - 3x(x + 5) - 9(x + 5)$
40. $3y^2(y - 1) + 10y(y - 1) - 8(y - 1)$

[C]
41. $4x^2(x^2 - 9) - 16x(x^2 - 9) + 15(x^2 - 9)$
42. $1 - z^2 - 5z(1 - z^2) + 6z^2(1 - z^2)$

43. $(3x^2 - 2)^2 - x^2$
44. $(x^2 - 6)^2 - 6x(x^2 - 6) + 5x^2$
45. $5bz^2 - bw^2 + bz^2 - 5bw^2$
46. $k^2t^2 - 9s^2 - 9t^2 + k^2s^2$
47. $-20x^2 + 43xy - 14y^2$

48. $c^4 - 7c^2 + 6$
49. $x^4 + x^2 - 42$
50. $x^3 - x^2 + x - 1$
51. $n^3 + n^2 - n - 1$
52. $3x^4 - 288$

In Exercises 53–56, the given binomial is a factor of the trinomial over the set of polynomials with integral coefficients. Determine c in each case.

53. $2x - 3$; $10x^2 - 3x + c$
54. $3y + 2$; $21y^2 - y + c$

55. $5w + 1$; $cw^2 + 3w - 1$
56. $n - 3$; $cn^2 - 5n - 21$

APPLICATIONS OF FACTORING

7–12   Working with Factors Whose Product Is Zero

If you know that the product of two numbers is zero, what can you say about the numbers?

First, if $ab = 0$ and $a \neq 0$, you can show that $b = 0$ as follows:

Since $a \neq 0$, the reciprocal of a, $\dfrac{1}{a}$, exists and is not zero. Using the multiplication property of equality (page 123), multiply each of the terms ab and 0 by $\dfrac{1}{a}$:

$$\frac{1}{a}(ab) = \frac{1}{a} \cdot 0.$$

$$\frac{1}{a}(ab) = \frac{1}{a}(0)$$

On the left, use the associative axiom, axiom of reciprocals (page 97), and the multiplicative axiom of 1 (page 92).

$$\left(\frac{1}{a} \cdot a\right) b = 0$$

$$1 \cdot b = 0$$

$$b = 0$$

On the right, use the multiplicative property of 0 (page 92).

Similarly, if $ab = 0$ and $b \neq 0$, you can show that $a = 0$.

On the other hand, if either $a = 0$ or $b = 0$, then $ab = 0$ by the multiplicative property of 0. Thus, you have:

Zero-Product Property of Real Numbers

For all real numbers a and b, $ab = 0$ if and only if $a = 0$ or $b = 0$.

You can use this property to find solutions of equations in which one member is 0 and the other member is in factored form. For example, the solutions of the equation

$$(x - 3)(x + 4) = 0$$

are those real numbers for which one or the other factor in the left-hand member is 0. These values are, by inspection, 3 and -4. If you could not determine these values by inspection, you could have written the equivalent compound sentence

$$x - 3 = 0 \quad \text{or} \quad x + 4 = 0$$

and solved each equation for x. The solution set in either case is $\{3, -4\}$.

Oral Exercises

State all values of x for which each sentence becomes a true statement, and justify your answer.

SAMPLE. $x(x - 2) = 0$.

Solution: 0 and 2, because for $x = 0$ the statement is "$0 \cdot (-2) = 0$," which is true, and for $x = 2$ the statement is "$2 \cdot (0) = 0$," which is true.

1. $2(x - 5) = 0$

2. $3(y - 4) = 0$

3. $z(z - 3) = 0$

4. $0(t - 1) = 0$

5. $(t - 2)(t - 3) = 0$

6. $(k + 1)(k - 1) = 0$

7. $(r + 2)(r - 3) = 0$

8. $(a + 1)(a + 2) = 0$

9. $(b + 4)(b + 3) = 0$

10. $(d + 6)(d - 6) = 0$

11. $0(n + 1)(n - 2) = 0$

12. $-5(z + 3)(z - 4) = 0$

Written Exercises

Solve each equation.

A

1. $x(x - 5) = 0$

2. $3z(z + 7) = 0$

3. $(t - 6)(t - 8) = 0$

4. $(p - 10)(p - 3) = 0$

5. $(k + 2)(k - 7) = 0$

6. $(y + 6)(y - 8) = 0$

7. $(n + 4)(2n - 3) = 0$

8. $(m - 6)(3m - 1) = 0$

9. $(2r - 1)(3r - 7) = 0$

10. $(4a - 3)(7a - 2) = 0$

11. $(2b + 7)(2b + 5) = 0$

12. $(9d + 2)(6d + 1) = 0$

13. $2x(x - 1)(x + 3) = 0$

14. $3r(r + 6)(r - 5) = 0$

15. $0(p + 7)(3p - 2) = 0$

16. $0(m + 6)(5m - 8) = 0$

SAMPLE. $\left(\dfrac{1}{x} - \dfrac{2}{3}\right)\left(\dfrac{3}{x} + \dfrac{1}{2}\right) = 0$

Solution: For the given equation to become a true statement either

$$\frac{1}{x} - \frac{2}{3} = 0 \quad \text{or} \quad \frac{3}{x} + \frac{1}{2} = 0. \text{ Thus:}$$

$$\frac{1}{x} - \frac{2}{3} = 0 \qquad\qquad \frac{3}{x} + \frac{1}{2} = 0$$

$$\frac{1}{x} = \frac{2}{3} \qquad\qquad \frac{3}{x} = -\frac{1}{2}$$

Taking reciprocals, $x = \frac{3}{2}$

Taking reciprocals, $\dfrac{x}{3} = -2$

$$x = -6$$

Check: $\dfrac{1}{\frac{3}{2}} - \dfrac{2}{3} = \dfrac{2}{3} - \dfrac{2}{3} = 0; \quad \dfrac{3}{-6} + \dfrac{1}{2} = -\dfrac{1}{2} + \dfrac{1}{2} = 0.$ ✓

$\therefore$ the solution set is $\{\frac{3}{2}, -6\}$. **Answer.**

B **17.** $4\left(\dfrac{1}{3} - \dfrac{2}{t}\right) = 0$

18. $-3\left(\dfrac{5}{4} + \dfrac{3}{k}\right) = 0$

19. $\left(\dfrac{2}{v} - 3\right)\left(\dfrac{1}{v} + 4\right) = 0$

20. $\left(\dfrac{3}{x} - 7\right)\left(\dfrac{1}{x} + 6\right) = 0$

21. $\left(\dfrac{2}{y} - \dfrac{1}{7}\right)\left(-\dfrac{1}{y} + \dfrac{3}{8}\right) = 0$

22. $\left(\dfrac{5}{a} + \dfrac{3}{7}\right)\left(\dfrac{1}{a} - \dfrac{5}{8}\right) = 0$

23. $\left(\dfrac{3}{5} - \dfrac{7}{n}\right)\left(\dfrac{5}{3} + \dfrac{2}{n}\right) = 0$

24. $\left(6 - \dfrac{2}{3x}\right)\left(5 + \dfrac{3}{2x}\right) = 0$

7–13 Solving Polynomial Equations by Factoring

A **polynomial equation** is an equation whose left and right members are polynomials. A polynomial equation is in **standard form** when one of its members is zero and the other is a polynomial in simple form (page 206) in which all similar terms have been combined and the terms have been arranged in descending powers of the variable. Thus, the standard form for

$$y^2 - 10y = 24$$

is

$$y^2 - 10y - 24 = 0.$$

This equation is of degree two and is called a **quadratic equation**. The **degree of a polynomial equation** is the greatest of the degrees of the terms of the equation when written in standard form. An equation of degree one, like

$$3x + 2 = x - 5,$$

is called a **linear equation**, while an equation like

$$z^3 = 2z - 3z$$

whose degree is three, is a **cubic equation**. If you transform a polynomial equation into standard form, and if you can factor the left member, then you can obtain its roots by finding the numbers for which at least one of those factors is zero.

EXAMPLE 1. Solve $y^2 - 10y = 24.$

Solution:

1. Transform the equation into standard form.

2. Factor the left-hand member.

3. Determine solutions by inspection (12 and −2) or

3a. Set each factor equal to zero and solve the resulting linear equations.

$$y^2 - 10y = 24$$
$$y^2 - 10y - 24 = 0$$

$$(y - 12)(y + 2) = 0$$

$$\begin{array}{c|c} y - 12 = 0 & y + 2 = 0 \\ y = 12 & y = -2 \end{array}$$

(*cont. on p. 278*)

4. Check in original equation: $y^2 - 10y = 24$

$$(12)^2 - 10\,(12) \stackrel{?}{=} 24 \qquad\qquad (-2)^2 - 10\,(-2) \stackrel{?}{=} 24$$
$$144 - 120 \stackrel{?}{=} 24 \qquad\qquad 4 + 20 \stackrel{?}{=} 24$$
$$24 = 24 \checkmark \qquad\qquad 24 = 24 \checkmark$$

∴ the solution set is $\{12, -2\}$. **Answer.**

Several situations may arise when you try to solve a polynomial equation by factoring. First, the polynomial may have a common numerical factor. Since such a factor would be a nonzero number, you should eliminate it by transforming the equation by division (page 127). Second, two or more factors may be identical. Such factors will yield a *double* or *multiple root*, which should be written only once in the roster of the solution set.

Of course, not all polynomial equations can be solved in this way, because it may not be possible to factor the nonzero polynomial member.

EXAMPLE 2. Solve $5r^2 - 30r + 45 = 0$.

Solution: The equation is in standard form. $5r^2 - 30r + 45 = 0$

1. Divide each member by 5. $r^2 - 6r + 9 = 0$
2. Factor the left-hand member. $(r - 3)(r - 3) = 0$
3. Determine solution by inspection or
3a. Set each factor equal to zero and solve $r - 3 = 0 \quad | \quad r - 3 = 0$
     the resulting linear equations. $r = 3 \quad | \quad\quad r = 3$
4. Check in original equation: $5\,(3)^2 - 30\,(3) + 45 \stackrel{?}{=} 0$
                                      $45 - 90 + 45 \stackrel{?}{=} 0$
                                                $0 = 0 \checkmark$

∴ the solution set is $\{3\}$. **Answer.**

If you have a common monomial factor which contains a variable, you should not eliminate it by division. Such a factor may be zero and give you a root.

EXAMPLE 3. Solve $x^3 = 2x^2 + 8x$.

Solution: $x^3 = 2x^2 + 8x$

1. Transform the equation into stan- $x^3 - 2x^2 - 8x = 0$
     dard form.
2. Factor the left-hand member. $x(x^2 - 2x - 8) = 0$
                                    $x\,(x - 4)(x + 2) = 0$
3. Determine solutions by inspection
     $(0, 4, -2)$, or

3a. Set each factor equal to 0 and $\quad x = 0 \mid x - 4 = 0 \mid x + 2 = 0$
solve the resulting equations. $\qquad\qquad\qquad x = 4 \mid \quad x = -2$

4. Checkin the original equation: $\qquad x^3 = 2x^2 + 8x$

$$(0)^3 \overset{?}{=} 2\,(0)^2 + 8\,(0) \mid \quad (4)^3 \overset{?}{=} 2\,(4)^2 + 8\,(4) \mid \quad (-2)^3 \overset{?}{=} 2\,(-2)^2 + 8\,(-2)$$

$$0 \overset{?}{=} 0 + 0 \qquad\qquad 64 \overset{?}{=} 32 + 32 \qquad\qquad -8 \overset{?}{=} 8 - 16$$

$$0 = 0 \ \checkmark \qquad\qquad 64 = 64 \ \checkmark \qquad\qquad -8 = -8 \ \checkmark$$

$\therefore$ the solution set is $\{0, 4, -2\}$. **Answer.**

Written Exercises

Find the solution set of each equation.

A

1. $x^2 + x - 6 = 0$
2. $y^2 - 2y + 1 = 0$
3. $r^2 + 2r - 3 = 0$
4. $t^2 - 3t - 10 = 0$
5. $k^2 - 16 = 0$
6. $p^2 - 25 = 0$
7. $x^2 - 5x = 0$
8. $s^2 + 3s = 0$
9. $n^2 = 6n + 7$
10. $q^2 - 8 = 2q$
11. $h^2 + h = 56$

12. $w^2 - 2w = 15$
13. $r^2 + 15 = -8r$
14. $z^2 + 18 = -11z$
15. $4n^2 + 4n = -1$
16. $9t^2 - 6t + 1 = 0$
17. $2s^2 = s + 6$
18. $3x^2 + 5x = 2$
19. $2n^2 + 9n + 10 = 0$
20. $3t^2 + 13t = -14$
21. $3v^2 = 198 + 15v$
22. $2t^2 = 216 + 6t$

23. $6z^2 = 34z - 20$
24. $20x^2 = 22x - 6$
25. $10 = 17n - 3n^2$

26. $11q = 3 + 10q^2$
27. $10y^2 = 75 - 35y$
28. $8c^2 = 22c + 6$

29. $4y = y^2$
30. $6x^2 = -x$
31. $r^2 + 9 = 6r$

B

32. $p^4 - 5p^2 + 4 = 0$
33. $t^4 - 13t^2 + 36 = 0$
34. $2d^3 - d^2 = 10d$

35. $10c^3 = 18c - 3c^2$
36. $4k^3 - 12k^2 + 9k = 0$
37. $3a^3 - 6a^2 + 3a = 0$

C

38. $(z - 4)(z + 3) = -10$
39. $(b - 5)(b + 2) = -12$

40. $(r - 2)(r + 1) = r(2 - r)$
41. $p(3p + 2) = (p + 2)^2$

Find an equation of the lowest degree having the given solution set.

SAMPLE. $z \in \{2, -1\}$.

Solution: Since $z = 2$ or $z = -1$, you have $z - 2 = 0$ or $z + 1 = 0$.
$\therefore (z - 2)(z + 1) = 0$ and $z^2 - z - 2 = 0$. **Answer.**

42. $x \in \{3, 6\}$
43. $t \in \{5, -7\}$

44. $p \in \{0, 2, 5\}$
45. $q \in \{-3, 0, 3\}$

46. $p \in \{-1, 1, 3\}$
47. $y \in \{-3, -2, 2, 3\}$

7–14   Using Factoring in Problem Solving

With the ability to solve polynomial equations by factoring, you can solve a wider variety of problems. However, because polynomial equations usually have more than one solution, you must exercise your judgment and reject answers (even when they are solutions of the equation you have set up) which are not sensible in the light of the conditions of the problem.

EXAMPLE 1.   Mr. Carlton wishes to make a pan by cutting squares from each corner of a 16-inch by 26-inch rectangular sheet of tin and folding up the sides. What should be the length of the side of each square if the base of the pan is to have an area of 200 square inches?

Solution:

1 ▶   Let x = length (in inches) of edge of square.

Then $26 - 2x$ = length (in inches) of base of pan,

and $16 - 2x$ = width (in inches) of base of pan.

2 ▶ $(26 - 2x)(16 - 2x) = 200$

3 ▶ $416 - 84x + 4x^2 = 200$
$4x^2 - 84x + 216 = 0$
$x^2 - 21x + 54 = 0$
$(x - 18)(x - 3) = 0$

$x - 18 = 0 \mid x - 3 = 0$
$\quad x = 18 \mid \quad x = 3$
(Rejected)

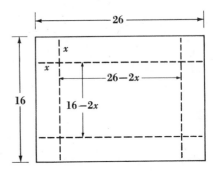

Although 18 is a solution of the equation, you reject it because you cannot cut an 18-inch square from a rectangle only 16 inches wide.

4 ▶   *Check:*   If 3-inch squares are cut from each corner and the sides folded up, will the base have an area of 200 square inches?

$(26 - 6)(16 - 6) \overset{?}{=} 200$

$(20)(10) \overset{?}{=} 200$

$200 = 200 \checkmark$

∴ the length of the sides of each square should be 3 inches.   **Answer.**

The next problem also has only one solution. The problem is especially interesting because it employs a most important rule:

$$d = rt + 16t^2$$

This rule gives a good approximation to the distance (in feet) covered in t seconds by an object falling freely toward the ground with an initial velocity of r feet per second.

EXAMPLE 2. From the top of a 200-foot building, an object is thrown toward the ground with an initial velocity of 40 feet per second. After how many seconds will the object hit the ground?

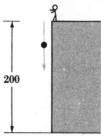

200

Solution:

1▶ Let t = number of seconds it takes the object to reach the ground,

d = distance fallen = 200 (feet),

r = rate at which object starts to fall = 40 (feet per second).

2▶ $\quad d = rt + 16t^2$

$\quad 200 = 40t + 16t^2$

3▶ $16t^2 + 40t - 200 = 0$

$\quad 2t^2 + 5t - 25 = 0$

$\quad (2t - 5)(t + 5) = 0$

$2t - 5 = 0$	$t + 5 = 0$	The solution -5 is rejected because the
$2t = 5$	$t = -5$	object could not have hit the ground
$t = \frac{5}{2}$	(Rejected)	before it was thrown.

4▶ Does an object take $\frac{5}{2}$ seconds to fall 200 feet when it starts falling at the rate of 40 feet per second?

$\quad d = rt + 16t^2$

$\quad 200 \overset{?}{=} 40(\frac{5}{2}) + 16(\frac{5}{2})^2$

$\quad 200 \overset{?}{=} 100 \ \ + 16(\frac{25}{4})$

$\quad 200 \overset{?}{=} 100 \ \ + 100$

$\quad 200 = 200 \ \checkmark$

∴ the object strikes the ground after $2\frac{1}{2}$ seconds. **Answer.**

Remember that you solve a problem by reasoning that if a number satisfies the requirements stated in the problem, then that number must satisfy the equation obtained in Step 2. On the other hand, just because a number satisfies the equation, you cannot conclude that the number will satisfy the problem. The solution set of the equation gives the *possible solutions* of the problem. By checking these possibilities in the statement of the problem, you find the *actual solutions* of the problem.

Problems

Solve each problem, rejecting solutions that do not meet the conditions of the problem.

1. Find two consecutive positive integers whose product is 56.

2. Find two consecutive positive integers whose product is 132.

3. The sum of the squares of two consecutive negative integers is 113. Find the integers.

4. The sum of the squares of two consecutive negative odd integers is 130. Find the integers.

5. If the length of a rectangle is 3 feet greater than the width and it has an area of 28 square feet, find its dimensions.

6. The length of a rectangle is 2 inches greater than twice its width, and its area is 60 square inches. Find its dimensions.

7. An object is thrown downward from the top of a 280-foot tower at a rate of 24 feet per second. In how many seconds does it hit the ground?

8. From an airplane flying at an altitude of 2560 feet, an object is thrown downward at a rate of 96 feet per second. In how many seconds will it strike the ground?

9. The front of a house is in the shape of a triangle on top of a rectangle. If the rectangle is twice as long as it is tall, the altitude of the triangular part is 5 feet less than the length of its base, and the total area of the front is 1500 square feet, find the width of the house.

10. The rectangular base of the Mark VII computer is 3 times as long as it is wide. The Mark VII is an improved version of the old Mark VI which was 1 foot longer and 2 feet wider than the Mark VII. If the base area of the Mark VII is 13 square feet less than that of the Mark VI, find the dimensions of the Mark VII.

11. The perimeter of a rectangle is 60 inches and the area is 161 square inches. Find the dimensions of the rectangle.

12. The sum of the squares of three consecutive integers is 77. Find the integers.

The equation $h = rt - 16t^2$ is needed to solve the next four problems. It gives the height h, in feet, that an object will reach in t seconds when it is projected upward with a starting speed of r feet per second.

13. An object is projected upward at 160 feet per second. In how many seconds will the object be 400 feet above the ground?

14. A ball is thrown upward at 80 feet per second. In how many seconds will the object be 100 feet above the ground?

B **15.** A ball is thrown upward at 64 feet per second. John is on top of a building 48 feet in height and catches the ball on its way down. How many seconds had the ball been in the air when John caught it?

16. A projectile is fired upward at 1600 feet per second. In how many seconds will the projectile hit the ground?

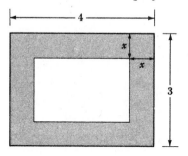

Ex. 17

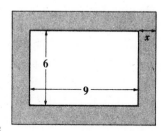

Ex. 18

17. A strip of masking tape is placed around the edges of a rectangular window prior to painting its frame. If the window measures 3 feet by 4 feet, and the masking tape covers $\frac{1}{2}$ the area of the window, how wide is the tape?

18. The area of a concrete walk around a rectangular fishpond is equal to the area of the pond. If the pond measures 6 yards by 9 yards, find the width of the walk.

19. Let f be a function with domain $\Re$ such that $f: x \rightarrow 2x^2 + 5x + 8$. Determine the least value of x such that $f(x) = 11$.

20. Let g be a function whose domain is the set of positive numbers. Given that $g: t \rightarrow 6t^2 + t - 2$, determine the value of t such that $g(t) = 0$.

21. The sum S of the first n consecutive natural numbers is given by the formula $S = \frac{1}{2}n(n + 1)$. How many such natural numbers must be added to give a sum of 28?

22. In a plane, consider a set of p points no three of which lie on a line. The number N of segments that can be drawn connecting all possible pairs of these points is given by the formula $N = \frac{1}{2}p(p - 1)$. How many points are there in the particular set for which the total number of segments joining pairs of points is 21?

23. What is the error in the following argument? The equation

$$x^2 + 4x + 3 = 1$$

is equivalent to

$$(x + 1)(x + 3) = 1 \cdot 1$$

Hence, the given equation is equivalent to:

$$x + 1 = 1 \quad \text{or} \quad x + 3 = 1$$
$$x = 0 \qquad\qquad x = -2$$

∴ its solution set is $\{0, -2\}$.

24. A picture 15 inches wide and 20 inches long is enclosed in a frame of uniform width and whose area is two-thirds that of the picture. Find the width of the frame.

25. The sides of 2 cubes differ by 2 inches and their volumes differ by 152 cubic inches. Find the length of a side of the smaller cube.

26. A farmer makes a rectangular enclosure using a stone wall for one side and 100 feet of fence for the other three sides. Find the dimensions of the enclosure if the area enclosed is 1200 square feet.

$\boxed{\text{C}}$ **27.** Show that the sum of the squares of any two consecutive integers is 1 more than a multiple of 4. (*Hint:* Let n and $n + 1$ denote the integers. Also use the fact that one of every two consecutive integers is even.)

28. Show that the square of an odd integer is 1 more than a multiple of 8. (*Hint:* If n denotes an integer, then $2n + 1$ denotes an odd integer. Square $2n + 1$ and use the fact that one of every two consecutive integers is even.)

● CHAPTER SUMMARY ●

Inventory of Structure and Method

1. To find the greatest common factor of a number of integers, factor each as a product of prime numbers. The factors of a polynomial with integral coefficients usually are limited to positive integers and polynomials with integral coefficients.

2. To factor a polynomial, use the distributive axiom to form a product of the greatest monomial factor, if any, and the remaining polynomial factor. Next, consider the possibilities of factoring this polynomial.

3. Certain **special products** should be read and factored at sight:

The sum of two numbers times their difference:

$$(a + b)(a - b) = a^2 - b^2$$

The square of a binomial sum: $\quad (a + b)^2 = (a^2 + 2ab + b^2)$

The square of a binomial difference: $(a - b)^2 = (a^2 - 2ab + b^2)$

4. **To factor trinomial products** such as $ax^2 + bx + c, a > 0$:
   If b and c are positive, both binomial factors are sums; if b is negative and c is positive, both binomial factors are differences; if c is negative, the binomial factors are a sum and a difference. By inspection and trial, find factors of the quadratic and constant terms which produce binomials whose product contains a linear term with coefficient b.

5. **Factoring** must be complete; each polynomial factor must be prime over the set of polynomials with appropriate coefficients. The correctness of factoring should be checked by multiplication.

6. **To solve a polynomial equation by factoring:** Transform the equation into standard form with the right member zero and the left member a polynomial in descending powers of the variable. Factor the left member. Set each factor equal to zero, applying the principle that a product is zero if and only if at least one of its factors is zero. Solve the resulting linear equations. Check each possible root in the original equation. Write the solution set, listing multiple roots only once.

7. Problems leading to quadratic equations may have two answers. However, some problems have only one answer even though the equation has two roots. Therefore, all possible answers must be checked against the wording of the problem.

Vocabulary and Spelling

Review the meaning of each term by reference to the page listed.

factoring a number (over a set of numbers) (*p. 249*)
prime number (*p. 249*)
prime factors (*p. 250*)
positive integral factors (*p. 250*)
greatest common factor (of two integers) (*p. 250*)
polynomial factoring (*p. 251*)
monomial factor (*p. 253*)
greatest monomial factor (of a polynomial) (*p. 253*)
factoring by grouping terms (*p. 253*)
trinomial square (*p. 260*)
quadratic term (*p. 265*)

linear term (*p. 265*)
constant term (*p. 265*)
quadratic polynomial (*p. 265*)
irreducible polynomial (over a set of polynomials) (*p. 268*)
prime polynomial (*p. 268*)
polynomial equation (*p. 277*)
standard form (*p. 277*)
degree of polynomial equation (*p. 277*)
linear equation (*p. 277*)
quadratic equation (*p. 277*)
cubic equation (*p. 277*)
multiple root (*p. 278*)

Chapter Test

7–1 **1.** Find the greatest common factor of 60 and 450.

2. $27a^2bc^2 = (-3abc^2)(\underline{\quad ?\quad})$

7–2 **3.** Write $45t^3 - 15t^2$ in factored form.

4. Write $z(z + 2) + 3(z + 2)$ in factored form.

5. Factor $x^3 - 15 - 3x^2 + 5x$.

7–3 **6.** $(-7y^4)^2 = \underline{\quad ?\quad}$ **7.** $(xy - 3)(xy + 3) = \underline{\quad ?\quad}$

Factor each expression.

7–4 **8.** $27x^2 - 48$ **9.** $-121 + z^2$

7–5 **10.** $(2z + 3u)^2 = \underline{\quad ?\quad}$ **11.** $(4a - 3b)^2 = \underline{\quad ?\quad}$

7–6 **12.** Factor $9c^2 + 12cd + 4d^2$.

7–7 **13.** Solve and check: $(4x + 3)(x - 2) = (2x + 1)^2 + 2$.

Factor each expression.

7–8 **14.** $x^2 + 5x + 6$ **15.** $x^2 - 8xy + 7y^2$

7–9 **16.** $t^2 - 4t - 21$ **17.** $p^2 + 4p - 12$

7–10 **18.** $3r^2 + 20r + 12$ **19.** $6a^2 + ab - 12b^2$

7–11 **20.** $20n^2 - 22n - 12$

Solve each equation and check.

7–12 **21.** $(y + 3)(y - 9) = 0$ **22.** $3z(3z + 8) = 0$

7–13 **23.** $t^2 = 88 - 3t$ **24.** $64k^2 - 25 = 0$

7–14 **25.** Find the dimensions of a rectangle with area 24 square feet if its length is 2 feet greater than twice its width.

Chapter Review

7–1 **Factoring in Algebra**   *Pages 249–252*

1. Express 276 as the product of its prime factors.

2. $-85t^2s = -5t(\underline{\quad ?\quad})$

3. The greatest common factor of 116 and 124 is $\underline{\quad ?\quad}$.

4. The greatest power of $3rs^2$ that is a factor of $54r^3s^7$ is $\underline{\quad ?\quad}$.

7–2 **Identifying Monomial Factors** *Pages 253–256*

 5. Factor $7a^2b + 14ab^2 - 28$. **6.** Factor $3z^4 + 3z^2t - 6z$.

 7. $y(y^2 + 2) + 3(y^2 + 2) = (y^2 + 2)(\underline{\ ?\ } + \underline{\ ?\ })$

Factor each expression.

 8. $z(z + 2) + 7(z + 2)$ **10.** $(3r + 2)(5r - 1) + (3r + 2)$

 9. $p^2 + pq + 2p + 2q$ **11.** $2uw - 6ux - 3vx + vw$

7–3 **Multiplying the Sum and Difference of Two Numbers**
    Pages 256–258

 12. $(-11)^2 = \underline{\ ?\ }$ **13.** $(x^2y^3)^2 = \underline{\ ?\ }$ **14.** $(-y^3)^2 = \underline{\ ?\ }$

 15. $(2x - 3)(2x + 3) = \underline{\ ?\ }$ **16.** $(h + \frac{1}{3}t)(h - \frac{1}{3}t) = \underline{\ ?\ }$

7–4 **Factoring the Difference of Two Squares** *Pages 258–259*

Factor each expression.

 17. $y^2 - 64$ **18.** $36t^2 - 1$ **19.** $4d^2 - 9$ **20.** $81t^4 - 1$

7–5 **Squaring a Binomial** *Pages 260–262*

 21. $(x + z)^2 = \underline{\ ?\ }$ **23.** $(3y - 2)^2 = \underline{\ ?\ }$

 22. $(x - z)^2 = \underline{\ ?\ }$ **24.** $(4u + 7t)^2 = \underline{\ ?\ }$

7–6 **Factoring a Trinomial Square** *Pages 263–264*

Factor each expression.

 25. $t^2 - 10t + 25$ **27.** $36k^2 - 60k + 25$

 26. $r^2 + 14r + 49$ **28.** $9p^2 + 42pq + 49q^2$

7–7 **Multiplying Binomials at Sight** *Pages 265–266*

 29. In $7t^2 - 8t + 4$, the linear term is $\underline{\ ?\ }$, the quadratic term is $\underline{\ ?\ }$, and the constant term is $\underline{\ ?\ }$.

 30. $(2y + 3)(y + 4) = \underline{\ ?\ }$

 31. $(7p + q)(2p - 3q) = \underline{\ ?\ }$

 32. Solve: $(2x - 1)(3x + 5) = 4(x + 1)(x - 3) + 2x^2 + 34$

7–8 **Factoring the Product of Binomial Sums or Differences**
    Pages 267–269

 33. To factor $y^2 + 10y + 16$ into the form $(y + r)(y + s)$, you must find integers r and s whose product is $\underline{\ ?\ }$ and whose sum is $\underline{\ ?\ }$.

Factor each expression.

34. $y^2 + 10y + 16$ **35.** $z^2 - 7z + 12$ **36.** $t^2 + 15t + 54$

7–9 **Factoring the Product of a Binomial Sum and a Binomial Difference**   *Pages 270–271*

37. To factor $n^2 + 5n - 14$ into the form $(n + r)(n + s)$, you must find integers r and s whose product is __?__ and whose sum is __?__.

Factor each expression.

38. $n^2 + 5n - 14$ **39.** $r^2 - 8r - 20$ **40.** $x^2 + 13x - 48$

7–10 **General Method of Factoring Quadratic Trinomials**   *Pages 271–273*

Factor each expression.

41. $3n^2 + 7n + 2$ **43.** $8z^2 - 14z + 3$
42. $5t^2 - 2t - 7$ **44.** $35x^2 - 22x + 3$

7–11 **Combining Several Types of Factoring**   *Pages 273–274*

Factor each expression.

45. $4t^3 - 36t$ **47.** $by^2 - 5byz - 50bz^2$
46. $-z^2 + 4z - 4$ **48.** $a^4 - 5a^2 + 4$

7–12 **Working with Factors Whose Product is Zero**   *Pages 275–277*

Solve each equation.

49. $5(n - 7) = 0$ **51.** $(m - 5)(m + 11) = 0$
50. $2t(t + 3) = 0$ **52.** $(3x - 7)(2x + 1) = 0$

7–13 **Solving Polynomial Equations by Factoring** *Pages 277–279*

Solve each equation.

53. $n^2 + n = 90$ **55.** $3b^2 = 12b - 12$
54. $y^2 - 20y - 300 = 0$ **56.** $n^3 = 4n^2 + 5n$

7–14 **Using Factoring in Problem Solving**   *Pages 280–283*

57. The sum of the squares of two consecutive positive even integers is 340. Find the integers.

58. Find two numbers whose sum is 13 and the sum of whose squares is 125.

 *Ancient Egyptian Problems*

Ancient Egyptians sometimes had to solve problems similar to some of those that you are learning to solve in this course. They did not have any general rules (or if they did have, such rules have not survived). What we do know of their work has come down to us as a handbook of special problems — each with its solution written out in great detail. This handbook (now known as the Rhind papyrus after a former owner) was put together about 3500 years ago by a scribe named Ahmes (meaning "child of the moon"). Here is one of Ahmes' number problems:

Heap, its two-thirds, its one-half, and its three-sevenths, added together, becomes thirty-three. What is the quantity?

Other problems dealt with everyday affairs, with bread and beer, with feeding livestock and storing grain. Some of these were practical; some were clearly just for fun. Here is one of the latter sort:

There are seven houses; in each are seven cats. Each cat kills seven mice. Each mouse would have eaten seven ears of spelt [wheat]. Each ear of spelt will produce seven hekats of grain. What is the total of these? [That is, how much grain was saved?]

A portion of the Rhind Papyrus *is shown below. This ancient book is now in the British Museum.*

Just for Fun

In ancient and medieval times, learned men called 6 a "perfect" number, whereas 8 was called "deficient" and 12 "excessive," depending on the sum of their *aliquot parts*. The **aliquot parts** of a number are all its factors except itself. Notice the results when you add the aliquot parts of each of the three numbers mentioned above:

6          $1 + 2 + 3 = 6$ → The sum of the aliquot parts equals the number, so the number is called "perfect."

8          $1 + 2 + 4 = 7$ → The sum of the aliquot parts is less than the number, so the number is called "deficient."

12    $1 + 2 + 3 + 4 + 6 = 16$ → The sum of the aliquot parts is greater than the number, so the number is called "excessive."

Now identify each of the adjoining four consecutive numbers as perfect, deficient, excessive, or prime: **27, 28, 29, 30**

The Greek mathematician Euclid developed a rule for finding perfect numbers:

$$N = 2^{p-1}(2^p - 1),$$

in which p is a prime number. The rule doesn't give all the perfect numbers, but it works with these values of p: 2, 3, 5, 7, 13, 17, 19, 31, 61, 89, 107, 127. Try it with some of the smaller values. Check the perfection of your result.

The ancients called 220 and 284 "friends" or "amicable" because the aliquot parts of 220 total 284, and the aliquot parts of 284 total 220.

220 →	1		284 →	1	
	2	110			
	4	55		2	142
	5	44			
	10	22		4	71
	11	20			
	$\overline{33} + \overline{251} = 284$			$\overline{7} + \overline{213} = 220$	

In 1636, Fermat told a friend that he had found another pair: 17,296 and 18,416. Using the factors shown, check this.

$17{,}296 \rightarrow 2 \cdot 2 \cdot 2 \cdot 2 \cdot 23 \cdot 47$

$18{,}416 \rightarrow 2 \cdot 2 \cdot 2 \cdot 2 \cdot 1151$

In 1866, the Italian mathematician Paganini, who was then 16 years old, found a pair between those given above: 1184 and 1210. If he could find them, surely you can show that they are amicable!

EXTRA FOR EXPERTS

Scientific Notation

Scientists use very large and very small numbers.

The speed of light is 29,900,000,000 centimeters per second;
the mass of a proton is 0.000,000,000,000,000,000,000,001,65 grams.

It is customary to express such numbers in a shorter way in scientific notation (or standard notation), as the product of a whole number or decimal between 1 and 10 and an integral power of 10. Thus, $29,900,000,000 = 2.99 \times 10^{10}$ and $0.00000000000000000000000165 = 1.65 \times 10^{-24}$.

To determine a method of transforming a number from ordinary decimal form to scientific notation, study the change in the exponent of ten in the following:

$$
\begin{aligned}
0.00194 &= 1.94 \times 0.001 = 1.94 \times 10^{-3} \\
0.0194 &= 1.94 \times 0.01 = 1.94 \times 10^{-2} \\
0.194 &= 1.94 \times 0.1 = 1.94 \times 10^{-1} \\
1.94 &= 1.94 \times 1 = 1.94 \times 10^{0} \\
19.4 &= 1.94 \times 10 = 1.94 \times 10^{1} \\
194 &= 1.94 \times 100 = 1.94 \times 10^{2} \\
1940 &= 1.94 \times 1000 = 1.94 \times 10^{3}
\end{aligned}
$$

The effect of multiplying or dividing a number in the decimal system by 10 is to shift the position of the decimal point. Therefore, changing from one form to the other becomes a matter of counting the number of places you must shift the decimal point.

These examples illustrate a procedure for changing a number from one form to the other.

EXAMPLE 1. **A starfish lays an average of 2,520,000 eggs annually. Express this number in scientific notation.**

Solution: **$2,520,000 = 2.52 \times 10^{n}$. To find n, place a caret ($\wedge$) to correspond to the position of the decimal point in the answer: $2_{\wedge}520,000$. Count the number of places from the caret to the decimal point. You count 6 to the right.**

$\therefore 2,520,000 = 2.52 \times 10^{6}$. Answer.

EXAMPLE 2. The charge of an electron is 0.00000000048 electrostatic units. Express this number in scientific notation.

Solution: $0.00000000048 = 4.8 \times 10^n$
Place the caret sign as above: $0.0000000004_\wedge 8$. Count the number of places from the caret sign to the decimal point. You count 10 to the left.

∴ $0.00000000048 = 4.8 \times 10^{-10}$. Answer.

EXAMPLE 3. Express 8.0×10^{-4} without exponents.

Solution: Since $n = -4$, count 4 places to the left of the caret to locate the decimal point.

$8._\wedge 0 \times 10^{-4} = 0.0008$. Answer.

Two numbers expressed in scientific notation can be multiplied or divided readily. Thus,

$$(4.3 \times 10^{-12})(1.92 \times 10^8) = (4.3)(1.92) \times (10^{-12})(10^8)$$
$$= 8.3 \times 10^{-4}$$

Exercises

Express each number in scientific notation.

1. The diameter of the earth's orbit: 186,000,000 miles
2. The diameter of a large molecule: 0.00000017 centimeter
3. The length of the largest virus (parrot fever): 0.000025 centimeter
4. The number of molecules in 22.4 liters of a gas (Avogadro's number): 602,000,000,000,000,000,000,000
5. The diameter of the sun: 130,000,000,000 centimeters
6. The electronic charge: 0.00000000000000000016 coulomb

Express each number without using exponents.

7. 9.3×10^7 miles
8. 1.86×10^5 miles per second
9. 9.6×10^{22} centimeters
10. 9.5×10^{-6} centimeter
11. 6.67×10^{-8} cgs unit
12. 1.6×10^{-19} coulomb

Express the result of each operation in standard notation.

13. $(6.9 \times 10^{-6}) \div (2.3 \times 10^{-2})$
14. $(5.83 \times 10^{-9}) \times (1.39 \times 10^{-8})$
15. $(9.72 \times 10^8) \times (4.8 \times 10^{-20})$
16. $\dfrac{1.82 \times 10^5}{9.1 \times 10^{17}}$

Who Uses Mathematics?

The computer finds use in many unexpected places. A very specialized use of mathematics, particularly as identified with the computer, is suggested by this photograph. Here an assistant curator of Egyptian Art at The Metropolitan Museum of Art is shown with a graphic display unit that she uses to classify pottery by its shape and decoration.

Information about the pottery is entered on the TV-like screen by drawing pictures with a "light pen." Once the image data is stored in the computer, it may be enlarged, reduced, rotated, and so on, as one studies details of the object.

... *magnetic cores used in memory*
units of electronic computers

left, ... a pattern showing the cores strung together

Operations with Fractions

Learning to handle fractions is important preparation for later work. You will notice that the rules for operations with fractions are just an outgrowth of rules for handling fractions in arithmetic.

FRACTIONS AND RATIOS

8–1 Defining Fractions

Any indicated quotient of two mathematical expressions, such as $\frac{3}{1}$, $\frac{7}{13}$, $-\frac{11}{3}$, $\frac{t}{2}$, $\frac{5}{z}$, and $\frac{n^2 + 2n - 3}{2n + 1}$, is called a **fraction**. In a fraction $\frac{r}{s}$ you call r, the **numerator,** and s, the **denominator.** Since division by zero is not permitted, a *fraction is defined only when its denominator is not zero.* In the fractions below, do you see why the indicated numbers must be excluded from the replacement set of x? To find such excluded values, set the denominator of each fraction equal to zero, and solve the resulting equation.

Fraction	$\dfrac{5}{x}$	$\dfrac{2}{x - 1}$	$\dfrac{3x + 5}{x + 7}$	$\dfrac{2}{x^2 - 1}$	$\dfrac{5x - 2}{3}$
Excluded values of the variable	0	1	-7	1 and -1	No exclusions

Oral Exercises

State the value of the variable for which the fraction is not defined.

SAMPLE. $\dfrac{2z}{2z + 6}$ *Solution:* -3, because when $z = -3$, $2z + 6 = 0$.

1. $\dfrac{3}{4t}$

2. $\dfrac{-7}{6r}$

3. $\dfrac{2}{x - 5}$

4. $\dfrac{-3}{y + 2}$

5. $\dfrac{b}{2b - 4}$

6. $\dfrac{3r}{15 - 3r}$

7. $\dfrac{k - 8}{k - 8}$

8. $\dfrac{2n + 1}{2n + 1}$

9. $\dfrac{x - 3}{x^2}$

10. $\dfrac{m + 2}{m^2}$

11. $\dfrac{2x - 8}{8 - 2x}$

12. $\dfrac{3z - 12}{12 - 3z}$

Written Exercises

Express as a fraction. State any values of the variable for which the fraction is not defined.

A 1. $6 \div x$ 5. $0.5y$ 9. $h \div (3h - 6)$

2. $-3 \div b$ 6. $7z$ 10. $n \div (5n + 15)$

3. 0.23 7. $(x - 1) \div x$ 11. $(7z^2 + 2) \div 5$

4. 0.7 8. $t \div (t - 2)$ 12. $(8r^2 - 16) \div 4$

13. $(p - 3) \div (7p + 14)$ 15. $1 \div z(z - 7)$

14. $(t - 8) \div (10t - 30)$ 16. $1 \div k(k + 1)$

Give the set of excluded values of the variable.

B 17. $\dfrac{2z + 3}{z^2 - 8z + 15}$ 20. $\dfrac{1}{r^2 + 5r - 14}$ 23. $\dfrac{k + 7}{k^2 - 49}$

18. $\dfrac{3x - 8}{x^2 + 8x + 12}$ 21. $\dfrac{2n}{3n^2 - 5n - 2}$ 24. $\dfrac{a - 8}{a^2 - 64}$

19. $\dfrac{-2}{t^2 - 3t - 28}$ 22. $\dfrac{-2r + 4}{5r^2 - 11r + 6}$

SAMPLE. $\dfrac{3}{2r(r - s)}$

Solution: You cannot have $r = 0$ or $r - s = 0$. $\therefore r \neq 0, r \neq s$. **Answer.**

C 25. $\dfrac{-2}{c(c - d)}$ 27. $\dfrac{x - 2y}{x^2 - 2xy + y^2}$ 29. $\dfrac{p - 3r}{2p^2 + pr - r^2}$

26. $\dfrac{4t}{(t - s)(t - 2s)}$ 28. $\dfrac{3u + v}{u^2 - 3uv - 18v^2}$ 30. $\dfrac{a^2 - 2a + 4}{3a^2 - 11ab + 6b^2}$

8–2 Reducing Fractions to Lowest Terms

Do you recall why the fractions $\frac{4}{3}$ and $\frac{12}{9}$ name the same number? Using the property of quotients (page 226), you have

$$\frac{12}{9} = \frac{4 \cdot 3}{3 \cdot 3} = \frac{4}{3} \cdot \frac{3}{3} = \frac{4}{3} \cdot 1 = \frac{4}{3}.$$

Similarly, any fraction of the form $\dfrac{4c}{3c}$ $(c \neq 0)$ equals $\dfrac{4}{3}$ because if $c \neq 0$, then $\dfrac{c}{c}$ equals 1.

This example illustrates the following property:

Multiplication Property of Fractions

Dividing or multiplying the numerator and denominator of a fraction by the same nonzero number produces a fraction equal to the given one. That is:

$$\frac{ac}{bc} = \frac{a}{b}, \text{ provided } c \neq 0$$

Thus, $-\dfrac{24}{56} = -\dfrac{3 \cdot 8}{7 \cdot 8} = -\dfrac{3}{7}$ and $\dfrac{15z}{20z^2} = \dfrac{3 \cdot 5z}{4z \cdot 5z} = \dfrac{3}{4z}$ if $z \neq 0$.

A fraction whose numerator and denominator are polynomials is said to be **in lowest terms** when the numerator and denominator have no common factor other than 1 and -1. **Reducing a fraction to lowest terms** is the process of dividing the numerator and denominator by their *greatest common factor* (page 250).

EXAMPLE 1. Reduce $\dfrac{4x - 12}{2x^2 - 5x - 3}$ to lowest terms.

Solution: **Factor numerator** $\rightarrow \dfrac{4x - 12}{2x^2 - 5x - 3} = \dfrac{4(x - 3)}{(2x + 1)(x - 3)}$
     and denominator.

What values of x are excluded? $\rightarrow$ $-\frac{1}{2}$ and 3

Divide numerator and denominator by their greatest common factor, $x - 3$. $\rightarrow \dfrac{4(x - 3) \div (x - 3)}{(2x + 1)(x - 3) \div (x - 3)}$

Simplify the result. $\rightarrow = \dfrac{4}{2x + 1}$ if $x \notin \{-\frac{1}{2}, 3\}$.   **Answer.**

EXAMPLE 2. Simplify $\dfrac{5 - y}{y^2 - 25}$.

Solution:

  Factor numerator $\rightarrow \dfrac{5 - y}{y^2 - 25} = \dfrac{5 - y}{(y + 5)(y - 5)}$ $y \notin \{-5, 5\}$
  and denominator.

  To show the common factor, express the numerator as a product having -1 as a factor. $\rightarrow = \dfrac{-1(y - 5)}{(y + 5)(y - 5)}$

  Simplify. $\rightarrow = \dfrac{-1}{y + 5}$ if $y \notin \{-5, 5\}$.   **Answer.**

The fraction $\dfrac{-1}{y+5}$ in Example 2 on the preceding page also can

be written in the form $-\dfrac{1}{y+5}$, because

$$\frac{-1}{y+5} = (-1) \cdot \frac{1}{y+5} = -\frac{1}{y+5}.$$

Note that you can reduce a fraction only when the numerator and denominator have a common *factor*. Compare the fractions below:

$$\frac{5 \cdot 7}{5} = \frac{7}{1} \qquad\qquad \frac{5 + 7}{5}$$

$$\frac{a\,b}{a} = \frac{b}{1} = b, \ \text{if } a \neq 0. \qquad\qquad \frac{a+b}{a}, \ \text{if } a \neq 0.$$

a and *b* are factors of the numerator. This fraction can be reduced because *a* is a common factor of the numerator and denominator.	*a* and *b* are *not* factors of the numerator. This fraction can *not* be reduced, for no factor (other than 1 or −1) is common to both numerator and denominator.

Written Exercises

Write each fraction in lowest terms, noting all necessary restrictions on values of the variables.

A

1. $\dfrac{15a}{3}$

2. $\dfrac{28b^2}{7}$

3. $\dfrac{14}{21x}$

4. $\dfrac{15}{10y}$

5. $\dfrac{24a^2b}{-24ab}$

6. $\dfrac{-8xy^2}{24xy}$

7. $\dfrac{2c+2d}{5c+5d}$

8. $\dfrac{3x-3y}{3x+3y}$

9. $\dfrac{7a-7b}{a^2-b^2}$

10. $\dfrac{z^2-9}{z-3}$

11. $\dfrac{9p^2q}{3pq^2+6p^2q}$

12. $\dfrac{8rt-2r}{2rt^2}$

13. $\dfrac{k^2-9}{3-k}$

14. $\dfrac{4-r^2}{r-2}$

15. $\dfrac{x^2-9}{x^2+6x+9}$

16. $\dfrac{y^2+8y+16}{y^2-16}$

17. $\dfrac{p-p^2q}{q-pq^2}$

18. $\dfrac{7t^2-28}{t+2}$

19. $\dfrac{2z^2+4}{2z+4}$

20. $\dfrac{kr^2+k}{kr+k}$

21. $\dfrac{x^2-3x}{x^2-2x-3}$

22. $\dfrac{y^2+y-6}{3y^2-27}$

23. $\dfrac{3x^2+15x+18}{3x^2-12}$

24. $\dfrac{(x-3)^2}{x^2-9}$

B **25.** $\dfrac{x^2 + 6xy + 9y^2}{x^2 - 9y^2}$

26. $\dfrac{r^2 + rs - 6s^2}{r^2 - 4s^2}$

27. $\dfrac{y^2 - 2y - 8}{y^2 - 4y}$

28. $\dfrac{3x^2 - 9x}{x^2 - 5x + 6}$

29. $\dfrac{n^2 - 5n + 6}{n^2 - 4n + 4}$

30. $\dfrac{y^2 - 8y + 15}{y^2 + 4y - 21}$

31. $\dfrac{n^2 + n - 6}{n^2 - 7n + 10}$

32. $\dfrac{z^2 - 2z - 15}{z^2 + 3z - 40}$

Explain why each of the following fractions cannot be reduced.

33. $\dfrac{3 + y}{y}$ **34.** $\dfrac{3 - n}{2 - n}$ **35.** $\dfrac{t^2 - 1}{t + 3}$ **36.** $\dfrac{z^2}{z + 4}$

Write each fraction in lowest terms, noting all necessary restrictions on the values of the variables.

C **37.** $\dfrac{2y^3 - y^2 - 10y}{y^3 - 2y^2 - 8y}$

38. $\dfrac{2z^3 + z^2 - 3z}{6z^3 + 5z^2 - 6z}$

39. $\dfrac{4r^4 + 2r^3 - 6r^2}{4r^4 + 26r^3 + 30r^2}$

40. $\dfrac{3x^3 + 2x^2 - 8x}{3x^4 - x^3 - 4x^2}$

41. $\dfrac{18x^3 + 3x^2 - 36x}{12x^3 - 31x^2 + 20x}$

42. $\dfrac{3n^4 + 27n^3 + 60n^2}{6n^2 + 6n - 72}$

43. $\dfrac{x^2 - x - 6}{x^2 + 2a + ax + 2x}$

44. $\dfrac{rt - us - ur + st}{rt - 2us + 2st - ur}$

8–3   Ratio

To compare the enrollments at two schools, one having 800 students and the other 200 students, you can say that the first school has four times as many students as the second. This comparison is made by computing the quotient $\frac{800}{200} = 4$. You can also say that the enrollments are in the *ratio* of 4 to 1.

A **ratio** of one number to another one (not zero) is the quotient of the first number divided by the second. You can express the ratio 7 to 5 by:

1. An indicated quotient using the division sign $\div$ $\rightarrow$ 7 $\div$ 5

2. An indicated quotient using the ratio sign : $\rightarrow$ 7 : 5

3. A fraction $\rightarrow$ $\frac{7}{5}$

4. A fraction in decimal notation $\rightarrow$ 1.4

By the multiplication property of fractions (page 297), the ratio 7 : 5 compares not only the numbers 7 and 5, but also 14 and 10, 21 and 15,

-28 and -20, and $7n$ and $5n$, where $n \neq 0$. However, if you wish to compare a 2-pound weight to a 10-ounce weight, you must change the 2 pounds to 32 ounces and then use the ratio $\frac{32}{10}$ or $16:5$.

> To find the ratio of two quantities of the same kind:
>
> 1. Find the measures in the same unit.
>
> 2. Then divide these measures.

EXAMPLE.   **In an alloy, the ratio of copper to tin is 2 : 5. How many pounds of each metal are in 140 pounds of the alloy?**

Solution:

1▶   Let $2n =$ the number of pounds of copper.
Then $5n =$ the number of pounds of tin.

2▶ $2n + 5n = 140$

3▶ $7n = 140$
$n = 20$

$\therefore 2n = 40,\ 5n = 100$

4▶   *Check:* Are the weights in the $\frac{40}{100} \stackrel{?}{=} \frac{2}{5},\ \frac{2}{5} = \frac{2}{5}\ \checkmark$
ratio of 2 to 5?

Do the weights of copper
and tin total 140 pounds? $40 + 100 \stackrel{?}{=} 140,\ \ 140 = 140\ \checkmark$

$\therefore$ there are 40 pounds of copper and 100 pounds of tin in the alloy.   **Answer.**

Any real number that is the ratio of two integers (the second integer not zero) is called a **rational number**. Thus, the following are rational numbers:

$$\frac{3}{4}, \qquad 3 = \frac{3}{1}, \qquad 2\frac{1}{2} = \frac{5}{2}, \qquad 0.7 = \frac{7}{10}, \qquad -\frac{2}{3} = \frac{-2}{3} = \frac{2}{-3}$$

Rational numbers may be represented by fractions. Fractions are often called **rational expressions**. Thus, $\dfrac{x}{2}$ might be called a "rational expression" although it may not represent a rational number.

Oral Exercises

Give each ratio in its lowest terms.

1. $3:6$ **4.** $\dfrac{rst}{ust}$ **7.** $\dfrac{6t}{6v}$ **10.** $7z$ to $2z$ **13.** y^2 to $3y^2$

14. $6z^2$ to $2z^2$

2. $7:21$ **5.** $\dfrac{100}{20}$ **8.** $\dfrac{12x}{12y}$ **11.** $\dfrac{.7}{7}$ **15.** $\dfrac{8h}{40h}$

3. $\dfrac{xy}{xz}$ **6.** $\dfrac{90}{45}$ **9.** $3r$ to $5r$ **12.** $\dfrac{3.5}{7}$ **16.** $\dfrac{4k^2}{6k^3}$

17. $(z+2):(z+2)^2$ **23.** 3 quarts to 1 gallon
18. $(n^2+1)^3:(n^2+1)$ **24.** 3 ounces to 1 pound
19. 5 inches to 15 inches **25.** 2 pints to 2 quarts
20. 6 feet to 3 feet **26.** 15 minutes to 1 hour
21. 3 inches to 1 foot **27.** 2 years to 2 months
22. 2 feet to 18 inches **28.** 80 cents to 2 dollars

Written Exercises

Give each ratio in its lowest terms.

1. The area of a 3-inch by 4-inch rectangle to that of one 2 by 3 inches.
2. The area of a 7-inch by 10-inch rectangle to that of one 5 by 7 inches.
3. The area of a 2-inch by 3-foot rectangle to that of one 10 by 20 inches.
4. The area of a 6-inch square to that of a 0.75-foot square.
5. A basketball player's 24 free throws made to his 72 attempted.
6. The cost per ounce of flower seed to the cost of $32 per pound.
7. 384 students to 12 teachers.
8. The ratio of miles to hours on a trip of 496 miles completed in 8 hours.
9. Boys to girls in a school of 2400 students with 1800 boys.
10. Wins to losses in a season of 38 games with 8 losses.

In Exercises 11–14, use the rule that in a triangle

$$\text{Area} = \tfrac{1}{2}(\text{Base} \times \text{Altitude}).$$

11. The area of a triangle with a 10-yard base and a 12-yard height to that of one with a 16-yard base and an 8-yard height.
12. The area of a triangle with a 12-meter base and a 20-meter height to that of one with a 30-meter base and a 4-meter height.
13. The area of a triangle with a 3-foot base and an 8-inch height to that of a rectangle measuring 6 inches by 18 inches.
14. The area of a triangle with a 24-inch base and a $1\tfrac{2}{3}$-foot height to that of a square with sides each measuring 1 yard.

Find the ratio $x : y$ in each case.

SAMPLE. $5x = 7y$

Solution: $5x = 7y$

$$\frac{5x}{5y} = \frac{7y}{5y}$$

$$\frac{x}{y} = \frac{7}{5}$$

$$\therefore x : y = 7 : 5. \quad \textbf{Answer.}$$

15. $5x = 9y$ **17.** $7y = 14x$ **19.** $4x - 3y = 0$

16. $3x = 3y$ **18.** $3y = 12x$ **20.** $-7x + 2y = 0$

B **21.** $\dfrac{2x + 3y}{3y} = \dfrac{3}{4}$ **23.** $\dfrac{3x + 2y}{2y} = \dfrac{7}{2}$

22. $\dfrac{5x - y}{y} = \dfrac{4}{3}$ **24.** $\dfrac{5x - 3y}{3y} = -\dfrac{12}{7}$

C **25.** $\dfrac{x^2 + 2y^2}{y^2} = \dfrac{2x + y}{y}$ **26.** $\dfrac{x^2 + 5y^2}{y^2} = \dfrac{y - 4x}{y}$

Problems

A **1.** Find the greater of two numbers in the ratio of 7 to 2, whose difference is 25.

2. Find the lesser of two numbers in the ratio of 2 to 5, whose sum is -14.

3. How many of the 28 members of the Mathematics Club are boys if the ratio of girls to boys is 2 to 5?

4. How many pages of a 34-page newspaper are classified advertisements if the ratio of classified advertisements to other material in the newspaper is 3 to 14?

5. If a car goes 52 miles on 4 gallons of gasoline, how far will it travel on 7 gallons?

6. If 38 ounces of a salt solution contain 15 ounces of salt, how much salt will 30 ounces of the solution contain?

7. A mutual fund invests in bonds and stocks in the ratio of 4 to 5. How much of $27,000 invested will go into bonds?

8. In the Acme Manufacturing Company, 4 out of every 5 dollars expended by the company goes to labor costs. How much of an expenditure of $100,000 will go to labor costs?

9. A 90-foot rope is cut into two pieces whose lengths are in the ratio of 26 to 19. How long is the shorter piece of rope?

10. Mr. Fisher plants wheat and alfalfa in the ratio of 5 to 3. How many acres of a 160-acre plot are devoted to alfalfa?

11. Which is a better buy on a canned vegetable, a 16-ounce can at 72 cents or a 12-ounce can at 57 cents?

12. Evelyn can type 2000 words in 50 minutes, while Michael can type 738 words in 19 minutes. Which one is the faster typist?

B 13. If 2 of every 9 trees in a forest containing 831,762 trees are cedars, how many trees in the forest are not cedars?

14. If 7 out of every 11 dollars collected by Central City in taxes are spent on education, how much of the $24,026,343 collected goes to items other than education?

15. In a dry concrete mixture the ratio of sand to cement is 4:1 and the ratio of gravel to sand is 5:4. How many pounds of each are in 1100 pounds of the concrete?

16. A casting is made from an alloy containing 4 parts lead, 3 parts copper, and 2 parts tin. How many pounds of each does a 117-pound casting contain?

17. A profit of $1800 is divided among 3 persons in the ratio of 8:5:2. How much does each person receive?

18. Adjoining lots on a street have frontages of 70, 80, and 100 feet. How much of an assessment of $2000 should be assigned the owner of each lot?

8–4 Percent and Percentage Problems

The ratio of one number to another is often expressed as a *percent*. The word **percent** (denoted by %) stands for "divided by 100" or "hundredths." Hence:

$$7\% \text{ is another way of writing } \tfrac{7}{100} \text{ or } 0.07.$$
$$150\% \text{ is another name for } \tfrac{150}{100} \text{ or } 1.5.$$
$$1\% = \tfrac{1}{100} \quad \text{and} \quad 100\% = \tfrac{100}{100} = 1.$$

To write a ratio as a percent:

1. Write the ratio as a fraction with denominator 100.
2. Then write the numerator followed by a percent sign.

EXAMPLE 1. Express each number as a percent: $\frac{3}{8}$, 3.4

Solution:
$$\frac{3}{8} = \left(\frac{3}{8} \cdot 100\right)\frac{1}{100} = \frac{37\frac{1}{2}}{100} = 37\frac{1}{2}\%. \text{ Answer.}$$

$$3.4 = (3.4)(100)\frac{1}{100} = \frac{340}{100} = 340\%. \text{ Answer.}$$

A **percentage** is a number equal to the product of the percent and another number, called the **base**. Since percent is the ratio of the percentage to the base, it is often called the **rate** to avoid confusion with *percentage*. The key to percent and percentage problems is this basic relationship:

Percentage = Rate × Base   or $p = rb$, $b \neq 0$.

$$\frac{\text{Percentage}}{\text{Base}} = \text{Rate} \qquad \text{or} \qquad \frac{p}{b} = r, \quad b \neq 0.$$

EXAMPLE 2. How much is a 15% discount on an item whose price is $40?

Solution:

1▶ Let p = discount (percentage)   2▶ $p = rb$ or $\frac{p}{b} = r$
    $r = 15\%$ $p = (0.15)(40)$
    $b = 40$ $\frac{p}{40} = \frac{15}{100}$

3–4▶ Show that the discount (percentage) is $6.

Written Exercises

Determine each of the following.

A

1. 12% of 180
2. 3% of 3.2
3. 42% of 18.5
4. 80% of 1000

5. 25% of 16
6. 100% of 83
7. 200% of 15
8. 150% of 44

9. 400% of 1
10. 3.25% of 48
11. $\frac{3}{5}\%$ of 820
12. 0.02% of 1000

Find the number.

13. 18 is 60% of the number.
14. 23 is 25% of the number.
15. 4% of the number is 3.4.
16. 75% of the number is 9.75.

17. 100% of the number is 218.
18. 150% of the number is 84.
19. $\frac{1}{5}\%$ of the number is 1.23.
20. $1\frac{1}{2}\%$ of the number is 30.2.

Determine each rate.

21. What % of 64 is 48?
22. What % of 56 is 24?
23. What % of 8 is 24?
24. What % of 12 is 40?

25. 2 is what % of 400?
26. 5 is what % of 900?
27. 80 is what % of 5?
28. 270 is what % of 30?

Problems

A 1. If 4% of 2400 persons polled expressed no opinion, how many of the persons did express an opinion?

2. If Jupiter Airlines Flight 203 was filled to 65% of capacity, how many of the 120 seats were occupied?

3. How many minutes out of an hour's TV program are taken up by commercials if 15% of the program is alloted to commercials?

4. How much zinc is in 30 pounds of an alloy containing 28% zinc?

5. Miss Tamura paid $124 in sales tax on her new car. If this represents 4% of the price of the car, what was the price of the car?

6. Jack received 462 votes for president of Union High School. If this represented 55% of the votes cast for president, how many votes were cast?

7. Mrs. McGee receives a commission of 15% for selling a house. If she received $1860 as commission for a sale, what was the price of the house she sold?

8. During a sale, a coat sells for $77.50. If this is 62% of the usual price, what is the usual price of the coat?

9. The sales tax on $140 is $6.30. What is the rate of sales tax?

10. Out of a shipment of 12,000 bolts, 360 are defective. What percent of the shipment are defective?

11. The salesman's commission on an $11,000 home is $1540. What is his rate of commission?

12. The list price of a camera is $150. If a discount of $7.50 is given for cash, what percent of the list price is the discount?

B 13. The price of one share of Acme Motors Company stock rose from $64.20 to $67.41. By what percent of the first price did the price of the stock increase?

14. For tax purposes, a house worth $14,000 one year was worth $13,440 the next year. By what percent of the initial value had the value of the house depreciated?

15. Mrs. Fisher received $1136 as trade-in for her old car. What was the original price of the old car if it had depreciated by 60% of its original purchase price?

16. If an ore contains 15% copper, how many tons of ore are necessary to obtain 18 tons of copper?

17. A dealer pays $190 for a TV set. He has overhead (expenses) totaling 15% of the selling price and wishes to make 40% profit on the selling price. What price should he charge for the set?

18. An article is marked $24 and an 18% discount on that price is given. What profit is made if the article cost $12?

SAMPLE. Find the number of degrees in each central angle of this graph, called a **circle graph**.

Solution: The sum of all the adjacent angles around a point is 360°. Thus,

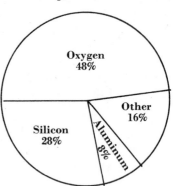

Oxygen, $\frac{48}{100} \times 360° = 172.8° \doteq 173°$

Silicon, $\frac{28}{100} \times 360° = 100.8° \doteq 101°$

Aluminum, $\frac{8}{100} \times 360° = 28.8° \doteq 29°$

Other, $\frac{16}{100} \times 360° = 57.6° \doteq 58°$

Average Chemical Composition of the Earth's Crust

Check: 173° + 101° + 29° + 58° = 361°. (We have 1° too many, because we rounded each measurement to a whole number of degrees. To compensate, we can replace 58° by 57°.

19. Of the registered voters in Valley City, 43% are registered Democratic, 29% Republican, 15% Independent, and the remainder decline to state a party.

 a. Make a circle graph, using a protractor to draw the central angles.
 b. If 540 voters decline to state a party, how many registered voters are there in Valley City?

20. A survey found that at a given hour in Central City, of the TV sets in operation, 38% were tuned to channel 2, 35% to channel 5, 16% to channel 7, 5% to channel 9, and the rest to channel 11.

 a. Make a circle graph.
 b. If 980 sets were tuned to channel 5, how many sets in all were in operation?

Make a circle graph from the data given in each table. Label each graph.

21.

Ages of Licensed Drivers in U.S.	Under 20	20–25	26–35	36–45	46–65	Over 65
% of Licensed Drivers in U.S.	10	10	25	25	25	5

22.

Ages of U.S. population in 1967	Under 5	5–19	20–44	45–64	65 and over
% of population of given age to nearest 1%	10	29	31	20	10

MULTIPLYING AND DIVIDING FRACTIONS

8–5 Multiplying Fractions

When you read the property of quotients (see page 226)

$$\frac{xy}{cd} = \frac{x}{c} \cdot \frac{y}{d}$$

from right to left, you have the following:

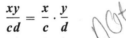

Rule for Multiplying Fractions

For any real numbers x, y, c, and d, if $c \neq 0$ and $d \neq 0$, then

$$\frac{x}{c} \cdot \frac{y}{d} = \frac{xy}{cd}$$

That is, when fractions are multiplied, the product is a fraction whose numerator is the product of the numerators and whose denominator is the product of the denominators of the given fractions.

Thus:

$$\frac{(x-4)}{(x-3)} \cdot \frac{(x+5)}{(x+3)} = \frac{(x-4)(x+5)}{(x-3)(x+3)} = \frac{x^2 + x - 20}{x^2 - 9}, \quad x \notin \{3, -3\}$$

$$7t\frac{5t}{r} = \frac{7t}{1} \cdot \frac{5t}{r} = \frac{35t^2}{r}, \quad r \neq 0$$

A product that is not in lowest terms should be reduced. Thus:

$$\frac{a}{b} \cdot \frac{b}{a} = \frac{ab}{ba} = \frac{ab}{ab} = 1, \quad a \neq 0, b \neq 0$$

$$\frac{x+y}{x-y} \cdot \frac{x-y}{5} = \frac{(x+y)(x-y)}{5(x-y)} = \frac{x+y}{5}, \quad x \neq y$$

You can simplify the multiplication of fractions by first factoring where possible:

$$\frac{4y-6}{3y+5} \cdot \frac{9y^2-25}{2y^2+y-6} = \frac{2(2y-3)}{(3y+5)} \cdot \frac{(3y+5)(3y-5)}{(2y-3)(y+2)}, \quad y \notin \{-\tfrac{5}{3}, \tfrac{3}{2}, -2\}$$

$$= \frac{2(3y-5)(2y-3)(3y+5)}{(y+2)(2y-3)(3y+5)}$$

$$= \frac{2(3y-5)}{y+2}, \text{ or } \frac{6y-10}{y+2}, \quad y \notin \{-\tfrac{5}{3}, \tfrac{3}{2}, -2\}$$

Hereafter, in the sets of exercises it will be assumed that the replacement sets of the variables include no value for which the denominator is zero.

Oral Exercises

Express each product as a single fraction in lowest terms.

1. $\frac{1}{2} \cdot \frac{1}{8}$

2. $\frac{1}{3} \cdot \frac{1}{7}$

3. $\frac{2}{3} \cdot \frac{5}{7}$

4. $\frac{6}{5} \cdot \frac{2}{11}$

5. $(-\frac{1}{3})(\frac{5}{2})$

6. $\frac{2}{5}(-\frac{1}{9})$

7. $\frac{a}{2} \cdot \frac{b}{5}$

8. $\frac{x}{4} \cdot \frac{x}{6}$

9. $5 \cdot \frac{3}{8}$

10. $7 \cdot \frac{2}{5}$

11. $x \cdot \frac{x}{6}$

12. $n \cdot \frac{n}{10}$

13. $\left(-\frac{1}{u}\right)\left(\frac{2}{v}\right)$

14. $\left(-\frac{3}{a}\right)\left(-\frac{5}{b}\right)$

15. $\frac{3t}{2} \cdot \frac{t}{5s}$

16. $\frac{5a}{6b} \cdot \frac{a}{3}$

17. $\left(-\frac{1}{4t}\right)\left(\frac{1}{3t}\right)$

18. $\left(\frac{2}{3z}\right)\left(-\frac{2}{3z}\right)$

19. $\frac{x^2}{2z} \cdot \frac{x}{2z}$

20. $\frac{p}{3r} \cdot \frac{2p^2}{3r}$

21. $\frac{c-d}{c}(c+d)$

22. $\frac{2r+s}{3}(r+s)$

23. $\frac{1}{(x-1)} \cdot \frac{2}{(x-1)}$

24. $\frac{b+2}{3} \cdot \frac{b+2}{3}$

25. $\frac{2}{x^2-2} \cdot \frac{1}{x^2+2}$

26. $\frac{1}{t^2+1} \cdot \frac{1}{t^2+1}$

27. $\frac{a+b}{2} \cdot \frac{3}{a+b}$

Written Exercises

Express each product as a single fraction in lowest terms.

A

1. $\frac{3}{5} \cdot \frac{2}{11} \cdot 3$

2. $\frac{1}{3} \cdot \frac{5}{4} \cdot (-5)$

3. $\frac{2}{9} \cdot \frac{3}{5}$

4. $\frac{4}{9} \cdot \frac{3}{8}$

5. $\frac{2}{3} \cdot \frac{3}{5} \cdot \frac{5}{4}$

6. $\frac{3}{8} \cdot \frac{4}{9} \cdot \frac{12}{5}$

7. $\frac{24}{30} \cdot \frac{20}{36} \cdot \frac{3}{4}$

8. $\frac{9}{15} \cdot \frac{6}{8} \cdot \frac{2}{10}$

9. $\frac{8a}{13b} \cdot \frac{26ab}{4a}$

10. $\frac{-6rs}{5} \cdot \frac{10r}{3r^2s}$

11. $\frac{2}{3} \cdot \frac{9z^2}{4}$

12. $6a^2b \cdot \frac{2}{3a^2}$

13. $\frac{-16xy^2}{8x} \cdot \frac{14x^2y}{14y}$

14. $\frac{21a^2b}{8c} \cdot \frac{-3c^2}{7ab}$

15. $\frac{3x+15}{2x} \cdot \frac{4x}{4x+40}$

16. $\frac{2t+14}{6t} \cdot \frac{9t^2}{t^2+7t}$

17. $\frac{y-3}{8y-4} \cdot \frac{10y-5}{5y-15}$

18. $\frac{2z-4}{3z+6} \cdot \frac{2z+3}{z-2}$

B

19. $\frac{a^2-b^2}{a^2-16} \cdot \frac{a+4}{a+b}$

20. $\frac{y^2-4}{y^2-1} \cdot \frac{y-1}{y-2}$

21. $\frac{z^2-2z-3}{3z^2} \cdot \frac{6z}{z+1}$

22. $\frac{t^2-2t+1}{4t} \cdot \frac{8t^2}{t-1}$

23. $\frac{x^2+5x+6}{2x-2} \cdot \frac{x^2-x}{x+3}$

24. $\frac{n^2-3n-4}{n^2-2n} \cdot \frac{n-2}{n+1}$

25. $\frac{r^2-r-20}{r^2+7r+12} \cdot \frac{r^2+9r+18}{r^2-7r+10}$

26. $\frac{p^2+p-2}{p^2-3p+2} \cdot \frac{p^2-p-2}{p^2+5p+6}$

27. $\frac{x-y}{x^2+xy} \cdot \frac{x^2-y^2}{x^2-xy}$

28. $\frac{r^2+s^2}{r^2-s^2} \cdot \frac{r-s}{r+s}$

29. $\frac{n^2-11n+30}{n^2-6n+9} \cdot \frac{n^2-3n}{n^2-5n}$

30. $\frac{t^2-2t-3}{t^2-9} \cdot \frac{t^2+5t+6}{t^2-1}$

31. $\frac{a^2-4}{a^2-5a+6} \cdot \frac{a^2-2a-3}{a^2+3a+2}$

32. $\frac{c^2-d^2}{c^2+4cd+3d^2} \cdot \frac{c^2+cd-6d^2}{c^2+cd-2d^2}$

33. $\frac{2a^2-a-3}{6a^2-13a+6} \cdot \frac{3a^2-2a}{a+1}$

34. $\frac{z^2-z-6}{z^3-9z} \cdot \frac{z+3}{3z+9}$

35. $\frac{u^2+3u+2}{u^2+u} \cdot \frac{u^2+3u}{u^2+5u+6}$

36. $\frac{b^2+5bc+4c^2}{bc+4c^2} \cdot \frac{b^2+5bc}{b^2+6bc+5c^2}$

C **37.** $\dfrac{n^2 + 4n + 3}{n^2 - 1} \cdot \dfrac{n^2 - 2n + 1}{n + 3} \cdot \dfrac{n + 1}{n - 1}$

38. $\dfrac{3t^2 - 27}{t^2 + t - 6} \cdot \dfrac{t^2 + 3t}{6} \cdot \dfrac{2t - 4}{t - 3}$

39. $\dfrac{20 + y - y^2}{y^2 - 6y + 5} \cdot \dfrac{6 - 5y - y^2}{y^2 + 7y + 12} \cdot \dfrac{y^2 - 9}{36 - y^2}$

40. $\dfrac{12 + r - r^2}{9 - r^2} \cdot \dfrac{r + 2}{r^2 + r} \cdot \dfrac{3 + 2r - r^2}{8 + 2r - r^2}$

41. $\dfrac{k^2 + 4k + 3}{k^2 - 8k + 7} \cdot \dfrac{35 + 2k - k^2}{k^2 - 7k - 8} \cdot \dfrac{k^2 - 9k + 8}{k^2 + 8k + 15}$

42. $\dfrac{2b^2 - b - 3}{4b^2 - 5b + 1} \cdot \dfrac{b^2 - 1}{(b + 1)^2} \cdot \dfrac{1 - 3b - 4b^2}{3 - 5b + 2b^2}$

8–6 Dividing Fractions

A quotient can be expressed as the product of the dividend and the reciprocal of the divisor (page 125). Thus:

$$12 \div 4 = 12 \times \tfrac{1}{4}; \qquad 8 \div \tfrac{1}{5} = 8 \times 5; \qquad \tfrac{2}{3} \div \tfrac{4}{9} = \tfrac{2}{3} \times \tfrac{9}{4}$$

Since the reciprocal of $\dfrac{c}{d}$ is $\dfrac{d}{c}$, you have the following:

Rule for Dividing Fractions

For any real numbers a, b, c, and d, if $b \neq 0$, $c \neq 0$, and $d \neq 0$, then

$$\frac{a}{b} \div \frac{c}{d} = \frac{a}{b} \cdot \frac{d}{c} = \frac{ad}{bc}$$

That is, to divide fractions, multiply the dividend by the reciprocal of the divisor.

EXAMPLE. Simplify $\dfrac{x^2 - 16}{x + 4} \div \dfrac{x^2 - 8x + 16}{4 - x}$.

Solution:

$$\frac{x^2 - 16}{x + 4} \div \frac{x^2 - 8x + 16}{4 - x} = \frac{x^2 - 16}{x + 4} \cdot \frac{4 - x}{x^2 - 8x + 16}$$

$$= \frac{(x + 4)(x - 4)}{(x + 4)} \cdot \frac{4 - x}{(x - 4)(x - 4)}$$

$$= \frac{(x + 4)(x - 4)\,(-1)(x - 4)}{(x + 4)(x - 4)(x - 4)} = -1. \textbf{ Answer.}$$

Written Exercises

Simplify each expression.

A

1. $\frac{2}{5} \div \frac{7}{10}$

2. $\frac{4}{9} \div \frac{2}{15}$

3. $\frac{x}{y^2} \div \frac{x^2}{y}$

4. $\frac{r^2}{s^2} \div \frac{r}{s^3}$

5. $\frac{p^2}{2q} \div \frac{p^4}{4q^3}$

6. $\frac{n^2}{m^3} \div \frac{3n}{m^4}$

7. $\frac{3t}{8s^2} \div \frac{12t^2}{4s^3}$

8. $\frac{81k^2}{28k} \div \frac{9k}{7k^3}$

9. $(-16z^2) \div \frac{4z}{3}$

10. $\frac{3ab}{4} \div (-12b^2)$

11. $\frac{r+s}{18} \div \frac{r+s}{3}$

12. $\frac{3z-1}{36} \div \frac{3z-1}{9}$

13. $\frac{y^2-4}{2y} \div (y+2)$

14. $\frac{t^2-2t+1}{t^2} \div (t-1)$

15. $\frac{z+2}{z^2-9} \div \frac{1}{z-3}$

16. $\frac{k^3}{k^2+4k+4} \div \frac{k}{k+2}$

17. $\frac{4n-8}{3n+9} \div \frac{2n-4}{6n+18}$

18. $\frac{r^2+2rs}{2rs+s^2} \div \frac{r^3+2r^2s}{rs+s^2}$

19. $\frac{3a+3z}{4a^2} \div \frac{a^2-z^2}{2a^2}$

20. $\frac{x^2-4}{x^3} \div \frac{x^2-4x+4}{x^2}$

21. $\frac{n^2-m^2}{n^2-3n-4} \div \frac{n-m}{n^2+n}$

22. $\frac{y^2-9}{y^2-6y+9} \div \frac{3y+9}{7y-21}$

B

23. $\frac{9-a^2}{3a-3b} \div \frac{9-6a+a^2}{b^2-a^2}$

24. $\frac{4z^2+8z+3}{2z^2-5z+3} \div \frac{1-4z^2}{6z^2-9z}$

25. $\frac{1-4t^2}{t^2-4} \div \frac{4t+2}{t^2+2t}$

26. $\frac{c^2+2c^3}{9-c^2} \div \frac{c-4c^3}{3c+c^2}$

27. $\frac{2n^2-18}{n^2+6n-7} \div \frac{8n^2+4n-24}{n^2-1}$

28. $\frac{20+r-r^2}{r^2+7r+12} \div \frac{(r-5)^2}{(r+3)^2}$

29. $\frac{3s^2-14s+8}{2s^2-3s-20} \div \frac{6-25s+24s^2}{15-34s-16s^2}$

30. $\frac{2x^2-5x-3}{3x^2-10x-8} \div \frac{9-x^2}{12+x-x^2}$

C

31. $\frac{ab-3a+b-3}{a-2} \div \frac{a+1}{a^2-4}$

32. $\frac{2rs+4r+3s+6}{2r+3} \div \frac{s+2}{r-1}$

33. $\frac{ac-bc+bt-at}{3x^3-3xy^2} \div \frac{ac-at}{y^2-2xy+x^2}$

34. $\frac{ux+2uy-vx-2vy}{x^2+xy-2y^2} \div \frac{u^2+uw-2v^2}{x^2-2xy+y^2}$

8-7   Expressions Involving Multiplication and Division

In the absence of parentheses, the rule for order of performing multiplications and divisions (page 41) is applied to an expression containing fractions. You replace only the fraction immediately following a division sign by its reciprocal.

EXAMPLE.   Simplify $\dfrac{x^2 - x - 2}{x^2 + 2x + 1} \div \dfrac{x - 2}{7} \cdot \dfrac{4}{x}$.

Solution: $\dfrac{x^2 - x - 2}{x^2 + 2x + 1} \div \dfrac{x - 2}{7} \cdot \dfrac{4}{x} = \dfrac{x^2 - x - 2}{x^2 + 2x + 1} \cdot \dfrac{7}{x - 2} \cdot \dfrac{4}{x}$

$$= \frac{(x + 1)(x - 2)(7)(4)}{(x + 1)(x + 1)(x - 2)x}$$

$$= \frac{28}{x(x + 1)}, \text{ or } \frac{28}{x^2 + x} \cdot \text{ Answer.}$$

Check: **Let x have the value 3. The check is left to you.**

Written Exercises

Simplify each expression and check by substitution.

A   **1.** $\dfrac{2}{y^2} \cdot \dfrac{y}{6} \div \dfrac{x}{9}$

2. $\dfrac{z^3}{8} \cdot \dfrac{2}{z^4} \div \dfrac{z}{6}$

3. $\dfrac{rs^2}{t} \cdot \dfrac{st^2}{r} \div rst$

4. $\dfrac{4ab^3}{3c} \cdot \dfrac{6bc}{5a} \div \dfrac{abc}{10}$

5. $\dfrac{y^2 - 4}{y^2} \cdot \dfrac{y}{y + 2} \div \dfrac{y - 2}{2y}$

6. $\dfrac{4x}{4x - 3} \cdot \dfrac{8x - 6}{6x^2} \div \dfrac{x + 1}{3}$

7. $\dfrac{3t + 4}{8st} \div \dfrac{9t + 12}{12s^2} \cdot \dfrac{4t^2}{9}$

8. $\dfrac{x - 3y}{3x} \div \dfrac{8x - 24y}{9x^2} \cdot \dfrac{16y}{3x}$

9. $\dfrac{p^2}{p^2 - q^2} \cdot \dfrac{p + q}{p - q} \div \dfrac{p}{(p - q)^2}$

10. $\dfrac{k^2 + 4k + 4}{3k} \cdot \dfrac{k - 2}{k + 2} \div \dfrac{k^2 - 4}{4k^3}$

11. $\dfrac{x}{x + 3} \div \dfrac{3x^2}{3x + 9} \cdot \dfrac{x^2 + 4x + 3 \cdot}{x^2 - 9}$

12. $\dfrac{2y - 1}{4y^2} \div \dfrac{4y + 2}{y^3} \cdot \dfrac{4y^2 + 4y + 1}{4y^2 - 1}$

13. $\dfrac{t^2}{4t} \div \dfrac{s^2t^2 - 4}{2t} \cdot \dfrac{st + 2}{st}$

14. $\dfrac{5a}{a^2b^2 - 9} \div \dfrac{20}{ab} \cdot \dfrac{3ab + 9}{a^2b}$

B **15.** $\dfrac{x^2 + 9x + 14}{x^2 - 3x} \cdot \dfrac{2x^2 + 2x}{x^2 + 6x - 7} \div \dfrac{x + 2}{x - 3}$

16. $\dfrac{y^2 + 2y - 15}{6y^2} \cdot \dfrac{24y}{y^2 + 7y + 10} \div \dfrac{y - 3}{y + 2}$

17. $\dfrac{4n^2}{2n - m} \div \dfrac{12n^3}{4n^2 - m^2} \cdot \dfrac{2n^2}{6n^2 - 3nm}$

18. $\dfrac{a^2 c^2}{a^3 - a^2 c} \div \dfrac{4ac^3}{a^2 - c^2} \cdot \dfrac{2a + 2c}{ac}$

19. $\dfrac{y^2 - yc - 2c^2}{10y + 5c} \cdot \dfrac{4y^2 - c^2}{3y - 6c} \div \dfrac{y^2 - c^2}{15y - 15c}$

20. $\dfrac{r^2 - r}{r^2 - 2r - 3} \cdot \dfrac{r^2 + 2r + 1}{r^2 + 4r} \div \dfrac{r^2 - 3r - 4}{r^2 - 16}$

ADDING AND SUBTRACTING FRACTIONS

8–8 Sums and Differences of Fractions with Equal Denominators

Consider the sum $\dfrac{a}{b} + \dfrac{c}{b}$. Since $\dfrac{a}{b} = a\left(\dfrac{1}{b}\right)$ and $\dfrac{c}{b} = c\left(\dfrac{1}{b}\right)$

(page 126), by the distributive axiom you know that

$$\frac{a}{b} + \frac{c}{b} = a\left(\frac{1}{b}\right) + c\left(\frac{1}{b}\right) = (a + c)\left(\frac{1}{b}\right) = \frac{a + c}{b}.$$

Similarly,

$$\frac{a}{b} - \frac{c}{b} = a\left(\frac{1}{b}\right) - c\left(\frac{1}{b}\right) = (a - c)\frac{1}{b} = \frac{a - c}{b}.$$

These chains of equalities suggest the following theorem:

Rule for Adding and Subtracting Fractions with Equal Denominators

For any real numbers a, b, and c, if $b \neq 0$, then

$$\frac{a}{b} + \frac{c}{b} = \frac{a + c}{b} \qquad \text{and} \qquad \frac{a}{b} - \frac{c}{b} = \frac{a - c}{b}$$

That is, the sum of fractions with equal denominators is a fraction whose numerator is the sum of the numerators and whose denominator is the common denominator of the given fractions. The difference of two fractions with equal denominators is a fraction whose numerator is the difference of the numerators and whose denominator is the common denominator of the given fractions.

EXAMPLE 1. $\dfrac{6}{11} + \dfrac{8}{11} - \dfrac{9}{11} = \dfrac{6 + 8 - 9}{11} = \dfrac{5}{11}$

EXAMPLE 2. $\dfrac{n}{3n + 1} + \dfrac{n + 3}{3n + 1} - \dfrac{5 - n}{3n + 1} = \dfrac{n + (n + 3) - (5 - n)}{3n + 1}$

$$= \dfrac{3n - 2}{3n + 1}.$$

EXAMPLE 3. $\dfrac{3x}{2x^2 + 3x} + \dfrac{5 - x}{2x^2 + 3x} - \dfrac{2}{2x^2 + 3x}$

$$= \dfrac{3x + (5 - x) - 2}{2x^2 + 3x} = \dfrac{2x + 3}{2x^2 + 3x} = \dfrac{2x + 3}{x(2x + 3)} = \dfrac{1}{x}$$

Oral Exercises

State a fraction in lowest terms equivalent to each expression.

1. $\frac{4}{11} + \frac{2}{11}$

2. $\frac{5}{13} + \frac{7}{13}$

3. $\frac{3}{5} - \frac{1}{5}$

4. $\frac{7}{3} - \frac{5}{3}$

5. $\dfrac{3}{x} - \dfrac{6}{x}$

6. $\dfrac{10}{y} - \dfrac{5}{y}$

7. $\dfrac{a}{2b} + \dfrac{a}{2b}$

8. $\dfrac{c}{3d} + \dfrac{5c}{3d}$

9. $\dfrac{x}{7} + \dfrac{2y}{7}$

10. $\dfrac{z}{8} - \dfrac{5t}{8}$

11. $\dfrac{x + y}{2} - \dfrac{y}{2}$

12. $\dfrac{r - s}{2} + \dfrac{r}{2}$

Written Exercises

Find a fraction in lowest terms equivalent to each expression.

A

1. $\frac{3}{17} + \frac{8}{17}$

2. $\frac{9}{23} + \frac{14}{23}$

3. $\frac{2}{7} + \frac{8}{7} - \frac{4}{7}$

4. $\frac{3}{8} - \frac{5}{8} + \frac{7}{8}$

5. $\dfrac{4}{3x} - \dfrac{5}{3x} + \dfrac{2}{3x}$

6. $\dfrac{7}{10z} + \dfrac{9}{10z} - \dfrac{19}{10z}$

7. $\dfrac{x + 4}{2} + \dfrac{2x - 1}{2}$

8. $\dfrac{3z}{5} + \dfrac{z + 4}{5}$

9. $\dfrac{4x}{x + y} + \dfrac{4y}{x + y}$

10. $\dfrac{y}{y - 7} - \dfrac{7}{y - 7}$

11. $\dfrac{x^2}{x - y} - \dfrac{y^2}{x - y}$

12. $\dfrac{r^2}{r + 3} - \dfrac{9}{r + 3}$

13. $\dfrac{2a - 3b}{3ab} + \dfrac{4a + 2b}{3ab} + \dfrac{3a + b}{3ab}$

14. $\dfrac{4x + y}{4xy} - \dfrac{2x - 3y}{4xy} + \dfrac{10y - 2x}{4xy}$

B **15.** $\dfrac{3ab}{a + 2b} + \dfrac{a^2 + 2b^2}{a + 2b}$

18. $\dfrac{p + 1}{p^2 - 3p - 10} - \dfrac{6}{p^2 - 3p - 10}$

16. $\dfrac{r^2 - 3s^2}{r + s} - \dfrac{2rs}{r + s}$

19. $\dfrac{3z}{z^2 - 2z - 15} - \dfrac{2z + 5}{z^2 - 2z - 15}$

17. $\dfrac{k^2 + k}{k^2 - 9} + \dfrac{k - 3}{k^2 - 9}$

20. $\dfrac{b^2 + 2b}{b^2 + 4b - 12} - \dfrac{b + 6}{b^2 + 4b - 12}$

C **21.** Find a fraction whose sum with $\dfrac{a - a^2}{a^3 + 9a}$ is $\dfrac{1}{a^2 + 9}$.

22. Find a fraction whose sum with $\dfrac{x^3 - 3x^2}{r^3 + 2r^2 + 3r}$ is $\dfrac{x}{r^2 + 2r + 3}$.

8–9 Sums and Differences of Fractions with Unequal Denominators

To add $\frac{5}{4}$ and $\frac{7}{18}$, you first express them as fractions with equal denominators. Then you use the method developed in the preceding section. As a common denominator, you may use any positive integer having 4 and 18 as factors, but for convenience you usually seek the least common denominator (L.C.D.). To find the L.C.D. systematically, you write 4 and 18 as products of primes (recall page 250):

$$4 = 2 \cdot 2 = 2^2 \qquad 18 = 2 \cdot 3 \cdot 3 = 2 \cdot 3^2$$
$$\therefore \text{ the L.C.D. } = 2^2 \cdot 3^2 = 36.$$

To convert $\frac{5}{4}$ and $\frac{7}{18}$ to fractions with denominator 36, you note that

$$36 \div 4 = 9 \qquad \text{and} \qquad 36 \div 18 = 2.$$

Thus,

$$\frac{5}{4} = \frac{5 \cdot 9}{4 \cdot 9} = \frac{45}{36} \qquad \text{and} \qquad \frac{7}{18} = \frac{7 \cdot 2}{18 \cdot 2} = \frac{14}{36}.$$

You then have

$$\frac{5}{4} + \frac{7}{18} = \frac{45}{36} + \frac{14}{36} = \frac{45 + 14}{36} = \frac{59}{36}.$$

EXAMPLE 1.   Simplify: $\frac{5}{27} - \frac{11}{36} + \frac{7}{30}$

Solution:

1. To find the L.C.D., first factor each denominator.

$$\begin{aligned} 27 &= 3^3 \\ 36 &= 2^2 \cdot 3^2 \\ 30 &= 2 \cdot 3 \cdot 5 \end{aligned}$$

Then take each prime factor the greatest number of times it appears in any denominator. → L.C.D. $= 2^2 \cdot 3^3 \cdot 5$

2. Replace each fraction with an equal fraction having the L.C.D., apply the rule for adding and subtracting fractions, and simplify:

$$\frac{5}{27} - \frac{11}{36} + \frac{7}{30} = \frac{5 \cdot 2^2 \cdot 5}{(3^3) \cdot 2^2 \cdot 5} - \frac{11 \cdot 3 \cdot 5}{(2^2 \cdot 3^2) \cdot 3 \cdot 5} + \frac{7 \cdot 2 \cdot 3^2}{(2 \cdot 3 \cdot 5) \cdot 2 \cdot 3^2}$$

$$= \frac{100 - 165 + 126}{4 \cdot 27 \cdot 5}$$

$$= \frac{61}{540}. \quad \text{Answer.}$$

EXAMPLE 2.   Simplify: $\dfrac{n+10}{n^2-2n} + \dfrac{2}{n} - \dfrac{6}{n-2}$

Solution:

1. To find the L.C.D., first factor each denominator.

$$\begin{aligned} n^2 - 2n &= n(n-2) \\ n &= n \\ n - 2 &= n - 2 \end{aligned}$$

Then take each prime factor the greatest number of times it appears in any denominator: → L.C.D. $= n(n-2)$

2. Replace each fraction with an equal fraction having the L.C.D.:

$$\frac{n+10}{n(n-2)} + \frac{2}{n} - \frac{6}{n-2} = \frac{n+10}{n(n-2)} + \frac{2(n-2)}{n(n-2)} - \frac{6n}{n(n-2)}$$

3. Apply the rule for adding and subtracting fractions, and simplify:

$$\frac{n+10+2(n-2)-6n}{n(n-2)} = \frac{n+10+2n-4-6n}{n(n-2)}$$

$$= \frac{-3n+6}{n(n-2)}$$

$$= \frac{-3(n-2)}{n(n-2)} = -\frac{3}{n}. \quad \text{Answer.}$$

Check: Let *n* have the value 3. The check is left to you.

Oral Exercises

Give the L.C.D. of these denominators.

1. 4, 6
2. 3, 5
3. 3, x

4. 5, b
5. 12, 8
6. 10, 5

7. xy, xz
8. a^2b, ab
9. ab, bc, ac

10. c, d, cd
11. $x + y$, $y + x$
12. $r - t$, $t - r$

Give the L.C.D.

13. $\dfrac{2}{x + 2} - \dfrac{5}{x^2 - 4}$

14. $\dfrac{3}{x + y} + \dfrac{2}{(x + y)^2}$

15. $\dfrac{n}{3} - \dfrac{2}{6x + 6y}$

16. $\dfrac{5}{a^2 + ab} - \dfrac{3}{a + b}$

17. $\dfrac{x}{x + 3} - \dfrac{3}{x + 1}$

18. $\dfrac{7}{b + 2} + \dfrac{3}{b + 3}$

19. $\dfrac{3}{a^2 - b^2} + \dfrac{3}{a - b} + \dfrac{2}{a + b}$

20. $\dfrac{t}{t^2 - 4} + \dfrac{3}{2 - t} - \dfrac{5}{t + 2}$

Written Exercises

Find a fraction in lowest terms equivalent to each expression

A

1. $\dfrac{2}{a} + \dfrac{1}{3}$

2. $\dfrac{1}{4} - \dfrac{a}{x}$

3. $\dfrac{3}{2a} - \dfrac{1}{a}$

4. $\dfrac{5}{3b} + \dfrac{2}{b}$

5. $\dfrac{x + 2}{6} + \dfrac{2}{3}$

6. $\dfrac{3}{5} - \dfrac{x + 1}{10}$

7. $\dfrac{2z + 1}{3} - \dfrac{z - 1}{9}$

8. $\dfrac{3x - 2}{4} + \dfrac{2x - 1}{6}$

9. $\dfrac{3t + 4}{2} + \dfrac{4t - 1}{3}$

10. $\dfrac{2 - x}{6} + \dfrac{3 + x}{2}$

11. $\dfrac{2}{x} + \dfrac{3}{x^2} - \dfrac{1}{x^3}$

12. $\dfrac{3}{b^3} - \dfrac{1}{b^2} + \dfrac{2}{b^3}$

13. $\dfrac{5c + 1}{6c} + \dfrac{3}{2c}$

14. $\dfrac{3n - 2}{2n} - \dfrac{1}{n}$

15. $\dfrac{x + 7}{ax} + \dfrac{3}{a}$

16. $\dfrac{2}{b^2} - \dfrac{6x + 5}{b^2x}$

17. $\dfrac{2x - y}{4y} - \dfrac{x - 3y}{6x}$

18. $\dfrac{r - s}{rs} - \dfrac{s - t}{st}$

19. $\dfrac{2}{c^2 - d^2} - \dfrac{3}{c + d}$

20. $\dfrac{6}{p^2 - q^2} + \dfrac{p}{p - q}$

21. $\dfrac{5}{6r + 6} - \dfrac{3}{2r + 2}$

22. $\dfrac{6}{5x - 10} + \dfrac{7}{3x - 6}$

23. $\dfrac{y}{y + 2} - \dfrac{y}{y - 2}$

24. $\dfrac{3}{z + 3} - \dfrac{3}{z - 3}$

25. $\dfrac{2}{t + 2} + \dfrac{3}{t + 3}$

26. $\dfrac{3}{3b - 4} - \dfrac{5}{5b + 6}$

B **27.** $\dfrac{y+1}{y+2} - \dfrac{y+2}{y+3}$

28. $\dfrac{z-1}{z+1} - \dfrac{z+1}{z-1}$

29. $\dfrac{3x}{x^2-4x+3} + \dfrac{2}{x-3}$

30. $\dfrac{3z-4}{z^2-z-20} + \dfrac{2}{z-5}$

31. $\dfrac{2x-3}{16x^2} - \dfrac{2-x}{8x} + \dfrac{3}{4x}$

32. $\dfrac{2y+1}{3y} - \dfrac{y-5}{2y} + \dfrac{y+4}{18y^2}$

33. $\dfrac{1}{z^2-z-2} - \dfrac{3}{z^2+2z+1}$

34. $\dfrac{3y}{y^2+3y-10} - \dfrac{2y}{y^2+y-6}$

35. $\dfrac{3}{z+2} + \dfrac{5}{z-2} + \dfrac{2z-5}{4-z^2}$

36. $\dfrac{4}{k^2-25} - \dfrac{2}{k+5} - \dfrac{k+2}{5-k}$

C **37.** $\dfrac{2}{a^2-9} - \dfrac{3}{a^2-1} + \dfrac{1}{a^2+2a+3}$

38. $\dfrac{n+2}{(n-2)^2} - \dfrac{n}{n^2-4} + \dfrac{2}{n-2}$

39. $\dfrac{1}{t^2-5t+6} - \dfrac{1}{4-t^2} + \dfrac{1}{6+t-t^2}$

40. $\dfrac{p+1}{p^2-2p-3} - \dfrac{1}{p^2+p} - \dfrac{3}{p^2-3p}$

8–10 Mixed Expressions

A **mixed numeral** like $3\frac{2}{5}$ denotes the sum of an integer and a fraction. When you transform it into a fraction, you write the integer as a fraction with denominator 1 and add the fractions:

$$3\tfrac{2}{5} = \tfrac{3}{1} + \tfrac{2}{5} = \tfrac{15}{5} + \tfrac{2}{5} = \tfrac{17}{5}.$$

Similarly, $-3\frac{2}{5} = -(3 + \frac{2}{5}) = -3 - \frac{2}{5} = -\frac{17}{5}$.

The sum or difference of a polynomial and a fraction is called a **mixed expression**. A mixed expression can be written as a single fraction, as shown below:

$$y + \frac{5}{y} = \frac{y}{1} + \frac{5}{y} = \frac{y^2}{y} + \frac{5}{y} = \frac{y^2+5}{y}$$

$$3 - \frac{x-2z}{x+z} = \frac{3}{1} - \frac{x-2z}{x+z} = \frac{3(x+z)}{x+z} - \frac{x-2z}{x+z} = \frac{2x+5z}{x+z}$$

If the numerator is a polynomial, you can change a fraction to a mixed expression by applying the division algorithm (page 235):

$$\frac{6n^2+5}{2n} = 3n + \frac{5}{2n}$$

$$\frac{x^2-3x-10}{x+1} = x - 4 - \frac{6}{x+1}$$

Oral Exercises

Read each expression as a fraction in lowest terms.

1. $3\frac{1}{2}$

2. $4\frac{1}{3}$

3. $-2\frac{2}{5}$

4. $-6\frac{3}{4}$

5. $x + \frac{2}{y}$

6. $5 - \frac{a}{b}$

7. $t - \frac{2}{3t}$

8. $z + \frac{5}{2z}$

9. $4 + \frac{n}{n+1}$

10. $2 - \frac{r}{s-1}$

11. $3 + \frac{t}{r+s}$

12. $6 - \frac{pq}{p-q}$

Read each fraction as a mixed expression.

13. $\frac{n+3}{n}$

14. $\frac{b-2}{b}$

15. $\frac{t^2 - 2}{t}$

16. $\frac{r^3 + 5}{r}$

17. $\frac{x^2 + 2x - 1}{x}$

18. $\frac{3t^2 - 4t + 2}{t}$

Written Exercises

Express each mixed expression as a fraction in lowest terms.

A **1.** $a + \frac{2}{a+3}$

2. $t + \frac{2r}{t+r}$

3. $2 + \frac{x+2y}{x-y}$

4. $3 + \frac{a-4b}{a+b}$

5. $y - 2 + \frac{1}{y+2}$

6. $z + 3 + \frac{1}{z-3}$

7. $\frac{4}{n+2} + 1$

8. $\frac{5}{n-3} + 1$

9. $2 + \frac{a}{b} + \frac{b}{a}$

10. $\frac{p}{q} + 2 + \frac{q}{p}$

11. $y + 3 + \frac{2y-1}{y-2}$

12. $z + 2 - \frac{z+1}{z-1}$

Change each fraction to a mixed expression.

13. $\frac{27}{4}$

14. $\frac{231}{18}$

15. $\frac{12 + 18z^3}{6z}$

16. $\frac{12 - 6t^2}{2t}$

17. $\frac{14p^3 - 3}{7p^2}$

18. $\frac{20t^3 - 5}{4t^3}$

19. $\frac{16x^2y^2 + 12xy}{16xy}$

20. $\frac{12a^2b^2 - 4ab}{4a^2b^2}$

21. $\frac{y^2 - 3y + 2}{y + 3}$

22. $\frac{b^2 + 5b - 2}{b + 2}$

23. $\frac{9t^2 - 6t + 5}{3t - 2}$

24. $\frac{15n^2 - 2n + 8}{3n - 1}$

8–11 Complex Fractions (Optional)

A **complex fraction** is a fraction whose numerator or denominator contains one or more fractions. Complex fractions may be changed to simple ones by two methods.

> **Method I:** Multiply the numerator and denominator by the L.C.D. of all fractions within them.
>
> **Method II:** Express the fraction as a quotient, using the sign ÷, and apply the rule for dividing fractions.

EXAMPLE 1. Simplify: $\dfrac{\frac{2}{3}}{\frac{5}{7}}$

Solution:

Method I

$$\frac{\frac{2}{3}}{\frac{5}{7}} = \frac{\frac{2}{3}(21)}{\frac{5}{7}(21)}$$

$$= \frac{14}{15}$$

Method II

$$\frac{\frac{2}{3}}{\frac{5}{7}} = \frac{2}{3} \div \frac{5}{7}$$

$$= \frac{2}{3} \cdot \frac{7}{5}$$

$$= \frac{14}{15}$$

EXAMPLE 2. Simplify: $\dfrac{\dfrac{x + 3y}{2y}}{\dfrac{2x - y}{4y^2}}$

Solution:

Method I

$$\frac{\dfrac{x + 3y}{2y}}{\dfrac{2x - y}{4y^2}} = \frac{\dfrac{x + 3y}{2y}(4y^2)}{\dfrac{2x - y}{4y^2}(4y^2)}$$

$$= \frac{2y(x + 3y)}{2x - y}$$

Method II

$$\frac{\dfrac{x + 3y}{2y}}{\dfrac{2x - y}{4y^2}} = \frac{x + 3y}{2y} \div \frac{2x - y}{4y^2}$$

$$= \frac{x + 3y}{2y} \cdot \frac{4y^2}{2x - y}$$

$$= \frac{4y^2(x + 3y)}{2y(2x - y)}$$

$$= \frac{2y \cdot 2y(x + 3y)}{2y(2x - y)}$$

$$= \frac{2y(x + 3y)}{2x - y}$$

Written Exercises

Simplify each fraction.

A **1.** $\dfrac{\frac{3}{4}}{\frac{9}{8}}$

5. $\dfrac{\dfrac{10x^2y^2}{9z}}{\dfrac{5xy^2}{3z}}$

9. $\dfrac{\dfrac{y^2-9}{y}}{y+3}$

13. $\dfrac{\dfrac{x+3}{x-3}}{\dfrac{3x+9}{x^2-9}}$

2. $\dfrac{\frac{12}{27}}{\frac{2}{9}}$

6. $\dfrac{\dfrac{18a^2}{5ab^2}}{\dfrac{9ab}{25b^4}}$

10. $\dfrac{\dfrac{t^2-4}{t-2}}{t}$

14. $\dfrac{\dfrac{cy-cz}{y^2-z^2}}{\dfrac{y-c}{y+c}}$

3. $\dfrac{\dfrac{x}{y}}{\dfrac{x}{y}}$

7. $\dfrac{\dfrac{x+y}{x}}{\dfrac{x-y}{y}}$

11. $\dfrac{\frac{2}{3}+\frac{1}{4}}{2-\frac{1}{6}}$

15. $\dfrac{\dfrac{a}{b}+2}{1-\dfrac{a}{b}}$

4. $\dfrac{\dfrac{a}{b^2}}{\dfrac{a}{b}}$

8. $\dfrac{\dfrac{a+3}{6a}}{\dfrac{a-2}{3a^2}}$

12. $\dfrac{\frac{7}{8}+\frac{5}{6}}{\frac{5}{12}-2}$

16. $\dfrac{\dfrac{p}{q}-2}{1+\dfrac{p}{q}}$

B **17.** $\dfrac{\dfrac{x^2+y^2}{xy}-2}{\dfrac{4x^2-4y^2}{2xy}}$

19. $\dfrac{x+2-\dfrac{12}{x+3}}{x-5+\dfrac{16}{x+3}}$

21. $\dfrac{\dfrac{x^2+y^2}{x^2-y^2}}{\dfrac{x-y}{x+y}-\dfrac{x+y}{x-y}}$

18. $\dfrac{\dfrac{4a^2-b^2}{3ab}}{\dfrac{2a^2-b^2}{ab}+1}$

20. $\dfrac{n-\dfrac{2}{n+1}}{n+\dfrac{n-3}{n+1}}$

22. $\dfrac{x+\dfrac{2x+1}{x-1}}{x+\dfrac{2}{x-1}}$

C **23.** $2-\dfrac{2}{3+\frac{1}{2}}$

24. $1-\dfrac{1}{1-\dfrac{1}{x-2}}$

25. $2+\dfrac{1}{1+\dfrac{2}{x+\frac{1}{x}}}$

Determine each solution set.

26. $1+\dfrac{2+\dfrac{12}{y}}{\dfrac{y}{2}+3}=\dfrac{2}{y}$

27. $1+\dfrac{2-\dfrac{2}{x}}{x-1}=\dfrac{1}{2x}$

● CHAPTER SUMMARY ●

Inventory of Structure and Method

1. The **Multiplication Property of Fractions**: For each a, each b, and each c other than zero, $\dfrac{ac}{bc} = \dfrac{a}{b}$. This property permits you to **reduce a fraction to lowest terms** by dividing its numerator and denominator by their **greatest common factor**.

2. From the **Property of Quotients**, $\dfrac{xy}{ab} = \dfrac{x}{a} \cdot \dfrac{y}{b}$, comes the rule for **multiplying fractions**: The product is the fraction whose numerator is the product of the numerators and whose denominator is the product of the denominators of the fractions. The product should be expressed in lowest terms. By first factoring numerators and denominators, you may be able to compute the product of fractions more readily.

3. To **divide fractions**, multiply the dividend by the reciprocal of the divisor; thus, $\dfrac{a}{b} \div \dfrac{c}{d} = \dfrac{a}{b} \cdot \dfrac{d}{c} = \dfrac{ad}{bc}$.

4. To find the **least common denominator** of several fractions, factor each denominator, and find the product of the different prime factors, each taken the greatest number of times it appears in any denominator.

5. To **add and subtract fractions**, use the multiplication property of fractions to replace each fraction by one equal to it and having as its denominator the least common denominator of the given fractions. The **sum of fractions with equal denominators** is the fraction whose numerator is the sum of the numerators and whose denominator is the common denominator of the fractions.

6. To change a **mixed expression** to a fraction, write the polynomial as a fraction whose denominator is 1, and add this fraction to the fractional part of the expression. To change a **rational expression** to a mixed expression, divide the numerator by the denominator.

Vocabulary and Spelling

Review the meaning of each term by reference to the page listed.

fraction (*p. 295*)
reducing a fraction (*p. 297*)
fraction in lowest terms (*p. 297*)
ratio (*p. 299*)
rational number (*p. 300*)
rational expression (*p. 300*)
percent (*p. 303*)

percentage (*p. 304*)
base (*p. 304*)
rate (*p. 304*)
least common denominator (L.C.D.) (*p. 315*)
mixed expression (*p. 318*)
complex fraction (*p. 320*)

Who Uses Mathematics?

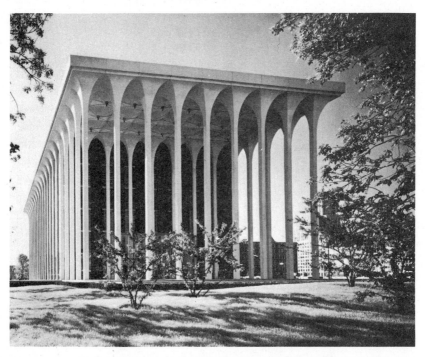

Northwestern National Life Insurance Company building, Minneapolis, Minnesota

Eero Saarinen

Minoru Yamasaki

The architect combines in a unique way many areas of study — design, sociology, engineering, and the fine arts, to name just a few. A study of mathematics is essential preparation for such a career. The architect Saarinen was responsible for the design of the Gateway Arch in St. Louis, Missouri, pictured on page 328. The beautiful buildings pictured here and on page 62 are the work of Yamasaki.

Chapter Test

8–1 **1.** For what values of t is $\dfrac{t - 3}{t^2 - 1}$ not defined?

8–2 Reduce to lowest terms.

2. $\dfrac{8x + 16y}{3x + 6y}$ **3.** $\dfrac{n^2 - 7n}{n^2 - 8n + 7}$ **4.** $\dfrac{r^2 - 4r + 4}{4 - r^2}$

8–3 **5.** Express the ratio of 3 feet to 8 inches in lowest terms.

6. If a 20-foot string is cut into two pieces whose lengths are in the ratio $3:2$, how long is each of the two pieces?

8–4 **7.** What would be the sale price on an item regularly priced at $4.50 if a 30% discount is given?

8. Draw a circle graph, showing the following use of the Berry family's income: Housing 20%, Food 30%, Savings 10%, Other 40%.

Express as a single fraction in lowest terms.

8–5 **9.** $\dfrac{4z}{9z^2} \cdot \dfrac{3z}{2z}$ **10.** $\dfrac{p^2 - q^2}{r^2 - s^2} \cdot \dfrac{r + s}{p - q}$

8–6 **11.** $\dfrac{6r - 3s}{4r^2 - s^2} \div \dfrac{3}{2r + s}$ **12.** $\dfrac{n^2 + n}{n^2} \div \dfrac{n^2 - 1}{3n - 3}$

8–7 **13.** $\dfrac{3p - 1}{3p} \div \dfrac{3p + 1}{3p^2} \cdot \dfrac{p^2 + 2p - 3}{p^2 - p}$

8–8 **14.** $\dfrac{3a - 3b}{2ab} - \dfrac{2a + 5b}{2ab} + \dfrac{8b - a}{2ab}$

8–9 **15.** $\dfrac{2z + 1}{6} - \dfrac{3z - 5}{9}$ **16.** $\dfrac{1}{x + y} + \dfrac{x}{x^2 - y^2}$

17. $\dfrac{r}{r^2 - 25} - \dfrac{1}{2r + 10}$

8–10 **18.** $t - 3 + \dfrac{5t - 6}{t - 2}$

19. Change to a mixed expression: $\dfrac{4c^2 + 6c - 8}{2c}$

8–11 **(Optional)** Simplify.

20. $\dfrac{\dfrac{8x^2y}{9z}}{\dfrac{4xy}{3z}}$ **21.** $\dfrac{\dfrac{t + 1}{t - 1}}{\dfrac{2t + 2}{t^2 - 1}}$ **22.** $\dfrac{\dfrac{x^2 + y^2}{xy} + 2}{\dfrac{x^2 - y^2}{3}}$

Chapter Review

8–1 **Defining Fractions** *Pages 295–296*

1. A fraction is not defined if its denominator is __?__.

State all values of the variables for which each fraction is undefined.

2. $\dfrac{3}{2x - 1}$ **3.** $\dfrac{5}{x^2 - 4}$ **4.** $\dfrac{x + 3}{x^2 - 5x - 14}$

8–2 **Reducing Fractions to Lowest Terms** *Pages 296–299*

Reduce each fraction to lowest terms.

5. $\dfrac{18a^2b^2}{-3ab^3}$ **6.** $\dfrac{r + s}{r^2 - s^2}$ **7.** $\dfrac{7t + 28}{3t + 12}$ **8.** $\dfrac{y^2 - 3y + 2}{1 - y}$

8–3 **Ratio** *Pages 299–303*

Express each ratio as a fraction in lowest terms.

9. $12:2$ **10.** $13:42$ **11.** 8 ounces to $1\frac{1}{2}$ pounds

12. The area of a 5-inch square to that of a triangle with base 1 foot and altitude 4 inches.

8–4 **Percent and Percentage Problems** *Pages 303–307*

13. $27\% = \dfrac{?}{100}$ **14.** $\frac{8}{5} = $ __?__ $\%$

15. Make a circle graph picturing the kinds of majors in Gentry High School: academic, 60%; agriculture, 8%; industrial, 10%; business, 18%; other, 4%.

16. How much silver is in 160 pounds of an alloy containing 18% silver?

In Exercises 17–38, write each expression as a fraction in lowest terms.

8–5 **Multiplying Fractions** *Pages 307–310*

17. $\dfrac{2a}{b} \cdot \dfrac{a^2b}{c}$ **19.** $\dfrac{n^2 + 2n + 1}{5n - 5} \cdot \dfrac{15}{n + 1}$

18. $\dfrac{2x^2y^2}{9u^2v^2} \cdot \dfrac{27uv}{6x^2y}$ **20.** $\dfrac{3z^2 - 75}{z^2 - 16} \cdot \dfrac{2z + 16}{3z - 15}$

8–6   Dividing Fractions

Pages 310–311

21. $\dfrac{3k}{4n^2} \div \dfrac{15k^2}{16n^2}$

23. $\dfrac{2a+4}{3a+9} \div \dfrac{4a+18}{5a+15}$

22. $\dfrac{r}{r^2+6r+9} \div \dfrac{r-3}{r+3}$

24. $\dfrac{c^2+c-2}{c^2+c-12} \div \dfrac{c^2-c-6}{c^2+3c-4}$

8–7   Expressions Involving Multiplication and Division

Pages 312–313

25. $\dfrac{9}{n^3} \cdot \dfrac{n^2}{5} \div \dfrac{6}{n}$

27. $\dfrac{x}{x+1} \div \dfrac{2x^2}{2x+6} \cdot \dfrac{x^2-2x-3}{x^2-9}$

26. $\dfrac{6a^2b^3}{c} \div 9a^2b^4 \cdot \dfrac{3c^2}{b^2}$

28. $\dfrac{r^2-s^2}{4r+s} \cdot \dfrac{4r^2+4rs+s^2}{r-s} \div \dfrac{r+s}{3}$

8–8   Adding and Subtracting Fractions with Equal Denominators

Pages 313–315

29. $\dfrac{8}{5z} - \dfrac{2}{5z} + \dfrac{4}{5z}$

31. $\dfrac{k^2}{k+n} - \dfrac{n^2}{k+n}$

30. $\dfrac{2x}{9y} - \dfrac{3-7x}{9y}$

32. $\dfrac{x^2+y^2}{x+y} + \dfrac{2xy}{x+y}$

8-9   Adding and Subtracting Fractions with Unequal Denominators

Pages 315–318

33. $\dfrac{1}{10z} - \dfrac{2z+5}{2z}$

35. $\dfrac{2y-5}{2-y} + \dfrac{y}{2y-4}$

34. $\dfrac{3}{x^3} - \dfrac{2}{x^2} + \dfrac{1}{x}$

36. $\dfrac{3}{n^2-25} - \dfrac{1}{5+n} - \dfrac{n+1}{5-n}$

8–10   Mixed Expressions

Pages 318–319

37. $z + \dfrac{x}{x+z}$

38. $n - 3 + \dfrac{5n-6}{n-2}$

Change to a mixed expression.

39. $\dfrac{4x^2-32x+7}{2x}$

40. $\dfrac{n^2+3n+6}{n+1}$

8–11   Complex Fractions (Optional)

Pages 320–321

Simplify each fraction.

41. $\dfrac{\frac{7}{8}}{\frac{35}{16}}$

42. $\dfrac{\frac{x-y}{x}}{\frac{x+y}{2x}}$

43. $\dfrac{\frac{2}{x}+\frac{1}{2x}}{x+\frac{x}{2}}$

D. N. Lehmer,
from Tables to Songs

Derrick Norman Lehmer (**Lay**-mer) was what is called in football a "triple threat." During his career he made notable achievements in three fields: mathematics, literature, and music.

Born in Indiana, Dr. Lehmer was educated at the University of Nebraska and the University of Chicago, and he spent most of his working life at the University of California. He was regarded as a leading authority on the theory of numbers. His "Factor Tables for the First Ten Millions," published by the Carnegie Institution in 1909, set a record for completeness and accuracy. They have been used by scholars all over the world, as have his "List of Primes from 1 to 10,006,721" and his "Factor Stencils."

He collaborated with his son, Derrick Henry Lehmer, in devising an electronic calculating machine which is capable of determining whether any given number, no matter how large, is a prime. The testing of that machine in Pasadena, California, was described by the father in an article "Hunting Big Game in the Theory of Numbers," which appeared in *Scripta Mathematica,* Vol. 1 (1932), pages 229–235.

This charmingly written article bears witness to Dr. Lehmer's literary skill. He was a frequent contributor to poetry magazines, and ten of his best ballads were collected in a volume titled "Fightery Dick and Other Poems," published in New York in 1936. For ten years he served as editor of the *University of California Chronicle*, a literary magazine.

In 1920 this versatile mathematician began an exhaustive study of the music of the American Indians. He traveled extensively through the southwestern United States, making hundreds of valuable phonograph records of Indian songs. He wrote songs based on Indian melodies, and also two operas, "The Harvest" and "The Necklace of the Sun," which were performed in California in 1933 and 1935.

Derrick Norman Lehmer (1867–1938)

. . . Gateway Arch in St. Louis, Missouri (The architect, Eero Saarinen, based his design on an inverted catenary curve.)

Using Fractions

Many equations and inequalities used to solve problems involve fractions. In this chapter you will have an opportunity to study some special applications.

OPEN SENTENCES WITH FRACTIONAL COEFFICIENTS

9–1 Solving Equations and Inequalities

Transformations previously used to solve open sentences (pages 131 and 166) may be used also when the numerical coefficients are fractions. Two methods are shown in the following Example. You will need to find the least common denominator (L.C.D.) of the fractional coefficients in applying either method.

EXAMPLE. $\dfrac{3y}{2} + \dfrac{8 - 4y}{7} = 3$

Solution 1: $\quad \dfrac{3y}{2} + \dfrac{8 - 4y}{7} = 3$

Solution 2: $\quad \dfrac{3y}{2} + \dfrac{8 - 4y}{7} = 3$

Replace each term in each member by an equivalent fraction having the L.C.D. as denominator:

Multiply each member by the L.C.D., 14

L.C.D. = 14

$$14\left(\frac{3y}{2} + \frac{8 - 4y}{7}\right) = 14\,(3)$$

$$\frac{21y}{14} + \frac{2(8 - 4y)}{14} = 3$$

$$14\left(\frac{3y}{2}\right) + 14\left(\frac{8 - 4y}{7}\right) = 14(3)$$

$$\frac{21y + 16 - 8y}{14} = 3$$

$$21y + 16 - 8y = 42$$

$$\frac{13y + 16}{14} = 3$$

$$13y + 16 = 42$$

$$13y = 26$$

$$y = 2$$

The check is left to you.

Oral Exercises

State the L.C.D., and read each open sentence after multiplying all its terms by the L.C.D.

SAMPLE. $\dfrac{2x}{3} + \dfrac{x}{2} = 7$ *Solution:* The L.C.D. is 6; $4x + 3x = 42$

1. $\dfrac{y}{2} + \dfrac{2y}{5} = 1$

2. $\dfrac{2k}{3} + \dfrac{5k}{4} = 2$

3. $\dfrac{n}{5} - n < \dfrac{7}{2}$

4. $\tfrac{2}{3}u - 2 > \tfrac{1}{2}u + 1$

5. $\tfrac{1}{6}t + \tfrac{1}{2}t = 3 - t$

6. $\tfrac{1}{4}y + \tfrac{1}{2}y = \tfrac{1}{8}y + 1$

7. $\dfrac{n}{5} \geq 6 + \dfrac{n}{10}$

8. $\dfrac{p}{4} \leq \dfrac{2p}{5} + 1$

9. $\dfrac{n^2}{4} - \dfrac{n}{3} + \dfrac{5}{6} = 0$

10. $\dfrac{r^2}{3} + \dfrac{r}{15} - \dfrac{2}{5} = 0$

11. $k^2 + \dfrac{2k}{12} - \dfrac{k}{6} = 0$

12. $x^2 - \dfrac{3x}{7} + \dfrac{2}{21} = 0$

Written Exercises

Solve. If the sentence is an inequality, graph its solution set.

A

1. $\dfrac{x}{2} + \dfrac{x}{5} = 7$

2. $\dfrac{y}{3} - \dfrac{y}{6} = 1$

3. $\dfrac{5z}{2} - z < \dfrac{3}{2}$

4. $\dfrac{4t}{5} - \dfrac{3t}{10} > \dfrac{3}{2}$

5. $\tfrac{3}{4}z - \tfrac{3}{2}z = 3$

6. $\tfrac{2}{3}n - \tfrac{5}{9}n = -1$

7. $0.03b - 0.01b \geq 0.2$

8. $0.5a - 0.2a \leq 1.5$

9. $\tfrac{3}{4}t - \tfrac{2}{5}t = \tfrac{7}{20}$

10. $\tfrac{1}{3}s + \tfrac{2}{5}s = \tfrac{11}{15}$

11. $\tfrac{3}{4}x - \tfrac{1}{4}x > \tfrac{3}{2}$

12. $\tfrac{1}{6}y \geq \tfrac{2}{3} + \tfrac{1}{3}y$

B

13. $\dfrac{t}{2} = \dfrac{3 - t}{4}$

14. $\dfrac{x + 1}{4} - \dfrac{3}{2} = \dfrac{2x - 9}{10}$

15. $\dfrac{z}{6} - \dfrac{20 - z}{8} = 1$

16. $\dfrac{n + 1}{10} - \dfrac{n}{3} = \dfrac{19}{15}$

17. $\dfrac{3x - 14}{6} \leq \dfrac{2x}{9} + \dfrac{x}{4}$

18. $\dfrac{5x - 2}{2} + \dfrac{x + 1}{4} \geq 2$

19. $\tfrac{1}{10}(10y - 3) - \tfrac{3}{5}(y + 1) = \tfrac{1}{10}$

20. $\tfrac{1}{3}(x - 3) + \tfrac{2}{5}(x + 10) = \tfrac{56}{15}$

21. $\dfrac{z + 2}{2} + \dfrac{3(28 - z)}{8} = 11$

22. $\dfrac{x + 8}{16} - \dfrac{x - 4}{12} = 1$

23. $0.08y + 0.12(10{,}000 - y) = 960$

24. $0.03n + 0.05(2000 - n) = 68$

Ⓒ **25.** $\dfrac{4x + 3}{15} - \dfrac{2x - 3}{9} = \dfrac{3x + 2}{3} - x$

26. $5z + \dfrac{3z - 4}{7} + \dfrac{5z + 3}{3} = 43$

27. $\dfrac{2t}{3} - \dfrac{t + 5}{2} = \dfrac{3t - 3}{4}$

28. $\dfrac{3n}{2} - \dfrac{n + 3}{3} = 8 - \dfrac{n + 2}{4}$

29. $0.12x - 0.02(x - 3) = 0.03x - 0.03(3x - 9)$

30. $0.06t - 0.03(3 - t) = 0.06 - 0.03(t + 2)$

9–2 Percent Mixture Problems

An interesting type of problem involving percent is the percent mixture problem. Recall (page 304) that the basic percentage equation is

$$p = rb$$

and that percents are equal to fractions with denominator 100.

EXAMPLE. How many ounces of water must be added to 12 ounces of an 8% salt solution to produce a 6% solution?

Solution:

1 ▶ Let x = number of ounces of water to be added.

Amount of original solution:	12 ounces
Amount of final solution:	$(12 + x)$ ounces
Salt in original solution:	8% of 12
Salt in final solution:	6% of $(12 + x)$

2 ▶

Amount of salt in original solution	=	Amount of salt in final solution
$0.08(12)$	=	$0.06(12 + x)$

L.C.D. = 100

3 ▶
$$100(0.08)(12) = 100(0.06)(12 + x)$$
$$8(12) = 6(12 + x)$$
$$96 = 72 + 6x$$
$$24 = 6x$$
$$4 = x$$

4 ▶ The check is left for you.

Problems

A 1. How many pounds of water must be added to 10 pounds of a 10% salt solution to produce a 4% solution?

2. How many ounces of water must be added to 4 ounces of a 50% antiseptic solution to produce a 40% solution?

3. How many pounds of water must be added to 50 pounds of a 90% acid solution to produce an 80% acid solution?

4. How many ounces of water must be added to 2 ounces of a 30% antifreeze solution to produce a 20% solution?

5. How many pounds of water must be evaporated from 40 pounds of a 10% salt solution to produce a 25% solution?

6. How many pounds of water must be evaporated from a barrel containing 80 pounds of a 6% brine (salt and water) to obtain a 10% brine?

7. How many pounds of pure alcohol must be added to 20 pounds of an 80% pure alcohol to produce an 85% pure alcohol?

8. How many ounces of pure acid must be added to 20 ounces of a 20% acid solution to produce a 50% solution?

SAMPLE. How many ounces of a 75% acid solution must be added to 30 ounces of a 15% acid solution to produce a 50% acid solution?

Solution:

1▶ Let x = number of ounces of 75% acid solution to be added.

Amount of original 15% acid solution:	30 ounces
Amount of final 50% acid solution:	$(30 + x)$ ounces
Acid in 75% solution:	75% of x
Acid in *original* 15% solution:	15% of 30
Acid in *final* 50% solution:	50% of $(30 + x)$

2▶

$$\underbrace{\text{Amount of acid in 75\% acid solution}}_{0.75x} + \underbrace{\text{Amount of acid in } \textit{original } 15\% \text{ acid solution}}_{0.15(30)} = \underbrace{\text{Amount of acid in final 50\% acid solution}}_{0.50(30 + x)} \quad \text{L.C.D.} = 100$$

3▶
$$100(0.75)x + 100(0.15)(30) = 100(0.50)(30 + x)$$
$$75x + 450 = 1500 + 50x$$
$$25x = 1050$$
$$x = 42$$

4▶ The check is left for you.

B

9. How many pounds of a 30% solution of acid must be added to 40 pounds of a 12% solution to produce a 20% solution?

10. How many ounces of a 5% antiseptic solution must be added to 30 ounces of a 10% solution to produce an 8% solution?

11. How many pounds of a 35% silver alloy must be melted with how many pounds of a 65% silver alloy to obtain 20 pounds of a 41% silver alloy?

12. How many pounds of a 70% copper alloy must be melted with how many pounds of a 90% copper alloy to obtain 100 pounds of an 81% copper alloy?

C

13. At most, how many quarts of an antifreeze solution containing 40% glycerine should be drawn from a radiator containing 32 quarts and replaced with water in order that the radiator be filled with at least a 20% glycerine solution?

14. An automobile radiator contains 20 quarts of a 25% antifreeze solution. At least, how many quarts of this solution should be drawn off and replaced with pure antifreeze to fill the radiator with at least a 40% antifreeze solution?

9–3 Investment Problems

The amount of interest, i dollars, paid on an investment of P dollars at the interest rate r per year for 1 year is found by applying the percentage equation,

$$\textbf{Percentage = Rate} \times \textbf{Base.}$$

But here the percentage is i, the rate of interest is r, and the base is P:

$$i = rP$$

To find the **simple interest** for t years, you multiply rP by t. Thus:

> Simple interest, i dollars, paid on P dollars for t years at rate r per year is given by
>
> $$i = Prt.$$

Thus, the simple interest on $1000 invested at 4% per year for 3 months is $10, since

$$i = Prt = 1000(\tfrac{4}{100})(\tfrac{3}{12}) = 10.$$

Investment problems may concern money invested at different rates of interest.

EXAMPLE.   **Mrs. Crawford has $8000 invested, part at 3% and the remainder at 4% annual interest. If her yearly return on these investments is $275, how much does she have invested at each rate?**

Solution:

1▶   Let x = number of dollars invested at 3%.

Then $8000 - x$ = number of dollars invested at 4%.

Income from 3% investment	+	Income from 4% investment	=	Total income

2▶ $(0.03)(x)$ + $(0.04)(8000 - x) = 275$ L.C.D. $= 100$

3▶ $100 \ (0.03)(x)$ $+ 100 \ (0.04)(8000 - x) = 100 \ (275)$

$$3x + 4(8000 - x) = 27{,}500$$

$$3x + 32{,}000 - 4x = 27{,}500$$

$$-x = -4500$$

$$x = 4500$$

$$8000 - x = 3500$$

4▶   Thecheck is left for you.

Problems

A

1. If $700 is invested at 4% per year, how much simple interest is earned in 2 years?

2. What is the simple interest for 3 years on $500 invested at 6% per year?

3. Miss James received $120 as interest for 1 year on a sum of money she invested at 6% per year. How much had she invested?

4. An investment at 4% simple annual interest returned $576 in 4 years. How much was invested?

5. Mrs. Stevens borrowed $700 at simple interest of 3% per year. Three years later she paid back the $700, together with the amount of interest. What was the total amount she paid?

6. If $800 is borrowed at simple interest of 5% per year, how much money must be paid all together after 5 years?

7. Mr. Lopez has some money invested at 4% annual interest. If he adds $2000 more to his investment, his annual interest will amount to $260. How much did Mr. Lopez originally invest?

8. Mrs. Lee had $5200 in an account at 3% annual interest. After withdrawing some money to buy a car, what remained in her account drew $72 annual interest. How much did she withdraw?

9. Mrs. Ulrich invested twice as much money at 5% per year as she did at 4% per year. How much did she invest at each rate if her annual return totaled $168?

10. Miss Mooney invested a sum of money at 6% per year, and 3 times as much at 4% per year. How much did she invest at each rate if her annual return totaled $144?

11. Mr. Daniels has some money invested at 5% per year. If he adds $200 to what he has, the new total will return the same amount each year at 4% as his original investment does at 5%. How much does he have invested at 5%?

12. Mrs. Cohen withdrew all of her savings from an account. The savings had been earning 3% per year. After spending $400 of the money, she reinvested what remained at 5% per year.' She then earned $4 more in interest each year than she had on the original account. How much did she have in her original account?

13. Mr. Krishna invested $8000, part at 4% and the rest at 5% per year. How much did he invest at each rate if his total return per year on the investment was $380?

14. A total of $9000 is invested, part at 6% and the rest at 3% per year. If the annual return from both investments is $396, how much is invested at each rate?

B 15. An investment fund has $3000 more invested at 4% per year than it does at 5%, and the interest on the amount invested at 4% is $30 per year greater than the annual interest on the amount invested at 5%. How much does the fund have invested at each rate?

16. Mrs. Thoma withdrew all of her money from an account paying 4% per year. $2000 of the money she invested at 5% per year and the remainder at 6%. If her investments paid $100 more per year than she used to receive from her account, how much did she invest at each rate?

17. Mr. Conte invests $\frac{1}{2}$ of his money at 5% per year and $\frac{1}{5}$ of it at 4%. Also, the amount invested at 3% is $1000 more than that invested at 4%. If his annual interest is $420, how much has he invested at each rate?

18. Mrs. Danton invests some money at 7% per year, $\frac{3}{4}$ as much at 6% as she does at 7%, and $150 less at 5% than she does at 6%. If her yearly income from these investments is $633, how much has she invested at each rate?

C 19. The Omer Fund invested part of $150,000 at 6% and the remainder at 4%. If it had invested twice as much at 6% and the rest at 4%, it would have increased its income by $1200. How much was invested at 6%?

FRACTIONAL EQUATIONS

9–4 Solving Fractional Equations

An equation which has a variable in the denominator of one or more terms is called a **fractional equation**.

EXAMPLE. Solve $\dfrac{30}{x^2 - 9} + 2 = \dfrac{5}{x - 3}$.

Solution: **Factor the denominators:** $\dfrac{30}{(x - 3)(x + 3)} + 2 = \dfrac{5}{x - 3}$

L.C.D. $= (x - 3)(x + 3)$. $x \notin \{3, -3\}$ **(Recall page 127.)**

$$(x - 3)(x + 3)\,\dfrac{30}{(x - 3)(x + 3)} + (x - 3)(x + 3)(2)$$
$$= (x - 3)(x + 3)\,\dfrac{5}{x - 3}$$

$$30 + 2(x^2 - 9) = 5(x + 3)$$
$$30 + 2x^2 - 18 = 5x + 15$$
$$2x^2 - 5x - 3 = 0$$
$$(2x + 1)(x - 3) = 0$$

$x = -\tfrac{1}{2}$ | $x = 3$ **Excluded above, this cannot be a root of the original equation.**

You now check $-\tfrac{1}{2}$ **in the original equation:**

$$\dfrac{30}{x^2 - 9} + 2 = \dfrac{5}{x - 3}$$

$$\dfrac{30}{(-\tfrac{1}{2})^2 - 9} + 2 \stackrel{?}{=} \dfrac{5}{(-\tfrac{1}{2}) - 3}$$

$$\dfrac{30}{-\tfrac{35}{4}} + 2 \stackrel{?}{=} \dfrac{5}{-\tfrac{7}{2}}$$

$$-\tfrac{120}{35} + 2 \stackrel{?}{=} -\tfrac{10}{7}$$

$$-\tfrac{24}{7} + \tfrac{14}{7} \stackrel{?}{=} -\tfrac{10}{7}$$

$$-\tfrac{10}{7} = -\tfrac{10}{7} \checkmark$$

∴ **the solution set is** $\{-\tfrac{1}{2}\}$. **Answer.**

In the Example above, notice that multiplying the given equation by $(x - 3)(x + 3)$ led to an equation that was *not equivalent* to the given one. This new equation had the extra root 3, a number for which the multiplier $(x - 3)(x + 3)$ represents **zero**. Observe this caution:

Multiplying an equation by a variable expression which can represent zero may produce an equation having roots not satisfying the original equation. Only values producing true statements when substituted in the original equation belong to the solution set.

Written Exercises

Solve each equation. Check your solutions.

A

1. $\dfrac{12}{z} = \dfrac{4 + 4z}{z}$

2. $\dfrac{3}{n} - 2 = \dfrac{5}{2n} - \dfrac{3}{2}$

3. $\dfrac{t - 2}{t} = \dfrac{14}{3t} - \dfrac{1}{3}$

4. $\dfrac{y - 2}{5y} = \dfrac{1}{6} - \dfrac{4}{15y}$

5. $\dfrac{n}{n + 2} = \dfrac{3}{5}$

6. $\dfrac{2}{3n} = \dfrac{2}{n + 4}$

7. $\dfrac{6 - x}{6x} = \dfrac{1}{x + 1}$

8. $\dfrac{r + 1}{r - 1} = \dfrac{2}{r(r - 1)}$

9. $\dfrac{y - 3}{2} = \dfrac{4y}{y + 3}$

10. $\dfrac{x - 5}{8x} = \dfrac{3}{x + 5}$

11. $\dfrac{4}{s} - 3 = \dfrac{5}{2s + 3}$

12. $\dfrac{4}{3a} + \dfrac{3}{3a + 1} = -2$

13. $1 + \dfrac{2}{b - 1} = \dfrac{2}{b^2 - b}$

14. $\dfrac{1}{k^2 - k} = \dfrac{3}{k} - 1$

B

15. $\dfrac{14}{y - 6} = \dfrac{1}{2} + \dfrac{6}{y - 8}$

16. $\dfrac{2}{r - 3} + 1 = \dfrac{6}{r - 8}$

17. $\dfrac{7}{p - 3} - \dfrac{1}{2} = \dfrac{3}{p - 4}$

18. $\dfrac{4}{q - 2} - \dfrac{2}{15} = \dfrac{7}{q - 3}$

19. $\dfrac{3z - 1}{z + 3} + 3 = \dfrac{4z}{z - 3}$

20. $\dfrac{k + 2}{k - 2} - \dfrac{2}{k + 2} = -\dfrac{7}{3}$

C

21. $\dfrac{2x + 11}{x + 4} + \dfrac{x - 2}{x - 4} - \dfrac{12}{x^2 - 16} = \dfrac{7}{2}$

22. $\dfrac{2c}{2c - 3} = \dfrac{15 - 32c^2}{4c^2 - 9} + \dfrac{3c}{2c + 3}$

23. $\dfrac{z - 2}{z^2 - z - 6} = \dfrac{1}{z^2 - 4} + \dfrac{3}{2z + 4}$

24. $\dfrac{y - 4}{2y^2 + 5y - 3} = \dfrac{4y - 1}{4y^2 + 13y + 3} - \dfrac{2y + 7}{8y^2 - 2y - 1}$

9–5   Rate-of-Work Problems

To solve problems about work, you use the formula

$$w = rt,$$

where w is the amount of work done, r is the rate of doing work, and t is the time worked. When two or more persons work on and complete a job, each does a fractional part of the job. Since together they complete a job, the sum of their fractional parts is 1.

EXAMPLE 1.   Janet can key-punch a number of computer cards in 6 hours, while Martha requires 8 hours to punch the same number. How long will it take both girls to punch that number of cards if they work together at the same rates at which they work individually?

Solution:

1▶   Let x = number of hours for both to complete the work together.

$\frac{1}{6}x$ = fractional part of the job done by Janet ($\frac{1}{6}$ of the job in 1 hour)

$\frac{1}{8}x$ = fractional part of the job done by Martha ($\frac{1}{8}$ of the job in 1 hour)

2▶

Part of work done by Janet	+	Part of work done by Martha	=	Whole job done together	
$\frac{1}{6}x$	$+$	$\frac{1}{8}x$	$=$	1	L.C.D. $= 24$

3▶ $24\left(\frac{1}{6}x + \frac{1}{8}x\right) = 24\,(1)$

$$4x + 3x = 24$$
$$7x = 24$$
$$x = \tfrac{24}{7}$$

4▶   *Check:*   In $\frac{24}{7}$ hours, Janet finishes $\frac{1}{6}\left(\frac{24}{7}\right)$, or $\frac{4}{7}$, of the job.

In $\frac{24}{7}$ hours, Martha finishes $\frac{1}{8}\left(\frac{24}{7}\right)$, or $\frac{3}{7}$, of the job.

Does $\frac{4}{7} + \frac{3}{7} = 1$? Yes. ✓

∴ it takes $3\frac{3}{7}$ hours for both girls working together to complete the job.   **Answer.**

Sometimes those doing a job may not work for the same length of time. In such cases, the values substituted for time in the equation may differ.

EXAMPLE 2.   How long would it take to punch all the cards in Example 1, if they started at the same time, but Janet stopped work after 2 hours?

Solution:

1▸ Let t = number of hours Martha works. Janet works 2 hours.

2▸ $\frac{1}{6}(2) + \frac{1}{8}t = 1$

Steps 3 and 4 are left for you.

Problems

A 1. The main engine alone on a rocket can consume the fuel supply in 60 seconds, while the auxiliary engine alone can consume the fuel in 80 seconds. How long can both engines be fired together?

2. One spillway can empty the reservoir behind Beaver Creek Dam in 5 days and a second spillway can empty it in 7 days. How long will it take to empty the reservoir if both spillways are used at the same time?

3. Working alone, Mr. Golden can paint his house in 3 days, while his son can paint it in 5 days. How long will it take them to paint the house if they work together?

4. One pipe can fill a tank in 12 hours and another can fill the tank in 8 hours. How long will it take both pipes together to fill the tank?

5. A heater raises the temperature 15 degrees in 24 minutes. With a second heater also in operation, the change takes place in 6 minutes. How long would it take the second heater working alone to produce the same temperature change?

6. One pipe can fill a small reservoir in 15 hours, while with a second pipe also in operation, the reservoir can be filled in 6 hours. How long would it take the second pipe alone to fill the reservoir?

7. One electronic reader can read a deck of punched cards in $\frac{1}{2}$ the time of another reader. Together, they can read the deck in 8 minutes. How long would it take each reader alone to read the deck?

8. A battery can operate one radio receiver for 4 times as long as it can operate another radio receiver. If both receivers are operated together, the battery will last 16 hours. How long would the battery operate each receiver alone?

B 9. A filler pipe can fill a tank in 10 hours, while an outlet pipe can empty the tank in 15 hours. How long will it take to fill the empty tank with both pipes operating?

10. One pipe can fill a tank in 6 hours while another can empty it in 2 hours. How long will it take to empty the full tank if both pipes are open at once?

11. Mr. Johnson paints $\frac{2}{3}$ of his house in 10 hours, and is then joined on the job by his neighbor, Mr. Prima. Together, they finish painting the house in 3 hours. How long would it have taken Mr. Prima to do the entire job by himself?

12. Doris and Julie addressed all the invitations to a graduation party in 2 hours. Doris completed 3 invitations in the time it took Julie to do 2. How long would it take Julie to address all the invitations?

13. The reservoir behind Buford Dam can be emptied in 15 days by opening both of its spillways. With the reservoir full, one spillway is opened. Then after 5 days, the second spillway is opened, and the reservoir is then emptied by both spillways in 13 days more. How long would it take each spillway alone to empty the reservoir?

C 14. Jason can paint the fence around his house in 15 hours, while his brother Amos can do it in 18 hours. If Jason paints for 7 hours alone and then turns the rest of the job over to Amos, how long will it take Amos to finish painting the fence?

15. An outlet pipe can empty a cistern in 18 hours. With the cistern full, this pipe and a second pipe are opened, and together they empty $\frac{3}{5}$ of the cistern in 6 hours. If the first pipe is then shut off, how long will it take the second pipe to empty the cistern?

16. Joe started out to paint the family garage alone. After $1\frac{1}{3}$ hours he coaxed his younger brother into helping him and they finished in $2\frac{2}{3}$ hours more. If Joe had worked 2 hours before calling in his brother, it would have taken them $2\frac{2}{7}$ hours to complete the job. How long would it take each boy to paint the garage alone?

9–6   Motion Problems

You can solve certain motion problems by using fractional equations. Recall that the basic motion equation is

$$d = rt,$$

where d is the distance traveled, r is the rate (speed), and t is the time.

EXAMPLE.   **The riverboat Memphis Belle sailing at the rate of 18 miles per hour in still water can go 63 miles down the river in the same time it takes it to go 45 miles up the river. What is the speed of the current in the river?**

Solution:

1▶   Let r = the speed of the current.
     Since the boat's speed in still water is 18 miles per hour:
     $18 + r$ = speed downstream   Distance downstream = 63 miles
     $18 - r$ = speed upstream   Distance upstream = 45 miles

2 ▶

	r	d	$t = \dfrac{d}{r}$
Down-stream	$18 + r$	63	$\dfrac{63}{18 + r}$
Upstream	$18 - r$	45	$\dfrac{45}{18 - r}$

$$\underbrace{\text{Time} \atop \text{downstream}} \biggl| \underbrace{\text{Time} \atop \text{upstream}}$$

$$\frac{63}{18 + r} \biggl| \frac{45}{18 - r}$$

L.C.D. $= (18 + r)(18 - r).$
$$r \notin \{18, -18\}$$

3 ▶
$$(18 - r)(18 + r)\frac{63}{18 + r} = (18 - r)(18 + r)\frac{45}{18 - r}$$
$$63(18 - r) = 45(18 + r)$$
$$7(18 - r) = 5(18 + r)$$
$$126 - 7r = 90 + 5r$$
$$36 = 12r$$
$$3 = r$$

4 ▶ Is the speed of the current 3 miles per hour?

The speed of the boat downstream: $18 + 3 = 21$ (miles per hour)

The speed of the boat upstream: $18 - 3 = 15$ (miles per hour)

Since $t = \dfrac{d}{r}$: time downstream $= \dfrac{63}{21} = 3$ (hours)

time upstream $= \dfrac{45}{15} = 3$ (hours)

Time downstream $\overset{?}{=}$ time upstream; $3 = 3$ ✓

∴ the speed of the current is 3 miles per hour. **Answer.**

Problems

A

1. A motorboat goes 24 miles upstream in the same length of time it takes to go 36 miles downstream. If the current is flowing at 3 miles per hour, what is the boat's rate in still water?

2. Water flows down the Chino River at 2 miles per hour. Rowing steadily, Mr. McCoy can go 12 miles downstream in the same time it would take him to go 4 miles upstream. What is his rate of rowing in still water?

3. The riverboat Lucky Piece can travel 12 miles per hour in still water. It takes the Lucky Piece as long to move 27 miles upstream as it does to move 45 miles downstream. What is the rate of the current?

4. An airplane whose cruising speed in still air is 220 miles per hour can travel 520 miles with the wind in the same length of time it travels 360 miles against the wind. What is the speed of the wind?

5. Jeremy can row in still water at a rate twice that of the current in the Juta River. What is the rate of the current in the river if it takes Jeremy 2 hours less to row 2 miles up the river than it does to row 9 miles down the river?

6. One day Mr. Kimbel found that his light airplane cruised at 5 times the rate of the wind. If he flew 132 miles against the wind in one-half hour less time than he flew 396 miles with the wind, what was the speed of the wind?

7. Julie's motorboat cruises at 20 miles per hour in still water. It takes her twice as long to go 90 miles upstream as it does to return 75 miles downstream. What is the speed of the current?

8. Paul can row 3 miles per hour in still water. If it takes him twice as long to row 8 miles upstream as it does the same distance downstream, what is the rate of the current?

B 9. Mrs. Sigura drove 90 miles to visit her brother. She averaged 15 miles per hour more on the return trip than she did on the trip going. If her total travel time was $3\frac{1}{2}$ hours, what was her average rate on the return trip?

10. It takes Jack an hour longer to walk his 4-mile paper route than it does to ride his bicycle over the route. If he averages 2 miles per hour more riding than walking, what is his rate walking?

11. Jane sailed 6 miles across a lake in $1\frac{1}{2}$ hours less than it took Sally to walk 12 miles around the lake to meet her. If Jane's rate was 6 miles per hour greater than Sally's rate, what was the rate of each?

12. Miss Egbert had driven 20 miles at a constant speed, but found that she had to increase her speed by 20 miles per hour in order to cover the last 30 miles in time to make an appointment. If her total traveling time was 1 hour, what was her original rate?

C 13. Fred gave Bill a five-yard head start in a 100-yard dash, and Fred was beaten by $\frac{1}{4}$ yard. In how many yards more would Fred have overtaken Bill?

14. Two cars race on a 4-mile oval track. The sum of the rates at which they travel is 200 miles per hour. Find the rate of each if the faster car gains one lap in 40 minutes.

● CHAPTER SUMMARY ●

Inventory of Structure and Method

1. Equations whose numerical coefficients are fractions and fractional equations having the variable in the denominator of a fraction may be solved by multiplying both members by the least common denominator (L.C.D.) of the terms of the equation.

2. Whenever the L.C.D. may represent zero, the roots of the resulting equation may not satisfy the original equation. Check all roots in the original equation.

3. Fractions often occur in the solution of problems involving percent mixtures, investments, work, or motion. You use these equations:

$$p = rb, \qquad i = Prt, \qquad w = rt, \qquad d = rt$$

Vocabulary and Spelling

Review the meaning of each term by reference to the page listed.

simple interest (*p. 333*) fractional equation (*p. 336*)

Chapter Test

9–1   **1.** Solve and graph the solution set: $3x - \dfrac{7x}{3} \le 1$

9–2   **2.** How many ounces of water must be added to 16 ounces of a 25% salt solution to obtain a 10% solution?

9–3   **3.** A sum of $10,000 is invested part at 4% per year and part at 6%. If the annual return from both investments is $500, how much is invested at each rate?

9–4   **4.** Solve: $\dfrac{4x}{x-3} - 3 = \dfrac{3x-1}{x+3}$

9–5   **5.** A pipe can fill a tank in 5 hours while an outflow pipe can empty it in 8 hours. How long would it take to fill the tank if both pipes are opened together?

9–6   **6.** Tom can row 9 miles downstream in the same length of time it takes him to row 3 miles upstream. If the current in the river flows at 6 miles per hour, how fast does Tom row in still water?

Chapter Review

9–1   **Solving Equations and Inequalities**   *Pages 329–331*

Find the solution set. If the sentence is an inequality, graph the solution set.

1. $\dfrac{n}{4} - \dfrac{n}{8} = 2$ **3.** $\tfrac{1}{4}y + \tfrac{1}{5}y = 9$

2. $\dfrac{3z}{2} + \dfrac{8 - 4z}{7} = 3$ **4.** $\dfrac{x+3}{2} - 1 \le \dfrac{x-8}{5}$

9–2 Percent Mixture Problems   *Pages 331–333*

5. How many quarts of water must be added to 10 quarts of a 60% antifreeze mixture to obtain a 25% mixture?

6. How many ounces of alcohol must be added to 8 ounces of a 10% iodine solution to produce a 4% solution?

9–3 Investment Problems   *Pages 333–335*

7. Mr. Adams invested twice as much money at 4% per year as he did at 5%. If his yearly income is $19.50, how much has he invested at each rate?

8. Mr. Smith had $3000 invested at 5% per year. How much must he invest at 6% in order to make his annual income from both investments $300?

9. Mrs. Jeffers invested $700 more at 6% per year than she did at 4%. If her annual return from both investments is $162, how much has she invested at each rate?

10. Mr. Taylor invested some money at 4% per year. If he had invested the same amount at 6%, his annual income would have been $84 greater. How much has he invested?

9–4 Solving Fractional Equations   *Pages 336–337*

Solve each equation.

11. $\dfrac{12}{t+2} = \dfrac{4}{t-2}$

13. $x - \dfrac{2}{x-3} = \dfrac{x-1}{3-x}$

12. $\dfrac{5}{n} = \dfrac{n-3}{2}$

14. $\dfrac{60}{y^2-36} + 1 = \dfrac{5}{y-6}$

9–5 Rate-of-Work Problems   *Pages 338–340*

15. Pam and her father together can do a job in $7\frac{1}{2}$ minutes. Working alone, Pam takes 20 minutes to do the same job. How long would it take her father to do the job by himself?

16. One pipe can fill a tank in 40 hours, while a second pipe can fill the same tank in 32 hours. How long would it take both pipes together to fill the tank?

9–6 Motion Problems   *Pages 340–342*

17. An airplane that cruises at 130 miles per hour in still air flies 495 miles with the wind in the same time it would fly 285 miles against the wind. What is the speed of the wind?

18. Arlene and Gwen row at the same speed in still water. On a river running at 3 miles per hour, Arlene can row 9 miles upstream in the same time that it takes Gwen to row 27 miles downstream. How fast can the girls row in still water?

Who Uses Mathematics?

A large research hospital requires the services of many kinds of persons — doctors, nurses, dieticians, biologists, chemists, and others. All must include mathematics in their preparation. If you are interested in any of the professions associated with medicine, you should continue to study mathematics at least through your high school years.

The doctor pictured above is using a laboratory weighing device which measures small amounts in grams. Scientists generally use the metric system in making their measurements.

EXTRA FOR EXPERTS

Loops and Subscripts in Flow Charts

The flow chart below pictures a program to compute and print the **compound amount** A (principal plus interest) of 1 unit of principal (say \$1) at the end of n interest periods at interest rate x per period, where

$$A = (1 + x)^n.$$

In the program, x is taken to be 1%, and A is computed for values of n from 1 to 50 in steps of 1.

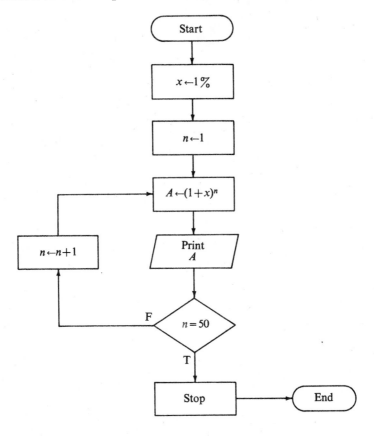

This flow chart as well as those on pages 58, 106, 107, and 108 involves a **loop**, which is a set of steps that are to be done over and over again.

Each loop has four parts:

1. One or more steps that set up the **initial conditions** to start the loop. In the compound amount flow chart, there are two such **initialization steps**:

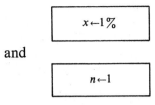

and

2. One or more steps that are to be repeatedly executed. These are called the **iteration steps**. In the preceding flow chart there are two iteration steps:

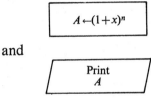

and

3. One or more **test steps** used to decide when to *exit from*, or break off, the loop. The flow chart on page 346 has one test step:

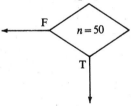

4. One or more steps that **update** the loop, that is, prepare the iteration steps for the next time around. The step

$$n \leftarrow n+1$$

updates the loop on page 346.

You should now look back at the flow charts on pages 58, 106, 107, and 108, and identify the steps that form the four parts of the loops in those flow charts.

Often a program contains a loop inside another loop (a **nested loop**). For instance, the flow chart below shows the program to compute the compound amount for n varying from 1 to 50 in steps of 1, first with $x = 1\%$, then with $x = 1.5\%$, and so on, with x varying from 1% to 8% in steps of 0.5%.

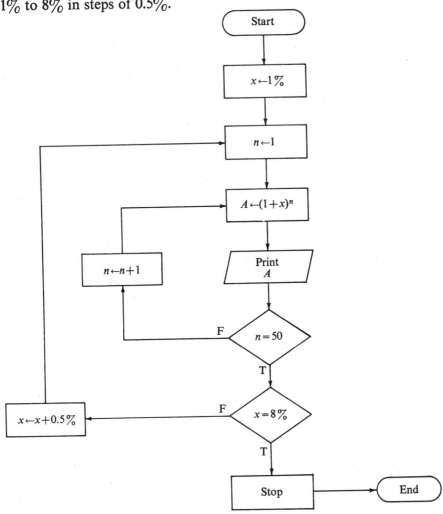

Many loops involve computations with long lists, or arrays, of data. Suppose, for instance, that you want to write a program to compute the sum of the squares of the ten numbers:

$$5.6, \; -2, \; 3, \; 1.25, \; -8, \; 6, \; 4.5, \; 0.4, \; -2.1, \; 15$$

For convenience in referring to this array, you might call it V. You can then refer to any number in the array V by writing the array name followed by a numeral in parentheses (called a *subscript*) that shows the position of the number in the list. For example, the first number in the array V is 5.6; therefore,

$$V(1) = 5.6,$$

read "the value of V-sub-one is five and six tenths." Similarly, since -8 is the fifth number in the array, $V(5) = -8$. In general, if I denotes any one of the integers from 1 to 10, inclusive, then the Ith number in array V is $V(I)$. We call $V(I)$ a *subscripted variable.* Notice that in the ordinary notation of algebra, V_1 is written in place of $V(1)$, V_5 in place of $V(5)$, and V_I in place of $V(I)$.

Do you see that the array V is really a function whose domain is the set of natural numbers $\{1, 2, 3, 4, 5, 6, 7, 8, 9, 10\}$ and whose range is the numbers in the array?

EXAMPLE. Draw a flow chart of a program to read an array V of ten numbers, and to compute and write the sum of the squares of the numbers in the array.

Solution: **Let I denote the subscript and let S denote the sum of the squares.**

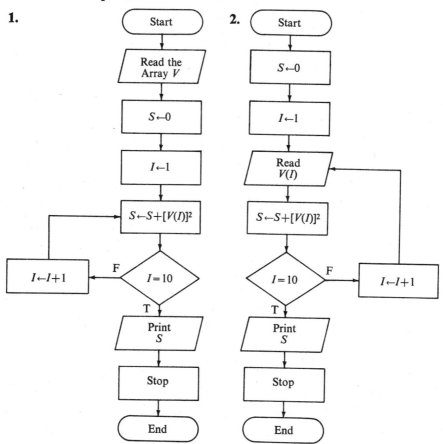

Exercises

If $D(1)$ refers to the first number in an array D of 50 numbers, to which number in the array does each of the following refer?

1. $D(3)$　　　　**2.** $D(30)$　　　　**3.** $D(50)$　　　　**4.** $D(60)$

Exercises 5–8 refer to the loop shown in the first flow chart in the Example on page 349.

5. What steps initialize the loop?　　**7.** What is the test step?

6. What is (are) the iteration step(s)?　**8.** What step updates the loop?

9–12. Answer the questions in Exercises 5–8 for the second flow chart in the Example on page 349.

Draw a flow chart of the program described in each of the following exercises.

13. Read an array R of 50 numbers and compute and write the arithmetic mean, or average, of the numbers in the array.

14. Read an array G of 20 numbers and compute and write the product of the numbers in the array.

15. Read an array V of 25 numbers and an array W of 25 numbers and compute and write the value of the sum of products:

$$V(1) \times W(1) + V(2) \times W(2) + \cdots + V(25) \times W(25)$$

16. Read two arrays C and D each containing 20 numbers, and compute and print the values of the sums

$$C(1) + D(1), \quad C(2) + D(2), \quad \ldots, \quad C(20) + D(20).$$

17. Read an array X of 30 numbers and write an array Y of 30 numbers when the values in the array Y are computed by the following rule:

$$Y(I) = X(I) \text{ if } X(I) \geq 0, \quad Y(I) = -X(I) \text{ if } X(I) < 0$$

18. Read an array X of 40 numbers and compute and write the values of $\overline{X}$ and V where

$$\overline{X} = \frac{X(1) + X(2) + \cdots + X(40)}{40},$$

$$V = \frac{(X(1) - \overline{X})^2 + (X(2) - \overline{X})^2 + \cdots + (X(40) - \overline{X})^2}{39}.$$

19. Read an array B containing 100 numbers and compute and write the sum P of the positive numbers in B and the sum N of the negative numbers.

Hermann Weyl, Mathematician Extraordinary

In 1904 Hermann Weyl (Vīl) entered Göttingen University (in central Germany) at the age of eighteen. Since he took with him a letter of recommendation to the famous geometer David Hilbert (1862–1942), the young man chose to take the course that Hilbert was giving that term — on the notion of number and the quadrature of the circle. He later said that, as a result, "The doors of a new world swung open for me, and I had not sat long at Hilbert's feet before the resolution formed itself in my young heart that I must by all means read and study whatever this man had written."

It has been said that of all twentieth century mathematicians, Hermann Weyl made major contributions in the greatest number of fields. Among the fields to which he contributed early in his career were the theory of numbers, functions of a complex variable, logical foundations of mathematics, and a fusion of function-theory and geometry. He also assisted in the development of Einstein's theory of relativity. He created a theory of matrix representation of continuous groups and applied group theory to quantum mechanics.

He was at the Institute of Technology in Zurich, Switzerland, from 1913 to 1930, when he returned to Göttingen as successor to Hilbert. He was not to stay there long, however. This very human mathematician left Göttingen in 1933 because he felt that he could not stay in Germany after the dismissal of his colleagues by the Nazis. He accepted an offer of permanent membership in the Institute for Advanced Study in Princeton, New Jersey, where he worked until his retirement in 1951. After that, he spent half of each year in Zurich and half in Princeton.

Hermann Weyl (1885–1955)

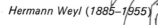

Cumulative Review: Chapters 1–9

1. Given $A = \{a, b, c, d\}$ and $B = \{b, c, f, g\}$, specify **(a)** $A \cap B$ and **(b)** $A \cup B$ by roster.

2. Write $3aaabbbb$ in exponential form.   **3.** Simplify $\dfrac{3 \times 8}{2} + 5 \cdot 3$.

4. Graph over {the natural numbers}, $1 \leq x < 8$.

5. Given $g: x \rightarrow 2x - 3$, $D = \{3, 4, 5, 6\}$, specify the range of g.

Justify each statement in Exercises 6–9 by citing a property of equality or a property of real numbers.

6. $7(3 + 2) = 7 \cdot 3 + 7 \cdot 2$ **8.** If $k + 3 = 5$, then $5 = k + 3$.

7. $[7(-2)] \cdot 4 = 4 \cdot [7(-2)]$ **9.** $(3 + 6) + (-7) = 3 + [6 + (-7)]$

Simplify each expression.

10. $(-5) + (-3)$ **12.** $(-2)(5)(-1) + 1$ **14.** $(-7) - (-9)$

11. $(-6) + (-3) + 7$ **13.** $12 - (-3)$ **15.** $\dfrac{-20 + 2}{-6}$

16. If $f(x) = 3x + 5$, then $f(-2) = \underline{\ ?\ }$.

17. If $g: x \rightarrow x^2 + 1$, then $g(-1) = \underline{\ ?\ }$.

18. Simplify $-3n^2 + 4n + n^2 - 6n + 2$.

19. If $-x > x$, then $x \underline{\ ?\ } 0$.   **20.** If $|x| = x$, then $x \underline{\ ?\ } 0$.

Solve each equation over $\mathcal{R}$.

21. $4n + 3 = 18 - 3n$ **23.** $\dfrac{y - 3}{2} + 1 = 7$

22. $4(x - 1) = x + 11$ **24.** $2(x - 3) = 5(x + 9)$

25. Specify the solution set over $\mathcal{R}$ of $4(t + 3) \leq 20$.

26. Graph the solution set of $-1 < x \leq 2$ for $x \in \mathcal{R}$.

27. Find three consecutive odd integers whose sum is 75.

28. Find an angle whose measure is $3°$ greater than twice the measure of its complement.

Write each expression as a polynomial in which no two terms are like terms.

29. $(n^2 + 2n + 3) + (n^2 - 4n)$ **32.** $(-6x^2y^3z)^3$

30. $(t^2 - 3t + 5) - (2t^2 + 5t - 1)$ **33.** $(n + 3)(2n - 4)$

31. $3xz(x - 2z + 3)$ **34.** $\dfrac{8x^2 + 10x - 3}{4x - 1}$

35. Find two consecutive even integers the sum of whose squares is 164.

36. The length of the side of a square is 4 inches greater than the length of the side of another, and the area of the larger exceeds that of the smaller by 80 square inches. Find the dimensions of each square.

Factor each expression.

37. $14x^2y + 28xy - 21xy^2$

38. $n^2 - 5n + 4$

39. $3t^2 - 20t + 12$

40. $12z^2 + 2z - 24$

41. $36p^2 - 49q^2$

42. $ar - 2br + at - 2bt$

Solve each equation and check your result.

43. $4n^2 = 12n$

44. $(r + 3)(2r - 1) = 0$

45. $18k^2 = 48k$

46. $p^2 - 4p = 21$

47. Find the dimensions of a rectangle having an area of 35 square feet if its length is 3 feet less than twice its width.

48. One negative integer is 5 greater than 2 times another, and the difference of their squares is 13. Find the integers.

Simplify to a single fraction in lowest terms.

49. $\dfrac{2n^2 - 2r^2}{6n + 6r}$

50. $\dfrac{2}{5} - \dfrac{3}{t^2} + \dfrac{5}{2}$

51. $\dfrac{3x - 2y}{4x + 4y} \cdot \dfrac{(x + y)^2}{3x^2 + xy - 2y^2}$

52. $\dfrac{x^2 - 9}{2x + 6} \div \dfrac{x - 3}{x + 2}$

53. $\dfrac{n^2 - 1}{3n + 3} - \dfrac{n^2 - 1}{4n + 4}$

54. $\dfrac{27}{z^2 - 81} + \dfrac{3}{2z + 18}$

Solve and check.   **55.** $\dfrac{4}{3x - 2} + \dfrac{1}{3x} = \dfrac{1}{x}$ **56.** $\dfrac{3z - 4}{z - 4} = 2 + \dfrac{z + 4}{z + 1}$

57. If Mrs. Thomas had $1000 less invested at 5% than she now does at 4%, her annual return would be the same. How much does she now have invested at 4%?

58. How many pounds of an alloy containing 10% copper must be melted with how many pounds of an alloy containing 60% copper to make 250 pounds of an alloy containing 50% copper?

59. John can complete a job in 3 hours. His brother Peter can also do it in 3 hours, but his brother Walter needs 4 hours. How long would it take the three brothers to do the job if they worked together?

60. In still water, Maureen's motorboat is 6 miles per hour faster than Lorna's. In a current flowing at 4 miles per hour, Maureen can travel 78 miles upstream in the same length of time Lorna goes 84 miles downstream. What is the speed of Lorna's boat in still water?

CHAPTER 10

. . . Old Faithful Geyser in Yellowstone National Park, Wyoming

Functions, Relations, and Graphs

Old Faithful Geyser in Yellowstone National Park in Wyoming was given this name because of the regularity of its eruptions. However, there are variations, as shown by the graph. In 1878, nearly 50% of the observed intervals were about 65 minutes. However, in 1965, nearly 10% were about 45 minutes and close to 25% were about 70 minutes.

From The Physics Teacher, *April, 1969. Redrawn by permission of the publisher.*

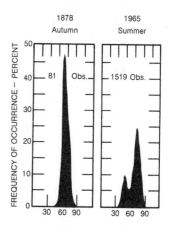

INTERVAL BETWEEN ERUPTIONS — MINUTES

GRAPHING FUNCTIONS AND RELATIONS

10–1   Functions Described by Tables

The table shown below reports the average daily circulation of the five newspapers in Central County. The contents of this table can also be presented as a *correspondence* or as a list of **ordered pairs**:

CENTRAL COUNTY

Newspaper	Average Daily Circulation
Times	17,500
Examiner	16,000
Courier	25,000
Journal	9,000
Blade	12,000

Times ⟶ **17,500**   (*Times*, **17,500**)

Examiner ⟶ **16,000**   (*Examiner*, **16,000**)

Courier ⟶ **25,000**   (*Courier*, **25,000**)

Journal ⟶ **9,000**   (*Journal*, **9,000**)

Blade ⟶ **12,000**   (*Blade*, **12,000**)

Since corresponding to each newspaper, there is one and only one value, you see that this table describes a *function* (page 146). The *domain D* of this function is the set of first elements in the ordered pairs above,

{Times, Examiner, Courier, Journal, Blade},

and the *range R* is the set of second elements in the ordered pairs above,

{17,500, 16,000, 25,000, 9,000, 12,000}.

You can see from the table on page 355 that the *Courier* has the greatest average daily circulation, while the *Journal* has the least. However, comparisons can be made more easily when the numbers in the range are represented by lengths in a diagram. One way of doing this is by drawing a *bar graph* as shown in Figure 10–1.

Average Daily Newspaper Circulation in Central County

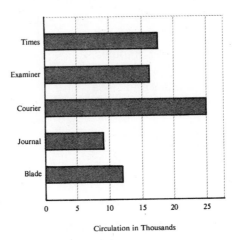

Figure 10–1

In this graph the elements of the domain are listed down the left-hand side of the graph. For each element of the domain, a horizontal bar is drawn to represent the corresponding element of the range. The length of each bar is determined by the horizontal scale at the bottom of the diagram. From this bar graph you can easily see how the circulations of the newspapers compare.

Pictographs or *pictorial graphs* like Figure 10–2 are special bar graphs in which rows of uniform symbols replace the bars.

Average Daily Newspaper Circulation in Central County

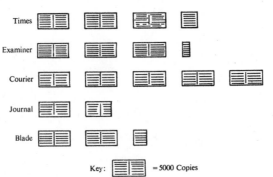

Figure 10–2

The adjoining table gives the numbers of college graduates in the United States at 5-year intervals from 1940 through 1965. The domain of this function is

{1940, 1945, 1950, 1955, 1960, 1965}.

The range (in hundred thousands) is

{2, 2.5, 3, 4, 5.5}.

Year of Graduation	United States College Graduates (nearest 50,000)
1940	200,000
1945	250,000
1950	400,000
1955	300,000
1960	400,000
1965	550,000

This function is pictured as a bar graph in Figure 10–3. Note that in this figure the elements of the domain are listed across the bottom of the graph.

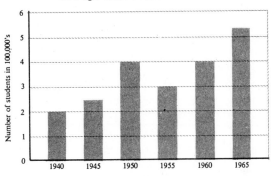

Figure 10–3

Sometimes when the elements of the domain of a function form a numerical succession, the bars of a vertical bar graph are replaced by dots located where the tops of the bars are. Then these dots are connected by line segments, giving a *broken-line graph* as shown in Figure 10–4.

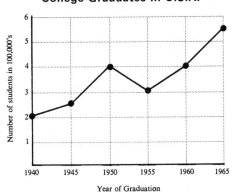

Figure 10–4

Notice carefully that the line segments in Figure 10–4 do not show the number of graduates for "in-between" years. They do, however, help you to visualize the changes or trends over periods of 5 years.

In working with ordered pairs of numbers, such as (1940, 200,000), you call the first number, 1940, the **first component** or **first coordinate** and you call the second number, 200,000, the **second component** or **second coordinate**. Two ordered pairs of numbers are defined to be **equal** when *both* their first components *and* their second components are equal. Thus, $(1940, 200,000) = (1940, 2 \times 10^5)$, but $(1940, 200,000) \neq (1940, 200,001)$.

Written Exercises

Make a bar graph for the facts shown in each table and give the graph a title. Give the domain and the range of each function.

A   1.

Name of Satellite	Discoverer 1	Tiros 1	Courier 1	Ranger 1
Satellite weight in hundreds of pounds	2.5	2.7	5.00	6.75

2.

Computer Program Language	Fortran G	Fortran H	PL/1	Cobol F	RPG
Running time of Program T in seconds	70	80	115	85	110

Make a broken-line graph for the facts shown in each table, and give the graph a title. Give the domain and the range of each function.

3.

Year	1920	1930	1940	1950	1960
Population of Central City in thousands	30	32	35	46	52

4.

Year	1950	1955	1960	1965
Male High School Graduates in U.S. during year (nearest 100,000)	6	7	9	13

5–8. Make a pictograph for the facts shown in the table in Exercises 1–4 above. Give each pictograph a title.

Find all real values of *a* and *b* for which the given ordered pairs are equal.

SAMPLE. $(a + 2, 3b + 5)$; $(2a - 1, b - 3)$

Solution: $(a + 2, 3b + 5) = (2a - 1, b - 3)$ if and only if

$$a + 2 = 2a - 1 \quad \text{and} \quad 3b + 5 = b - 3$$
$$3 = a \qquad\qquad\qquad 2b = -8, \text{ or } b = -4$$

The check is left to you.

∴ the values of a and b are 3 and -4, respectively. **Answer.**

9. $(2a - 3, b);\ (9, 3)$ 12. $(3a + 9, 4b);\ (2a + 11, -4)$

10. $(3a, b - 7);\ (15, -2)$ 13. $(a, b + 5);\ (2a, 2b - 13)$

11. $(-a, 7b + 1);\ (3a - 6, 15)$ 14. $(3a + 8, b + 2);\ (7a, 8 - b)$

B   15. $(1 - a, 4);\ (2 + a, |b|)$ 18. $(3 - a^2, b^2);\ (2a, 25)$

16. $(|a| + 1, b);\ (4, 5b)$ 19. $(|a + 1|, b^2);\ (0, -1)$

17. $(2a + 5, b^2);\ (5a + 2, b)$ 20. $(3 - a, b^2 - 4);\ (1 - a, 0)$

10–2   Coordinates in a Plane

The functions that you deal with most often have sets of numbers as domains and ranges. To work with them, you need to know how to **graph** *ordered pairs of numbers* as points in a plane.

Draw a horizontal number line, called the *horizontal axis*, and draw a second number line intersecting it at right angles such that both number lines have the same zero point, called the *origin (O)*. The second number line is called the *vertical axis* (Figure 10–5). The positive direction (indicated by the single arrowhead) is usually to the right on the horizontal axis and upward on the vertical axis.

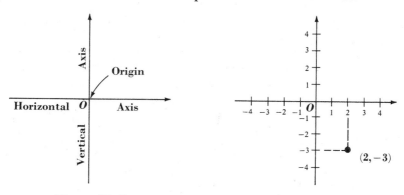

Figure 10–5   Figure 10–6

To locate the *graph of the ordered pair* $(2, -3)$, find the graph (page 8) of **2** on the horizontal axis (Figure 10–6), and draw a vertical line through it. Then find the graph of -3 on the vertical axis, and draw a horizontal line through that point. The point of intersection of these lines is the graph of $(2, -3)$. Mark the point with a dot. Marking a point in this way is called *plotting the point*.

It is convenient to draw the axes on squared paper, using the length of the side of a square as the unit on each axis (Figure 10–7).

The axes separate the plane into four regions, called **quadrants,** numbered as shown in Figure 10–7.

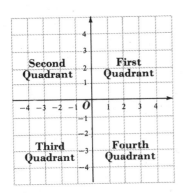

Figure 10–7

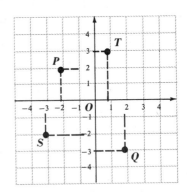

Figure 10–8

From point *P* in Figure 10–8, draw a vertical line to meet the horizontal axis. The coordinate (page 8) of the point where it meets this axis is called the **abscissa** (ab-**sis**-a) of *P*, -2.

Draw a horizontal line from *P* to meet the vertical axis. The coordinate of this meeting point is called the **ordinate** (or-**din**-et) of *P*, 2.

Together, the abscissa and ordinate of *P* are called the **coordinates** of *P*. The coordinates are written as an ordered pair, with the abscissa first, $(-2, 2)$.

Verify the coordinates of the other points graphed in Figure 10–8:

$$T(1, 3), \quad S(-3, -2), \quad Q(2, -3), \quad O(0, 0)$$

Notice that in the first quadrant, both coordinates are positive; in the second quadrant, the abscissa is negative but the ordinate is positive; in the third quadrant, both coordinates are negative; in the fourth quadrant, the abscissa is positive but the ordinate is negative.

When a coordinate system is set up on a plane as we have just done, the axes are called **coordinate axes** and the plane is called a **coordinate plane.** In working with a coordinate plane, you take the following facts for granted:

1. There is exactly one point in the coordinate plane paired with each ordered pair of real numbers.

2. There is exactly one ordered pair of real numbers paired with each point in the coordinate plane.

Thus, there is a one-to-one correspondence (page 21) between ordered pairs of real numbers and points of a coordinate plane. This correspondence is called a **plane rectangular coordinate system.**

Oral Exercises

Give the coordinates of each numbered point.

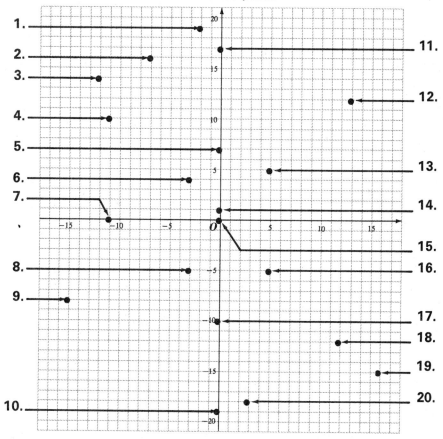

In each of Exercises 21–32, name the quadrants or axes containing the specified points.

21. The ordinate is 3.

22. The ordinate is −4.

23. The abscissa is −2.

24. The abscissa is 5.

25. The ordinate is positive.

26. The ordinate is negative.

27. The abscissa is positive.

28. The abscissa is negative.

29. The ordinate equals the abscissa.

30. The ordinate equals the negative of the abscissa.

31. The ordinate equals 0.

32. The abscissa equals 0.

Written Exercises

Plot the graph of each ordered pair.

A
1. $(2, 3)$	**4.** $(0, -3)$	**7.** $(-4, 2)$	**10.** $(-3, -3)$
2. $(5, 0)$	**5.** $(-2, -3)$	**8.** $(0, 6)$	**11.** $(5, -5)$
3. $(1, -4)$	**6.** $(-5, 0)$	**9.** $(7, 7)$	**12.** $(-6, 6)$

Each of Exercises 13–18 lists three vertices of a rectangle. Graph these, determine the coordinates of the fourth vertex, and sketch the rectangle.

B
13. $(1, 1), (1, -1), (-1, -1)$	**16.** $(1, 6), (-2, 6), (-2, -3)$
14. $(2, 6), (0, 0), (2, 0)$	**17.** $(8, -2), (2, -2), (8, -5)$
15. $(-2, -3), (5, 1), (-2, 1)$	**18.** $(-6, -1), (-6, -5), (-1, -1)$

Plot three points in at least two quadrants whose coordinates are integers satisfying the given requirement.

19. The abscissa equals the ordinate.

20. The abscissa is half the ordinate.

21. The ordinate is one greater than the abscissa.

22. The ordinate is two greater than twice the abscissa.

10–3 Relations

The diagram at the right shows how each number in the set D where $D = \{0, 1, 2, 3\}$ is paired with one or more numbers in the set R, $R = \{1, 2, 3, 4\}$. The same pairing is shown in the adjoining table, and in the following roster of the set of ordered pairs of numbers:

$$\{(0, 1), (1, 2), (1, 4), (2, 3), (3, 2)\}$$

D	R
0	1
1	2
1	4
2	3
3	2

Does this pairing define a function with domain D and range R? No! In a function, each member of the domain is assigned *exactly one* partner in the range. The given pairing, however, assigns to the number 1, two range elements, namely, 2 *and* 4.

The pairing in the preceding example is a *relation*. A **relation** is any set of ordered pairs of elements. The set of first elements in the ordered pairs is called the **domain** of the relation, and the set of second elements is called the **range**. The domain of the relation described above is

$$\{0, 1, 2, 3\},$$

and the range is

$$\{1, 2, 3, 4\}.$$

Recall (page 16) that in the roster of a set, no element is listed more than once. The listing {(0, 1), (1, 2), (1, 4), (2, 3), (3, 2)} is called a *roster* of the relation.

    You now see that a function is a special kind of relation. A function is a relation such that each element of the domain is paired with *one and only one* element of the range.

    Figure 10–9 shows the graphs in a coordinate plane of all the ordered pairs that form the relation described above. We call this set of points the **graph** of the relation. Notice that domain elements are shown along the horizontal axis and range elements along the vertical axis.

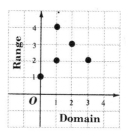

Figure 10–9

Oral Exercises

State the roster of the relation graphed in each diagram. Give the domain and the range of the relation. Is the relation a function?

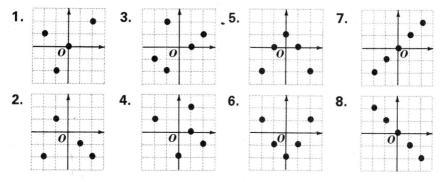

Give the domain and range of each relation. Is the relation a function?

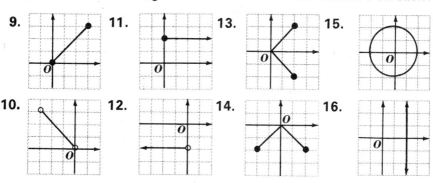

17. 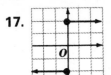   **18.**   **19.**   **20.**

Written Exercises

Graph the relation whose ordered pairs are shown in the given table or roster. State the domain and the range of the relation. Is the relation a function?

A

1.

1	2
2	4
3	6
4	8
5	10

3.

1	2
2	4
3	3
4	4
5	2

5.

−2	−1
−1	−0.5
0	0
1	1.5
2	1
3	1.5

7.

−2	4
−1	1
0	0
1	1
2	4
3	9

2.

1	3
2	2
3	9
4	12
5	15

4.

1	5
2	4
3	3
4	4
5	5

6.

−2	−0.7
−1	−0.3
0	0
1	0.3
2	0.7
3	1

8.

−2	−8
−1	−1
0	0
1	1
2	8
3	27

9.

1	0
2	3
3	4
1	2

10.

0	1
1	2
2	1
1	3

11. $\{(-2, 2), (-1, 1), (0, 0), (1, 1), (2, 2)\}$

12. $\{(0, 0), (1, 1), (1, -1), (2, 2), (2, -2)\}$

13. $\{(-4, 1), (-1, 2), (4, 3), (4, -3), (-1, -2), (-4, -1), (-5, 0)\}$

14. $\{(0, 1), (1, 2), (2, 5), (3, 10), (-1, 2), (-2, 5), (-3, 10)\}$

10–4 Open Sentences in Two Variables

Have you ever had this kind of problem? The Davis Music Club had $36 to buy two kinds of recordings. One kind cost $3 each, and the other kind cost $4 each. If the club is to buy some of each, how many combinations are possible?

Let x = number of $3 recordings; then $3x$ = cost, in dollars, of $3 recordings.

Let y = number of $4 recordings; then $4y$ = cost, in dollars, of $4 recordings.

Total cost of two purchases = total amount to be spent

$$3x + 4y = 36$$

Any combination of whole-number values of x and y which make the preceding equation a true statement gives a solution of the buying problem. For instance, you can check that the ordered pair of numbers $(8, 3)$, with the value of x written first, makes the equation a true statement:

$$3 \cdot 8 + 4 \cdot 3 \stackrel{?}{=} 36$$
$$24 + 12 \quad = 36 \checkmark$$

Thus, the Club could buy 8 three-dollar and 3 four-dollar recordings. Another acceptable way to spend the money is shown by the ordered pair $(4, 6)$ since

$$3 \cdot 4 + 4 \cdot 6 = 36$$

is a true statement. On the other hand, $(2, 5)$ does not give an acceptable spending plan because the statement

$$3 \cdot 2 + 4 \cdot 5 = 36$$

is false.

We call equations or inequalities that involve two variables, such as x and y, **open sentences in two variables**. To **solve an open sentence in two variables**, you must find all the ordered pairs of numbers (chosen from the replacement sets of the two variables) that make the sentence a true statement. Each such ordered pair is called a **solution** or **root** of the sentence and is said to **satisfy** the sentence. The set of all solutions of the open sentence is called the **solution set** over the given replacement sets of the variables.

EXAMPLE 1.   Find the solution set of $3x + 4y = 36$ if the replacement set of both x and y is the set of whole numbers.

Solution:

1. Transform the given sentence into an equivalent one having y as its left member.

$$3x + 4y = 36$$
$$y = \tfrac{1}{4}(36 - 3x)$$
$$y = 9 - \tfrac{3}{4}x$$

2. Replace x with each member of its replacement set in turn and determine the corresponding value of y. Since y must be a whole number, $\tfrac{3}{4}x$ must also be a whole number. Therefore, only multiples of 4 are acceptable replacements for x.

3. If the value of y determined in Step 2 belongs to the replacement set of y, then the pair of corresponding values is a root of the sentence. As shown in the table, values of x greater than 12 will yield negative numbers for y; therefore, 12 is the greatest acceptable value of x.

x	$y = 9 - \tfrac{3}{4}x$	y
0	$9 - \tfrac{3}{4} \cdot 0$	9
4	$9 - \tfrac{3}{4} \cdot 4$	6
8	$9 - \tfrac{3}{4} \cdot 8$	3
12	$9 - \tfrac{3}{4} \cdot 12$	0
16	$9 - \tfrac{3}{4} \cdot 16$	-3

$\therefore$ the solution set is $\{(0, 9), (4, 6), (8, 3), (12, 0)\}$.   **Answer.**

Do you see that the solution set of the equation in Example 1 is a function with domain $\{0, 4, 8, 12\}$ and range $\{9, 6, 3, 0\}$? In general, the solution set of any open sentence in two variables is a relation whose domain is the set of first elements and whose range is the set of second elements in the ordered pairs satisfying the sentence. In Example 2, below, the solution set of the given open sentence is a relation, but *not* a function.

EXAMPLE 2.   Find the solution set of $x - 2y \geq 6$ if $x \in \{-2, 0, 2\}$ and $y \in \{-1, -2, -3, -4\}$.

Solution:

$$x - 2y \geq 6$$
$$-2y \geq 6 - x$$
$$y \leq \tfrac{x}{2} - 3$$

x	$\tfrac{x}{2} - 3$	$y \leq \tfrac{x}{2} - 3$	y
-2	$\tfrac{-2}{2} - 3$	$y \leq -4$	-4
0	$\tfrac{0}{2} - 3$	$y \leq -3$.	$-4, -3$
2	$\tfrac{2}{2} - 3$	$y \leq -2$	$-2, -3, -4$

∴ the solution set is

$\{(-2, -4), (0, -4), (0, -3), (2, -2), (2, -3), (2, -4)\}$.   **Answer.**

Oral Exercises

Is the given ordered pair of numbers a root of the open sentence? Why?
Assume that $\mathcal{R}$ is the replacement set of each variable.

SAMPLE 1. $4x - 3y = 1$; $(2, 3)$

Solution: Not a root, because $4 \cdot 2 - 3 \cdot 3 \neq 1$.

1. $x - y = 8$; $(12, 4)$
2. $3x + y = 10$; $(3, 1)$
3. $2x - y = 6$; $(2, -4)$
4. $x + 2y = -1$; $(-5, 2)$
5. $3x + 5y = 6$; $(2, 0)$

6. $-2x + 5y = 4$; $(1, 1)$
7. $8x - y > -1$; $(1, -9)$
8. $-3x + 4y \geq -7$; $(0, -2)$
9. $x^2 + y = 11$; $(-3, 2)$
10. $y - xy = 9$; $(-2, 3)$

Transform each open sentence into an equivalent one having y as one
member.

SAMPLE 2. $2x + 3y = 9$ *Solution:* $y = 3 - \frac{2}{3}x$. **Answer.**

11. $5x - y = 0$
12. $x - y = -3$

13. $4x + 2y = 6$
14. $12x - 4y = 1$

15. $x + y \leq 2$
16. $x - 2y \geq 4$

State the domain and the range of the function whose ordered pairs are
given in the table. Then give a formula for the function.

SAMPLE 3.

x	1	2	3	4	5	6
y	−1	0	1	2	3	4

Domain: $\{1, 2, 3, 4, 5, 6\}$;

Range: $\{-1, 0, 1, 2, 3, 4\}$;   *Solution:* $y = x - 2$. **Answer.**

17.

x	1	2	3	4	5
y	1	2	3	4	5

18.

x	1	2	3	4	5
y	−1	−2	−3	−4	−5

19.

x	1	2	3	4	5
y	4	5	6	7	8

20.

x	1	2	3	4	5
y	−2	−4	−6	−8	−10

21.

x	1	2	3	4	5
y	-3	-6	-9	-12	-15

22.

x	1	2	3	4	5
y	-3	-2	-1	0	1

Written Exercises

Find the solution set of each equation given that $\{-2, -1, 0, 1, 2\}$ is the replacement set of x and $\mathcal{R}$, the replacement set of y. Graph the solution set.

A

1. $y = x$

2. $y = -x$

3. $y = x + 1$

4. $y = -x - 1$

5. $y = -2x$

6. $y = \frac{3}{2}x$

7. $y = x - 1$

8. $y = -x + 1$

9. $y = 2x + 2$

10. $y = 2x - 2$

11. $y = -x + 4$

12. $y = -x - 4$

13. $y = 2x^2$

14. $y = -x^2$

15. $y = x^2 + 3$

16. $y = x^2 - 5$

17. $y = x^2 - 3x$

18. $y = x^2 + 4x$

Find the solution set of each inequality given that $\{-1, 0, 1\}$ is the replacement set of x and $\{-2, -1, 0, 1, 2\}$ is the replacement set of y. Graph the solution set.

B

19. $y > x$

20. $y < x$

21. $y + 1 \leq 2x$

22. $y - 1 \leq 3x$

23. $x - y < x + y$

24. $1 - y > 2x + 1$

Find the solution set over the given replacement sets for x and y.

C

25. $|x| + 3y = 2y + 4$; $x \in \{-3, 0, 4\}$, $y \in \{\text{positive integers}\}$

26. $|x| - 5y = 12 - y$; $x \in \{-1, 0, 4\}$, $y \in \{\text{negative integers}\}$

27. $y = x^2 - 4x + 3$; $y \in \{0, -1, 3\}$; $x \in \mathcal{R}$

28. $y = x^2 + 6x$; $y \in \{0, -9, 7\}$; $x \in \mathcal{R}$

For each problem write an equation in two variables. Restrict the replacement sets to the conditions of the problem and find the solution set.

29. Miss Novak spent $1.50 for stamps, buying some 6¢ stamps and some 10¢ stamps. How many of each did she buy?

30. Amy Jorgensen sent $16 to a hatchery for chicks and ducklings. She specified that all the money be used and that she receive at least a dozen of each kind of fowl. The chicks cost 15¢ each and the ducklings 40¢ each. How many of each did she get?

LINEAR EQUATIONS AND FUNCTIONS

10–5   The Graph of a Linear Equation in Two Variables

Every root of the equation

$$-2x + y = 1$$

is an ordered pair of numbers represented by (x, y). The graph of one such root, $(0, 1)$, is the point P in Figure 10–10. Note that it is customary to take the horizontal axis as the x-axis and the vertical axis as the y-axis. To find other roots of this equation, substitute values for x and obtain corresponding values for y, as shown in the table.

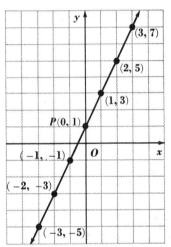

$-2x + y = 1$		
x	**y = 1 + 2x**	**y**
-3	$1 + 2(-3)$	-5
-2	$1 + 2(-2)$	-3
-1	$1 + 2(-1)$	-1
0	$1 + 2(0)$	1
1	$1 + 2(1)$	3
2	$1 + 2(2)$	5
3	$1 + 2(3)$	7

Figure 10–10

Figure 10–10 suggests that the points corresponding to these roots lie on a straight line, part of which is shown in the diagram. In fact, if the set $\Re$ (of real numbers) is the replacement set for both x and y, then each root of the equation does give the coordinates of a point on this line, and the coordinates of each point of the line satisfy the equation.

Because this line is the set of *all those points* and *only those points* whose coordinates satisfy the equation, the line is called the *graph of the equation* in the coordinate plane, and

$$-2x + y = 1$$

is called *an equation of the line*.

In general:

> In the coordinate plane, the graph of any equation equivalent to one of the form
>
> $$Ax + By = C, \qquad x \in \mathcal{R}, \qquad y \in \mathcal{R}$$
>
> where A, B, and C are real numbers with A and B not both zero is a straight line. Any such equation is called a **linear equation in two variables**, x and y.

Notice that in a linear equation, each term is a constant or a monomial of degree 1. Thus, "$3x - 2y = 1$" is linear, but "$x + \dfrac{2}{y} = 5$," "$x^2 + y^2 = 3$," and "$xy = 7$," are not.

Although you need plot *only two points* to graph a linear equation, it is good practice to plot a third point, as a check. Sometimes it is helpful to find roots of the form $(0, b)$ and $(a, 0)$. You obtain the latter by replacing y with "0" and finding the corresponding value of x.

In the following examples and throughout the rest of this book, you may assume, unless otherwise directed, that $\mathcal{R}$ is the replacement set for each variable in an open sentence in two variables.

EXAMPLE 1. Graph $x + 3y = 9$ in the coordinate plane.

Solution:

$3y = 9 - x$

$y = 3 - \tfrac{1}{3}x$

x	$3 - \tfrac{1}{3}x$	y
-3	$3 - \tfrac{1}{3}(-3)$	4
0	$3 - \tfrac{1}{3}(0)$	3
3	$3 - \tfrac{1}{3}(3)$	2
9	$3 - \tfrac{1}{3}(9)$	0

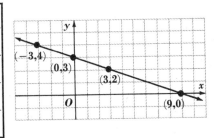

EXAMPLE 2. Graph $y = 2$ in the coordinate plane.

Solution: Since the equation places no restrictions on x, every point having ordinate 2 corresponds to a root, regardless of its first coordinate.

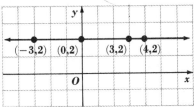

A function whose ordered pairs satisfy a linear equation is called a **linear function.** Thus,

$$f: x \rightarrow y = 2x - 4$$

is a linear function.

Oral Exercises

State whether or not the equation is linear.

1. $3x - 2y = 7$ **5.** $2x - y = 0$ **9.** $\dfrac{2}{x} + y = 5$

2. $x = 5y$ **6.** $xy = 7$ **10.** $x = 5$

3. $\dfrac{y}{3} = 2x - 5$ **7.** $\frac{1}{2}x + \frac{3}{4}y = x^2$ **11.** $y = 2$

4. $\dfrac{x}{2} = y^2 - 4$ **8.** $5x - 3xy = 2$ **12.** $xy = 0$

Solve each equation for y in terms of x.

13. $x + y = 2$ **17.** $2x + 3y = 0$
14. $y - x = 3$ **18.** $3x - 2y = 0$
15. $3x + y = 6$ **19.** $3x + 2y = 5$
16. $2x - y = 5$ **20.** $2x - 3y = 7$

State the relationship between the ordinate and abscissa of points on the graph of the given equation.

SAMPLE. $y = 2x - 3$

Solution: The ordinate is 3 less than two times the abscissa.

21. $y = \dfrac{1}{3x} + 1$ **25.** $2x + 3y = 7$

22. $y = \frac{1}{2}x - 1$ **26.** $x - 2y = 3$
23. $y = 3x + 5$ **27.** $xy = 7$
24. $y = 5x - 3$ **28.** $y = x^2 + 5$

Tell which of the given pairs of points belong to the graph of the given equation.

29. $x + y = 7$; $(3, -4)$, $(6, 1)$
30. $2x - y = 3$; $(3, 3)$, $(-3, 3)$
31. $5x + 3y = 0$; $(0, 2)$, $(3, -5)$
32. $4x - 3y = 12$; $(2, -1)$, $(3, 0)$

Written Exercises

Graph each equation in the coordinate plane.

1. $y = 4$ 4. $x = -2$ 7. $3x + y = 5$ 10. $3x - y = 6$
2. $y = -2$ 5. $y = x + 1$ 8. $2x + y = 6$ 11. $2x - 3y = 6$
3. $x = 3$ 6. $y = x - 2$ 9. $4x - y = 2$ 12. $3x + 4y = 12$

Write a formula and then graph the function defined by each rule. In each case, let the domain be {the positive real numbers}.

13. The number of inches is 12 times the number of feet.
14. The number of feet is 3.3 times the number of meters.
15. The number of U.S. dollars is 2.4 times the number of British pounds.
16. The pressure of water (in pounds per square foot) on the bottom of a tank is 62.4 times the depth (in feet) of water.
17. The total number of dollars to be repaid on $100 borrowed at 7% per year is 100 more than 7 times the number of years of the loan.
18. Bradley's Rent-A-Car Service makes the following daily charge in dollars for a standard model automobile: 7 plus 0.07 times the number of miles driven.

Graph the function with the indicated domain.

19. $f: x \rightarrow y = \frac{1}{2}x - 7$; $x \in \mathcal{R}$

20. $g: x \rightarrow y = 4 - \dfrac{x}{2}$; $x \in \mathcal{R}$

21. $P(l) = 2(l + 3)$; $l \in$ {the nonnegative numbers}
22. $f(c) = \frac{9}{5}c + 32$; $c \in \mathcal{R}$
23. $C: r \rightarrow 2\pi r$; $0 \le r \le 14$ (Use $\frac{22}{7}$ for π.)
24. $C: d \rightarrow \pi d$; $0 \le d \le 7$ (Use $\frac{22}{7}$ for π.)

Find the coordinates of the point where the graph of each equation crosses (a) the x-axis and (b) the y-axis.

25. $7x + 5y = 35$ 27. $5x = 50 - 10y$ 29. $2x = 9y$
26. $4x - 6y = 24$ 28. $7x = 56 + 4y$ 30. $4y = -15x$

31. Show that the function $f: x \rightarrow y = (x - 4)(x + 3) - x^2 + 6$ is a linear function.
32. Show that the function $g: x \rightarrow y = (x - 1)(x + 1) - (x + 2)^2$ is a linear function.

Graph each pair of equations on the same set of axes. Name the co-ordinates of the point where the graphs intersect, and show by substitution that the coordinates satisfy both equations.

C **33.** $x + y = 4$; $y = 2x + 1$ **35.** $x - 2y = 6$; $2x - 3y = 5$
  34. $2x + y = 4$; $y = x + 1$ **36.** $x - y = 6$; $x + y = -2$

Graph each equation. Is it a linear equation?

37. $y = |x| + 1$ **39.** $y = -|x| + 1$
38. $y = |x + 1|$ **40.** $y = -|x| - 11$

Graph each function. Is it a linear function?

41. The function which assigns the number 2 to each nonnegative number, and the number -1 to each negative number.

42. The function which assigns the number 1 to each positive number, and the number 3 to each nonpositive number.

43. The function which assigns to each number twice its absolute value.

44. The function which assigns to each number half its absolute value.

10–6 Slope of a Line

To describe the steepness, or grade, of a hill, you may determine the vertical *rise* for every 100 feet of horizontal *run*. For example, if a hill rises 20 feet for every 100 feet of horizontal distance, its grade is the ratio $\frac{20}{100}$, or 20% (Figure 10–11).

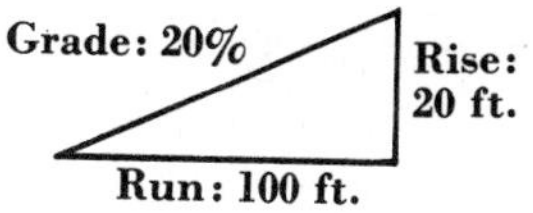

Similarly, to describe the steepness, or *slope*, of a straight line, you choose two points on it and compute the quotient

Grade: 20%   Rise: 20 ft.   Run: 100 ft.

Figure 10–11

$$\text{slope} = \frac{\text{rise}}{\text{run}} = \frac{\text{vertical change}}{\text{horizontal change}}$$

Because the vertical change in moving from one point to another is the difference of the ordinates, and the horizontal change is the *corresponding* difference of abscissas,

$$\text{slope} = \frac{\text{difference of ordinates}}{\text{difference of abscissas}}.$$

Thus, to find the slope of the line through $P(3, 2)$ and $Q(4, 5)$, notice that

$$\text{ordinate of } Q - \text{ordinate of } P = 5 - 2$$

$$\text{abscissa of } Q - \text{abscissa of } P = 4 - 3$$

Thus, using m to denote slope, you have

$$m = \frac{5 - 2}{4 - 3} = \frac{3}{1} = 3.$$

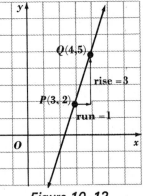

Figure 10–12

One way of checking the slope is to move on a line from left to right. On a line with slope 3, each horizontal change of 1 unit produces a positive change of 3 units in the vertical direction. For the line joining S and T in Figure 10–13,

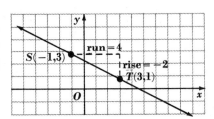

$$m = \frac{1 - 3}{3 - (-1)} = \frac{-2}{4} = -\frac{1}{2}.$$

Figure 10–13

Check by counting units. From S to T are 4 units of horizontal change and -2 units of vertical change. For each positive change of one horizontal unit, therefore, there is a negative change of half a vertical unit, a rate of change equal to $-\frac{1}{2}$.

Whenever a line falls from left to right, its slope is a negative number. When it rises from left to right, its slope is a positive number. Can the slope of a line be 0? The slope of the line joining $K(-2, -2)$ and $M(3, -2)$ in Figure 10–14 is

$$m = \frac{-2 - (-2)}{3 - (-2)}$$

$$= \frac{-2 + 2}{3 + 2}$$

$$= \frac{0}{5} = 0.$$

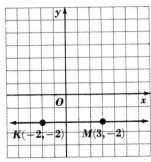

Do you see that the slope of every horizontal line is 0?

Figure 10–14

If you use the formula on page 373 to try to compute the "slope" of the line pictured in Figure 10–15, you find

$$\frac{3 - (-2)}{3 - 3} = \frac{5}{0}.$$

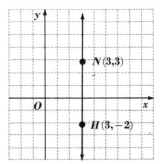

Since you cannot divide by 0, the formula does not apply, and this line, like *every vertical line, has no slope.*

Figure 10–15

A basic property of a line is that its slope is constant. Thus, you may use *any* two of its points in computing its slope.

Oral Exercises

In Exercises 1–8, give the slope of each line.

1.

3.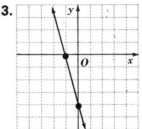

5.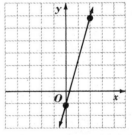

2.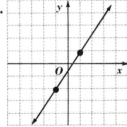

4.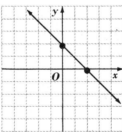

6.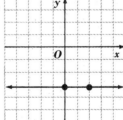

7.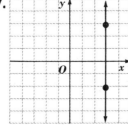

8.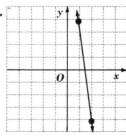

Do the points specified in each table lie on a line? If so, tell its slope.

SAMPLE.

	1	1	1	
x	0	1	2	3
y	5	7	9	11
	2	2	2	

Solution: The points lie on a line because equal changes in the value of *x* produce equal changes in the value of *y*. The slope is $\frac{2}{1}$ or 2.

9.

x	0	1	2	3
y	3	4	5	6

13.

x	−1	0	1	2
y	3	6	3	6

10.

x	0	1	2	3
y	5	4	3	2

14.

x	−2	0	2	4
y	2	0	−2	−4

11.

x	0	1	2	3
y	5	2	4	3

15.

x	1	4	7	11
y	6	8	11	15

12.

x	0	1	2	3
y	−2	0	2	4

16.

x	−2	5	12	19
y	3	3	3	3

Written Exercises

Plot each pair of points, draw the line containing the points, and determine the slope of the line from the graph. Check by finding the slope algebraically.

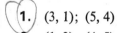

A

1. (3, 1); (5, 4)   **3.** (−2, 3); (0, 2)   **5.** (4, 2); (−3, 2)

2. (1, 3); (4, 5)   **4.** (3, −1); (3, 4)   **6.** (2, 4); (−1, −1)

Through the given point, draw a line with the given slope.

SAMPLE. (2, −1); slope, $-\frac{3}{2}$

Solution: From (2, −1) measure 2 units to the right and 3 units down. Connect the point reached with (2, −1) to determine the line.

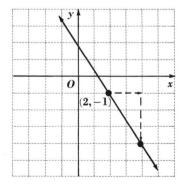

7. (3, 2); slope, 2   **9.** (−3, 1); slope, $\frac{3}{4}$ **11.** (−3, −2); slope, −$\frac{1}{2}$

8. (0, −2); slope, 1   **10.** (2, −2); slope, $\frac{3}{5}$ **12.** (1, 3); slope, 0

Determine a value for b so that the slope m of the line through each pair of points has the given value. Check your solution by graphing the line through the points.

B   **13.** (4, −1); (6, b); $m = 1$ **16.** (8, 3b); (b, 3); $m = \frac{1}{2}$

    14. (4, b); (9, 1); $m = -2$ **17.** (2b, 3); (6, b); $m = -\frac{1}{2}$

    15. (3, b); (2b, 7); $m = \frac{3}{5}$ **18.** (1, b); (−b, 7); $m = 5$

10–7   The Slope-Intercept Form of a Linear Equation

The graph of "$y = 2x$" is the straight line (Figure 10–16) containing the points whose coordinates are given in the table. Do you see that when the abscissas of two points on the line differ by 1 their ordinates differ by 2, the slope of the line? Notice that the line passes through the origin.

	1	1	1	
x	−1	0	1	2
y	−2	0	2	4
	2	2	2	

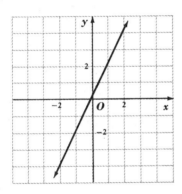

Figure 10–16   Figure 10–17

Can you guess the slope of the line whose equation is "$y = -2x$" (Figure 10–17)? It is −2, because an increase of 1 in the abscissa produces a change of −2 in the ordinate. This line also contains the origin. In general:

> For every real number m, the graph in the coordinate plane of the equation
>
> $$y = mx$$
>
> is the line that has slope m and passes through the origin.

In Figure 10–18, compare the graphs of "$y = 2x + 4$" and "$y = 2x$." They have equal slopes, but they cross the y-axis at different points. The ordinate of the point where a line crosses the y-axis is called the line's **y-intercept**. To determine the y-intercept, replace x with "0" in the equation of each line:

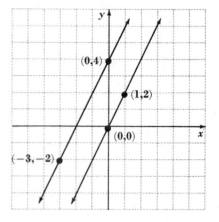

$$y = 2x \qquad\qquad y = 2x + 4$$
$$y = 2 \cdot 0 \qquad\qquad y = 2 \cdot 0 + 4$$
$$y = 0 \leftarrow y\text{-intercepts} \rightarrow y = 4$$

If you write "$y = 2x$" as "$y = 2x + 0$," you can see that the constant term in these equations is the y-intercept of each graph:

$$y = 2x + 0 \quad \text{and} \quad y = 2x + 4.$$

Figure 10–18

For all real numbers m and b, the graph in the coordinate plane of the equation

$$y = mx + b$$

is the line whose slope is m and y-intercept is b.

One way to describe a straight line is to write its equation in the form "$y = mx + b$," and then read the values of the slope m and the y-intercept b. This is called the **slope-intercept form**.

Equation	Transforming to $y = mx + b$	Describing the line	
		Slope	y-intercept
$x + 2y = 4$	$2y = -x + 4,\ y = -\frac{1}{2}x + 2$	$-\frac{1}{2}$	2
$6x - 3y = 8$	$3y = 6x - 8,\ \ y = 2x - \frac{8}{3}$	2	$-\frac{8}{3}$
$2y - 10 = 0$	$2y = 10,\qquad y = 0x + 5$	0	5

EXAMPLE. Draw the line with $m = \frac{2}{3}$, $b = 1$; then find its equation.

Solution: The y-intercept is 1; so you label $(0, 1)$. Since the slope is $\frac{2}{3}$, you move from (0, 1) 3 units to the right and 2 units up to locate a second point on the line. Draw the line containing the two points.

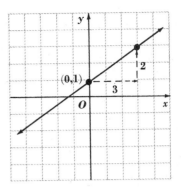

$$y = mx + b$$
$$\downarrow \qquad \downarrow$$
$$y = \tfrac{2}{3}x + 1, \text{ or}$$
$$3y = 2x + 3. \quad \text{Answer.}$$

Oral Exercises

State the slope and y-intercept of the line whose equation is given.

1. $y = 5x + 7$
2. $y = x - 3$
3. $y = -2x - 8$
4. $y = -\tfrac{1}{2}x + 3$
5. $y - 3 = 0$
6. $y + 7 = 0$
7. $3y = 6x - 1$

8. $4y = -8x - 3$
9. $3 + 2x = y$
10. $5 - 2x = y$
11. $5x + y = 7$
12. $2x - 2y = 1$
13. $x = -3$
14. $x = 2$

[handwritten: m = 3, b = 5, y = 2x + 5]

[handwritten: m = slope, b = y intercept]

Written Exercises

Write a linear equation with integral coefficients whose graph has the given slope and y-intercept.

 A

1. $m = 2, b = 5$
2. $m = -4, b = 1$ *[handwritten: y = -4x + 1]*
3. $m = -2, b = -3$ *[handwritten: y = -2x - 3]*
4. $m = 5, b = -4$ *[handwritten: y = 5x - 4]*
5. $m = \tfrac{1}{2}, b = 7$ *[handwritten: y = \tfrac{1}{2}x + 7]*

6. $m = -\tfrac{1}{3}, b = 2$
7. $m = 0, b = 2$ *[handwritten: y = 2]*
8. $m = 0, b = -7$ *[handwritten: y = -7]*
9. $m = -\tfrac{2}{3}, b = -\tfrac{1}{6}$ *[handwritten: y = -\tfrac{2}{3}x - \tfrac{1}{6}]*
10. $m = -\tfrac{4}{5}, b = \tfrac{3}{10}$ *[handwritten: y = -\tfrac{4}{5}x + \tfrac{3}{10}]*

Use only the y-intercept and slope to graph each equation.

11. $y - x = 2$
12. $y - 2x = -2$
13. $2x - y = 3$
14. $3x + y = 1$

15. $2x + y = 0$
16. $-3x + y = 0$
17. $6x + 2y + 1 = 0$
18. $5y + 3 = 0$

10–8   Determining an Equation of a Line

The line in Figure 10–19 has slope -2 and passes through the point $(2, 1)$. The slope-intercept form of the equation of this line is

$$y = -2x + b.$$

Since the point $(2, 1)$ is on the line, its coordinates must satisfy the equation; that is,

$$1 = -2(2) + b$$
$$1 = -4 + b, \quad \text{or} \quad 5 = b.$$

Thus, an equation of the line is

$$y = -2x + 5.$$

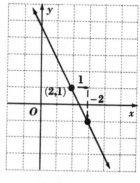

Figure 10–19

To determine an equation of a line containing two given points, find the slope of the line, and then find the y-intercept, as above. The following example illustrates the method.

EXAMPLE.   **Find an equation of the line which passes through the points whose coordinates are $(5, 2)$ and $(2, -1)$.**

Solution: **1. Slope $= m = \dfrac{-1 - 2}{2 - 5} = \dfrac{-3}{-3} = 1$**

2. The slope-intercept form of the equation is $y = mx + b$. Thus:

$$y = 1x + b$$

Choose one point, say $(5, 2)$. Since it lies on the line:

$$2 = 1 \cdot 5 + b, \quad \text{or} \quad 2 = 5 + b$$
$$\therefore -3 = b.$$

3. To check, show that the coordinates of the other point $(2, -1)$ satisfy the equation:

$$y = x - 3$$
$$-1 \stackrel{?}{=} 2 - 3$$
$$-1 = -1 \checkmark$$

$\therefore$ **an equation of the line is $y = x - 3$.   Answer.**

Written Exercises

Find an equation of the line through the given point having the given slope.

1. $(1, 2)$; 2

2. $(3, 2)$; 1

3. $(-1, 2)$; -2

4. $(3, -4)$; -3

5. $(2, 0)$; $\frac{2}{3}$

6. $(0, 4)$; $-\frac{1}{2}$

7. $(0, 0)$; $-\frac{3}{4}$

8. $(-2, -6)$; $\frac{4}{3}$

Find an equation of the line through the given points.

9. $(1, 4)$; $(4, 7)$

10. $(3, 2)$; $(5, 6)$

11. $(2, 1)$; $(2, 3)$

12. $(-1, 3)$; $(2, 3)$

13. $(-3, 2)$; $(5, -2)$

14. $(6, -5)$; $(1, 10)$

15. $(0, 0)$; $(-4, -2)$

16. $(-5, -3)$; $(0, 0)$

Determine the value of *a* so that the graph of the given equation contains the given point.

B **17.** $ax + 2y = 3$; $(1, 2)$

18. $ax + 2y = 8$; $(0, 4)$

19. $5x + ay = 13$; $(2, -1)$

20. $-5x + ay = 4$; $(-2, 3)$

21. $6x - 5y + a = 0$; $(3, 4)$

22. $2x - ay + 2 = 0$; $(-5, -1)$

Find an equation of the line parallel to the given line containing the given point. (Parallel lines have the same slope.)

23. $x + y = 2$; $(1, 2)$

24. $x - y = 7$; $(2, -1)$

25. $2x - y = 5$; $(2, 2)$

26. $2x + 3y = 5$; $(-3, 1)$

Determine the coordinates of the point where the lines intersect.

27. $7x - 2y + 10 = 0$; the x-axis

28. $-4x + 3y - 8 = 0$; the y-axis

29. $3x - 6y = 27$; $x = 3$

30. $5x + 2y = 14$; $y = 2$

EXTRA PROBLEMS

Draw a flow chart for each problem.

1. Read each number in an array of 35 numbers. After each number is read, write the number, its square, and, if the number is not negative, its positive square root.

2. Read in arrays A and B for 20 linear equations (see page 370). Compute $-A/B$ for each equation where $B \neq 0$, and write A, B, $-A/B$ for each equation.

10–9   Direct Variation and Proportion

The table shows the distance, d miles, an automobile would travel in t hours if it were able to maintain a constant speed. The ratio $\dfrac{d}{t}$ for every pair of numbers is the same, that is,

$$\frac{d}{t} = 60,$$

or

$$d = 60t.$$

t (in hours)	d (in miles)	$\dfrac{d}{t}$ (in miles per hour)
1	60	$\frac{60}{1} = 60$
2	120	$\frac{120}{2} = 60$
3	180	$\frac{180}{3} = 60$
4	240	$\frac{240}{4} = 60$
5	300	$\frac{300}{5} = 60$

Such a formula describes a function that is called a *linear direct variation*.

A **linear direct variation** (or simply, a **direct variation**) is a function in which the ratio between a number y of the range and the corresponding number x of the domain is the same for all pairs of the function other than $(0, 0)$; that is, $\dfrac{y}{x} = k$, for $x \neq 0$. Thus, in a direct variation

$$y = kx, \text{ where } k \text{ is a nonzero constant.}$$

You can say that y *varies directly as* x or y *is directly proportional to* x or y *varies with* x. k is the **constant of proportionality** or the **constant of variation**.

Figure 10–20 shows the graph of

$$y = kx$$

with $k = 2$. The line has slope 2 and passes through the origin.

In general, the graph of a linear direct variation with $\mathcal{R}$ as domain and range is a straight line passing through the origin and having a slope equal to the constant of proportionality.

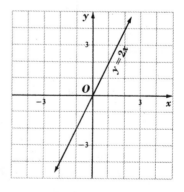

Figure 10–20

EXAMPLE 1. Given that r varies directly as s and that the value of r is 6 when the value of s is 9, find:

    a. the constant of proportionality.

    b. the value of r when 24 is the value of s.

Solution: Let $r = ks$

    a. Replacing r with "6" and s with "9," you find

$$6 = k \cdot 9; \quad \therefore k = \tfrac{6}{9} = \tfrac{2}{3}. \quad \text{Answer.}$$

    b. $r = \tfrac{2}{3}s$;

    $\therefore$ if $s = 24$, then

$$r = \tfrac{2}{3} \cdot 24 = 16.$$

    $\therefore$ when 24 is the value of s, 16 is the value of r.   Answer.

If one ordered pair of a direct variation is (x_1, y_1) (read "x sub 1, y sub 1") and another of the same function is (x_2, y_2), neither $(0, 0)$, then

$$y_1 = kx_1, \quad \text{and} \quad y_2 = kx_2$$

or

$$\frac{y_1}{x_1} = k \quad \text{and} \quad \frac{y_2}{x_2} = k.$$

Therefore,

$$\frac{y_1}{x_1} = \frac{y_2}{x_2}.$$

Such an equality of ratios is called a **proportion** and can be read "y_1 is to x_1 as y_2 is to x_2." In this proportion, x_1 and y_2 are called the **means,** and y_1 and x_2 are called the **extremes.** Multiplying both members by $x_1 x_2$ gives

$$(x_1 x_2)\left(\frac{y_1}{x_1}\right) = (x_1 x_2)\left(\frac{y_2}{x_2}\right).$$

Then:

$$y_1 x_2\left(\frac{x_1}{x_1}\right) = x_1 y_2\left(\frac{x_2}{x_2}\right) \qquad \text{Commutative and associative axioms of multiplication}$$

$$\therefore y_1 x_2 = x_1 y_2. \qquad \text{Multiplicative axiom of 1}$$

In any proportion, the product of the means equals the product of the extremes.

EXAMPLE 2. If the cost of some kinds of fruit varies directly with the weight and if 6 pounds cost $1.10:

  a. How much will 12 pounds cost?
  b. How much will 7 pounds cost?
  c. How much can be bought for $1.00?

Solution: **a. Let** c = cost in dollars,

  w = weight in pounds.

$$\frac{c_1}{w_1} = \frac{c_2}{w_2}; \; c_1 = 1.10, \; w_1 = 6, \; w_2 = 12$$

$$\frac{1.10}{6} = \frac{c_2}{12}$$

$$6c_2 = 13.20$$

$$c_2 = 2.20 \quad \therefore \text{ cost is \$2.20.   Answer.}$$

  b. $c_1 = 1.10, \; w_1 = 6, \; w_2 = 7$

$$\frac{1.10}{6} = \frac{c_2}{7}$$

$$6c_2 = 7.70$$

$$c_2 \doteq 1.283 \quad \therefore \text{ cost is \$1.29.   Answer.}$$

  c., $c_1 = 1.10, \; w_1 = 6, \; c_2 = 1.00$

$$\frac{1.10}{6} = \frac{1.00}{w_2}$$

$$1.10w_2 = 6.00$$

$$w_2 \doteq 5.5 \quad \therefore \text{ about 5.5 pounds can be bought.   Answer.}$$

Notice that in solving Example 2, it was not necessary to find a constant of proportionality because a proportion was used.

Oral Exercises

State whether or not each formula or table expresses direct variation. For each direct variation, state the constant of proportionality.

1. $p = 5b$ **3.** $xy = 4$ **5.** $m = \frac{1}{4}n$ **7.** $ab = -3$

2. $c = \frac{1}{2}d$ **4.** $\frac{y}{x} = 2$ **6.** $p = \frac{1}{2q}$ **8.** $-7x = y$

9.

x	1	2	3	4
y	1	3	5	7

10.

x	1	2	3	4
y	4	8	12	16

Read each proportion in two ways.

SAMPLE. $\dfrac{b}{3} = \dfrac{5}{9}$

Solution: b divided by 3 equals five-ninths, and b is to 3 as 5 is to 9.

11. $\dfrac{3}{5} = \dfrac{y}{15}$ **14.** $\dfrac{5r}{5s} = \dfrac{r}{s}$ **17.** $\dfrac{15}{y} = \dfrac{33}{5}$ **20.** $\dfrac{5}{7} = \dfrac{25}{x}$

12. $\dfrac{y}{4} = \dfrac{18}{12}$ **15.** $\dfrac{xy}{x} = \dfrac{yz}{y}$ **18.** $\dfrac{24}{7} = \dfrac{4}{x}$ **21.** $\dfrac{x+1}{5} = \dfrac{x-1}{2}$

13. $\dfrac{c}{d} = \dfrac{2c}{2d}$ **16.** $\dfrac{ca}{da} = \dfrac{cb}{db}$ **19.** $\dfrac{y}{5} = \dfrac{15}{10}$ **22.** $\dfrac{y-3}{7} = \dfrac{y+2}{4}$

State whether or not each formula expresses direct variation.

23. $\dfrac{x_1}{y_1} = \dfrac{x_2}{y_2}$ **24.** $\dfrac{x_1}{x_2} = \dfrac{y_1}{y_2}$ **25.** $\dfrac{y_1}{x_2} = \dfrac{y_2}{x_1}$ **26.** $\dfrac{y_2}{x_2} = \dfrac{y_1}{x_1}$

Written Exercises

A

1. y varies directly as x. y is 28 when x is 4. Find y when:
  a. x is 1   **b.** x is 20   **c.** x is -2

2. w is directly proportional to t. w is 6 when t is 30. Find w when:
  a. t is 15   **b.** t is -1 **c.** t is -10

In these direct variations, find the value of the indicated variable.

3. $x_2 = 10$, $y_1 = 12$, $x_1 = 5$, $y_2 = \underline{}$
4. $x_1 = 4$, $x_2 = 16$, $y_2 = 36$, $y_1 = \underline{}$
5. $n_2 = 35$, $n_1 = 14$, $m_1 = -10$, $m_2 = \underline{}$
6. $y_1 = 4$, $x_1 = 1$, $y_2 = -16$, $x_2 = \underline{}$
7. $s_1 = 6.5$, $r_1 = 3.9$, $r_2 = 3.6$, $s_2 = \underline{}$
8. $u_1 = \frac{3}{10}$, $v_1 = 1\frac{1}{4}$, $u_2 = 1\frac{4}{5}$, $v_2 = \underline{}$

Find all values of the variable for which each proportion is true.

9. $\dfrac{x-4}{x} = \dfrac{7}{9}$ **11.** $\dfrac{3w}{w+2} = \dfrac{5}{2}$ **13.** $\dfrac{10y}{12y+7} = \dfrac{8}{11}$

10. $\dfrac{y+2}{y} = \dfrac{4}{3}$ **12.** $\dfrac{6x}{x+7} = \dfrac{9}{5}$ **14.** $\dfrac{3w}{10w+2} = \dfrac{2}{7}$

15. $\dfrac{7z - 2}{4z + 13} = \dfrac{6}{5}$

16. $\dfrac{8x - 5}{5x - 4} = \dfrac{13}{8}$

B **17.** $\dfrac{32}{x} = \dfrac{x}{2}$

19. $\dfrac{x - 1}{x} = \dfrac{x + 1}{x + 3}$

18. $\dfrac{27}{y} = \dfrac{y}{3}$

20. $\dfrac{x + 2}{x + 1} = \dfrac{x}{x - 2}$

21. If x varies directly as $y + 4$, and $x = 8$ when $y = 6$, find y when $x = 12$.

22. If y is proportional to $4x - 1$, and $y = 3$ when $x = 2$, find x when $y = 11$.

23. If $2y$ is directly proportional to $3x - 1$ and $y = 1$ when $x = 2$, find x when $y = 0.40$.

24. If $3x - 5$ and $y + 2$ are in a direct proportion, and $x = 3$ when $y = 1$, find x when $y = -5$.

Translate into formulas expressing direct variation.

SAMPLE.   The circumference of a circle varies directly as its diameter. The constant of proportionality is π.

Solution: Let C = circumference, and let d = diameter. Then $\dfrac{C}{d} = \pi$, or

$$C = \pi d, \text{ or } \dfrac{C_1}{d_1} = \dfrac{C_2}{d_2}.$$

25. The time required to complete a job varies with the amount of work to be done.

26. The interest on a mortgage varies with the principal.

27. The distance traveled varies with the rate of speed.

28. The elongation of a coil spring varies with the weight suspended from it.

29. The pressure in a container of gas varies with the temperature.

30. The velocity of a freely falling body varies with the length of time it falls.

Problems

A **1.** The ratio of an object's weight on Earth to its weight on Mars is $5:2$. How much would a man who weighs 145 pounds here weigh on Mars?

2. The ratio of oil to vinegar in a certain brand of salad dressing is $7:3$. How much oil must be blended with 51 quarts of vinegar for that recipe?

3. Fourteen gallons of heavy cream will yield 9 pounds of butter. How many gallons of cream are needed to make 2 pounds of butter?

4. Twelve grams of calcium chloride can absorb 5 cubic centimeters of water. How much calcium chloride is needed to absorb 138 cubic centimeters of water?

5. In a local election the winning candidate defeated his opponent by a margin of 8 to 5. If the loser's share of the votes was 7,425, how many votes were cast for the winner?

6. When an electric current is 35 amperes, the electromotive force is 315 volts. Find the force when the current is 50 amperes if the force varies directly as the current.

7. Find the resistance of 700 feet of wire having 0.00042 ohm resistance per foot if resistance varies directly as the length.

8. How heavy is a 500-foot reel of cable if a 1-foot section weighs 0.87 pound?

9. What length represents 288 miles on a map scaled at $\frac{3}{16}$ inch = 15 miles?

10. What is the scale of a blueprint on which a 111-foot ceiling beam is drawn $9\frac{1}{4}$ inches long?

B 11. Rod A has 180 equal divisions, and rod B has 100, although both rods have the same length. A length equal to 66.6 divisions on rod A is equal to a length of how many divisions on rod B?

12. On a business trip Mr. Wilson decided to test the accuracy of his automobile's odometer. For the 220-mile trip from Oakdale to Alton the odometer registered only 216.7 miles. On the return trip Mr. Wilson had to detour for road repairs. If the odometer registered 453.1 miles for the round trip, how many actual miles was the detour?

13. One cubic centimeter of gold weighs 19.3 grams, while a cubic centimeter of silver weighs 10.5 grams. Which is heavier and by how much — a cube of gold 1.2 centimeters on an edge or a cube of silver 1.4 centimeters on an edge?

14. One cubic foot of mahogany wood weighs 32.2 pounds, while a cubic foot of white pine weighs 23.3 pounds. Which is heavier and by how much — a mahogany table top 6 feet by $3\frac{1}{2}$ feet by 3 inches, or a pine door $8\frac{1}{2}$ feet by 4 feet by $1\frac{1}{2}$ inches?

15. The cost of boring an automobile cylinder varies directly as the circumference of the cylinder. If it costs $14.20 to bore each cylinder with a 1.5-inch radius for the standard engine, how much more expensive is it to bore each cylinder with a radius of 1.9 inches for the high performance engine?

16. The length of a shadow of a vertical object at a given time and location varies with the height of the object casting the shadow. A boy 5 feet 6 inches tall casts a shadow of 12 feet 9 inches. If the shadow of a nearby tree measures 153 feet at the same time, how tall is the tree?

17. If 1 inch represents 45 miles on a map, and Colorado is shown by a rectangle $6\frac{3}{4}$ inches by $8\frac{1}{8}$ inches, calculate its area to the nearest 100 square miles.

18. The Forestry Bureau plans to plant 1600 trees per square mile in a tract of land shown on a map as a rectangle $1\frac{3}{8}$ inches by $\frac{3}{4}$ inch. The scale of the map is 1 inch = 3 miles. How many trees will be needed for the area?

OTHER FUNCTIONS AND EQUATIONS

10–10 Quadratic Functions

Several points on the graph of the quadratic equation "$y = x^2$" have been plotted in Figure 10–21, and connected by a smooth curve.

$y = x^2$		
x	x^2	y
0	0^2	0
1	1^2	1
2	2^2	4
3	3^2	9
-1	$(-1)^2$	1
-2	$(-2)^2$	4
-3	$(-3)^2$	9

$y = x^2$

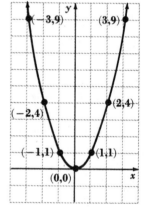

Figure 10–21

In Figure 10–22, you see the graph of another quadratic equation, "$y = -2x^2$."

$y = -2x^2$		
x	$-2x^2$	y
0	$-2(0)^2$	0
1	$-2(1)^2$	-2
$\frac{3}{2}$	$-2(\frac{3}{2})^2$	$-\frac{9}{2}$
2	$-2(2)^2$	-8
-1	$-2(-1)^2$	-2
$-\frac{3}{2}$	$-2(-\frac{3}{2})^2$	$-\frac{9}{2}$
-2	$-2(-2)^2$	-8

$y = -2x^2$

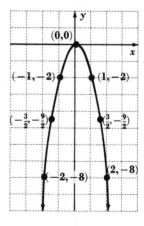

Figure 10–22

Sometimes a statement such as this is made: "The area of a circle *varies directly as the square* of its radius." The formula for this *quadratic direct variation* is

$$A = \pi r^2.$$

In general, a *quadratic direct variation* is a function in which each number x in the domain and the corresponding number y in the range satisfy an equation of the form

$$y = kx^2, \text{ where } k \text{ is a nonzero constant.}$$

EXAMPLE.   The value of a diamond varies as the square of its weight. If a 2-carat diamond is worth \$1,600, what would be the value of a diamond weighing $1\frac{1}{2}$ carats?

Solution: Let d = value in dollars, and
                        c = weight in carats.

Method I	Method II

Method I

Use: $d = kc^2$

$1600 = k \cdot 2^2; \quad 1600 = 4k$

$400 = k$

$\therefore d = 400c^2 \cdot$

$d = 400(\frac{3}{2})^2 = 400 \cdot \frac{9}{4}$

$d = 900$

Method II

Use: $\dfrac{d_1}{c_1^2} = \dfrac{d_2}{c_2^2}$

$\dfrac{1600}{2^2} = \dfrac{d_2}{(\frac{3}{2})^2}$

$\dfrac{1600}{4} = \dfrac{d_2}{\frac{9}{4}}$

$900 = d_2$

$\therefore$ a $1\frac{1}{2}$-carat diamond would be worth \$900.   Answer.

A quadratic direct variation is a special kind of quadratic function. A **quadratic function** is a function whose ordered pairs (x, y) satisfy a quadratic equation of the form

$$y = ax^2 + bx + c, \quad a \neq 0.$$

Consider the function

$$f: x \rightarrow y = x^2 - x - 6.$$

You can plot the graph of this function by finding the coordinates of selected points as shown on the next page.

To plot the graph of

$$f: x \rightarrow y = x^2 - x - 6,$$

assume that the domain is $\mathcal{R}$ and that the range is the set of corresponding values of y.

$y = x^2 - x - 6$		
x	$x^2 - x - 6$	y
-3	$9 + 3 - 6$	6
-2	$4 + 2 - 6$	0
-1	$1 + 1 - 6$	-4
0	$0 - 0 - 6$	-6
1	$1 - 1 - 6$	-6
2	$4 - 2 - 6$	-4
3	$9 - 3 - 6$	0
4	$16 - 4 - 6$	6

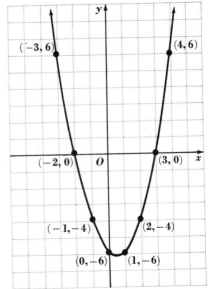

Figure 10–23

Notice that the graphs of "$y = x^2$" (Figure 10–21) and "$y = x^2 - x - 6$" (Figure 10–23) open upward so that each has a lowest point, while the graph of "$y = -2x^2$" (Figure 10–22) opens downward and has a highest point.

Notice also, that in these examples the points, except the lowest or highest points, occur in pairs that have the same ordinate. Be sure to plot enough such points to enable you to draw a smooth curve and to show whether the curve opens upward or downward.

A curve such as those in Figures 10–21, 10–22 and 10–23 is called a **parabola** (pa-**rab**-oh-luh).

The graph of every quadratic equation of the form

$$y = ax^2 + bx + c, \qquad a \neq 0, \qquad x \in \mathcal{R}$$

is a parabola.

The path of a projectile moving in a vacuum, the cable supporting a suspension bridge, and certain cross sections of the reflector on a searchlight are examples of parabolas.

Oral Exercises

Which of the following functions with domain $\Re$ is a quadratic function?

1. $f: x \to y = -3x^2$

2. $g: x \to y = -x + 4$

3. $k: x \to y = \frac{1}{2}x^2 - 7$

4. $m: x \to y = 2x^2 - 6x + 8$

5. $f(x) = \dfrac{1}{x^2}$

6. $g(x) = x^3 + x^2 - 1$

Which of these quadratic functions with domain $\Re$ have a graph opening downward and which have a graph opening upward?

7. $T: x \to x^2 + 8$

8. $S: x \to -x^2 + 6$

9. $r: x \to 7 - x^2$

10. $p: x \to \frac{2}{3}x^2$

Complete these statements.

11. The graph of each quadratic function with domain $\Re$ is a __?__.

12. The graph of each quadratic function with domain $\Re$ has a __?__ point or a __?__ point, but not both.

Written Exercises

Graph each equation in the coordinate plane.

A

1. $y = 2x^2$

2. $y = 4x^2$

3. $y = \frac{1}{2}x^2$

4. $y = \frac{1}{3}x^2$

5. $y = -2x^2$

6. $y = -3x^2$

7. $y = x^2 - 1$

8. $y = x^2 - 4$

9. $y = x^2 + 1$

10. $y = x^2 + 4$

11. $y = 2x^2 + 1$

12. $y = 1 - 2x^2$

Graph each function. Assume that the domain is $\Re$.

B

13. $f: x \to y = x^2 - 2x$

14. $g: x \to y = x^2 + 2x$

15. $k: x \to y = 4x - x^2$

16. $r: x \to y = 4x + x^2$

17. $g(x) = x^2 - 2x - 3$

18. $t(x) = x^2 + 2x - 3$

19. $p(x) = x^2 + 2x + 1$

20. $q(x) = 3 - 2x - x^2$

Problems

1. The radii of two circles are 5 and 2, respectively. Find the ratio of their areas.

2. What is the ratio of the areas of two squares if one is 4 inches on a side and the other is 6 inches on a side?

3. If the distance needed to stop an automobile varies as the square of its speed, how much distance is needed to bring the car to a stop from 50 miles per hour, if it requires 22 feet to stop at 10 miles per hour?

4. The distance which a freely falling body falls varies directly as the square of the time it falls. If it falls 144 feet in 3 seconds how far will it fall in 8 seconds?

5. Wind pressure on a flat surface varies as the square of the wind velocity. If 0.35 pounds per square foot results when the wind blows at 8 miles per hour, how much pressure is exerted by a gust of 40 miles per hour?

6. A diamond's price varies as the square of its weight. If one weighing $\frac{3}{8}$ carat is worth $360, find the cost of a similar diamond of $\frac{7}{8}$ carat.

7. A basketball has a radius 4 times larger than that of a tennis ball. If surface area varies as the square of the radius, find the surface area of the tennis ball if the surface area of the basketball is 144π inches.

8. The lift on an airplane wing is directly proportional to the square of the speed of the air moving over it. If the lift is 732 pounds per square foot when the air speed is 320 miles per hour, find the lift when the speed is increased by 80 miles per hour.

B 9. Find the ratio of the areas of two circular table tops if the circumference of the larger is 132 inches and that of the other is 88 inches.

10. Two spheres have a surface area of 1256 square inches and 113.04 square inches, respectively. If the radius of the larger sphere is 10 inches, find the radius of the smaller sphere. (See Problem 7 above.)

11. A pilot flying at an altitude of 14,400 feet released an object which fell to an altitude of 12,800 feet after 10 seconds. How many feet will the object have fallen 30 seconds after it is released? (See Problem 4 above.)

12. The pressure from a 20-mile-per-hour wind registered 0.028 grams per square centimeter on a very sensitive gauge. (See Problem 5 above.) Find the velocity of the wind which registered a 0.035-gram increase on the gauge.

10–11 Inverse Variation

Three rectangles whose lengths and widths are (15, 2), (10, 3), and (6, 5) have the same area:

$$15 \cdot 2 = 30, \qquad 10 \cdot 3 = 30, \qquad 6 \cdot 5 = 30,$$

or

$$lw = 30.$$

Such a formula describes a function that is called an *inverse variation*.

An **inverse variation** is a function in which the product of the co-ordinates of its ordered pairs is a nonzero constant. For any ordered pair (x, y) of the function,

$$xy = k \quad \text{or} \quad y = \frac{k}{x}, \quad \text{where } k \text{ is a nonzero constant.}$$

You say that y *varies inversely as* x or y *is inversely proportional to* x, because $y = k\left(\dfrac{1}{x}\right)$, or y varies *directly* as the *inverse* of x.

You would not expect the graph of an inverse variation to be a straight line, because its equation,

$$xy = k,$$

is not linear; one term, xy, is of the second degree. The graph of $xy = 1$ is shown in Figure 10–24.

$$xy = 1$$

x	y
$\frac{1}{4}$	4
$\frac{1}{2}$	2
1	1
2	$\frac{1}{2}$
4	$\frac{1}{4}$

x	y
-4	$-\frac{1}{4}$
-2	$-\frac{1}{2}$
-1	-1
$-\frac{1}{2}$	-2
$-\frac{1}{4}$	-4

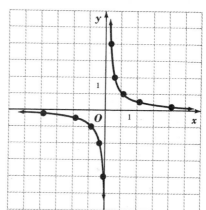

Figure 10–24

As x increases, y decreases so that the product is always 1. Neither x nor y can have the value 0. Notice that this graph consists of two separate branches neither of which intersects an axis.

For every nonzero value of k, the graph of "$xy = k$" has this shape and is called a **hyperbola**(hy-**pur**-bo-la). The curve is in the first and third quadrants if k is positive and in the second and fourth quadrants if k is negative. If k were 0, what would be the limitation on the range and domain?

When negative answers are meaningless, as they often are in practical problems, the range and domain are limited to positive numbers. The graph of such an inverse variation has only one branch — the one in the first quadrant.

If (x_1, y_1) and (x_2, y_2) are ordered pairs of an inverse variation,

$$x_1y_1 = k \quad \text{and} \quad x_2y_2 = k.$$

Therefore,

$$x_1y_1 = x_2y_2.$$

Since neither y_1 nor x_2 is 0, you can divide both members by x_2y_1, obtaining

$$\frac{x_1y_1}{x_2y_1} = \frac{x_2y_2}{x_2y_1} \quad \text{or} \quad \frac{x_1}{x_2} = \frac{y_2}{y_1}.$$

One instance of inverse variation is the law of the lever (**lee**-ver), a bar pivoted at a point called the fulcrum (**ful**-krum) (Figure 10–25). If weights w_1 and w_2 are placed at distances d_1 and d_2 from the fulcrum, and the lever is in balance, then

or

$$d_1w_1 = d_2w_2$$

$$\frac{d_1}{d_2} = \frac{w_2}{w_1}.$$

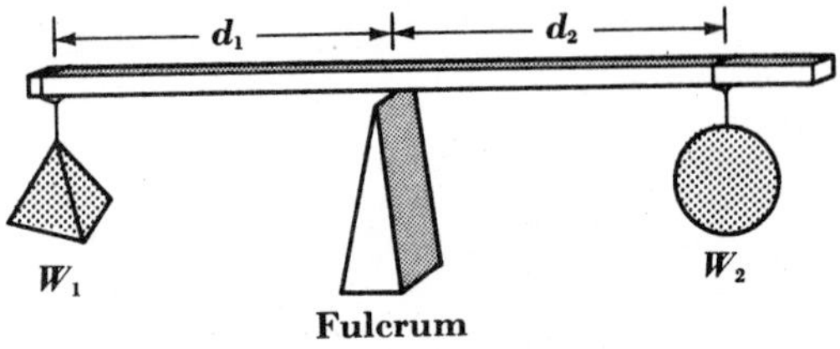

Figure 10–25

EXAMPLE 1. If an eight-pound weight is 72 centimeters from the fulcrum of a lever, how far from the fulcrum is a nine-pound weight which balances it?

Solution: Let $w_1 = 8,\ d_1 = 72,\ w_2 = 9.$ *Check:*

$$d_1w_1 = d_2w_2$$

$$72(8) = d_2 9$$

$$64 = d_2$$

$$\frac{8}{9} \overset{?}{=} \frac{64}{72}$$

$$\frac{8}{9} = \frac{8}{9} \checkmark$$

∴ distance of nine-pound weight from fulcrum is 64 centimeters. **Answer.**

Several physical quantities vary *inversely as the square* of another quantity. We say that y varies inversely as x^2, or y is *inversely proportional to* x^2, if

$$y = \frac{k}{x^2} \quad \text{or} \quad x^2y = k, \quad k \neq 0.$$

If $x_1^2y_1 = k$ and $x_2^2y_2 = k$, then

$$\frac{x_1^2y_1}{x_1^2y_2} = \frac{x_2^2y_2}{x_1^2y_2} \quad \text{or} \quad \frac{y_1}{y_2} = \frac{x_2^2}{x_1^2}.$$

EXAMPLE 2. The brightness of the illumination of an object varies inversely as the square of the distance from the source of light to the object. If the illumination of a book 9 feet from a lamp is 4 foot-candles, find the illumination of the book 3 feet closer to the lamp.

Solution: If I is the amount of illumination and d is the distance from the light source to the object,

$$\frac{I_1}{I_2} = \frac{d_2^2}{d_1^2}.$$

Let $I_1 = 4$, $d_1 = 9$, $d_2 = 6$

$I_1 d_1^2 = I_2 d_2^2$ *Check:* $\frac{9}{4} \overset{?}{=} \frac{(9)^2}{(6)^2}$

$4(9)^2 = I_2(6)^2$

$9 = I_2$ $\frac{9}{4} = \frac{81}{36}$

∴ in the second position the illumination is 9 foot-candles.   **Answer.**

Oral Exercises

Tell whether or not each formula or table expresses inverse variation.

1. $xy = 3$

2. $t = 4v$

3. $\dfrac{l_2}{l_1} = \dfrac{w_1}{w_2}$

4. $p = \dfrac{1}{q}$

5. $y = \dfrac{k}{x}$

6. $t = \dfrac{50}{r}$

7. $\dfrac{p_1}{p_2} = \dfrac{s_2}{s_1}$

8. $a_1 b_1 = a_2 b_2$

9. $\dfrac{y}{x} = 10$

10.

x	1	2	3	4
y	1	$\frac{1}{2}$	$\frac{1}{3}$	$\frac{1}{4}$

11.

x	2	4	6	8
y	1	$\frac{1}{2}$	$\frac{1}{3}$	$\frac{1}{4}$

12.

x	5	10	15	20
y	1	2	3	4

Translate each statement into a formula expressing inverse variation.

SAMPLE. The base of a rectangle of constant area varies inversely as its height.

Solution: Let b = base and h = height.

$$\therefore bh = k, \text{ or } b = \frac{k}{h}, \text{ or } \frac{b_1}{b_2} = \frac{h_2}{h_1}, \text{ or } b_1 h_1 = b_2 h_2.$$

13. The force F necessary to remove a spike varies inversely as the length L of the crowbar used.

14. The time t required to go a given distance varies inversely as the rate of speed, r.

15. At a fixed temperature, the volume V of a gas varies inversely as the pressure P.

16. The amount of current I flowing through a circuit is inversely proportional to the amount of resistance R of the circuit.

17. The height h of a right circular cylinder of given volume is inversely proportional to the square of the radius r.

18. The force of attraction F between two objects is inversely proportional to the square of the distance d between them.

Written Exercises

Graph each of the following equations if the domain and range elements are limited to the set of positive numbers.

[A] 1. $xy = 4$ 2. $2xy = 1$ 3. $x = \frac{3}{y}$ 4. $\frac{x}{4} = \frac{3}{y}$

In these inverse variations, find the value of the indicated variable.

5. $x_1 = 18$, $x_2 = 4$, $y_1 = 52$, $y_2 = $ __?__

6. $x_1 = \frac{4}{5}$, $y_1 = 15$, $y_2 = 24$, $x_2 = $ __?__

7. $p_2 = 3.90$, $q_2 = 0.35$, $q_1 = 0.65$, $p_1 = $ __?__

8. $q_2 = \frac{3}{14}$, $p_2 = \frac{8}{15}$, $p_1 = \frac{12}{5}$, $q_1 = $ __?__

9. If $w = rt$ and r is tripled while w remains constant, how does t change?

10. If $Fl = k$ and l is doubled while k remains constant, how does F change?

11. If $E = mc^2$, and c is tripled while E remains constant, how does m change?

12. If $Id^2 = k$, and d is halved while k remains constant, how does I change?

13. If x varies inversely as $t - 1$, and $x = 8$ when $t = 10$, find t when $x = 18$.

14. If y varies inversely as $3w + 2$, and $y = 24$ when $w = 1$, find w when $y = 15$.

B **15.** How far from a lamp does a book receive 9 times as much illumination as a book 6 feet from the lamp? (See Example 2, page 395.)

16. If T varies inversely as s^2, and $T = 256$ when $s = 50$, find T when $s = 80$.

17. If P varies inversely as Q^2, what value of Q causes P to become one-sixteenth as much as it is when $Q = 10$?

18. If V varies inversely as the cube of s, and $V = 297$ when $s = 2$, what is V when $s = 3$?

C **19.** Plot the graph of $y = \dfrac{12}{x^2}$ for $-4 \le x < 0$ and $0 < x \le 4$.

Problems

A **1.** At 60 miles per hour, how long does a journey take if it takes 8 hours at 45 miles per hour?

2. If 6 men do a job in 12 days, how long do 18 men take, working at the same rate?

3. How far from the seesaw support must John sit to balance Mary, who sits 6 feet from it, if he weighs 90 pounds and she weighs 60 pounds?

4. Tom, sitting 6 feet from the seesaw support, balances a friend who weighs 120 pounds and sits 7 feet from the support. How heavy is Tom?

5. At what rate does $9000 yield the same annual income as $15,000 at 3%?

6. What sum at 4% yields the same yearly income as $800 at 5%?

7. The altitude of a triangle is 24 inches, and the base is 4 inches. Find the altitude of a triangle of equal area whose base is 6 inches.

8. A rectangle has a base of 42 inches and a height of 12 inches. Find the base of another rectangle of equal area whose height is 14 inches.

9. The volume of a gas is 75 cubic feet under 7 pounds pressure. What is its volume at the same temperature when the pressure is 15 pounds?

10. If the current through a circuit is 24 amperes when the resistance is 15 ohms, what is the current when the resistance is reduced to 6 ohms?

11. A 12-inch pulley runs at 240 revolutions per minute (r.p.m.). How fast does the 8-inch pulley it drives revolve if the number of r.p.m. varies inversely as the diameter?

12. A gear with 28 teeth makes 45 r.p.m. and meshes with a gear having 20 teeth. What is the speed of the second gear if the number of r.p.m. varies inversely with the number of teeth?

B **13.** Paul weighs 162 pounds and Philip weighs 135. How far from Paul, on a seesaw 12.1 feet long, is the support balancing them?

14. A meter stick is placed on a fulcrum at the 50-centimeter mark. If a 20-gram weight is suspended from the 15-centimeter mark and a 55-gram weight is suspended from the 90 centimeter mark, how much weight must be suspended at the 25 centimeter mark to bring the meter stick into balance?

15. The weight of a body at or above the earth's surface varies inversely as the square of the body's distance from the earth's center. What does a 445.5-pound projectile weigh 500 miles out from the earth's surface? (Use 4000 miles as the earth's radius.)

16. A three-eighths-inch wire has 48 ohms resistance. How much has the same length of half-inch wire if resistance varies inversely as the square of the diameter?

For the wave motion of sound, the following formula holds:

$$fl = v,$$

where f is the frequency (number of waves per second), l is the wave-length (in feet), and v is the speed of sound (about 1100 feet per second in air). Use this information in the following problems.

17. The frequency of a note an octave above a given note is twice that of the given note. How does the wavelength of the higher note compare with that of the lower note?

18. If the wavelength of a note is $\frac{3}{2}$ that of a given note, how do the frequencies compare?

19. An open organ pipe (see picture on page 30) produces a sound wave that has a length that is twice the length of the pipe. Find the length of an open pipe that will produce the note A with the frequency 440.

20. A stopped organ pipe produces a sound wave that has a length that is four times the length of the pipe. What is the frequency of the sound produced by a stopped organ pipe $4\frac{1}{4}$ feet long?

EXTRA PROBLEMS

1. Read a number X and an array S of 100 different numbers. Print the number X and then test X against each number in the array S until a match, if any, is found. If X is equal to some number in the array, then the message "In the table" should be printed; otherwise, the output message should be "Not in the table." Draw a flow chart.

2. Do Exercise 1 for each of the *ten* numbers in an *array X*. (*Hint:* Use a nested loop with J as the subscript for array X and I, the subscript for array S.)

10–12 Joint Variation and Combined Variation (Optional)

The area A of a triangle depends upon its altitude a and its base b. If a and b are measured in the same units,

$$A = \frac{1}{2}\,ab \quad \text{or} \quad \frac{A}{ab} = \frac{1}{2}.$$

The area is directly proportional to the altitude and to the base, and you say that the area of a triangle *varies jointly* as its base and altitude.

Joint variation occurs when a variable z varies directly as the product of variables x and y. We say z *varies jointly as x and y*, and for a nonzero constant k, write

$$\frac{z}{xy} = k \quad \text{or} \quad z = kxy.$$

Therefore,

$$\frac{z_1}{x_1 y_1} = \frac{z_2}{x_2 y_2} \quad \text{or} \quad \frac{z_1}{z_2} = \frac{x_1 y_1}{x_2 y_2}.$$

EXAMPLE 1. **The volume of a right circular cylinder varies jointly as its height and the square of its radius. If a right circular cylinder of height 10 inches and radius 4 inches has a volume of 160π cubic inches, find the volume of one with a height of 8 inches and a radius of 3 inches.**

Solution: **Let $h_1 = 10$, $r_1 = 4$, $h_2 = 8$, $r_2 = 3$, $V_1 = 160\pi$.**

$$\frac{V_1}{h_1 r_1^2} = \frac{V_2}{h_2 r_2^2} \qquad \textit{Check:} \quad \frac{160\pi}{72\pi} \stackrel{?}{=} \frac{10(4)^2}{8(3)^2}$$

$$\frac{160\pi}{10(4)^2} = \frac{V_2}{8(3)^2} \qquad\qquad\qquad \frac{20}{9} = \frac{20}{9} \ \checkmark$$

$$72\pi = V_2$$

∴ **the volume of the second cylinder is 72π cubic inches.   Answer.**

Another variation involving three variables is called *combined variation*. **Combined variation** is indicated when a variable z varies directly as one variable x and inversely as another y. For a nonzero constant k,

$$z = \frac{kx}{y} \quad \text{or} \quad zy = kx \quad \text{or} \quad \frac{zy}{x} = k.$$

Therefore,

$$\frac{z_1 y_1}{x_1} = \frac{z_2 y_2}{x_2} \quad \text{or} \quad \frac{z_1}{z_2} = \frac{x_1 y_2}{x_2 y_1}.$$

EXAMPLE 2.   If everyone available works at the same speed at a given task, then the number of persons needed to finish a given amount of work varies directly as the amount of work to be done and inversely as the amount of time desired.   If 2 typists can type 210 pages of manuscript in 3 days, how many typists will be needed to type 700 pages in 2 days?

Solution: Let $t_1 = 2$, $p_1 = 210$, $d_1 = 3$, $p_2 = 700$, $d_2 = 2$.

$$\frac{t_1 d_1}{p_1} = \frac{t_2 d_2}{p_2} \qquad 2t_2 = \frac{4200}{210}$$

$$\frac{(2)(3)}{210} = \frac{t_2(2)}{700} \qquad t_2 = 10$$

∴ **10 typists will be needed to type 700 pages in 2 days.   Answer.**

Oral Exercises

Express in words. Assume that k is a nonzero constant.

SAMPLE 1. $\dfrac{E}{IR} = k$ *Solution:* E varies jointly as I and R.

SAMPLE 2. $PV = kT$

Solution: P varies directly as T and inversely as V.

1. $PV = k$

2. $C = k\dfrac{Q}{V}$

3. $\dfrac{V_1}{V_2} = \dfrac{M_2}{M_1}$

4. $E = kmc^2$

5. $l = k\dfrac{A}{w}$

6. $Q = kIt$

7. $\dfrac{E_1}{E_2} = \dfrac{I_1 R_1}{I_2 R_2}$

8. $a = k\dfrac{V^2}{r}$

9. $\dfrac{I_1}{I_2} = \dfrac{P_1 r_1 t_1}{P_2 r_2 t_2}$

10. $D = \dfrac{12S}{\pi R}$

11. $P = k\dfrac{V^2}{R}$

12. $F = k\dfrac{m_1 m_2}{s^2}$

Written Exercises

Translate into formulas.

A

1. The rate of speed varies directly as the distance traveled and inversely as the time traveled.

2. The volume of a rectangular container varies jointly as the length, the width, and the depth.

3. The amount of time necessary to complete a job varies directly as the amount of work and inversely as the rate at which it is done.

4. The area of a trapezoid varies jointly as its altitude and the sum of its bases.

5. The temperature of a gas varies jointly as the volume and the pressure.

6. The area of a triangle varies jointly as its base and altitude.

7. The volume of a right circular cylinder varies jointly as its height and the square of the radius of its base.

8. The volume of a pyramid varies jointly as the altitude and the area of the base.

9. The force between two electrical charges varies jointly as the charges on the bodies and inversely as the square of the distance between them.

10. Centrifugal force varies directly as the square of the velocity of a moving body and inversely as the radius of its circular path.

Problems

A 1. In the formula $H = \dfrac{I^2 Rt}{4}$, R remains constant. If I is tripled, and t is made 4 times as large, how is H changed?

2. In the formula $F = \dfrac{mv^2}{r}$, m remains constant, v is quadrupled, and r is made $\frac{1}{3}$ as large. How does F change?

3. W varies jointly as x and y and inversely as the square of z. If $W = 189$, $x = 28$, $y = 16$, and $z = 8$, find (a) the constant k of variation, (b) the equation, and (c) W when $x = 24$, $y = 4$, and $z = 6$.

4. R varies directly as the cube of s and inversely as t and the square of u. If $R = 1$, $s = 4$, $t = 8$, and $u = 2$, find (a) the constant k of variation, (b) the equation of relation, and (c) t when $R = 12$, $s = 6$, and $u = 3$.

5. If 14 boys pick 294 crates of apples in 7 hours, how many boys pick 513 boxes in 3 hours?

6. A rod's weight varies jointly as its length and the area of its cross section. If a rod $5\frac{1}{3}$ feet long with a $\frac{3}{4}$-inch-square cross section is 5.60 pounds, what weight has a similar rod $3\frac{3}{4}$ feet long whose cross section is a half-inch square?

7. When a mass moves at 18 feet per second in a circle whose radius is 3 feet, the centrifugal force is 108 pounds. Find the force when that mass moves at 24 feet per second in a circle whose radius is 8 feet. (See Exercise 10, above.)

8. The cost of operating an appliance varies jointly as the number of watts drawn, the hours of operation, and the cost per kilowatt-hour. A thousand-watt waffle iron operates for 45 minutes for 3¢ at 4¢ per kilowatt-hour. What is the cost of cooking 30 waffles 4 minutes each, if the iron uses 875 watts?

9. The safe load on a horizontal beam supported at its ends varies directly as the square of the beam's depth and inversely as its length between supports. A beam 9.6 meters long and 4 centimeters deep bears 2170 grams. What load can one 3.5 meters long and 5 centimeters deep bear?

10. The heat developed in an electric wire varies jointly as the wire's resistance, the time the current flows, and the square of the current. In 8 minutes a current of 7 amperes develops 140 heat units in a wire of 0.1 ohm resistance. What resistance has a similar wire which develops 42,000 heat units with a current of 14 amperes in 2 minutes?

B 11. The wind pressure on a plane varies jointly as the surface area and the square of the wind's velocity. With a velocity of 12 miles per hour, the pressure on a 4-foot by $1\frac{1}{2}$ foot rectangle is 20 pounds. What is the velocity when the pressure on a surface 2 feet square is 30 pounds?

12. The heat lost through a windowpane varies jointly as the difference of the inside and outside temperatures and the window area, and inversely as the thickness of the pane. If 198 heat calories are lost through a pane 40 by 28 centimeters, $\frac{4}{5}$ centimeter thick, in one hour when the temperature difference is 44°C, how many are lost in one hour through a pane $\frac{1}{2}$ centimeter thick having $\frac{1}{4}$ the area, when the temperature difference is 40°C?

● CHAPTER SUMMARY ●

Inventory of Structure and Method

1. Bar and broken-line graphs and pictographs are employed for the visual presentation of statistics to display comparisons and trends in data.

2. To set up a **rectangular coordinate system in a plane**, choose a vertical and a horizontal line, and scale them as number lines intersecting at zero. Each point in the coordinate plane corresponds to exactly one ordered pair of real numbers, and each ordered pair of real numbers corresponds to exactly one point in the plane.

3. The ordered pairing of the members of two sets is a **relation** that can be shown by table, graph, roster, or rule. The domain of definition (domain) and the range of values (range) of the relation must be specified in each case. Thus, a **function** is a relation which assigns only one element of the range to each element of the domain.

4. A plane coordinate system enables you to picture the **solution set of an open sentence in two variables** as the set of points whose coordinates satisfy the open sentence. To graph a linear equation in two variables, each having the set of real numbers as its replacement set, draw the straight line determined by plotting any two roots of the equation.

5. To measure the **slope** of a nonvertical straight line, choose two different points on the line, and compute the ratio of the difference between the

ordinates of the points to the corresponding difference between the abscissas of the points. It is a property of a straight line that this ratio is the same for every pair of distinct points on the line. Vertical lines have no slope.

6. A line with slope m and y-intercept b is the graph of the equation $y = mx + b$. This **slope-intercept form** of a linear equation can be used to find an equation for a line

a. with given slope and passing through a given point;

b. passing through two different points.

7. **Direct variation** and **inverse variation** are special types of functions. If k is a nonzero constant, equations like

$$y = kx \quad \text{and} \quad y = \frac{k}{x}$$

are associated with, respectively, a direct and an inverse variation. In either case, you find the constant of proportionality, k, by substituting in the equation a pair of values for the variable. Direct and inverse variation as the square are given by the equations

$$y = kx^2 \quad \text{and} \quad y = \frac{k}{x^2}.$$

Vocabulary and Spelling

Review the meaning of each term by reference to the page listed.

ordered pair (*p. 355*)
bar graph (*p. 356*)
pictograph (*p. 356*)
broken-line graph (*p. 357*)
components (coordinates) (*p. 358*)
horizontal axis (*p. 359*)
origin (*p. 359*)
vertical axis (*p. 359*)
graph of an ordered pair (*p. 359*)
plotting a point (*p. 359*)
quadrant (*p. 360*)
abscissa (*p. 360*)
ordinate (*p. 360*)
coordinates of a point (*p. 360*)
coordinate axes (*p. 360*)
coordinate plane (*p. 360*)
plane rectangular coordinate system (*p. 361*)
relation (*p. 362*)
domain of a relation (*p. 362*)
range of a relation (*p. 362*)
open sentence in two variables (*p. 365*)

solution set of an open sentence in two variables (*p. 365*)
the graph of an equation (*p. 369*)
an equation of a line (*p. 369*)
linear equation in two variables (*p. 370*)
linear function (*p. 371*)
slope of a line (*p. 373*)
y-intercept (*p. 378*)
slope-intercept form (*p. 378*)
direct variation (*p. 382*)
constant of proportionality (*p. 382*)
proportion (*p. 383*)
means (*p. 383*)
extremes (*p. 383*)
quadratic direct variation (*p. 389*)
quadratic function (*p. 389*)
parabola (*p. 390*)
inverse variation (*p. 393*)
hyperbola (*p. 393*)
joint variation (*p. 399*)
combined variation (*p. 399*)

Just for Fun

Suppose that you draw a silhouette on a sheet of graph paper as shown in the figure below. By noting the points at which the outline changes direction, you can make a list of coordinates which represent the picture. Someone else can take your list, plot your number pairs, and connect them in the given order with line segments to reproduce your picture.

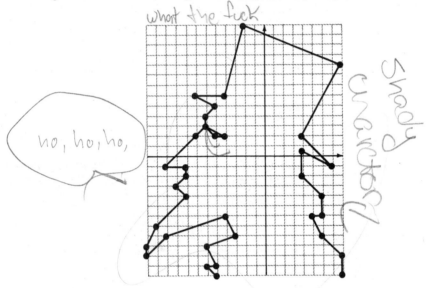

Can you give the list of coordinate pairs to represent the picture in the given figure? Starting on the left at the bottom of the picture, the first four pairs are: $(-5, -12)$, $(-6, -11)$, $(-5, -11)$, $(-6, -9)$.

You need not confine your artistry to human profiles; animals, plants, and cartoon characters also are suitable for coordinated pictures. See if you can develop the picture represented by the following number pairs:

$(4, -13)$, $(5, -10)$, $(5, -7)$, $(3, -6)$, $(1, -2\frac{1}{2})$, $(0, -3)$, $(-1, 0)$, $(0, 4)$, $(-2, 5)$, $(-4, 4)$, $(-9, 1)$, $(-6, 4)$, $(-2, 6)$, $(-\frac{1}{2}, 6\frac{1}{2})$, $(0, 6)$, $(1, 6)$, $(-\frac{1}{2}, 6\frac{1}{2})$, $(0, 7)$, $(1, 7)$, $(2, 6)$, $(1\frac{1}{2}, 5)$, $(\frac{1}{2}, 2)$, $(1, 0)$, $(3, \frac{1}{2})$, $(5, 0)$, $(7, -1)$, $(10, -3)$, $(12, -6)$, $(13, -9)$, $(12\frac{1}{2}, -8\frac{1}{2})$, $(12, -9)$, $(11\frac{1}{2}, -8\frac{1}{2})$, $(11, -9)$, $(10, -7)$, $(9, -7)$, $(9\frac{1}{2}, -10)$, $(9\frac{1}{2}, -12)$; [Start a new broken line]: $(9, -13)$, $(9, -10)$, $(8\frac{1}{2}, -7)$, $(5\frac{1}{2}, -7)$, $(5\frac{1}{2}, -10)$, $(4\frac{1}{2}, -13)$.

Chapter Test

10–1 **1.** Make a bar graph for the sales in millions of shares of stock: Monday 14, Tuesday 12, Wednesday 0, Thursday 9, Friday 11.

2. Make a broken-line graph from the table:

Time of Day	6:00 A.M.	10:00 A.M.	2:00 P.M.	4:00 P.M.
Temperature in Degrees Fahrenheit	45	55	75	70

10–2 **3.** Find all values of a and b for which $(a + 5, b - 2)$ is equal to $(2a - 3, 4 - b)$.

4. Give the coordinates of each point labeled in the adjoining figure.

5. Graph the following points in the coordinate plane.

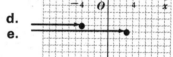

   a. $(4, 0)$

   b. $(3, 6)$

   c. $(-3, 4)$

   d. $(-1, -1)$

   e. $(4, -2)$

10–3 Plot points to represent the ordered pairs listed in these tables. State the domain and the range of each relation. Is the relation a function?

6.

1	4
2	3
3	2
4	1

7.

0	5
1	4
2	4
3	2

8.

0	2
1	3
2	1
1	0

10–4 **9.** If the ordered pairs of numbers $(3, b)$ and $(a, -1)$ are equal, then $a =$ _?_ and $b =$ _?_.

10. The solution set of $2x - y = 8$ _?_ (does/does not) contain $(3, -2)$.

10–5 **11.** Graph the equation that is linear.

$$y = x^2 + 2, \qquad 3x - xy = 2, \qquad 2x - y = 1$$

12. Determine which of the points $(6, 1)$, $(3, 2)$, and $(-3, 6)$ belong to the graph of $2x + 3y = 12$.

10–6 **13.** Determine the slope of the line containing $(-2, -3)$ and $(1, -1)$.

14. Draw the line through $(2, -1)$ having slope -1.

15. Find the value of a for which $(1, -3)$ is on the graph of $2x + ay = 8$.

10–7 **16.** Find the slope and y-intercept of the graph of $4x - 2y = 7$.

17. Write an equation for the line through $(0, 3)$ with slope -2.

10–8 **18.** Write an equation for the line through $(2, -2)$ and having slope $\frac{2}{3}$.

19. Write an equation for the line containing $(3, -2)$ and $(-2, 8)$.

10–9 **20.** Find the missing value in this direct variation:

$$x_1 = 35, \qquad y_1 = 28, \qquad x_2 = 5, \qquad y_2 = \underline{\quad ? \quad}$$

21. In a local high school the girls outnumber the boys 5 to 4. If there are 212 boys in the school, how many girls are there?

10–10 **22.** Graph $y = 3x^2 - 3$.

10–11 **23.** Find the missing value in this inverse variation:

$$x_1 = 14, \qquad y_2 = 3, \qquad x_2 = 21, \qquad y_1 = \underline{\quad ? \quad}$$

24. If 3 farmers can harvest their crop in 24 days, how many days would be required to complete the harvest if 5 additional workers were hired?

10–12 **(Optional)**

25. If $I = prt$, and p is halved, r is made 3 times as large, and t is made $\frac{1}{4}$ as large, how is I changed?

26. If $P = k\dfrac{V^2}{d}$, and $P = 54$, $V = 12$, and $d = 4$, find:

  a. k, the constant of proportionality
  b. d when $P = 18$ and $V = 6$.

Who Uses Mathematics?

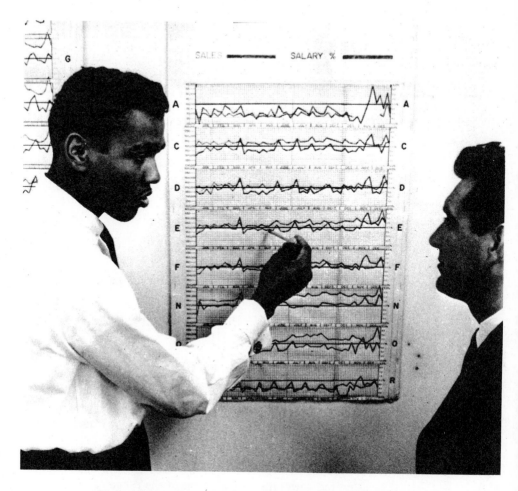

No matter what vocation you eventually choose, you are likely to find charts and graphs very useful. They are especially helpful in business, where large amounts of data must be considered and compared. The charts shown here are being studied by two businessmen with evident concern for what it tells them about sales and salaries. One needs to be able to interpret the graphs as well as to draw them.

You might like to assemble a collection of graphs from newspapers. You will find various types — pictographs, circle graphs, bar graphs, as well as line graphs of the type shown here. Perhaps you know someone who is a nurse. She might show you the kind of graph she keeps for the doctor's inspection.

Chapter Review

10–1   Functions Described by Tables   *Pages 355–359*

1. If relative lengths are to be correct, the scale of the bars on a bar graph must start at __?__.

2. Make a bar graph of the data in the following table:

Year	1966	1967	1968	1969
Number of Students in Acme High School	520	600	710	750

3. Make a broken-line graph of the data in the preceding table.

10–2   Coordinates in a Plane   *Pages 359–362*

4. The first coordinate of $P(a, b)$ is called the __?__ of P and the second coordinate is called the __?__ of P.

5. A point with a positive abscissa and a negative ordinate lies in the __?__ quadrant.

6. All points with abscissa -2 lie __?__ units from the __?__ axis and to the __?__ of that axis.

Graph each point on the coordinate plane.

7. $(-5, 0)$ 8. $(3, -8)$ 9. $(3, 3)$

10–3   Relations   *Pages 362–365*

10. A set of ordered pairs of elements is called a __?__.

11. A function is a relation such that each element of the domain is paired with only __?__ element of the range.

Does the table describe a function or not?

12.

1	3
2	2
3	1
2	0

13.

1	2
2	3
3	3
4	2

14.

1	6
2	5
3	4
4	3

10–4   Open Sentences in Two Variables   *Pages 365–368*

15. Each ordered pair whose components are a solution of an open sentence in two variables is called a __?__ of the open sentence.

16. $(4, \underline{\ ?\ })$ is a root of the equation "$6x + y = 17$."

17. The set of all points whose coordinates satisfy a given equation is called the $\underline{\ ?\ }$ of the given equation.

18. Using $\{2, 1, 0, -1, -2\}$ as the replacement set for x and $\Re$, the replacement set for y, solve $y = x^2 - 2x$.

10–5   The Graph of a Linear Equation in Two Variables
Pages 369–373

19. Each term in a linear equation is either a constant or a monomial of degree $\underline{\ ?\ }$.

20. The graph of a linear equation in two variables is a $\underline{\ ?\ }$ in the plane.

21. Graph $y = 3x + 2$.   **22.** Graph $y + 5 = 0$.

10–6   Slope of a Line   *Pages 373–377*

23. If a line in the coordinate plane rises from left to right, then its slope is $\underline{\ ?\ }$, and if it falls from left to right its slope is $\underline{\ ?\ }$.

24. The slope of the line containing $(-1, 2)$ and $(3, 8)$ is $\underline{\ ?\ }$.

25. While a vertical line has $\underline{\ ?\ }$ slope, a horizontal line has slope $\underline{\ ?\ }$.

10–7   The Slope-Intercept Form of a Linear Equation
Pages 377–379

26. The slope of the line with equation $y = -3x + 2$ is $\underline{\ ?\ }$ and its y-intercept is $\underline{\ ?\ }$.

27. The slope-intercept form of the equation for the graph of $2x + y = 5$ is $\underline{\ ?\ }$.

28. The graph of $x - 2y = 4$ crosses the y-axis at $(0, \underline{\ ?\ })$ and has slope $\underline{\ ?\ }$.

29. An equation of the line with slope 5 and y-intercept -2 is $\underline{\ ?\ }$.

10–8   Determining an Equation of a Line   *Pages 380–381*

30. If the graph of $y = 3x + b$ contains the point $(8, 2)$, then $b = \underline{\ ?\ }$.

31. Find an equation of the line with slope -2 that passes through $(2, 1)$.

32. Find an equation of the line containing points $(5, 1)$ and $(1, -7)$.

33. Find an equation of the line parallel to $2y - 6x = 7$ and containing point $(0, 0)$.

10-9   Direct Variation and Proportion   *Pages 382–388*

34. A function in which corresponding members of the domain and range are related in a fixed ratio is known as a __?__.

35. A direct variation may be shown by $y = kx$ or $k = $ __?__.

36. The fixed ratio k is called the __?__ of __?__.

37. In graphing the line represented by the equation $y = kx$ the letter __?__ stands for the slope of the line.

38. An equality of two ratios is a __?__.

39. In the proportion $\dfrac{w}{x} = \dfrac{y}{z}$, the means are __?__ and __?__; the extremes are __?__ and __?__.

40. If a is directly proportional to b, and $a = 15$ when $b = 22$, find a when $b = 88$.

10-10   Quadratic Functions   *Pages 388–392*

41. Graph $y = 2x^2$.

42. Find the coordinates of the points on the graph of $y = x^2 - 2$ having the least ordinate.

43. Find the coordinates of the point on the graph of $y = 3 - x^2$ having the greatest ordinate.

10-11   Inverse Variation   *Pages 392–398*

44. An inverse variation is a function in which the product of the coordinates of ordered pairs is a __?__.

45. If x varies inversely as y, then $\dfrac{x_1}{x_2} = \dfrac{?}{?}$.

46. When you graph an inverse variation, the resultant figure is a __?__.

47. If r is inversely proportional to s and $r_1 = 27$ when $s_1 = 8$ find r_2 when $s_2 = 3$.

10-12   Joint Variation and Combined Variation (Optional)   *Pages 399–402*

48. Joint variation takes place when one variable varies __?__ as the __?__ of other variables.

49. The centripetal force f on a body varies jointly as its mass m and the square of its velocity v. If $f = 12,800$ when $m = 160$ and $v = 80$, find m when $f = 7,500$ and $v = 50$.

50. Combined variation occurs when a variable varies __?__ as one variable and __?__ as another variable.

Descartes, Who Used Algebra with Geometry

"My advice," said the school principal to frail, young René Descartes (Re-nay Day-cart) "is to lie in bed as late as you like each morning." Descartes acted on this advice, not only while he was a sickly boy in school, but all the rest of his life.

As a young man, Descartes drifted. After several years in Paris, he traveled to Holland, where he served for a time as a volunteer soldier. While he was in Holland, something happened. One day, Descartes saw a poster in Flemish, a language he could not read. Curious, he asked a passerby to translate it for him. His reply was, "The poster bears a challenge. It asks whether anyone can solve a certain problem in mathematics." The man, who happened to be a college president, continued, "I'll read you the problem on one condition. You must promise me you will try to solve it."

Descartes was intrigued. He promised to try. And he found a solution. It was work, and took time, but he enjoyed it.

When Descartes discovered the pleasure in study, he left the army, and for the rest of his life devoted himself to learning. He became a great scientist, a great philosopher, and a great mathematician. He still stayed in bed in the morning. There he was undisturbed, and he could use this time to think. He once watched a fly crawl across the ceiling, and figured out how to describe its path by an equation.

Perhaps his greatest contribution to mathematics was his work in geometry. He thought of ways to apply algebra to geometry and in this way laid the foundations of analytic geometry. A rectangular coordinate system is sometimes called a Cartesian coordinate system in his honor.

It is not where a person is that counts so much as what he does!

René Descartes (1596–1650) after he had gained renown as scientist, philosopher, and mathematician.

Diophantine Equations

Can you find a solution of $x + 2y = 3$ in the set of real numbers? Of course you can; $(0, 1.5)$ is a solution, as is $(-1, 2)$. In fact, the number of solutions is unlimited. Can you see, however, that if the replacement set for x and for y is {the positive integers}, the only solution is $(1, 1)$? Since $y = \dfrac{3 - x}{2}$, x must be positive, less than 3, and odd, and so the only value it can have is 1. If the replacement set were {the nonnegative integers}, then $(3, 0)$ would also be a solution.

How many solutions of $x - 2y = -3$ over {the positive integers} can you find? Here $y = \dfrac{3 + x}{2}$, and so x can have the values 1, 3, 5, and so on. Thus, the solution set is infinite: $\{(1, 2), (3, 3), (5, 4), \ldots\}$.

Because a system of one or more equations with more variables than equations may have an infinite solution set, the equations are called *indeterminate*. When the replacement sets of the variables are restricted to subsets of {the integers}, the equations are called *Diophantine* (di′o-fan-tin) equations, after the Greek algebraist Diophantus. The solutions must be so restricted in many practical situations.

EXAMPLE.   **How many quarters and how many dimes together can be chosen to make up \$1.60?**

Solution: **Let d = the number of dimes and q = the number of quarters, where d and $q \in$ {the nonnegative integers}.**

$$10d + 25q = 160 \to 2d + 5q = 32 \to q = \frac{2(16 - d)}{5}$$

For q to be a nonnegative integer, $(16 - d)$ must represent a nonnegative multiple of 5:

$$16 - d = 5t, \text{ where } t \in \text{\{the nonnegative integers\}}.$$

Substituting $5t$ in the expression for q,

$$q = \frac{2 \cdot 5t}{5} = 2t.$$

Thus, d and q are expressed in terms of t by the equations

$$d = 16 - 5t$$

and

$$q = 2t,$$

where $t \in$ {the nonnegative integers}. Specific values for t give corresponding pairs (d, q):

t	0	1	2	3
d	16	11	6	1
q	0	2	4	6

Additional choices of t result in negative values of d, so that the chart gives all the acceptable pairs (d, q). Check these values in the problem.

Exercises

If possible, graph the solution set of the equation over {the positive integers}.

1. $x + 2y = 3$ 3. $x + 2y = -3$ 5. $3x + 4y = 24$

2. $x - 2y = 3$ 4. $x - 2y = -3$ 6. $5x + 2y = 30$

Solve these problems.

7. A 55-yard cloth is cut into pieces $3\frac{1}{2}$ and $4\frac{1}{2}$ yards long, without remnants. How many pieces of each length are there?

8. If a baker arranges his almost 6 dozen loaves of bread in groups of 4, 1 is left over; in groups of 5, 4 are left over. How many loaves has he?

9. Find the smallest positive integer which when divided by 2, 3, and 7 leaves remainders of 1, 2, and 6, respectively.

10. This "Chinese Problem of a Hundred Fowl" dates at least to the sixth century: If a rooster is worth 5 yuan, a hen is worth 3 yuan, and 3 chicks are worth 1 yuan, how many of each, 100 in all, would be worth 100 yuan? Assume that at least 5 roosters are required.

11. If at least one coin of each kind is used, how can you change a dollar into 15 coins, each less than a quarter in value?

12. Solve in positive integers:

$$\begin{cases} 4a - 11b + 12c = 22 \\ a + 5b - 4c = 17 \end{cases}$$

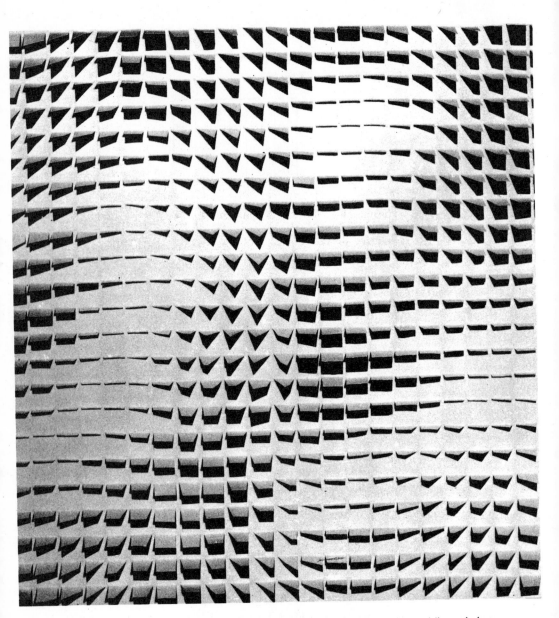

. . . *a pattern obtained by cutting triangular and quadrilateral shapes from a grid of one-inch squares and bending them into relief*

Systems of Open Sentences in Two Variables

Sometimes it takes more than one open sentence to help solve a problem. In this chapter you will discover how to use two sentences containing two variables. Does it surprise you to know that with the use of large computers we can solve problems requiring a great many variables and equations?

SOLVING SYSTEMS OF LINEAR EQUATIONS

11–1 The Graphic Method

You saw in section 10–5 that the graph of a linear equation in two variables is a straight line. When the graphs of two such equations in the same variables are drawn in the same coordinate system, the resulting lines may have in common:

A. No point — the lines are *parallel*. (*Parallel lines* are lines that lie in the same plane, but have no point in common.)

B. All their points — the lines *coincide*.

C. Just one point — the lines *intersect* and their common point is called their *point of intersection*.

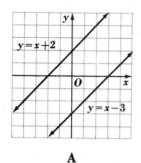
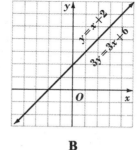
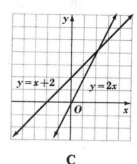

A	B	C
$y = x + 2$	$y = x + 2$	$y = x + 2$
$y = x - 3$	$3y = 3x + 6$	$y = 2x$

Figure 11–1

Because two equations impose two conditions on the variables at the same time, they are called a **system of simultaneous equations.** To solve such a system, you seek the ordered pairs of numbers that satisfy *both* equations of the system. Each such ordered pair is called a **solution of the system**; the set of all solutions is called the **solution set of the system.**

The graphs in Figure 11–1 show that:

$$\textbf{A.} \quad y = x + 2$$
$$y = x - 3$$

has no solution; the graphs do not intersect.

$$\textbf{B.} \quad y = x + 2$$
$$3y = 3x + 6$$

has an unlimited number of solutions; the graphs coincide.

$$\textbf{C.} \quad y = x + 2$$
$$y = 2x$$

has just one solution, (2, 4); the graphs intersect at one point.

To understand why the solution set of System **A** is ∅ (the empty set), notice that if "$y = x + 2$" and "$y = x - 3$" were *both* true statements for some ordered pair (x, y), then by substitution

$$x + 2 = x - 3,$$

and

$$2 = -3, \text{ a false statement.}$$

Simultaneous equations having no common root are called **inconsistent.** Because the equations of Systems **B** and **C** do have common roots, they are called **consistent equations.**

You can tell that the equations in System B have the same line as their graph by noticing that the slope-intercept form of each equation is

$$y = x + 2.$$

Thus, the solution set of System B is equal to the solution set of "$y = x + 2$."

You can check that the coordinates (2, 4) of the point of intersection of the graphs of the equation in System C satisfy both equations:

$y = x + 2$	$y = 2x$
$4 \overset{?}{=} 2 + 2$	$4 \overset{?}{=} 2 \cdot 2$
$4 = 4 \checkmark$	$4 = 4 \checkmark$

No other ordered pair satisfies both equations because no point other than the point (2, 4) lies on both graphs. Thus, the solution set of System C is $\{(2, 4)\}$.

> A pair of linear equations can be solved by graphing the equations in the same coordinate system and determining the coordinates of all points common to the graphs.

Examine Figure 11–2. Do you see that $(2, 4)$ is the common root of any pair of linear equations whose graphs pass through that point? In particular, the pair of heavy red lines in the figure pass through it. One of these red lines is the horizontal line whose equation is "$y = 4$," and the other is the vertical line with equation "$x = 2$."

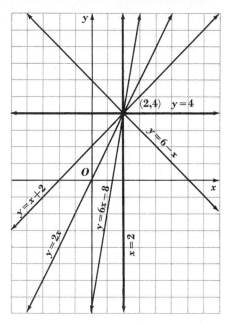

Because the system of equations

$$x = 2$$
$$y = 4$$

has the same solution set as the system

Figure 11–2

$$y = x + 2$$
$$y = 2x$$

these systems are said to be *equivalent systems*. The system $\begin{cases} x = 2 \\ y = 4 \end{cases}$ is also equivalent to the systems

$$\begin{array}{lll} y = 2x & y = 2x & y = 6 - x \\ y = 6x - 8 & y = 6 - x & y = 6x - 8 \end{array} \quad \textbf{and so on.}$$

Oral Exercises

Determine the coordinates of the point of intersection.

1. 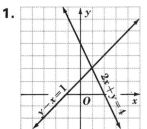   **2.** 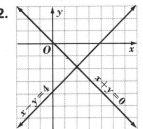   **3.**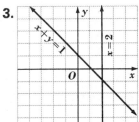

4.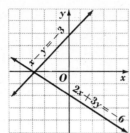

5.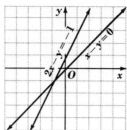

6.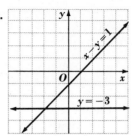

Do the equations in each system have one and only one common root? Explain.

SAMPLE. $x + y = 2$
$2x + 2y = 4$

Solution: No; they have an unlimited number of solutions. The slope-intercept form of each equation is $y = -x + 2$.
∴ their graphs coincide.

7. $x + y = 3$
$x - y = 2$

8. $x + y = 2$
$2x + y = 4$

9. $x - y = 2$
$x - y = 1$

10. $x + y = 5$
$2x + 2y = 10$

11. $x + y = 3$
$x + 2y = 6$

12. $3x - 2y = 5$
$2x + 3y = 8$

13. Are two equations consistent or inconsistent when their graphs are lines that

a. coincide?   **b.** intersect?   **c.** are parallel?

14. Given a system of linear equations that has at least two solutions, how are the graphs of the equations related?

Written Exercises

Graph the system and from your graph determine the solution set of the system.

A **1.** $y = x$
$y = 2 - x$

2. $y = 2x$
$y = 6 - x$

3. $x + y = 3$
$x - y = 1$

4. $x + y = 4$
$x - y = 2$

5. $x + y = 0$
$x + 2y = 2$

6. $2x + y = 3$
$x + 2y = 0$

7. $y = 3 - x$
$x + y = 5$

8. $y = x - 2$
$2x - 2y = 4$

9. $y = 2 - x$
$x = 2 + y$

10. $x = y - 1$
$y = x - 1$

11. $y = 2x + 1$
$x + y = -2$

12. $y = \frac{2}{3}x + 1$
$y = -\frac{2}{3}x + 5$

Solve graphically and estimate the coordinates of the point of intersection to the nearest tenth.

B **13.** $x + 2y = 7$
$x - y = 5$

14. $2x + y = 8$
$x - 2y = 1$

15. $2x + 3y = -2$
$2x - y = -9$

16. $3x + 2y = 4$
$x - 2y = 6$

17. Where on the graph of $2x + 3y = 5$ is the abscissa equal to the ordinate?

18. Where on the graph of $x - 2y = 9$ is the ordinate twice the abscissa?

$\boxed{C}$ **19.** Find the area of the triangle whose vertices are determined by the graphs of $y = x + 4$, $y = 10 - x$, $y = 2$.

20. Find the area of the triangle whose vertices are determined by the graphs of $2x + y = -2$, $x - 2y = -6$, $x = 2$.

11–2 The Addition or Subtraction Method

When the solution of a system of equations is an ordered pair of integers, it can usually be found by the graphic method of the preceding section as in the left-hand diagram below. However, there are algebraic methods that enable you to compute the solution for any pair of simultaneous equations.

EXAMPLE 1. Solve: $x + 3y = 19$
$x - y = -1$

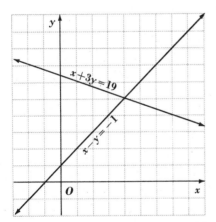
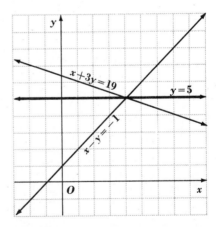

Solution: You can use the addition property of equality (page 111) to obtain the equivalent system made up of the equations of the horizontal and vertical lines through the point of intersection.

1. To obtain an equation that does not involve x, subtract (add the opposite of) each member of the second given equation from the corresponding member of the first equation:

$$\begin{array}{r} x + 3y = 19 \\ x - y = -1 \\ \hline 4y = 20 \\ y = 5 \end{array}$$

(horizontal line through the intersection, right above)

(*cont. on next page*)

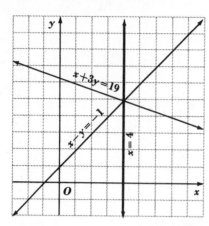

Now, substitute "5" for y in either of the original equations:

$x + 3y = 19$
$x + 3(5) = 19$
$x + 15 = 19$
$x = 4$ (vertical line through the intersection)

Check: Substitute "4" for x and "5" for y in both original equations.

$\therefore$ the solution set is $\{(4, 5)\}$.
Answer.

EXAMPLE 2. Solve: $3a + 4b = 7$
$\qquad\qquad\qquad a - 4b = 5$.

Solution:

1. Add the corresponding members of the given equations.

$\begin{array}{rl} 3a + 4b &= 7 \\ a - 4b &= 5 \\ \hline 4a &= 12 \\ a &= 3 \end{array}$

2. Substitute "3" for a in one of the given equations.

$\begin{array}{rl} 3a + 4b &= 7 \\ 3 \cdot 3 + 4b &= 7 \\ 4b &= -2 \\ b &= -\frac{1}{2} \end{array}$

Check:

$3a + 4b = 7$
$3(3) + 4(-\frac{1}{2}) \overset{?}{=} 7$
$9 - 2 \overset{?}{=} 7$
$7 = 7$ ✓

$a - 4b = 5$
$(3) - 4(-\frac{1}{2}) \overset{?}{=} 5$
$3 + 2 \overset{?}{=} 5$
$5 = 5$ ✓

$\therefore$ the solution set is $\{(3, -\frac{1}{2})\}$. **Answer.**

Written Exercises

Solve by addition or subtraction.

1. $x + y = 7$
$\quad x - y = 9$

2. $r - s = -5$
$\quad r + s = 25$

3. $2t + u = 7$
$\quad 2t - u = 13$

4. $m + 3n = -26$
$\quad m - 3n = 22$

5. $x - 3y = 2$
$\quad x + 4y = 16$

6. $7w - z = 18$
$\quad -5w + z = -14$

7. $2A - 3B = 20$
$\quad A - 3B = 13$

8. $5x + 3y = 8$
$\quad -7x - 3y = -10$

9. $6r + 5s = -8$
$\quad 2r - 5s = -16$

10. $3m - 7n = 16$
$\quad 5m - 7n = 36$

11. $7w + 11z = -25$
$\quad w - 11z = 9$

12. $5x + 3y = 10$
$\quad 2x - 3y = 4$

13. $3C + 2D = -6$
$\quad C + 2D = -6$

14. $3k - 7g = 15$
$\quad 3k + 2g = 15$

15. $46 = 4x + 3z$
$\quad 14 = 2x - 3z$

16. $32 = 5s - 3t$
$\quad -8 = 5s + 7t$

17. $8g + 7h = 26$
$\quad 8g - 10h = 60$

18. $12x - 9y = 126$
$\quad 12x + 13y = 170$

Clear the equations of fractions before adding or subtracting.

B **19.** $\frac{1}{8}(x + y) = 1$
$x - y = 4$

20. $3y - 2x = 4$
$\frac{1}{6}(3y - 4x) = 1$

21. $\frac{x}{3} - y = 0$
$\frac{x}{5} + \frac{2y}{5} = 1$

22. $\frac{2u}{5} - \frac{v}{2} = 1$
$\frac{2u}{5} + v = -2$

23. $0.3(x + y) = 22.2$
$0.4(x - y) = 6.4$

24. $0.5(x - y) = 2$
$0.75(x + y) = 9$

25. $\frac{5a}{6} + \frac{b}{4} = 7$
$\frac{2a}{3} - \frac{b}{8} = 3$

26. $\frac{2r}{5} + \frac{6s}{20} = \frac{4}{5}$
$\frac{2r}{3} + \frac{5s}{12} = \frac{7}{6}$

11–3 Problems with Two Variables

Problems concerning two numbers can be solved by using one or two variables. A solution using two variables to form two open sentences is often the more direct.

EXAMPLE. **Cathy spent 40 minutes longer on her algebra homework than she did on her English homework. If she spent 1 hour and 50 minutes studying both subjects, how long did she spend on each?**

Solution:

1▶ Choose two variables to represent the desired numbers.

Let x = number of minutes spent on algebra and y = number of minutes spent on English.

2▶ Form two open sentences using the facts of the problem.

$x + y = 110$ $\left(\begin{array}{l}\text{minutes spent study-}\\ \text{ing both subjects}\end{array}\right)$

$x - y = 40$ $\left(\begin{array}{l}\text{difference in time}\\ \text{spent on each subject}\end{array}\right)$

3▶ Solve the equations.

$$\begin{array}{r} x + y = 110 \\ x - y = 40 \\ \hline 2x = 150 \\ x = 75 \end{array}$$

$75 + y = 110$
$y = 35$

4▶ Check your results in the words of the problem.

75 minutes is 40 minutes more than 35 minutes.
Total time is $75 + 35$, or 110, minutes, or 1 hour and 50 minutes.

∴ Cathy spent 1 hour and 15 minutes on algebra and 35 minutes on English. Answer.

Oral Exercises

Translate into a system of equations in two variables.

1. One number is 3 more than another. Their sum is 27.
2. The sum of two numbers is 15. One number is three times the other.
3. The sum of two numbers is 14 and their difference is 6.
4. One number is twice another. Their difference is 16.
5. A 27-foot rope is cut into two pieces. One piece is 3 feet longer than the other.
6. An amount of $340 is divided into two parts. One part contains $80 less than the other.
7. Three apples and two peaches cost 55¢. Four apples and one peach cost 60¢.
8. Two malts and two sundaes cost $2.20. Three malts and one sundae cost $2.00.
9. An algebra class contains 31 students. There are 3 more boys than girls in the class.
10. The perimeter of a rectangle is 400 feet. It is 40 feet longer than it is wide.

Problems

Use two variables and a system of two equations to solve each problem.

1. Half the perimeter of a rectangular lot, which is 50 feet longer than it is wide, is 350 feet. What are the dimensions of the lot?
2. Mr. Smith's house has 3 rooms more than Mr. Tripp's. The two houses together contain 17 rooms. How many rooms are in each house?
3. The difference between three times one number and a smaller one is 23. The sum of the smaller and twice the larger is 27. Name the numbers.
4. If Jane were 10 years older, she would be twice as old as Jim, and their combined ages would be 36. How old are Jane and Jim?
5. Fred and Bill bowl together and have a combined score of 425. Twice the difference between Fred's score and Bill's is 50. Find their scores.
6. In a game of cards, Judy scored 2 points more than twice the number of points Ann scored. If a total of 26 points were scored, how many points did each score?
7. Large boxes of a certain kind of tea sell for 82¢ and small boxes for 56¢. Ted buys several boxes for a total of $3.58. If he spent $1.34 more for the large boxes than for the small boxes, how many boxes of each size did he buy?
8. A shoe store is selling all shoes for $12 and all slippers for $8. If Linda spent $44 more on shoes than on slippers, and spent a total of $76, how many pairs of each did she buy?

9. Three hamburgers and four hot dogs cost a total of $2.15. If the hamburgers cost $.55 more than the hot dogs, what is the cost of each hamburger and each hot dog?

10. A store received $823 one month from the sale of 5 tape recorders and 7 radios. If the receipts from the tape recorders exceeded the receipts from the radios by $137, what is the cost of a tape recorder?

B 11. A girl has 15 coins, all nickels and dimes, with a total value of $1.20. Find the number of each kind of coin.

12. A shipment of 18 cars, some weighing 3,000 pounds apiece and the others 5,000 pounds each, has a total weight of 30 tons. Find the number of each kind of car.

11–4 Multiplication in the Addition or Subtraction Method

Sometimes adding or subtracting the members will not eliminate either variable because the coefficients of a pair of corresponding terms do not have the same absolute value. You then can use the multiplication property of equality (page 123) to make the coefficient of a variable in one equation have the same absolute value as the corresponding coefficient in the other.

EXAMPLE 1. Solve: $2r + 3s = 12$
$$r - 4s = -5$$
Solution:

1. **Multiply** both members of the second equation by **2**.

$$2r + 3s = 12$$
$$2r - 8s = -10$$

2. Subtract the second equation from the first and solve for s.

$$11s = 22$$
$$s = 2$$

3. Find the value of r by substituting "**2**" for s in one of the given equations.

$$r - 4(2) = -5$$
$$r - 8 = -5$$
$$r = 3$$

4. *Check:* Substitute in original equations. (This is left to you.)

EXAMPLE 2. Solve: $5x - 2y = -5$
$$3x - 7y = -32$$
Solution:

$$7(5x - 2y) = 7(-5) \longrightarrow 35x - 14y = -35 \qquad 5(1) - 2y = -5$$
$$-2(3x - 7y) = -2(-32) \longrightarrow -6x + 14y = 64 \qquad -2y = -10$$
$$29x = 29 \qquad y = 5$$
$$x = 1$$

Check: $5(1) - 2(5) \overset{?}{=} -5 \qquad 3(1) - 7(5) \overset{?}{=} -32$
$$-5 = -5 \checkmark \qquad -32 = -32 \checkmark$$

∴ the solution set is $\{(1, 5)\}$. **Answer.**

Oral Exercises

By what number would you multiply one equation in each pair to eliminate one variable? Give the transformed equation.

1. $x + y = 7$
$3x + 2y = 18$

2. $m - n = 2$
$2m + 5n = 11$

3. $2r + s = 6$
$3r + 2s = 9$

4. $u - 3v = 5$
$3u + 2v = 4$

5. $5a + 2b = -12$
$2a - b = -3$

6. $6t + w = 5$
$5t - 3w = 8$

7. $5x + 9y = 13$
$3x + 3y = 3$

8. $4m + 3n = 5$
$2m - 5n = 14$

By what number would you multiply each equation in the system to eliminate a variable?

9. $3t - 2s = 3$
$2t + 5s = 21$

10. $6n + 5k = 2$
$4n - 2k = 10$

11. $4x - 5y = 7$
$10x + 3y = -29$

12. $2p + 9q = 20$
$9p + 2q = 13$

13. $4r - 4t = 0$
$5r + 6t = 11$

14. $7a + 2b = 3$
$2a - 5b = -27$

Written Exercises

Solve each system of equations algebraically.

A

1. $d + f = 3$
$3d - 5f = 17$

2. $4a - 3b = -1$
$a - b = -1$

3. $\dfrac{m}{6} + \dfrac{n}{4} = \dfrac{3}{2}$
$\dfrac{2m}{3} - \dfrac{n}{2} = 0$

4. $\dfrac{u}{5} + \dfrac{2v}{5} = 2$
$\dfrac{u}{2} - v = 1$

5. $2a + 3b = -1$
$3a + 5b = -2$

6. $2w - 3z = -1$
$3w + 4z = 24$

7. $2m + 3n = 0$
$5m - 2n = -19$

8. $5a - 2b = 0$
$2a - 3b = -11$

9. $\dfrac{5x}{4} + y = \dfrac{11}{2}$
$x + \dfrac{y}{3} = 3$

10. $2r - \dfrac{5s}{2} = 13$
$\dfrac{r}{3} + \dfrac{s}{5} = \dfrac{14}{15}$

11. $3c - 2d = 13$
$7c + 3d = 15$

12. $7p + 5q = 2$
$8p - 9q = 17$

B

13. $\dfrac{1}{x} + \dfrac{1}{y} = 7$
$\dfrac{2}{x} + \dfrac{3}{y} = 16$

Hint: Rewrite: $\dfrac{1}{x} + \dfrac{1}{y} = 7$

$2\left(\dfrac{1}{x}\right) + 3\left(\dfrac{1}{y}\right) = 16$

Let $a = \dfrac{1}{x}$ and $b = \dfrac{1}{y}$. Solve for a and b.

Then $x = \dfrac{1}{a}$ and $y = \dfrac{1}{b}$.

14. $\dfrac{1}{a} + \dfrac{2}{b} = 11$

$\dfrac{1}{a} - \dfrac{2}{b} = -1$

15. $\dfrac{5}{c} - \dfrac{6}{d} = -3$

$\dfrac{10}{c} + \dfrac{9}{d} = 1$

16. $\dfrac{1}{r} - \dfrac{1}{s} = 4$

$\dfrac{2}{r} - \dfrac{1}{2s} = 11$

Note: The equations in Exercises 13–16 are not linear in the original variables.

17. $\dfrac{a-1}{3} + \dfrac{b-1}{3} = 2$

$\dfrac{a-1}{2} + \dfrac{b-1}{6} = \dfrac{5}{3}$

18. $\dfrac{2s+1}{7} + \dfrac{3t+2}{5} = \dfrac{1}{5}$

$\dfrac{3s-2}{2} + \dfrac{t+4}{4} = 4$

Problems

Solve, using a system of two equations in two variables.

A

1. Mr. Waite's rent and utilities bills each month total $160. If his utilities bill increases $8 per month, it will be $\frac{1}{5}$ of his rent. What is his rent?

2. A certain recipe requires a total of 5 cups of sugar and flour together. If the recipe had called for $\frac{1}{4}$ cup more sugar, there would be twice as much flour as sugar. How much sugar does the recipe call for?

3. The ages of Kim and her father total 57 years. If Kim's age were doubled, Kim's father would be 12 years older than Kim. How old is Kim?

4. The federal tax on a $10,000 salary was $500 less than 10 times the state tax. If the taxes total $2800, find the state's share.

5. The side of a square house is 24 feet long, and the house is located on a lot which is 50 feet longer than it is wide. The perimeter of the lot is 20 feet more than 5 times the perimeter of the house. Find the length of the lot.

6. A rectangular rug which is 3 feet longer than it is wide is in a room of perimeter 54 feet. The perimeter of the rug is 12 feet less than the perimeter of the room. Find the dimensions of the rug.

7. Judy buys 2 bags of potato chips and 3 boxes of pretzels for $2.35. She then buys another bag of potato chips and 2 more boxes of pretzels for $1.37. Find the cost of potato chips and pretzels.

8. A group of 4 couples are going out for refreshments. If 4 people have ice cream sodas and 4 people have sundaes, the bill will total $3.60. However, if only 2 people have sundaes and 6 people have sodas, the bill will be $3.20. What is the cost of each soda and each sundae?

9. Mrs. Britten's income from two stocks each year totals $280. Stock A pays dividends at the rate of 5% and stock B at the rate of 6%. If she has invested a total of $5000, how much capital is invested in each stock?

10. Mr. Towne takes loans from two banks. He borrows $300 more from the bank which charges 7% interest than from the bank which charges 8% interest. If his interest payments for one year are $126, how much does he borrow at each rate?

11–5 The Substitution Method

You can solve either equation of a system of two equations for one variable in terms of the other, and use the substitution principle to obtain a third equation involving only one variable. This method is sometimes easier to use than the addition and subtraction method.

EXAMPLE. Solve: $x - 2y = 4$
$$3x + 4y = 2$$

Solution:

1. Solve for x in the first equation.

$$x - 2y = 4$$
$$x = 4 + 2y$$

2. Substitute this expression for x in the other equation.

$$3x + 4y = 2$$
$$3(4 + 2y) + 4y = 2$$

3. Solve for y.

$$12 + 6y + 4y = 2$$
$$10y = -10$$
$$y = -1$$

Solving for x and checking are left for you. The solution set is $\{(2, -1)\}$. **Answer.**

Written Exercises

Solve each system of equations by substitution.

A 1. $3x + y = 5$
$y = 2x$

2. $z + 5r = 2$
$z = -3r$

3. $-a + b = 1$
$a + b = -5$

4. $m - 3n = -4$
$2m + 6n = 5$

5. $x + y = 2$
$3x + 2y = 5$

6. $5a - 3b = -1$
$a + b = 3$

7. $x + 3y = 2$
$2x + 3y = 7$

8. $3t - 2s = 5$
$t + 2s = 15$

9. $3c - 2d = 3$
$2c - d = 2$

10. $3r - 5s = 8$
$r + 2s = 1$

11. $3a - 4b = 5$
$a + 7b = 10$

12. $x - 2y = 0$
$4x - 3y = 15$

B 13. $\frac{1}{5}(x + y) = 2$
$\frac{1}{2}(x - y) = 1$

14. $\frac{s}{3} - t = 2$
$s - t = 20$

15. $x + y = 7$
$x - \frac{y}{2} = 4$

16. $x - y = 16$
$\frac{1}{2}(x + y) = 37$

17. $3a - 2b = 11$
$a - \frac{b}{2} = 4$

18. $\frac{1}{3}(x + y) = 2$
$\frac{1}{5}(x - y) = 2$

Problems

Solve, using a system of two equations in two variables and the substitution method.

A 1. Half the sum of two numbers is $\frac{15}{2}$. Half their difference is $-\frac{3}{2}$. Find the two numbers.

2. Steve and Harry live 250 miles apart. They decide to meet at a town which is 30 miles further from Steve's house than it is from Harry's. How far will each travel?

3. Janet and Lynn live 8 blocks apart in opposite directions from their office. If Lynn lives 1 block less than twice as far from the office as Janet does, how far does each girl live from the office?

4. A mother took her 3 children on an airplane flight. Her ticket cost $2 more than twice each of the children's. If the total cost of the tickets was $53.25, find the mother's fare and the fare for each of the children.

5. On a jury there are 3 fewer men than twice the number of women. If there were 2 more women on the jury, there would be an equal number of men and women. How many men are on the jury?

6. Mrs. Birch invested $1200, some at 6%, the rest at $4\frac{1}{2}$% per year. The return from the $4\frac{1}{2}$% investment exceeded that from the 6% investment by $12. How much was invested at each rate?

B 7. The average of two numbers is $\frac{11}{24}$. One-third of their difference is $\frac{1}{12}$. Find the two numbers.

8. One sum invested at 6% and another at 5% yield a total of $37.50. If the investments were interchanged, their income would increase by $2.00. Find the sums.

9. Mrs. Bowen receives a total of $135 a year interest from a regular savings account, paying 5% per year, and from a special notice account, paying $5\frac{1}{2}$% per year. If she had interchanged the amounts deposited in each type of account, her income would have decreased by $7.50. Find the amount she deposited in each type of account.

10. A certain laundromat has washing machines available for $.25 per load and $.35 per load. Using both types of machines, several loads can be laundered for $2.65. If only the $.35-per-load type of machines is used, the laundry could be done in 2 fewer loads and cost $.20 less. Find the number of loads of laundry done if only the $.35-per-load machines are used.

EXTRA PROBLEM

Draw a flow chart of a program to determine and print all positive two-digit numbers, if any, which are equal to twice the product of the two digits.

ADDITIONAL PROBLEMS

11–6   Digit Problems

The digits 0, 1, 2, 3, 4, 5, 6, 7, 8, 9 not only represent different values themselves, but represent different values in different positions within a numeral:

$$76 = 7 \cdot 10 + 6 \cdot 1; \qquad 67 = 6 \cdot 10 + 7 \cdot 1$$

All two-digit decimal numerals have the same form in general:

$$10t + u,$$

where t denotes the value of the tens digit and u denotes the value of the ones (units) digit. Thus,

$$t \in \{1, 2, 3, 4, 5, 6, 7, 8, 9\} \quad \text{and} \quad u \in \{0, 1, 2, 3, 4, 5, 6, 7, 8, 9\}.$$

If you wish to represent a number with the same digits in reverse order, you write $10u + t$. In either case, the sum of the values of the digits themselves is represented by $t + u$.

Frequently, to avoid clumsy wording, you refer to "the sum of the digits" rather than "the sum of the values of the digits." Similarly, you may say "reverse the digits of the number" instead of "reverse the digits of the numeral."

EXAMPLE.   **The sum of the digits in a two-digit numeral is 8. When the digits are interchanged, the number designated is 18 more than the original number. Find the original number.**

Solution:

1▶   Let t = the value of the tens digit in the original numeral
and u = the value of the units digit in the original numeral.

Then $10t + u$ = the original number
and $10u + t$ = the new number.

2▶   The sum of the values of the digits is 8:   The new number is 18 more
$$t + u = 8$$ than the original number.
$$10u + t = 18 + 10t + u$$
$$(10u + t) - (10t + u) = 18$$

3▶ $u + t = \ 8$ $9u - 9t = 18$
$\dfrac{u - t = \ 2}{\ }$ ⟵————————— $u - t = \ 2$
$\quad 2u = 10$ ——➤ $5 - t = 2$
$\qquad u = 5$ ——➤ $t = 3$

4▶   *Check:*   Is the sum of the digits 8? $3 + 5 = 8$ ✓

Is 53 eighteen more than 35? $53 - 35 = 18$ ✓

∴ the original number was 35. Answer.

Problems

A **1.** The sum of the digits of a two-digit numeral is 11. If 45 is added to the number, the result is the number with its digits reversed. Find the original number.

2. The sum of the digits of a two-digit numeral is 9. If the order of the digits is reversed, the result names a number exceeding the original by 9. Find the original number.

3. The sum of the digits of a two-digit numeral is 12. The value of the number is 13 times the tens digit. Find the number.

4. The sum of the digits of a two-digit numeral is 8. The number with its digits interchanged is 11 times the original units digit. Find the original number.

5. The units digit of a two-digit numeral is three times the tens digit. The sum of the digits is 12. Find the number.

6. The tens digit of a two-digit numeral exceeds three times the units digit by 2. The sum of the digits is 10. Find the number.

7. The sum of the digits of a two-digit numeral is 7. The number with the digits interchanged is 5 times the tens digit of the original number. Find the original number.

8. The sum of the digits of a two-digit numeral is 10. The number with the digits in reverse order is 16 times the original tens digit. Find the original number.

9. A clerk mistakenly reversed the two digits in the price of a paperback book, overcharging the customer 18¢. If the sum of the digits is 16, determine the correct price of the paperback book.

10. Find a number less than 100 whose tens digit exceeds twice its units digit by 1 and whose digits in reverse order give a number which is 7 more than 3 times their sum.

B **11.** Find a three-digit number whose hundreds digit is twice its tens digit and three times its units digit, and whose digits total 11.

12. A three-digit number is 198 more than itself reversed. The hundreds digit is three more than the tens digit, and the sum of the digits is 16. Find the original number.

13. If a two-digit number is divided by its tens digit, the quotient is 12 and the remainder is 1. If the number with its digits interchanged is divided by its original units digit, the quotient is 10 and the remainder is 4. Find the original number.

14. Show that the difference between a three-digit number and the number with the order of the digits reversed is always divisible by 99.

Problems 15–18 refer to two-place decimal fractions between 0 and 1.

C **15.** The sum of the digits of a two-place fraction is 9. When its digits are reversed, the new fraction exceeds the original by 0.27. Find the original fraction.

16. When the digits of a two-place fraction are reversed, the new fraction is $\frac{4}{7}$ the original fraction. If the sum of the digits is 12, find the original fraction.

17. The sum of the digits of a two-place fraction is 7. The fraction with its digits reversed is 0.02 more than twice the original fraction. Find the original fraction.

18. The tenths digit of a two-place fraction exceeds twice the hundredths digit by 1. If the digits are reversed, the original is 0.02 more than twice the new fraction. Find the original fraction.

11–7 Motion Problems

You can solve some motion problems conveniently by using a system of two equations in two variables.

EXAMPLE. **Lisa took 45 minutes to go 6 miles down Taylor's River in a motorboat, and it took her $1\frac{1}{2}$ hours to return. What was the speed (in miles per hour) of Lisa's boat in still water, and what was the speed of the current in the river?**

Solution:

1 ▶ Let m = the speed, in m.p.h., of Lisa's boat
   and r = the speed, in m.p.h., of the river's current.

2 ▶

	r	·	t	=	d	
Downstream	$m + r$		$\frac{3}{4}$		6	$\longrightarrow \frac{3}{4}(m + r) = 6$
Upstream	$m - r$		$\frac{3}{2}$		6	$\longrightarrow \frac{3}{2}(m - r) = 6$

3 ▶ Solve the equations. ⎫
                                     ⎬ Left to you.
4 ▶ Check the roots.   ⎭

The speed of the boat is 6 m.p.h.

The speed of the current is 2 m.p.h.

Problems

A **1.** A motorboat goes 15 miles downstream in 45 minutes. The return trip against the current takes $1\frac{1}{2}$ hours. Find the boat's speed in still water.

2. A cyclist rode 5 miles in 15 minutes with the wind, and returned in 20 minutes against the same wind. Find her speed without a wind.

3. A speed boat traveled 60 miles with the current in $1\frac{1}{2}$ hours. The return trip took 2 hours against the current. What was the speed of the current?

4. It required $1\frac{1}{3}$ hours for a 400-mile plane trip and $1\frac{3}{5}$ hours for the return against the same wind. What would have been the speed of the plane without wind?

5. Nick took 36 minutes to row 3 miles. When he returned, he took 2 hours. What was the river's current?

6. A fish swims 12 miles downstream in $2\frac{2}{5}$ hours and returns in 6 hours. At the same rate, how fast does he go in still water?

B 7. A man rows 3 miles upstream and 3 miles back in $2\frac{1}{4}$ hours. He rows 1 mile against the current in the time he rows 2 miles with it. At what rate does he row in still water? What is his average rate of travel?

8. A swimmer takes $1\frac{1}{4}$ hours on a 1-mile round trip. On the return trip against the current he did $\frac{1}{8}$ mile in the time that he did $\frac{1}{2}$ mile on the trip downstream. Find his average rate. What was the rate of the current?

9. A round trip flight of 1037.5 miles takes $7\frac{1}{2}$ hours. The part of the flight with the wind takes $1\frac{1}{2}$ hours less than the other part of the trip. Find the speed of the plane in still air and the speed of the wind.

10. A motorboat races a distance up the river in the time it races $1\frac{1}{4}$ that distance downstream. If the speed of the boat is s and that of the current is c, find the relationship between s and c.

11. A boat can move upstream only three-fifths as fast as it can move downstream. To go 30 miles upstream and 30 miles downstream requires one-half hour more time than to go 60 miles in still lake water. Find the rate of the boat (in still water) and the rate of the current.

12. Two boys are camped at a spot where a river enters a big lake. One boy is injured so severely that every minute counts. His companion can use an outboard motorboat to get a doctor by going 3 miles down the lake and back, or by going 3 miles up the river and back. Show that even though the boy does not know the speed of either the boat or the current, he should choose the lake.

EXTRA PROBLEM

Draw a flow chart to compute and print the solution of the system $\begin{cases} ax + by = c \\ dx + ey = f \end{cases}$. Assume that $ae - bd \neq 0$.

(*Hint:* The system is equivalent to $x = \dfrac{ce - bf}{ae - bd}$ and $y = \dfrac{af - cd}{ae - bd}$.)

11–8   Age Problems

You can simplify the solution of age problems by using two variables and by organizing the facts in chart form.

EXAMPLE.   **Five years ago, Cliff was $\frac{2}{3}$ as old as Judith. Ten years from now, he will be $\frac{5}{6}$ as old as Judith. How old is each now?**

Solution:

Time	Cliff	Judith
5 years ago	$x - 5$	$y - 5$
This year	x	y
10 years hence	$x + 10$	$y + 10$

$$x - 5 = \tfrac{2}{3}(y - 5)$$

$$x + 10 = \tfrac{5}{6}(y + 10)$$

Solve these equations and check.

Cliff is 15 years old; $\Big\}$ **Answer.**
Judith is 20 years old.

Problems

A

1. A man is 13 times as old as his son. In ten years he will be 3 times as old as his son will be then. How old is the son now?

2. Karen's mother is twice as old as Karen is. Eleven years ago she was 3 times as old as Karen was. Find Karen's present age.

3. Two years ago, Rick's age was 1 year less than twice Christopher's. Four years from now, Rick will be 8 years more than half Christopher's age. How old is Rick?

4. Five years ago, Barbara was $\frac{4}{5}$ as old as Fred. Ten years from now, she will be $\frac{7}{8}$ as old as Fred. How old is each now?

5. Ann is $\frac{3}{4}$ as old as Judy. Four years ago Ann was $\frac{2}{3}$ as old as Judy. How old is each?

6. A man said, "My son is four times as old as my daughter. My wife is 3 times as old as the combined ages of both, and I am as old as my wife and daughter together. My father, who is as old as all of us together, is 72." How old is the speaker's son?

B

7. Nick said, "If I were $\frac{1}{2}$ as old as I am, and Linda were $\frac{3}{4}$ as old as she is, we would be 3 years older together than I am alone. But if I were $\frac{2}{3}$ as old as I am, and Linda were $\frac{1}{4}$ as old as she is, together we would be 2 years younger than I am alone." How old is Nick?

8. Laura is 3 times as old as Maria was when Laura was as old as Maria is now. In 2 years, Laura will be twice as old as Maria was 2 years ago. Find their present ages.

9. Mary is 3 times as old as Linda was when Mary was as old as Linda is now. Find the relationship between Mary's present age (m) and Linda's (l).

10. Meg is twice as old as Peg will be when Meg is 5 times as old as Peg is now. Find the relationship between Meg's present age (m) and Peg's (p).

C 11. Mary is twice as old as Jane was at the time when Mary was as old as Jane is now. The sum of the present ages of Mary and Jane is 28 years. How old is each person now?

12. A man is three times as old as his son was at the time when the father was twice as old as his son will be 2 years from now. Find the present age of each person if the sum of their ages is 55 years.

11–9 Problems about Fractions

Among the problems you can solve by using two variables are those about fractions, like this one:

EXAMPLE. The value of a fraction is $\frac{3}{4}$. When 7 is added to its numerator, the resulting fraction is equal to the reciprocal of the original fraction. Find the original fraction.

Solution:

1 ▶ Let $\dfrac{n}{d}$ = the original fraction.

2 ▶ $\dfrac{n}{d} = \dfrac{3}{4}$ and $\dfrac{n+7}{d} = \dfrac{4}{3}.$

3 ▶ Multiply by d:

$$d\left(\frac{n}{d}\right) = d\left(\frac{3}{4}\right)$$

$$n = \frac{3}{4}d$$

Multiply by L.C.D., $3d$:

$$3d\left(\frac{n+7}{d}\right) = 3d\left(\frac{4}{3}\right)$$

$$3(n+7) = d(4)$$

$$3n + 21 = 4d$$

$$3\left(\frac{3}{4}d\right) + 21 = 4d$$

$$9d + 84 = 16d$$

$$-7d = -84$$

$$d = 12$$

$$n = \frac{3}{4}(12)$$

$$n = 9$$

4 ▶ Check is left to you.   ∴ the original fraction is $\frac{9}{12}$. Answer.

Problems

Using two variables, find the original fraction.

A   **1.** The denominator is 4 more than the numerator. If each is increased by 1, the value of the resulting fraction is $\frac{1}{2}$.

2. The denominator is 2 more than the numerator. If 1 is subtracted from each, the value of the resulting fraction is $\frac{1}{2}$.

3. The denominator exceeds the numerator by 1. If 1 is subtracted from the numerator, and the denominator is unchanged, the resulting fraction has value $\frac{3}{4}$.

4. The denominator exceeds the numerator by 3. If 1 is added to the denominator, a fraction is obtained whose value is $\frac{2}{3}$.

5. A fraction has value $\frac{2}{3}$. When 15 is added to its numerator, the resulting fraction equals the reciprocal of the value of the original fraction.

6. A fraction's value is $\frac{4}{5}$. When its numerator is increased by 9, the new fraction equals the reciprocal of the value of the original fraction.

B   **7.** The two digits in the numerator of a fraction whose value is $\frac{2}{9}$ are reversed in its denominator. The reciprocal of the fraction is the value of the fraction obtained when 27 is added to the original numerator and 71 is subtracted from the original denominator.

8. The numerator equals the sum of the two digits in the denominator. The value of the fraction is $\frac{1}{4}$. When both numerator and denominator are increased by 3, the resulting fraction has the value $\frac{1}{3}$.

9. The two digits in the numerator of a fraction are reversed in its denominator. If 1 is subtracted from both the numerator and the denominator, the value of the resulting fraction is $\frac{1}{2}$. The fraction whose numerator is the difference and whose denominator is the sum of the units and tens digits equals $\frac{2}{5}$.

10. The numerator is a three-digit number whose hundreds digit is 4. The denominator is the numerator with the digits reversed. If 31 is subtracted from the numerator, the value of the fraction is $\frac{1}{2}$. If 167 is subtracted from the denominator, the resulting fraction equals $\frac{2}{3}$.

List all possible members of each solution set.

C   **11.** The numerator is a two-digit number and the denominator is that number with the digits reversed. The value of the fraction is $\frac{7}{4}$.

12. The numerator of a fraction whose value is $\frac{334}{667}$ is a four-digit number whose hundreds and tens digits are 0. The denominator contains the same digits in reverse order.

INEQUALITIES

11–10 Graph of an Inequality in Two Variables

In Figure 11–3 the graph (line *l*) of "$y = 2$" separates the coordinate plane into two regions. If you start at any point on line *l*, say (1, 2) and move vertically upward, the *y*-coordinate *increases* as you move. If you move vertically downward from this point, the value of *y* *decreases*. In either case, the value of *x* remains 1.

The equation "$y = 2$" is the boundary of two **half-planes**. In Figure 11–3 the half-plane above the line consists of all points for which

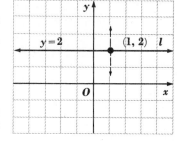

$$y > 2,$$

and is the **graph** of that inequality. The half-plane below the line is the graph of

$$y < 2.$$

Figure 11–3

The half-plane above the line together with the **boundary line** forms the graph of

$$y \geq 2,$$

while the boundary line together with the half-plane below it is the graph of

$$y \leq 2.$$

A half-plane without its boundary is called an *open half-plane*, while the union (page 169) of an open half-plane and its boundary is called a *closed half-plane*.

These graphs are indicated by shading. If the graph is a closed half-plane, the boundary line is drawn as a solid line. If the graph is an open half-plane, a dashed line is used for the boundary line. See the graphs in Figure 11–4.

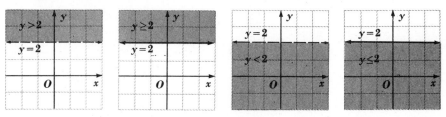

Figure 11–4

The inequalities "$y > 2$" and "$x > 3$" are graphed on the same coordinate plane in Figure 11–5. The points in the upper right-hand section of the plane represent those points whose coordinates satisfy *both* inequalities. That is, these are the points for which "$y > 2$" *and* "$x > 3$," and so this region is the graph of the solution set of the **system of inequalities**:

$$y > 2$$
$$x > 3$$

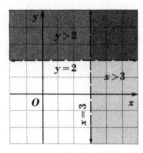

Figure 11–5

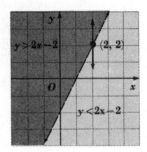

Figure 11–6

Figure 11–6 above shows the graph of "$y = 2x - 2$" separating the plane into two half-planes. For each x, all the points on the line satisfy the equation "$y = 2x - 2$." All the points in the half-plane above the line satisfy the inequality "$y > 2x - 2$," and all the points in the half-plane below the line satisfy the inequality "$y < 2x - 2$."

$y = 2x - 2$

x	3	2	1	0	−1	−2	−3
y	4	2	0	−2	−4	−6	−8

EXAMPLE.   **Graph the inequality $2x - y < 1$.**

Solution: **1. Transform this into an equivalent inequality (page 165) having y as one member:**

$$2x - y < 1$$
$$-y < 1 - 2x$$
$$y > 2x - 1$$

2. Graph $y = 2x - 1$ and show it as a *dashed line*.

3. Shade the half-plane *above* the line.

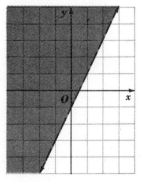

Oral Exercises

Transform each open sentence into an equivalent one having y alone as one member.

1. $x + y < 2$	**5.** $4x + 2y > 0$	**9.** $2x - y \leq 0$
2. $-2x + y > 3$	**6.** $12x + 4y < 0$	**10.** $9x - 3y \leq 0$
3. $6x + y \geq 7$	**7.** $3y < x$	**11.** $x - y > 2$
4. $3x + y \leq -2$	**8.** $2x > 3y$	**12.** $3x - y < 5$

Which of the given points belong to the graph of the given inequality?

13. $x + y < 0$; $(1, -1)$, $(1, 2)$ **15.** $3x + y \leq 2$; $(0, 0)$, $(1, -1)$

14. $x - y \geq 0$; $(3, 3)$, $(4, 5)$ **16.** $x - 2y > 4$; $(1, 2)$, $(0, -3)$

Written Exercises

Graph each inequality in the coordinate plane.

A

1. $y \leq 4$	**5.** $y \leq x$	**9.** $y \leq x + 2$
2. $y \geq -2$	**6.** $y \geq 3x$	**10.** $y > 3 - x$
3. $x > 0$	**7.** $y \geq -x$	**11.** $x + 2y < 4$
4. $y < 1$	**8.** $y \leq -\dfrac{x}{3}$	**12.** $2x + y \geq 1$

In the coordinate plane, indicate the region consisting of all points whose coordinates satisfy both inequalities.

B

13. $y \geq 0$ and $x \leq 0$	**16.** $x + y \leq 3$ and $y \geq 1$
14. $y < 3$ and $x > -2$	**17.** $y \leq 2x + 1$ and $x > 0$
15. $x + y > 0$ and $x > 1$	**18.** $y > 2 - x$ and $y \geq 0$

C

19. $|x| \leq 1$	**21.** $y \geq |x|$	**23.** $-1 < x \leq 2$
20. $|y| \geq 2$	**22.** $y + |x| \leq 0$	**24.** $-3 \leq y < 1$

11–11   Graphs of Systems of Linear Inequalities (Optional)

Not only can graphs be used to solve systems of equations; they can also be employed in determining the solution sets of systems of simultaneous inequalities such as:

$$x + y > 4$$
$$2x - y > 2$$

First draw the graphs of "$x + y = 4$" and "$2x - y = 2$" (Figure 11–7) on the same axes. Use broken lines here, since the graphs of the given inequalities are both open half-planes.

Since "$x + y > 4$" is equivalent to "$y > 4 - x$," the graph of the solution set of "$x + y > 4$" consists of all points in the open half-plane *above* the graph of "$x + y = 4$." Since "$2x - y > 2$" is equivalent to "$y < 2x - 2$," the graph of the solution set of "$2x - y > 2$" consists of all points in the open half-plane *below* the graph of "$2x - y = 2$." The graph of the *intersection* (common points) of the solution sets is the double-shaded region which contains all, and only those, points with coordinates satisfying both inequalities. Some points in the graph of the common solution set are $(4, 2)$, $(5, 0)$, and $(7, -1)$.

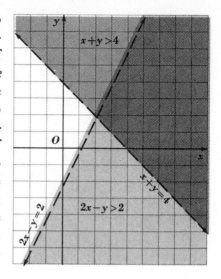

Figure 11–7

Written Exercises

Graph each pair of inequalities, indicating their solution set with cross-hatching.

A

1. $y \geq 0$
$\quad x \geq 0$

2. $y \leq 1$
$\quad x \geq -1$

3. $y < x$
$\quad x > 1$

4. $y > 2x$
$\quad x < 3$

5. $y \geq x$
$\quad y \leq x + 2$

6. $y \leq x - 1$
$\quad y \geq 1 - x$

7. $y > 2x - 4$
$\quad y < 3x + 6$

8. $y < 3x + 3$
$\quad y > 3 - 3x$

B

9. $y \leq 3$
$\quad y \geq 0$

10. $x + 2 > 0$
$\quad x - 3 < 0$

11. $2x + y \geq 1$
$\quad x - 2y \geq 2$

12. $2x + y \geq -1$
$\quad 2x + y \leq 3$

13. $2x + y \leq 3$
$\quad 4x + 2y \leq 6$

14. $x + 2y \geq 3$
$\quad 4y \geq 6 - 2x$

Graph each inequality in the given system. Show the solution set of the system as points in a three-way shaded region.

SAMPLE 1. $y \leq x$
$\quad y \geq -x$
$\quad x \leq 5$

Solution:

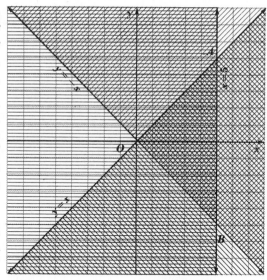

a. The graph of the solution set of "$y \leq x$" consists of points on the graph of "$y = x$" and in the diagonally shaded region below it.

b. The graph of the solution set of "$y \geq -x$" consists of points on the graph of "$y = -x$" and in the diagonally shaded region above it.

c. The graph of the solution set of "$x \leq 5$" consists of points on the graph of "$x = 5$" and in the horizontally shaded region to the left of it.

d. The intersection of these three sets is the three-way shaded region, triangle *AOB*, including points on its sides as well as in its interior.

C **15.** $x + y \leq 2$
$\quad\quad x \geq 0$
$\quad\quad y \geq 0$

16. $y \leq 2 - x$
$\quad\quad y \leq x + 2$
$\quad\quad y \geq -1$

17. $y \geq x$
$\quad\quad y \leq -x$
$\quad\quad x \geq -2$

18. $y \geq -1$
$\quad\quad y \leq 1$
$\quad\quad x + y \leq 2$

19. $2y \geq x + 2$
$\quad\quad 2y + x \leq 8$
$\quad\quad x > 0$

20. $2x - y \leq 2$
$\quad\quad x \geq 0$
$\quad\quad y > 1$

In Exercises 21–24, solve each pair graphically (**a**), and check by solving algebraically (**b**).

SAMPLE 2. $\quad\quad y = 2x$
$\quad\quad\quad\quad\quad x + y \geq 3$

Solution:

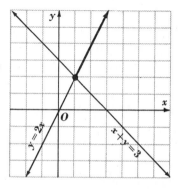

a. The heavy red ray including $(1, 2)$ is the graph of the solution set.

b. Substitute $2x$ for y in $x + y \geq 3$:

$$x + 2x \geq 3$$

Solve for x: $\quad 3x \geq 3$
$\quad\quad\quad\quad\quad x \geq 1$

Since $y = 2x$, $x = \tfrac{1}{2}y$.

(cont. on next page)

Substitute $\frac{1}{2}y$ for x in $x \geq 1$: $\frac{1}{2}y \geq 1$, or $y \geq 2$

$\therefore$ the given system is equivalent to the system: $\begin{cases} y = 2x \\ x \geq 1 \\ y \geq 2 \end{cases}$ **Answer.**

21. $y = x$
$x + y \leq 2$

22. $y \geq 2 - x$
$y = x + 1$

23. $y = 2 - x$
$x < 0$

24. $2x - y = 4$
$y \geq 1$

● CHAPTER SUMMARY ●

Inventory of Structure and Method

1. The **solution set** of a system of open sentences in two variables consists of **ordered pairs** of numbers.

2. If the graphs of the two equations of a system of linear equations in two variables **intersect** in exactly one point, then the solution set is **one ordered pair of numbers** and the equations in the system are said to be **consistent**;

if the graphs are **two parallel lines**, then the solution set is the **empty set** and the equations in the system are said to be **inconsistent**;

if the graphs are the same line, then the solution set is an **infinite set** and the equations in the system are said to be **consistent**.

3. When the coefficients of one variable have the same absolute value, use the **addition** or **subtraction property of equality** to eliminate that variable; then solve for the other variable. When the coefficients of both variables have different absolute values in the two equations, use the **multiplication property of equality** before adding or subtracting.

4. A system of simultaneous linear equations in the same variables can be solved by applying the **substitution principle**.

5. To solve a system of linear inequalities, graph both in one coordinate system; the intersection of their regions contains all points which satisfy both.

6. By using two variables to form two equations, you can solve **digit** problems, **motion** problems, **age** problems, and problems about **fractions**.

Vocabulary and Spelling

Review the meaning of each term by reference to the page listed.

graphic method (*p. 415*)
parallel lines (*p. 415*)
intersection (*p. 415*)

system of simultaneous equations
  (*p. 416*)
inconsistent equations (*p. 416*)

consistent equations (*p. 416*)   half-plane (open, closed) (*p. 435*)
equivalent systems (*p. 417*)   boundary line (*p. 435*)
addition or subtraction method   graph of an inequality in two
   (*p. 419*)   variables (*p. 435*)
substitution method (*p. 426*)   system of inequalities (*p. 436*)

Chapter Test

11–1   **1.** Solve "$x - y = 4$ and $x + y = 6$" graphically.

11–2   Solve each system by addition or subtraction.

    2. $x + y = 12$ **3.** $2z + 3t = 7$ **4.** $5a + 2b = 9$
       $x - y = -4$ $z - 3t = 8$ $5a - b = 3$

11–3   **5.** Two packages, weighed together, total 42 pounds. If one package weighs 4 pounds more than the other, what is the weight of each?

11–4   Solve by using multiplication with addition or subtraction.

    6. $r + 2s = -5$ **7.** $2p + 5q = 9$
       $3r - s = -1$ $3p - 2q = 4$

11–5   Solve by substitution.

    8. $m - 2n = 0$ **9.** $3a + b = 4$ **10.** $x + 3y = 1$
       $2m + 3n = 14$ $2a - 3b = 10$ $3x + y = 11$

11–6   **11.** The sum of the digits of a two-digit numeral is 6. If the order of the digits is reversed, the result names a number 6 less than twice the original number. Find the original number.

11–7   **12.** Two trains left Endicott and Central City, which are 300 miles apart, at the same time, moving toward each other on parallel tracks. When they met, the train from Endicott had traveled 40 miles farther than the train from Central City. How far from Central City did they meet?

11–8   **13.** Maria is 16 years older than Carl. In 4 years, she will be twice as old as Carl. How old is each person now?

11–9   **14.** If 6 is added to the numerator of a fraction, the resulting fraction equals 2. The sum of the numerator and denominator of the original fraction is 9. Find the original fraction.

11–10 **15.** Graph: $y - 3x \leq 2$ **16.** Graph: $x + 2y > 5$

11–11 (Optional) **17.** Solve the system $\begin{array}{l} y \leq x + 2 \\ x - y < 1 \end{array}$ graphically.

Chapter Review

11–1   The Graphic Method   *Pages 415–419*

1. To solve a system of two simultaneous equations, you seek an ordered pair that satisfies __?__ equations.

2. The graphs of two inconsistent linear equations are __?__ lines.

3. The solution set of two __?__ equations whose graphs are the same line is __?__ (finite/infinite).

Exercises 4–6 refer to the figure at the right, which shows the graphs of "$y - x = 2$" and "$4x - y = 4$."

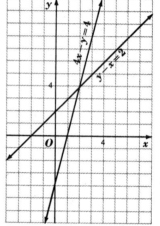

4. Give the coordinates of a point on the graph of "$y - x = 2$" but not on the graph of "$4x - y = 4$."

5. Name an ordered pair satisfying "$4x - y = 4$" but not "$y - x = 2$."

6. The coordinates of the point __?__ satisfy both equations.

11–2   The Addition or Subtraction Method   *Pages 419–421*

Solve each system of equations by addition or subtraction.

7. $3a + b = 7$
    $3a - b = 5$

8. $3x + y = 2$
    $4x + y = 1$

9. $m - 4n = -5$
    $m + 4n = 11$

10. In solving a system by addition or subtraction, you use the addition or subtraction property of __?__.

11–3   Problems with Two Variables   *Pages 421–423*

Translate each statement into a pair of equations.

11. One number is 3 greater than another, and their sum is 49.

12. The base of an isosceles triangle is 2 inches longer than each of the other two sides. The perimeter of the triangle is 26 inches.

Solve using two variables and a system of two equations.

13. A 110-foot cable is cut into two pieces, one of which is 14 feet longer than twice the other. How long is each piece of cable?

11–4 **Multiplication in the Addition or Subtraction Method**

Pages 423–426

Solve by using multiplication with addition or subtraction.

14. $r + 2s = 3$ **15.** $3x - 2y = 10$ **16.** $5t - 3s = -4$
 $3r + 5s = 7$ $5x + 3y = 4$ $4t + 7s = 25$

11–5 **The Substitution Method**   *Pages 426–427*

Solve by substitution.

17. $m + n = 0$ **18.** $2p - q = 4$ **19.** $a - 3b = 7$
 $m - 2n = 15$ $3p + 2q = -1$ $2a + 5b = -19$

11–6 **Digit Problems**   *Pages 428–430*

20. The numeral whose tens digit is t and whose units digit is u names the number represented by __?__ .

21. The sum of the digits of a two-digit numeral is 14 and the tens digit is 4 greater than the units digit. What is the number named?

22. The units digit of a numeral is 3 greater than the tens digit. If the digits are reversed, the numeral formed names a number 27 greater than the number named by the original numeral. What is the original numeral?

11–7 **Motion Problems**   *Pages 430–431*

23. If s represents the speed of a boat in still water, then, in a river flowing at a rate r, the speed of the boat upstream is __?__ and downstream is __?__ .

24. It takes 2 hours for a boat to go 18 miles down a river, and 3 hours to return. What is the rate of flow of the river and the speed of the boat in still water?

25. A small plane travels 60 miles in 20 minutes with the wind and returns in 30 minutes against the wind. What is the rate of the plane and the speed of the wind?

11–8 **Age Problems**   *Pages 432–433*

26. Ten years ago, Mr. Endo was 7 times as old as his son, while today he is 3 times as old. How old is each today?

27. Seven years ago, Mrs. Thomas was 4 times as old as her daughter. Seven years from now, she will be twice as old as her daughter. How old is each now?

11–9   Problems about Fractions   *Pages 433–434*

28. A fraction is equal to $\frac{3}{5}$, and its numerator is 14 less than its denominator. What is the fraction?

29. A fraction is equal to $\frac{9}{7}$. If 4 is subtracted from its numerator and 4 is added to its denominator, the resulting fraction equals $\frac{7}{9}$. Find the original fraction.

11–10   Graph of an Inequality in Two Variables   *Pages 435–437*

30. The graph of a linear equation in two variables separates the plane into two __?__.

31. The graph of "$y < 3x - 1$" consists of all points __?__ the graph of the equation "$y = 3x - 1$."

32. The graph of "$y \geq x - 4$ __?__" (does/does not) include the graph of "$y = x - 4$."

33. Graph: $3x + y > -2$.

11–11   Graphs of Systems of Linear Inequalities (Optional)
Pages 437–440

Exercises 34–36 refer to the graphs of "$y \leq 2x + 2$" and "$2x + 3y \geq 6$" pictured at the right.

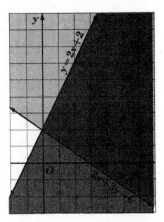

34. State the coordinates of a point in the graph of "$y \leq 2x + 2$" but not in the graph of "$2x + 3y \geq 6$."

35. Name an ordered pair satisfying "$2x + 3y \geq 6$" but not "$y \leq 2x + 2$."

36. Name an ordered pair satisfying both "$y \leq 2x + 2$" and "$2x + 3y \geq 6$."

Who Uses Mathematics?

Mathematics is essential to many persons engaged in the printing industry. The pages of a book, for example, are carefully planned as to size, width of columns, size of type used, and so on. In the photograph a newspaper pressman is examining a new type of printing plate to see that everything seems ready for the printing to take place.

The printing and publishing industries have good openings for persons with both high school and college training. You may find it interesting to investigate some of the many positions in these industries, for example, copy editors, editorial writers, designers, proofreaders, compositors, pressmen.

Linear Programming with Convex Polygonal Regions

Consider the following system of simultaneous inequalities:

$$y \leq 2x + 4$$

$$y \geq -x - 2$$

$$y \leq 4 - 4x.$$

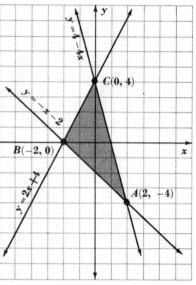

The graph of the solution set is the shaded region ABC.

Any plane region, such as region ABC, which is the intersection of a finite number of closed half-planes is called a **convex polygonal region**.

A region is **convex** when it contains every line segment joining any two of its points. For example, in the following figures, the square and the triangle enclose convex regions, but the star does not.

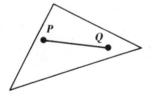

Convex polygonal regions in the plane are important in studying the values of linear expressions in the form $mx + ny$, where m and n are any real numbers. Let us take $2x + 3y$ as an example. Suppose that you want to find the greatest or least values of $2x + 3y$ over the set of ordered pairs (x, y) satisfying the inequalities

$$y \leq 2x + 4, \quad x + y + 2 \geq 0, \quad \text{and} \quad y + 4x \leq 4.$$

This means that you want to *maximize* or *minimize* $2x + 3y$ over the triangular region ABC on the graph above.

A remarkable fact, not proved here, is that over convex polygonal regions any maximum or minimum values of any linear expression occur at the vertices (corner points) of the region. In particular, over the triangular region ABC, the greatest or least values of $2x + 3y$ must occur at one or another of the three vertices: $A(2, -4)$, $B(-2, 0)$, $C(0, 4)$. Evaluating $2x + 3y$ at each of these points, you see that over the triangle ABC the maximum, 12, occurs at C and the minimum, -8, occurs at A.

Point	$2x + 3y$
$A(2, -4)$	-8
$B(-2, 0)$	-4
$C(0, 4)$	12

It is possible that maximum or minimum values may also occur at other points besides vertices. What matters is that by testing values at the vertices, you can in a finite number of steps determine the greatest or least values of any linear expression over any closed convex polygon.

Development of the ideas above has led to the formulation of a relatively new branch of mathematics called *linear programming*, which uses graphs of linear inequalities to solve practical problems like the following:

Each week the McKay Trucking Company needs at least 650 gallons of diesel fuel, 324 gallons of gasoline, and 48 gallons of oil to keep its fleet of trucks in operation. Pacific Petroleum Company can deliver 130 gallons of diesel fuel, 36 gallons of gasoline, and 4 gallons of oil for a bulk wholesale rate of $60. A similar plan, costing $75, is available from Overseas Oil Company for 65 gallons of diesel fuel, 54 gallons of gasoline, and 12 gallons of oil. How many standing orders should the McKay Company place with each firm in order to meet its minimum weekly petroleum needs at the smallest cost?

Let x = number of weekly orders from Pacific Petroleum Company,

and y = number of weekly orders from Overseas Oil Company.

If C = total weekly cost, in dollars,

$$C = 60x + 75y, \quad \text{or} \quad y = -\tfrac{4}{5}x + \frac{C}{75}$$

You are trying to minimize C (find its smallest value) within the limits of these inequalities (*constraints*):

1. $130x + 65y \geq 650$, or $2x + y \geq 10$ ⎫ **The total amount of each**

2. $36x + 54y \geq 324$, or $2x + 3y \geq 18$ ⎬ **petroleum product must equal**

3. $4x + 12y \geq 48$, or $x + 3y \geq 12$ ⎭ **at least the weekly need.**

4. $x \geq 0$ ⎫ **The McKay Company cannot purchase a negative amount**

5. $y \geq 0$ ⎭ **from either firm.**

The graph of the system of inequalities on the preceding page is shown below. The points in the solution set are represented by the shaded region. Because the points satisfying all the constraints lie within or on its boundary, this region is called the *feasible region*.

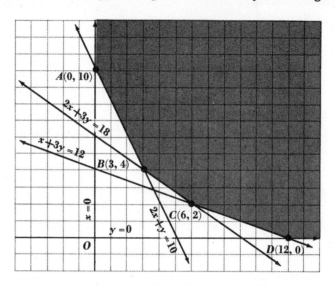

As we have said earlier, any maximum or minimum values for a linear expression occur at the corner points of the region. Therefore, by substituting the coordinates of the corner points in

$$C = 60x + 75y,$$

we find that point $B(3, 4)$ gives the least value, $C = 480$, since at the other corners C has the values 750, 510, and 720.

Thus, the least expensive combination is 3 orders from Pacific Petroleum Company and 4 orders from Overseas Oil Company, with a total weekly cost of $480.

Exercises

1. Graph the set of points defined by $y \geq \frac{1}{3}x + 2$, $y \leq x + 8$, and $y \leq -3x + 12$.

2. Over the polygon obtained in Exercise 1, determine the points where $1.6x - 1.3y$ has its maximum and minimum values.

3. Find x and y, maximizing $T = 3x + y$ subject to the constraints, $x \geq 1$, $y \geq 2$, $y \geq -2x + 8$, $y \geq -x + 6$.

4. Each day the Auburndale Post Office handles at least 3120 first-class letters and 1890 second-class advertising brochures. The cancelling machine now in use can handle 390 letters and 315 brochures per hour at an hourly cost of $2.10. The manufacturer of the machine is about to release an improved model which can accommodate 520 letters and 210 brochures each hour at a cost of $2.70 per hour. Neither machine can be run for more than 10 hours due to internal heating.

a. How would the expense of handling the mail be affected if the post office can use both machines?

b. Would the use of both machines be practical if the post office were to reduce the cost of operating the old machine by $0.30 an hour?

Just for Fun

8	1	6
3	5	7
4	9	2

A **magic square** is a square array of integers such that the sum of each row, of each column, and of each diagonal is the same. A magic square of the third order has three rows and three columns. Illustrated is a pure magic square of the *third order* in a 3 × 3 table containing nine spaces, or *cells*.

A *pure magic square* is a magic square containing consecutive integers. There are eight ways to arrange the numbers 1 to 9 in a pure magic square of the third order. The number 5 is always in the center, and even numbers are in the four corners. You can easily make a magic square of the third order which is not pure by multiplying the number in each cell by −3 or 2 or any other number (except −1). How does the distributive axiom assure you that such a square will still be magic?

You may construct a magic square of third, fifth, seventh, or any odd order by following these rules.

1. Write the numerals in order, putting each in a separate cell. Begin by writing 1 in the middle cell of the top row.

2. Move from cell to cell by going up and to the right one step at a time. If you find yourself going out of the square, or getting into a cell that is already filled, make the move and then proceed as follows:

a. When a move takes you out at the top of the square, drop down to the lowest cell in that column. When a move takes you out at the right of the square, shift to the cell farthest left in that row.

b. When a move takes you to a cell already filled, drop down one row, instead. When a move takes you out the upper right-hand corner, drop down one row, instead.

Using these rules to construct a pure magic square of the third order, as the figure shows, your very first move takes you out at the top of the square, so you drop down to the bottom of that column, and put 2 in the lowest cell. Your second move takes you out at the right of the square, so you shift to the left of that row, and put 3 in the left-hand cell.

Your next move also leads to difficulty; it takes you to a cell already filled. So you drop down one row, and put 4 directly beneath 3. Your next two moves are unobstructed.

You are now at the upper right-hand corner of the square. Therefore, you drop down one row, and put 7 beneath 6. The next move takes you out at the right again, so you shift left. And the final move takes you out at the top, so you drop to the bottom!

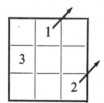 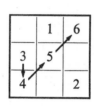

Of course, the reason your moves take you out so often is that the square is small. Try building a magic square of the fifth order, and one of the seventh order.

In a pure magic square of the third order, the sum of each row, column, and diagonal is 15, as you can readily check. In a pure magic square of the fifth order the sum is 65, and in one of the seventh order it is 175. You can find this sum for any pure magic square if you know how many cells are on each side. If n represents this number, the sum is

$$\tfrac{1}{2}(n^3 + n):$$

Third order:	$\tfrac{1}{2}(3^3 + 3) = \tfrac{1}{2} \cdot 30 =$	**15**
Fifth order:	$\tfrac{1}{2}(5^3 + 5) = \tfrac{1}{2} \cdot 130 =$	**65**
Seventh order:	$\tfrac{1}{2}(7^3 + 7) = \tfrac{1}{2} \cdot 350 =$	**175**

Of course, if the square is not pure you multiply this result by the smallest number in the square.

So far, nothing has been said about magic squares containing an even number of cells. But there are such squares, and you can find the sum of their columns, rows, and diagonals by the same formula.

Fourth order: $\tfrac{1}{2}(4^3 + 4) = \tfrac{1}{2} \cdot 68 = 34$

16	3	2	13
5	10	11	8
9	6	7	12
4	15	14	1

You cannot construct even magic squares by the rules given above, however. Such squares are based on an entirely different principle.

Ramanujan, Who Felt Numbers Were His Friends

A member of a poor Brahman family in southern India, Srinivasa Ramanujan Aiyangar (1887–1920) was noticed in his early years at school as a meditative boy with an unusual memory. He often entertained his friends by repeating for them approximations to π and of $\sqrt{2}$ to large numbers of decimal places.

Ramanujan (Rah-**mah**-noo-jan) attended the Town High School at Kumbakonam on a scholarship and later entered the Government College there, but did not stay. However, when he was about fifteen years old, someone had loaned him a copy of a book containing some 6,000 theorems of algebra, trigonometry, calculus, and analytical geometry. This aroused his interest to such an extent that he set about deriving them on his own. He felt that his patron goddess, Namagiri, inspired him in his dreams, because many times upon rising in the morning, he would be able to write down results and verify them.

Even with his limited formal education, Ramanujan kept up independent work in mathematics. In 1911 he published an article on "Some Properties of Bernoulli's Numbers" in the *Journal of the Indian Mathematical Society*. His greatest opportunity came in 1913 when he began a correspondence with the famous mathematician G. H. Hardy (1877–1947) of Trinity College, Cambridge, England, who was very much impressed with his work. Ramanujan was able to go to England in 1914, where Hardy helped him to fill in and strengthen his background in mathematics.

Ramanujan was especially interested in numbers — it has been said that "numbers were his friends." The story is told that one day when he was ill in England, Hardy visited him, remarking that he had arrived in taxicab number 1729, and that the number seemed rather a dull one. "No," Ramanujan is said to have replied, "it is a very interesting number. It is the smallest number expressible as a sum of two cubes in two different ways."

Srinivasa Ramanujan died in India of tuberculosis in 1920, at the age of thirty-three. But he had been able to make many brilliant contributions to the development of mathematics.

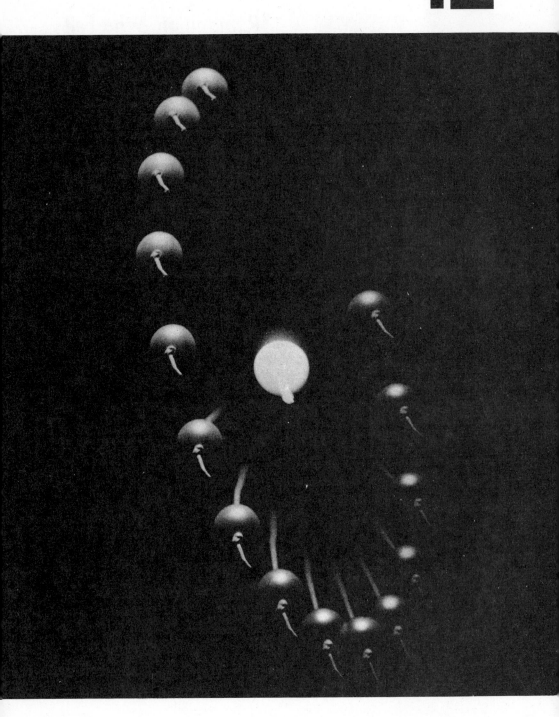

. . . the path of a pendulum set in elliptical motion

Rational and Irrational Numbers

What does the word "irrational" mean to you? In this chapter you will learn about numbers called "irrational numbers." However, they are really not at all irrational in the everyday sense!

THE SYSTEM OF RATIONAL NUMBERS

12–1 The Nature of Rational Numbers

The set $\mathcal{R}$ of real numbers, together with the operations of addition and multiplication, is a *number system* — the **real number system**. You define a **number system** by specifying a set of numbers and telling how to add and multiply the numbers.

For example, the set $N = \{1, 2, 3, 4, \ldots\}$ (page 21), together with the operations of addition and multiplication, forms the **system of natural numbers** (or **positive integers**). This system is closed under addition and multiplication, but not under subtraction or division.

The system of positive numbers named by fractions is closed under addition, multiplication, and division. When you extend your idea of number to include zero, the negative integers, and the negative numbers named by fractions, you have a system of numbers that is closed under subtraction, too. This is the **system of rational numbers,** and you learned how to operate with these numbers in Chapter 8. Because the system of rational numbers is closed under addition, subtraction, multiplication, and division (except by zero), these operations are called the **rational operations**.

Recall that a rational number can be expressed in an unlimited number of ways:

$$0 = \frac{0}{8} = \frac{0}{-3} \cdots \qquad 7 = \frac{7}{1} = \frac{-7}{-1} \cdots \qquad -\frac{4}{5} = \frac{-4}{5} = \frac{8}{-10} \cdots$$

$$\frac{3}{14} = \frac{-3}{-14} = \frac{9}{42} \cdots \qquad 2.3 = \tfrac{23}{10} = \tfrac{69}{30} \cdots \qquad 26\% = \tfrac{26}{100} = \tfrac{13}{50} \cdots$$

Furthermore, you always can tell which of two rational numbers is the greater by writing them with the same positive denominator and comparing their numerators. For example, to compare $-\frac{3}{4}$ and $-\frac{2}{3}$, you write $-\dfrac{3}{4} = \dfrac{-9}{12}$ and $-\dfrac{2}{3} = \dfrac{-8}{12}$. Then

$$-\tfrac{3}{4} < -\tfrac{2}{3} \qquad \text{because} \qquad -9 < -8.$$

Similarly,

$$\tfrac{7}{3} > \tfrac{13}{6} \qquad \text{because} \qquad \tfrac{7}{3} = \tfrac{14}{6} \text{ and } 14 > 13.$$

This test can be developed in another form. Let a and b be integers and c and d be positive integers. Then if

$$\frac{a}{c} > \frac{b}{d},$$

you have

$$\frac{a}{c}(cd) > \frac{b}{d}(cd)$$

and so

$$ad > bc.$$

On the other hand, if

$$ad > bc,$$

then since $cd > 0$,

$$\frac{ad}{cd} > \frac{bc}{cd}$$

and

$$\frac{a}{c} > \frac{b}{d}.$$

For all integers a and b and all positive integers c and d:

$$\frac{a}{c} > \frac{b}{d} \qquad \text{if and only if} \qquad ad > bc.$$

Thus,

$$\tfrac{5}{6} > \tfrac{3}{4} \qquad \text{because} \qquad 5(4) > 3(6);$$
$$-\tfrac{1}{2} > -\tfrac{3}{2} \qquad \text{because} \qquad -1(2) > -3(2).$$

For each integer, there is a next larger one. For example, -4 follows -5, 0 follows -1, and 4 follows 3. This is not true for the set of rational numbers. There is no "next larger" rational number after $\tfrac{2}{3}$, for instance. Instead, the set of rational numbers has a property which the set of integers does not have, namely:

See TM p. 51, 12-1(2).

The Property of Density

Between every pair of different rational numbers there is another rational number.

EXAMPLE.   Find a rational number between $\frac{5}{4}$ and $\frac{4}{3}$.

Solution:

1. Find the difference of the numbers: $\frac{4}{3} - \frac{5}{4} = \frac{16}{12} - \frac{15}{12} = \frac{1}{12}$

2. Add half this difference to the smaller: $\frac{5}{4} + \frac{1}{2}(\frac{1}{12}) = \frac{31}{24}$

3. *Check:*   Is $\frac{5}{4} < \frac{31}{24} < \frac{4}{3}$?

$$5(24) \overset{?}{<} 4(31) \qquad 3(31) \overset{?}{<} 4(24)$$

$$120 < 124 \qquad\qquad 93 < 96$$

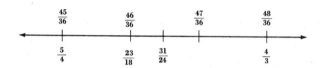

∴ a rational number between (exactly halfway between) $\frac{5}{4}$ and $\frac{4}{3}$ is $\frac{31}{24}$.

Answer.

Another way of finding the rational number that was given as the answer to the preceding Example is to take the average of the given numbers:

$$\frac{1}{2}\left(\frac{5}{4} + \frac{4}{3}\right) = \frac{1}{2}\left(\frac{15 + 16}{12}\right) = \frac{31}{24}$$

However, the method used in the solution of the Example suggests a way of finding other rational numbers between $\frac{5}{4}$ and $\frac{4}{3}$. For example, you can add $\frac{1}{3}$ the difference to $\frac{5}{4}$:

$$\frac{5}{4} + \frac{1}{3}(\frac{1}{12}) = \frac{45}{36} + \frac{1}{36} = \frac{46}{36} = \frac{23}{18}$$

Check that $\frac{5}{4} < \frac{23}{18} < \frac{4}{3}$.

Do you see that the number of rational numbers between $\frac{3}{4}$ and $\frac{5}{6}$ is unlimited? The property of density implies that between every pair of rational numbers there is an infinite set of rational numbers.

Oral Exercises

Express each number as a quotient of integers.

SAMPLE. 2.7   *Solution:* 27 divided by 10.

1. 4.2	**5.** 0.09	**9.** -3	**13.** $(-3)(-\frac{1}{3})$
2. 15.7	**6.** 0.003	**10.** -5	**14.** $\frac{1}{3} \div \frac{1}{3}$
3. $-2\frac{1}{3}$	**7.** 10%	**11.** $\frac{1}{5} + (-\frac{2}{5})$	**15.** $1\frac{1}{5} + \frac{4}{5}$
4. $-5\frac{1}{2}$	**8.** 20%	**12.** $\frac{5}{9} - \frac{3}{9}$	**16.** $0 \cdot (-\frac{1}{3})$

State which number is greater.

17. $\frac{4}{5}, \frac{6}{5}$	**19.** $-1, \frac{1}{2}$	**21.** $-\frac{2}{5}, -\frac{4}{5}$	**23.** $4, \frac{25}{6}$
18. $\frac{21}{8}, \frac{19}{8}$	**20.** $\frac{2}{3}, -5$	**22.** $-\frac{4}{3}, -\frac{7}{3}$	**24.** $8, \frac{47}{6}$

If $x \in \{1, 2, 3, 4\}$, taking each value in succession, state whether the given fraction increases in value or decreases in value.

25. $\dfrac{x}{2}$	**27.** $\dfrac{3}{x+2}$	**29.** $\dfrac{x+3}{2}$	**31.** $\dfrac{1}{2x-1}$
26. $\dfrac{2}{x}$	**28.** $\dfrac{5}{x-10}$	**30.** $\dfrac{5}{5-x}$	**32.** $\dfrac{2}{1-2x}$

Written Exercises

Replace the __?__ with =, <, or > to make a true statement.

A

1. $\frac{7}{8}$ __?__ $\frac{11}{14}$	**3.** $\frac{3}{14}$ __?__ $\frac{5}{24}$	**5.** $\frac{23}{47}$ __?__ $\frac{41}{83}$
2. $\frac{3}{5}$ __?__ $\frac{8}{13}$	**4.** $-\frac{7}{16}$ __?__ $-\frac{11}{25}$	**6.** $\frac{215}{103}$ __?__ $\frac{311}{148}$

7. $-18\frac{1}{5}$ __?__ $-\frac{127}{7}$ **8.** $\frac{312}{12}$ __?__ $28\frac{1}{2}$

Arrange the members of each set in increasing order.

9. $\{\frac{2}{3}, -\frac{3}{4}, \frac{5}{9}\}$	**11.** $\{-2.1, -\frac{4}{3}, -2.0\}$	**13.** $\{\frac{4}{15}, \frac{5}{16}, \frac{7}{24}, \frac{1}{4}\}$
10. $\{\frac{4}{7}, \frac{3}{5}, -\frac{3}{5}\}$	**12.** $\{-1.6, -\frac{33}{20}, -\frac{37}{22}\}$	**14.** $\{\frac{7}{8}, \frac{9}{7}, \frac{19}{18}, \frac{13}{12}\}$

Find the number halfway between the given numbers.

15. $\frac{2}{3}, \frac{3}{5}$	**17.** $-\frac{2}{25}, -\frac{3}{100}$	**19.** $4\frac{1}{6}, 5\frac{1}{8}$
16. $\frac{4}{7}, \frac{5}{9}$	**18.** $-\frac{7}{1000}, -\frac{7}{100}$	**20.** $2\frac{3}{5}, 3\frac{5}{8}$

B **21.** Find the number one-fourth of the way from $\frac{5}{6}$ to $1\frac{1}{4}$.

22. Find the number one-third of the way from $-\frac{3}{2}$ to $-\frac{3}{4}$.

23. Show that the number halfway between x and y is $\dfrac{x+y}{2}$.

24. What number is one-fourth of the way from p to q:

a. if $p < q$?   **b.** if $p > q$?

Explain why each statement is true.

25. 5 is the smallest integer greater than 4.

26. There is no smallest rational number greater than 0.

In each case, tell whether the given statement is true with blanks filled as indicated.

27. If a and b are different __(x)__, then there are as many __(y)__ between a and b as you please.

   a. (x) integers; (y) integers

   b. (x) integers; (y) rational numbers

   c. (x) rational numbers; (y) rational numbers

   d. (x) rational numbers; (y) integers

28. If a and b are different __(x)__, then the number halfway between a and b is always a(n) __(y)__.

   a. (x) integers; (y) integer

   b. (x) integers; (y) rational number

   c. (x) rational numbers; (y) rational number

   d. (x) rational numbers; (y) integer

In Exercises 29–32, a, b, c, and d are nonzero integers. Explain why each expression represents a rational number.

29. $\dfrac{a}{b} \cdot \dfrac{c}{d}$ **30.** $\dfrac{a}{c} + \dfrac{b}{d}$ **31.** $\dfrac{a}{b} - \dfrac{c}{d}$ **32.** $\dfrac{a}{b} \div \dfrac{c}{d}$

12–2   Decimal Forms for Rational Numbers

In arithmetic you learned to change common fractions to decimals and decimals to common fractions. To change a common fraction to a decimal, you carry out the indicated division.

$$\tfrac{5}{16} = 5 \div 16 \qquad \tfrac{1}{6} = 1 \div 6 \qquad \tfrac{3}{11} = 3 \div 11$$

```
    0.3125            0.1666             0.2727
16)5.0000         6)1.0000         11)3.0000
   48                 6                 22
   ──                 ─                 ──
    20                40                 80
    16                36                 77
    ──                ──                 ──
     40               40                  30
     32               36                  22
     ──               ──                  ──
      80              40                   80
      80              36                   77
      ──              ──                   ──
       0              4                    3
```

A decimal with a finite number of places, like 0.3125 on the preceding page, is called **terminating, ending, or finite.** Such a decimal represents a rational number; for example,

$$0.3125 = \tfrac{3125}{10000} \quad \text{or} \quad 0.3125 = \tfrac{5}{16}.$$

In the division of 1 by 6, however, you never have a remainder of 0, but the remainder 4 repeats step after step, and 6 repeats in the quotient. A decimal which continues indefinitely is called **nonterminating** or **unending.** A nonterminating decimal like the one for $\tfrac{1}{6}$ is called **repeating** or **periodic,** because the same digit (or block of digits) repeats unendingly. You may write

$$\tfrac{1}{6} = 0.1666\ldots \quad \text{or} \quad \tfrac{1}{6} = 0.1\overline{6},$$

where the dots and the bar indicate "continue unendingly."

When 3 is divided by 11, the successive remainders are 8, 3, 8, 3, ... and the quotient is a repeating decimal:

$$\tfrac{3}{11} = 0.272727\ldots \quad \text{or} \quad \tfrac{3}{11} = 0.\overline{27}$$

When you divide an integer by 11, the remainder at each step belongs to {0, 1, 2, 3, 4, 5, 6, 7, 8, 9, 10}. Within no more than ten steps after only zeros are left in the dividend, either the remainder is 0 and the division terminates, or a sequence of other remainders repeats unendingly. This sort of reasoning can be applied to division by any positive integer and thus leads to the following result.

For every integer r and every positive integer s, the decimal numeral of the rational number $\dfrac{r}{s}$ either terminates or eventually repeats in a block of fewer than s digits.

On the other hand, the following statement is also true.

All terminating decimals and all repeating decimals represent rational numbers which can be written in the form $\dfrac{r}{s}$ where r is an integer and s is a positive integer.

The preceding conversion of 0.3125 to $\frac{5}{16}$ shows how a terminating decimal can be written as a common fraction. The following examples show how to convert a repeating decimal into a common fraction.

EXAMPLE 1. Write $0.5\overline{16}$ as a common fraction.

Solution: Let N = the number.

$$100N = 51.61\overline{616}$$

Subtract: $N = 0.51\overline{616}$

$$99N = 51.1000\overline{0}$$

$$N = \frac{51.1}{99} = \frac{511}{990}$$

EXAMPLE 2. Write $0.\overline{234}$ as a common fraction.

Solution: Let N = the number.

$$1000N = 234.\overline{234}$$

Subtract: $N = 0.\overline{234}$

$$999N = 234.00\overline{0}$$

$$N = \frac{234}{999} = \frac{26}{111}$$

In general, if the number of digits in the block of repeating digits is p, multiply the given number N by 10^p, producing a number with the same repeating block as the given number. Then subtracting the given number from this product yields a terminating decimal.

It often is convenient to break off a lengthy decimal, leaving an approximation of the number represented. You may write, for example,

$$\frac{1}{12} \doteq 0.08333 \quad \text{or} \quad \frac{1}{12} \doteq 0.083 \quad \text{or} \quad \frac{1}{12} \doteq 0.08.$$

To round a decimal, add 1 to the value of the last digit kept if the first digit dropped is 5 or more; otherwise, leave the digits unchanged.

Thus,

$$\frac{2}{3} = 0.666\ldots \quad \text{or} \quad \frac{2}{3} \doteq 0.67 \quad \text{or} \quad \frac{2}{3} \doteq 0.7;$$

$$\frac{5}{9} = 0.555\ldots \quad \text{or} \quad \frac{5}{9} \doteq 0.56 \quad \text{or} \quad \frac{5}{9} \doteq 0.6.$$

$$\frac{161}{110} = 1.4\overline{63} \quad \text{or} \quad \frac{161}{110} \doteq 1.5 \quad \text{or} \quad \frac{161}{110} \doteq 1.$$

Oral Exercises

Approximate each number to the nearest tenth.

1. 3.14 **4.** -3.554 **7.** $-15.2\overline{5}$ **10.** $0.09\overline{5}$

2. 2.76 **5.** $0.21\overline{6}$ **8.** $-31.66\ldots$ **11.** $\frac{2}{3}$

3. -8.21 **6.** $0.83\overline{3}$ **9.** $0.04\overline{8}$ **12.** $\frac{5}{4}$

Give a second numeral naming the same number.

13. $\frac{1}{2}$ **16.** 3.4 **19.** $-\frac{5}{4}$ **22.** 0.125

14. 3 **17.** $2.199\ldots$ **20.** $-\frac{16}{8}$ **23.** -0.0083

15. 0.2 **18.** $12.\overline{9}$ **21.** $2.3\overline{3}$ **24.** -5.013

Written Exercises

Write as terminating or repeating decimals.

A **1.** $\frac{7}{50}$ **4.** $\frac{11}{8}$ **7.** $\dfrac{-3}{7}$ **10.** $\frac{48}{70}$

2. $\frac{6}{25}$ **5.** $-\frac{9}{11}$ **8.** $\dfrac{-19}{80}$ **11.** $-\frac{3}{16}$

3. $\frac{3}{32}$ **6.** $-\frac{4}{3}$ **9.** $\frac{41}{20}$ **12.** $-\frac{10}{21}$

Write as common fractions.

13. 0.33 **15.** $0.11\overline{8}$ **17.** $0.21212121\ldots$ **19.** $-3.\overline{148}$

14. 0.6 **16.** $0.1\overline{18}$ **18.** $0.202202202\ldots$ **20.** $-1.30\overline{4}$

Find the difference of the given numbers, and name a number between them.

B **21.** 0.18 and $0.\overline{18}$ **24.** 0.14 and $0.\overline{14}$

22. 0.66 and $0.\overline{66}$ **25.** 0.126 and $\frac{1}{8}$

23. 0.8 and $0.\overline{8}$ **26.** 0.101 and $\frac{1}{9}$

Compare the decimal forms of the members of each set.

C **27.** $\{\frac{1}{7}, \frac{2}{7}, \frac{3}{7}, \ldots, \frac{6}{7}\}$ **29.** $\{\frac{1}{11}, \frac{2}{11}, \frac{3}{11}, \ldots, \frac{10}{11}\}$

28. $\{\frac{1}{9}, \frac{2}{9}, \frac{3}{9}, \ldots, \frac{8}{9}\}$ **30.** $\{\frac{1}{15}, \frac{2}{15}, \frac{3}{15}, \ldots, \frac{14}{15}\}$

IRRATIONAL NUMBERS

12–3 Roots of Numbers

Recall (page 37) that the power of a number is the product of factors each equal to that number:

$$5^2 = 5(5), \quad 5^3 = 5(5)(5), \quad \text{and} \quad 5^n = 5(5) \cdots (5), \text{ } n \text{ factors}$$

This operation is called *raising to a power*.

Just as addition and multiplication have inverse operations, so has raising to a power. Its inverse operation is called *extracting a root*. For any positive integer n, a number x is an nth **root** of the number a if it satisfies

$$x^n = a.$$

For example, since $3^4 = 81$, 3 is a *fourth root* of 81.

To indicate the nth root of a, you use the expression $\sqrt[n]{a}$, which is called a **radical** (in Latin *radix* means "root"). The symbol $\sqrt{}$ indicates that a root is to be extracted; n is the **root index,** signifying the root to be taken; the bar, usually incorporated in the radical symbol, covers the **radicand** (rad'i-**cand**), the expression for the number whose root is to be extracted. With no root index, $\sqrt{}$ indicates square root:

$$\sqrt{81} = 9, \quad \sqrt[3]{125} = 5, \quad \sqrt[4]{81} = 3$$

When you square a positive or a negative number, you get a positive result. That is, $5^2 = 25$ and $(-5)^2 = 25$. Thus, every positive number has two square roots, one positive and the other negative. Zero, however, has only one square root, zero. You use the expression $\sqrt{25}$ to indicate the positive root 5 (the *principal square root*), $-\sqrt{25}$ to indicate the negative root -5, and $\pm\sqrt{25}$ (read "positive and negative square root of 25") to represent both roots. Thus,

$$\sqrt{\tfrac{4}{9}} = \tfrac{2}{3}, \quad -\sqrt{\tfrac{4}{9}} = -\tfrac{2}{3}, \quad \pm\sqrt{\tfrac{4}{9}} = \pm\tfrac{2}{3}.$$

Since the square of every real number is either positive or zero, negative numbers do not have square roots in the set of real numbers.

One method of finding the square root of a large number is to determine its factors, and then to express it as a product of powers, and take the square roots of the powers.

EXAMPLE 1. Evaluate $\sqrt{3969}$.

Solution: $\quad 3969 = 9(441) = 9(9)(49) = 9^2(7^2)$

$\qquad\qquad \sqrt{3969} = \sqrt{9^2(7)^2} = 9(7) = 63$

Check: $\quad 63(63) = 3969 \checkmark \quad \therefore \sqrt{3969} = 63.$ **Answer.**

This method of solution just shown is based on the following:

Product Property of Square Roots

For any real numbers a and b:

$$\text{if } a \geq 0 \text{ and } b \geq 0, \text{ then } \sqrt{ab} = \sqrt{a} \cdot \sqrt{b}.$$

To prove this property, we show that $\sqrt{a} \cdot \sqrt{b}$ is a nonnegative number and that its square is ab. Notice that only principal roots are used.

To show that $\sqrt{a} \cdot \sqrt{b} \geq 0$:	To show that $(\sqrt{a} \cdot \sqrt{b})^2 = ab$:
If $a \geq 0$, and $b \geq 0$,	$(\sqrt{a} \cdot \sqrt{b})^2 = (\sqrt{a} \cdot \sqrt{b})(\sqrt{a} \cdot \sqrt{b})$
then $\sqrt{a} \geq 0$, $\sqrt{b} \geq 0$,	$= \underbrace{(\sqrt{a} \cdot \sqrt{a})(\sqrt{b} \cdot \sqrt{b})}$
and $\sqrt{a} \cdot \sqrt{b} \geq 0$.	$= \qquad a \qquad \cdot \qquad b$
	$\therefore (\sqrt{a} \cdot \sqrt{b})^2 = \qquad\qquad ab$

Similarly, you can prove (Exercise 27, page 464) the following.

Quotient Property of Square Roots

For any real numbers a and b:

$$\text{if } a \geq 0 \text{ and } b > 0, \text{ then } \sqrt{\frac{a}{b}} = \frac{\sqrt{a}}{\sqrt{b}}.$$

EXAMPLE 2.   Evaluate $\sqrt{\frac{64}{2025}}$.

Solution: $64 = 8^2; \quad 2025 = (25)(81) = 5^2(9^2)$

$$\sqrt{\frac{64}{2025}} = \sqrt{\frac{8^2}{5^2(9^2)}} = \frac{8}{5 \cdot 9} = \frac{8}{45}$$

Check: $\frac{8}{45} \cdot \frac{8}{45} = \frac{64}{2025} \checkmark \qquad \therefore \sqrt{\frac{64}{2025}} = \frac{8}{45}.$ **Answer.**

EXAMPLE 3.   What is the principal square root of $49x^2$, if $x \in \mathcal{R}$?

Solution: $49 = 7^2; \quad \therefore \sqrt{49x^2} = 7|x|.$

Check: For every real number x, $7|x| \geq 0$.

Also $(7|x|)^2 = 49|x|^2 = 49x^2$.

$\therefore \sqrt{49x^2} = 7|x|.$ **Answer.**

Notice that in Example 3, "$7x$" would *not* be an acceptable answer unless you knew that $x \geq 0$. Remember that the principal square root of a number is *never* a negative number.

Oral Exercises

Give the principal square root.

1. 49

2. 64

3. $\frac{100}{9}$

4. $\frac{4}{25}$

5. $144x^2$

6. $81y^4$

7. $36a^2b^2$

8. $121n^4p^4$

9. $0.16t^6$

10. $0.09r^8$

11. $\frac{9t^2}{s^6}$

12. $\frac{25p^8}{q^{10}}$

Simplify each expression.

13. $\sqrt{9}$

14. $\sqrt{1}$

15. $\sqrt{\frac{25}{36}}$

16. $\sqrt{\frac{1}{4}}$

17. $\sqrt{(-1)^2}$

18. $\sqrt{(-5)^2}$

19. $-\sqrt{49a^2}$

20. $-\sqrt{81t^4}$

21. $-\sqrt{64r^2s^4}$

22. $-\sqrt{81a^8b^2}$

23. $\pm\sqrt{\frac{n^2}{144}}$

24. $\pm\sqrt{\frac{k^4}{16}}$

25. $(\sqrt{7})^2$

26. $(\sqrt{15})^2$

27. $\sqrt{5^2 - 3^2}$

28. $\sqrt{3^2 + 4^2}$

29. $\pm\sqrt{6^2 + 8^2}$

30. $\pm\sqrt{10^2 - 8^2}$

Written Exercises

Evaluate each expression.

1. $\sqrt{225}$

2. $\sqrt{324}$

3. $\sqrt{676}$

4. $\sqrt{1024}$

5. $-\sqrt{1296}$

6. $-\sqrt{1600}$

7. $-\sqrt{\frac{256}{49}}$

8. $-\sqrt{\frac{576}{25}}$

9. $\pm\sqrt{\frac{1}{256}}$

10. $\pm\sqrt{\frac{1}{784}}$

11. $\pm\sqrt{\frac{25}{484}}$

12. $\pm\sqrt{\frac{36}{729}}$

Solve. Use {the rational numbers} as the replacement set of the variable.

SAMPLE 1. $t^2 = 25$

Solution: $t^2 = 25$ *Check:* $(5)^2 \stackrel{?}{=} 25$ $(-5)^2 \stackrel{?}{=} 25$

$t = \pm\sqrt{25} = \pm 5$ $25 = 25 \checkmark$ $25 = 25 \checkmark$

∴ the solution set is $\{5, -5\}$. **Answer.**

13. $n^2 = 16$

14. $r^2 = 36$

15. $9x^2 - 4 = 0$

16. $25t^2 - 49 = 0$

17. $5a^2 - 80 = 0$

18. $7z^2 - 175 = 0$

SAMPLE 2. If $r^2 + s^2 = 12$ and $rs = 2$, find the positive value of $r + s$.

Solution: Multiply each member of $rs = 2$ by 2. $2rs = 2 \cdot 2$

Add left- and right-hand members
of $2rs = 4$ and $r^2 + s^2 = 12$: $r^2 + 2rs + s^2 = 12 + 4$

Factor the left-hand member. $(r + s)^2 = 16$

$\therefore r + s = \pm\sqrt{16} = \pm 4$.

$\therefore$ the positive value of $r + s$ is 4. **Answer.**

B 19. If $r^2 + s^2 = 15$ and $rs = 5$, find the positive value of $r + s$.

20. If $x^2 + y^2 = 20$ and $xy = 8$, find the negative value of $x + y$.

21. If $p - q = 5$ and $pq = 3$, find the value of $p^2 + q^2$.

22. If $(a - b)^2 = 5$ and $ab = 1$, find the positive value of $a + b$.

23. If $r + s = 8$ and $r^2 + s^2 = 40$, find the positive value of $r - s$.

24. If $c - d = 3$ and $c^2 + d^2 = 29$, find the positive value of $c + d$.

C 25. Solve the equation $\sqrt{a^2} - a = 6$.

26. Solve the equation $n - \sqrt{n^2} = -18$.

27. Prove the quotient property of square roots (page 462).

28. Prove that if $a > b > 0$, then $a^2 > b^2$.
    Hint: Show that $a^2 > ab$, and $ab > b^2$.

29. Use the result of Exercise 28 to explain why a positive number cannot have two different positive square roots.

30. Find the fallacy in this "proof" that every real number is 1.
    Let r be any real number. Then:

$$r - 1 = -(1 - r)$$
$$\therefore (r - 1)^2 = (1 - r)^2.$$
$$\therefore r - 1 = 1 - r.$$
$$\therefore 2r = 2.$$
$$\therefore r = 1.$$

12–4 Properties of Irrational Numbers

Rational numbers, like 25, 36, and $\frac{49}{16}$, which are squares of rational numbers are called **perfect squares**. However, not every positive rational number is a perfect square.

Do those integers which are not squares of integers have rational square roots? Consider some positive integer n. Assume that its square root is named by a fraction $\frac{a}{b}$ in lowest terms; that is, $\sqrt{n} = \frac{a}{b}$, where a, b, and n are positive integers, and a and b have no common integral factors.

If $\sqrt{n} = \dfrac{a}{b}$, then $n = \dfrac{a^2}{b^2}$. Since a^2 has the same prime factors as a, and b^2 has the same prime factors as b, if a and b have no factors in common, neither do a^2 and b^2, and $\dfrac{a^2}{b^2}$ is in lowest terms. *If a fraction in lowest terms is equal to an integer, the denominator of the fraction must be 1.* Thus, since n is an integer, and $\dfrac{a^2}{b^2}$ is in lowest terms, $b^2 = 1$, and $b = 1$, which means that $\dfrac{a}{b} = \dfrac{a}{1} = a$. Therefore, if the square root of a positive integer is a rational number, $\dfrac{a}{b}$, the root is in fact an integer, $\dfrac{a}{1}$. Thus, only integers which are squares of integers can have rational square roots.

Since integers such as 3, 5, and 7 are not the squares of integers, you must seek numbers like $\sqrt{3}$, $\sqrt{5}$, and $\sqrt{7}$ outside the set of rational numbers. You find such numbers in another major subset of the real numbers called the set of *irrational numbers*. **Irrational numbers** are real numbers which cannot be expressed in the form $\dfrac{r}{s}$, where r and s are integers. Thus, the set of real numbers is the union of the set of rational numbers and the set of irrational numbers.

Since every rational number is a real number, the real numbers share with the set of rational numbers the property of density (page 455). In addition, the set of real numbers has the following property:

Property of Completeness

Every decimal represents a real number, and every real number has a decimal representation.

Terminating and repeating decimals represent rational numbers; therefore, the decimals for irrational numbers must neither terminate nor repeat. One method of finding successive digits in the decimal approximations of irrational numbers which are square roots is based on the following.

Property of Pairs of Divisors of Any Real Number

If you divide a positive number by a positive number which is smaller than the positive square root of that number, the quotient will be larger than the square root.

Consider 100 and its square root 10:

$$100 \div 10 = 10;$$

but if the divisor is less than 10, then the quotient is greater than 10:

$$100 \div 2 = 50, \qquad 100 \div 4 = 25, \qquad 100 \div 5 = 20.$$

Of course, if the divisor is greater than 10, then the quotient is less than 10:

$$100 \div 50 = 2, \qquad 100 \div 25 = 4, \qquad 100 \div 20 = 5.$$

EXAMPLE 1. Find the decimal approximation of $\sqrt{15}$ to 4 digits.

Solution:

1. As your first approximation select the integer whose square is nearest 15.

2. Divide 15 by a.
   Carry the quotient to twice as many digits as are in the divisor.

3. From the property of pairs of divisors, you know that $\sqrt{15}$ is between a and $\dfrac{15}{a}$. Take their average to find a better approximation to $\sqrt{15}$.

4. Use this average as your new a. Repeat Steps 2, 3, 4 until you have as close an approximation as you wish.

   Your approximation is accurate to at least as many digits as match in a and $15 \div a$.

Let a be a number such that

$$a^2 \doteq 15.$$

$$\text{First } a = 4 \qquad (1)$$
$$15 \div 4 \doteq 3.7 \qquad (2)$$
$$2\overline{)7.7} \qquad (3)$$
$$\text{Second } a = 3.8 \qquad (4)$$
$$15 \div 3.8 \doteq 3.947 \qquad (2)$$
$$2\overline{)7.747} \qquad (3)$$
$$\text{Third } a = 3.873 \qquad (4)$$

$$15 \div 3.873 \doteq 3.8729666$$

Since $3.87296 < \sqrt{15} < 3.873,$

$$\sqrt{15} \doteq 3.873 \text{ to 4 digits.} \quad \textbf{Answer.}$$

Check: **Continue:**

$$\text{Fourth } a = \tfrac{1}{2}(3.873 + 3.8729666)$$
$$= 3.8729833$$

$$\begin{array}{r} 3.87298339 \\ 3.8729833\overline{)15.00000000} \end{array}$$

$$\therefore \sqrt{15} \doteq 3.8729833.$$

The product and quotient properties of square roots, too, may be useful in finding the decimal approximation for roots of numbers less than 1 and numbers greater than 100. Notice how even powers of 10 are used in Example 2.

EXAMPLE 2. Evaluate: a. $\sqrt{13924}$ b. $\sqrt{0.013924}$

Solution: a. $13924 = 10^4(1.3924)$; $\sqrt{13924} = 100\sqrt{1.3924}$

b. $0.013924 = \dfrac{1}{10^2}(1.3924)$; $\sqrt{0.013924} = \frac{1}{10}\sqrt{1.3924}$

Both solutions require you to find $\sqrt{1.3924}$. To find this:

1. First approx. = 1.2	1. Second approx. = 1.180
2. $1.3924 \div 1.2 \doteq 1.160$	2. $1.3924 \div 1.180 = 1.180$
3. Second approx. $= \dfrac{2.360}{2}$	$\therefore$ $\sqrt{1.3924} = 1.18$, the true root, since the last remainder was 0.

Substituting this value in the given expressions gives:

a. $\sqrt{13924} = 100(1.18) = 118.$ Answer.

b. $\sqrt{0.013924} = \frac{1}{10}(1.18) = 0.118.$ Answer.

The next example shows how you can use the values in the table of square roots in the Appendix to solve some square root problems.

EXAMPLE 3. Approximate the square roots of: a. 0.39   b. 390

Solution: Use the table of square roots in the Appendix.

a. $0.39 = \dfrac{39}{100}$ b. $390 = 39(10)$

$\sqrt{\dfrac{39}{100}} \doteq \dfrac{6.245}{10}$ $\sqrt{(39)(10)} \doteq (6.245)(3.162)$

$\therefore$ $\sqrt{0.39} \doteq 0.6245.$ Answer. $\therefore$ $\sqrt{390} \doteq 19.75.$ Answer.

Oral Exercises

State whether the number named is rational or irrational. If the number is rational, give a simpler name for it.

SAMPLE. $\sqrt[3]{8}$ *Solution:* Rational; 2

1. $\sqrt{5}$	4. $\sqrt{\frac{25}{2}}$	7. $\sqrt[3]{27}$	10. $\sqrt{0.64}$
2. $-\sqrt{16}$	5. $2\sqrt{10}$	8. $\sqrt[3]{\frac{1}{8}}$	11. $\sqrt[3]{64}$
3. $\sqrt{\frac{9}{49}}$	6. $-3\sqrt{3}$	9. $-\sqrt{0.25}$	12. $\sqrt[3]{2}$

13. $\sqrt{25} - \sqrt{36}$ **15.** $\sqrt{6} - \sqrt{6}$ **17.** $\sqrt{81} - \sqrt{49}$

14. $\dfrac{\sqrt{10}}{\sqrt{10}}$ **16.** $-\sqrt{28} + \sqrt{28}$ **18.** $\dfrac{\sqrt{27}}{\sqrt{3}}$

Name the integer closest to the square root of the given number.

19. 22   **21.** 8.1   **23.** 51.22   **25.** 1.27

20. 45   **22.** 34.8   **24.** 75.02   **26.** 18.31

Express as the product of a number between 1 and 100 and a power of 100.

27. 700   **29.** 415.7   **31.** 2176   **33.** 1600

28. 1500   **30.** 736.9   **32.** 6385   **34.** 4900

Express as the quotient of a number between 1 and 100 divided by a power of 100.

35. 0.45   **37.** 0.1715   **39.** 0.6   **41.** 0.000517

36. 0.83   **38.** 0.618   **40.** 0.3   **42.** 0.000826

Written Exercises

Find the indicated square roots.

A **1.** $\sqrt{2.89}$ **3.** $\sqrt{12.96}$ **5.** $\sqrt{1849}$ **7.** $-\sqrt{309.76}$ **9** $\sqrt{28{,}224}$

2. $\sqrt{5.29}$ **4.** $\sqrt{33.64}$ **6.** $\sqrt{5184}$ **8.** $-\sqrt{416.16}$ **10.** $\sqrt{110{,}224}$

Find each square root to the nearest hundredth.

11. $\sqrt{3}$ **13.** $\sqrt{40.7}$ **15.** $-\sqrt{273}$ **17.** $\sqrt{190}$

12. $\sqrt{5}$ **14.** $\sqrt{11.9}$ **16.** $-\sqrt{408}$ **18.** $\sqrt{230}$

Find both roots to the nearest tenth.

B **19.** $r^2 = 840$ **21.** $k^2 - 5.7 = 0$ **23.** $600 = 5x^2$

20. $t^2 = 382$ **22.** $n^2 - 11.2 = 0$ **24.** $900 = 4u^2$

25. Find $\sqrt{41}$ by taking $a = 6$ and by taking $a = 7$.

26. Find $\sqrt{72}$ by taking $a = 8$ and by taking $a = 9$.

Solve to the nearest tenth.

C **27.** $0.7r^2 = 5.81$ **29.** $12x^2 = 38$

28. $(y + 1)^2 + (y - 1)^2 = 50$ **30.** $11z^2 - 9 = 0$

Problems

 Find each answer to the nearest tenth, unless otherwise directed.

1. Find the side of a square whose area is 68 square inches.
2. The area of a square is 51 square feet. How long is one side?
3. The area of a circle is $A \doteq 3.14r^2$. Find the radius, correct to hundredths, of a circle whose area is 74.34 square centimeters.
4. The area of a circle is $A \doteq 0.7854d^2$. Find the diameter, correct to hundredths, of a circle whose area is 13.636 square centimeters.
5. Find the side of a square whose area is $\frac{43}{25}$ square meters.
6. The area of a square is $\frac{46}{9}$ square meters. Find its side.
7. A rectangle whose area is 174 square meters has a length four times its width. Find the length and width of this rectangle.
8. The width of a rectangle is $\frac{1}{3}$ its length. Its area is 1783 square centimeters. Find the dimensions of the rectangle.

12–5   Geometric Interpretation of Square Roots

Is it possible to locate irrational square roots on the number line without using approximations? Pythagoras (Pith-**ag**-uh-ras) proved the existence of distances which could not be measured by rational numbers in the *Pythagorean theorem* (Pith-ag'uh-**re**-an **the**-uh-rem).

Pythagorean Theorem

In any right triangle, the square of the length of the hypotenuse equals the sum of the squares of the lengths of the other two sides.

The **hypotenuse** of a right triangle is the longest side and is opposite the right angle.

Figure 12–1 illustrates the Pythagorean theorem, $c^2 = a^2 + b^2$, where c is the length of the hypotenuse, and a and b are the lengths of the other two sides.

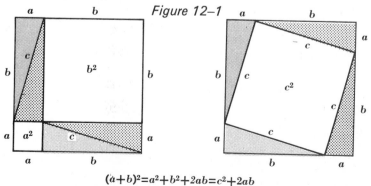

Figure 12–1

$$(a+b)^2 = a^2 + b^2 + 2ab = c^2 + 2ab$$

To find a length equal to $\sqrt{2}$, draw a square whose sides are 1 unit long (Figure 12–2). The diagonal $\overline{OP}$ separates it into two right triangles in which $a = 1$ and $b = 1$.

$$c^2 = a^2 + b^2$$
$$c^2 = 1^2 + 1^2$$
$$c^2 = 1 + 1$$
$$c^2 = 2$$
$$c = \sqrt{2}$$

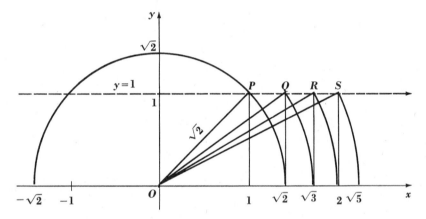

Figure 12–2

Figure 12–3 combines this square with the coordinate axes.   The semicircle has the origin as its center and $\sqrt{2}$ as its radius.

Figure 12–3

Points Q, R, and S are on the line $y = 1$ at distances of $\sqrt{3}$, $\sqrt{4}$, and $\sqrt{5}$ from the origin.   Each can be found by using the previously constructed square root and drawing perpendiculars to form new right triangles. If OQ, OR, and OS represent lengths, then:

$(OQ)^2 = (\sqrt{2})^2 + 1^2$	$(OR)^2 = (\sqrt{3})^2 + 1^2$	$(OS)^2 = (\sqrt{4})^2 + 1^2$
$(OQ)^2 = 2 + 1$	$(OR)^2 = 3 + 1$	$(OS)^2 = 4 + 1$
$(OQ)^2 = 3$	$(OR)^2 = 4$	$(OS)^2 = 5$
$(OQ) = \sqrt{3}$	$(OR) = \sqrt{4} = 2$	$(OS) = \sqrt{5}$

The Example on the opposite page applies the *converse* of the Pythagorean theorem.   You obtain the **converse** of a theorem by interchanging the hypothesis and conclusion.

Converse of the Pythagorean Theorem

If the sum of the squares of the lengths of the two shorter sides of a triangle is equal to the square of the length of the longest side, then the triangle is a right triangle, with the right angle opposite the longest side.

EXAMPLE. Is a triangle whose sides measure 3, 4, and 5 units a right triangle?

Solution: $c^2 = a^2 + b^2$

$5^2 \overset{?}{=} 3^2 + 4^2$

$25 = 25 \checkmark$ A 3-4-5 triangle is a right triangle. **Answer.**

Written Exercises

Determine whether or not each triangle described is a right triangle.

A

1. The three sides measure 5, 12, and 13 inches.
2. The three sides measure 12, 16, and 20 feet.
3. The three sides measure 10, 24, and 26 inches.
4. The three sides measure 9, 12, and 14 centimeters.

In each right triangle, find the missing dimension to the nearest hundredth of a unit.

5. $a = 6$ feet; $b = 8$ feet
6. $a = 12$ meters; $b = 9$ meters
7. $a = 12$ yards; $b = 3\frac{1}{2}$ yards
8. $a = 5$ feet; $b = 2\frac{3}{4}$ feet
9. $b = 5$ miles; $c = 13$ miles
10. $a = 12$ yards; $c = 22$ yards

Problems

Make a sketch for each problem. If the number asked for is irrational, approximate it to the nearest hundredth.

A

1. If the bottom of a 17-foot ramp is 15 feet from a loading platform, how high is the platform?
2. A rope from the top of a mast on a sailboat attached to a point 7 feet from the mast is 25 feet long. How high is the mast?
3. A rectangular flower garden is 30 feet wide and 50 feet long. How long is a straight path running from one corner to the corner diagonally opposite?

4. Two sides of a plastic draftsman's triangle are 9 inches long. How long is the third side?

5. The length of one side of a right triangle, expressed in inches, is one inch less than twice the length of the other. The hypotenuse is one inch more than twice the length of the latter side. Find the length of each side.

6. The length of the longer side of a right triangle, expressed in inches, is 3 more than the height of the shorter side, and the length of the hypotenuse is 3 more than the length of the longer side. Find the length of each side.

B 7. The lengths of the sides of a right triangle have a ratio of 8:15. The hypotenuse is 34 centimeters in length. Find the length of each side.

8. A group of hikers walks 6 miles due west from their base camp, then north for 2 miles, then due east. They spend the night at a point 4 miles northwest of base camp. How far east did they walk?

C 9. An arched doorway is a rectangle 4 feet wide by 8 feet high, surmounted by a semicircular arch. How high a cabinet, $2\frac{1}{2}$ feet deep, can be passed through the doorway upright?

10. Can a 40-inch long fencing foil be stored in a box 35 inches long by 15 inches wide by 6 inches deep?

RADICAL EXPRESSIONS

12–6 Multiplication, Division, and Simplification of Square-Root Radicals

The product and quotient properties of square roots (page 462) together with the commutative and associative axioms enable you to multiply, divide, and simplify square-root radicals quickly.

$$\sqrt{5} \cdot \sqrt{6} = \sqrt{5 \cdot 6} = \sqrt{30} \qquad \sqrt{2} \cdot \sqrt{8} = \sqrt{2 \cdot 8} = \sqrt{16} = 4$$

$$(3 \cdot \sqrt{7}) \cdot (5 \cdot \sqrt{2}) = (3 \cdot 5)(\sqrt{7} \cdot \sqrt{2}) = 15\sqrt{14}$$

$$\frac{\sqrt{15}}{\sqrt{3}} = \sqrt{\frac{15}{3}} = \sqrt{5} \qquad \sqrt{\frac{5}{12}} = \sqrt{\frac{5 \cdot 3}{12 \cdot 3}} = \sqrt{\frac{15}{36}} = \frac{\sqrt{15}}{6}$$

An expression having a square-root radical is in **simplest form** when

1. no integral radicand has a square factor other than 1,
2. no fractions are under a radical sign, and
3. no radicals are in a denominator.

$$\sqrt{12} = \sqrt{4} \cdot \sqrt{3} = 2\sqrt{3}; \quad 2\sqrt{45} = 2\sqrt{9 \cdot 5} = 6\sqrt{5}$$

$$\sqrt{\frac{2}{3}} = \frac{\sqrt{2}}{\sqrt{3}} = \frac{\sqrt{2} \cdot \sqrt{3}}{\sqrt{3} \cdot \sqrt{3}} = \frac{\sqrt{6}}{3}; \quad \frac{1}{\sqrt{5}} = \frac{1 \cdot \sqrt{5}}{\sqrt{5} \cdot \sqrt{5}} = \frac{\sqrt{5}}{5}$$

$$\frac{3\sqrt{7}}{2\sqrt{32}} = \frac{3\sqrt{7} \cdot \sqrt{2}}{2\sqrt{32} \cdot \sqrt{2}} = \frac{3\sqrt{14}}{2\sqrt{64}} = \frac{3\sqrt{14}}{2 \cdot 8} = \frac{3\sqrt{14}}{16}$$

The process of changing the form of a fraction with an irrational denominator such as $\dfrac{3\sqrt{7}}{2\sqrt{32}}$ to an equal fraction with a rational denominator such as $\dfrac{3\sqrt{14}}{16}$ is called **rationalizing the denominator**. Rationalizing the denominator of a radical expression helps in approximating its value.

Oral Exercises

Express in simplest form.

1. $\sqrt{3} \cdot \sqrt{5}$ **5.** $\sqrt{3} \cdot 2\sqrt{7}$ **9.** $2\sqrt{3} \cdot \sqrt{3}$ **13.** $(2\sqrt{5})^2$

2. $\sqrt{5} \cdot \sqrt{7}$ **6.** $3\sqrt{2} \cdot \sqrt{5}$ **10.** $3 \cdot \sqrt{6} \cdot 2\sqrt{6}$ **14.** $(3\sqrt{2})^2$

3. $\dfrac{\sqrt{12}}{\sqrt{3}}$ **7.** $\sqrt{\frac{28}{7}}$ **11.** $2\sqrt{2} \cdot 3\sqrt{8}$ **15.** $\sqrt{\frac{1}{3}} \cdot \sqrt{\frac{1}{3}}$

4. $\dfrac{\sqrt{18}}{\sqrt{2}}$ **8.** $\sqrt{\frac{72}{2}}$ **12.** $3\sqrt{12} \cdot 2\sqrt{3}$ **16.** $\sqrt{\frac{1}{5}} \cdot \sqrt{\frac{1}{5}}$

17. $\sqrt{12}$ **21.** $\sqrt{32}$ **25.** $\sqrt{48}$ **29.** $\dfrac{1}{\sqrt{8}}$ **33.** $\dfrac{2}{\sqrt{x^3}}$

18. $\sqrt{20}$ **22.** $\sqrt{200}$ **26.** $\sqrt{75}$ **30.** $\dfrac{1}{\sqrt{12}}$ **34.** $\dfrac{3}{\sqrt{y^5}}$

19. $\sqrt{18}$ **23.** $\dfrac{1}{\sqrt{2}}$ **27.** $\sqrt{\frac{2}{3}}$ **31.** $\sqrt{\frac{2}{x}}$ **35.** $\sqrt{4x^3}$

20. $\sqrt{27}$ **24.** $\dfrac{1}{\sqrt{5}}$ **28.** $\sqrt{\frac{3}{5}}$ **32.** $\sqrt{\frac{5}{z}}$ **● 36.** $\sqrt{9y^5}$

Give two integral factors, one of which is the greatest possible perfect square.

SAMPLE. 50   *Solution:*   25 times 2.

37. 24   **39.** 48   **41.** 125   **43.** 98   **45.** 500

38. 28   **40.** 72   **42.** 128   **44.** 162   **46.** 800

Written Exercises

Express in simplest form. (Assume that all radicands are nonnegative real numbers.)

A

1. $2\sqrt{5} \cdot 3\sqrt{5}$ 5. $2\sqrt{3} \cdot \sqrt{5} \cdot \sqrt{7}$ 9. $\sqrt{\frac{3}{5}} \cdot \sqrt{\frac{25}{12}}$

2. $4\sqrt{7} \cdot 2\sqrt{7}$ 6. $3\sqrt{2} \cdot \sqrt{7} \cdot \sqrt{3}$ 10. $\sqrt{\frac{5}{9}} \cdot 2\sqrt{\frac{9}{20}}$

3. $\sqrt{2} \cdot \sqrt{5} \cdot \sqrt{10}$ 7. $\sqrt{\frac{2}{5}} \cdot \sqrt{\frac{5}{2}}$ 11. $\sqrt{5\frac{1}{7}} \cdot \sqrt{1\frac{3}{4}}$

4. $\sqrt{15} \cdot \sqrt{3} \cdot \sqrt{5}$ 8. $\sqrt{\frac{4}{3}} \cdot \sqrt{\frac{12}{4}}$ 12. $\frac{1}{2}\sqrt{\frac{4}{15}} \cdot \frac{1}{3}\sqrt{\frac{3}{20}}$

13. $\dfrac{12\sqrt{6}}{3\sqrt{2}}$ 18. $5\sqrt{75}$ 23. $\dfrac{12\sqrt{3}}{4\sqrt{27}}$ 28. $\dfrac{\sqrt{5x}}{\sqrt{x}}$

14. $\dfrac{4\sqrt{24}}{3\sqrt{4}}$ 19. $\dfrac{\sqrt{80}}{\sqrt{5}}$ 24. $\dfrac{\sqrt{x^7}}{\sqrt{x}}$ 29. $\dfrac{\sqrt{50}}{3\sqrt{10}}$

15. $\sqrt{150}$ 20. $\dfrac{\sqrt{7}}{\sqrt{63}}$ 25. $15\sqrt{\frac{8}{3}}$ 30. $\dfrac{\sqrt{72}}{2\sqrt{6}}$

16. $5\sqrt{24}$ 21. $3\sqrt{\frac{32}{9}}$ 26. $6\sqrt{\frac{5}{18}}$ 31. $\sqrt{54a^2}$

17. $3\sqrt{72}$ 22. $5\sqrt{\frac{45}{4}}$ 27. $8\sqrt{\frac{3}{50}}$ 32. $\sqrt{63x^5}$

B

33. $(-2\sqrt{x^3y})(4\sqrt{xy})$ 41. $(3x\sqrt{2x})^2$

34. $(-5\sqrt{np^2})(-3\sqrt{n})$ 42. $(4y\sqrt{3y})^2$

35. $\sqrt{a}(\sqrt{a} + 2)$ 43. $3\sqrt{2}(2\sqrt{6} + \sqrt{3})$

36. $\sqrt{b}(3 - \sqrt{b})$ 44. $5\sqrt{3}(-2\sqrt{6} + \sqrt{15})$

37. $(4\sqrt{3})(\sqrt{6})(-\sqrt{8})$ 45. $-3\sqrt{2\frac{1}{3}}$

38. $(-5\sqrt{28})(-\sqrt{14})(2\sqrt{2})$ 46. $4\sqrt{1\frac{1}{5}}$

39. $(\sqrt{14x})(2\sqrt{x})(\sqrt{7})$ 47. $-3\sqrt{1.2}$

40. $(\sqrt{2x})(\sqrt{3x})(\sqrt{6})$ 48. $2.38\sqrt{0.26}$

49. $\dfrac{2\sqrt{3} + 3\sqrt{6}}{\sqrt{3}}$ 51. $\dfrac{2\sqrt{5} - \sqrt{10}}{\sqrt{5}}$ 53. $\dfrac{5\sqrt{x^3} + \sqrt{x}}{\sqrt{x}}$

50. $\dfrac{4\sqrt{28}}{5\sqrt{7} - 3\sqrt{7}}$ 52. $\dfrac{\sqrt{7} + 2\sqrt{14}}{\sqrt{7}}$ 54. $\dfrac{\sqrt{y} - 5\sqrt{y^3}}{\sqrt{y}}$

Problems

Find answers to the nearest tenth unless otherwise directed.

B

1. One positive number is five times another, and the difference of their squares is 18. Find the numbers.

2. Find two positive numbers in the ratio of 3 to 2 whose squares differ by 10.

3. The length and width of a rectangle are in the ratio 4 to 3. If the area of the rectangle is 36 square inches, what are its dimensions?

4. Find the length of a diagonal of a square with area 81 square inches.

5. Use Heron's formula, $A = \sqrt{s(s - a)(s - b)(s - c)}$, where a, b, and c are lengths of sides and s is half the perimeter, to find the area of a triangle with sides of length 3 inches, 6 inches, and 7 inches.

6. If a circle is inscribed in a right triangle as shown in the figure at the right, $c = a + b - 2r$, and so the radius r of the circle is determined by $r = \frac{1}{2}(a + b - c)$, where a and b are the lengths of the shorter sides of the triangle and c is the length of the hypotenuse. Find r, if a is 8 feet and b is 10 feet.

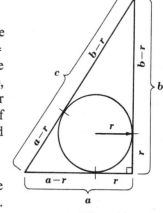

C 7. Find the length s of each side of a square if a diameter of the square is 5.3 feet long.

8. A square is inscribed in a circle as shown at the right. Find the radius of the circle if the area of the square is 36 square inches.

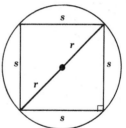

9. Will a square whose area is 36 square inches fit inside a circle whose area is 54 square inches? Support your answer with calculations.

10. Show that an equilateral triangle with sides of length 9 inches is smaller in area than a square inscribed in a circle with a diameter of 9 inches.

11. An altitude of an equilateral triangle separates the triangle into two congruent triangles as pictured at the right. Find the length h of the altitude if the length s of a side is 1 foot.

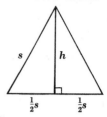

12. Express the length h of an altitude of an equilateral triangle in terms of the length s of a side of the triangle.

12–7 Addition and Subtraction of Square-Root Radicals

Because $3\sqrt{7}$ and $2\sqrt{7}$ have the common factor $\sqrt{7}$, you can simplify the expression for their sum by using the distributive axiom:

$$3\sqrt{7} + 2\sqrt{7} = (3 + 2)\sqrt{7} = 5\sqrt{7}$$

The sum or difference of square-root radicals having the same radicand is the sum or difference of the coefficients of the radicals, multiplied by the common radical. On the other hand, the addition or subtraction of radicals having unlike radicands can only be indicated.

$$3\sqrt{5} - 5\sqrt{11} + 2\sqrt{5} + \sqrt{11} = 5\sqrt{5} - 4\sqrt{11}$$

By reducing each radical to simplest form, you sometimes can combine terms in a sum of radicals.

EXAMPLE. Simplify: $4\sqrt{8} - 2\sqrt{50} + 3\sqrt{128}$

Solution:

$$
\begin{aligned}
4\sqrt{8} - 2\sqrt{50} + 3\sqrt{128} &= 4\sqrt{4 \cdot 2} - 2\sqrt{25 \cdot 2} + 3\sqrt{64 \cdot 2} \\
&= 4(2\sqrt{2}) - 2(5\sqrt{2}) + 3(8\sqrt{2}) \\
&= 8\sqrt{2} - 10\sqrt{2} + 24\sqrt{2} \\
&= 22\sqrt{2}. \quad \text{Answer.}
\end{aligned}
$$

> To simplify sums or differences of square-root radicals:
>
> 1. Express each radical in simplest form.
> 2. Use the distributive axiom to add or subtract radicals with like radicands.
> 3. Indicate the sum or difference of radicals with unlike radicands.

Oral Exercises

From each group select the radicals having the same radicand.

1. $3\sqrt{5}, 5\sqrt{3}, \sqrt{5}$
2. $\sqrt{6}, 4\sqrt{6}, \sqrt{12}$
3. $2\sqrt{15}, 3\sqrt{5}, -4\sqrt{15}$

4. $-\sqrt{7}, 2\sqrt{14}, 7\sqrt{14}$
5. $2\sqrt{8}, 5\sqrt{2}, \sqrt{5}, 3\sqrt{8}$
6. $2\sqrt{11}, 5\sqrt{22}, 11\sqrt{11}, 3\sqrt{2}$

Simplify each radical expression.

7. $2\sqrt{5} + 4\sqrt{5}$
8. $6\sqrt{3} + \sqrt{3}$
9. $7\sqrt{2} - 3\sqrt{2}$
10. $2\sqrt{6} - 5\sqrt{6}$
11. $3\sqrt{7} + 2\sqrt{7} - 5\sqrt{7}$

12. $7\sqrt{10} + 2\sqrt{10} - 3\sqrt{10}$
13. $2\sqrt{11} - 8\sqrt{11} - \sqrt{11}$
14. $7\sqrt{14} + \sqrt{14} - 10\sqrt{14}$
15. $3\sqrt{x} - 2\sqrt{x} + \sqrt{x}, \; x \geq 0$
16. $\sqrt{z} - 4\sqrt{z} + 3\sqrt{z}, \; z \geq 0$

Written Exercises

Simplify each expression.

A

1. $2\sqrt{3} + 3\sqrt{3} - \sqrt{3}$

2. $5\sqrt{6} - 8\sqrt{6} - 2\sqrt{6}$

3. $\sqrt{5} - 2\sqrt{7} + 3\sqrt{7} - \sqrt{5}$

4. $2\sqrt{3} + \sqrt{11} - 3\sqrt{11} + \sqrt{3}$

5. $2\sqrt{8} + \sqrt{2}$

6. $\sqrt{3} - \sqrt{27}$

7. $\sqrt{12} - 2\sqrt{3}$

8. $\sqrt{32} + 2\sqrt{2}$

9. $\sqrt{3} + \sqrt{\frac{1}{3}}$

10. $\sqrt{5} - \sqrt{\frac{1}{5}}$

11. $2\sqrt{54} + \sqrt{24}$

12. $5\sqrt{48} - 8\sqrt{27}$

13. $\sqrt{10} + \sqrt{\frac{2}{5}}$

14. $2\sqrt{21} - \sqrt{\frac{3}{7}}$

15. $\sqrt{200} - \frac{2}{3}\sqrt{162}$

16. $\sqrt{192} + \frac{1}{5}\sqrt{50}$

B

17. $2\sqrt{2} - \sqrt{32} + 2\sqrt{\frac{1}{2}}$

18. $2\sqrt{54} + \sqrt{96} - 9\sqrt{\frac{2}{3}}$

19. $15\sqrt{\frac{2}{5}} + 6\sqrt{\frac{5}{2}} - \sqrt{160}$

20. $8\sqrt{\frac{3}{2}} - 15\sqrt{\frac{2}{3}} + \sqrt{96}$

21. $6\sqrt{\frac{5}{4}} - 15\sqrt{\frac{1}{5}} + 5\sqrt{45}$

22. $2\sqrt{\frac{3}{8}} + \sqrt{\frac{8}{3}} - 4\sqrt{24}$

In Exercises 23–26, assume that all radicands are nonnegative real numbers, and simplify.

C

23. $3\sqrt{18y} - \frac{3y}{4}\sqrt{\frac{32}{y}}$

24. $x^3\sqrt{\frac{3}{x^3}} + 4x\sqrt{27x}$

25. $\sqrt{\frac{x^2}{16} + \frac{x^2}{9}}$

26. $\sqrt{\frac{3n^2}{5} - \frac{n^2}{20}}$

Solve each equation.

27. $x\sqrt{3} - 2\sqrt{12} = 2\sqrt{27} - x\sqrt{27}$

28. $\sqrt{288} - y\sqrt{18} = y\sqrt{72} + \sqrt{162}$

29. $3\sqrt{a} + 15 = 35 - \sqrt{a}$

30. $3(2 + \sqrt{b}) - \sqrt{b} = 14$

12–8 Multiplication of Binomials Containing Square-Root Radicals

Sometimes in dealing with radicals, you may wish to find a product like $(2 + \sqrt{5})(2 - \sqrt{5})$. Do you see that this product resembles $(a + b)(a - b) = a^2 - b^2$? Two binomials of the form $x + \sqrt{y}$ and $x - \sqrt{y}$ are called **conjugates** of each other. They differ only in the sign before the radical. In case x and y are rational numbers, their product is also a rational number, as this example shows.

EXAMPLE 1. $(2 + \sqrt{5})(2 - \sqrt{5})$

Solution: $(2 + \sqrt{5})(2 - \sqrt{5}) = 2^2 - (\sqrt{5})^2$

$$= 4 - 5 = -1. \quad \textbf{Answer.}$$

Consider the product $(3 + \sqrt{7})(3 + \sqrt{7})$ whose form is $(a + b) \times (a + b) = a^2 + 2ab + b^2$.

EXAMPLE 2. $(3 + \sqrt{7})(3 + \sqrt{7})$

Solution: $\quad (3 + \sqrt{7})(3 + \sqrt{7}) = 3^2 + 2(3\sqrt{7}) + (\sqrt{7})^2$
$$= 9 + 6\sqrt{7} + 7 = 16 + 6\sqrt{7}.$$
Answer.

Noting conjugates or their negatives can help you *rationalize a binomial denominator.*

EXAMPLE 3. Rationalize the denominator: $\dfrac{1}{3\sqrt{2} - 2}$

Solution: **Multiply the numerator and denominator by $3\sqrt{2} + 2$:**

$$\frac{1}{3\sqrt{2} - 2} = \frac{1(3\sqrt{2} + 2)}{(3\sqrt{2} - 2)(3\sqrt{2} + 2)} = \frac{3\sqrt{2} + 2}{(3\sqrt{2})^2 - (2)^2}$$

$$= \frac{3\sqrt{2} + 2}{18 - 4} = \frac{3\sqrt{2} + 2}{14}. \quad \textbf{Answer.}$$

Here the conjugate of $2 + 3\sqrt{2}$ is $2 - 3\sqrt{2}$, which is $-(3\sqrt{2} - 2)$.

Written Exercises

Express in simplest form.

A

1. $(3 + \sqrt{2})(3 - \sqrt{2})$
2. $(5 - \sqrt{7})(5 + \sqrt{7})$
3. $(\sqrt{5} - \sqrt{2})(\sqrt{5} + \sqrt{2})$
4. $(\sqrt{3} + \sqrt{6})(\sqrt{3} - \sqrt{6})$
5. $(3\sqrt{5} + 1)(\sqrt{5} - 2)$
6. $(2\sqrt{3} - 1)(3\sqrt{3} + 2)$

7. $(5 + \sqrt{5})^2$
8. $(3 - \sqrt{6})^2$
9. $(2\sqrt{3} - 3)^2$
10. $(4\sqrt{5} + 3)^2$
11. $3\sqrt{5}(2\sqrt{10} + \sqrt{5})$
12. $4\sqrt{6}(2\sqrt{3} + 5\sqrt{2})$

B

13. $(3\sqrt{5} + \sqrt{2})(2\sqrt{5} - \sqrt{2})$
14. $(4\sqrt{3} + 5)(3\sqrt{3} - 4)$

15. $(4\sqrt{2} + 3\sqrt{6})(2\sqrt{2} - \sqrt{6})$
16. $(2\sqrt{10} + \sqrt{5})(3\sqrt{10} - 2\sqrt{5})$

Rationalize the denominator of each fraction.

17. $\dfrac{1}{1 + \sqrt{2}}$

18. $\dfrac{2}{\sqrt{5} - 1}$

19. $\dfrac{\sqrt{3}}{\sqrt{3} - 2}$

20. $\dfrac{\sqrt{5}}{3 + \sqrt{5}}$

21. $\dfrac{2 + \sqrt{3}}{1 - \sqrt{3}}$

22. $\dfrac{3 + \sqrt{2}}{2 - \sqrt{2}}$

23. $\dfrac{5}{2\sqrt{7} + 3}$

24. $\dfrac{4}{3\sqrt{5} - 2}$

If $f(x) = x^2 - 4x + 1$, find:

25. $f(\sqrt{2})$ **26.** $f(\sqrt{2} - 1)$ **27.** $f(2 - \sqrt{3})$ **28.** $f(2 + \sqrt{3})$

29. Show that $1 + 2\sqrt{3}$ and $1 - 2\sqrt{3}$ are roots of the equation "$x^2 - 2x - 11 = 0$."

30. Write an expression in simplest form for the area of a square whose perimeter is $8\sqrt{5} + 4$ centimeters.

Simplify. Assume that the value of each variable is nonnegative.

C **31.** $(\sqrt{a} - b)(\sqrt{a} + b)$

32. $(x + 2\sqrt{3})^2$

33. $(2a\sqrt{b} - c)(3a\sqrt{b} + 4c)$

34. $2\sqrt{\dfrac{x}{y}} - 3\sqrt{\dfrac{y}{x}} + \sqrt{xy}$

12–9   Radical Equations

An equation having a variable in a radicand is a **radical equation**. The simplest kind of radical equation is one like $\sqrt{y} = 5$, which you solve by squaring each of its members:

$$\sqrt{y} = 5, \qquad (\sqrt{y})^2 = 5^2, \qquad y = 25$$

Check: $\sqrt{25} = 5$ $\therefore$ **the solution set is** $\{25\}$. **Answer.**

To solve radical equations which have several terms in each member but only one radical term, you first isolate the radical term in one member. Then you can square each member and solve the resulting equation.

EXAMPLE 1.   Solve $2 = 3\sqrt{x} - x$.

Solution:

1. **Isolate the radical term in one member of the equation.**

$$2 = 3\sqrt{x} - x$$
$$x + 2 = 3\sqrt{x}$$

2. **Square both members.**

$$(x + 2)^2 = (3\sqrt{x})^2$$
$$x^2 + 4x + 4 = 9x$$

3. **Solve the resulting equation.**

$$x^2 - 5x + 4 = 0$$
$$(x - 4)(x - 1) = 0$$

$x - 4 = 0$	$x - 1 = 0$
$x = 4$	$x = 1$

(*cont. on p. 480*)

4. *Check:*

Substitute.   Be sure to take the principal root of the number in the radicand.

$2 \stackrel{?}{=} 3\sqrt{4} - 4$	$2 \stackrel{?}{=} 3\sqrt{1} - 1$
$2 \stackrel{?}{=} 3 \cdot 2 - 4$	$2 \stackrel{?}{=} 3 \cdot 1 - 1$
$2 = 6 - 4 \checkmark$	$2 = 3 - 1 \checkmark$

$\therefore$ the solution set is $\{4, 1\}$.   **Answer.**

Can you explain why the "squared" equation in Step 2 may not be equivalent to the given equation? Notice that:

If $a = b$, then $a^2 = b^2$; but if $a^2 = b^2$, it need not be true that $a = b$.

For example, $5^2 = (-5)^2$, but $5 \neq -5$.

Thus, when you square the members of an equation, the most that you can say is that the solution set of the original equation is a *subset* of the solution set of the new equation. Therefore, you *must* check each root of the new equation in the original equation to see which, if any, satisfy the equation.

EXAMPLE 2.   Solve $10 = 3\sqrt{x} + x$.

Solution:
$$10 = 3\sqrt{x} + x$$
$$10 - x = 3\sqrt{x}$$
$$(10 - x)^2 = (3\sqrt{x})^2$$
$$100 - 20x + x^2 = 9x$$
$$x^2 - 29x + 100 = 0$$
$$(x - 4)(x - 25) = 0$$

$x - 4 = 0$	$x - 25 = 0$
$x = 4$	$x = 25$

Check:
$$10 \stackrel{?}{=} 3\sqrt{4} + 4$$
$$10 \stackrel{?}{=} 3 \cdot 2 + 4$$
$$10 = 10 \checkmark$$

$$10 \stackrel{?}{=} 3\sqrt{25} + 4$$
$$10 \stackrel{?}{=} 3 \cdot 5 + 4$$
$$10 \stackrel{?}{=} 19 \quad \text{No}$$

25 is not a root. $\therefore$ the solution set is $\{4\}$.   **Answer.**

Written Exercises

Solve each equation.

A 1. $\sqrt{3y} = 6$ 7. $\sqrt{x} - \frac{2}{3} = 3$ 13. $3\sqrt{2x} = 6$

2. $\sqrt{2z} = 8$ 8. $\sqrt{b} + \frac{3}{5} = 2$ 14. $5\sqrt{3x} = 15$

3. $\sqrt{7a} = \frac{1}{2}$ 9. $\sqrt{\dfrac{z}{3}} = 1$ 15. $\sqrt{2t} + 3 = 1$

4. $\sqrt{6t} = \frac{2}{3}$ 10. $\sqrt{\dfrac{k}{5}} = 2$ 16. $\sqrt{6n} + 5 = 2$

5. $\sqrt{n} - 2 = -1$ 11. $\sqrt{n+2} = 4$ 17. $\sqrt{3x+2} - 1 = 1$

6. $\sqrt{r} + 3 = 5$ 12. $\sqrt{m-3} = 3$ 18. $\sqrt{5y-2} + 3 = 6$

19. $\sqrt{\dfrac{4a}{3}} - 2 = 6$ 20. $\sqrt{\dfrac{7t}{2}} + 3 = 12$

B 21. $\sqrt{\dfrac{2n+6}{5}} = 4$ 27. Solve for m: $v = \sqrt{\dfrac{2E}{m}}$

22. $\sqrt{\dfrac{3t-1}{6}} = 3$ 28. Solve for v: $r = \sqrt{\dfrac{7v}{22h}}$

23. $\sqrt{n} = 3\sqrt{2}$ 29. $\sqrt{y^2 + 2} = 2 - y$

24. $2\sqrt{t} = 4\sqrt{3}$ 30. $\sqrt{x^2 - 2} = x + 10$

25. $3\sqrt{2t^2 - 28} = 6$ 31. $\sqrt{a} = -\dfrac{a}{4}$

26. $3\sqrt{5x^2 - 11} = 9$ 32. $\sqrt{b} = -\dfrac{b}{3}$

C 33. $\sqrt{y^2 + 11} - 1 = y$ 37. $\sqrt{7t - 3} = 2t - 3$

34. $\sqrt{z^2 - 13} + 1 = z$ 38. $\sqrt{3b + 10} = b + 4$

35. $\sqrt{y + 4} = y + 2$ 39. $\sqrt{n - 3} + 5 = 0$

36. $\sqrt{x + 2} = x - 4$ 40. $\sqrt{r + 2} + 3 = 0$

Problems

A 1. Twice the square root of a number is 22. Find the number.

2. One-fifth the square root of a number is 2. Find the number.

3. The square root of 5 less than one third a number is 10. What is the number?

4. When 7 is added to three times a certain number, the square root of the result is 5. Find the number.

5. The diameter of a circle in terms of its area is $d \doteq \sqrt{\dfrac{14A}{11}}$. Solve for A in terms of d, and find the area of a circle of diameter 7 inches.

6. The distance in miles to the horizon from a submarine's periscope that is h feet above a calm sea is $d = \sqrt{\dfrac{3h}{2}}$. Solve this for h in terms of d, and determine how far above the surface the periscope is if the lookout sees 3 miles to the horizon.

7. Solve this form of the Pythagorean theorem for the positive value of b: $c = \sqrt{a^2 + b^2}$. Find b when $c = 10$ and $a = 6$.

8. The current I (measured in amperes) which flows through an electrical appliance is expressed by $I = \sqrt{\dfrac{P}{R}}$, where P is power consumed (in watts) and R is the resistance of the appliance (in ohms). If an electric iron has a resistance of 20 ohms and draws 8 amperes of current, how much power does it consume?

B 9. A 1-carat diamond costs $700. The weight in carats of a diamond of equal quality may be found by $w = \sqrt{\dfrac{C}{700}}$, where C is the cost in dollars. Using this formula, find the cost of a 1.7 carat diamond.

10. The number of times a pendulum swings in one second is given by the formula $f \doteq \dfrac{1}{2\pi}\sqrt{\dfrac{32}{l}}$, where l is its length in feet. If a pendulum completes half a swing in each second, how long is it? (Use $\pi \doteq 3.14$.)

11. The velocity of sound in air, in meters per second, at a temperature of t degrees, is $V = 333\sqrt{14.0037t}$. At what temperature will sound travel at 11,544 meters per second?

12. $s = 16t^2$ gives the approximate distance (in feet) traveled by a falling object in t seconds. How long does it take a rock to fall 900 feet?

13. The thickness (in inches) of a beam of fixed width and length in terms of the weight (in pounds) which the beam can support is $t = \dfrac{1}{5}\sqrt{\dfrac{w}{6}}$. How much weight can a 2-inch-thick beam support?

14. The acceleration in meters/sec^2 of an object moving in a circular path is expressed by $a = \dfrac{v^2}{r}$, where v is velocity in meters/sec and r is the radius of the path in meters. How fast does an object tied to a 12-meter string need to move in order to have the same acceleration as an object tied to a 10-meter string and moving at 10 meters/sec?

15. Let f be the function with domain {3 and the real numbers greater than 3} such that $f(x) = \sqrt{x-3} - 5$. For what value of x is $f(x) = 2$?

16. Two positive numbers x and y are related as follows: $x = \sqrt{y^2 - 5y - 1}$. Find y when x is 7.

● CHAPTER SUMMARY ●

Inventory of Structure and Method

1. A **rational number** can be expressed as a fraction in an unlimited number of ways, and as either a **terminating decimal** or a **repeating decimal**. Between every pair of rational numbers is another rational number (**Property of Density**).

2. To round a decimal, you retain the digits unchanged if the first digit dropped is less than 5; you increase the value of the last digit by one if the first digit dropped is 5 or more.

3. If $a \geq 0$ and $b > 0$, then $\sqrt{ab} = \sqrt{a} \cdot \sqrt{b}$ and $\sqrt{\dfrac{a}{b}} = \dfrac{\sqrt{a}}{\sqrt{b}}$.

4. In any right triangle, if c is the length of hypotenuse, and a and b are the lengths of the other sides, then $a^2 + b^2 = c^2$. This is the **Pythagorean theorem**.

5. Roots of rational numbers are not all rational numbers. **Irrational numbers** are represented by **unending, nonrepeating decimals**. The set of real numbers is the union of the set of rational numbers and the set of irrational numbers.

6. If you divide a positive number by a number which is smaller in absolute value than the square root of the number, the quotient is larger in absolute value than the square root. (**Property of Pairs of Divisors**)

7. Sums and differences of square roots having the same radicand can be simplified by applying the distributive axiom.

8. Squaring both members of an equation produces a new equation whose solution set includes the solution set of the given equation.

Vocabulary and Spelling

Review the meaning of each term by reference to the page listed.

real number system (*p. 453*)
number system (*p. 453*)
system of rational numbers (*p. 453*)
rational operations (*p. 453*)
terminating (*p. 458*)
nonterminating (*p. 458*)
repeating, periodic (*p. 458*)
raising to a power (*p. 461*)
extracting a root (*p. 461*)
*n*th root (*p. 461*)
radical (*p. 461*)
root index (*p. 461*)

radicand (*p. 461*)
principal square root (*p. 461*)
perfect square (*p. 464*)
irrational numbers (*p. 465*)
property of completeness (*p. 465*)
hypotenuse (*p. 469*)
converse (*p. 470*)
radical in simplest form (*p. 472*)
rationalizing the denominator
  (*p. 473*)
conjugate (*p. 477*)
radical equation (*p. 479*)

Chapter Test

12–1 Arrange in order, from greatest to least.

1. $\frac{3}{20}, \frac{4}{23}, \frac{7}{25}$ **2.** $\frac{77}{32}, \frac{56}{25}, \frac{64}{27}$

Find a number halfway between the given pair.

3. $\frac{23}{24}, 1$ **4.** $-\frac{11}{7}, 3$

12–2 Write as a terminating or repeating decimal.

5. $\frac{3}{40}$ **6.** $\frac{8}{9}$ **7.** $-\frac{5}{11}$ **8.** $3\frac{2}{7}$

Write as a common fraction

9. $0.1818\ldots$ **10.** $0.\overline{5}$ **11.** $3.\overline{13}$ **12.** $5.\overline{234}$

12–3 Evaluate each expression using the product and quotient properties.

13. $\sqrt{1600}$ **14.** $-\sqrt{\frac{1}{1296}}$

Find each solution set over $\Re$.

15. $x^2 = 2500$ **16.** $5z^2 - 405 = 0$

12–4 Compute the given square root to the nearest hundredth.

17. $\sqrt{3.18}$ **18.** $-\sqrt{0.285}$

12–5 Find the length of the third side of right triangle *ABC* if its hypotenuse has length *AB*. $\angle C$ is the right angle.

19. $BC = 16$, $AB = 20$ **20.** $AC = 20$, $BC = 15$

12–6 Express each product or quotient in simplest form.

21. $2\sqrt{11} \cdot 3\sqrt{11}$ **23.** $2\sqrt{5} \cdot \sqrt{10} \cdot 3\sqrt{8}$

22. $\dfrac{5\sqrt{6}}{2\sqrt{75}}$ **24.** $\dfrac{6\sqrt{x^3y}}{\sqrt{9xy}}$

12–7 Simplify each expression.

25. $2\sqrt{7} + \sqrt{7} - 5\sqrt{7}$ **27.** $7\sqrt{8} - 2\sqrt{\frac{1}{2}}$

26. $4\sqrt{\frac{1}{12}} + \sqrt{\frac{1}{3}}$ **28.** $\frac{1}{3}\sqrt{\frac{2}{27}} - \frac{1}{6}\sqrt{\frac{1}{3}}$

12–8 Express in simplest form.

29. $(2 + \sqrt{3})(1 - \sqrt{3})$ **30.** $(4 - \sqrt{2})^2$ **31.** $\dfrac{\sqrt{5} + 1}{1 - \sqrt{5}}$

12–9 Find the solution set.   **32.** $\sqrt{2x} - 4 = 0$ **33.** $\sqrt{t} = t - 6$

Who Uses Mathematics?

Foresters examine trees as part of their work in protecting and directing the use and conservation of forest lands. Our state and national parks all require trained men to care for their forests. Industries also employ foresters to maintain and cultivate the forests on which their business depends.

Many universities today offer courses in forestry. To prepare for work in this interesting area, your high school course should include the mathematics specified for entrance to the institution where you wish to study.

Chapter Review

12–1 **The Nature of Rational Numbers** *Pages 453–457*

1. The set of real numbers is the union of two disjoint sets, the set of __?__ numbers and the set of __?__ numbers.
2. Of the numbers $\frac{7}{8}$ and $\frac{43}{48}$, the greater is __?__.
3. The number halfway between $\frac{2}{7}$ and $\frac{3}{8}$ is __?__.

12–2 **Decimal Forms for Rational Numbers** *Pages 457–460*

Write as decimals.

4. $3\frac{1}{8}$ 5. $\frac{8}{7}$ 6. $-\frac{2}{9}$ 7. $\frac{23}{32}$

Write as common fractions.

8. 3.375   9. 0.242424 . . .   10. $3.1\overline{3}$ 11. $0.\overline{234}$

12–3 **Roots of Numbers** *Pages 461–464*

12. In $\sqrt[5]{6x}$, the root index is __?__ and the radicand is __?__.
13. The positive square root of 7 is represented by __?__, and the negative square root of 7 is represented by __?__.

Evaluate each expression.

14. $\sqrt{1296}$ 15. $\sqrt{\frac{81}{25}}$ 16. $-\sqrt{\frac{1}{324}}$ 17. $-\sqrt{196}$

Find each solution set.

18. $x^2 - 49 = 0$ 20. $(x - 1)^2 = 16$
19. $6n^2 - 54 = 0$ 21. $3(t + 2)^2 = 48$

12–4 **Properties of Irrational Numbers** *Pages 464–469*

22. The decimal representation of an irrational number is a __?__ and __?__ numeral.

Compute to the nearest hundredth.

23. $\sqrt{28}$ 24. $\sqrt{4.283}$ 25. $-\sqrt{0.7162}$

26. Find, to the nearest hundredth of a foot, the length of a side of a square window whose area is 32 square feet.

12–5 **Geometric Interpretation of Square Roots** *Pages 469–472*

27. If c is the length of the hypotenuse of a right triangle and a and b are the lengths of the other two sides, then the __?__ theorem asserts that $c^2 = a^2 + b^2$.

The hypotenuse of right triangle ABC is $\overline{AB}$. How long is the side not given?

28. $AC = 12$ inches, $BC = 16$ inches

29. $AC = 9$ feet, $AB = 41$ feet

30. $BC = 12$ yards, $AB = 13$ yards

Determine whether the given numbers are the lengths of sides of a right triangle.

31. 10, 24, 26 **32.** 8, 10, 13

12–6 Multiplication, Division, and Simplification of Square-Root Radicals *Pages 472–475*

Simplify each expression.

33. $3\sqrt{5} \cdot 5\sqrt{5}$ **35.** $7\sqrt{27} \div 3\sqrt{3}$ **37.** $\sqrt{6}(2\sqrt{5} + 3\sqrt{6})$

34. $\dfrac{8\sqrt{64}}{2\sqrt{16}}$ **36.** $\dfrac{\sqrt{36x^2y^3z}}{3\sqrt{4x^2yz}}$ **38.** $\dfrac{\sqrt{12} + 4\sqrt{48}}{2\sqrt{3}}$

39. $2 + \sqrt{3}$ and $2 - \sqrt{3}$ are called __?__ of each other.

40. To simplify $\dfrac{\sqrt{3}}{1 - \sqrt{2}}$, you would multiply the numerator and denominator by __?__.

Simplify each expression.

41. $\frac{3}{5}\sqrt{75}$ **42.** $-3\sqrt{\frac{4}{3}}$ **43.** $\dfrac{2}{\sqrt{12}}$ **44.** $\dfrac{3}{2\sqrt{27}}$

12–7 Addition and Subtraction of Square-Root Radicals *Pages 475–477*

Simplify.

45. $\sqrt{3} - 2\sqrt{3} + 5\sqrt{3}$ **47.** $\sqrt{4} + \sqrt{5} + \sqrt{40} + \sqrt{100}$

46. $7\sqrt{12} - 5\sqrt{18} + \sqrt{48}$ **48.** $2\sqrt{8} - \sqrt{\frac{1}{2}} + 6\sqrt{\frac{2}{9}}$

12–8 Multiplication of Binomials Containing Square-Root Radicals *Pages 477–479*

Simplify.

49. $(3\sqrt{7} + 2)^2$ **51.** $(2\sqrt{3} + 2)(\sqrt{3} - 5)$

50. $(4\sqrt{3} - 3)(4\sqrt{3} + 3)$ **52.** $\dfrac{1}{\sqrt{5} - 2}$

12–9 Radical Equations *Pages 479–482*

Solve and check.

53. $\sqrt{3x} = 6$ **55.** $2\sqrt{x} = x - 3$

54. $3\sqrt{5y} = 15$ **56.** $\sqrt{3x + 1} + 1 = x$

EXTRA FOR EXPERTS

The Distance Formula

How do you find the distance PT between two points such as P and T on the number line below?

You compute the absolute value of the difference between the co-ordinates of the points on the number line:

$$PT = |3 - (-2)| = |3 + 2| = |5| = 5$$

Similarly: $MP = |-6 - (-2)| = |-6 + 2| = |-4| = 4$

Now look at the figure below, which shows the three points $A(4, -1)$, $B(-3, 5)$, and $C(-3, -1)$ in a coordinate plane. Notice that A and C are on the same horizontal line, while B and C are on the same vertical line. Since A and C have the same y-coordinate, you can find the distance AC by computing the absolute value of the difference between the x-coordinates of A and C:

$$AC = |4 - (-3)| = 7$$

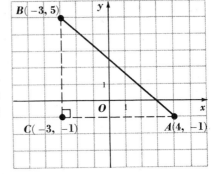

Similarly, the distance BC between B and C is the absolute value of the difference between the y-coordinates of B and C:

$$BC = |5 - (-1)| = 6$$

What is the distance between A and B? It is the length of the hypotenuse of $\triangle ABC$. Using the Pythagorean theorem (page 469), you find

$$(AB)^2 = (AC)^2 + (BC)^2 = 7^2 + 6^2 = 85.$$
$$\therefore AB = \sqrt{85}.$$

This example shows how to derive a formula for the distance between any two points $P_1(x_1, y_1)$ and $P_2(x_2, y_2)$ in a coordinate plane. In the figure at the top of the next page, you have:

$$P_1C = |x_2 - x_1|$$
$$P_2C = |y_2 - y_1|$$

Since $\triangle P_1 P_2 C$ is a right triangle,

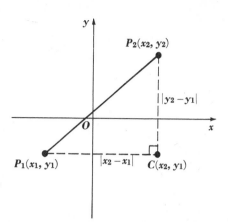

$$(P_1P_2)^2 = (P_1C)^2 + (P_2C)^2$$
$$= |x_2 - x_1|^2 + |y_2 - y_1|^2.$$

But $\quad |x_2 - x_1|^2 = (x_2 - x_1)^2$

and $\quad |y_2 - y_1|^2 = (y_2 - y_1)^2.$

Therefore,

$$(P_1P_2)^2 = (x_2 - x_1)^2 + (y_2 - y_1)^2,$$
$$P_1P_2 = \sqrt{(x_2 - x_1)^2 + (y_2 - y_1)^2}.$$

Distance Formula in the Plane

For any point $P_1(x_1, y_1)$ and $P_2(x_2, y_2)$,

$$P_1P_2 = \sqrt{(x_2 - x_1)^2 + (y_2 - y_1)^2}.$$

EXAMPLE. Find the distance between $A(3, 7)$ and $B(0, 11)$.

Solution:

1. $AB = \sqrt{(3 - 0)^2 + (7 - 11)^2}$
   $= \sqrt{3^2 + (-4)^2} = \sqrt{25} = 5.$ **Answer.**

2. $AB = \sqrt{(0 - 3)^2 + (11 - 7)^2}$
   $= \sqrt{(-3)^2 + 4^2} = \sqrt{25} = 5.$ **Answer.**

The two solutions show that the distance does not depend on which point is considered (x_1, y_1) and which point, (x_2, y_2).

Exercises

Find the distance between the two points having the given coordinates.

1. $(0, 0), (8, -15)$ 3. $(-2, 6), (3, -6)$ 5. $(-5, -2), (8, -2)$
2. $(3, 1), (-1, 4)$ 4. $(-3, 4), (4, -3)$ 6. $(0, -1), (-4, -3)$

7. Show that the points $(-3, -2)$, $(3, 2)$ and $(-2\sqrt{3}, 3\sqrt{3})$ are the vertices of an equilateral triangle.

8. Find the values of x such that $(x, 3)$ is 5 units from $(-2, -1)$.

EXTRA PROBLEM

Given the two arrays A and B of ten numbers each. Draw a flow chart of a program to read the two arrays and to compute and print the value of

$$\sqrt{[A(1) - B(1)]^2 + [A(2) - B(2)]^2 + \cdots + [A(10) - B(10)]^2}.$$

Just for Fun

You can make a person repeat himself, whether or not he wishes to do so.

You say	If he selects 28	If he selects 63
Multiply any two-digit number by 15.	$15 \times 28 = 420$	$15 \times 63 = 945$
Now multiply by 7.	$7 \times 420 = 2940$	$7 \times 945 = 6615$
Subtract 4 times the original number from the product. Why are you repeating yourself?	$4 \times 28 = 112$ $2940 - 112 = 2828$	$4 \times 63 = 252$ $6615 - 252 = 6363$
Let's start over: Multiply the original number by 13.	$13 \times 28 = 364$	$13 \times 63 = 819$
Now multiply by 8.	$8 \times 364 = 2912$	$8 \times 819 = 6552$
Subtract three times the original number — You're repeating yourself again!	$3 \times 28 = 84$ $2912 - 84 = 2828$	$3 \times 63 = 189$ $6552 - 189 = 6363$

The person repeats himself because he is multiplying by 101. Any two-digit number multiplied by 101 gives a four-digit number containing the same digits in the same order.

Let n represent the number, and carry out the computations above to show that the result in each case is $101n$.

Sir Arthur Stanley
Eddington, Astrophysicist

Could you state from memory the products of all pairs of counting numbers through 24 × 24? Not many people can, but Sir Arthur Stanley Eddington, the distinguished British astrophysicist, is said to have been able to perform that feat at the age of five. Before he was ten, he was experienced in the use of the telescope.

Eddington distinguished himself in mathematics at Cambridge University, standing first in his class, but his primary interest was in astronomy. He made major contributions to the study of the interiors of stars and was among the earliest to recognize the importance of Einstein's theory of relativity. However, he is probably better known to the general public for his semi-popular books on scientific subjects, the best known of which are *The Nature of the Physical World* (1928) and *The Expanding Universe* (1933). He was knighted in 1930, and in 1938 he received the Order of Merit.

This brilliant scientist was a very shy person, who had great difficulty in speaking extemporaneously in public. However, his prepared speeches and his published writings were notable for their dramatic contrasts, their humor, and their apt examples. For instance, he illustrated the process of abstraction used in the exact sciences by citing the problem of an elephant sliding down a grassy hillside. He complained that, to the scientist, this exploit loses all its charm and becomes merely an exercise involving a *mass* of two tons, an *angle* of 60°, and a *coefficient of friction*.

At the time of his death, Eddington had nearly completed a book dealing with what he called *The Fundamental Theory*. This was concerned with the unity of the forces of nature, working on the cosmic and the atomic scale.

Cumulative Review: Chapters 1–12

Given that a has the value 3, b has the value -2, and c has the value 0, evaluate:

1. $\dfrac{2a + 5b}{b}$

3. $(a - 2b)c$

2. $(a + b)(a - b)$

4. $\dfrac{4a^2 - 2b^2}{b^2 + 2c}$

5. If $f(x) = 3x^2 - 2x + 5$, and if the domain of f is $\{-2, 0, 2\}$, find the range of f.

6. If $g(x) = 2x^2 - x + 5$, find: **a.** $g(-1)$ **b.** $g(0)$ **c.** $g(1)$

Express as a polynomial in simple form.

7. $(2y^2 - 3y + 7) + (y^2 - y - 8)$

9. $z(3z^2 - 2z + 1)$

8. $(x^3 + 3x^2 - 7) - (4x^2 + x^3 - 7)$

10. $(z + 3)(2z - 1)$

Express as a single fraction in lowest terms.

11. $\dfrac{3x^2 + 2x}{5x}$

14. $\dfrac{x + 1}{x - 3} \cdot \dfrac{x^2 - x - 6}{x^2 + 4x + 3}$

12. $\dfrac{2c}{3} - \dfrac{c - 1}{2}$

15. $\dfrac{a^2 - 4a}{2a + 1} \div \dfrac{a - 4}{4a^2 - 1}$

13. $\dfrac{3xy^2}{2z} \cdot \dfrac{5z^2}{15xy}$

16. $\dfrac{2 + \dfrac{r}{s}}{3 - \dfrac{2r}{s}}$

Solve and check each equation.

17. $3x + 2 = x - 6$

20. $r^2 - 3r = 0$

18. $\dfrac{n}{2} + \dfrac{2n}{3} = n - 5$

21. $k^2 - 5k - 14 = 0$

19. $\dfrac{t + 2}{3} - \dfrac{t - 1}{2} = t - 7$

22. $(t + 1)^2 = 25$

Graph the solution set of each inequality on the number line.

23. $2y - 7 \le 13$

24. $4n + (3n - 2) > n - 5$

Graph each sentence.

25. $x - y = 5$ **27.** $2x + y \leq 7$ **29.** $y = 2x^2$

26. $3x + 4y = 12$ **28.** $x - y < 0$ **30.** $y = x^2 - 4$

31. Solve the system

$$2x + y = 3$$
$$x - y = 9$$

by addition or subtraction.

32. Solve the system

$$3a + 2b = 13$$
$$2a - b = 11$$

by substitution.

Simplify.

33. $\sqrt{64n^2}$ **35.** $\sqrt{2z} \cdot \sqrt{8z^3}$

34. $-\sqrt{0.25r^4}$ **36.** $\dfrac{2}{\sqrt{11}}$

Solve these problems.

37. A freight train left Central City at 6 A.M. traveling at 30 miles per hour. At 8 A.M., a passenger train traveling 50 miles per hour left the same station along a parallel track. When did the passenger train overtake the freight train?

38. Find two complementary angles one of which measures 18° less than 3 times the other.

39. The product of two consecutive integers is 13 greater than the square of the lesser of the two integers. Find the integers.

40. How much water must be added to 2 quarts of a 30% salt solution to obtain a 20% solution?

41. One pipe can fill a reservoir in 5 days while another pipe can fill the same reservoir in 3 days. How long will it take both pipes together to fill the reservoir?

42. Mr. Roberts is 5 times as old as his daughter. In 5 years, he will be 3 times as old as his daughter. How old is his daughter now?

*. . . two 90-foot parabolic antennas in California,
used to locate radio sources in space*

Quadratic Equations and Inequalities

As in the study of a language, mathematics becomes more interesting after the basic skills have been acquired. You will find this to be true in this chapter where you will study about quadratic equations and inequalities. With such open sentences you will increase your power to solve problems.

GENERAL METHODS OF SOLVING QUADRATIC EQUATIONS

13–1 The Square-Root Property

A quadratic equation can be put into the **standard form**

$$ax^2 + bx + c = 0,$$

where a, b, and c are real numbers and $a \neq 0$. At present your chief tool in solving such equations is factoring (page 273). If the equation is of the form $ax^2 + c = 0$, it is a *pure quadratic* and may be solved by using the following:

Property of Square Roots of Equal Numbers

If r and s are any real numbers, $r^2 = s^2$ if and only if $r = s$ or $r = -s$.

EXAMPLE 1. Solve $t^2 - 18 = 0$.

Solution:
$$t^2 - 18 = 0$$
$$t^2 = 18$$

$$t = \sqrt{18} \quad \text{or} \quad t = -\sqrt{18}$$
$$t = 3\sqrt{2} \qquad\qquad t = -3\sqrt{2}$$

Check:
$$(3\sqrt{2})^2 - 18 \stackrel{?}{=} 0 \qquad (-3\sqrt{2})^2 - 18 \stackrel{?}{=} 0$$
$$18 - 18 = 0 \checkmark \qquad\qquad 18 - 18 = 0 \checkmark$$

$\therefore$ the solution set is $\{3\sqrt{2},\ -3\sqrt{2}\}$. **Answer.**

EXAMPLE 2. Solve $36r^2 + 9 = 0$.

Solution:
$$36r^2 + 9 = 0$$
$$36r^2 = -9$$
$$r^2 = -\tfrac{9}{36}$$

Since negative numbers have no square roots in the set of real numbers, $36r^2 + 9 = 0$ is not solvable in the real number system.

This method also solves quadratic equations having a trinomial square as one member and a nonnegative constant as the other.

EXAMPLE 3. Solve $x^2 - 4x + 4 = 16$.

Solution:
$$x^2 - 4x + 4 = 16$$
$$(x - 2)^2 = 16$$
$$\therefore x - 2 = \pm\sqrt{16}.$$

$$x - 2 = 4 \quad \text{or} \quad x - 2 = -4$$
$$x = 6 \qquad\qquad x = -2$$

Do the elements of $\{-2, 6\}$ check as the roots of the given equation?

Oral Exercises

Give the roots of each equation.

1. $n^2 = 1$
2. $m^2 = 16$
3. $t^2 = \tfrac{1}{4}$
4. $r^2 = \tfrac{1}{25}$

5. $p^2 - 4 = 0$
6. $t^2 - 9 = 0$
7. $x^2 - 3 = 0$
8. $y^2 - 12 = 0$

9. $9z^2 = 1$
10. $36r^2 = 1$
11. $49n^2 = 9$
12. $25t^2 = 4$

13. $x^2 + 2x + 1 = 0$
14. $y^2 - 2y + 1 = 0$

15. $9y^2 - \tfrac{1}{4} = 0$
16. $10t^2 - \tfrac{1}{10} = 0$

Written Exercises

Solve each equation.

A

1. $t^2 = 121$
2. $r^2 = 144$
3. $4x^2 = 81$

4. $49y^2 = 64$
5. $12 - x^2 = 0$
6. $32 - a^2 = 0$

7. $50k^2 - 2 = 0$
8. $72n^2 - 2 = 0$
9. $6t^2 - \tfrac{1}{24} = 0$

10. $3n^2 - \frac{1}{27} = 0$ **15.** $(x - 1)^2 = 25$ **20.** $(t + \frac{1}{3})^2 = \frac{4}{9}$

11. $\frac{1}{4}x^2 - 81 = 0$ **16.** $(y + 1)^2 = 49$ **21.** $n^2 + 2n + 1 = 9$

12. $\frac{4}{9}z^2 - 1 = 0$ **17.** $9(z + 3)^2 = 81$ **22.** $k^2 - 4k + 4 = 36$

13. $(t + 2)^2 = 9$ **18.** $4(k - 5)^2 = 64$ **23.** $t^2 - 10t + 25 = 4$

14. $(s - 3)^2 = 16$ **19.** $(x - \frac{2}{5})^2 = \frac{9}{25}$ **24.** $r^2 + 14r + 49 = 100$

B **25.** $(y - 4)^2 = 3$ **29.** $(x + \frac{1}{2})^2 = \frac{1}{2}$ **33.** $\frac{1}{3}p^3 - 3p = 0$

26. $(t - 2)^2 = 5$ **30.** $(x - \frac{2}{3})^2 = \frac{1}{3}$ **34.** $7y - \frac{1}{7}y^3 = 0$

27. $(s + 5)^2 = 7$ **31.** $n^3 - n = 0$ **35.** $x^3 = 5x$

28. $(n + 3)^2 = 6$ **32.** $4k - k^3 = 0$ **36.** $s^3 = 3s$

C **37.** $r^2 - 2\sqrt{5}\,r + 5 = 0$ **39.** $a^2 + 2\sqrt{6}\,a + 6 = 0$

38. $z^2 + 2\sqrt{2}\,z + 2 = 0$ **40.** $b^2 - 2\sqrt{7}\,b + 7 = 0$

41. Explain why $x^2 + 8 = 0$ is not solvable over $\Re$.

42. Explain why $x^4 + 1 = 0$ is not solvable over $\Re$.

13–2   Sum and Product of the Roots of a Quadratic Equation

If r and s are the roots of a quadratic equation in x, then you know that the equation is equivalent to the disjunction:

$$x - r = 0 \quad \textbf{or} \quad x - s = 0$$

Therefore, by the zero-product property (page 275) the equation is also equivalent to

$$(x - r)(x - s) = 0$$

or

$$x^2 - (r + s)x + rs = 0.$$

This latter equation has the form "$x^2 + bx + c = 0$" where $-(r + s) = b$ and $rs = c$. Thus, you have:

The Property of the Sum and Product of the Roots of a Quadratic Equation

If the roots of a quadratic equation of the form

$$x^2 + bx + c = 0$$

are r and s, then

$$r + s = -b \quad \text{and} \quad rs = c.$$

EXAMPLE 1. Is $\{2, 7\}$ the solution set of $y^2 - 9y + 14 = 0$?

Solution: $\qquad y^2 - 9y + 14 = 0;\qquad b = -9,\qquad c = 14$

$\qquad\qquad\quad r + s = 2 + 7 = 9 = -(-9) = -b\ \checkmark$

$\qquad\qquad\qquad rs = 2 \cdot 7 = 14 = c\ \checkmark$

$\qquad\qquad \therefore\ \{2, 7\}$ is the solution set of $y^2 - 9y + 14 = 0$.   **Answer.**

EXAMPLE 2. Is $\{5 + \sqrt{2}, 5 - \sqrt{2}\}$ the solution set of

$$n^2 - 10n + 23 = 0?$$

Solution:

Is the sum of the roots 10?	Is the product of the roots 23?
$5 + \sqrt{2} + 5 - \sqrt{2} \overset{?}{=} 10$	$(5 + \sqrt{2})(5 - \sqrt{2}) \overset{?}{=} 23$
$10 = 10\ \checkmark$	$25 - 2 = 23\ \checkmark$

$\therefore\ \{5 + \sqrt{2}, 5 - \sqrt{2}\}$ is the solution set of $n^2 - 10n + 23 = 0$.   **Answer.**

The expressions $5 + \sqrt{2}$ and $5 - \sqrt{2}$ in Example 2 may be written as the single expression $5 \pm \sqrt{2}$ (read "5 plus or minus $\sqrt{2}$").

Oral Exercises

State the sum and the product of the roots of each equation.

1. $x^2 - 8x + 9 = 0$
2. $y^2 + 3y - 8 = 0$
3. $z^2 + 7z - 6 = 0$
4. $t^2 - t + 3 = 0$
5. $r^2 + r - 7 = 0$

6. $n^2 + 3n - 5 = 0$
7. $3k^2 + 6k - 3 = 0$
8. $4n^2 + 20n - 16 = 0$
9. $p^2 + 3p = 8$
10. $t^2 - 5t = -3$

Is the given set the solution set of the given equation?

11. $y^2 - 3y - 28 = 0$ $\{4, -7\}$
12. $n^2 + 5n - 6 = 0$ $\{2, 3\}$
13. $k^2 - 3k = 0$ $\{0, 3\}$
14. $t^2 + 7t = 0$ $\{0, -7\}$

15. $18 - 3n + n^2 = 0$ $\{6, -3\}$
16. $r^2 = 2r + 8$ $\{-2, 4\}$
17. $16 = k^2$ $\{4, -4\}$
18. $4m^2 = 36$ $\{6, -6\}$

Written Exercises

Determine whether or not the given set is the solution set of the given equation.

A

1. $x^2 - 8x - 20 = 0$ $\{10, -2\}$
2. $t^2 + 12t - 28 = 0$ $\{4, -7\}$
3. $2s^2 - 9s - 5 = 0$ $\{-\frac{1}{2}, 5\}$
4. $3n^2 - n - 10 = 0$ $\{-\frac{5}{3}, 2\}$

5. $4z^2 + 8z + 3 = 0$ $\{-\frac{3}{2}, -\frac{1}{2}\}$ **7.** $6k^2 - 11k + 3 = 0$ $\{\frac{1}{3}, \frac{3}{2}\}$

6. $7t^2 - 33t - 10 = 0$ $\{-\frac{2}{7}, 5\}$ **8.** $4t^2 + 4t + 1 = 0$ $\{-\frac{1}{2}, \frac{1}{2}\}$

9. $x^2 - 2x - 1 = 0$ $\qquad \{1 \pm \sqrt{2}\}$

10. $y^2 + 6y - 1 = 10$ $\qquad \{-3 \pm \sqrt{10}\}$

11. $5n^2 - 8n + 1 = 0$ $\qquad \left\{\dfrac{4 \pm \sqrt{10}}{5}\right\}$

12. $3t^2 - 2t - 9 = 0$ $\qquad \left\{\dfrac{1 \pm \sqrt{7}}{2}\right\}$

Find a quadratic equation having the given solution set.

SAMPLE. $\{\sqrt{3}, -\sqrt{3}\}$

Solution: $(x - \sqrt{3})[x - (-\sqrt{3})] = 0$
$$(x - \sqrt{3})(x + \sqrt{3}) = 0$$
$$x^2 - 3 = 0. \quad \textbf{Answer.}$$

B **13.** $\{1, 3\}$ **17.** $\{5, 0\}$ **21.** $\{\sqrt{11}\}$

14. $\{7, 5\}$ **18.** $\{0, -7\}$ **22.** $\{3\sqrt{2}\}$

15. $\{-3, 2\}$ **19.** $\{\sqrt{6}, -\sqrt{6}\}$ **23.** $\{2 - \sqrt{3}, 2 + \sqrt{3}\}$

16. $\{-6, -3\}$ **20.** $\{2\sqrt{5}, -2\sqrt{5}\}$ **24.** $\{5 - \sqrt{2}, 5 + \sqrt{2}\}$

13–3   Solution by Completing a Trinomial Square

If you can transform a quadratic equation into one having a trinomial square as a member, you can find its solution set.

EXAMPLE 1.   Solve $x^2 + 4x - 12 = 0$.

Solution:

1. Write an equivalent equation with the constant term as right member.

$$x^2 + 4x - 12 = 0$$
$$x^2 + 4x \quad\quad = 12$$

2. Add to both members the number making the left member a trinomial square.

$$x^2 + 4x + 4 = 12 + 4$$
$$(x + 2)^2 = 16$$

3. Use the property of square roots.

$$x + 2 = \pm 4$$

4. Form two linear equations.

$$x + 2 = 4 \qquad \text{or} \qquad x + 2 = -4$$

5. Solve.

$$x = 2 \qquad\qquad\qquad x = -6$$

6. *Check.*

$$2^2 + 4(2) - 12 \stackrel{?}{=} 0 \qquad (-6)^2 + 4(-6) - 12 = 0$$
$$0 = 0 \checkmark \qquad\qquad\qquad 0 = 0 \checkmark$$

$\therefore$ the solution set is $\{2, -6\}$.   **Answer.**

The only unfamiliar step in this solution is the second, called **completing a trinomial square**. To apply the method of this example to any quadratic equation in the form $x^2 + bx = k$, you must be able to determine what to add to $x^2 + bx$ to produce a trinomial square.

Analyze the following trinomials, which are squares of binomials.

$$(x + 7)^2 = x^2 + 2(7)x + 7^2 \qquad (x - n)^2 = x^2 + 2(-n)x + (-n)^2$$

$$(x - 5)^2 = x^2 + 2(-5)x + (-5)^2 \qquad \left(x + \frac{b}{2}\right)^2 = x^2 + 2\left(\frac{b}{2}\right)x + \left(\frac{b}{2}\right)^2$$

Do you see that in each case, the *constant term is the square of half the coefficient of the linear term?*

EXAMPLE 2. What value of c makes $t^2 - \frac{3}{4}t + c$ a trinomial square?

Solution: Half the coefficient of the linear term is

$$\tfrac{1}{2}(-\tfrac{3}{4}) = -\tfrac{3}{8}.$$
$$\therefore c = (-\tfrac{3}{8})^2 = \tfrac{9}{64}.$$

Check: Is $t^2 - \frac{3}{4}t + \frac{9}{64}$ a trinomial square?

$$t^2 - \tfrac{3}{4}t + \tfrac{9}{64} = (t - \tfrac{3}{8})(t - \tfrac{3}{8})$$
$$= (t - \tfrac{3}{8})^2 \checkmark$$
$$\therefore c = \tfrac{9}{64}. \quad \text{Answer.}$$

To solve an equation whose quadratic term has a coefficient other than 1, you first can use the multiplication property of equality (page 123) and multiply each term by the reciprocal of the coefficient of the quadratic term.

EXAMPLE 3. Solve $2x^2 - 3x - 3 = 0$.

Solution:
$$2x^2 - 3x - 3 = 0$$

Multiply by $\frac{1}{2}$ $\qquad x^2 - \frac{3}{2}x - \frac{3}{2} = 0$

(or divide by 2): $\qquad x^2 - \frac{3}{2}x \qquad = \frac{3}{2}$

$$x^2 - \tfrac{3}{2}x + \tfrac{9}{16} = \tfrac{3}{2} + \tfrac{9}{16}$$
$$(x - \tfrac{3}{4})^2 = \tfrac{33}{16}$$
$$x - \tfrac{3}{4} = \pm\sqrt{\tfrac{33}{16}}$$

$$x - \tfrac{3}{4} = \sqrt{\tfrac{33}{16}} \quad \bigg| \quad x - \tfrac{3}{4} = -\sqrt{\tfrac{33}{16}}$$

$$x = \frac{3}{4} + \frac{\sqrt{33}}{4} \quad \bigg| \quad x = \frac{3}{4} - \frac{\sqrt{33}}{4}$$

$$x = \frac{3 + \sqrt{33}}{4} \quad \bigg| \quad x = \frac{3 - \sqrt{33}}{4}$$

Check:

Is the sum of the roots $-(-\frac{3}{2})$?	Is the product of the roots $-\frac{3}{2}$?
$$\frac{3+\sqrt{33}}{4} + \frac{3-\sqrt{33}}{4} \overset{?}{=} -\left(\frac{-3}{2}\right)$$	$$\left(\frac{3+\sqrt{33}}{4}\right)\left(\frac{3-\sqrt{33}}{4}\right) \overset{?}{=} -\frac{3}{2}$$
$$\frac{3}{2} = \frac{3}{2} \checkmark$$	$$\frac{9-33}{16} \overset{?}{=} -\frac{3}{2}$$
	$$-\frac{3}{2} = -\frac{3}{2} \checkmark$$

$\therefore$ the solution set is $\left\{ \dfrac{3+\sqrt{33}}{4},\ \dfrac{3-\sqrt{33}}{4} \right\}$.   Answer.

For computational purposes, you sometimes need decimal approximations of such roots (section 12–4). To approximate them to the nearest tenth, use a two-decimal-place approximation of $\sqrt{33}$ from the table in the Appendix, and perform the indicated operations:

$$\frac{3+\sqrt{33}}{4} \doteq \frac{3+5.75}{4} = \frac{8.75}{4} \doteq 2.19 \doteq 2.2$$

$$\frac{3-\sqrt{33}}{4} \doteq \frac{3-5.75}{4} = \frac{-2.75}{4} \doteq -0.69 \doteq -0.7$$

$\therefore$ to the nearest tenth, the roots are 2.2 and -0.7.   Answer.

Oral Exercises

For what value of c will the given trinomial be the square of a binomial?

1. $x^2 + 6x + c$
2. $y^2 + 4y + c$
3. $n^2 - 10n + c$
4. $t^2 - 16t + c$
5. $r^2 + r + c$
6. $t^2 - 3t + c$

7. $z^2 + 5z + c$
8. $k^2 - 7k + c$
9. $n^2 - 0.4n + c$
10. $x^2 + 0.2x + c$
11. $y^2 - 1.4y + c$
12. $a^2 + 1.6a + c$

13. $b^2 + \frac{1}{2}b + c$
14. $d^2 - \frac{1}{3}d + c$
15. $y^2 + \frac{2}{3}y + c$
16. $m^2 - \frac{4}{5}y + c$
17. $x^2 + bx + c$
18. $x^2 - bx + c$

Written Exercises

Solve by completing the square. Give irrational roots in radical form and also approximate them to the nearest tenth.

1. $n^2 + 2n = 24$
2. $t^2 - 4t = 21$
3. $y^2 - 8y = 4$

4. $z^2 - 4z = 2$
5. $x^2 + 2x - 1 = 0$
6. $a^2 + 2a - 7 = 0$

7. $t^2 - 5t = 0$
8. $r^2 + 3r = 0$
9. $s^2 - s - 3 = 0$

10. $u^2 - 5u + 3 = 0$

11. $2z^2 - 6z - 5 = 0$

12. $4p^2 + 4p - 3 = 0$

13. $2x^2 = x + 2$

14. $2y^2 = 3y + 1$

15. $3n^2 + n = 1$

16. $4p^2 - 2p = 1$

B **17.** $x^2 - \frac{4}{3}x = 1$

18. $a^2 - \frac{5}{2}a = 1$

19. $3y^2 + y - \frac{1}{2} = 0$

20. $\frac{1}{3}n^2 + \frac{3}{2}n = 3$

21. $5z = \dfrac{1 - 3z}{z - 1}$

22. $3y = \dfrac{y + 2}{y - 1}$

23. $x - 1 = \dfrac{-2x}{x + 1}$

24. $2y + 2 = \dfrac{-y}{y + 2}$

Solve for x in terms of a, b, or c.

C **25.** $x^2 - 2x + c = 0$

26. $x^2 - bx - 1 = 0$

27. $x^2 + bx + c = 0$

28. $ax^2 + bx + c = 0$

Problems

A **1.** The dimensions of a sheet of paper can be represented by consecutive odd integers. Its area is 99 square inches. Find its dimensions.

2. A chalk board is two feet wider than it is high. Its area is 24 square feet. Find its length and height.

3. A large package of brownie mix made 154 brownies cut into 1-inch squares. If the pan was 3 inches longer than it was wide, find the dimensions of the pan.

4. A bookshelf is 5 times longer than it is deep. If the area of the surface of the bookshelf is 625 square inches, find the dimensions of the surface.

5. Two (square) checkerboards together have an area of 169 square inches. One has a side that is 7 inches longer than the other. Find the side of each.

6. To lay wall-to-wall carpeting in a living room and dining room takes 612 square feet of carpet. The living-room floor is 3 feet longer than it is wide. The dining-room floor is 6 feet wider than the width of the living room, and its length is twice the width of the living room. Find the dimensions of each room.

7. The members of a certain organization decided to donate 2000 dollars to charity, and to share the cost of the contribution equally. If the club had 20 more members, each would have contributed 5 dollars less. How many members now belong to the organization?

8. Each year a certain company divides 7200 dollars equally among its employees. This year the company employs 6 more people than last year, and therefore each employee received 60 dollars less. How much did each employee receive last year?

9. Marla and Kay live 13 miles apart. If Marla drives directly south, and Kay drives directly west, they will meet. If Kay will have driven 7 miles more than Marla when they meet, how far will each have driven?

10. The Boutique Fashion Shop bought some dresses for 240 dollars. The owners kept 2 of the dresses for themselves and sold the rest at a gain of 3 dollars each for a total profit of 30 dollars. How many did they sell?

13–4 Solution by Using the Quadratic Formula

For a given set of coefficients a, b, and c, $a \neq 0$, the quadratic equation $ax^2 + bx + c = 0$ can be transformed to express the variable x directly in terms of a, b, and c by completing the square. Study carefully the following parallel treatment of the *standard quadratic equation* and of a special quadratic equation.

$$ax^2 + bx + c = 0 \qquad\qquad 2x^2 - 5x + 1 = 0$$

$$x^2 + \frac{b}{a}x + \frac{c}{a} = 0 \qquad\qquad x^2 - \tfrac{5}{2}x + \tfrac{1}{2} = 0$$

$$x^2 + \frac{b}{a}x \;\;= -\frac{c}{a} \qquad\qquad x^2 - \tfrac{5}{2}x \;\;= -\tfrac{1}{2}$$

$$x^2 + \frac{b}{a}x + \left(\frac{b}{2a}\right)^2 = -\frac{c}{a} + \left(\frac{b}{2a}\right)^2 \qquad\qquad x^2 - \tfrac{5}{2}x + (\tfrac{5}{4})^2 = -\tfrac{1}{2} + (\tfrac{5}{4})^2$$

$$\left(x + \frac{b}{2a}\right)^2 = -\frac{c}{a} + \frac{b^2}{4a^2} \qquad\qquad (x - \tfrac{5}{4})^2 = -\tfrac{1}{2} + \tfrac{25}{16}$$

$$\left(x + \frac{b}{2a}\right)^2 = \frac{b^2 - 4ac}{4a^2} \qquad\qquad (x - \tfrac{5}{4})^2 = \tfrac{17}{16}$$

$$x + \frac{b}{2a} = \pm\sqrt{\frac{b^2 - 4ac}{4a^2}}\;{}^* \qquad\qquad x - \tfrac{5}{4} = \pm\sqrt{\tfrac{17}{16}}$$

$$x = -\frac{b}{2a} \pm \sqrt{\frac{b^2 - 4ac}{4a^2}} \qquad\qquad x = \tfrac{5}{4} \pm \sqrt{\tfrac{17}{16}}$$

$$x = -\frac{b}{2a} \pm \frac{\sqrt{b^2 - 4ac}}{2a} \qquad\qquad x = \frac{5}{4} \pm \frac{\sqrt{17}}{4}$$

$$x = \frac{-b \pm \sqrt{b^2 - 4ac}}{2a} \qquad\qquad x = \frac{5 \pm \sqrt{17}}{4}$$

*If $b^2 - 4ac \geq 0$.

The last sentence in the preceding proof is actually a disjunction of two linear equations and is called the **quadratic formula**. If the root of either linear equation is taken as the value of x and substituted in the original quadratic equation, the resulting statement is $0 = 0$. In developing the quadratic formula, notice the assumptions that $a \neq 0$ and that $\sqrt{b^2 - 4ac}$ is a real number ($b^2 - 4ac \geq 0$).

To solve any quadratic equation of the form

$$ax^2 + bx + c = 0,$$

substitute the coefficients in the quadratic formula,

$$x = \frac{-b \pm \sqrt{b^2 - 4ac}}{2a},$$

and evaluate.

EXAMPLE.   **Solve $2x^2 - 5x + 1 = 0$ by using the quadratic formula.**

Solution:

$$2x^2 - 5x + 1 = 0$$

$$x = \frac{-b \pm \sqrt{b^2 - 4ac}}{2a} ; \quad a = 2, \quad b = -5, \quad c = 1$$

$$x = \frac{-(-5) \pm \sqrt{(-5)^2 - 4(2)(1)}}{2(2)}$$

$$x = \frac{5 \pm \sqrt{25 - 8}}{4} = \frac{5 \pm \sqrt{17}}{4}$$

Check: Is the sum of the roots $-(-\frac{5}{2})$? Is the product of the roots $\frac{1}{2}$? Checking that each answer is "Yes" is left to you.

$\therefore$ the solution set is $\left\{ \dfrac{5 + \sqrt{17}}{4}, \dfrac{5 - \sqrt{17}}{4} \right\}$.   **Answer.**

Oral Exercises

State the values of a, b, and c for each equation.

1. $x^2 + 3x + 2 = 0$

2. $y^2 - 3y + 3 = 0$

3. $2z^2 + z - 5 = 0$

4. $3u^2 - 5u - 8 = 0$

5. $6 - 3v^2 = 2v$

6. $2 + 4n = n^2$

7. $x - 2x^2 = -3$

8. $3y + 2y^2 = 5$

9. $x^2 = 3x$

10. $y^2 + 2y = 0$

11. $3z^2 + 5 = 0$

12. $2s^2 = 3$

13. $r^2 = 0$

14. $3n^2 = 0$

15. $t = 4t^2$

16. $0 = 6y - 5y^2$

Written Exercises

Use the quadratic formula to solve each equation. Give irrational roots in simplest radical form and also approximate them to the nearest tenth.

1. $t^2 - 9t + 20 = 0$

2. $r^2 + 9r - 10 = 0$

3. $x^2 + 10x - 2 = 0$

4. $y^2 + 6y - 1 = 0$

5. $2n^2 + 4n + 1 = 0$

6. $3p^2 - 7p - 3 = 0$

7. $t^2 - 2t - 5 = 0$

8. $r^2 + 4r + 1 = 0$

9. $3y^2 = 4y + 2$

10. $3s = 1 - 2s^2$

11. $5x^2 + 2x = 2$

12. $5y - 2 = 3y^2$

13. $5t^2 = 5t$

14. $3k^2 = 14$

Factor each polynomial over $\mathcal{R}$.

SAMPLE. $x^2 - 2x - 2$

Solution: Use the fact that if r_1 and r_2 are roots of $x^2 - 2x - 2 = 0$, then $(x - r_1)$ and $(x - r_2)$ are factors of $x^2 - 2x - 2$.

Solve $x^2 - 2x - 2 = 0$.

By the quadratic formula,

$$x = \frac{2 \pm \sqrt{4 + 8}}{2} = \frac{2 \pm \sqrt{12}}{2} = \frac{2 \pm 2\sqrt{3}}{2} = 1 \pm \sqrt{3}.$$

$\therefore x^2 - 2x - 2 = (x - 1 - \sqrt{3})(x - 1 + \sqrt{3})$, as you can check by multiplication. **Answer.**

B 15. $x^2 - 2x - 1$

16. $n^2 - 4n - 6$

17. $s^2 - 6s - 1$

18. $r^2 + 4r - 4$

Show that the given equation has no real roots.

19. $x^2 + 2x + 8 = 0$

20. $3x^2 - 2x + 5 = 0$

21. $\sqrt{z} = z + 3$

22. $3\sqrt{z} = z + 5$

Problems

Give irrational answers to the nearest tenth. Reject inappropriate roots.

A **1.** A one-room apartment of 490 square feet has folding doors such that it can be divided into a square kitchen area and a rectangular living room area (see diagram). The ratio of the length of the living room to its width is $3:2$. Find the dimensions of each division.

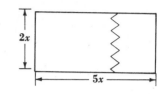

2. A square section of wood floor is 144 square inches in area. The section has 6 rectangular pieces, 4 outside pieces of equal area, and 2 smaller inside pieces of equal area (see diagram). The length of each outside piece is 3 times its width. Find dimensions of the pieces.

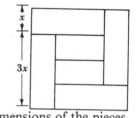

3. A square picture has a two-inch frame. If the area of the picture is $\frac{2}{3}$ of the total area, what are the dimensions of the frame?

4. A quilt is made from 150 small squares. It is possible to make a quilt of the same size using 100 squares 1 inch longer on a side. How long is each small square?

5. The perimeter of a triangle is 3 feet. Two sides form a right angle and are in the ratio of $3:4$. Find the lengths of all 3 sides.

6. A sailboat heads east from a dock at the same time that a motorboat heads north from the dock. The motorboat travels 7 miles per hour faster than the sailboat. The boats are 13 miles apart at the end of one hour. Find the rate of each boat.

7. A jet plane flying 3000 miles cross country ran into a strong tail wind that increased the plane's speed by 100 miles per hour and thus shortened its flying time by 1 hour. What was its ground speed?

8. A rectangular ottoman having a volume of 2592 cubic inches is to be covered on its top and sides with heavy fabric. The covering is made by cutting a 12-inch square from each corner of a rectangular piece of fabric that is 6 inches longer than it is wide. Find the dimensions of the ottoman.

9. At Hillsdale High School 1000 students buy lunch every day for 25 cents each. If the cafeteria raises the price, for each increase of 1 cent, 4 students will bring their own lunches. After a price increase, 44 dollars more than usual was taken in by the cafeteria. How many students had stopped buying lunch?

10. A book club has a bonus of 16 dollars worth of books per year for each of its 1000 members. The bonus is increased by 1 cent for each new member. How many new members would increase the total bonus money by approximately 900 dollars?

B **11.** A boat takes 1 hour longer to go 36 miles up a river than to return. If the river flows at 3 miles per hour, find the rate at which the boat travels in still water.

12. The average speed of a plane in still air is 425 miles per hour. With a constant wind blowing, the plane flies 900 miles into the wind and returns. The round trip takes $4\frac{1}{4}$ hours of flying time. Find the speed of the wind.

13. A workman earned $180 in a certain number of days. If his daily wage had been $2 less, he would have taken one more day to earn the same amount. Find how many days he worked at the higher rate.

14. One car starts traveling west along a road. At the same time, from the same point, another car starts traveling south at a speed 15 miles per hour faster than that of the first car. After one hour and twenty minutes the cars are 100 miles apart. At what speeds are they traveling?

EXTRA PROBLEMS

1. Draw a flow chart of a program to read and then print three positive integers a, b, and c, and to determine whether or not these numbers are the measures of the sides of a right triangle. The output message should be "right triangle" or "not a right triangle" as the case may be. (*Hint:* You have a right triangle if $a^2 + b^2 = c^2$, or $a^2 + c^2 = b^2$, or $b^2 + c^2 = a^2$.)

2. Draw a flow chart of a program to read and print three numbers a, b, and c, and to determine and print the real roots of

$$ax^2 + bx + c = 0.$$

Assume that *not both a* and *b* are zero. (*Hint:* If $a = 0$, the equation is linear and has one root. If $a \neq 0$, the equation is quadratic and has either two or no real roots, depending on the value of $b^2 - 4ac$.)

13–5 **The Nature of the Roots of a Quadratic Equation (Optional)**

In Figure 13–1 on the next page, the parabola at the far left is the graph of the function $f: x \to y = x^2 + 22x + 120$, $x \in \mathcal{R}$. The figure also shows the graphs of the functions $x \to y = -x^2 - 4x - 4$ and $x \to y = x^2 - 12x + 40$, $x \in \mathcal{R}$. (Recall section 10–10.)

The y-coordinate of every point on the x-axis is 0. Therefore, by replacing y with "0" in the formula for any of the functions and solving the resulting quadratic equation, you can determine the abscissa of any point where the graph intersects the x-axis. Such an abscissa is called an ***x*-intercept**.

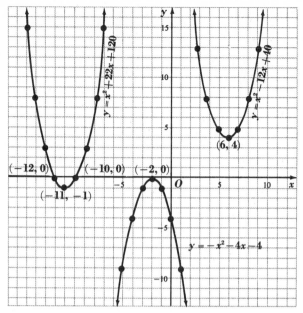

Figure 13–1

Case 1	*Case 2*	*Case 3*
$y = x^2 + 22x + 120$	$y = -x^2 - 4x - 4$	$y = x^2 - 12x + 40$
$0 = x^2 + 22x + 120$	$0 = -x^2 - 4x - 4$	$0 = x^2 - 12x + 40$
$x = \dfrac{-22 \pm \sqrt{484 - 480}}{2}$	$x = \dfrac{4 \pm \sqrt{16 - 16}}{-2}$	$x = \dfrac{12 \pm \sqrt{144 - 160}}{2}$
$x = -11 \pm 1$	$x = -2 \pm 0$	$x = \dfrac{12 \pm \sqrt{-16}}{2}$
$x = -10$ or $x = -12$	$x = -2$	But $\sqrt{-16}$ is not a real
$\therefore$ there are *two* x-intercepts, -10 and -12.	$\therefore$ -2 is a double root (page 278) so that there is *one* x-intercept, -2.	number and so neither is $\dfrac{12 \pm \sqrt{-16}}{2}$.
		$\therefore$ there is *no* x-intercept.

The three cases are analyzed in the following chart:

	Number of points in common with the x-axis	Number of different real roots of the equation	Value of $b^2 - 4ac$
Case 1	2	2	a positive number
Case 2	1	1 (a double root)	zero
Case 3	0	0	a negative number

Do you see that the value of $b^2 - 4ac$ is the key to these cases? If $b^2 - 4ac > 0$, then $\sqrt{b^2 - 4ac}$ is positive. Thus, "$ax^2 + bx + c = 0$" has two different roots, because

$$\frac{-b + \sqrt{b^2 - 4ac}}{2a} \neq \frac{-b - \sqrt{b^2 - 4ac}}{2a}.$$

But if $b^2 - 4ac = 0$, then $\sqrt{b^2 - 4ac} = 0$ and you find that $\frac{-b + 0}{2a} = \frac{-b - 0}{2a} = \frac{-b}{2a}$, so that there is only one root. But, for $b^2 - 4ac < 0$, no real root exists, because square roots of negative numbers do not exist in the real number system (page 461).

A quadratic equation with real coefficients can have

1. two different real roots ($b^2 - 4ac > 0$)
2. one (double) real root ($b^2 - 4ac = 0$), or
3. no real roots ($b^2 - 4ac < 0$).

Because the value of $b^2 - 4ac$ distinguishes the three cases, it is called the **discriminant** of the quadratic equation.

Written Exercises

Determine the nature of the roots of each equation (a) graphically and (b) by use of the discriminant.

A

1. $x^2 - 3x - 4 = 0$
2. $x^2 + 5x - 6 = 0$
3. $3x^2 + 5x + 3 = 0$
4. $-2x^2 - 4x + 6 = 0$
5. $-\frac{1}{3}x^2 - 3x + 4 = 0$

6. $\frac{1}{2}x^2 - 6x + 5 = 0$
7. $-x^2 - 2x - 2 = 0$
8. $-x^2 + 2x - 2 = 0$
9. $2x^2 - 3x + 2 = 0$
10. $3x^2 + 4x + 1 = 0$

Determine whether or not each polynomial can be factored over $\mathcal{R}$. If it can be factored, find the factors.

B

11. $x^2 + 4 - 5x$
12. $x^2 + 6x - 9$
13. $-3x^2 + 5x - 2$
14. $-2x^2 + 6x + 3$

15. $y^2 - \frac{1}{4}y + \frac{1}{3}$
16. $t^2 - \frac{1}{12}t - \frac{1}{12}$
17. $\frac{1}{9}y - \frac{1}{9}y^2 - \frac{2}{3}y^3$
18. $\frac{1}{6}n + \frac{1}{3}n^2 - \frac{5}{3}n^3$

Problems

Find the roots in the most efficient way, and reject inappropriate roots. Approximate irrational roots to the nearest tenth. Use the given formulas.

A

1. The motion of a freely falling body is described approximately by $h = vt - 16t^2$, where h represents the height above the ground, v the initial velocity of the body (positive if the body is propelled away from the earth and negative if propelled toward the earth), and t the elapsed time of fall. In how many seconds will an object thrown upward from the ground with an initial velocity of 64 feet per second first reach a height of 32 feet? When will it again be 32 feet above the ground? When will it strike the ground?

2. If an object is thrown downward with a velocity of 8 feet per second from the top of a building 250 feet high, in how many seconds will it strike the ground? (Use the formula in Problem 1 with $h = -250$.)

3. The sum of the first n positive integers is represented by $\dfrac{n(n + 1)}{2}$. How many positive integers yield a sum of 78?

4. How many positive integers yield a sum of 171? (Use the formula in Problem 3.)

5. The formula for the surface area of a cube with edges of length s is $A = 6s^2$. What is the length of each edge of a cube with surface area 600 square inches?

6. The number of straight lines l determined by n points, no three of which lie on the same line, is given by $l = \dfrac{n(n - 1)}{2}$. How many such points determine 21 lines?

The distance d between two points (x_1, y_1) and (x_2, y_2) is given by $d^2 = (x_2 - x_1)^2 + (y_2 - y_1)^2$.

7. Find the distance between the points $(3, 2)$ and $(5, 1)$.

8. Find the distance between the points $(-5, 1)$ and $(4, -6)$.

B

9. Find the abscissas of the two points on the line $y = 3$ that are 13 units from the point $(6, -2)$.

10. Find the ordinate of the two points on the line $x = 6$ that are 10 units from the point $(-2, -2)$.

11. Show that the points $(-5, 0)$, $(-3, 4)$, and $(5, 0)$ are the vertices of a right triangle.

12. Show that the points $(-1, -2)$, $(7, 2)$, and $(1, 4)$ are the vertices of an isosceles triangle.

THE SOLUTION OF QUADRATIC INEQUALITIES

13–6 Solving Quadratic Inequalities (Optional)

To solve quadratic equations by factoring, you use the zero-product property. To solve a **quadratic inequality,** you use:

The Property of the Nonzero Product of Two Real Numbers

A product is greater than zero if and only if both factors are greater than zero or both are less than zero, and a product is less than zero if and only if one factor is greater than zero and the other is less than zero.

EXAMPLE 1. Graph the solution set of $x^2 + x > 6$.

Solution:
$$x^2 + x > 6$$
$$x^2 + x - 6 > 0$$
$$(x + 3)(x - 2) > 0$$

Both factors are negative	or	Both factors are positive

Both factors are negative

$x + 3 < 0$ and $x - 2 < 0$

$x < -3$ and $x < 2$

The only numbers which satisfy *both* conditions satisfy $x < -3$, whose solution set is the intersection (page 169) of their solution sets:

or Both factors are positive

$x + 3 > 0$ and $x - 2 > 0$

$x > -3$ and $x > 2$

The only numbers which satisfy *both* conditions satisfy $x > 2$, whose solution set is the intersection of their solution sets:

∴ the graph of the solution set is the union (page 169) of these graphs:

Answer.

EXAMPLE 2. Graph the solution set of $x^2 + x \leq 6$.

Solution:
$$x^2 + x - 6 \leq 0$$
$$(x + 3)(x - 2) \leq 0$$

(*cont. on next page*)

$x + 3 \geq 0$ and $x - 2 \leq 0$ or $x + 3 \leq 0$ and $x - 2 \geq 0$
$x \geq -3$ and $x \leq 2$ $x \leq -3$ and $x \geq 2$

The numbers satisfying *both* conditions satisfy	The intersection of their solution sets is the empty set.

$$-3 \leq x \leq 2,$$

whose solution set is the intersection
of their solution sets:

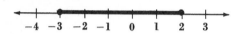

∴ the graph of the solution set is the union of these graphs:

                                                                Answer.

Oral Exercises

1. Consider $(x + 5)(x - 2) > 0$.
    a. If $x + 5 > 0$, then $x - 2$ _?_ 0.
    b. If $x + 5 < 0$, then $x - 2$ _?_ 0.
    c. If $x - 2 > 0$, then $x + 5$ _?_ 0, or $x >$ _?_.
    d. If $x - 2 < 0$, then $x + 5$ _?_ 0, or $x <$ _?_.

2. Consider $(x - 3)(x - 4) > 0$.
    a. If $x - 3 < 0$, then $x - 4$ _?_ 0.
    b. If $x - 3 > 0$, then $x - 4$ _?_ 0.
    c. If $x - 4 < 0$, then $x - 3$ _?_ 0, or $x <$ _?_.
    d. If $x - 4 > 0$, then $x - 3$ _?_ 0, or $x >$ _?_.

3. Consider $x^2 - 4x - 5 < 0$, or $(x - 5)(x + 1) < 0$.
    a. If $x - 5 > 0$, then $x + 1$ _?_ 0.
    b. If $x - 5 < 0$, then $x + 1$ _?_ 0.
    c. If $x + 1 > 0$, then $x - 5$ _?_ 0, or $x <$ _?_.
    d. If $x + 1 < 0$, then $x - 5$ _?_ 0, or $x >$ _?_.

4. Consider $x^2 + 4x \geq 0$, or $x(x + 4) \geq 0$.
    a. If $x \geq 0$, then $x + 4$ _?_ 0.
    b. If $x \geq 0$, and $x \geq -4$, then $x \geq$ _?_.
    c. If $x \leq 0$, then $x + 4$ _?_ 0.
    d. If $x \leq 0$, and $x \leq -4$, then $x \leq$ _?_.

5. Consider $x^2 - 4 \leq 0$, or $(x - 2)(x + 2) \leq 0$.

  a. If $x - 2 \geq 0$, then $x + 2$ _?_ 0.

  b. If $x - 2 \geq 0$, and $x + 2 \leq 0$, then $x \leq$ _?_ and $x \geq$ _?_.

  c. If $x - 2 \leq 0$, then $x + 2$ _?_ 0.

  d. If $x - 2 \leq 0$, and $x + 2 \geq 0$, then _?_ $\leq x \leq$ _?_.

Written Exercises

Graph the solution set of each inequality.

|A|
1. $x^2 - 3x - 4 < 0$	**5.** $x^2 - x < 2$	**9.** $a^2 \leq 4a$
2. $x^2 - 3x - 4 > 0$	**6.** $x^2 - x > 2$	**10.** $b^2 \geq 5b$
3. $t^2 + 5t + 6 > 0$	**7.** $2y^2 - 3y < 2$	**11.** $n^2 \geq 4$
4. $t^2 + 5t + 6 < 0$	**8.** $3z^2 > 2 - z$	**12.** $m^2 \leq 16$

|B|
| **13.** $t^2 - 2t + 1 > 0$ | **15.** $n^2 + 8n + 16 \leq 0$ | **17.** $y^2 > 0$ |
| **14.** $r^2 + 4r + 4 \leq 0$ | **16.** $x^2 - 6x + 9 \geq 0$ | **18.** $z^2 < 0$ |

Find the values of x for which each expression represents a real number.

|C|
| **19.** $\sqrt{2x^2 + x}$ | **21.** $\sqrt{x^2 - 3x - 28}$ |
| **20.** $\sqrt{3x^2 - 27}$ | **22.** $\sqrt{x^2 + 12x + 27}$ |

13–7 Using Graphs of Equations to Solve Inequalities (Optional)

Figure 13–2 below shows the graph of "$y = x^2 + x - 6$." The abscissas of points at which $y = 0$ form the solution set of "$x^2 + x - 6 = 0$." The values of x for which $y > 0$ give the solution set of "$x^2 + x - 6 > 0$," and the values of x for which $y < 0$ give the solution set of "$x^2 + x - 6 < 0$."

Figure 13–2

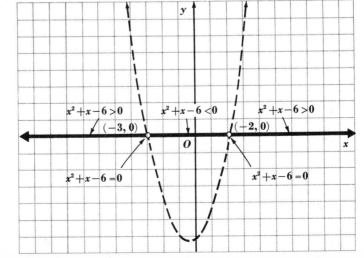

Do you see that you can find the solution sets of these open sentences by determining the values of x for which the graph of the equation is on, above, or below the x-axis?

Compare the solution above with the solutions of Examples 1 and 2 in section 13–6.

Figure 13–3 shows the graph of

$$y = x^2 - 4x + 4.$$

How many x-intercepts does it have? Does the point $(2, 0)$ satisfy $y = 0$, $y > 0$, or $y < 0$? Which sentence is satisfied by values of x to the left of $(2, 0)$? to the right of $(2, 0)$? Do you see that no value of x will make $y < 0$, since the graph does not go below the x-axis?

Figure 13–3

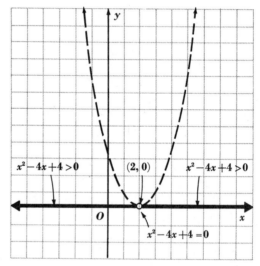

In general, the values of x for which the graph of "$y = ax^2 + bx + c$" lies *above* the x-axis form the solution set of "$ax^2 + bx + c > 0$," while the x-coordinates of the points on the graph *below* the x-axis form the solution set of "$ax^2 + bx + c < 0$."

Oral Exercises

1.   Consider $y = x - 2$.
  a.   If $x = 2$, then $x - 2$ __?__ 0.
  b.   If $x > 2$, then $x - 2$ __?__ 0.

2.   Consider $y = x + 3$.
  a.   If $x = -3$, then $x + 3$ __?__ 0.
  b.   If $x < -3$, then $x + 3$ __?__ 0.

3. Consider $y = (x - 2)(x - 5)$.
   a. State the x-intercepts of the graph of the equation.
   b. If $x < 2$, then $(x - 2)(x - 5)$ __?__ 0.
   c. If $x > 5$, then $(x - 2)(x - 5)$ __?__ 0.
   d. If $2 < x < 5$, then $(x - 2)(x - 5)$ __?__ 0.

4. Consider $y = (x - 2)^2$.
   a. State the x-intercepts of the graph of the equation.
   b. If $x < 2$, then $(x - 2)^2$ __?__ 0.
   c. If $x > 2$, then $(x - 2)^2$ __?__ 0.
   d. If $x \neq 2$, then $(x - 2)^2$ __?__ 0.

5. Consider $y = x^2 - 4$, or $y = (x - 2)(x + 2)$.
   a. State the x-intercepts of the graph of the equation.
   b. If $x < -2$, then $(x - 2)(x + 2)$ __?__ 0.
   c. If $-2 < x < 2$, then $(x - 2)(x + 2)$ __?__ 0.
   d. If $x > 2$, then $(x - 2)(x + 2)$ __?__ 0.

6. Consider $y = x^2 - 2x$, or $y = x(x - 2)$.
   a. State the x-intercepts of the graph of the equation.
   b. If $x < 0$, then $x(x - 2)$ __?__ 0.
   c. If $0 < x < 2$, then $x(x - 2)$ __?__ 0.
   d. If $x > 2$, then $x(x - 2)$ __?__ 0.

Written Exercises

Graph each equation and mark the section of the x-axis it determines as solution sets for $y = 0$, $y > 0$, and $y < 0$.

A
1. $x^2 - 4 = y$
2. $x^2 - 1 = y$
3. $x^2 + 2x = y$
4. $x^2 - 4x = y$
5. $x^2 - 3x - 4 = y$
6. $x^2 + 3x - 4 = y$

7. $x^2 - 4x + 3 = y$
8. $x^2 + 4x + 3 = y$
9. $4x^2 - 8x + 3 = y$
10. $2x^2 + x - 3 = y$
11. $4 - x^2 = y$
12. $3x - x^2 = y$

B
13. $x^2 + 2x + 1 = y$
14. $x^2 - 4x + 4 = y$

15. $9 + 6x + x^2 = y$
16. $9 - 6x + x^2 = y$

Find the values of x for which each expression represents a real number.

C
17. $\sqrt{x^2 - 3x - 4}$

18. $\sqrt{x^2 + 2x}$

● CHAPTER SUMMARY ●

Inventory of Structure and Method

1. A quadratic equation containing no linear term can be solved by using the Property of Square Roots of Equal Numbers: If r and s are real numbers, $r^2 = s^2$ if and only if $r = s$ or $r = -s$.

2. In a quadratic equation of the form "$x^2 + bx + c = 0$," the **sum of the roots** is equal to $-b$, the opposite of the coefficient of the linear term, and **the product of the roots** is equal to the constant term c. These facts may be used to check the solution set of a quadratic equation.

3. To solve a quadratic equation in one variable by the method of **completing the square**: transform it into an equivalent equation whose quadratic term has coefficient 1; write it in the form "$x^2 + bx = -c$"; add to each member $\left(\dfrac{b}{2}\right)^2$, making the left member a square; apply the property of square roots of equal numbers; solve the resulting linear equations.

4. A **decimal approximation** of an irrational root can be calculated by substituting a decimal approximation for each radical which is accurate to one more place than desired in the root and performing the operations.

5. The roots of the **standard quadratic equation** "$ax^2 + bx + c = 0$" are given by the **quadratic formula**: $x = \dfrac{-b \pm \sqrt{b^2 - 4ac}}{2a}$.

6. To solve a quadratic equation in one variable graphically, write it in the standard form "$ax^2 + bx + c = 0$," and find ordered pairs (x, y) satisfying "$ax^2 + bx + c = y$." Graph the parabola and determine the abscissas of the points of intersection of the parabola with the x-axis.

7. To solve a quadratic inequality in one variable, first transform it into an inequality whose right member is zero, and then factor the left member L. (If $L > 0$, the factors must be both positive or both negative; if $L < 0$, the factors must be opposite in sign.) Solve the resulting linear inequalities.

8. The solution set of "$ax^2 + bx + c > 0$" is the set of values of x for which the graph of "$y = ax^2 + bx + c$" lies above the x-axis. The solution set of "$ax^2 + bx + c < 0$" is the set of values of x for which the graph of "$y = ax^2 + bx + c$" lies below the x-axis.

Vocabulary and Spelling

Review the meaning of each term by reference to the page listed.

standard form (*p. 495*)
pure quadratic (*p. 495*)
completing a trinomial square (*p. 500*)
quadratic formula (*p. 504*)
discriminant (*p. 509*)
quadratic inequality (*p. 511*)

Who Uses Mathematics?

The construction of a new building, a bridge, or a space capsule is a complicated undertaking. Before any work can begin, exact specifications must be drawn up to ensure the successful completion of the project. The draftsman is the person responsible for translating the ideas and rough sketches into a working plan, or blueprint.

The draftsman relies on many mathematical tools to obtain precision in his work. Since he usually works on a scale model of the actual product, the properties of proportions play an important part in his work. Elements of geometry are also used in drafting; compasses, protractors, and T-squares are an essential part of the draftsman's equipment.

The need for draftsmen is not limited to architectural or engineering fields. Almost every industry today has openings for qualified men and women. Technical and design schools provide excellent programs for training in this field.

Chapter Test

13–1   Solve, using the property of square roots of equal numbers.

1. $2x^2 - 50 = 0$ **3.** $(x - \frac{3}{5})^2 = \frac{9}{25}$

2. $3y^2 = \frac{1}{27}$ **4.** $5(z + 3)^2 = 125$

13–2   Is the given set the solution set of the given equation?

5. $x^2 + 4x - 3$; $\{-2 \pm \sqrt{7}\}$ **6.** $x^2 + 7 = 0$; $\{\sqrt{7}, -\sqrt{7}\}$

13–3   **7.** Find the value of c that will make the left member of $x^2 - 0.2x + c = 0$ the square of a binomial, and write an equivalent equation using the square of a binomial.

8. Transform "$y^2 + 5y + 6 = 0$" into an equivalent equation of the form $(y - a)^2 = b$.

Solve by completing the square. Express each root in simplest radical form and also to the nearest tenth.

9. $r^2 + 6r + 4 = 0$ **10.** $s^2 + 4s = 7$

13–4   **11.** Use the quadratic formula to solve "$x^2 + 6x + 7 = 0$." Express each root in simplest radical form and also to the nearest tenth.

12. A path of uniform width was constructed around the border of a rectangular flower garden measuring 40 feet by 60 feet. If the path added an area of 438 square feet to the garden, find the width of the path.

13–5   **(Optional)** Determine the nature of the roots of the given equation.

13. $y^2 + 4y = 5$ **14.** $3t^2 - 4t = -2$

13–6   **(Optional)**   **15.** Graph the solution set of "$s^2 + s \leq 2$."

13–7   **(Optional)**   **16.** Graph "$x^2 - 2x - 8 = y$" and, from the graph, find the solution set of "$x^2 - 2x < 8$."

Chapter Review

13–1   **The Square-Root Property**   *Pages 495–497*

1. The standard form for "$2x = 3 - x^2$" is __?__.

2. For real numbers x and y, $x^2 = y^2$ if and only if $x = $ __?__ or $x = $ __?__.

Solve by using the property of square roots of equal numbers.

3. $3t^2 = 108$ **4.** $(s - 4)^2 = 81$

13–2 Sum and Product of the Roots of a Quadratic Equation
Pages 497–499

5. For the equation "$x^2 + bx + c = 0$," the sum of the roots is __?__, and the product of the roots is __?__.

Use the sum and product method to check each solution set.

6. $2r^2 - r - 6 = 0$ $\{2, -\frac{3}{2}\}$

7. $t^2 - 18t = 7$ $\{9 \pm 2\sqrt{11}\}$

8. $x^2 - x - 3 = 0$ $\left\{\dfrac{1 \pm \sqrt{13}}{2}\right\}$

13–3 Solution by Completing a Trinomial Square *Pages 499–503*

State the value of c which makes each trinomial the square of a binomial. Express the trinomial equivalently as the square of a binomial.

9. $t^2 - 14t + c$ **10.** $s^2 - 0.6s + c$

Solve by completing the square. Express irrational roots in simplest radical form, and approximate them to the nearest tenth.

11. $p^2 + p = 6$ **13.** $r^2 - 5r + 3 = 0$

12. $n^2 - 8n = -2$ **14.** $2t^2 - 10t - 2 = 8$

15. A rectangle is 2 feet longer than it is wide, and its area is 224 square feet. Find its dimensions.

16. What is the rate in still air of an airplane that travels 600 miles downwind in a 30-mile-per-hour wind in $\frac{1}{2}$ hour less time than it returns against the wind?

13–4 Solution by Using the Quadratic Formula *Pages 503–507*

17. The equation "$ax^2 + bx + c = 0$" is a quadratic equation in __?__ form.

18. If r and s are roots of "$ax^2 + bx + c = 0$," then $r = $ __?__ and $s = $ __?__.

Solve by using the quadratic formula. Express irrational roots in simplest radical form, and approximate them to the nearest tenth.

19. $2y^2 + 4y + 1 = 0$ **21.** $3x^2 - 7x = 3$

20. $t^2 + 12t - 9 = 0$ **22.** $5z^2 - 8z = 2$

23. A square picture has a frame 2 inches wide. If the picture has an area $\frac{2}{3}$ that of the picture and frame together, what is the length of a side of the picture?

24. Mr. Timothy regularly drives a truck 400 miles from Central City to Placertown during the day. He found that by driving at night, he could save 2 hours because he averaged 10 miles per hour more in speed. What was his regular average speed during the day?

13–5 The Nature of the Roots of a Quadratic Equation (Optional) *Pages 507–510*

25. The real-number roots of "$ax^2 + bx + c = 0$" are the __?__ of the graph of "$y = ax^2 + bx + c$."

26. The x-intercepts of the graph of "$y = x^2 - 2x - 15$" are __?__ and __?__.

State the nature of the roots of each equation.

27. $y^2 + 4y - 5 = 0$ 29. $6x + 8 = 2x^2$

28. $z^2 + 2z + 1 = 0$ 30. $2r^2 + 6r + 1 = 0$

13–6 Solving Quadratic Inequalities (Optional) *Pages 511–513*

31. If $(x - 3)(x + 4) > 0$, then for values of x in the solution set of the inequality, either $x - 3 > 0$ and $x + 4$ __?__ 0, or else $x - 3 < 0$ and $x + 4$ __?__ 0.

32. If $(y + 2)(y - 5) \leq 0$, then for values of x in the solution set of the inequality, either $y + 2 \geq 0$ and $y - 5$ __?__ 0, or else $y + 2 \leq 0$ and $y - 5$ __?__ 0.

Graph the solution set of each inequality.

33. $y^2 - 5y + 4 > 0$ 35. $2x^2 \leq x + 15$

34. $t^2 + 4t + 3 < 0$ 36. $x^2 + 4x \leq 0$

13–7 Using Graphs of Equations to Solve Inequalities (Optional) *Pages 513–515*

37. The portion(s) of the x-axis over which the graph of "$ax^2 + bx + c = y$" is below the axis represent(s) the solution set of the inequality "$ax^2 + bx + c$ __?__ 0."

Solve each inequality by graphing a quadratic equation in two variables of the form $y = ax^2 + bx + c$.

38. $x^2 - 4x + 3 < 0$ 40. $x^2 - 2x \leq 0$

39. $x^2 + 3x + 2 > 0$ 41. $x^2 - 1 \geq 0$

Omar Khayyám and His Algebra

It was a great honor to study with the Imam Mowaffek. Did not all Persia know that everyone who did so attained fame and fortune, honor and happiness? Any boy would be proud to be accepted as his student. Surely Nizam and Hasan and Omar were proud.

But the three boys couldn't quite believe that they were all destined for success. So one day they made a friendship pact, pledging each other, as Nizam later reported in his autobiography, "that to whomsoever this fortune falls, he shall share it equally with the rest." Fortune favored Nizam. About the year 1050, he became Vizier to the Sultan, that is, the chief administrative officer in all Persia. True to his boyhood pact, he shared his good fortune with Hasan and Omar.

Hasan asked for and was given a position in the government.

Omar's request was also granted — a place to live and freedom to study. He used his freedom well. He made thousands of observations of the heavens, recorded the results in tables that other astronomers could use, and reformed the calendar. And he wrote a really excellent book on algebra for his time. He gave rules for finding one root of each of the quadratic equations

$$x^2 + px = q, \qquad x^2 + q = px, \qquad px + q = x^2.$$

When Omar died, about 1123, he was famous as a mathematician and a scientist.

Omar is still famous today — but primarily as a poet. For he was the Omar Khayyám (Ky-**yahm**) who wrote the well-known *Rubaiyat*.

Do you recognize the problem in the multiplication of polynomials on this page of Omar Khayyám's algebra?

Here, also, is some of his poetry:

Ah, but my computa-
tions, people say,
Reduced the year to
better reckoning?
Nay
'Twas only striking
from the calendar
Unborn tomorrow and
dead yesterday.

... the pattern created when a beam of electrons is diffracted by zinc oxide

Geometry and Trigonometry

As you look into your own future, can you see the role mathematics may play in it? Space engineers require a knowledge of mathematics greater than that you now possess. They did not learn their mathematics as part of their jobs. They learned it in order to get their jobs. Since many occupations which are challenging require a knowledge of mathematics, you should plan to include it in your education.

GEOMETRY

14–1 The Structure of Geometry

Up to this time, all of your study in this book has been concerned directly or indirectly with the properties of various sets of *numbers:* natural numbers, directed numbers, rational numbers, real numbers. To help you understand some of these properties, you often used sets of *points.* You first associated numbers with points on the number line (pages 8–9). Later, when you made graphs, you associated a pair of numbers (x, y) with a point P (page 359).

You used points, lines, and other sets of points (parabolas, for example) to help you understand the properties of sets of numbers, but of course it is perfectly possible to have as your aim the study of the properties of sets of points themselves, without being particularly concerned with sets of numbers of any kind. This is the object of the study of *Geometry:* to learn about the properties of points, lines, triangles, squares, rectangles, circles, and other figures made up of points. Just as your aim in algebra is to learn about the properties of *sets of numbers*, so your aim in studying geometry would be to learn about the properties of *sets of points.*

Fortunately, whether you are learning about sets of numbers or sets of points, you do not have to list and memorize all the properties in which you are interested. The various properties are related to one another, and if you know certain basic properties, others can be worked out. In other words, in both algebra and geometry you deal with a *structure*, not just a miscellaneous collection of observations.

Like numbers, geometric points and sets of points such as lines, planes, and circles, are abstract concepts, not concrete objects. However, every mathematician helps his thinking by representing points by dots, lines by strokes, and planes by flat surfaces, as shown in Figure 14–1.

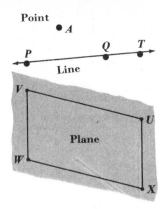

Figure 14–1

14–2 Geometric Assumptions

Your study of geometry begins by stating certain relationships that will be taken for granted. These statements are called *axioms*, and they are assumed to hold for the points and sets of points you will be studying. Other properties and relationships will be proved on the basis of the axioms. Such proved relationships, as you know, are called *theorems*. Here are the first two of seven axioms you will need:

AXIOM I. Every line is a set of points containing at least two different points.

AXIOM II. Any two different points belong to one and only one line.

From Axioms I and II, you know at once that you can identify any line by naming any two of its points. There is no other line that contains them both. Thus, you can call the line shown in Figure 14–1: line *PQ* or line *QT* or line *PT* or line *TP* or line *TQ* or line *QP*. Points that belong to or lie on the same line are called **collinear** (ko-**lin**-e-ar). Thus, *P*, *Q*, and *T* are collinear points.

From these two axioms it follows that *two different lines cannot have more than one point in common.* For if points *H* and *K* lie on line *l* and also lie on line *m*, then *l* and *m* must be two names for the same line, by Axiom II. The next two axioms concern planes:

AXIOM III. Every plane is a set of points containing at least three points not all on the same line (that is, containing three *noncollinear* points).

AXIOM IV. Any three noncollinear points belong to one and only one plane.

From Axioms III and IV, you know at once that you can identify any plane by naming any three noncollinear points in it. There is no other plane that contains all three. Thus, you can call the plane shown in Figure 14–1 plane *UVW* or plane *UXW* or plane *XUV*. Points or lines that belong to or lie on the same plane are called **coplanar** (ko-**plain**-ar) points or lines. Thus, *U*, *V*, *W*, and *X* are coplanar points.

The next two axioms relate lines and planes:

AXIOM V. If two points of a line are in a plane, every point of the line is in that plane.

This axiom immediately tells you two things: (1) that a plane does indeed contain lines; (2) that, since the lines it contains extend indefinitely, a plane also extends indefinitely.

AXIOM VI. If two planes have one point in common, they have two points in common.

From Axioms V and VI, it follows that *if two planes have one point in common, they have a line in common.*

From Axioms III and IV, it follows that *two different planes cannot have more than one line in common.* For if lines *l* and *m* lie on plane *M* and also lie on plane *N*, there must be three distinct points, say *A* and *B* on *l* and *C* on *m*, all three of which belong to *M* and also to *N*. By Axiom IV, therefore, *M* and *N* must be two names for the same plane.

You already know that it is important to be able to put coordinates on a number line. This is the way you used sets of points to help you understand the properties of sets of numbers. You therefore assumed (pages 9, 21, and 79) the content of the following axiom:

AXIOM VII. There is a one-to-one correspondence between real numbers and points of a line such that if *A* and *B* are points on the line with coordinates *a* and *b*, the *distance* between *A* and *B* (denoted by *AB*) is the absolute value of the difference of their coordinates, that is (see Figure 14–2),

$$AB = |a - b|.$$

Figure 14–2

From Axiom VII you know that a line extends indefinitely in both directions without holes or gaps. You know this because of the properties of real numbers you have learned. If you have a point B with coordinate b, you can always find a real number larger than b. The point belonging to this number must be to the right of B. Thus, since the set of real numbers has no largest number, the set of points being paired with the real numbers, that is, the line, must extend indefinitely to the right. Since the set of real numbers has no smallest number, the line must extend indefinitely to the left. Since the real numbers have the Property of Completeness (see page 465), there can be no gaps or holes in the line.

You can use Axiom VII also to define precisely what is meant when you say one point is *between* two others (refer to Figure 14–2): If point C lies on number line AB, then C is **between** A and B if

$$a < c < b \quad \text{or} \quad b < c < a,$$

where the real numbers a, b, and c are coordinates of points A, B, and C, respectively. You can also define the **line segment** determined by points A and B as the set of points consisting of A and B and the points on the line between them. A and B are the **endpoints** of the line segment. The symbol naming the segment is $\overline{AB}$.

The **length** of a line segment is the distance between its endpoints. Thus, the length of $\overline{AB}$ is denoted by AB, as in Axiom VII.

Written Exercises

State the axiom or definition that justifies each statement.

[A] 1. If A and B are different points, then there is a line l containing A and B.

2. If line l contains different points P and Q, and line m contains P and Q, then lines l and m are the same line.

3. If on a number line a is the coordinate of A, and b the coordinate of B, then $AB = |b - a|$.

4. If A, B, and C are noncollinear points, then there is a plane containing A, B, and C.

5. If A and B are points in a plane, then all points between A and B are in the plane.

6. If A, B, and C are noncollinear points in a plane, and D is a point not in the plane, then ABD and BCD designate different planes.

Exercises 7–10 refer to the figure shown. Use the name of a point to make the sentence a true statement.

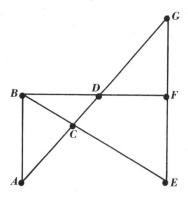

7. Points *B, C,* and __?__ are collinear.

8. Point __?__ lies between points *B* and *F.*

9. Points *G, D,* and __?__ are noncollinear.

10. Points *A, C,* __?__, and __?__ are collinear.

Given collinear points with coordinates as shown. Find each distance.

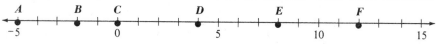

11. *AD*	13. *CF*	15. *AD* + *DE*	17. *CE* − *DE*
12. *EB*	14. *BD*	16. *BE* + *EF*	18. *AD* − *BD*

Sketch a number line showing the points *R, S, T, U* on a line in the given relationship. In each case, at least two orders are possible.

19. $RS + ST = RT,\ U \in \overline{RS}$	21. $T \in \overline{SU},\ RS < RU$
20. $RT + RU = TU,\ S \in \overline{RU}$	22. $RT > RS,\ \overline{RS} \subset \overline{RU}$

14–3   Rays and Angles

A line is a set of points. Clearly there are many subsets that can be selected from this set of points. For instance, $\overline{QR}$ in Figure 14–3 is one such subset; so is any other segment, say $\overline{TS}$. But

Figure 14–3

you do not need to limit yourself to segments. You can make up a subset consisting only of the three particular points *P, R,* and *S.* Another possibility is the subset consisting of point *Q* and all points to its right.

This last subset is an example of a particularly important idea: the set consisting of a point on a line and all the points on one side of it. A subset of this sort is called a **ray**. A segment has two endpoints; a line has no endpoint, and extends indefinitely in both directions; a ray has one endpoint and extends indefinitely in one direction.

Clearly, if you take a particular point on a line, say R, there are two rays having R as endpoint: the subset including R, S, T and all other points to the right of R is one such ray; the other is the subset including R, Q, P, and all other points to the left of R. To distinguish them, the first is called the "ray RS," represented by $\overrightarrow{RS}$, and the other is $\overrightarrow{RP}$. Do you see that $\overrightarrow{RS}$ and $\overrightarrow{RT}$ are two names for the same ray?

In the study of geometry, it is considered very important not merely to describe a set of points or a figure that is being named, but to give a formal definition that distinguishes the entity being defined from everything else under discussion. Here is a definition of a ray: If a point P with coordinate p is taken on a line, then the set of points consisting of P and all points whose coordinates equal or exceed p is called a **ray starting from P**. Similarly, the set of points consisting of P and all points whose coordinates equal or are less than p is a **ray starting from P**.

The expression "a ray having P as endpoint," means exactly the same thing as "a ray starting from P."

Another important set of points in geometry is the set called an *angle:* An **angle** is a set of points consisting of two rays starting from the same point. The point is called the **vertex** of the angle and the rays are called the **sides**. Either of the rays may be called the initial ray or initial side, and the other one the terminal ray or terminal side.

The union (recall page 169) of the two rays may or may not be a line. (See Figure 14–4.) If it is a line, the angle is called a *straight angle*.

To name an angle, use the symbol $\angle$ (read "angle") followed by a letter naming its vertex, as $\angle G$ or $\angle K$ in Figure 14–4. When two or more angles have the same vertex, use $\angle$ followed by three letters, naming first a point on the initial side, then the vertex and finally, a point on the terminal side, as $\angle MHP$, or $\angle MHB$; $\angle RHP$, or $\angle BHA$, and so on. Why would the designation $\angle H$ be ambiguous? Note that any point on the straight angle pictured in Figure 14–4 may be taken as the vertex.

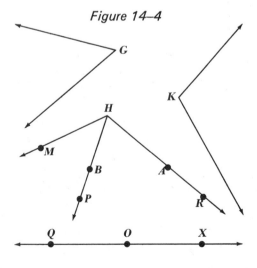

Figure 14–4

Written Exercises

Exercises 1–10 refer to the figure shown.

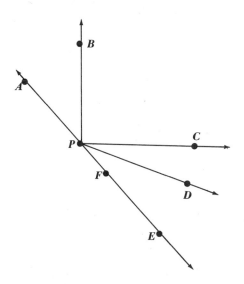

A 1. Name the angle having $\overrightarrow{PE}$ as initial side and $\overrightarrow{PC}$ as terminal side.

  2. Name the angle having $\overrightarrow{PD}$ as initial side and $\overrightarrow{PA}$ as terminal side.

  3. Name an angle having $\overrightarrow{PB}$ as its terminal side and another having $\overrightarrow{PB}$ as its initial side.

  4. Is $\overrightarrow{PA}$ the same ray as $\overrightarrow{PF}$?   7. Is $\angle FPC$ the same angle as $\angle CPF$?

  5. Is $\overrightarrow{PF}$ the same ray as $\overrightarrow{PE}$?   8. What kind of angle is $\angle APF$?

  6. Is $\overrightarrow{PE}$ the same ray as $\overrightarrow{FE}$?   9. Is $\angle EPB$ the same angle as $\angle BPF$?

 10. Name $\overrightarrow{AP}$ in two other ways.

On a number line, graph the solution set of each sentence, and identify the graph as a ray, a point, a line segment, a line, or none of these.

 11. $|x| = 0$ 13. $x \leq 2$ 15. $|x| \geq 0$ 17. $|x| \geq 1$

 12. $0 \leq x \leq 2$ 14. $x > 3$ 16. $|x| \leq 1$ 18. $2 < x \leq 3$

14–4 The Measurement of Angles

AXIOM VIII. If a line is drawn in a plane, the set of points comprising the plane is separated into three subsets: the points on one side of the line, the points on the other side of the line, and the line itself.

In any plane, draw a line PN and choose a fixed point Q on it. Choose one of the closed half-planes into which line PN separates the plane. Since it is closed, that is, contains the edge PN, the half-plane contains the point Q, and a set of rays starting from Q, such as $\overrightarrow{QN}$, $\overrightarrow{QL}$, $\overrightarrow{QK}$, and many more. By placing a protractor as indicated in Figure 14–5, each ray can be associated with a number.

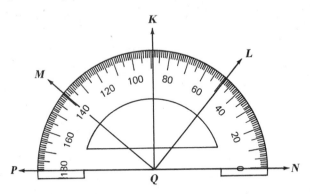

Figure 14–5

The important matter for geometry is not the protractor; it is the one-to-one correspondence between the rays and certain real numbers. This is emphasized in the following axiom:

AXIOM IX. In a closed half-plane, the set of rays with a common endpoint in the edge of the half-plane can be put into one-to-one correspondence with the set of real numbers between 0 and 180, inclusive, in such a way that any angle whose sides are rays of the given set has a measure equal to the absolute value of the difference between the numbers corresponding to its sides.

To see more clearly what this means, look closely at Figure 14–5. The table at the right shows the numbers corresponding to certain rays.

What is the measure of angle LQK (in symbols, $m\angle LQK$)?

Ray	Number
$\overrightarrow{QN}$	0
$\overrightarrow{QL}$	50
$\overrightarrow{QK}$	90
$\overrightarrow{QM}$	140
$\overrightarrow{QP}$	180

$\overrightarrow{QK}$ corresponds to 90 and $\overrightarrow{QL}$ to 50;

$m\angle LQK = 90 - 50 = 40.$

Look now at the set of angles having as sides $\overrightarrow{QN}$ and any other ray proceeding from Q. Since the number corresponding to $\overrightarrow{QN}$ is 0, the measure of any one of these angles will be the number corresponding to the other ray. Thus:

For $\angle NQM$, $\overrightarrow{QM}$ corresponds to 140, $\overrightarrow{QN}$ corresponds to 0, and $m\angle NQM = 140 - 0 = 140$.

Do you see that you can draw an angle, one side of which is $\overrightarrow{QN}$, having as its measure any specified number between 0 and 180? Moreover, $\angle NQP$, which as you have already learned is a straight angle, since the union of its sides is a line, has measure 180. It is agreed also to call $\overrightarrow{QN}$ an angle with measure 0. By making this agreement, you can say that the set of measures of the angles having $\overrightarrow{QN}$ as one side is the set of all real numbers r such that

$$0 \leq r \leq 180.$$

An angle of measure 90 is called a **right angle**; an angle whose measure is between 90 and 180 is called an **obtuse angle**; an angle whose measure is greater than 0 and less than 90 is called an **acute angle**.

Protractors often have a second number scale with 0 corresponding to $\overrightarrow{QP}$ and 180 corresponding to $\overrightarrow{QN}$, as shown in Figure 14–6. This scale is convenient for some measuring situations, but we shall use only the scale with 0 corresponding to $\overrightarrow{QN}$ in our work here.

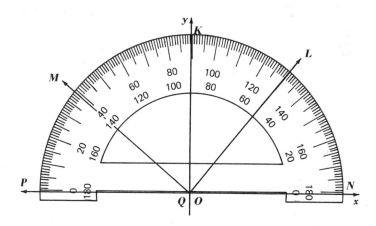

Figure 14–6

Now superimpose on Figure 14–5 a rectangular coordinate system with Q at the origin, $\overrightarrow{QN}$ as the positive x-axis, and $\overrightarrow{QK}$ as the positive y-axis (Figure 14–6). Any angle with $\overrightarrow{QN}$ as one side is said to be

in standard position. In other words, an angle is *in standard position* if its vertex is at the origin of a rectangular coordinate system, and if the initial side is the ray which is the positive *x*-axis. The terminal side falls in Quadrant I or II (page 360), or on an axis, since all the angles discussed here have measure 180 or less.

Oral Exercises

Exercises 1–10 refer to the figure shown. Tell whether the given statement is true or false, and give a reason for your answer.

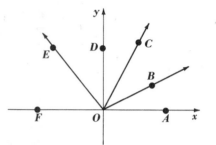

1. $\angle AOB$ is a right angle.
2. $\angle COA$ is an acute angle.
3. $\angle FOD$ is an obtuse angle.
4. $m\angle AOB < m\angle AOC$
5. $m\angle AOD = 90$
6. $m\angle FOE < 90$
7. $m\angle AOB + m\angle BOD = 90$
8. $m\angle AOB + m\angle BOC > 90$
9. $\angle BOA$ is in standard position.
10. $\angle BOC$ is in standard position.

14–5 Triangles

You will have a good deal to do with triangles in the work of this chapter. You know, of course, what a triangle looks like, but in geometry, figures must be defined, even those you can already recognize. The definition of a triangle is as follows: If A, B, and C are three noncollinear points, the union of the segments $\overline{AB}$, $\overline{BC}$, and $\overline{AC}$ is a **triangle.** The segments $\overline{AB}$, $\overline{BC}$ and $\overline{AC}$ are called the **sides** of the triangle and the angles having rays $\overrightarrow{AB}$ and $\overrightarrow{AC}$, $\overrightarrow{BA}$ and $\overrightarrow{BC}$, $\overrightarrow{CA}$ and $\overrightarrow{CB}$, respectively, as sides are called the **angles** of the triangle.

If one of the angles of a triangle is a right angle, the triangle is called a *right triangle*. The side opposite the right angle is called the *hypotenuse*. In your earlier courses, you have probably used one of the most important properties of a right triangle, the **Pythagorean Theorem** (page 469). This theorem states:

THEOREM. In any right triangle, the square of the length of the
14-4   hypotenuse equals the sum of the squares of the lengths
             of the other two sides.

You will need this theorem repeatedly.

A number assigned by the protractor method is called the **degree measure** of the angle. Generally, such measures of angles will be labeled as degrees (°): $m\angle A = 40°$.

You probably have also used this property of a triangle (page 183):

THEOREM. The sum of the degree measures of the angles of a triangle is 180.

Written Exercises

In Exercises 1–6 use the Pythagorean Theorem to determine which of the given triangles are right triangles. For each exercise, draw a rough sketch.

1. $\triangle ABC$; $AB = 3$, $BC = 4$, $AC = 6$
2. $\triangle DEF$; $DE = 6$, $EF = 8$, $DF = 10$
3. $\triangle GHJ$; $GH = 5$, $HJ = 12$, $GJ = 13$
4. $\triangle KLM$; $KL = 1$, $LM = 2$, $KM = 3$
5. $\triangle XYZ$; $XY = 3$, $YZ = 3$, $XZ = 2\sqrt{3}$
6. $\triangle BDK$; $BD = 1$, $DK = 1$, $BK = \sqrt{2}$

7. Given: $\triangle ABC$ is a right triangle with $AC = BC$ and $AB = 4$. Find AC and BC.
8. Given: $\triangle ABC$ is a right triangle with $AC = 2(BC)$ and $AB = \sqrt{3}$. Find AC and BC. (Two possible answers)
9. In $\triangle XYZ$, $\angle X$ measures 50° and $\angle Y$ measures 40°. What is the measure of $\angle Z$?
10. In $\triangle MNO$, $\angle M$ measures 30° and $\angle N$ measures 22°. What is the measure of $\angle O$?
11. Why can there not be a triangle whose angles measure 40°, 50°, and 60°? 60°, 70°, and 80°?
12. If each angle of a triangle has the same measure, what is the measure of each?

TRIGONOMETRY

14–6 Tangent of an Angle

In section 14–4, we set up a one-to-one correspondence between a set of real numbers and a particular set of rays through the origin. Since each one of the rays through the origin (except $\overrightarrow{OY}$) can be identified by the slope of its line (page 373) it is possible to set up another one-to-one correspondence, as shown on the next page. In

Figure 14–7, $\overrightarrow{OA}$, for example, passes through the point (5, 3). Its slope is, therefore,

$$\frac{3-0}{5-0} = \frac{3}{5}.$$

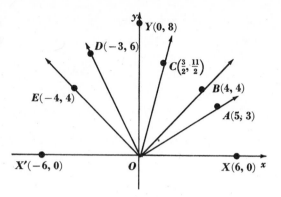

There is no other ray in the upper half-plane starting from O with this particular slope. The ray is, therefore, completely identified by giving its slope.

Figure 14–7

Since the slope of a line was defined to be

difference of ordinates

difference of abscissas

for two points on the line, and since all the rays in which you are interested have (0, 0) as one such point, the slope of any of these rays is $\dfrac{y}{x}$, where (x, y) is any point on the ray.

You will recall (page 374) that the slope of any ray in Quadrant I is positive; the slope of $\overrightarrow{OX}$ is 0, the slope of $\overrightarrow{OB}$ is 1; the slopes of the rays between $\overrightarrow{OX}$ and $\overrightarrow{OB}$, like $\overrightarrow{OA}$, are less than 1; the slopes of the rays between $\overrightarrow{OB}$ and $\overrightarrow{OY}$ are greater than 1; $\overrightarrow{OY}$ itself has no slope.

Similarly, the rays in the second quadrant all have negative slopes; those between $\overrightarrow{OY}$ and $\overrightarrow{OE}$ are less than -1, that is, negative and in absolute value greater than 1, for example, -2. Those between $\overrightarrow{OE}$ and $\overrightarrow{OX'}$ fall between -1 and 0.

Thus, for every negative or positive real number there is in the upper half-plane one and only one ray starting from the origin and having that number as its slope. However, there are two rays, $\overrightarrow{OX}$ and $\overrightarrow{OX'}$, having 0 slope, and there is one ray, $\overrightarrow{OY}$, having no slope.

The two procedures for assigning numbers to rays in the upper half-plane starting from the origin may profitably be compared. In the table at the top of the next page, the degree measures and the slopes assigned to certain rays are listed.

Ray	Angle measure	Slope		Ray	Angle measure	Slope
$\overrightarrow{OX}$	0°	0		$\overrightarrow{OR}$	105°	−3.73
$\overrightarrow{OM}$	15°	0.27		$\overrightarrow{OS}$	120°	−1.73
$\overrightarrow{ON}$	30°	0.58		$\overrightarrow{OE}$	135°	−1
$\overrightarrow{OB}$	45°	1		$\overrightarrow{OT}$	150°	−0.58
$\overrightarrow{OP}$	60°	1.73		$\overrightarrow{OU}$	165°	−0.27
$\overrightarrow{OQ}$	75°	3.73		$\overrightarrow{OX'}$	180°	0
$\overrightarrow{OY}$	90°	−				

It is clear that the last two columns of this table can be related directly; in other words a correspondence can be set up directly between the measure of an angle in standard position and the slope of its terminal ray. Since corresponding to each angle measure, there is one and only one real number, this correspondence is a *function* (see page 146). The name given to this function is *tangent*. The **tangent** of an angle in standard position is the slope of its terminal ray. To indicate that the tangent of 45° is 1, we write "tan 45° = 1."

Since any angle with measure between 0° and 180° can be put into standard position, this definition will enable you to compute the tangent of any such angle *A*. Place the angle in standard position, choose any point (x_1, y_1) on the terminal ray, or if more convenient, two points (x_1, y_1) and (x_2, y_2), not both (0, 0), and compute the slope:

$$\tan \angle A = \frac{y_1}{x_1} \quad \text{or} \quad \tan \angle A = \frac{y_2 - y_1}{x_2 - x_1}$$

Now draw on the coordinate axes a circle with center at the origin and radius 1 (called a *unit circle*), and the vertical line through the point $C(1, 0)$ as in Figure 14–8.

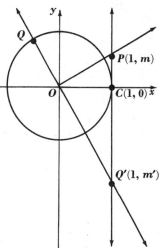

Since any point on a ray through the origin can be used to find the slope of the ray, you can agree to use the point P where the ray intersects the vertical line. The coordinates of this point are $(1, m)$, where m is the slope of the ray.

You can see this either by writing the equation of a line through (0, 0) with slope m,

$$y = mx,$$

and letting x have the value 1 in this

Figure 14–8

equation, or by noting that for point $P(1, y)$,

$$m = \frac{y - 0}{1 - 0} = y;$$

that is, the ordinate of P, which is y, equals m.

In Figure 14–8, then, there is a line segment, $\overline{CP}$, which has as its length the same number as the slope of $\overrightarrow{OP}$. This number is also the *tangent of* $\angle COP$. Therefore, $\overline{CP}$ is a picture of the tangent of $\angle COP$.

You can see how the lengths of the line segments above the x-axis cut off on the vertical line $x = 1$ by rays from the origin would agree with the numbers listed in the table on page 535. Angles less than 45° clearly have tangents less than 1, and angles between 45° and 90° have tangents greater than 1; the greater the angle, the greater the tangent.

If the angle is greater than 90°, for example $\angle COQ$, the ray $\overrightarrow{OQ}$ does not cut the line $x = 1$. But the line QQ' of which $\overrightarrow{OQ}$ is a part does cut the line $x = 1$, and of course line OQ' and ray $\overrightarrow{OQ}$ necessarily have the same slope. You can therefore use the point Q' where the *line OQ* cuts the line $x = 1$ to find the slope of *ray* $\overrightarrow{OQ}$, even though Q' is not a point of the ray. The coordinates of Q' are $(1, m')$, where m' is negative and equal in absolute value to the length of the segment $\overline{CQ'}$.

You can now see that the ordinate of every point on the vertical line $x = 1$ is the tangent of some angle, namely, the angle formed by the positive x-axis and the ray lying in the upper half-plane along the line joining the point in $x = 1$ to the origin.

Oral Exercises

State the tangent of the given angle.

1. $\angle POA$

2. $\angle POB$

3. $\angle POC$

4. $\angle POD$

5. $\angle POE$

6. $\angle POF$

7. $\angle POG$

8. $\angle POH$

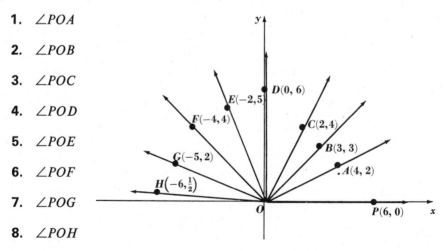

Exercises 9–12 refer to the figure shown. In each case give a reason for your answer.

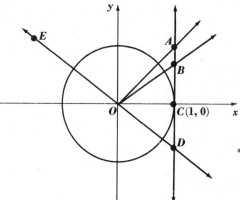

9. In the figure shown $AC =$ tan $\angle AOC$. How long is $\overline{OC}$?

10. For what angle is BC the tangent?

11. What segment has a length equal to tan $\angle EOC$?

12. If $m\angle AOC = 45°$, what are the coordinates of point A?

Written Exercises

In Exercises 1–10, the point with given coordinates lies on the terminal side of an angle in standard position. In each case, give the tangent of the angle.

A

1. (3, 5)	**3.** (−5, 2)	**5.** (50, 15)	**7.** (−2, 0)	**9.** (a, b)
2. (6, 6)	**4.** (−7, 7)	**6.** (3, 81)	**8.** (−3, 39)	**10.** (−a, b)

In Exercises 11–16, tell whether the given statement is true or false. If it is false, give an example showing that it is false.

11. If $\angle A$ and $\angle B$ are acute angles, and $m\angle A > m\angle B$, then tan $\angle A >$ tan $\angle B$.

12. If $\angle A$ is an obtuse angle, then tan $\angle A > 0$.

13. If $\angle A$ is an acute angle, then tan $\angle A > 0$.

14. If $\angle A$ and $\angle B$ are acute angles, and tan $\angle A >$ tan $\angle B$, then $m\angle A > m\angle B$.

15. If $\angle A$ and $\angle B$ are any angles, then if $m\angle A > m\angle B$, tan $\angle A >$ tan $\angle B$.

16. If $\angle A$ and $\angle B$ are any angles, then if tan $\angle A <$ tan $\angle B$, $m\angle A < m\angle B$.

14–7 Sine and Cosine of an Angle

When you wanted a line segment equal in length to the tangent of an angle so that you could, so to speak, picture the tangent, you took a particular point on the terminal ray of the angle, namely, the point where the ray (or the line containing it) cut the vertical line $x = 1$. By taking a different point on the terminal ray, two other very important line segments can be found.

Consider any angle in standard position, for example, $\angle XOV$ or $\angle XOW$. This time consider the point where the ray intersects the unit circle, P or P'. The line segments in which you are interested are $\overline{OM}$ and $\overline{MP}$, or for $\angle XOW$, $\overline{OM'}$ and $\overline{M'P'}$. The lengths of these line segments are nothing but the coordinates of P or P'.

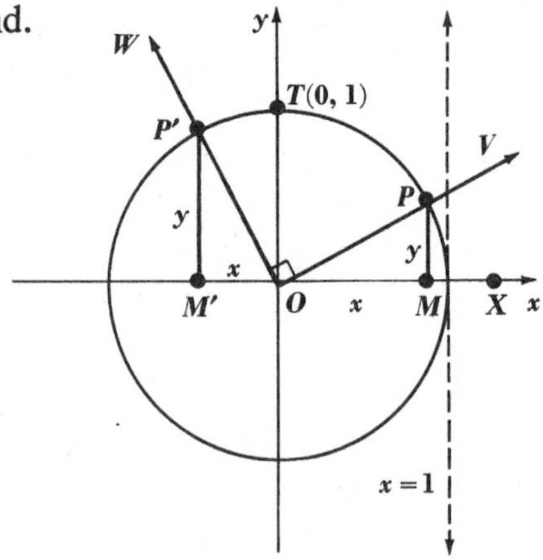

Figure 14–9

Again, you see that correspondences can be set up between the angle measures and these coordinates. These correspondences are functions and are given special names. y is called the *sine* of the angle and x is called the *cosine* of the angle.

In general, the **sine** of an angle in standard position is the ordinate of the point on the terminal ray whose distance from the origin is 1. The **cosine** of an angle in standard position is the abscissa of the point on the terminal ray whose distance from the origin is 1.

To indicate that the sine of 30° is 0.5, we write "sin 30° = 0.5." To indicate that the cosine of 120° is −0.5, we write "cos 120° = −0.5."

From these definitions you can immediately note five very important facts:

1. The sine of an angle is never greater than 1.

You see this because every ordinate except the ordinate of $T(0, 1)$ is less than the radius of the circle.

Similarly, you can see that:

2. The cosine of an angle is never greater than 1.

3. The sine and the cosine of any angle between 0° and 90° are both greater than 0 (positive).

You see this because the coordinates of any point in the first quadrant are positive.

4. sin 90° = 1 and cos 90° = 0.

You see this by using the coordinates of point T.

5. The sine of any angle between 90° and 180° is greater than 0 (positive), and the cosine of any angle between 90° and 180° is less than 0 (negative).

You see this because in the case of (x, y), any point in the second quadrant, $x < 0$ and $y > 0$.

In Figure 14–10, $OM = \cos A$ and $MP = \sin A$, and so the co-ordinates of point P may be written

$$P(\cos A, \sin A).$$

Now, by the Pythagorean Theorem, you have in right triangle OMP

$$(MP)^2 + (OM)^2 = (OP)^2.$$

But

$$MP = \sin A, \quad OM = \cos A, \quad OP = 1.$$

Therefore

$$(\sin A)^2 + (\cos A)^2 = 1.$$

This result, which for simplicity may also be written

$$\sin^2 A + \cos^2 A = 1,$$

holds for every angle without exception.

Now, using points $P(\cos A, \sin A)$ and $O(0, 0)$ to find the slope of $\overrightarrow{OV}$, you have:

$$\text{slope } \overrightarrow{OV} = \frac{\sin A}{\cos A}.$$

But you already know that

$$\text{slope } \overrightarrow{OV} = \tan A.$$

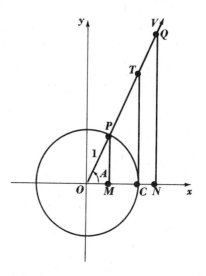

Figure 14–10

Therefore

$$\tan A = \frac{\sin A}{\cos A}.$$

This result is true for every angle A, except that it does not hold when $\cos A = 0$, that is, when $m\angle A = 90°$.

Moreover, any point on $\overrightarrow{OV}$ may be used to compute its slope. Thus you may write

$$\tan A = \frac{NQ}{ON},$$

where Q is any point whatsoever on $\overrightarrow{OV}$.

The *tangent* of an angle in standard position is *ordinate divided by abscissa* for any point on the terminal ray.

It is not hard to see that similar statements can be made about the sine and the cosine. First, for simplicity, write

$$OM = p, \quad MP = m, \quad ON = q, \quad NQ = n.$$

Then by the Pythagorean Theorem

$$OP = \sqrt{p^2 + m^2} \quad \text{and} \quad OQ = \sqrt{q^2 + n^2}.$$

Moreover, since $\tan A$ may be written either as $\dfrac{MP}{OM} = \dfrac{m}{p}$ or as $\dfrac{NQ}{ON} = \dfrac{n}{q}$, you know that

$$\frac{m}{p} = \frac{n}{q}, \quad \text{or} \quad m = \frac{pn}{q}.$$

Now, by definition, $\sin A = MP$. Since $OP = 1$, this can be written

$$\sin A = MP = \frac{MP}{1} = \frac{MP}{OP} = \frac{m}{\sqrt{p^2 + m^2}}.$$

Now substitute $\dfrac{pn}{q}$ for m:

$$\sin A = \frac{\dfrac{pn}{q}}{\sqrt{p^2 + \dfrac{p^2 n^2}{q^2}}}$$

For simplicity, multiply numerator and denominator by $\dfrac{q}{p}$:

$$\sin A = \frac{\dfrac{q}{p} \cdot \dfrac{pn}{q}}{\sqrt{\dfrac{q^2}{p^2}\left(p^2 + \dfrac{p^2n^2}{q^2}\right)}} = \frac{n}{\sqrt{q^2 + n^2}} = \frac{NQ}{OQ}$$

In other words, the *sine* of an angle in standard position is *ordinate divided by distance from the origin* for any point on the terminal ray.

Now there is an easy way to find the cosine. You know that

$$\sin A = \frac{NQ}{OQ} \quad \text{and that} \quad \tan A = \frac{NQ}{ON}.$$

You also know that

$$\frac{\sin A}{\cos A} = \tan A.$$

Therefore,

$$\cos A = \frac{\sin A}{\tan A}$$

$$= \frac{\dfrac{NQ}{OQ}}{\dfrac{NQ}{ON}} = \frac{NQ}{OQ} \cdot \frac{ON}{NQ} = \frac{ON}{OQ}.$$

In other words, the *cosine* of an angle in standard position is *abscissa divided by distance from the origin* for any point on the terminal ray. Of course, for angles whose terminal sides lie in the second quadrant the abscissas $OM = p$ and $ON = q$ are negative.

To summarize, in Figure 15–11, you have

$$\sin A = \frac{y}{r} \quad \cos A = \frac{x}{r} \quad \tan A = \frac{y}{x}.$$

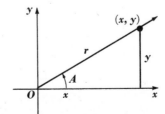

Figure 14–11

Oral Exercises

Exercises 1–10 refer to the figure shown. In each exercise, state the given value.

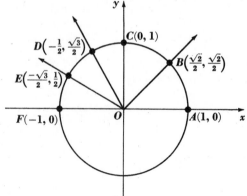

1. $\sin \angle AOB$
2. $\cos \angle AOB$
3. $\sin \angle AOC$
4. $\cos \angle AOC$
5. $\cos \angle AOD$
6. $\sin \angle AOD$
7. $\cos \angle AOE$
8. $\sin \angle AOE$
9. $\cos \angle AOF$
10. $\sin \angle AOF$

Use the figure above to determine each of the following.

11. $\sin 0°$ 13. $\sin 90°$ 15. $\cos 180°$
12. $\cos 0°$ 14. $\cos 90°$ 16. $\sin 180°$

Written Exercises

Exercises 1–8 refer to the figure shown. In each exercise, find the required value.

A
1. $\cos \angle AOC$
2. $\sin \angle AOC$
3. $\cos \angle AOB$
4. $\sin \angle AOB$
5. $\sin \angle AOD$
6. $\cos \angle AOD$
7. $\sin \angle AOE$
8. $\cos \angle AOE$

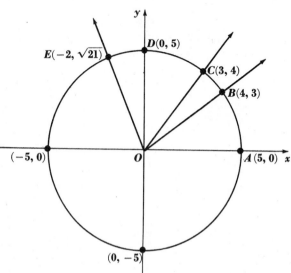

Use the figure shown to find the requested values.

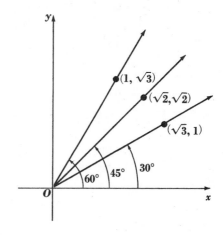

9. sin 30°   **14.** cos 60°

10. cos 30°   **15.** tan 30°

11. sin 45°   **16.** tan 45°

12. cos 45°   **17.** tan 60°

13. sin 60°

18. $\sin^2 60° + \cos^2 60°$

19. $\sin^2 30° + \cos^2 30°$

20. $\sin^2 45° + \cos^2 45°$

The results of Exercises 18–20 verify that for all angles A,

$$\sin^2 A + \cos^2 A = 1.$$

Use this fact to do Exercises 21–24.

B **21.** Find $\cos A$ given that $\sin A = \frac{3}{5}$.

22. Find $\sin A$ given that $\cos A = \frac{12}{13}$.

C **23.** Find $\tan A$ given that $\cos A = \dfrac{3}{\sqrt{10}}$.

24. Find $\tan A$ given that $\sin A = \dfrac{1}{\sqrt{17}}$.

14–8 Function Values

Since the sine is a function, you can make a table including at least some of the ordered pairs. You will find such a table as part of Table 5 in the Appendix. Since the cosine and the tangent are also functions, they too can be tabulated. To save space, the tables for all three functions are printed together in Table 5. The table does not extend beyond 90°, although there are larger angles, and you saw how to work out the sine, cosine, and tangent for angles between 90° and 180°. For the use you will make of these functions, this table is sufficient. In Table 5 what are the values listed for sin 90° and cos 90°?

$$\textbf{sin } 90° = 1, \quad \textbf{cos } 90° = 0$$

Ninety degrees is not in the domain of the tangent function. Values for functions of 0° are:

$$\textbf{sin } 0° = 0, \quad \textbf{cos } 0° = 1, \quad \textbf{tan } 0° = 0.$$

With the preceding information, you see, as you look down the sine column, that as an angle increases from 0° to 90°, the sine increases from 0 to 1. How do the cosine and tangent change as the angle increases?

If the value of one of its trigonometric functions is given, the measure of an acute angle can be estimated. For example, the table indicates that an angle whose cosine is approximately 0.7660 has a measure of 40°.

Suppose that tan A = 2.5101, a number not listed in your table. To find the approximate measure of ∠A, locate in the tangent column the entries between which 2.5101 lies:

$$\text{tan } 68° \doteq 2.4751 \quad \text{and} \quad \text{tan } 69° \doteq 2.6051.$$

Thus,

$$68° < m\angle A < 69°.$$

Since 2.5101 is much closer to 2.4751 than it is to 2.6051,

$$m\angle A \doteq 68°, \text{ to the nearest degree.}$$

Oral Exercises

From Table 5 in the Appendix, find the requested value.

1. cos 22°	**3.** sin 42°	**5.** tan 89°	**7.** cos 45°
2. tan 15°	**4.** cos 74°	**6.** sin 1°	**8.** sin 45°

Find the measure of the acute ∠A to the nearest degree.

9. sin A = 0.6018	**13.** cos A = 0.9945
10. cos A = 0.5299	**14.** tan A = 0.0699
11. tan A = 1.1504	**15.** sin A = $\frac{1}{2}$
12. sin A = 0.9998	**16.** cos A = $\frac{2}{3}$

Written Exercises

From Table 5 in the Appendix, give the (a) sine, (b) cosine, and (c) tangent of the angle with given measure.

A

1. 10°	**3.** 21°	**5.** 44°	**7.** 60°	**9.** 83°
2. 12°	**4.** 38°	**6.** 50°	**8.** 75°	**10.** 30°

Find the measure of the acute $\angle A$ to the nearest degree.

11. $\cos A = 0.9272$ **14.** $\cos A = 0.7071$ **17.** $\cos A = \frac{4}{5}$

12. $\sin A = 0.9272$ **15.** $\sin A = 0.0523$ **18.** $\sin A = \frac{1}{10}$

13. $\tan A = 1.5399$ **16.** $\tan A = 0.6009$

Use Table 5 in the Appendix to find the necessary function values and then compute each of the following. Round your result to the nearest tenth.

SAMPLE. $24.2 \sin 51°$

Solution: From the table, $\sin 51° = 0.7771$

$$(24.2) \times (0.7771) = 18.80582 \doteq 18.8. \quad \textbf{Answer.}$$

19. $18.1 \tan 71°$ **21.** $\frac{2}{3} \sin 81°$ **23.** $\dfrac{102}{\tan 60°}$

20. $50.2 \cos 47°$ **22.** $\frac{4}{5} \tan 35°$ **24.** $\dfrac{403}{\sin 18°}$

14–9 Numerical Trigonometry

There are many practical problems that can be solved easily by the use of these functions. Many of these problems involve triangles. It is for this reason that the sine, cosine, and tangent are called **trigonometric functions.** The word *trigonometry* means "triangle measure."

EXAMPLE 1. How long a support rope (to the nearest foot) is needed to help anchor a ship's mast if the rope is attached to the mast 25 feet above the deck of the ship, and if the rope forms an angle of 75° with the deck of the ship?

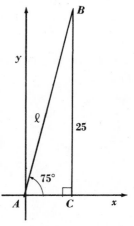

Solution: You see in the diagram that you must deal with the triangle *ABC*, and that what you want to find is the length of the line *AB*.

To see how the functions about which you have just learned can help, think of coordinate axes being drawn so that the *X*-axis lies along the deck, the origin is at point *A*, and the *Y*-axis is upright, like the mast of the ship.

Then angle *CAB* is in standard position, and we may write $\sin 75° = \dfrac{25}{l}$. Then $l \sin 75° = 25$.

$$l = \frac{25}{\sin 75°} \doteq \frac{25}{0.9659} \doteq 25.9.$$

You would need a 26-foot rope.   Answer.

In order to save yourself the trouble of drawing a set of coordinate axes in every problem, you can work out once and for all a very simple relation and remember it.

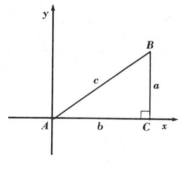

Figure 14–12

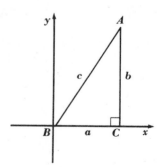

Figure 14–13

Place the right triangle ABC (in which $\angle C$ is the right angle) on a set of coordinate axes so that $\angle A$ is in standard position as in Figure 14–12. Let $AB = c$, $AC = b$, and $BC = a$. Then

$$\sin A = \frac{a}{c}, \quad \cos A = \frac{b}{c}, \quad \tan A = \frac{a}{b}.$$

If $\angle B$ is in standard position as in Figure 14–13, you have

$$\sin B = \frac{b}{c}, \quad \cos B = \frac{a}{c}, \quad \tan B = \frac{b}{a}.$$

Therefore, you can say the following:

For either acute angle of a right triangle:

The sine is the length of the side opposite the angle divided by the length of the hypotenuse.

The cosine is the length of the side adjacent to the angle divided by the length of the hypotenuse.

The tangent is the length of the side opposite the angle divided by the length of the side adjacent to the angle.

EXAMPLE 2. In diving, a submarine travels at a steady rate of 880 feet per minute and at a constant angle of 6°. How far (to the nearest foot) beneath the surface of the water will the submarine be after starting at the surface and diving for 5 minutes?

Solution: In 5 minutes, the submarine will have traveled 5 × 880, or 4400 feet. From the figure, you see that you want to find *a*, knowing angle *A* and *c*, the hypotenuse of the triangle.

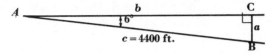

Remembering that the sine of angle *A* is the length of the side opposite divided by the length of the hypotenuse, you write

$$\sin 6° = \frac{a}{4400}.$$

You do not need to use coordinate axes and standard position.

From Table 5 in the Appendix, sin 6° ≐ 0.1045. Then

$$0.1045 ≐ \frac{a}{4400}$$

or

$$a ≐ (0.1045)(4400) ≐ 459.80.$$

The submarine will be approximately 460 feet beneath the surface. **Answer.**

EXAMPLE 3. If the submarine described in Example 2 has traveled from its point of dive to a place beneath a ship located 1 mile (5280 feet) from its point of dive:

a. How deep is the submarine at that point?

b. How far has it traveled through the water?

Solution: a. Here you know *b* and *A* and you want to find *a* and *c*. To find *a*, you notice that it is the side opposite the angle, and you know the side adjacent to the angle. You therefore write

$$\tan 6° = \frac{a}{5280}.$$

From the table, tan 6° ≐ 0.1051.

Then $a = 5280 \tan 6° ≐ 554.9.$

The depth of the submarine will be 555 feet. **Answer.**

b. To find c, you can write

$$\cos 6° = \frac{5280}{c}.$$

From the table, $\cos 6° \doteq 0.9945$

$$c = \frac{5280}{\cos 6°} \doteq \frac{5280}{0.9945} \doteq 5309.2.$$

The submarine will have traveled approximately 5309 feet from its point of dive.   Answer.

Problems

Solve each problem, drawing a sketch for each.   Express distances to the nearest foot. Use Table 5 in the Appendix as needed.

A **1.** A loading ramp is 40 feet long and forms an angle measuring 12° with the level ground. How high is the top end of the ramp?

2. A telephone pole casts a shadow 18 feet long when the sun's rays strike the ground at an angle of 48°. How tall is the pole?

3. How long must a brace to a TV antenna be if it is attached to the antenna 23 feet above the ground and forms an angle of 58° with the antenna?

4. The bed of a lake is a flat plane making an angle of 16° with the surface of the lake.   How far from shore is the depth of the water 15 feet?

5. A rectangular vacant lot is 200 feet long.   How long is a straight path cutting diagonally across the lot from one corner to the opposite corner, if the path forms an angle of 38° with the 200 foot side?

6. A patio roof makes an angle of 84° with the back wall of a house. If the roof itself is 16 feet long, how far from the wall of the house does the roof extend?

7. A 45-foot gangplank is attached to a pier at a distance of 35 feet from the side of a ship. How high above the pier is the deck of the ship?

8. Find the height of a skyscraper if you know that its top is 1000 feet from a point on the ground and its base is 200 feet from the same point.

In the following problems, the term *angle of elevation*, and a related term, *angle of depression*, will be used. The exact meaning of these terms is illustrated in the accompanying diagram. $\angle CAB$ is an **angle of ele-**

vation; the point B is *elevated* with respect to the observer at A and the horizontal line AC through A. ∠SRQ is an **angle of depression**; the point Q is *depressed* with respect to the observer at R and the horizontal line SR through R.

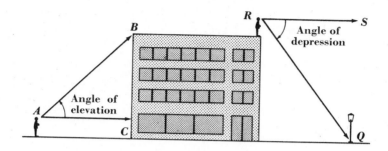

Give each answer to the nearest tenth unless otherwise specified. Use the table on page 580 as needed.

9. An observer notes that the angle of elevation from a spot 10,000 feet from the launch pad of a rocket to the ascending rocket is 56°. How high is the rocket at that time?

10. The 300-foot tall Adams building is located 400 feet from the Duncan building. If the angle of elevation from the top of the Adams building to the top of the Duncan building is 29°, how tall is the Duncan building?

11. From a point 310 feet from the ground in a control tower, the angle of depression to an airplane taxiing along the ground is 33°. How far from the base of the tower is the airplane?

12. An oil well is drilled on a slant line making an angle of depression of 23° with the level surface. How long is the shaft when the tip of the drill is 150′ below the surface?

13. The angle of elevation from an observer on the ground to a weather balloon 70,000 feet above the ground is 63°. How far from the observer is the point on the ground directly beneath the balloon?

14. The angle of elevation from a sailboat to the top of an 800-foot cliff on the coast is 31°. How far from the coast is the boat?

15. An airplane located 6000 feet above a marker beacon glides along a straight path with an angle of depression of 8°. How far from the marker beacon does the airplane contact the ground?

16. From a window in the Charles Hotel located 140 feet above the ground, the angle of elevation to the roof of the Hook building is 51°. If the Hook building is located 3000 feet from the Charles Hotel, how tall is the Hook building?

Sometimes a problem requires that you find the measure of an angle.

SAMPLE.   The shadow of a 200-foot tower is 180 feet long. What is the angle of elevation of the sun?

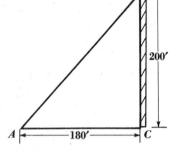

Solution: You can see at once that

$$\tan A = \tfrac{200}{180} = 1.1111.$$

Referring to the tables, you have

$$\tan 48° \doteq 1.1106$$
$$\tan 49° \doteq 1.1504$$

To the nearst degree, therefore, the angle of elevation of the sun is 48°.   **Answer.**

Give answers to tenths or to the nearest degree.

17. A pilot wishes to take off and climb along a straight path so that he will be 2000 feet above the ground by the time he reaches a distance of 1 mile (5280 feet) along the ground from his point of takeoff. What angle of elevation should his flight path have?

18. A submarine dives, it maintains a constant angle of descent. What is the angle of descent if the submarine has traveled a distance of 1000 yards across the surface of the sea while descending 80 yards?

19. A balloon on a 500-foot cable is blown to one side by the wind. If the balloon is 475 feet above the ground, what angle does the cable make with the ground?

20. What is the angle of elevation from a point 120 feet from the base of a 420-foot building to the top of the building?

21. A ship leaves harbor and sails on a constant heading in a general northeasterly direction. If the seacoast runs directly north and south, what angle does the path of the ship make with the coast if the ship is 80 miles from the coast after it has sailed 110 miles?

22. An 80-foot escalator raises a passenger 28 feet from the first to the second floor of the Shoppers' Mart. What angle does the escalator make with the first floor?

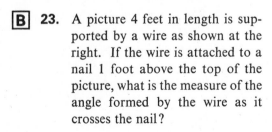

B **23.** A picture 4 feet in length is supported by a wire as shown at the right. If the wire is attached to a nail 1 foot above the top of the picture, what is the measure of the angle formed by the wire as it crosses the nail?

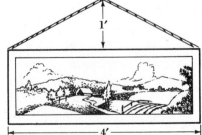

24. Two support cables to a TV antenna are anchored to the same spot on the ground 40 feet from the base of the tower. If one cable is fastened to the tower 40 feet above the ground and the other is fastened to the tower 60 feet above the ground, what is the measure of the angle between the cables?

14–10   Similar Triangles

Triangles ABC and $A'B'C'$ have the same shape, but differ in size. Clearly, you must first know precisely what is meant by "having the same shape." This means that

$$m\angle A = m\angle A', \quad m\angle B = m\angle B', \quad m\angle C = m\angle C'.$$

Such triangles are called **similar triangles**.

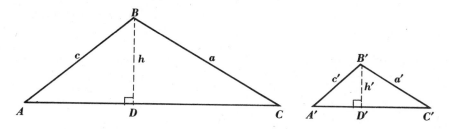

Figure 14–14

What can be said about the lengths of the sides of triangles ABC and $A'B'C'$? Draw $\overline{BD}$ and $\overline{B'D'}$. Call their lengths h and h', respectively. Then, since $m\angle A = m\angle A'$,

$$\sin A = \frac{h}{c} = \sin A' = \frac{h'}{c'};$$

$$\therefore \frac{h}{c} = \frac{h'}{c'}, \quad \text{or} \quad \frac{h}{h'} = \frac{c}{c'}.$$

Using triangles BDC and $B'D'C'$,

$$\sin C = \frac{h}{a} = \sin C' = \frac{h'}{a'};$$

$$\therefore \frac{h}{a} = \frac{h'}{a'}, \quad \text{or} \quad \frac{h}{h'} = \frac{a}{a'}.$$

Then

$$\frac{a}{a'} = \frac{c}{c'},$$

since each is equal to $\dfrac{h}{h'}$.

Similarly, by drawing perpendicular lines from C and C' to $\overline{AB}$ and $\overline{A'B'}$ you can show that $\dfrac{a}{a'} = \dfrac{b}{b'}$. Thus,

$$\frac{a}{a'} = \frac{b}{b'} = \frac{c}{c'}.$$

THEOREM. The sides of two similar triangles are proportional.

Written Exercises

A

1. Two angles of a triangle measure 80° and 72°. What is the measure of the smallest angle in a similar triangle?

2. Two angles of a triangle measure 30° and 40°. What is the measure of the largest angle in a similar triangle?

Exercises 3–6 refer to the adjoining figure. Assume that triangles ABC and $A'B'C'$ are similar.

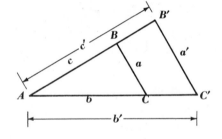

3. If $a' = 10$ inches, $c' = 14$ inches, and $a = 4$ inches, find c.

4. If $c = 12$ yards, $b' = 26$ yards, and $c' = 20$ yards, find b.

5. If $a' = 8$ centimeters, $b' = 15$ centimeters, and $a = 3$ centimeters, find b.

6. If $a = 12$ feet, $b = 15$ feet, $b' = 25$ feet, and $c = 14$ feet, find a' and c'.

Exercises 7–9 refer to the figure shown, which has right angles at B, C, and D.

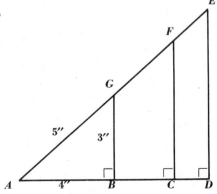

7. What is the ratio of ED to AD?

8. What is the ratio of FC to AF?

9. If $\overline{AE}$ and $\overline{AD}$ were extended to the right to points E' and D', respectively, to form a right triangle $AE'D'$, what would be the ratio of AD' to AE'?

Problems

Similar triangles can be used in practical problems also.

SAMPLE 1. An airplane takes off and climbs on a path making a constant angle with the ground. If the airplane is at an altitude of 1000 feet when it crosses an inner marker beacon located 6000 feet from the take-off point, at what altitude will it be when it crosses an outer marker beacon located 30,000 feet from the take-off point?

Solution: By trigonometry, you would say:

$$\tan A = \tfrac{1000}{6000} = \tfrac{1}{6}$$

$$\tan A = \frac{h}{30,000}$$

$$h = 30,000 \tan A$$

$$= 30,000 \cdot \tfrac{1}{6}$$

$$= 5000$$

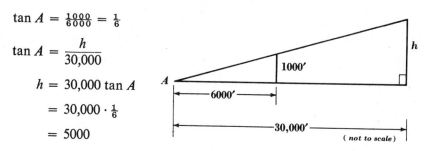

By similar triangles, you say:

$$\frac{h}{30,000} = \frac{1000}{6000} \quad \text{or} \quad \frac{h}{30,000} = \frac{1}{6}$$

$$h = \frac{30,000 \cdot 1}{6} = 5000$$

∴ the altitude of the airplane is 5000 feet.   **Answer.**

Do you see that the two methods used in Sample 1 are virtually identical? But there are problems that are much easier to do by similar triangles.

SAMPLE 2. Assuming that the triangles shown in the diagram are similar, use the distances given to find the width of the lake.

Solution: $\dfrac{W}{60} = \dfrac{4000}{300}$

$W = \tfrac{4000}{300} \cdot 60 = 800$

∴ the width of the lake is 800 feet.
   Answer.

A   **1.** A man 6 feet tall casts a shadow 5 feet in length. How tall is a flag-pole beside the man if its shadow is 35 feet in length?

2. A 48 foot tree casts a shadow 60 feet long. A boy 5 feet tall stands in the shade of the tree so that the end of his shadow is even with the end of the tree's shadow. How far is the boy from the tree?

3. When a stepladder with legs 8 feet long is standing erect, the legs are 3 feet apart at the bottom. How long is a brace of the ladder parallel to the ground if the brace is located 3 feet down each leg from the top?

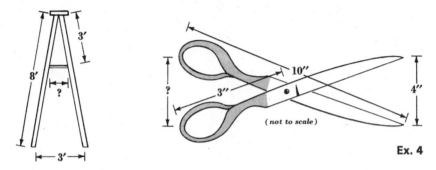

Ex. 3   Ex. 4

4. The blades of a pair of shears are 10″ long and are connected 3 inches from one end. How far apart are the ends of the handles when the tips of the blades are 4 inches apart?

5. The figure below represents a method of finding the distance across a river. If the measurements are as given, how wide is the river at the point indicated?

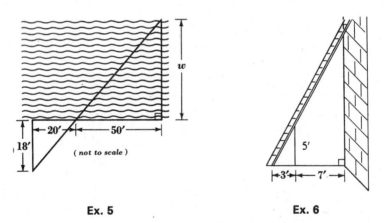

Ex. 5   Ex. 6

6. A ladder is placed across the top of a 5-foot wall to the side of a build-ing 7 feet from the wall. If the base of the ladder is 3 feet from the wall, how far up the building does the ladder touch the wall?

B **7.** A steel ramp runs from level ground to the top of a 12-foot platform. The base of the ramp is 22 feet from the foot of the platform. How far from the base of the ramp would a 4 foot support bar be placed?

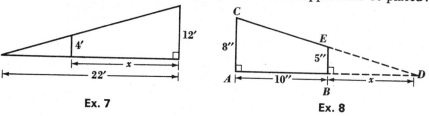

Ex. 7   Ex. 8

8. How far must the segment $\overline{AB}$ shown at the right be extended to form a triangle ACD?

VECTORS

14–11 Working with Vectors

In the town where Arthur lives, Main Street is laid out in a straight line for five miles. Arthur lives on Main Street $1\frac{1}{2}$ miles from the Post Office, downtown. If you are told that Arthur started out at noon to go downtown and that he walks at the rate of 3 miles per hour, you can easily compute just where he is at any time.

On the other hand, if you are told that an airplane left the St. Louis Airport at noon traveling at the rate of 300 miles per hour, you cannot possibly tell where it is at any time. You could say that at 1:00 P.M. it was 300 miles away, but you would not know whether it was over Arkansas, Mississippi, Tennessee, Kentucky, Indiana, Illinois, Wisconsin, Iowa, Kansas, or Oklahoma.

Arthur traveled only in a straight line, and it was sufficient to know his speed. The airplane can fly in any direction, and to be able to locate it you have to know both its speed and the direction in which it was traveling. Speed in a given direction is called *velocity*, which is a good example of a *vector* quantity.

A **vector** is a quantity that has both magnitude and direction. A vector quantity is represented by a directed line segment or arrow. On the following page are a few examples. Units of length on the arrow indicate the units of magnitude of the vector, and the direction of the arrow indicates the direction of the vector.

In Figure 14–15 vectors represent:

a. A velocity of 30 miles per hour in a northeasterly direction.
b. A force of 100 pounds exerted to the left and 20° upward.
c. Motion in a straight line from $A(1, 0)$ to $B(-3, 3)$.
d. Motion from the origin to $C(-4, 3)$.

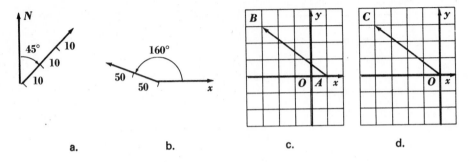

a.   b.   c.   d.

Figure 14–15

In order to deal adequately with vectors the concept of angle presented earlier must be somewhat extended. The notion of angle as

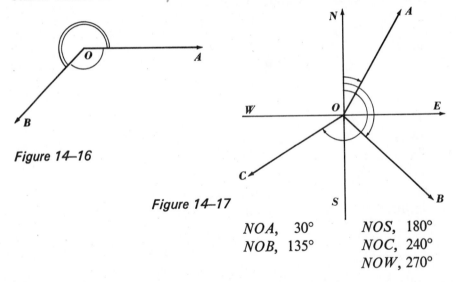

Figure 14–16

Figure 14–17

NOA, 30°	*NOS*, 180°
NOB, 135°	*NOC*, 240°
	NOW, 270°

the set of points formed by two rays starting from the same point does not enable you to distinguish between angle *AOB* less than 180°, marked with a single arc, and the angle *AOB* marked with a double arc. In working with vectors it is convenient to be able to make such a distinction. In navigation, for instance, angles are always measured clockwise from the north. Thus, Figure 14–17 shows *headings*, or *bearings* as navigators call them, as indicated.

Similarly, mathematicians often measure angles counterclockwise from the positive *x*-axis. A few examples are shown in Figure 14–18.

It does not seem necessary or desirable to give a formal redefinition of angle. The only essential point is to understand that angles can now exceed 180°, and, in any particular problem, to be sure you know where the initial ray of the angle is. As stated, in most problems of pure mathematics, the initial ray is the positive *x*-axis; in navigation problems, it is north; in other problems it should be clear from the context.

Now that the idea of angle has been extended to include angles greater than 180°, do you see that a vector may be specified by giving its magnitude and direction as a number pair, for example, (100, 200°) or by giving its initial and terminal points, for example, *A*(1, 0) to *B*(−3, 3)?

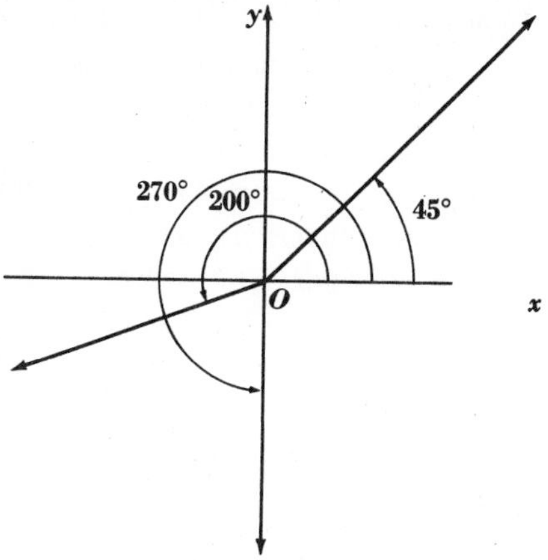

Figure 14–18

A short way to represent a vector is to place a half-headed arrow above the names of its endpoints, thus: $\overrightarrow{AB}$ represents the vector from *A* to *B* and $\overrightarrow{BA}$ represents the vector from *B* to *A*. $\overrightarrow{AB}$ and $\overrightarrow{BA}$ are *opposite vectors* because they have the same magnitude, *AB*, and are collinear but have opposite directions; therefore, you may write $\overrightarrow{AB} = -\overrightarrow{BA}$.

Vectors, like $\overrightarrow{AB}$ and $\overrightarrow{OC}$ in Figure 14–15, that have the same magnitude and act in the same direction are **equivalent vectors**. You can see that *AB* = *OC*, and $\overrightarrow{AB}$ is parallel to $\overrightarrow{OC}$ with the same direction.

The vector representing the **sum** of two or more vectors is their **resultant**. For example, the resultant of the forces exerted by a man pulling horizontally to the right with a force of 14 pounds and by a boy pushing in the same direction with a force of 10 pounds is a horizontal force of 24 pounds to the right (Figure 14–19, left). If the boy pushes to the left, the resultant is a force of 4 pounds to the right.

Figure 14–19

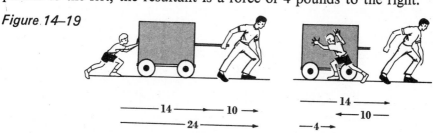

When the vectors are not parallel, the resultant may be found as shown in the following:

EXAMPLE. Find the resultant velocity $\vec{V}$ of an airplane flying due north at 120 miles per hour, $\vec{V_A}$, through a wind blowing toward the east at 35 miles per hour, $\vec{V_W}$.

Solution 1: To add $\vec{V_A}$ and $\vec{V_W}$, construct to scale a right triangle having $\vec{V_A}$ as one side and a vector $\vec{V_B}$ equivalent to $\vec{V_W}$ as the other side. In an hour, the plane would have traveled 120 miles due north through air that has itself moved 35 miles due east. From the drawing, you can estimate that the plane is actually moving at 125 miles per hour on a heading of 16°.

Answer.

$\frac{1''}{8} = 10$ mi.

Solution 2: You can also use trigonometry to solve the problem.

Direction of $\vec{V}$ is $\angle QPR$

$$\tan \angle QPR = \frac{QR}{PQ} = \frac{35}{120} \doteq 0.2917$$

$$m\angle QPR \doteq 16°$$

Magnitude of $\vec{V}$ is PR.

$$\sin \angle QPR = \frac{QR}{PR}$$

$$PR = \frac{QR}{\sin \angle QPR}$$

$$\doteq \frac{35}{0.2756}$$

$$\doteq 1.27$$

∴ the plane is flying at approximately 127 miles per hour on a heading of about 16°. **Answer.**

Written Exercises

State whether or not the given quantity is a vector quantity.

1. The size of your shoe
2. Your waist measure
3. An east wind at 12 miles per hour
4. Your weight
5. A speed of 6 miles per hour due west
6. The temperature at a point in your classroom
7. A horizontal force of 200 pounds
8. Your age

Name a vector in parallelogram *ABCD* equivalent to the given vector.

9. $\overrightarrow{AD}$ **11.** $-\overrightarrow{CB}$

10. $\overrightarrow{BA}$ **12.** $-\overrightarrow{DC}$

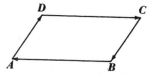

Complete each statement so that it is a true statement about the figure shown at the right.

13. $\overrightarrow{AB} + \overrightarrow{BF} = \underline{}$

14. $\overrightarrow{AC} + \overrightarrow{CB} = \underline{}$

15. $\overrightarrow{AE} + \underline{} = \overrightarrow{AD}$

16. $\overrightarrow{AF} + \underline{} = \overrightarrow{AC}$

17. $\overrightarrow{AE} + \underline{} = \overrightarrow{AF} + \overrightarrow{FD}$

18. $\overrightarrow{AB} + \overrightarrow{BD} = \overrightarrow{AC} + \underline{}$

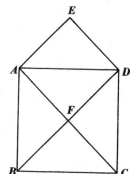

Find each resultant using **(a)** a scale drawing and **(b)** trigonometry.

19. Forces of 80 pounds up and 60 pounds to the right.

20. Forces of 150 pounds down and 200 pounds to the left.

21. Velocities of 50 miles per hour north and 120 miles per hour west.

22. Velocities of 7 feet per second south and 15 feet per second east.

Problems

For each problem, draw a sketch and find the answer to the nearest whole number using trigonometry.

A

1. Two men push a crate across a smooth surface. One man pushes with a force of 80 pounds due north and the other with a force of 100 pounds due east. Describe the force acting on the crate.

2. A boat moves due west at a speed of 10 miles per hour in a current flowing due south at a rate of 3 miles per hour. Describe the speed and direction the boat is moving over the surface of the earth.

3. A balloon rises at 24 feet per minute in a wind blowing at a rate of 10 feet per minute due east. Describe the speed and direction the balloon is moving.

4. An airplane flies at a rate of 200 miles per hour heading due south in a wind blowing 40 miles per hour due west. Describe the speed and direction of the airplane over the ground.

5. A woman walks from one side of a train to the other. If the woman is walking west at 4 miles per hour and the train is moving north at 50 miles per hour, describe the speed and direction of the woman over the ground.

6. A stone sinks steadily at a rate of 2 miles per hour in a stream of water moving at 3 miles per hour. Describe the speed and direction of the stone's motion.

14–12   Resolving a Vector

Two vectors, such as $\vec{V_1}$ and $\vec{V_2}$ in Figure 14–20, whose sum is $\vec{V}$ are called **components** of $\vec{V}$. Of particular interest are the horizontal and vertical components of a vector because they refer to a rectangular coordinate system.

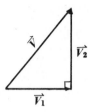

Figure 14–20

EXAMPLE 1.   Mr. Clark pulls on a rope attached to the bow of his boat with a force of 75 pounds. What is the horizontal force moving the boat if the rope makes an angle of 48° with the horizontal?

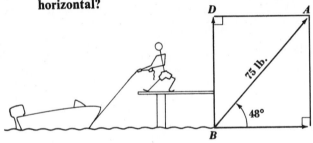

Solution:

1. **Draw a right triangle and label it to represent the known forces and angles.**

2. $\cos 48° = \dfrac{BC}{75}$

$$BC = 75 \cos 48° \doteq 75(0.6691) \doteq 50.2$$

∴ **the horizontal force is about 50 pounds.   Answer.**

By using sin 48° in Example 1, you can find the vertical component (force pulling the boat out of the water) to be approximately 56 pounds.

Can you find the resultant of two vectors whose horizontal and vertical components are known? The component of the resultant in each direction is the sum of the components of the vectors in that direction.

EXAMPLE 2. Two trucks pull a ship through a canal by means of cable attached to it. One truck exerts a force of 2000 pounds at 40° south of east and the other exerts a force of 2500 pounds at 32° north of east. If the boat is moving due east through the canal, what is the force moving it in that direction?

Solution:

Let $\overrightarrow{x_N}$ = the horizontal component of the force to the north of east.

$\overrightarrow{x_S}$ = the horizontal component of the force to the south of east.

$\overrightarrow{x}$ = the total force moving the ship east.

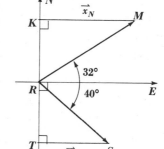

In $\triangle RKM$: $\sin 58° = \dfrac{\overrightarrow{x_N}}{2500}$ In $\triangle RTS$: $\sin 50° = \dfrac{\overrightarrow{x_S}}{2000}$

$\therefore \overrightarrow{x_N} = 2500 \sin 58°$ $\overrightarrow{x_S} = 2000 \sin 50°$

$\doteq 2500(0.848)$ $\doteq 2000(0.766)$

$\overrightarrow{x_N} \doteq 2120$ $\overrightarrow{x_S} \doteq 1532$

$$\overrightarrow{x} \doteq 2120 + 1532 \doteq 3652$$

$\therefore$ the total force due east is approximately 3652 pounds. **Answer.**

Problems

A

1. Karen pushes on a window pole with a force of 20 pounds at an angle of 28° with the vertical. How great a force raises the window?

2. Mr. Rogers pulls a rope making an angle of 35° from the vertical with a force of 120 pounds. What is the lifting force on a stump attached to the other end of the rope?

3. A kite pulls on a taut string with a force of 36 pounds. If the string makes an angle of 58° with the horizontal, what is the force acting on the kite in the direction of the wind?

4. In Problem 3, what is the vertical force acting on the kite?

5. A man on a pier pulls on a rope attached to a boat in the water with a force of 75 pounds. If the rope makes an angle of 72° with the surface of the water, what is the force propelling the boat through the water?

6. Lori is walking Sam, holding the leash at an angle of 43° with the horizontal. If the dog tugs forward with a force of 30 pounds, with how much force must she pull on the leash to hold the dog still?

B 7. The tugboat Mary Jane pulls on a steamer with a force of 2000 pounds in a direction 45° west of north, while the tugboat Starfish pulls on the same boat with a force of 2400 pounds in a direction of 45° east of north. If the steamer is steering due north, what force is acting on the steamer in that direction?

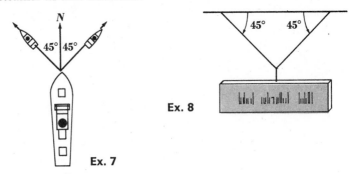

Ex. 8

Ex. 7

8. A 400-pound sign is suspended by two cables, each making an angle of 45° with the horizontal. Find the pull on each cable.

● CHAPTER SUMMARY ●

Inventory of Structure and Method

1. **Geometry** deals with the properties of sets of points. **Theorems** stating properties of geometric figures are proved on the basis of axioms stating assumptions for numbers, points, lines, and planes. Once a theorem is proved, you can use it in proving other theorems.

2. **Every line segment** has a length, and every angle has a measure. In a triangle the sum of the measures of the angles is 180°.

3. The **tangent** of an angle in standard position is the slope of the terminal ray. It may be pictured by the length cut off by the terminal ray above (or below) the x-axis on the line $x = 1$.

4. The **sine** of an angle in standard position is the ordinate of the point on the terminal ray whose distance from the origin is 1. The abscissa of the point is the **cosine** of the angle.

5. In any right triangle, if you know two sides, or one side and one angle, you can find the parts you do not know by using the tangent, sine, or cosine.

6. **Similar triangles** are triangles that have the same shape, that is, all of whose angles respectively have the same measure. Sides of similar triangles are proportional.

7. The **resultant of vectors** acting in the same or opposite directions at a point may be found by adding or subtracting their magnitudes. To find the resultant of two vectors acting at right angles to each other, find the hypotenuse of a right triangle whose sides represent the vectors.

8. To find the **vertical and horizontal components** of a vector, determine the sides of a right triangle whose hypotenuse represents the vector.

Vocabulary and Spelling

Review the meaning of each term by reference to the page listed.

collinear (*p. 524*)
coplanar (*p. 525*)
distance (*p. 525*)
between (*p. 526*)
line segment (*p. 526*)
ray (*p. 527*)
angle (*p. 528*)
standard position (*p. 532*)
triangle (*p. 532*)
degree measure (*p. 534*)
tangent function (*p. 535*)

unit circle (*p. 535*)
sine function (*p. 538*)
cosine function (*p. 538*)
trigonometric function (*p. 545*)
angle of elevation (*p. 548*)
angle of depression (*p. 549*)
similar triangles (*p. 552*)
vector (*p. 555*)
equivalent vectors (*p. 557*)
resultant (*p. 557*)
components (*p. 560*)

Chapter Test

14–2 1. The coordinates of points *A*, *B*, and *C* are 7, 6, and 12, respectively. Which point is between the other two?

14–3 State whether the graph of the given sentence is a ray, a line segment, a point, a line or none of these.

2. $|x| \leq 2$ 3. $x \leq 2$

14–4 4. In triangle *ABC*, *AB* = 6, *BC* = 8, and *AC* = 9. Is the triangle a right triangle?

14–5 5. If $\angle COA$ is in standard position, and $\overrightarrow{OA}$ lies in the second quadrant, what kind of an angle is $\angle COA$?

14–6 6. What is the tangent of an angle in standard position, if the terminal side of the angle contains the point (5, 1)?

14–7 7. If the terminal side of an angle *A* in standard position contains the point (6, 8), what is sin *A* and what is cos *A*?

14–8   Here is an excerpt from the table of trigonometric functions. Use it as necessary for the remainder of this test.

Angle	Sine	Cosine	Tangent
21°	0.3584	0.9336	0.3839
22°	0.3746	0.9272	0.4040
23°	0.3907	0.9205	0.4245

  8. What is cos 23°?

  9. If tan $A = 0.3839$, what is the degree measure of $\angle A$?

14–9   **10.** Find the height of a flagpole casting a 100-foot shadow if the sun's rays strike the ground at an angle of 21°.

14–10   **11.** How high is a tree with a 42-foot shadow if a 6-foot man casts a 5-foot shadow?

14–11   **12.** What is the magnitude of the resultant of two forces acting at right angles to each other if the forces are 50 pounds and 120 pounds?

14–12   **13.** Tom pushes a lawn mower with a force of 50 pounds at an angle of 23° from the vertical. What is the force moving the lawn mower forward?

Chapter Review

14–2   **Geometric Assumptions**   *Pages 524–527*

  1. Any three points lie in a __?__.

  2. Any __?__ points are collinear.

  3. If point B is between points A and C, then $AB + BC =$ __?__.

  4. If a, b, and c are the coordinates of collinear points A, B, and C, respectively, and if $a < b < c$, then point __?__ is between points __?__ and __?__.

14–3   **Rays and Angles**   *Pages 527–529*

Identify the graph of each sentence as a ray, a point, a line segment, a line, or none of these.

  5. $2 \leq x \leq 7$ **7.** $x \geq 5$

  6. $|x| \leq 3$ **8.** $|x| \leq 0$

14–4   **The Measurement of Angles**   *Pages 529–532*

  9. The measure of an obtuse angle lies between __?__ and __?__.

  10. If an angle is in standard position, its vertex lies at the __?__ of a rectangular coordinate system.

14–5   **Triangles**   *Pages 532–533*

11.   The sum of the measures of the angles of a triangle is __?__ .

12.   In $\triangle ABC, m\angle B = 90°, AB = 5, BC = 12$, and $AC =$ __?__ .

14–6   **Tangent of an Angle**   *Pages 533–537*

13.   If the slope of the terminal side of an angle in standard position is $\frac{3}{2}$, then the tangent of the angle is __?__ .

14.   If the point $(-2, 5)$ is in the terminal side of an angle in standard position, then the tangent of the angle is __?__ .

14–7   **Sine and Cosine of an Angle**   *Pages 537–543*

15.   The cosine of an angle is a number between __?__ and __?__ , inclusive.

16.   If $\sin A = \frac{3}{5}$ and $\cos A = \frac{4}{5}$, then $\tan A =$ __?__ .

14–8   **Function Values**   *Pages 543–545*

Use the table on page 580 to complete the sentences in Exercises 17 and 18.

17. $\cos 48° \doteq$ __?__   **18.** $\sin$ __?__ $\doteq 0.9336$

14–9   **Numerical Trigonometry**   *Pages 545–551*

19.   Find the height of a tree (to the nearest foot) casting a 32 foot shadow when the sun's rays make a 48° angle with the ground.

20.   How long (to the nearest inch) is the diagonal of a rectangle if the rectangle is 18 inches wide and the diagonal forms an angle measuring 40° with the longer side?

14–10   **Similar Triangles**   *Pages 551–555*

21.   The sides of two similar triangles are __?__ .

22.   A tree casts a 30-foot shadow at the same time a 6-foot man casts a 5-foot shadow. How tall is the tree?

14–11   **Working with Vectors**   *Pages 555–560*

23.   Find the magnitude to the nearest pound and the direction angle to the nearest degree of the resultant of a force of 200 pounds acting downward and a force of 150 pounds acting to the right.

14–12   **Resolving a Vector**   *Pages 560–564*

24.   Jack pulls a wagon with a force of 32 pounds along a handle making an angle of 32 degrees with the horizontal. To the nearest pound, what is the force propelling the wagon along the ground?

Complex Numbers

In a plane, a point like $P(3, 2)$ determines a vector $(\overrightarrow{OP})$ from the origin to the point. To pair a number with each such vector, begin with the real numbers as the partners of the horizontal vectors from O, as shown below.

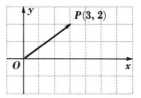

Point	Vector	Number
(3, 0)	$\overrightarrow{ON}$	3
(−2, 0)	$\overrightarrow{OM}$	−2
(0, 0)	$\overrightarrow{OO}$ (length 0)	0

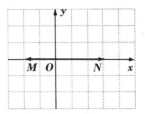

Since you use all the real numbers as partners of the horizontal vectors, you need *new* numbers as partners of the vertical vectors. Use the letter i to designate the partner of $\overrightarrow{OR}$, $R(0, 1)$, and, in general, ai to name the partner of the vector to $(0, a)$, as shown below. By agreement, $0i = 0$.

Point	Vector	Number
(0, 1)	$\overrightarrow{OR}$	i
(0, 2)	$\overrightarrow{OS}$	$2i$
(0, −3)	$\overrightarrow{OW}$	$-3i$

The vector $\overrightarrow{OP}$ at the right has $\overrightarrow{ON}$ as its horizontal component and $\overrightarrow{OS}$ as its vertical component. Since $\overrightarrow{OP} = \overrightarrow{ON} + \overrightarrow{OS}$ (page 557), pair $\overrightarrow{OP}$ with the sum of the partners of $\overrightarrow{ON}$ and $\overrightarrow{OS}$: $3 + 2i$. In general, pair the vector from O to (a, b) with the sum $a + bi$.

Point	Vector	Number
(−2, 1)	$\overrightarrow{OL}$	$-2 + i$
(−2, −3)	$\overrightarrow{OH}$	$-2 - 3i$
(4, −1)	$\overrightarrow{OJ}$	$4 - i$

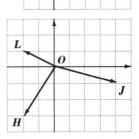

Expressions of the form $a + bi$, where a and b are real numbers, represent the elements of the *set of complex numbers*. You add two complex numbers just as you add vectors whose horizontal and vertical components you know:

$$(2 + 3i) + (4 - 7i) = (2 + 4) + (3 - 7)i = 6 - 4i$$

In general, if $a + bi$ and $c + di$ are complex numbers, then

$$(a + bi) + (c + di) = (a + c) + (b + d)i.$$

The identity element for addition is $0 + 0i$, or 0. Because

$$(a + bi) + (-a - bi) = 0 + 0i,$$

the additive inverse of $a + bi$ is $-a - bi$.

To multiply complex numbers, first define

$$i^2 = -1.$$

Then, multiply (as you multiply binomials) as follows:

$$(a + bi)(c + di) = ac + i^2 bd + adi + bci$$

Thus:

$$(a + bi)(c + di) = (ac - bd) + (ad + bc)i$$

For example:

$$(2 + 3i)(4 - 7i) = 8 - i^2 \cdot 21 - 14i + 12i$$
$$= (8 + 21) + (-14 + 12)i$$
$$= 29 - 2i$$

The identity element for multiplication is $1 + 0i$, or 1. To find the reciprocal of a complex number such as $3 + 2i$, proceed as follows:

$$\frac{1}{3 + 2i} = \frac{1}{3 + 2i} \cdot \frac{3 - 2i}{3 - 2i} = \frac{3 - 2i}{9 + 4}$$

$$\therefore \frac{1}{3 + 2i} = \frac{3}{13} - \frac{2}{13}i.$$

Numbers like $3 + 2i$ and $3 - 2i$ are *conjugate complex numbers*. The product of a complex number and its conjugate is a real number:

$$(a + bi)(a - bi) = a^2 + b^2$$

The complex number system is closed under addition, subtraction, multiplication, and division (except by 0).

EXAMPLE. If $r = 3 + i$ and $s = 4 - 3i$, find $r + s$, $r - s$, $r \cdot s$, $r \div s$.

Solution:

$$r + s = (3 + i) + (4 - 3i) = 7 - 2i$$
$$r - s = (3 + i) - (4 - 3i) = (3 + i) + (-4 + 3i) = -1 + 4i$$
$$r \cdot s = (3 + i) \cdot (4 - 3i) = 12 - 3(-1) - 9i + 4i = 15 - 5i$$
$$r \div s = \frac{3 + i}{4 - 3i} = \frac{3 + i}{4 - 3i} \cdot \frac{4 + 3i}{4 + 3i} = \frac{9 + 13i}{25} = \frac{9}{25} + \frac{13}{25} i$$

The complex number system has the commutative and associative axioms of addition and multiplication and also the distributive axiom. Moreover, any polynomial equation of degree n having this system as the domain of its coefficients and variable has n roots in this system. For example, the solution set of $x^2 + 1 = 0$ is $\{i, -i\}$. These complex numbers are thus the square roots of -1: $i = \sqrt{-1}$, $-i = -\sqrt{-1}$. Similarly, $\sqrt{-4} = \sqrt{4} \cdot \sqrt{-1} = 2i$ and $\sqrt{-48} = 4i\sqrt{3}$.

Exercises

1. Express the following in a form with i as a factor.
   a. $\sqrt{-64}$ b. $\sqrt{-27}$ c. $\sqrt{-\frac{81}{25}}$ d. $\sqrt{-0.25}$

2. Name the additive inverse and the conjugate.
   a. $5 + 2i$ b. $6 - 7i$ c. $-3 - \sqrt{-1}$ d. $7 + \sqrt{-9}$

3. Let r be the first complex number and s, the second, in the following pairs. Compute $r + s$, $r - s$, $r \cdot s$, $r \div s$.
   a. $3 + 7i, i$ c. $-i, 1 - 2i$ e. $9 - 3i, 7 + 6i$
   b. $15 + i, 1 - i$ d. $i, -3 + 2i$ f. $-3 - 5i, 6 + i$

4. Simplify:
   a. i^3 b. i^4 c. $(-3 + 7i)^2$ d. $(x - yi)(x + yi)$
   e. $(5 + 3i) + (2 - 7i) - (3 - 8i)$ g. $(-i)(1 + 2i)(-3 + i)$
   f. $\dfrac{3 + 3i}{8 + 6i} - \dfrac{7 + 4i}{2 - 3i}$ h. $\dfrac{3 - 9i}{7 + 2i} \div \dfrac{3 - 4i}{8 + 3i}$

5. Solve the following equations if the domain of the variable is the set of complex numbers.
   a. $x^2 + 25 = 0$ c. $x^2 - 2x + 2 = 0$ e. $t^2 - 6t + 34 = 0$
   b. $y^2 + 75 = 0$ d. $z^2 - 4z + 13 = 0$ f. $t^2 + 6t + 34 = 0$

6. Graph the vectors that correspond to the given complex numbers. What do you discover?
   a. $1, i, i^2$ b. $3i, i(3i)$ c. $3 + 2i, i(3 + 2i)$

Comprehensive Review and Tests

A.   Properties of Numbers: Structure

Give a reason to justify each statement. You may use an axiom, definition, theorem, etc. Unless otherwise noted, the set of real numbers is the replacement set for the variable.

1. $\dfrac{6x - 9}{3} = 2x - 3$

2. $621 + (16 + 29) = 621 + (29 + 16)$

3. $x - y = x + (-y)$

4. If $w = -z$, then $w + z = 0$.

5. If $x = 6y$, then $\dfrac{x}{6} = y$.

6. If $xy = 0$ and $y \neq 0$, then $x = 0$.

7. $(x - y)(w - z) = x(w - z) - y(w - z)$

8. $(r + h)^3 = (r + h)(r + h)(r + h)$

9. If $r^2 - 10r + 4 = 0$, then $r^2 - 10r = -4$.

10. If $c \neq 0$ and $d \neq 0$, then $a \div \dfrac{c}{d} = a \cdot \dfrac{d}{c}$.

11. If $x \neq y$, then $x > y$ or $x < y$.

12. If p and q are integers, and $r = p + q$, then r is also an integer.

13. If $A = \{-2, 0, 2\}$ and $B = \{-1, 1\}$, then the only subset of both A and B is the empty set.

14. If $n = -n$, then the only possible value of n is 0.

15. If $\dfrac{x}{16}$ is an integer, then x is an integral multiple of 16.

16. If $a > b$ and $b > c$, then $a > c$.

17. $y - 4 = 1$ and $y + 5 = 10$ are equivalent equations.

In Exercises 18–24, if the statement is always true, answer "True." If not, answer "False."

18. If a set is closed under an operation, any subset (except $\emptyset$) of that set is closed under that operation.

19. {points on the moon} is infinite.

20. The solution set of $-1 < x < 2$ is shown by this graph.

21. The absolute value of 0 is 0.

22. The solution of $x + y = -5$ is a set of ordered number pairs.

23. If $xy > 0$, then $x > 0$.

24. In right triangle ABC, $\sin A = \frac{3}{5}$ if $a = 3$, $b = 4$, and $c = 5$.

Which reason in the right-hand column goes with the statement in the left-hand column?

25. $13 + (-8) = (5 + 8) + (-8)$ A.   Axiom of opposites

26. $\qquad\qquad = 5 + [8 + (-8)]$ B.   Additive axiom of zero and transitive property of zero

27. $\qquad\qquad = 5 + 0$ C.   Associative axiom of addition

28. $\therefore\ 13 + (-8) = 5$ D.   Substitution principle

B. Fundamental Operations

Simplify.

1. $6(x - 1) - 3(2x + 1)$

2. $mn^2(10m^2n - 3m^3)$

3. $(x - 2)(5x - 1)$

4. $(x^2 + 2xy + y^2)(x - y)$

5. $(3a + c)^8 \div (3a + c)^4$

6. $(1 - 2y)^2$

7. $(y^3 + 27) \div (y + 3)$

8. $(21by^3 - 18b^2y^2 + 3b^3y) \div (-3by)$

9. $(3t^3 + 13t^2 - 2t - 7) \div (t - 3)$

10. $4(a - 1) + 2[(a + b) - 6(b - 1)]$

11. $[5(2x - 1) + (x - 4)] - 2[12x - (-x + 1)] - 10$

12. $(2x - y)(x + z)$

13. $\dfrac{3c^2 - 27}{15} \cdot \dfrac{5}{c^2 - 3c}$

14. $\dfrac{3a^2y^4}{12x^4} \div \dfrac{9ay^3}{3x^4y}$

15. $\dfrac{(y - 1)^2}{y^2 - 1}$

16. $\dfrac{2b + 12}{b^2 + 10b + 24}$

17. $\dfrac{9x^2 - 1}{3x + 1} \div \dfrac{8c^2 + 2c}{8c - 2}$

Factor each expression, leaving it in its simplest form.

18. $24y^3 - 3y^2$

19. $9y^2 - 1$

20. $4\pi r^2 - 2\pi rh$

21. $a^2 - a - 6$

22. $y^2 - 12y + 36$

23. $p + prt$

24. $36x^2 - 5x - 1$

25. $x^2 - 0.09$

26. $\frac{1}{2}bh + \frac{1}{2}b'h$

27. $2x^6 - 18$

28. $x^4 - 25x^2 + 144$

29. $13r - 26r^2 - 65r^3$

Simplify.

30. $\dfrac{1}{x+y} - \dfrac{1}{x-y}$

31. $\dfrac{b}{b+1} + \dfrac{4}{4b+4}$

32. $\dfrac{a^2}{a^2-1} - \dfrac{1}{a+1}$

33. $\dfrac{3x+2y}{4z} - \dfrac{7x+5y}{12z}$

34. $1 - \dfrac{x-1}{x+1}$

35. $\dfrac{2x+5}{x^2-4} + \dfrac{x}{2-x}$

36. $\dfrac{\frac{r}{2}+1}{6+\frac{r}{3}}$

37. $\dfrac{d^2 - \frac{1}{9}}{5 + \frac{5}{d}}$

38. $\dfrac{\frac{r+1}{r-1} - 1}{\frac{r-1}{r+1} + 1}$

C. Radicals

Simplify.

1. $\sqrt{32}$

2. $\frac{1}{3}\sqrt{160y^4}$

3. $2\sqrt{\frac{1}{2}}$

4. $3\sqrt{\frac{7}{9}}$

5. $\frac{1}{4}\sqrt{16b^4}$

6. $\sqrt{\frac{2}{3}}$

7. $2\sqrt{9x^2 + 9y^2}$

8. $\dfrac{1}{\sqrt{2}}$

9. $\dfrac{\sqrt{3}}{2\sqrt{2}}$

10. $\dfrac{16}{\sqrt{32}}$

11. $\dfrac{2\sqrt{3}+4}{\sqrt{36}}$

12. $\dfrac{x}{\sqrt{4x}}$

13. $\dfrac{1}{\sqrt{3}-1}$

14. $\dfrac{2}{3-\sqrt{2}}$

15. $\sqrt{8} - \sqrt{64}$

16. $4\sqrt{72} - 3\sqrt{36}$

17. $2\sqrt{48} - \sqrt{9} - 6\sqrt{18}$

18. $\frac{1}{4}\sqrt{8} - \frac{1}{2}\sqrt{12} + \frac{3}{4}\sqrt{27}$

19. $\frac{2}{3}\sqrt{\frac{1}{4}} - 3\sqrt{50} + 2\sqrt{18}$

20. $15\sqrt{\frac{3}{5}} - \frac{2}{3}\sqrt{45}$

21. $(\sqrt{2} - 1)(\sqrt{8})$

22. $(4\sqrt{2})(2\sqrt{6} - 6\sqrt{3})$

23. $(2\sqrt{5} + 3)(2\sqrt{5} - 3)$

24. $(6\sqrt{\frac{2}{3}})(3\sqrt{15})$

Express the square root as a decimal to the nearest tenth.

25. $\sqrt{15}$

26. $\sqrt{452}$

27. $\sqrt{71.2}$

28. $\sqrt{5.64}$

D. Equations

Solve.

1. $2a - 1 = 3a + 4$

2. $4x = 3(4x - 3)$

3. $\dfrac{2b}{5} + \dfrac{3b}{5} + \dfrac{17}{10} = 0$

4. $\dfrac{w}{3} - \dfrac{w+1}{2} = 1$

5. $\dfrac{1}{2m} - \dfrac{1}{5m} = \dfrac{1}{10}$

6. $2(d + 5) - 4(d - 5) = 0$

7. $\dfrac{2}{2x+5} + 1 = \dfrac{5}{3}$

8. $\dfrac{5}{y-3} + \dfrac{6}{3-y} = \dfrac{1}{2}$

9. $\dfrac{16}{3x-1} - \dfrac{4}{1-3x} = 1$

10. $\dfrac{3}{x^2-1} + \dfrac{1}{x-1} = 0$

11. $3.2(x - 1) - 3(x - 2) = 0$ **13.** $2n^2 + 6n + 3 = 0$

12. $W^2 = 19W - 84$ **14.** $6 - n^2 = 0$

Solve for x.

15. $bx = 0, b \neq 0$ **16.** $cx = 1, c \neq 0$ **17.** $a - x^2 = 1, a \geq 1$

18. $\dfrac{1}{ax} - \dfrac{1}{bx} = \dfrac{1}{c}, a \neq 0, b \neq 0, c \neq 0$

Solve each system.

19. $m - n = 0$ **21.** $\dfrac{x}{2} + y = 19$ **22.** $0.2r + 0.3s = 6.0$

   $3m - 2n = 1$ $\dfrac{x}{4} - 3y = -8$ $0.4r + .05s = 12.0$

20. $x - 2y = 16$

   $y + x = 10$

Solve by use of graphs.

23. $3x - 2y = 1$ **24.** $2x + 3y = 5$ **25.** $x - 2y = 5$

   $x + y = 2$ $x - y = 6$ $x - 2y = 20$

26. Find the x-intercept of $3x - 3y = \text{·}19$.

27. Find the y-intercept of $2y - 5x = 0$.

28. For what value of a will the graph of $4x - ay = 5$ pass through the point $(3, 1)$?

29. For what value of k will the graph of $kx + 2y = 2$ pass through the point $(-1, 0)$?

In Exercises 30–35, find an equation of the line described.

30. Slope 2, passes through point $(-1, -1)$.

31. Slope -2, passes through point $(-1, -1)$.

32. Slope $\frac{2}{3}$, passes through point $(5, 0)$.

33. Slope $\frac{3}{4}$, passes through point $(0, 5)$.

34. Parallel to line $x - y = 5$, passes through point $(3, 3)$.

35. Parallel to line $x + y = 2$, passes through point $(0, -6)$.

E. Functions; Variation

1. If $f(x) = x + 2$, find $f(0)$; $f(2)$.

2. If $f(n) = n^2 + 1$, find $f(1)$; $f(3)$.

Solve for the variable indicated.

3. $V = lwh$ for h **5.** $A = \pi r^2$ for r

4. $V = \frac{1}{3}\pi r^2 h$ for h **6.** $F = \frac{9}{5}C + 32$ for C

Write a rule for the function shown by each table.

7.

x	6	7	8
y	3	4	5

8.

x	0	1	3
y	0	2	6

9.

x	1	2	3
y	5	8	11

10. Graph $y = 6x$ if $0 < y \le 30$. What is the domain of this function?

11. A flat-roofed garage has dimensions l, w, h. It has one door $c \times d$ and another door $a \times d$. Write a formula for the wall surface of the garage.

12. If $g = 32$ and $t = 4$, find the value of d in $2d = gt^2$.

13. Given $A = \frac{1}{2}h(B + b)$, find the value of A when $h = 16$, $B = 8$, $b = 6$.

Write as proportions.

14. w varies inversely as l.

15. x varies directly as y.

16. A varies jointly as w and l.

17. a varies directly as b and inversely as c.

18. $k = rt$ **19.** $x = ky$

Write as equations with the constant k.

20. F varies inversely as l.

21. d varies directly as t.

22. $d_1w_1 = d_2w_2$

23. $I_1d_1^2 = I_2d_2^2$

24. If I varies as d^2, and $I = 16$ when $d = 2$, find d when $I = 32$.

25. If y varies as x, and $y = 2$ when $x = 6$, what is the value of y when $x = -6$?

26. If y varies inversely as x^2, and $y = 2$ when $x = 9$, for what values of x will $y = 5$?

27. If l varies inversely as w, and $l = 3$ when $w = 1$, find w when $l = 9$.

28. A snowplow plows a street 6 yards wide and 200 yards long in 20 minutes. At that rate, how long would it take to plow one 12 yards wide and 300 yards long?

29. If 3 typists can do a job in h hours, how many girls, at the same rate, can do it in $(h - 4)$ hours?

F. Inequalities

Show the solution sets graphically.

1. $3 - 2y > 16$

2. $4a + 1 \ge 9$

3. $|2y + 3| > 5$

4. $|2x - 3| > 5$

5. $y^2 - 6y < 16$

6. $5x + y = 12$
    $x - 2y < 6$

7. $3x - y > 5$
    $3x + 5y \ge 0$

8. $\frac{1}{3}x < y + 5$
    $y \le \dfrac{1 - x}{2}$

G. Problems

1. The sum of the digits in a certain two-digit number is 12. When the order of the digits is reversed, the number obtained is $\frac{4}{7}$ as great. Find the number.

2. The difference of two numbers is 298. If the larger is divided by the smaller, the quotient and remainder are both 12. Find the numbers.

3. If the sides of a square are increased by 2 feet, its area is increased by 100 square feet. What is the area of the smaller square?

4. A woman has $11.50, consisting of a number of $1 bills, twice as many half dollars, and three times as many dimes as dollars. How many of each kind of money has she?

5. Mrs. Hume invested $5000, part at 6% and the rest at 4%. The average rate of interest on the $5000 was $5\frac{1}{2}$%. What amount did she invest at each rate?

6. Al and Bill can do a certain job in 10 days. At the end of the seventh day Al becomes ill, and Bill finishes the job working alone for 5 days. How long would it take each man to do a similar job, working alone for the entire time?

7. How long will it take two machines together to do a job which one does in 12 hours and the other in 18 hours?

8. Myra buys 2 pounds of peanuts and $1\frac{1}{2}$ pounds of cashews for $3.23. Her brother Fred spends $2.92 for 3 pounds of peanuts and $\frac{1}{2}$ pound of cashews. What is the price per pound of the peanuts; the cashews?

9. Make a circle graph based on this division of income: rent, 20%; food, 20%; clothing, 10%; insurance and savings, 15%; education, 25%; miscellaneous, 10%.

10. If a line 3 inches long represents 100 miles, how long a line represents 600 miles?

11. Ted's weight, 193 pounds, is at least 10 percent more than his father's. How much does his father weigh?

12. Fay has 4 times as much money as her sister. Fay gives her 39 cents and they then have equal amounts. What is that new amount?

13. Mary bicycled to her cousin's house at the rate of 8 miles per hour. On the return trip she rode 12 miles per hour. How far did she ride altogether if the combined trip took 5 hours?

14. Two consecutive odd numbers have a product which is 15 more than 4 times the smaller number. What are the numbers?

15. Find the dimensions of a rectangular garden whose area is 24 square feet and whose perimeter is 28 feet.

16. The square of a certain number is 91 more than 6 times the number. Find the number.

17. A grocer made a blend of two grades of coffee, one worth $1.00 per pound and the other worth $1.40 per pound. If 40 pounds of the blend is to sell for $1.10 per pound, how many pounds of each coffee should he use?

18. Tickets for a game sold at 25 cents each for students and 75 cents each for adults. If the box office took in $108.75 for a capacity crowd of 347 patrons, how many student tickets were sold?

19. The sum of the present ages of Karen and Linda is 30 years. Five years ago Linda was $\frac{2}{3}$ as old as Karen was then. What are their present ages?

20. Carol weighs 100 pounds. Her younger sister weighs 80 pounds. Each sits on the end of a seesaw 9 feet long, and it balances. How far is each girl from the balance point?

21. A canoe takes $1\frac{1}{2}$ hours to go 12 miles down river and 6 hours to return. Assuming that the canoe's still-water rate is the same for both directions, what is the speed of the current?

22. Find two consecutive even integers the sum of whose squares is 164.

23. The formula $n = \dfrac{p(p-1)}{2}$ gives the number (n) of straight lines that can connect p different points. If only 15 lines can be drawn connecting some points, how many points are there?

24. Given a triangle whose area is 42 square centimeters, find its base and height if together they measure 19 centimeters.

25. Find the degree measure of two complementary angles if their difference in degrees is 26.

26. Find the degree measure of two supplementary angles if the measure of one is 14 times that of the other.

27. The perimeter of a triangle is 30 centimeters. The lengths of its sides are three consecutive integers. Find the lengths.

28. The perimeter of a rectangular playground is 1260 feet. What is its area if its width is 50 feet less than its length?

29. A plane left Chicago at 12 noon, flying west at 250 miles per hour. At 2 P.M. another plane left in the same direction flying at 350 miles per hour. At what time did the second plane overtake the first?

30. A store sells two kinds of can openers, one at $4.50 and the other at $7.00. During one month $110 worth of can openers were sold. Receipts from the more expensive openers were just $2 more than from the others. How many of each kind were sold that month?

31. The movie theater has 1200 seats. The number of rows is 10 less than the number of seats in each row. How many seats are in a row?

32. A dealer pays $1800 for a new car. What should he charge the buyer if he wishes to make a profit of 8% of the selling price?

33. Ann bought a dress for $12 that originally sold for $15. What was the markdown rate?

34. A tank can be filled in 9 minutes when both intake pipes are open. When one of the pipes is open it takes 15 minutes. How long would it take to fill the tank if only the second pipe were open?

35. The sum of the digits in a 2-digit numeral is 12. The units digit is twice the tens digit. Find the numeral.

36. Two milkshakes and two ice creams cost $1.30. Three milkshakes and one ice cream cost $1.45. What does one ice cream cost?

37. A weight of 20 grams stretches a certain spring 6 centimeters. What is the smallest weight that would stretch it 10 centimeters if elongation varies directly as the weight?

38. A small boy has ten coins in nickels and dimes, together worth 70 cents. Find the number of dimes he has.

39. If the temperature at 6 A.M. is $-5°$ and it rises 30° by noon, what is the thermometer reading at noon?

40. Which is greater, $(2 - \sqrt{2})$ or $(3 - \sqrt{3})$?

Make a sketch, and solve each problem. Give answers to the nearest tenth.

41. In $\triangle ABC$, $m\angle C = 90$, $m\angle A = 40$, and $AB = 50$. Find BC.

42. In $\triangle ABC$, $m\angle C = 90$, $m\angle A = 16$, and $AB = 100$. Find AC.

43. In $\triangle ABC$, $m\angle C = 90$, $AB = 5$, and $BC = 4$. Find AC.

44. A new city building is 155 feet high. How far from its foot must I stand to make the angle of elevation to its top read 47°?

45. The top of a radio antenna is 125 feet above the ground. If I stand 20 feet from the base of the tower, what is the angle of elevation to the top?

46. The roof of the Empire State Building is 1252 feet above the ground. Looking from it at an angle of depression of 20°, I can see a bridge which is about how many feet from the base?

47. It is $\frac{3}{4}$ mile upgrade 5° from the railroad station to Mr. Murray's home. What is the difference in altitude of the two locations?

48. In a hilly city one street is connected with a parallel one by a long flight of steps. The steps ascend at an angle of 35° for a distance of 40 feet. What is the difference in level of the two streets?

49. Tom is pushing with a force of 50 pounds on a lawn mower whose handle is 40° from the horizontal. How great a force moves the mower forward?

50. A sailboat is blown by the wind at an angle of 48° from the direction of the boat's motion. The force of the wind against the sail is 450 pounds. How many pounds of force push the boat ahead?

APPENDIX

TABLE 1 FORMULAS

Circle	$A = \pi r^2,\ C = 2\pi r$	Cube	$V = s^3$
Parallelogram	$A = bh$	Rectangular Box	$V = lwh$
Right Triangle	$A = \frac{1}{2}bh,\ c^2 = a^2 + b^2$	Cylinder	$V = \pi r^2 h$
Square	$A = s^2$	Pyramid	$V = \frac{1}{3}Bh$
Trapezoid	$A = \frac{1}{2}h(b + b')$	Cone	$V = \frac{1}{3}\pi r^2 h$
Triangle	$A = \frac{1}{2}bh$	Sphere	$V = \frac{4}{3}\pi r^3$
Sphere	$A = 4\pi r^2$		

TABLE 2 WEIGHTS AND MEASURES

AMERICAN SYSTEM OF WEIGHTS AND MEASURES

LENGTH

12   inches = 1 foot
3   feet   = 1 yard
$5\frac{1}{2}$ yards = 1 rod
5280 feet   = 1 land mile
6076 feet   = 1 nautical mile

AREA

144 square inches = 1 square foot
9 square feet   = 1 square yard
160 square rods   = 1 acre
640 acres   = 1 square mile

VOLUME

1728 cubic inches = 1 cubic foot
27 cubic feet   = 1 cubic yard

WEIGHT

16 ounces   = 1 pound
2000 pounds = 1 ton
2240 pounds = 1 long ton

CAPACITY

Dry Measure

2 pints = 1 quart
8 quarts = 1 peck
4 pecks = 1 bushel

Liquid Measure

16 fluid ounces = 1 pint
2 pints   = 1 quart
4 quarts   = 1 gallon
231 cubic inches = 1 gallon

METRIC SYSTEM OF WEIGHTS AND MEASURES

LENGTH	10 millimeters (mm)	= 1 centimeter (cm)	$\doteq$	0.3937	inch
	100 centimeters	= 1 meter (m)	$\doteq$	39.37	inches
	1000 meters	= 1 kilometer (km)	$\doteq$	0.6	mile
CAPACITY	1000 milliliters (ml)	= 1 liter (l)	$\doteq$	1.1	quart
	1000 liters (l)	= 1 kiloliter (kl)	$\doteq$	264.2	gallons
WEIGHT	1000 milligrams (mg)	= 1 gram (g)	$\doteq$	0.035	ounce
	1000 grams	= 1 kilogram (kg)	$\doteq$	2.2	pounds

TABLE 3   SQUARES OF INTEGERS FROM 1 TO 100

Number	Square	Number	Square	Number	Square	Number	Square
1	1	26	676	51	2601	76	5776
2	4	27	729	52	2704	77	5929
3	9	28	784	53	2809	78	6084
4	16	29	841	54	2916	79	6241
5	25	30	900	55	3025	80	6400
6	36	31	961	56	3136	81	6561
7	49	32	1024	57	3249	82	6724
8	64	33	1089	58	3364	83	6889
9	81	34	1156	59	3481	84	7056
10	100	35	1225	60	3600	85	7225
11	121	36	1296	61	3721	86	7396
12	144	37	1369	62	3844	87	7569
13	169	38	1444	63	3969	88	7744
14	196	39	1521	64	4096	89	7921
15	225	40	1600	65	4225	90	8100
16	256	41	1681	66	4356	91	8281
17	289	42	1764	67	4489	92	8464
18	324	43	1849	68	4624	93	8649
19	361	44	1936	69	4761	94	8836
20	400	45	2025	70	4900	95	9025
21	441	46	2116	71	5041	96	9216
22	484	47	2209	72	5184	97	9409
23	529	48	2304	73	5329	98	9604
24	576	49	2401	74	5476	99	9801
25	625	50	2500	75	5625	100	10,000

TABLE 4 SQUARE ROOTS OF INTEGERS FROM 1 TO 100

Exact square roots are shown in red. For the others, rational approximations are given correct to three decimal places.

Number	Positive Square Root	Number	Positive Square Root	Number	Positive Square Root	Number	Positive Square Root
N	$\sqrt{N}$	N	$\sqrt{N}$	N	$\sqrt{N}$	N	$\sqrt{N}$
1	1	26	5.099	51	7.141	76	8.718
2	1.414	27	5.196	52	7.211	77	8.775
3	1.732	28	5.292	53	7.280	78	8.832
4	2	29	5.385	54	7.348	79	8.888
5	2.236	30	5.477	55	7.416	80	8.944
6	2.449	31	5.568	56	7.483	81	9
7	2.646	32	5.657	57	7.550	82	9.055
8	2.828	33	5.745	58	7.616	83	9.110
9	3	34	5.831	59	7.681	84	9.165
10	3.162	35	5.916	60	7.746	85	9.220
11	3.317	36	6	61	7.810	86	9.274
12	3.464	37	6.083	62	7.874	87	9.327
13	3.606	38	6.164	63	7.937	88	9.381
14	3.742	39	6.245	64	8	89	9.434
15	3.873	40	6.325	65	8.062	90	9.487
16	4	41	6.403	66	8.124	91	9.539
17	4.123	42	6.481	67	8.185	92	9.592
18	4.243	43	6.557	68	8.246	93	9.644
19	4.359	44	6.633	69	8.307	94	9.695
20	4.472	45	6.708	70	8.367	95	9.747
21	4.583	46	6.782	71	8.426	96	9.798
22	4.690	47	6.856	72	8.485	97	9.849
23	4.796	48	6.928	73	8.544	98	9.899
24	4.899	49	7	74	8.602	99	9.950
25	5	50	7.071	75	8.660	100	10

TABLE 5

VALUES OF SINE, COSINE, AND TANGENT FOR ANGLES A SUCH THAT
$1 \leq m\angle A \leq 90$

$m\angle A$	$\sin A$	$\cos A$	$\tan A$	$m\angle A$	$\sin A$	$\cos A$	$\tan A$
1	0.0175	0.9998	0.0175	46	0.7193	0.6947	1.0355
2	0.0349	0.9994	0.0349	47	0.7314	0.6820	1.0724
3	0.0523	0.9986	0.0524	48	0.7431	0.6691	1.1106
4	0.0698	0.9976	0.0699	49	0.7547	0.6561	1.1504
5	0.0872	0.9962	0.0875	50	0.7660	0.6428	1.1918
6	0.1045	0.9945	0.1051	51	0.7771	0.6293	1.2349
7	0.1219	0.9925	0.1228	52	0.7880	0.6157	1.2799
8	0.1392	0.9903	0.1405	53	0.7986	0.6018	1.3270
9	0.1564	0.9877	0.1584	54	0.8090	0.5878	1.3764
10	0.1736	0.9848	0.1763	55	0.8192	0.5736	1.4281
11	0.1908	0.9816	0.1944	56	0.8290	0.5592	1.4826
12	0.2079	0.9781	0.2126	57	0.8387	0.5446	1.5399
13	0.2250	0.9744	0.2309	58	0.8480	0.5299	1.6003
14	0.2419	0.9703	0.2493	59	0.8572	0.5150	1.6643
15	0.2588	0.9659	0.2679	60	0.8660	0.50	1.7321
16	0.2756	0.9613	0.2867	61	0.8746	0.4848	1.8040
17	0.2924	0.9563	0.3057	62	0.8829	0.4695	1.8807
18	0.3090	0.9511	0.3249	63	0.8910	0.4540	1.9626
19	0.3256	0.9455	0.3443	64	0.8988	0.4384	2.0503
20	0.3420	0.9397	0.3640	65	0.9063	0.4226	2.1445
21	0.3584	0.9336	0.3839	66	0.9135	0.4067	2.2460
22	0.3746	0.9272	0.4040	67	0.9205	0.3907	2.3559
23	0.3907	0.9205	0.4245	68	0.9272	0.3746	2.4751
24	0.4067	0.9135	0.4452	69	0.9336	0.3584	2.6051
25	0.4226	0.9063	0.4663	70	0.9397	0.3420	2.7475
26	0.4384	0.8988	0.4877	71	0.9455	0.3256	2.9042
27	0.4540	0.8910	0.5095	72	0.9511	0.3090	3.0777
28	0.4695	0.8829	0.5317	73	0.9563	0.2924	3.2709
29	0.4848	0.8746	0.5543	74	0.9613	0.2756	3.4874
30	0.50	0.8660	0.5774	75	0.9659	0.2588	3.7321
31	0.5150	0.8572	0.6009	76	0.9703	0.2419	4.0108
32	0.5299	0.8480	0.6249	77	0.9744	0.2250	4.3315
33	0.5446	0.8387	0.6494	78	0.9781	0.2079	4.7046
34	0.5592	0.8290	0.6745	79	0.9816	0.1908	5.1446
35	0.5736	0.8192	0.7002	80	0.9848	0.1736	5.6713
36	0.5878	0.8090	0.7265	81	0.9877	0.1564	6.3138
37	0.6018	0.7986	0.7536	82	0.9903	0.1392	7.1154
38	0.6157	0.7880	0.7813	83	0.9925	0.1219	8.1443
39	0.6293	0.7771	0.8098	84	0.9945	0.1045	9.5144
40	0.6428	0.7660	0.8391	85	0.9962	0.0872	11.4301
41	0.6561	0.7547	0.8693	86	0.9976	0.0698	14.3007
42	0.6691	0.7431	0.9004	87	0.9986	0.0523	19.0811
43	0.6820	0.7314	0.9325	88	0.9994	0.0349	28.6363
44	0.6947	0.7193	0.9657	89	0.9998	0.0175	57.2900
45	0.7071	0.7071	1	90	1	0	Undefined

GLOSSARY

Abscissa: The abscissa of a point P is the coordinate of the point where a vertical line from P meets the horizontal axis. (p. 360)

Absolute value: The positive number of any pair of opposite real numbers is the absolute value of each of the numbers. The absolute value of 0 is 0. (p. 79)

Acute angle: An angle with degree measure greater than 0 or less than 90. (p. 531)

Addition Axiom of Order: For all real numbers a, b, and c, (1) if $a < b$, then $a + c < b + c$; and (2) if $a > b$, then $a + c > b + c$. (p. 164)

Addition Property of Equality: If a, b, and c are any real numbers such that $a = b$, then $a + c = b + c$ and $c + a = c + b$. (p. 111)

Additive Axiom of Zero: The set of real numbers contains a unique element 0 having the property that for every real number a, $a + 0 = a$ and $0 + a = a$. (p. 73)

Additive inverse: See **Opposite of a number.**

Angle: A set of points consisting of two rays starting from the same point, called the *vertex* of the angle; the rays are called the *sides.* (p. 528) (See also **Directed angle.**)

Associative Axioms: For all real numbers a, b, and c:
　　(**Addition**)　　$(a + b) + c = a + (b + c)$　(p. 67)
　　(**Multiplication**)　　$(ab)c = a(bc)$.　　　　(p. 67)

Average: The sum of n numbers divided by n. (p. 129)

Axiom: A statement accepted as true without proof; an assumption. Also called *postulate.* (p. 63)

Axiom of Comparison: For all real numbers a and b, one and only one of the following statements is true: $a < b$, $a = b$, $b < a$. (p. 163)

Axiom of Opposites: For every real number a there is a unique real number $-a$ such that $a + (-a) = 0$ and $(-a) + a = 0$. (p. 77)

Axiom of Reciprocals: For every real number a except zero, there is a unique real number $\frac{1}{a}$ such that $a \cdot \frac{1}{a} = 1$ and $\frac{1}{a} \cdot a = 1$. (p. 97)

Axioms of Closure: For all real numbers a and b,
　　(**Addition**)　　the sum $a + b$ is a unique real number.　(p. 63)
　　(**Multiplication**)　the product ab is a unique real number.　(p. 64)

Axis: Two number lines intersecting at right angles and having the same zero point are called the *horizontal axis* and the *vertical axis.* (p. 359)

Base (in percent problems): See under **Percentage.**

Base (in a power): One of the equal factors. In the expression 5^4, 5 is the base. (p. 37)

Between: If point C lies on number line AB, then C is between A and B if $a < c < b$ or $b < c < a$, where the real numbers a, b, and c are coordinates of points A, B, and C, respectively. (p. 526)

Binary operation: An operation performed on just two numbers at a time. (p. 67)

Binomial: A polynomial of two terms. (p. 205)

Closed half-plane: The union of an open half-plane and its boundary. (p. 435)

Coefficient: In an expression such as $6yz$, each factor is the coefficient of the other factors. The *numerical coefficient* in $6yz$ is 6. (p. 36)

Coincide: Two lines coincide if they have all their points in common. (p. 415)

Collinear points: Points that belong to or lie on the same line. (p. 524)

Combined variation: When a variable z varies directly as one variable x and inversely as another variable y, the variation is called combined variation. (p. 399)

Commutative Axiom of Addition: For all real numbers a and b, $a + b = b + a$. (p. 66)

Commutative Axiom of Multiplication: For all real numbers a and b, $ab = ba$. (p. 66)

Complementary angles: Two angles whose degree measures have the sum 90. Each angle is the *complement* of the other. (p. 182)

Completing a trinomial square: Adding a term to an expression in the form "$x^2 + bx$" to produce a trinomial square. (p. 500)

Complex fraction: A fraction whose numerator or denominator contains one or more fractions. (p. 320)

Components (of an ordered pair): See **First component** and **Second component**.

Components (of a vector): Two vectors whose sum is $\overrightarrow{V}$ are components of $\overrightarrow{V}$. (p. 560)

Conclusion: A statement that follows from another statement assumed to be true; the "then" part of a statement in "if . . . , then . . ." form. (p. 111)

Conjugates: Two binomials of the form $x + \sqrt{y}$ and $x - \sqrt{y}$. (p. 477)

Conjunction: A sentence formed by joining two sentences by the word *and*. (p. 14)

Consecutive even integers: Obtained by counting by twos from an even integer. (p. 178)

Consecutive integers: Obtained by counting by ones from any given integer. (p. 177)

Consecutive odd integers: Obtained by counting by twos from an odd integer. (p. 178)

Consistent equations: Simultaneous equations that have a common root or common roots. (p. 416)

Constant: A variable with just one value. (p. 32)

Constant of proportionality: In a direct variation expressed by $y = kx$ or in an inverse variation expressed by $xy = k$ ($k \neq 0$), k is the constant of proportionality. Also called *constant of variation*. (pp. 382, 393)

Constant term: A numerical term with no variable factor. (p. 265)

Converse: A theorem formed by interchanging the hypothesis and conclusion of a given theorem. (p. 470)

Coordinate: The number paired with a point on the number line. (p. 8)

Coordinate axes: The axes of a coordinate system set up on a plane. (p. 360)

Coordinate plane: A plane on which a coordinate system has been set up. (p. 360)

Coordinates of a point: The abscissa and the ordinate of the given point, written as an ordered pair of numbers. (p. 360)

Coplanar points [lines]: Points [lines] that belong to or lie on the same plane. (p. 525)

Cosine of an angle: For an angle in standard position, the abscissa of the point on the terminal ray whose distance from the origin is 1. For either acute angle of a right triangle, the length of the side adjacent to the angle divided by the length of the hypotenuse. (pp. 538, 546)

Counting numbers: Members of the set $\{1, 2, 3, 4, 5, \ldots\}$. Also called *natural numbers*. (p. 21)

Cubic equation: An equation of degree three. (p. 277)

Degree: $\frac{1}{360}$ of a complete rotation of a ray about a point. (p. 182)

Degree of a monomial: The number of times that a variable occurs as a factor in a monomial is the degree of the monomial *in that variable*. The sum of the degrees in each of the variables is the degree of the monomial. $8m^3n^2$ is of degree 3 in m; the degree of the monomial is 5. A nonzero constant has degree 0. 0 has no degree. (p. 205)

Degree of a polynomial: For a polynomial having no two terms similar, the greatest of the degrees of its terms. (p. 206)

Degree of a polynomial equation: The greatest of the degrees of the terms of the equation when written in standard form. (p. 277)

Difference: For any two real numbers a and b, the difference $a - b$ is the number whose sum with b is a. (p. 116)

Direct variation: See **Linear direct variation**.

Directed angle: The figure composed of two rays drawn from a point, together with the rotation that sends one ray into the other. A directed angle formed by counterclockwise rotation is positive; one formed by clockwise rotation is negative. (p. 181)

Directed numbers: Positive and negative numbers. (p. 9)

Discriminant: The expression "$b^2 - 4ac$" is called the discriminant of the quadratic equation "$ax^2 + bx + c = 0$." (p. 509)

Disjoint sets: Sets that have no element in common. (p. 169)

Disjunction: A sentence formed by joining two sentences by the word *or*. (p. 174)

Distributive Axiom of Multiplication with Respect to Addition: For all real numbers a, b, and c, $a(b + c) = ab + ac$ and $(b + c)a = ba + ca$. (p. 88)

Domain of a relation: The set of first elements in the ordered pairs that form the relation. (p. 362)

Domain (of a variable): The set whose members may be used as replacements for the variable. Also called *replacement set*. (p. 32)

Element of a set: Any object in the set. (p. 16)

Empty set: The set with no members. Also called *null set*. (p. 18)

Equal ordered pairs: Two ordered pairs in which both the first components and the second components are equal. (p. 358)

Equal sets: Sets having the same members. (p. 20)

Equation: Any statement of equality. (pp. 1–2)

Equivalent equations [inequalities]: Equations [inequalities] having the same solution set over a given set. (pp. 113, 165)

Equivalent expressions: Expressions which represent the same number for all values of the variables that they contain. (p. 89)

Equivalent systems: Systems of simultaneous equations that have the same solution set. (p. 417)

Equivalent vectors: Vectors that have the same magnitude and act in the same direction. (p. 557)

Evaluating an expression: The process of replacing the variable in an open expression by the numeral for the given value and simplifying the result. (p. 32)

Exponent: In a power, the number of times the base occurs as a factor. In the expression 5^4, the base is 5, and the exponent is 4. (p. 37)

Exponential form of a power: The expression "n^5" is in exponential form. (p. 37)

Extremes of a proportion: In the proportion $\dfrac{y_1}{x_1} = \dfrac{y_2}{x_2}$, y_1 and x_2 are the extremes. (p. 383)

Factor: When two or more numbers are multiplied, each of the numbers is called a factor of the product. (p. 36)

Factored form of a power: The expression "$n \cdot n \cdot n \cdot n$" is in factored form. Also called *expanded form*. (p. 37)

Factoring: Factoring a number over a given set is finding numbers belonging to the given set and having their product equal to the given number. (p. 249)

Finite set: If there is a counting number which is the number of members in a set, or if the set is the empty set, then the set is finite. (p. 22)

First component: The first number of an ordered pair. Also called *first coordinate*. (p. 358)

Flow chart: A diagram that shows the steps in a program and the order in which they are to be performed. (p. 58)

Fraction: Any indicated quotient of two algebraic expressions. A fraction is defined only when its denominator is not zero. (p. 295)

Fractional equation: An equation which has a variable in the denominator of one or more terms. (p. 336)

Function: A function consists of two sets D and R together with a rule which assigns to each element of D exactly one element of R. The set D is called the *domain* of the function; the set R is called the *range* of the function. (pp. 146, 363)

Graph of an equation [inequality]: In the coordinate plane, the set of all those points and only those points whose coordinates satisfy the equation [inequality]. (p. 369)

Graph of a number: The point on the number line that is paired with the number. (p. 8)

Graph of an open sentence: The graph of the solution set of the sentence. (p. 44)

Graph of an ordered pair: The point in the coordinate plane paired with an ordered pair of real numbers. (p. 360)

Graph of a relation: The graphs in a coordinate plane of all the ordered pairs that form the relation. (p. 363)

Graph of a set: The set of points corresponding to a set of numbers. (p. 17)

Greatest common factor: The greatest integral factor of each of two or more given integers. (p. 250)

Grouping symbol (Symbol of inclusion): A pair of parentheses, brackets, or braces, or any other symbol that includes an expression for a particular number. (p. 4)

Half-plane: Part of a plane, bounded by a line in the plane. (p. 435)

Hyperbola: The graph of a function of the type $xy = k$, where k is a nonzero constant. (p. 393)

Hypotenuse: The longest side of a right triangle; the side opposite the right angle. (p. 469)

Hypothesis: A given assumption; the "if" part of a statement in "if . . . , then . . ." form. (p. 111)

Identity: An equation which is a true statement for every numerical replacement of the variable(s). (p. 140)

Identity element for addition: Zero. When 0 is added to any given number, the sum is identical with the given number. (p. 73)

Identity element for multiplication: One. When any given real number and 1 are multiplied, the product is the given real number. (p. 92)

Inconsistent equations: Simultaneous equations that have no common root. (p. 416)

Inequality: A statement that two numerical expressions do not have the same value. (p. 2)

Infinite set: If the process of counting the members of a set would never come to an end, the set is infinite. (p. 21)

Initial side (of a directed angle): The ray at which the rotation starts. (p. 181)

Integer: A member of the set $\{\ldots, -3, -2, -1, 0, 1, 2, 3, \ldots\}$. (p. 22)

Intersection: The set consisting of the elements belonging to both of two given sets. (p. 169)

Inverse operations: Operations that "undo" each other; for example, addition and subtraction. (p. 130)

Inverse variation: A function in which the product of the coordinates of its ordered pairs is a nonzero constant. The equation $y = \dfrac{k}{x}$ is associated with an inverse variation. (p. 393)

Irrational number: A real number which cannot be expressed in the form $\dfrac{r}{s}$, where r and s are integers. (p. 465)

Irreducible polynomial: A polynomial which cannot be factored into polynomials of lower degree belonging to a designated set. (p. 268)

Joint variation: When a variable z varies directly as the product of variables x and y, the variation is said to be joint. (p. 399)

Least common denominator (L.C.D.): The smallest nonzero common multiple of the denominators of two or more fractions. For $\frac{7}{10}$ and $\frac{4}{15}$ the L.C.D. is 30. (p. 315)

Length of a line segment: The distance between its endpoints. (p. 526)

Line segment: The line segment determined by points A and B is the set of points consisting of A and B and the points on the line between them. A and B are the *endpoints* of the segment. (p. 526)

Linear direct variation: A function in which the ratio between a number y of the range and the corresponding number x of the domain is the same for all pairs of the function other than $(0, 0)$. The equation $y = kx$ is associated with a direct variation. (p. 382)

Linear equation: An equation of degree one. Any equation equivalent to one of the form $Ax + By = C$ $(x, y \in \mathcal{R})$ where A, B, and C are real numbers with A and B not both 0 is a linear equation *in two variables;* its graph is a straight line. (pp. 277, 370)

Linear function: A function whose ordered pairs satisfy a linear equation. (p. 371)

Linear term: A term of degree one in the variable. (p. 265)

Mathematical expression: A variable expression or a numerical expression. (p. 32)

Means of a proportion: In the proportion $\dfrac{y_1}{x_1} = \dfrac{y_2}{x_2}$, x_1 and y_2 are the means. (p. 383)

Member of a set: Any object in the set. (p. 16)

Members of an equation [inequality]: The expressions joined by the symbol of equality [inequality]. (p. 112)

Mixed expression: The sum or difference of a polynomial and a fraction. (p. 318)

Mixed numeral: A numeral denoting the sum of an integer and a fraction. (p. 318)

Monomial: A term which is either a numeral or a variable or an indicated product of a numeral and one or more variables. (p. 205)

Monomial factor (of a polynomial): A monomial that is a factor of every term of the polynomial. (p. 253)

Multiple: The product of any real number and an integer is called a multiple of the real number. (p. 178)

Multiplication Axiom of Order: For all real numbers a, b, and c, (1) if $a < b$ and $c > 0$, then $ac < bc$; and (2) if $a > b$ and $c > 0$, then $ac > bc$. (p. 165)

Multiplication Property of Equality: If a, b, and c are any real numbers such that $a = b$, then $ac = bc$ and $ca = cb$. (p. 123)

Multiplication Property of Fractions: Dividing or multiplying the numerator and denominator of a fraction by the same nonzero number produces a fraction equal to the given ,one. That is $\dfrac{ac}{bc} = \dfrac{a}{b}$ $(c \neq 0)$. (p. 297)

Multiplicative Axiom of One: The set of real numbers has a unique element 1 having the property that for every real number a, $a \cdot 1 = a$ and $1 \cdot a = a$. (p. 92)

Multiplicative inverse: See **Reciprocal.**

Multiplicative Property of −1: For all real numbers a, $a(-1) = -a$ and $(-1)a = -a$. (p. 93)

Multiplicative Property of Zero: For each real number a, $a \cdot 0 = 0$ and $0 \cdot a = 0$. (p. 92)

Natural numbers: The numbers used in counting. Also called *counting numbers.* (p. 21)

Negative direction: On the number line, the direction from the origin to any point on the negative side of the line. (p. 9)

Negative of a number: See **Opposite of a number.**

Negative numbers: The numbers paired with points on the negative side of the number line. (p. 9)

Nonterminating decimal: A decimal which continues indefinitely, such as 0.151551555 . . . Also called an *unending decimal.* (p. 458)

Null set: The set with no members. (p. 18)

Numeral: A name, or symbol, for a number. Also called *numerical expression.* (p. 1)

Obtuse angle: An angle with degree measure between 90 and 180. (p. 531)

One-to-one correspondence: A pairing of the elements of two sets that assigns to each member of each set one and only one member of the other set. (p. 21)

Open expression: An expression which contains a variable. Also called a *variable expression.* (p. 32)

Open half-plane: A half-plane without its boundary. (p. 435)

Open sentence: An equation or an inequality which contains one or more variables. (p. 44)

Opposite of a number: For every real number a, the unique real number $-a$ such that $a + (-a) = 0$ and $(-a) + a = 0$. Also called *additive inverse*, or *negative*, *of a.* (p. 77)

Opposite vectors: Collinear vectors that have the same magnitude but opposite directions. (p. 557)

Ordered pair: A pair of elements in which the order is important. (p. 355)

Ordinate: The ordinate of a point P is the coordinate of the point where a horizontal line from P meets the vertical axis. (p. 360)

Origin: The starting point, labeled "0," on a number line; the zero point of both of two number lines that intersect at right angles. (pp. 8, 359)

Parabola: The graph of an equation of the form $y = ax^2 + bx + c$. (p. 390)

Parallel lines: Lines that lie in the same plane, but have no point in common. (p. 415)

Percent: Hundredths; divided by 100. The symbol for "percent" is "%." (p. 303)

Percentage: A number equal to the product of a *rate* (percent) and another number, called the *base*. (p. 304)

Perfect square: The square of a rational number. (p. 464)

Plane rectangular coordinate system: A one-to-one correspondence between ordered pairs of real numbers and points of a coordinate plane. (p. 361)

Polynomial: An indicated sum of monomials. (p. 205)

Polynomial equation: An equation whose left and right members are polynomials. (p. 277)

Polynomial factoring: Expressing a given polynomial as a product of polynomial factors. (p. 251)

Positive direction: On the number line, the direction from the origin to the point labeled "1." (p. 8)

Positive numbers: The numbers paired with points on the positive side of the number line. (p. 8)

Postulate: See Axiom.

Power: The number named by an expression in the form a^n, where n denotes the number of times a is used as a factor. The fourth power of $5(5^4)$ is equal to $5 \cdot 5 \cdot 5 \cdot 5$. (p. 37)

Prime factor: A factor that is a member of the set of prime numbers. The prime factors of 30 are 2, 3, and 5. (p. 250)

Prime number: An integer greater than one which has no positive integral factor other than itself and one. (p. 249)

Prime polynomial: An irreducible polynomial whose greatest monomial factor is 1. (p. 268)

Principal square root: The positive square root. (p. 461)

Product Property of Square Roots: For any real numbers a and b, if $a \geq 0$ and $b \geq 0$, then $\sqrt{ab} = \sqrt{a} \cdot \sqrt{b}$. (p. 462)

Program: A list of steps used to carry out a particular job. (p. 31)

Proof: Logical reasoning from known facts and given assumptions to conclusions. (p. 112)

Property of Completeness: Every decimal represents a real number, and every real number has a decimal representation. (p. 465)

Property of Density: Between every pair of different rational numbers there is another rational number. (p. 455)

Property of the Opposite of a Sum: The opposite of a sum of real numbers is the sum of the opposites of the numbers; that is, for all real numbers a and b, $-(a + b) = (-a) + (-b)$. (p. 83)

Property of Opposites in Products: For all real numbers a and b, $(-a)b = -ab$, $a(-b) = -ab$, $(-a)(-b) = ab$. (p. 93)

Property of Pairs of Divisors of Any Real Number: If you divide a number by a divisor which is smaller in absolute value than the square root of that number, the quotient will be larger in absolute value than the square root. (p. 466)

Property of Quotients: For all real numbers x and y, and nonzero real numbers c and d, $\dfrac{xy}{cd} = \dfrac{x}{c} \cdot \dfrac{y}{d}$. (p. 226)

Property of the Reciprocal of a Product: The reciprocal of a product of real numbers, each different from zero, is the product of the reciprocals of the numbers; that is, for all real numbers a and b such that $a \neq 0$ and $b \neq 0$, $\dfrac{1}{ab} = \dfrac{1}{a} \cdot \dfrac{1}{b}$. (p. 98)

Property of Square Roots of Equal Numbers: If r and s are any real numbers, $r^2 = s^2$ if and only if $r = s$ or $r = -s$. (p. 495)

Property of the Sum and Product of the Roots of a Quadratic Equation: If the roots of a quadratic equation of the form $x^2 + bx + c = 0$ are r and s, then $r + s = -b$ and $rs = c$. (p. 497)

Proportion: An equality of ratios of the form $\dfrac{y_1}{x_1} = \dfrac{y_2}{x_2}$. (p. 383)

Pure quadratic: A quadratic equation of the form "$ax^2 + c = 0$." (p. 495)

Pythagorean Theorem: In any right triangle, the square of the length of the hypotenuse equals the sum of the squares of the lengths of the other two sides. (p. 469)

Quadrant: One of the four regions into which the plane is separated by two number lines intersecting at right angles. (p. 360)

Quadratic direct variation: A function in which each number x in the domain and the corresponding number y in the range satisfy an equation of the form $y = kx^2$, where k is a nonzero constant. (p. 389)

Quadratic equation [inequality]: An equation [inequality] of degree two. (pp. 277, 511)

Quadratic formula: The equation $x = \dfrac{-b \pm \sqrt{b^2 - 4ac}}{2a}$. (pp. 503, 504)

Quadratic function: A function whose ordered pairs (x, y) satisfy a quadratic equation of the form $y = ax^2 + bx + c$, $a \neq 0$. (p. 389)

Quadratic polynomial: A polynomial in which the term of highest degree is a quadratic term. (p. 265)

Quadratic term: A term of degree two in the variable. (p. 265)

Quantifier: An expression involving the idea of "how many" or of "quantity." For example, *some*, *all*, and *every* are quantifiers. (p. 49)

Quotient: The quotient $a \div b$ of any real number a by any nonzero real number b is the number whose product with b is a. (p. 125)

Quotient Property of Square Roots: For any real numbers a and b, if $a \geq 0$ and $b > 0$, then $\sqrt{\dfrac{a}{b}} = \dfrac{\sqrt{a}}{\sqrt{b}}$. (p. 462)

Radical: An expression in the form $\sqrt[n]{a}$. (p. 461)

Radical equation: An equation having a variable in a radicand. (p. 479)

Radicand: An expression for a number whose root is to be extracted. (p. 461)

Range of a relation: The set of second elements in the ordered pairs that form the relation. (p. 362)

Ratio: The quotient of a first number divided by a second. (p. 299)

Rational expression: An algebraic fraction. (p. 300)

Rational number: Any real number that is the ratio of two integers (the second integer not zero). (p. 300)

Rational operations: Addition, subtraction, multiplication, and division (except by zero). (p. 453)

Rationalizing the denominator: The process of changing the form of a fraction with an irrational denominator to an equal fraction with a rational denominator. (p. 473)

Ray: A set of points consisting of a point on a line and all the points on one side of it. (p. 527)

Real number: Any number which is a positive number, a negative number, or 0. (p. 9)

Real number system: The set of real numbers, together with the operations of addition and multiplication. (p. 453)

Reciprocal: Two numbers whose product is 1 are called reciprocals of each other. The reciprocal of a is $\dfrac{1}{a}$. Also called *multiplicative inverse*. (p. 97)

Rectangular coordinate system: See **Plane rectangular coordinate system.**

Reducing to lowest terms: Dividing the numerator and denominator of a fraction by their greatest common factor. (p. 297)

Reflexive Property of Equality: $a = a$. (p. 64)

Relation: Any set of ordered pairs of elements. (p. 362)

Repeating decimal: A nonterminating decimal in which the same digit or block of digits repeats unendingly; for example, 0.272727 . . . Also called *periodic decimal*. (p. 458)

Replacement set: See **Domain of a variable.**

Resultant: The vector representing the sum of two or more vectors. (p. 557)

Right angle: An angle with degree measure 90. (p. 531)

Right triangle: A triangle one of whose angles is a right angle. (p. 532)

Root of an equation: A solution of the equation. (p. 44)

Root of a number: For any positive integer n, a number x is an nth root of the number a if it satisfies $x^n = a$. Since $2^5 = 32$, 2 is a fifth root of 32. (p. 461)

Root index: A numeral signifying the root to be taken; in $\sqrt[3]{125}$, it is 3. (p. 461)

Roster: A list of the members of a set. (p. 16)

Rules of Exponents: For all positive integers m and n.

      (**Multiplication**) $b^m \cdot b^n = b^{m+n}$. (p. 212)

      (**Power of a Power**) $(b^m)^n = b^{mn}$. (p. 214)

      (**Power of a Product**) $(ab)^m = a^m b^m$. (p. 214)

      For **Division:** For all positive integers m and n and nonzero b,

      if $m > n$, then $\dfrac{b^m}{b^n} = b^{m-n}$; and if $m < n$, then $\dfrac{b^m}{b^n} = \dfrac{1}{b^{n-m}}$. (p. 227)

Satisfy: Each member of the solution set of an open sentence satisfies that sentence. (p. 44)

Second component: The second number of an ordered pair. Also called *second coordinate*. (p. 358)

Set: A collection of objects so well described that it is always possible to tell whether or not an object belongs to the set. (p. 16)

Similar terms: Terms which are exactly alike or which differ only in their numerical coefficients. (p. 89)

Similar triangles: Triangles that have the same shape. The angles of similar triangles have the same measures, respectively, and the sides are proportional. (p. 551)

Simple interest: Simple interest, i dollars, paid on P dollars for t years at rate r per year is given by $i = Prt$. (p. 333)

Simplify: To replace a numerical expression by the simplest or most common numeral for the number named; to replace a given expression by an equivalent expression with as few terms as possible. (pp. 6, 89)

Simultaneous equations: See **System of simultaneous equations.**

Sine of an angle: For an angle in standard position, the ordinate of the point on the terminal ray whose distance from the origin is 1. For either acute angle of a right triangle, the length of the side opposite the angle divided by the length of the hypotenuse. (pp. 538, 546)

Slope of a line: The steepness of a nonvertical line as defined by the quotient:
$\dfrac{\text{rise}}{\text{run}} = \dfrac{\text{vertical change}}{\text{horizontal change}} = \dfrac{\text{difference of ordinates}}{\text{difference of abscissas}}$. A horizontal line has slope 0; a vertical line has no slope. (p. 373)

Slope-intercept form: An equation in the form "$y = mx + b$" is in the slope-intercept form. The value of the slope is given by m and that of the y-intercept by b. (p. 378)

Solution of an open sentence: Any ordered pair of numbers that makes an open sentence in two variables a true statement. (pp. 44, 365)

Solution of a system: Any ordered pair of numbers that satisfy both equations of a system of simultaneous equations. (p. 416)

Solution set of an open sentence: The set that consists of the members of the domain of the variable for which the sentence is true is called the solution set of the sentence over that domain. Also called *truth set*. (p. 44)

Solution set of a system: The set of all the ordered pairs of numbers that satisfy both equations of a system of simultaneous equations. (p. 416)

Solve: To determine the solution set of an open sentence over a given domain. (p. 44)

Square root: A number x is a square root of a number a if it satisfies $x^2 = a$. The positive square root of a is indicated by $\sqrt{a}$; the negative square root by $-\sqrt{a}$. (p. 461)

Standard form (of a polynomial equation): The form with one member zero and the other a polynomial in simple form with terms in descending powers of the variable. (p. 277)

Standard position (of an angle): An angle is in standard position if its vertex is at the origin of a rectangular coordinate system, and if the initial side is the ray which is the positive x-axis. (p. 532)

Standard quadratic equation: The equation $ax^2 + bx + c = 0$. (p. 503)

Subset: If every member of a set A is also a member of set U, then A is a subset of U. (p. 168)

Substitution Principle: Changing the numeral by which a number is named in an expression does not change the value of the expression. (p. 6)

Supplementary angles: Two angles whose degree measures have the sum 180. Each angle is the *supplement* of the other. (p. 182)

Symmetric Property of Equality: If $a = b$, then $b = a$. (p. 64)

System of inequalities: Inequalities that impose conditions on the same variables. (p. 436)

System of rational numbers: The set of rational numbers, together with the operations of addition, subtraction, multiplication, and division (except division by zero). (p. 453)

System of simultaneous equations: Two equations that impose two conditions on the variables at the same time. (p. 416)

Tangent of an angle: For an angle in standard position, the slope of its terminal ray. For either acute angle of a right triangle, the length of the side opposite the angle divided by the length of the side adjacent to the angle. (pp. 535, 546)

Term: A mathematical expression using numerals or variables or both to indicate a product or a quotient. (p. 33)

Terminal side (of a directed angle): The ray at which the rotation stops. (p. 181)

Terminating decimal: A decimal with a finite number of places, such as 0.875. Also called *ending decimal* or *finite decimal*. (p. 458)

Theorem: An assertion that is proved through logical reasoning from known facts and given assumptions. (p. 112)

Transform: To change a given sentence into an equivalent sentence. (pp. 113, 165)

Transitive Axiom of Order: For all real numbers a, b, and c, (1) if $a < b$ and $b < c$, then $a < c$; and (2) if $a > b$ and $b > c$, then $a > c$. (p. 164)

Transitive Property of Equality: If $a = b$ and $b = c$, then $a = c$. (p. 44)

Triangle: The union of the segments $\overline{AB}$, $\overline{BC}$, and $\overline{AC}$, if A, B, and C are three non-collinear points. (p. 532)

Trinomial: A polynomial of three terms. (p. 205)

Trinomial square: A trinomial obtained by squaring a binomial. The pattern of the terms is $a^2 + 2ab + b^2$ or $a^2 - 2ab + b^2$. (p. 260)

Union: The set of all the elements belonging to at least one of two given sets. (p. 169)

Unique: One and only one. (p. 63)

Universe: The overall set made up of all the elements in all the sets under consideration in a particular discussion. Also called *universal set*. (p. 168)

Value of a numerical expression: The number named by the expression. (p. 1)

Value of a variable: Any member of the replacement set of the variable. (p. 32)

Values of a function: Members of the range of the function. (p. 147)

Variable: A symbol which may represent any of the members of a specified set. (p. 32)

Vector: A quantity that has both magnitude and direction. (p. 555)

Vertex: The point from which the two rays that form an angle are drawn. (p. 181)

Whole number: A member of the set $\{0, 1, 2, 3, 4, \ldots\}$. (p. 21)

x-axis: Ordinarily, the horizontal axis. (See under **Axis**.) (p. 369)

x-intercept: The abscissa of the point where a graph intersects the x-axis. (p. 507)

y-axis: Ordinarily, the vertical axis. (See under **Axis**.) (p. 369)

y-intercept: The ordinate of the point where a graph intersects the y-axis. (p. 378)

Zero-Product Property of Real Numbers: For all real numbers a and b, $ab = 0$ if and only if $a = 0$ or $b = 0$. (p. 275)

INDEX

ANSWERS
FOR ODD-NUMBERED EXERCISES

MODERN
ALGEBRA Structure and Method
REVISED EDITION
Book 1

Dolciani / Wooton

HOUGHTON MIFFLIN COMPANY
BOSTON New York Atlanta Geneva, Illinois Dallas Palo Alto

1973 Impression

Page 3 **Written Exercises** **A 1.** = **3.** ≠ **5.** = **7.** = **9.** = **11.** = **13.** 7 **15.** Any no. except 4 **17.** 0 **19.** 0 **21.** 7 **23.** 8 **B 25.** 14 **27.** ½ **29.** 0.6 **31.** 1 **33.** 0

Pages 6–7 **Written Exercises** **A 1.** 29 **3.** 0 **5.** 65 **7.** 11 **9.** ⅚ **11.** 8 **13.** = **15.** = **17.** ≠ **19.** = **B 21.** ≠ **23.** ≠ **25.** = **27.** = **C 29.** = **31.** ≠

Pages 10–12 **Written Exercises**

A 1–7.

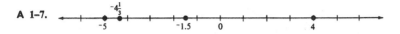

9. 8 **11.** 0 **13.** ⁻3 **15.** ½ **17.** 0 **19.** 3½ **21.** 0.5 **B 23.** ⁻5 **25.** ⁻1½ **27.** 1 **C 29.** 1

Pages 14–15 **Written Exercises** **A 1.** < **3.** > **5.** < **7.** > **9.** = **11.** < **13.** > **15.** < **17.** < **19.** < **21.** 0 **23.** 0 **25.** Any no. < 13 **27.** 2 **29.** Any no. > 5 **31.** Any no. **33.** $\frac{8}{15}$ **35.** Any no. < $\frac{9}{2}$ **B 37.** 12 **39.** Any no. > 4 and <6 **41.** 1 × 1 = 1 **43.** Any no. > $\frac{72}{14}$ and < $\frac{74}{14}$ **45.** Any no. > $\frac{2}{5}$ and < $\frac{3}{5}$ **47.** Any no. > 1 and < 1.2 **C 49.** Any no. > 3.14159 and < 3.15159 **51.** Any no. > 0 and < 1

Pages 19–20 **Written Exercises** **A 1.** {Truman, Johnson} **3.** {January, February, March, April, May} **5.** {Dolciani, Wooton} **7.** {The four "corner" states of the continental U.S.} **9.** {the two most populated cities in Texas} **11.** Answers will vary.

13.

15.

17.

19.

21.

23.

25.
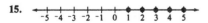

27.

B 29.
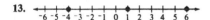

31. 4 **33.** ∈ **35.** ∈ **37.** Any positive no., e.g., 1

Pages 23–24 **Written Exercises** **A 1.** {6, 5, 4, 3, 2, 1}; finite **3.** {13, 14, 15, ...}; infinite **5.** {7, 9, 11 ... 39}; finite **7.** ∅; finite **9.** {the integers between 21 and 29, inclusive} **11.** {the positive odd integers less than 10} **13.** {the nonnegative integers that are multiples of 5}

15.
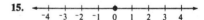

17.

B 19. {3, 5, 7} **21.** {1} **C 23.** {4, 6, 8, 9, 10, 11, ...}
25. Set of natural nos. = {1, 2, 3, 4, 5, 6, ...}

Set of even natural nos. = {2, 4, 6, 8, 10, 12, ...} Each natural no., *n*, is paired with its double, 2*n*.

Pages 26–27 **Chapter Test** **1. a.** ≠ **b.** = **3.** 12 **5. a.** < **b.** > **c.** < **7.** {The three Pacific coast states of the continental U.S.} **9. a.** equal **b.** not equal

Pages 27–28 **Chapter Review** **1.** num. **3.** = **5.** braces; brackets; grouping **7.** Subst.; value **9.** unit **11.** graph **13.** negative **15.** 6 < 8 **17.** conjunction **19.** set **21.** ∈ **23.** rule **25.** empty; null **27.** equal **29.** natural or counting **31.** finite

Chapter 2. The Language of Algebra

Page 34 Written Exercises A 1. One term; 6 **3.** Two terms; 6 **5.** Two terms; 0 **7.** One term; 18 **.** One term; 36 **11.** One term; 72 **13.** One term; 0 **15.** One term; 24 **17.** One term; 3 **B 19.** Two terms; 6 **21.** One term; 24 **23.** Two terms; 8

Pages 34–36 Problems (Answers to Problems involving π are approximations.) **A 1.** 5040 mi. **3.** 744 ft. **5.** 24 in. **7.** 93.75 sq. cm. **9.** 254 yd. **11.** 616 sq. in. **B 13.** 22.28 ft. **15.** 515.625 cu. in. **17.** 94.20 ft. per min. **19.** 3518 **C 21.** 8.7 cm.

Page 39 Written Exercises A 1. x^3 **3.** z^2 **5.** $10xy^2$ **7.** $23u^3(w+3)$ **9.** $(r+s)^2(r+t)$ **11.** $(x+8)^3$ **13.** $5(y+z)^3$ **15.** $(a+b)^4$ **17.** 36 **19.** 54 **21.** $\frac{2}{8}$ **23.** 36 **25.** 27 **27.** 50 **B 29.** $\frac{7}{8}$ **31.** 3 **33.** 37 **35.** 0

Pages 39–41 Problems (Answers to Problems involving π or g are approximations.) **A 1.** 54 cu. ft. **3.** 2552 sq. in. **5.** 616 sq. cm. **B 7.** 753.60 cu. in. **9.** 373.66 sq. ft. **11.** 12.8 watts **C 13.** 907,500 ft-lb. **15.** 3.27 ft.

Page 43 Written Exercises A 1. 3 **3.** 18 **5.** 9 **7.** 2 **9.** 1 **11.** 9 **13.** 600 **B 15.** 6 **17.** 1 **19.** 1 **21.** 3 **23.** 6 **25.** 6 **27.** $^-2$ **29.** 25 **31.** 11 **33.** 3 **35.** 1 **37.** 3 **C 39.** $\frac{44}{13}$ **41.** 0

Pages 46–47 Written Exercises A 1. True only for 4; $\{4\}$ **3.** True only for 5; $\{5\}$ **5.** True for 2, 3; $\{2, 3\}$ **7.** True only for 3; $\{3\}$ **9.** True for 1, 2, 3; $\{1, 2, 3\}$ **11.** True for 1, 2; $\{1, 2\}$ **13.** $\{6\}$ **15.** $\{3\}$

17. $\{6\}$ **19.** $\{5\}$ **21.** $\{2\}$ **23.**
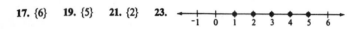

25.

27.
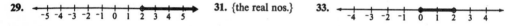

29. **31.** $\{$the real nos.$\}$ **33.**

35. $\{2\}$ **B 37.** True for $3 + 4 = 7$; $4 + 3 = 7$ **39.** True for $5 + 2(3) = 11$ **41.** True for $3 < 2(2)$ **43.** True for $1 + (2)(1) = 1(2 + 1)$ **C 45.** True for $3(5) - 2(3) = 9$ **47.** True for $3(5) + 2(6) > 26$; $3(6) + 2(5) > 26$; $3(6) + 2(6) > 26$ **49.** True for all except $0 + 3(0) \neq 2(0) + 0$

Page 50 Written Exercises A 1. $t = 3$ **3.** Any integer y such that $y > 2$ **5.** Any integer x such that $x \neq 1$ **7.** $m = 0$ **B 9.** $b = 5a$

Pages 52–53 Written Exercises 1. Let $k =$ amt. in Rick's account before the deposit. **3.** Let $g =$ no. of girls. **5.** Let $s =$ length of one side. **7.** Let $t =$ Margie's age now. **9.** Let $d =$ no. of dimes.

Page 55 Chapter Test 1. 12 **3.** $8\frac{1}{2}$ **5.** $\{t, 1\}$ **7.** $\{x, y, \frac{1}{2}, \frac{1}{2}x, \frac{1}{2}y, xy, 1\}$ **9.** $\frac{1}{8}$ **11.** $\frac{2}{8}$ **13.** 16 **15.** 8 **17.** 4 **19.** $\{2\}$ **21.** F **23.** F **25.** $l = 4w + 2$

Page 56 Chapter Review 1. variable **3.** 20 **5.** 3 **7.** 10 **9.** $\{$Any real no. $>$ or $= 0$ and $< 6\}$ **11.** F **13.** $7c - 7$ **15.** $x^2 + 4$

Page 60 Extra for Experts Exercises 1. Decision **3.** Start or end **5.** Arrows **7.** 4

Chapter 3. Addition and Multiplication of Real Numbers

Page 66 Written Exercises A 1. Not closed under add. or subt.; closed under mult. and div. **3.** Closed under add., subt., and mult.; not defined for div. **5.** Not closed under add. or subt.; closed under mult. and div. **7.** Not closed under add., subt., mult., or div. **9.** Closed under add. and mult.; not closed under subt. or div. **B 11.** Not closed under subt. or div.; closed under add. and mult. **13.** Closed under add., mult., and div.; not closed under subt.

Pages 69–70 Written Exercises A 1. 540 **3.** 3400 **5.** 15 **7.** 11 **9.** 24 **B 11.** {the real nos.} **13.** {6} **15.** ∅ **C 17. a.** 8 **b.** closed **c.** * is comm. and assoc. **19. a.** ⁻3 **b.** not closed **c.** * is neither assoc. nor comm.

Pages 74–75 Written Exercises A 1. a. ⁻8 **b.** ⁻4 + (3 + ⁻7) = ⁻4 + ⁻4 = ⁻8 **3. a.** ⁻6 **b.** 12 + (⁻24 + 6) = 12 + ⁻18 = ⁻6 **5. a.** 60 **b.** 38 + ⁻8 + 30 = 30 + 30 = 60 **7. a.** 0.6 **b.** (⁻2.3 + 1.3) + 1.6 = ⁻1 + 1.6 = 0.6 **9. a.** 3 **b.** $\frac{7}{2}$ + (⁻$\frac{1}{2}$ + 0) = $\frac{7}{2}$ + ⁻$\frac{1}{2}$ = 3 **11. a.** ⁻$\frac{2}{3}$ **b.** ⁻2 + (5 + ⁻3$\frac{1}{3}$) = ⁻2 + 1$\frac{1}{3}$ = ⁻$\frac{2}{3}$ **13. a.** ⁻12 **b.** ⁻2 + [(3 + ⁻5) + ⁻8] = ⁻2 + [⁻2 + ⁻8] = ⁻2 + ⁻10 = ⁻12 **15.** {⁻2} **17.** {2} **19.** {0} **21.** {7} **23.** {12} **25.** {⁻24} **27.** {⁻6} **29.** {0} **31.** {⁻2, ⁻1, 0, 1, 2} ; *A* is not closed under add. because 2 and ⁻2 are not elements of *A*.

Pages 75–76 Problems A 1. a. 42 + ⁻57 **b.** ⁻15 **c.** 15 mi. south of *A* **3. a.** 27,000 + ⁻8000 + 3500 **b.** 22,500 **c.** 22,500 ft. **5. a.** ⁻2.15 + ⁻3.05 + ⁻3.40 + ⁻2.85 + 2.25 + 2.85 + 3.15 + 2.75 **b.** ⁻0.45 **c.** She lost 45¢. **7. a.** 650 + ⁻75 + ⁻50 + 350 + ⁻125 **b.** 750 **c.** 750 shares **9. a.** 142 + 17 + ⁻22 + 8 **b.** 145 **c.** 3 points higher

Pages 78–79 Written Exercises A 1. 10 **3.** −5 **5.** −14 **7.** 1 **9.** −7.3 **11.** 3 **13.** −2 **15.** −$\frac{1}{2}$ **B 17. a.** True for −2 only **b.** {−2} **19. a.** True for 0 only **b.** {0} **21. a.** All false **b.** ∅ **23. a.** All false **b.** ∅ **25. a.** True for −2 only **b.** {−2} **27. a.** All false **b.** ∅ **29. a.** True for −2 **b.** {−2} **31. a.** True for −1 and 0 **b.** {−1, 0} **33. a.** True for 1 **b.** {1} **C 35.** 3$\frac{1}{4}$ **37.** −1$\frac{3}{4}$ **39.** $\frac{1}{2}$

Pages 81–82 Written Exercises A 1. 30 **3.** 12 **5.** 1 **7.** −2 **9.** 13 **11.** −8 **13.** {2, −2}

15. {5, −5} **17.** {5, −5} **B 19.**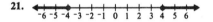

21.

23.

25. **C 27.** The statement is true. If *a* is a positive no. or zero,

then |*a*| = *a*. If *a* is negative no., then |*a*| equals the opposite of *a* or −*a*.

Page 86 Written Exercises A 1. 8 **3.** 1 **5.** −110 **7.** −5 **9.** −7 **11.** 20 **13.** −25 **15.** 6.7 **17.** 11 **B 19.** −3 **21.** −10 **23.** −3 **25.** −$\frac{7}{5}$

Page 87 Problems A 1. On the second floor **3.** 2 yd. **5.** 10 fewer patients **7.** 39 ft. below sea level

Page 87 Extra Problem −2, −4, 2, −4, 8

Pages 90–91 Written Exercises A 1. 47*x* **3.** 82*b* **5.** 52*z* **7.** 24*a*² + 14 **9.** 7*m* + 9*k* **11.** 4*m* + 24 **13.** 4*r* + 5*s* **15.** 7*c* + 9*d* **17.** 19*h*² + 12*h* + 6 **19.** 9*ab* + 5*a* **B 21.** 20*x* + 17*y* **23.** 15*a* + 39 **25.** 15*x*² + 3*x* + 24 **27.** 13*a* + 6*b* + 27 **29.** 78*x*² + 28*x* + 18 **31.** 9*a* + 11*b* **33.** *y*² + *y* + 3 **C 35.** 45*y* + 44 **37.** 120*p* + 164*q* + 234 **39.** 5400 **41.** 65 **43.** 35 **45.** 628,628 **47.** 370

Page 91 Extra Problem

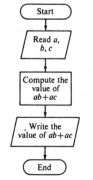

Pages 95–97 Written Exercises A 1. −36 **3.** −9 **5.** 0 **7.** −50 **9.** 21 **11.** 0 **13.** −350 **15.** −17 **17.** −18 **19.** −1.7 **21.** *x* + 3*y* **23.** 5*m* − 5*n* **25.** 2*t* − 4 **27.** −3*xy* + 5*yz* **29.** −4*x* − 2 **31.** 2*t*² + 3*t* **33.** 0.6*x* + 0.4*y* **35.** 2*xy* − $\frac{2}{4}$*xyz* **B 37.** −4*u* + *v* **39.** *a* − 9*b* **41.** *y* + 7*z* **43.** 2*x* − 26*y* **45.** 4 **47.** 0 **49.** −11 **51.** 2 **53.** 0.624 **C 55.** −0.648 **57.** 0.4 **59.** −0.512

Pages 100–101 Written Exercises A 1. 7 **3.** −17$\frac{1}{3}$ **5.** 3 **7.** −3 **9.** −*ab* **11.** 3*b*² **13.** −3*k*³ **15.** 5*y* **17.** −5 **19.** 5*x* + 4 **21.** 5*c* − 14*d* **23.** 9*mk* + *k* **25.** −*a*² + *b*² **B 27.** −*a* + 4*b* **29.** 2*s* **31.** −8*a*² **33.** *a*

Pages 102–103   Chapter Test   1. Ax. of closure for mult.   **3.** Symmetric prop. of equality   **5.** Assoc. ax.

of mult.   **7.** 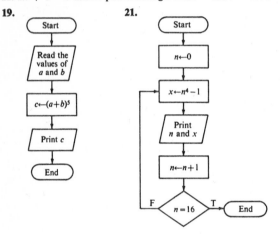   **9.** $-8\frac{3}{4}$ **11.** -20 **13.** 1   **15.** 27   **17.** 2; origin

19. -2 **21.** $19y$ **23.** identity   **25.** 1   **27.** -15 **29.** reciprocal

Pages 104–105   Chapter Review   1. symmetric; equality   **3.** 192   **5.** $^-7 + 42$ **7.** $^-5$ **9.** 7   **11.** $\frac{1}{4}$

13. $\frac{1}{4}; \frac{1}{4}$ **15.** 1   **17.** $x - 3y$ **19.** 630   **21.** 21   **23.** a **25.** $\frac{1}{4}$ **27.** $\dfrac{1}{ab}$

Pages 107–109   Extra for Experts   Exercises   1. 3, 6, 18   **3.** 650, $\frac{1}{2}$, 325   **5.** 50   **7.** 8, 11   **9.** 2

11. $ax + 1 = b$ has no positive integer root.   **13.** c **15.** b **17.** c

19.   **21.**   **23.**

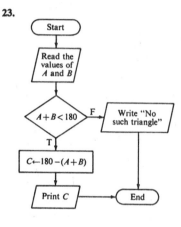

Chapter 4.   Solving Equations and Problems

Pages 115–116   Written Exercises   A 1. {37}   **3.** {72}   **5.** {0}
7. {50}   **9.** {-17}   **11.** {50}   **13.** {6.4}   **15.** {$\frac{18}{5}$}   **17.** {$\frac{2}{3}$}
B 19. {-21}   **21.** {0}   **23.** {-5}   **25.** {-1}   **27.** {9}
29. {-22}   **31.** {10}   **33.** {$-\frac{1}{2}$}   **C 35.** {5, -5}   **37.** {3, -3}

Page 122   Extra Problem

4; 3; 1;

Pages 120–122   Written Exercises   A 1. -8 **3.** -95 **5.** 8
7. $5\frac{1}{2}$ **9.** -2 **11.** 0.6   **13.** -6 **15.** 247   **17.** 10   **19.** {89}
21. {-41}   **23.** {0}   **25.** {-3}   **B 27.** {7}   **29.** {-1}
31. $-3 - 8 = -11$ **33.** $x - (x - 5) = 5$ **35.** $(3\pi - 2) -$
$(3\pi + 2) = -4$ **37.** $(-8 + 17) - (-6) = 15$ **C 43.** not
closed; $7 - 10 = -3$ **45.** closed

Page 122   Problems   A 1. 1014 ft.   **3.** 4 hr. 12 min.   **5.** 69 yr.
7. $67°$ **9.** 227 yd.

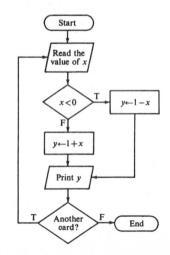

Page 125　Written Exercises　A 1. {136}　**3.** {−135}　**5.** {32}　**7.** {−4}　**9.** {−65}　**11.** {−40.7}
13. {−3}　**15.** {−12}　**17.** {1}　**B 19.** {13}　**21.** {−23}　**23.** {0}　**25.** {30}　**27.** {1}　**C 29.** {33}
31. ∅

Pages 129–130　Written Exercises　A 1. −5　**3.** 162　**5.** 0　**7.** −1.2　**9.** −0.07　**11.** −20　**13.** −0.29
15. 0　**17.** −21x　**19.** {20}　**21.** {13½}　**23.** {−6}　**25.** {−1.5}　**27.** −10　**29.** 0　**B 31.** 1　**33.** −3
35. −9　**37.** 9　**39.** 5　**41.** 1　**43.** 5　**45.** 1　**47.** −2

Page 132　Written Exercises　A 1. {5}　**3.** {18}　**5.** {−9}　**7.** {−1}　**9.** {2}　**11.** {1}　**13.** {8}
15. {20}　**17.** {10}　**19.** {9}　**21.** {8}　**23.** {−4}　**25.** {−3}　**27.** {−3}　**29.** {2}　**B 31.** {3}
33. {−16}　**35.** {−$\frac{3}{2}$}　**37.** {−13}　**39.** {1}　**41.** {39.6}　**C 43.** {−3}　**45.** {4}　**47.** {5}　**49.** {8, −8}

Pages 135–138　Problems　A 1. 13 yd.　**3.** 1308 students　**5.** 2549.5 ft.　**7.** *News*, 20¢; *Times*, 50¢
9. 353 people　**11.** 7 min.　**13.** 25 g.　**15.** 42 ft.; 51 ft.　**17.** 12　**19.** 18　**B 21.** 38　**23.** 36 ft.　**25.** Ann
made 1 more move than Barb.　**27.** 13 pt.　**29.** 1 dime, 3 nickels, 4 pennies, or 29¢　**31.** 25 nickels;
75 pennies; 150 dimes　**33.** X, 3060; Y, 1530; Z, 1580　**C 35.** 68 stitches　**37.** −115.90° F　**39.** 15 yr.

Pages 141–142　Written Exercises　A 1. {7}　**3.** {6}　**5.** {−6}　**7.** {7}　**9.** {14}　**11.** {−65}
13. {−6}　**15.** {15}　**17.** {−3}　**19.** {3}　**21.** {7}　**23.** {8}　**25.** {5$\frac{3}{5}$}　**27.** {$\frac{8}{3}$}　**29.** $w = \dfrac{P-1}{2}$

31. $u = 3w - 2t$　**33.** $x = \dfrac{1-3y}{2}$　**35.** $y = 3M - x - z$　**B 37.** {2}　**39.** {−5}　**41.** $h = \dfrac{T - 2\pi r^2}{2\pi r}$

43. $r = 1 - \dfrac{a}{S}$　**45.** {−5}　**47.** identity　**49.** ∅　**51.** {−64}　**C 53.** $x = \dfrac{7b}{4}$　**55.** {1}　**57.** {6}
59. {−$\frac{3}{2}$}　**61.** {−17½}

Page 142–146　Problems　A 1. 4　**3.** −15　**5.** 4　**7.** dimes　**9.** Ed, 150 pounds; Mike, 175 pounds;
Neil, 175 pounds　**11.** Faye, 14 yr.; Charles, 28 yr.　**13.** 4; 13　**15.** −5; 20　**17.** 9 yr.; 36 yr.　**19.** Sue,
3 moves; Judy, 4 moves　**21.** 8 yr. ago　**23.** 35 ft.; 38 ft.　**25.** base, 12 cm.; sides, 8 cm.　**27.** 75 cal.
B 29. 55,000; 750,000; 800,000　**31.** Panama, 1914; Suez, 1869　**33.** Jefferson, 7 yr.; Washington, 18 yr.
35. Dick, 12 yr.; Harry, 16 yr.; Tom, 24 yr.

Page 138　Extra Problem

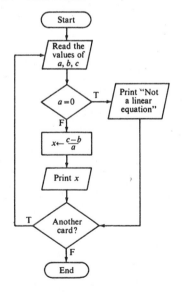

Page 146　Extra Problem

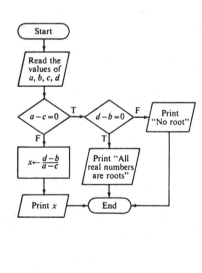

Pages 149–150　Written Exercises　A 1. $f\colon x \to 4x - 3$　**3.** $h\colon x \to x(x + 1)$　**5.** $g\colon x \to x(x^2 + x + 1)$
7. {5, 3, 9}　**9.** {4, 11, 20}　**11.** {2, 3, 4}　**13.** {0, 35, 80}　**15.** {51, 102, 123}　**17.** 4　**19.** 16　**21.** 0
23. 9　**B 25.** 4　**27.** 96　**29.** 49　**31.** 147　**33.** 17　**35.** 7　**C 37.** 3　**39.** 5　**41.** −3; 3; 3　**43.** −1; 0; 1

Pages 151–152 Chapter Test 1. {39} 3. {2} 5. {−48} 7. {3} 9. {−7} 11. {$\frac{1}{18}$} 13. {3}
15. {−24} 17. {−3} 19. {−3} 21. $1.35; $2.04 23. {−1} 25. $R = \{4, 1, 0\}$

Pages 152–154 Chapter Review 1. theorems 3. solution 5. {8} 7. subtrahend; add 9. {−10}
11. multiply; 3 13. zero 15. {$\frac{4}{3}$} 17. divisor 19. {−8} 21. add.; subt. 23. {$\frac{1}{3}$} 25. 10
27. {−6} 29. 388 people 31. one 33. $C = \frac{5}{9}(F − 32)$ 35. domain; range 37. a. 3 b. 1 c. 1 d. 3

Page 154 Extra Problem 1. a. −7, −5, −3, −1, 1, 3, 5, 7, 9, 11 b. 20

Pages 155–156 Cumulative Review 1–4 1. = 3. > 5. finite; {Alabama, Arkansas, Alaska, Arizona}

7. finite; {the letters of the English alphabet} 9.

11. {1, 2, 4, 6, 8, 10, 16} 13. 20 15. 7 17. {$\frac{1}{2}$, 3, 5} 19. {0, $\frac{1}{2}$, 3, 5} 21. $20 − y$ 23. $18 − 3s$
25. Comm. ax. of mult. 27. Distrib. ax. 29. closed 31. $2b + 6$ 33. $3s + t − 4$ 35. $8a + 3b$
37. {−10} 39. {$9\frac{31}{36}$} 41. $6.75 43. $R = \{0, 1, 2\}$ 45. $R = \{1, 4, 7\}$ 47. 5 49. 27

Page 158 Just For Fun

Page 160 Extra for Experts Exercises 1. $2023.33 3. −5860 ft.

Chapter 5. Solving Inequalities; More Problems

Pages 167–168 Written Exercises

A 1. $x < −60$ 3. $z \geq −7$;

5. $z > 6$; 7. $x \leq −10$;

9. $n < 5$; 11. $y > 0$;

13. $y \leq −3$; 15. $a < 5$;

17. $x \geq 1$; 19. $z \leq 1$;

21. $n \geq 4$;

B 23. $t < 7$ 25. $x \geq 33$ 27. $z \leq 5$ 29. Ø 31. ℛ **C** 33. $x < \dfrac{11a}{6}$ 35. $t \leq −44c$

Pages 171–172 Written Exercises A 1. {−5}; {0}; {10} 3. Ø 5. {−3, 5}; {−3, −1, 4, 5, 7}
7. {−3, 4}; {−3, 0, 3, 4} 9. Ø, disjoint; {0, 1, 2, 3, 4, 5} 11. {2}; {1, 2, 3, 4, 6, 8, . . .} 13. Ø, disjoint;
{the real nos. except 0}

15. a. 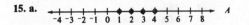 A

b. B

c. $A \cap B$

d. $A \cup B$

17. a. A

b. B

c. $A \cap B$

d. $A \cup B$

19. a. A

b. B

c. $A \cap B$

d. $A \cup B$

B 21. a. A

b. B

c. $A \cap B$

d. $A \cup B$

23. a. A

b. B

c. $A \cap B$

d. $A \cup B$

25. a. A

b. B

c. $A \cap B$

d. $A \cup B$

27.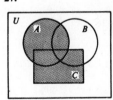

29.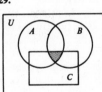

C 31.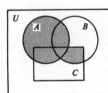

33.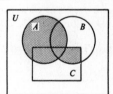

35. $S = \{3, 6\}$ **37.** $S = \{3, 6\}$ or $S = \{3, 5, 6\}$

Page 175   Written Exercises

A 1. $-5 \leq x < 1$;

3. $-3 \leq a \leq 2$;

5. $0 < t < 4$;

7. $y > 3$ or $y < -7$;

9. $r \leq 0$ or $r \geq 1$;

11. $-1 \leq p \leq 3$;

13. $c \leq -2$ or $c > 3$;

B 15. $1 < z \leq 4$;

17. $\Re$;

19. $\Re$;

21. $m < -1$;

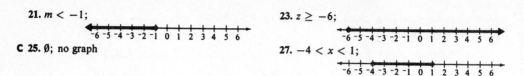

C 25. $\emptyset$; no graph

23. $z \geq -6$;

27. $-4 < x < 1$;

Page 177   Written Exercises

A 1. $\{-2, 6\}$;

3. $a \leq -3$ or $a \geq 3$;

5. $1 < t < 11$;

7. $1 \leq y \leq 3$;

9. $\{-\frac{1}{3}, 1\}$;

11. $4 \leq u \leq 5$;

13. $\mathcal{R}$;

15. $0 < p < 7$;

17. $\{2, -2\}$;

B 19. $\{6, -4\}$;

21. $-1 < y < 2$;

23. $s \geq 3$ or $s \leq -3$;

25. $\mathcal{R}$;

C 27. $\emptyset$; no graph

29. $t \geq 2$ or $t \leq \frac{1}{4}$;

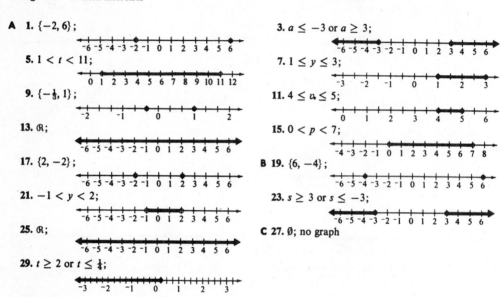

Pages 180–181   Written Exercises   A 1. 22, 23   **3.** $-12, -11, -10$ **5.** $-27, -26, -25, -24$ **7.** 72, 73, 74   **9.** 7 yr., 9 yr., 11 yr., 13 yr.   **11.** 9, 11   **13.** 8, 10   **B 15.** 6, 7, 8, 9   **17.** 4, 6   **19.** 8, 9   **C 21.** $-35, -30, -25, -20$ **23.** $\{-28, -24, -20\}$; $\{-24, -20, -16\}$; $\{-20, -16, -12\}$

Page 181   Extra Problem

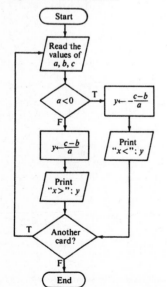

Pages 184–186   Written Exercises   A 1. $50°$ **3.** $90°$ **5.** $20°$ **7.** $(180 - 4n)°$ **9.** $[180 - (x + y)]°$ **11.** $(190 - 3x)°$ **13.** $270°$ **15.** $-180°$ **17.** $-180°$ **19.** $\{20\}$ **21.** $40°$ **23.** $200°$ **25.** $160°$

Pages 186–187   Problems   A 1. $70°$ **3.** $50°$ **5.** $62°$ **7.** $32°$; $64°$; $84°$ **9.** $58°$; $60°$; $62°$ **11.** $42°$; $42°$; $96°$ **13.** $44°$; $58°$; $78°$ **15.** $m\angle A \geq 24°$

Pages 190–192   Problems   A 1. 8 hr.   **3.** 2 hr.   **5.** 240 mi.   **7.** 2 mi.   **9.** 1000 mi.   **11.** $1\frac{1}{2}$ hr.   **13.** 50 m.p.h.; 60 m.p.h.   **B 15.** 300 mi.   **17.** 140 m.p.h.   **C 19.** 5:00 P.M. bus

Pages 194–196   Problems   A 1. 6 coins of each type   **3.** 12 first class passengers   **5.** 20 lb.   **7.** Part I, 11 questions; Part II, 7 questions   **9.** inconsistent   **11.** inconsistent   **13.** inconsistent   **B 15.** 8 thirty-cent stamps; 14 six-cent stamps; 42 ten-cent stamps   **17.** 20 nickels; 40 dimes; 60 quarters   **19.** insufficient information   **21.** insufficient information   **23.** 7 broken pieces   **C 25.** inconsistent   **27.** insufficient information

Page 197   Extra Problems

1.

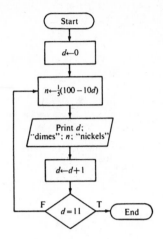

Page 198   Chapter Test

1. $x < -4\frac{3}{5}$;

3. $y > 2$ or $y < -\frac{1}{2}$;

5. $x < -1$ or $x > 6$ **7.** $70°$ **9.** 10:00 A.M.

Pages 198–199   Chapter Review   1. one   **3.** $>$ **5.** $c < 22$
7. $\{5\}$ **9.** $2 < x < 3$ **11.** $x < -3$ or $x > 7$ **13.** $i + 3$;
$i + 6$ **15.** $90°$ **17.** 24 mi.

Chapter 6.   Working with Polynomials

Pages 208–209   Written Exercises   A 1. $7m + n$ **3.** $-x - 7y$ **5.** $2x^2 + x$ **7.** $6rs - 20s$ **9.** $6.6y +$
$5.2x$ **11.** $-\frac{1}{2}t + \frac{3}{13}s$ **13.** $4x^2 + x + 5$ **15.** $3x^3 - 2x^2 + x + 7$ **17.** Correct   **19.** Correct   **21.** Correct   **23.** $3n + 8$ **25.** $\frac{3}{4}z - 1$ **27.** $4.3x^2 - 2.2$ **29.** $4z^3 - z^2 - 4z$ **B 31.** $5x^3 + x^2 - 2x$ **33.** $3a^4 -$
$a^3 - 2a^2 - 3$ **35.** $3t^6 + t^5 + t - 2$

Pages 210–212   Written Exercises   A 1. $2a + 3$ **3.** $2y + 8$ **5.** $7x - 3y$ **7.** $-x + 3$ **9.** $a^2 - 3a + 7$
11. $3ax$ **13.** $2r + s$ **15.** $-u + 2v$ **17.** $2z^2 - z$ **19.** $x^4 - x^2 + x - 1$ **21.** $\{-7\}$ **23.** $\{-6\}$
25. $\{6\}$ **27.** $\{21\}$ **29.** $\{2\}$ **31.** $\{-3\}$ **33.** $\{-10\}$ **B 35.** $\{10\}$ **37.** $\{8\}$ **39.** $\{17\}$ **41.** $8x^2 -$
$4x + 6$ **43.** $6 - 3x + x^2$ **45.** $4x$

Page 213   Written Exercises   A 1. $6y^3z$ **3.** $-2m^3n^4$ **5.** $-2x^3y^2$ **7.** $-8y^3$ **9.** $30a^3b^6$ **11.** $-x^4y^2z^3$
13. $\frac{1}{15}m^3n^6$ **15.** u^7v^8 **17.** $-27a^6b^6c^3$ **19.** x^{n+1} **21.** $2z^{n+2}$ **B 23.** $5r^6$ **25.** $-9h^3k^4$ **27.** $9m^4n^3p^2$
C 29. $5y^5 - 2y^4$ **31.** $2x^{m+n} + x^m$

Page 215   Written Exercises   A 1. $16a^4$ **3.** $16t^4$ **5.** $12z^3$ **7.** $-2s^3t^2$ **9.** x^7y^8 **11.** $4a^6b^8$ **13.** $4r^8s^6$
15. $-3c^{12}k^5$ **17.** $x^{n+2}z^{n+1}$ **B 19.** $32a^3b^6$ **21.** $5r^7s^2t$ **23.** 0 **C 25.** $-x^2y^2 + 6x^2y - 6xy^2$
27. $2x^{n+2} - x^{n+1}$

Page 217   Written Exercises   A 1. $3a^2 + 6ab + 6b^2$ **3.** $-12 + 8x + 12x^2$ **5.** $2x^3 + 2x^3y - 6x^2y^2$
7. $12x^2y + 6x^2y^2 - 3x^3y^3$ **9.** $-12p^3q + 8p^2q^2 - 6pq^3$ **11.** $21xz^2 + 15x^2z^2 - 9xz^3 + 6x^4z^3$
13. $-18p^1r + 24p^3r^2 - 42p^3r^3 + 12p^5r^3$ **15.** $\{9\}$ **17.** $\{-8\}$ **19.** $\{15\}$ **21.** $\{6\}$ **B 23.** $\{\frac{37}{10}\}$ **25.** $\{3\}$
27. $\{43\}$ **C 29.** $\{6\}$

Page 218   Problems   A 1. $w^2 + 5w$ (sq. in.)   **3.** $\frac{1}{2}b^2 - \frac{3}{2}b$ (sq. ft.)   **5.** $120 + x$ (mi.)   **7.** $520 + 7x$
B 9. $4v + 30$ (mi.)   **11.** $4x^2 + 128x + 960$ (sq. ft.)

Pages 219–220   Written Exercises   A 1. $a^2 + 3a + 2$ **3.** $x^2 - 4$ **5.** $z^2 + 3z - 18$ **7.** $2a^2 + 5a + 2$
9. $2n^2 - 7n - 15$ **11.** $3x^2 - 18x + 15$ **13.** $6r^2 + 13r + 6$ **15.** $18d^2 + 3d - 10$ **17.** $2x^2 + xy - y^2$
19. $4x^2 - 49z^2$ **21.** $4x^2 - 12xt + 9t^2$ **23.** $0.28z^2 + z - 2$ **25.** $x^4 - y^2$ **27.** $a^4 - 2a^2b^2 + b^4$
B 29. $x^3 + 4x^2 + x - 2$ **31.** $2x^3 + 5x^2 + 7x - 5$ **33.** $x^3 - y^3$ **35.** $5x^2 + x - 4$ **37.** $4a^2 +$
$6ab - 4b^2$ **C 39.** $x^4 + x^3 + 7x - 3$ **41.** $2r^2 + 3rs - rt - 2s^2 + 3st - t^2$ **43.** $t^5 - 1$

Pages 221–223   Problems   A 1. 6 in.; 12 in.   **3.** 11 in.; 14 in.   **5.** 10 in.; 12 in.   **7.** 12 in. by 12 in.
and 9 in. by 16 in.   **B 9.** 4 ft.; 7 ft.   **11.** 20 in.

Page 224 Written Exercises A 1. $x^2 + 2x + 1$ **3.** $a^2 - 6a + 9$ **5.** $a^2 + 2ab + b^2$ **7.** $4x^2 -$ $4xz + z^2$ **9.** $a^3 + 3a^2b + 3ab^2 + b^3$ **11.** $8x^3 + 12x^2z + 6xz^2 + z^3$ **13.** $2x^3 + 20x^2 + 50x$ **15.** $x^3 +$ $x^2y - xy^2 - y^3$ **17.** $5x^2 + 4x + 4$ **19.** $x^2 + x + \frac{1}{4}$ **21.** $a^2 - 0.6a + 0.09$ **B 23.** $x^2 + 2xy +$ $y^2 + 2xz + 2yz + z^2$ **25.** $x^2 + 2xy + y^2 - 2xz - 2yz + z^2$ **27.** $x^4 + 4x^3y + 6x^2y^2 + 4xy^3 + y^4$ **29.** $x^4 - 2x^2y^2 + y^4$ **C 31.** $16a^2b^2$ **33.** $6c^2d + 2d^3$ **35.** $x^{3n} + 9x^{2n} + 27x^n + 27$

Pages 224–225 Problems A 1. 7 in.; 10 in. **3.** 13, 14 **5.** 9, 11 **7.** 15, 16 **B 9.** 33 in.; 15 in. **11.** 2 in.; 4 in.

Pages 228–229 Written Exercises A 1. t^7 **3.** 3 **5.** $-4x^2y$ **7.** $\frac{n}{2}$ **9.** $\frac{8}{p^5q^3}$ **11.** $\frac{3}{r^{12}}$ **13.** $\frac{3x}{2y}$ **15.** $-\frac{2m^4}{n^2}$ **17.** $-\frac{1}{3x^3y^5}$ **B 19.** $7t$ **21.** $4c^2$ **23.** $-4x^4y^2$ **25.** cd **27.** $6a^2$ **29.** $-2m^4n^2$

Page 231 Written Exercises A 1. $\frac{x}{y^3}$ **3.** $\frac{1}{r^2s}$ **5.** $\frac{u^2}{z^2}$ **7.** 1 **9.** $\frac{r^6}{s^3}$ **11.** $\frac{z}{2}$ **13.** a^2b^{-2} **15.** $x^{-4}y^3$ **17.** $a^{-3}b^2c^{-1}d^4$ **19.** $4y^2$ **21.** 0 **23.** $5x^3y^3$ **25.** $-2x$ **B 27.** 2×10^9 **29.** $\frac{41}{9}$ **31.** $1 + x - y$

Pages 233–234 Written Exercises A 1. $2a + 4$ **3.** $2 - z$ **5.** $z + 2$ **7.** $4p - 1$ **9.** $3 + \frac{5}{t}$ **11.** $2 + \frac{1}{2k}$ **13.** $\frac{3m}{2n} - \frac{1}{2}$ **15.** $\frac{4}{y} + \frac{2}{x}$ **17.** $-4x^2 + 3x - 2$ **19.** $x + 2y - 3xy$ **21.** $-z + 4 - \frac{2}{z}$ **B 23.** $10x - 14$ **25.** $5k - 4t + 3$ **27.** $2x^2y + 4x - xy$ **29.** 1.6 **31.** $\emptyset$ **33.** $\{1\}$

Pages 236–237 Written Exercises A 1. $y + 2$ **3.** $x - 3$ **5.** $a - 5$ **7.** $x + 1 + \frac{2}{x + 1}$ **9.** $x + 4$ **11.** $m - 2$ **13.** $x + 2$ **15.** $3p + 3 + \frac{11}{2p - 3}$ **17.** $x^2 + 2xy + 4y^2$ **19.** $2t + 3s$ **21.** $16n^2 + 20mn + 25m^2$ **B 23.** $x^2 - 2x + 3$ **25.** $3r^2 - 4r + 5 + \frac{2}{2r + 3}$ **27.** $x^2 + 5x + 2$ **29.** $x^6 + x^4 + x^2 + 1$ **31.** $x^2 - 2x + 3$ **33.** no **C 35.** -21

Page 239 Chapter Test 1. $38y + 70$ **3.** $3a + b - c$ **5.** $\{4\}$ **7.** $3x^6y^3z^3$ **9.** $-27r^6s^3t^9$ **11.** $-15s^2 +$ $18s$ **13.** $t^2 - 3t - 4$ **15.** 8 in.; 11 in. **17.** $-\frac{4xy}{z^2}$ **19.** $\frac{x^5z^2}{y^2}$ **21.** $-2x^2 + 3x - 4$ **23.** $x^2 - 2x + 4$

Pages 240–242 Chapter Review 1. monomial **3.** 3 **5.** $2p^2 + 2p + 3$ **7.** $-7x + 2y - z$ **9.** $1 = 1$ **11.** $2m - 4n + p$; -3 **13.** sum **15.** x^5 **17.** $6x^6y^4$ **19.** a^mb^m **21.** $27x^3y^3$ **23.** $-54a^6b^7$ **25.** distrib. **27.** $-6y^3 + 15y^2 - 6y$ **29.** $\{\frac{11}{2}\}$ **31.** $(x + y)$; $(x + y)$ **33.** $2x^2 + 5xy - 3y^2$ **35.** $3x^2 + 16xy - 12y^2$ **37.** $x + 4$; $x(x + 4)$ **39.** $x^2 + 4x + 4$ **41.** $x^4 + 4x^3 + 2x^2 - 4x + 1$ **43.** b^{m-n}; $\frac{1}{b^{n-m}}$ **45.** $\frac{b^4}{2a^4}$ **47.** 1 **49.** $\frac{2}{z^4}$ **51.** $\frac{16}{3}x - 3$ **53.** $-3x + 2y - 1$ **55.** $y - 1$ **57.** $z^2 + 3z + 1$

Chapter 7. Special Products and Factoring

Page 252 Written Exercises A 1. $2 \cdot 17$ **3.** $3^2 \cdot 7$ **5.** $2^4 \cdot 3^2$ **7.** prime **9.** 1, 3, 5, 15 **11.** 1, 2, 3, 4, 6, 8, 12, 24 **13.** 1, 2, 3, 5, 6, 10, 15, 30 **15.** 1, 2, 3, 4, 6, 12, 37, 74, 111, 148, 222, 444 **17.** 12 **19.** 35 **21.** 63 **23.** $22ab$ **25.** $21x^2yz^2$ **27.** $16s^2$ **29.** ab **31.** $3x$ **33.** $-7uv$ **35.** $4s$ **B 37.** z^4 **39.** $(2t)^3$ **41.** $(5xy)^2$ **43.** $(4a^3b^2)^3$

Pages 254–255 Written Exercises A 1. $4(x^2 - 2)$ **3.** $a(4a + 5)$ **5.** $5z^2(2z - 1)$ **7.** $3ab(2a + b)$ **9.** $3(p^2 + p - 3)$ **11.** $5(n^2 - 3n + 4)$ **13.** $ax(a^2x^2 + ax - 1)$ **15.** $4b^2(y^2 - 2y + 6)$ **17.** $5xy(3x - 6 + 7y)$ **19.** $3x^3y^2(3x^2 - 2xy + y^2)$ **B 21.** $(n + 3)(n - 1)$ **23.** $(3a - b)(b + a)$ **25.** $(t^2 - 5)(y + 5)$ **27.** $(n^2 + 1)(2n + 1)$ **29.** $(a^2 + b)(a - b)$ **31.** $(5c - 1)(a^3 + b)$ **C 33.** $(n + p)(n + 2)$ **35.** $(k + 2)(k + 3)$ **37.** $(2x + 3)(x + 2)$ **39.** $(3y + p)(2y - 1)$ **41.** $n(m + 1)(n + 2)$

Pages 255–256 **Problems** **A 1.** $A = r^2(4 - \pi)$ **3.** $A = 2r^2(6 - \pi)$ **5.** $A = \pi(R^2 - r^2)$ **7.** $A = \pi(R^2 - 3r^2)$

Page 258 **Written Exercises** **A 1.** 96 **3.** 391 **5.** 375 **7.** 1599 **9.** 1564 **11.** 8096 **B 13.** 9975 **15.** $35\frac{8}{9}$ **17.** 999,600 **19.** 0.91

Page 259 **Written Exercises** **A 1.** $(t + 3)(t - 3)$ **3.** $(2m + 1)(2m - 1)$ **5.** $(t + u)(t - u)$ **7.** $(5v + 7)(5v - 7)$ **9.** $(9t + 10s)(9t - 10s)$ **11.** $(ab^2 + c)(ab^2 - c)$ **13.** $(2y + 1)(2y - 1)$ **15.** $(5x + 6y)(5x - 6y)$ **17.** $4(r + 4)(r - 4)$ **19.** $(x + 13)(x - 13)$ **21.** $(15a + b)(15a - b)$ **B 23.** $3(t + 3)(t - 3)$ **25.** $x^2(x + 5)(x - 5)$ **27.** $(c + b)(c - b)$ **29.** $3(7z + 5)(7z - 5)$ **31.** $t^2 + k^2)(t + k)(t - k)$ **33.** $(1 + n^n)(1 - n^n)$ **25.** $(x^n + 3)(x^n - 3)$ **37.** $(k + a^n)(k - a^n)$ **39.** $(l^3 + w^2h)(l^3 - w^2h)$ **C 41.** $(x^{2n} + y^{2n})(x^n + y^n)(x^n - y^n)$ **43.** $3(2x + 3)$ **45.** $4x$ **47. a.** $(n + 1)^2 - n^2 = 2n + 1 = n + (n + 1)$ **b.** $(2n + 3)^2 - (2n + 1)^2 = 2(4n + 4) = 2[(2n + 3) + (2n + 1)]$

Pages 261–262 **Written Exercises** **A 1.** $p^2 + 14p + 49$ **3.** $4x^2 - 4x + 1$ **5.** $16t^2 + 24t + 9$ **7.** $36r^2 + 60r + 25$ **9.** $4x^2 - 12xy + 9y^2$ **11.** $x^2y^2 - 2xy + 1$ **13.** $x^4 + 4x^2 + 4$ **15.** $4p^4 - 20p^2q^2 + 25q^4$ **B 17.** $x^2 - \frac{2}{3}x + \frac{4}{9}$ **19.** $\frac{1}{4} - m + m^2$ **21.** $n^2 - 0.6n + 0.09$ **23.** $0.36x^2 + 1.8x + 2.25$ **25.** $\frac{9}{16}y^2 + 2y + \frac{16}{9}$ **27.** $x^6 + 2x^3y^2z + y^4z^2$

Page 264 **Written Exercises** **A 1.** $(n - 1)^2$ **3.** $(k - 3)^2$ **5.** $(r + 5)^2$ **7.** $(2p - 1)^2$ **9.** $(4c + 1)^2$ **11.** $(2x - y)^2$ **13.** $(1 - 2t)^2$ **15.** $(8y - z)^2$ **17.** $(3 + 2p)^2$ **19.** $(2xy - 3z)^2$ **21.** $(x^2 + 1)^2$ **23.** $(5y^2 - x)^2$ **B 25.** $7x(x + 1)^2$ **27.** $x(x - 5)^2$ **29.** $6x(2 + x)^2$ **31.** $4(y + x)^2(y - x)^2$ **C 33.** $(x + y + 1)(x - y + 1)$ **35.** $(a + b - 1)(a - b + 1)$ **37.** 9 **39.** 4

Page 266 **Written Exercises** **A 1.** $n^2 + 9n + 18$ **3.** $x^2 + 5x - 50$ **5.** $2x^2 + 5x + 2$ **7.** $3t^2 + 11t - 4$ **9.** $6x^2 - 13x + 6$ **11.** $6r^2 - 7r - 5$ **13.** $6 + x - x^2$ **15.** $3 - 2s - 8s^2$ **17.** $-x^2 + 5x - 6$ **19.** $2z^2 + 5z + 3$ **21.** $x^3 + x^2 - 2x$ **23.** $6y^3 + 28y^2 - 10y$ **25.** $\{2\}$ **27.** $\{1\}$ **B 29.** $x^2 + \frac{1}{3}x - \frac{2}{9}$ **31.** $y^2 + \frac{2}{5}y - \frac{8}{25}$ **33.** $a^2 - 2.9a - 0.62$ **35.** $6.3z^2 - 2.97z - 0.34$ **C 37.** $\{2\}$ **39.** $\{-4\}$

Page 269 **Written Exercises** **A 1.** $(n + 7)(n + 1)$ **3.** $(y + 4)(y + 1)$ **5.** $(k - 6)(k - 1)$ **7.** $(a - 8)(a - 1)$ **9.** $(x + 5)(x + 2)$ **11.** $(n - 13)(n - 2)$ **13.** $(7 + k)(2 + k)$ **15.** $(7 - u)(6 - u)$ **17.** $(x + 7y)(x + y)$ **19.** $(m - 7n)(m - 4n)$ **21.** $(r - 4t)(r - 19t)$ **23.** $(a - 24b)(a - 2b)$ **B 25.** 11, 7, −11, −7 **27.** 21, 12, 9, −21, −12, −9 **29.** 2 **31.** 5, 8, 9 **C 33.** $(x + y - 3)(x + y - 1)$ **35.** $(x + 1)(x - 1)$ **37.** $5 = 5 \cdot 1, (-5)(-1); 5 + 1 \neq 3, -5 + (-1) \neq 3$ **39.** $1 = 1 \cdot 1, (-1)(-1); 1 + 1 \neq 0, -1 + (-1) \neq 0$

Page 271 **Written Exercises** **A 1.** $(a + 3)(a - 2)$ **3.** $(x - 3)(x + 1)$ **5.** $(c - 5)(c + 2)$ **7.** $(u + 9)(u - 2)$ **9.** $(z - 7)(z + 3)$ **11.** $(x + 8)(x - 7)$ **13.** $(a + 5)(a - 4)$ **15.** $(x - 10)(x + 6)$ **17.** $(a - 4b)(a + 2b)$ **19.** $(p - 8q)(p + 3q)$ **21.** $(r - 12s)(r + 2s)$ **23.** $(x - 12y)(x + 3y)$ **B 25.** −9, −3, 9, 3 **27.** −11, −4, −1, 1, 4, 11 **29.** −23, −10, −5, −2, 2, 5, 10, 23 **31.** −2, −6 **33.** −4, −10 **35.** −3, −8 **C 37.** $(s + t - 11)(s + t + 6)$ **39.** $(y + 7)(y - 7)$

Page 272 **Written Exercises** **A 1.** $(2x + 1)(x + 1)$ **3.** $(3t + 1)(t + 2)$ **5.** $(5r - 2)(r - 1)$ **7.** $(3y - 2)(y + 3)$ **9.** $(t - 3)(4t + 1)$ **11.** $(5n + 2)(n - 1)$ **13.** $(7x - 3)(x - 1)$ **15.** $(5k - 7)(k + 1)$ **17.** $(2y - 3x)(y + 2x)$ **B 19.** $(3x + 5)(4x - 3)$ **21.** $(3t + 2)(2t + 7)$ **23.** $(3u + 4)(2u - 3)$ **25.** $(10y - 9z)(y + 2z)$ **C 27.** $[2(x + y) + 5][4(x + y) - 3]$ **29.** $(4x - 7)(6x - 5)$

Page 274 **Written Exercises** **A 1.** $4(x + 1)(x - 1)$ **3.** $2(y + 2)(y + 1)$ **5.** $(7x - 1)(x + 2)$ **7.** $-3a(a^2 + b^2)$ **9.** $a(r - 4)(r + 1)$ **11.** $(6t - 5)(t - 1)$ **13.** $2(5r - 1)^2$ **15.** $(3y - 5)(y + 1)$ **17.** $(12y + 7x^2)(12y - 7x^2)$ **19.** $(2n - 3)(3n + 5)$ **21.** $(7 + s)(3 - s)$ **23.** $(4x + 9)(7x + 6)$ **B 25.** $2ab(3a + 2b)(a - 5b)$ **27.** $6n(7m + 3n)(m - n)$ **29.** $s^2(3s - 2)(2s - 5)$ **31.** $(z^2 + r^2)(z + r) \times (z - r)$ **33.** $(z - 1)(z^3 + z^2 + z - 9)$ **35.** $-3a(7 + z)(2 + z)$ **37.** $(u - 3)(u - 12)(u + 2)$ **39.** $(x + 5) \times (2x + 3)(x - 3)$ **C 41.** $(x + 3)(x - 3)(2x - 5)(2x - 3)$ **43.** $(3x - 2)(x + 1)(3x + 2)(x - 1)$ **45.** $6b(z + w)(z - w)$ **47.** $(-5x + 2y)(4x - 7y)$ **49.** $(x^2 - 6)(x^2 + 7)$ **51.** $(n + 1)^2(n - 1)$ **53.** −18 **55.** 40

Pages 276–277 **Written Exercises** **A 1.** $\{0, 5\}$ **3.** $\{6, 8\}$ **5.** $\{-2, 7\}$ **7.** $\{-4, \frac{3}{2}\}$ **9.** $\{\frac{1}{2}, \frac{7}{3}\}$ **11.** $\{-\frac{7}{2}, -\frac{5}{2}\}$ **13.** $\{0, 1, -3\}$ **15.** $\Re$ **B 17.** $\{6\}$ **19.** $\{\frac{2}{3}, -\frac{1}{4}\}$ **21.** $\{14, \frac{8}{3}\}$ **23.** $\{\frac{35}{3}, -\frac{6}{5}\}$

Page 279 **Written Exercises** **A** 1. $\{-3, 2\}$ 3. $\{-3, 1\}$ 5. $\{4, -4\}$ 7. $\{0, 5\}$ 9. $\{7, -1\}$ 11. $\{-8, 7\}$ 13. $\{-3, -5\}$ 15. $\{-\frac{1}{2}\}$ 17. $\{-\frac{3}{2}, 2\}$ 19. $\{-\frac{5}{2}, -2\}$ 21. $\{-6, 11\}$ 23. $\{\frac{2}{3}, 5\}$ 25. $\{\frac{2}{3}, 5\}$ 27. $\{\frac{3}{2}, -5\}$ 29. $\{0, 4\}$ 31. $\{3\}$ 33. $\{3, -3, 2, -2\}$ 35. $\{0, \frac{6}{5}, -\frac{3}{2}\}$ 37. $\{0, 1\}$ **C** 39. $\{2, 1\}$ 41. $\{2, -1\}$ 43. $t^2 + 2t - 35 = 0$ 45. $q^3 - 9q = 0$ 47. $y^4 - 13y^2 + 36 = 0$

Pages 282–284 **Problems** **A** 1. 7, 8 3. $-8, -7$ 5. 4 ft.; 7 ft. 7. $3\frac{1}{2}$ sec. 9. 40 ft. 11. 23 in.; 7 in. 13. 5 sec. **B** 15. 3 sec. 17. 6 in. 19. -3 21. 7 25. 4 in.

Page 286 **Chapter Test** 1. 30 3. $15t^2(3t - 1)$ 5. $(x^2 + 5)(x - 3)$ 7. $x^2y^2 - 9$ 9. $(z + 11) \times$ $(z - 11)$ 11. $16a^2 - 24ab + 9b^2$ 13. -1 15. $(x - 7y)(x - y)$ 17. $(p + 6)(p - 2)$ 19. $(3a - 4b) \times$ $(2a + 3b)$ 21. $\{-3, 9\}$ 23. $\{-11, 8\}$ 25. 3 ft.; 8 ft.

Pages 286–288 **Chapter Review** 1. $2^2 \cdot 3 \cdot 23$ 3. 4 5. $7(a^2b + 2ab^2 - 4)$ 7. $(y + 3)$ 9. $(p + 2) \times$ $(p + q)$ 11. $(2u + v)(w - 3x)$ 13. x^4y^6 15. $4x^2 - 9$ 17. $(y + 8)(y - 8)$ 19. $(2d + 3)(2d - 3)$ 21. $x^2 + 2xz + z^2$ 23. $9y^2 - 12y + 4$ 25. $(t - 5)^2$ 27. $(6k - 5)^2$ 29. $-8t, 7t^2, 4$ 31. $14p^2 -$ $19pq - 3q^2$ 33. 16; 10 35. $(z - 4)(z - 3)$ 37. $-14; 5$ 39. $(r - 10)(r + 2)$ 41. $(3n + 1)(n + 2)$ 43. $(2z - 3)(4z - 1)$ 45. $4t(t + 3)(t - 3)$ 47. $b(y - 10z)(y + 5z)$ 49. $\{7\}$ 51. $\{5, -11\}$ 53. $\{-10, 9\}$ 55. $\{2\}$ 57. 12, 14

Page 292 **Extra for Experts** **Exercises** 1. 1.86×10^8 mi. 3. 2.5×10^{-5} cm. 5. 1.3×10^{11} cm. 7. 93,000,000 mi. 9. 96,000,000,000,000,000,000,000 cm. 11. 0.0000000667 cgs unit 13. 3×10^{-4} 15. 4.6656×10^{-11}

Chapter 8. Operations with Fractions

Page 296 **Written Exercises** **A** 1. $\dfrac{6}{x}$; $x \ne 0$ 3. $\frac{23}{100}$ 5. $\dfrac{y}{2}$ 7. $\dfrac{x - 1}{x}$; $x \ne 0$ 9. $\dfrac{h}{3h - 6}$; $h \ne 2$ 11. $\dfrac{7z^2 + 2}{5}$ 13. $\dfrac{p - 3}{7p + 14}$; $p \ne -2$ 15. $\dfrac{1}{z(z - 7)}$; $z \ne 0, z \ne 7$ **B** 17. $\{3, 5\}$

19. $\{7, -4\}$ 21. $\{-\frac{1}{3}, 2\}$ 23. $\{7, -7\}$ **C** 25. $c \ne 0, c \ne d$ 27. $x \ne y$ 29. $p \ne \dfrac{r}{2}, p \ne -r$

Pages 298–299 **Written Exercises** **A** 1. $5a$ 3. $\dfrac{2}{3x}$; $x \ne 0$ 5. $-a$; $a \ne 0, b \ne 0$ 7. $\frac{2}{3}$; $c \ne -d$ 9. $\dfrac{7}{a + b}$; $a \ne -b$ 11. $\dfrac{3p}{q + 2p}$; $p \ne 0, q \ne 0, q \ne -2p$ 13. $-3 - k$; $k \ne 3$ 15. $\dfrac{x - 3}{x + 3}$; $x \ne -3$ 17. $\dfrac{p}{q}$; $q \ne 0, q = \dfrac{1}{p}$ 19. $\dfrac{z^2 + 2}{z + 2}$; $z \ne -2$ 21. $\dfrac{x}{x + 1}$; $x \ne 3, x \ne -1$ 23. $\dfrac{x + 3}{x - 2}$; $x \ne 2, x \ne -2$ **B** 25. $\dfrac{x + 3y}{x - 3y}$; $x \ne 3y, x \ne -3y$ 27. $\dfrac{y + 2}{y}$; $y \ne 0, y \ne 4$ 29. $\dfrac{n - 3}{n - 2}$; $n \ne 2$ 31. $\dfrac{n + 3}{n - 5}$; $n \ne 5, n \ne 2$ 33. y is not a factor of num. or denom. 35. t is not a factor of num. or denom. **C** 37. $\dfrac{2y - 5}{y - 4}$; $y \ne 4$, $y \ne -2, y \ne 0$ 39. $\dfrac{r - 1}{r + 5}$; $r \ne -5, r \ne -\frac{3}{2}$ 41. $\dfrac{3(2x + 3)}{4x - 5}$; $x \ne 0, x \ne \frac{4}{3}, x \ne \frac{1}{4}$ 43. $\dfrac{x - 3}{x + a}$; $x \ne -a$, $x \ne -2$

Pages 301–302 **Written Exercises** **A** 1. $\frac{2}{1}$ 3. $\frac{9}{25}$ 5. $\frac{1}{3}$ 7. $\frac{32}{1}$ 9. $\frac{3}{1}$ 11. $\frac{15}{16}$ 13. $\frac{4}{1}$ 15. $\frac{9}{5}$ 17. $\frac{1}{2}$ 19. $\frac{3}{4}$ **B** 21. $-\frac{3}{8}$ 23. $\frac{5}{3}$ **C** 25. $\frac{1}{1}$

Pages 302–303 **Problems** **A** 1. 35 3. 20 boys 5. 91 mi. 7. $12,000 9. 38 ft. 11. 16 oz. at 72¢ **B** 13. 646,926 trees 15. cement, 110 lb.; sand, 440 lb.; gravel, 550 lb. 17. first person, $960; second person, $600; third person, $240

Pages 304–305 **Written Exercises** **A** 1. 21.6 3. 7.77 5. 4 7. 30 9. 4 11. 4.92 13. 30 15. 85 17. 218 19. 615 21. 75% 23. 300% 25. 0.5% 27. 1600%

Pages 305–307 Problems A 1. 2304 persons **3.** 9 min. **5.** $3100 **7.** $12,400 **9.** 4.5% **11.** 14% **B 13.** 5%
15. $2840 **17.** $422.22

19. a. Registered Voters in Valley City   **b.** 4154   **21.**   Licensed Drivers in U.S.

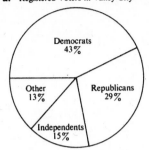

Pages 309–310 Written Exercises A 1. $\frac{18}{55}$ **3.** $\frac{2}{15}$ **5.** $\frac{1}{2}$ **7.** $\frac{1}{3}$ **9.** 4a   **11.** $\frac{3z^2}{2}$

13. $-2x^2y^2$ **15.** $\frac{3(x+5)}{2(x+10)}$ **17.** $\frac{1}{4}$ **B 19.** $\frac{a-b}{a-4}$ **21.** $\frac{2(z-3)}{z}$ **23.** $\frac{x(x+2)}{2}$ **25.** $\frac{r+6}{r-2}$

27. $\frac{x-y}{x^2}$ **29.** $\frac{n-6}{n-3}$ **31.** 1   **33.** a   **35.** 1   **C 37.** $n+1$ **39.** $\frac{y-3}{6-y}$ **41.** -1

Page 311 Written Exercises A 1. $\frac{4}{7}$ **3.** $\frac{1}{xy}$ **5.** $\frac{2q^2}{p^2}$ **7.** $\frac{s}{8t}$ **9.** $-12z$ **11.** $\frac{1}{6}$ **13.** $\frac{y-2}{2y}$

15. $\frac{z+2}{z+3}$ **17.** 4   **19.** $\frac{3}{2(a-z)}$ **21.** $\frac{n(n+m)}{n-4}$ **B 23.** $\frac{(a+b)(a+3)}{3(a-3)}$ **25.** $\frac{t(1-2t)}{2(t-2)}$

27. $\frac{(n+3)(n-3)(n+1)}{2(2n-3)(n+7)(n+2)}$ **29.** -1 **C 31.** $(a+2)(b-3)$ **33.** $\frac{(a-b)(x-y)}{3ax(x+y)}$

Pages 312–313 Written Exercises A 1. $\frac{3}{xy}$ **3.** $\frac{s^2}{r}$ **5.** 2   **7.** $\frac{2st}{9}$ **9.** p **11.** $\frac{x+1}{x(x-3)}$

13. $\frac{t}{2s(st-2)}$ **B 15.** $\frac{2(x+1)}{x-1}$ **17.** $\frac{2(2n+m)}{9(2n-m)}$ **19.** $2y-c$

Pages 314–315 Written Exercises A 1. $\frac{11}{17}$ **3.** $\frac{8}{7}$ **5.** $\frac{1}{3x}$ **7.** $\frac{3(x+1)}{2}$ **9.** 4   **11.** $x+y$

13. $\frac{3}{b}$ **B 15.** $a+b$ **17.** $\frac{k-1}{k-3}$ **19.** $\frac{1}{z+3}$ **C 21.** $\frac{a}{a^2+9}$

Pages 317–318 Written Exercises A 1. $\frac{6+a}{3a}$ **3.** $\frac{1}{2a}$ **5.** $\frac{x+6}{6}$ **7.** $\frac{5z+4}{9}$ **9.** $\frac{17t+10}{6}$

11. $\frac{2x^2+3x-1}{x^3}$ **13.** $\frac{5(c+2)}{6c}$ **15.** $\frac{4x+7}{ax}$ **17.** $\frac{6x^2-5xy+6y^2}{12xy}$ **19.** $\frac{2-3c+3d}{c^2-d^2}$

21. $-\frac{2}{3(r+1)}$ **23.** $-\frac{4y}{(y+2)(y-2)}$ **25.** $\frac{5t+12}{t^2+5t+6}$ **B 27.** $-\frac{1}{y^2+5y+6}$ **29.** $\frac{5x-2}{(x-3)(x-1)}$

31. $\frac{2x^2+10x-3}{16x^2}$ **33.** $-\frac{2z-7}{(z-2)(z+1)^2}$ **35.** $\frac{6z+9}{z^2-4}$ **C 37.** $\frac{-2a^3+12a^2+50a+84}{(a^2-9)(a^2-1)(a^2+2a+3)}$

39. $\frac{t+1}{(t-3)(t+2)(t-2)}$

Page 319 Written Exercises A 1. $\frac{(a+1)(a+2)}{a+3}$ **3.** $\frac{3x}{x-y}$ **5.** $\frac{y^2-3}{y+2}$ **7.** $\frac{n+6}{n+2}$ **9.** $\frac{(a+b)^2}{ab}$

11. $\frac{y^2+3y-7}{y-2}$ **13.** $6\frac{3}{4}$ **15.** $\frac{2}{z}+3z^2$ **17.** $2p-\frac{3}{7p^2}$ **19.** $xy+\frac{3}{4}$ **21.** $y-6+\frac{20}{y+3}$

23. $3t+\frac{5}{3t-2}$

Page 321 Written Exercises A 1. $\frac{2}{3}$ **3.** 1 **5.** $\frac{2x}{3}$ **7.** $\frac{xy + y^2}{x^2 - xy}$ **9.** $\frac{y - 3}{y}$ **11.** $\frac{1}{2}$ **13.** $\frac{x + 3}{3}$

15. $\frac{a + 2b}{b - a}$ **B 17.** $\frac{x - y}{2(x + y)}$ **19.** $\frac{x + 6}{x - 1}$ **21.** $-\frac{x^2 + y^2}{4xy}$ **C 23.** $\frac{1}{y}$ **25.** $\frac{3x^2 + 4x + 3}{(x + 1)^2}$ **27.** $\{-\frac{3}{2}\}$

Page 324 Chapter Test 1. $-1, 1$ **3.** $\frac{n}{n - 1}$ **5.** $\frac{9}{2}$ **7.** \$3.15 **9.** $\frac{2}{3z}$ **11.** 1 **13.** $\frac{3p^2 + 8p - 3}{3p + 1}$

15. $\frac{13}{18}$ **17.** $\frac{1}{2(r - 5)}$ **19.** $2c + 3 - \frac{4}{c}$ **21.** $\frac{t + 1}{2}$

Pages 325–326 Chapter Review 1. zero **3.** $-2, 2$ **5.** $-\frac{6a}{b}$ **7.** $\frac{7}{3}$ **15.**

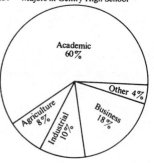

Majors in Gentry High School

Academic 60%

Other 4%

Business 18%

Industrial 10%

Agriculture 8%

9. $\frac{6}{1}$ **11.** $\frac{1}{3}$ **13.** 27 **17.** $\frac{2a^3}{c}$ **19.** $\frac{3(n + 1)}{n - 1}$ **21.** $\frac{4}{5k}$ **23.** $\frac{5(a + 2)}{6a + 27}$

25. $\frac{3}{10}$ **27.** $\frac{1}{x}$ **29.** $\frac{2}{z}$ **31.** $k - n$ **33.** $-\frac{5z + 12}{5z}$ **35.** $-\frac{3y - 10}{2(y - 2)}$

37. $\frac{xz + z^2 + x}{x + z}$ **39.** $2x - 16 + \frac{7}{2x}$ **41.** $\frac{2}{5}$ **43.** $\frac{5}{3x^2}$

Chapter 9. Using Fractions

Pages 330–331 Written Exercises A 1. $\{10\}$ **3.** $z < 1$; **5.** $\{-4\}$

7. $b \geq 10$; **9.** $\{1\}$

11. $x > 12$; **B 13.** $\{1\}$ **15.** $\{12\}$ **19.** $\{\frac{5}{2}\}$ **21.** $\{-4\}$

17. $x \leq 84$; **23.** $\{6000\}$ **C 25.** $\{3\}$ **27.** $\{-3\}$ **29.** $\{\frac{21}{16}\}$

Pages 332–333 Problems A 1. 15 lb. **3.** 6.25 lb. **5.** 24 lb. **7.** 6.66 lb. **B 9.** 32 lb. **11.** 35% silver alloy, 16 lb.; 65% silver alloy, 4 lb. **C 13.** 16 qt.

Pages 334–335 Problems A 1. \$56 **3.** \$2000 **5.** \$763 **7.** \$4500 **9.** \$1200 at 4%; \$2400 at 5% **11.** \$800 **13.** \$2000 at 4%; \$6000 at 5% **B 15.** \$9000 at 5%; \$12,000 at 4% **17.** \$5000 at 5%; \$2000 at 4%; \$3000 at 3% **C 19.** \$60,000

Page 337 Written Exercises A 1. $\{2\}$ **3.** $\{5\}$ **5.** $\{3\}$ **7.** $\{-3, 2\}$ **9.** $\{-1, 9\}$ **11.** $\{-2, 1\}$ **13.** $\{-2\}$ **B 15.** $\{10, 20\}$ **17.** $\{5, 10\}$ **19.** $\{-1, 12\}$ **C 21.** $\{2, 8\}$ **23.** $\{1, 4\}$

Pages 339–340 Problems A 1. $34\frac{2}{7}$ sec. **3.** $1\frac{7}{8}$ days **5.** 8 min. **7.** 12 min; 24 min. **B 9.** 30 hr. **11.** $10\frac{4}{5}$ hr. **13.** first spillway, $37\frac{1}{2}$ days; second spillway, 25 days **15.** 9 hr.

Pages 341–342 Problems A 1. 15 m.p.h. **3.** 3 m.p.h. **5.** $\frac{1}{2}$ m.p.h. **7.** 5 m.p.h. **B 9.** 60 m.p.h. **11.** Sally, 6 m.p.h.; Jane, 12 m.p.h. **C 13.** 5 yd.

Page 343 Chapter Test 1. $x \leq \frac{3}{2}$; **3.** \$5000 at 4%; \$5000 at 6% **5.** $13\frac{1}{3}$ hr.

Pages 343–344 Chapter Review 1. $\{16\}$ **3.** $\{20\}$ **5.** 14 qt. **7.** \$150 at 5%; \$300 at 4% **9.** \$1200 at 4%; \$1900 at 6% **11.** $\{4\}$ **13.** $\{-1\}$ **15.** 12 min. **17.** 35 m.p.h.

Page 350   Extra for Experts   Exercises   1. third   **3.** fiftieth   **5.** $S \leftarrow 0; I \leftarrow 1$ **7.** $I = 10$ **9.** $S \leftarrow 0$;
$I \leftarrow 1$ **11.** $I = 10$
13.   **15.**

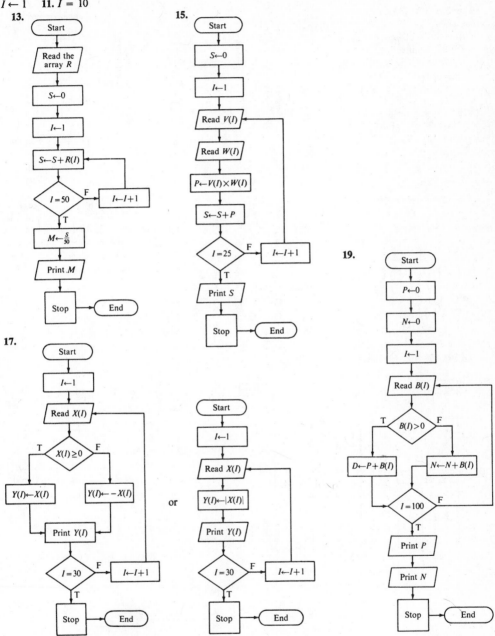

Pages 352–353   Cumulative Review 1–9   1. a. {b, c} ; **b.** {a, b, c, d, f, g}   **3.** 27   **5.** $R = \{3, 5, 7, 9\}$
7. Comm. ax. for mult.   **9.** Assoc. ax. for add.   **11.** -2 **13.** 15   **15.** 3   **17.** 2   **19.** $x < 0$ **21.** $\{\frac{15}{7}\}$
23. {15}   **25.** {the real nos. ≤ 2}   **27.** 23, 25, 27   **29.** $2n^2 - 2n + 3$ **31.** $3x^2z - 6xz^2 + 9xz$
33. $2n^2 + 2n - 12$ **35.** $-10, -8$ or 8, 10   **37.** $7xy(2x + 4 - 3y)$ **39.** $(3t - 2)(t - 6)$ **41.** $(6p + 7q) \times$
$(6p - 7q)$ **43.** {0, 3}   **45.** $\{0, \frac{8}{3}\}$ **47.** {5 ft.; 7 ft.}   **49.** $\dfrac{n - r}{3}$ **51.** $\frac{1}{4}$ **53.** $\dfrac{n - 1}{12}$ **55.** $\{-\frac{2}{3}\}$
57. $5000   **59.** $1\frac{1}{11}$ hr.

Chapter 10.   Functions, Relations, and Graphs

Pages 358–359   Written Exercises

A 1. Domain = {Discoverer I,
Tiros I, Courier I, Ranger I} ;
range = {250, 270, 500, 675}
(see right)

3. domain = {1920, 1930, 1940,
1950, 1960} ; range = {30,000,
32,000, 35,000, 46,000, 52,000}
(see right)

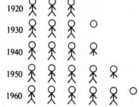

Ex. 1

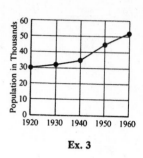

Ex. 3

5.   Weights of Satellites

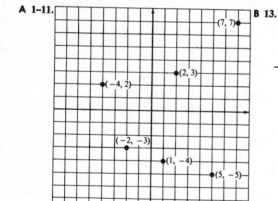

Key: ◯ = 100 pounds

7.   Population of Central City

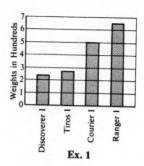

Key: ☂ = 10,000 persons

9. $a = 6; b = 3$ **11.** $a = \frac{3}{2}; b = 2$ **13** $a = 0; b = 18$ **B 15.** $a = -\frac{1}{2}; b = 4$ or $b = -4$ **17.** $a = 1; b = 0$ or $b = 1$ **19.** no solution

Page 362   Written Exercises

A 1–11.

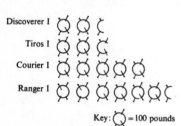

B 13.

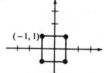

15.

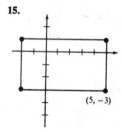

17.

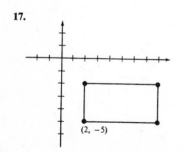

19.

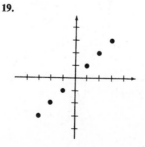

21.

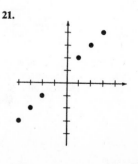

Pages 364–365 Written Exercises

A 1.

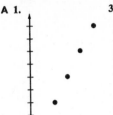

3.

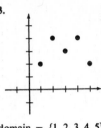

domain = {1, 2, 3, 4, 5};
range = {2, 3, 4}; yes

5.

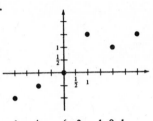

domain = {−2, −1, 0, 1, 2, 3}; range = {−1, −0.5, 0, 1, 1.5}; yes

7.

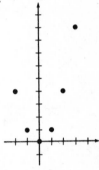

domain = {−2, −1, 0, 1, 2, 3};
range = {0, 1, 4, 9}; yes

domain = {1, 2, 3, 4, 5};
range = {2, 4, 6, 8, 10}; yes

9.

domain = {1, 2, 3};
range = {0, 2, 3, 4}; no

11.

domain = {−2, −1, 0, 1, 2};
range = {0, 1, 2}; yes

13.

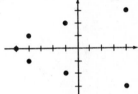

domain = {−5, −4, −1, 4};
range = {−3, −2, −1, 0, 1, 2, 3}; no

Page 368 Written Exercises

A 1.

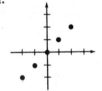

{(−2, −2), (−1, −1),
(0, 0), (1, 1), (2, 2)}

3.

{(−2, −1), (−1, 0),
(0, 1), (1, 2), (2, 3)}

5.

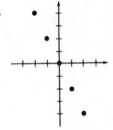

{(−2, 4), (−1, 2), (0, 0),
(1, −2), (2, −4)}

7.

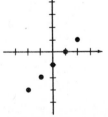

{(−2, −3), (−1, −2),
(0, −1), (1, 0), (2, 1)}

9.

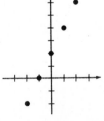

{(−2, −2), (−1, 0),
(0, 2), (1, 4), (2, 6)}

11.

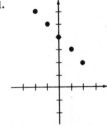

{(−2, 6), (−1, 5), (0, 4),
(1, 3), (2, 2)}

13.

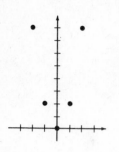

$\{(-2, 8), (-1, 2), (0, 0),$
$(1, 2), (2, 8)\}$

15.

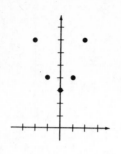

$\{(-2, 7), (-1, 4), (0, 3),$
$(1, 4), (2, 7)\}$

17.

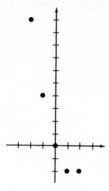

$\{(-2, 10), (-1, 4), (0, 0),$
$(1, -2), (2, -2)\}$

B 19.

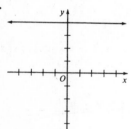

$\{(-1, 0), (-1, 1), (-1, 2),$
$(0, 1), (0, 2), (1, 2)\}$

21.

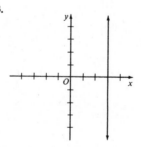

$\{(0, -1), (0, -2), (1, 1),$
$(1, 0), (1, -1), (1, -2)\}$

23.

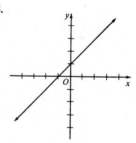

$\{(-1, 1), (-1, 2), (0, 1), (0, 2),$
$(1, 1), (1, 2)\}$

C 25. $\{-3, 1), (0, 4)\}$ **27.** $\{(3, 0), (1, 0), (2, -1), (0, 3), (4, 3)\}$ **29.** $\{(5, 12), (10, 9), (15, 6), (20, 3)\}$

Pages 372–373 Written Exercises

A 1.

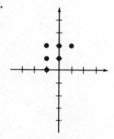

3.

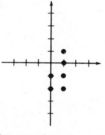

5.

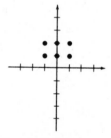

7.

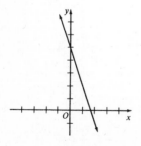

9.

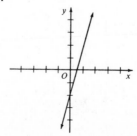

11.

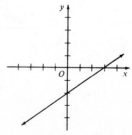

13.

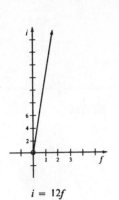

$i = 12f$

15.

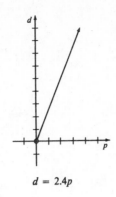

$d = 2.4p$

17.

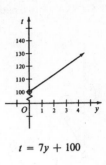

$t = 7y + 100$

B 19.

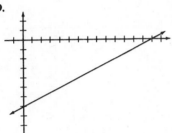

21.

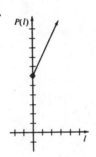

23.

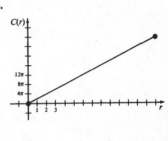

25. a. (5, 0) **b.** (0, 7)   **27. a.** (10, 0) **b.** (0, 5)   **29. a.** (0, 0) **b.** (0, 0)

C 33.

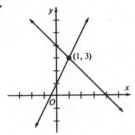

35.

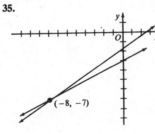

37. no;

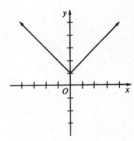

39. no;

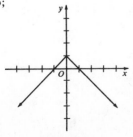

41. no;

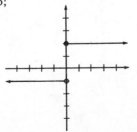

43. no;

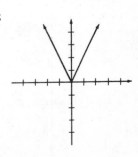

Pages 376–377 Written Exercises

A 1.

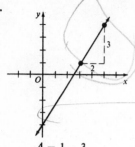

$$m = \frac{4-1}{5-3} = \frac{3}{2}$$

3.

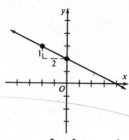

$$m = \frac{2-3}{0-(-2)} = -\frac{1}{2}$$

5.

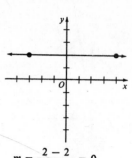

$$m = \frac{2-2}{-3-4} = 0$$

7.

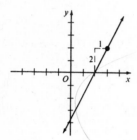

9.

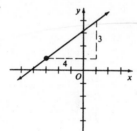

11.

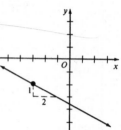

B 13. $b = 1$;

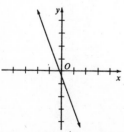

15. $b = 4$;

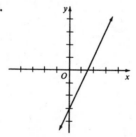

17. b is any real no.

Page 379 Written Exercises A 1. $-2x + y = 5$ **3.** $2x + y = -3$ **5.** $-x + 2y = 14$ **7.** $y = 2$
9. $4x + 6y = -1$

11.

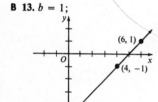

13.

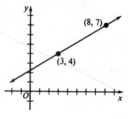

15.

17.

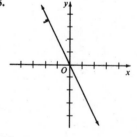

Page 381   Written Exercises   A 1. $y = 2x$
3. $y = -2x$ **5.** $3y = 2x - 4$ **7.** $y = -\frac{3}{4}x$
9. $y = x + 3$ **11.** $x = 2$ **13.** $2y = -x + 1$
15. $y = \frac{1}{2}x$ **B 17.** $a = -1$ **19.** $a = -3$
21. $a = 2$ **23.** $y = -x + 3$ **25.** $y = 2x - 2$
27. $(-\frac{10}{7}, 0)$ **29.** $(3, -3)$

Pages 385–386   Written Exercises   A 1. a. $y = 7$
b. $y = 140$ **c.** $y = -14$ **3.** $y_2 = 24$ **5.** $m_2 = -25$ **7.** $s_2 = 6$ **9.** $x = 18$ **11.** $w = 10$
13. $y = 4$ **15.** $z = 8$ **B 17.** $x = 8$ or $x = -8$
19. $x = 3$ **21.** $y = 11$ **23.** $x = 1$ **25.** $t = kw$
27. $d = kr$ **29.** $P = kT$

Pages 386–388   Problems   A 1. 58 lb.   **3.** $3\frac{1}{8}$
gal.   **5.** 11,880 votes   **7.** 0.294 ohm   **9.** $3\frac{2}{5}$ in.
B 11. 37 divisions   **13.** Cube of gold is heavier
by 4.5384 g.   **15.** $3.78   **C 17.** 111,059 sq. mi.

Page 381   Extra Problems

1.

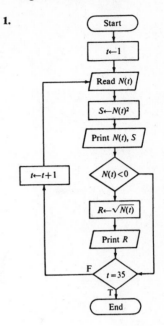

Page 391   Written Exercises

A 1.

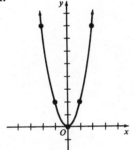

3.

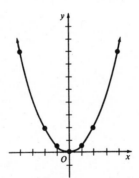

5.

7.

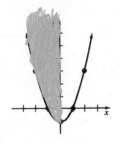

9.

11.

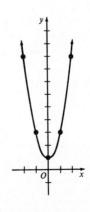

B 13

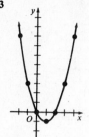

15.

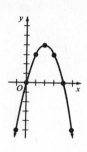

17.

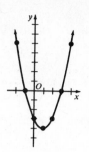

19.

Pages 391–392   Problems   A 1. 25:4   **3.** 550 ft.   **5.** 8.75 lb. per sq. ft.   **7.** 9π sq. in.   **B 9.** 9:4
11. 14,400 ft.

Pages 396–397   Written Exercises

A 1.

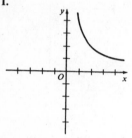

3.

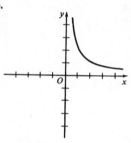

C 19.

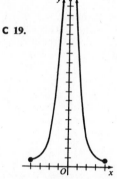

5. $y_2 = 234$ **7.** $p_1 = 2.10$ **9.** t is reduced to $\frac{1}{3}t$.   **11.** m is reduced to $\frac{1}{8}m$.   **13.** $t = 5$ **B 15.** 2 ft.
17. $Q = 40$

Page 398   Extra Problems

1.

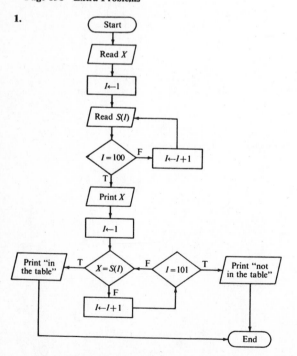

Pages 397–398   Problems   A 1. 6 hr.
3. 4 ft.   **5.** 5%   **7.** 16 in.   **9.** 35 cu. ft.
11. 360 r.p.m.   **B 13.** 5.5 ft.   **15.** 352 lb.
17. Wavelength of higher note is half that
of lower note.   **19.** 1.25 ft.

Pages 400–401 Written Exercises A 1. $r = k\dfrac{d}{t}$ **3.** $t = k\dfrac{w}{r}$ **5.** $T = kVP$ **7.** $V = khr^2$

9. $F = k\dfrac{q_1 q_2}{d^2}$

Pages 401–402 Problems A 1. H is multiplied by 36. **3. a.** $k = 27$ **b.** $W = \dfrac{27xy}{z^2}$ **c.** $W = 72$

5. 57 boys **7.** 72 lb. **9.** 9300 g. **B 11.** 18 m.p.h.

Page 404 Just For Fun

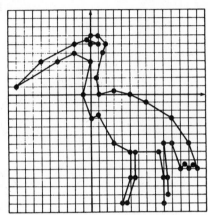

Pages 405–406 Chapter Test

1.

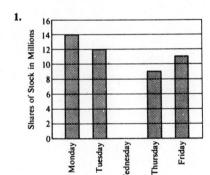

3. $a = 8; b = 3$ **5.**

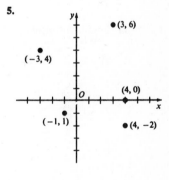

7.

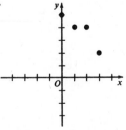

9. $3; -1$ **11.**

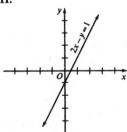

13. $\frac{2}{3}$ **15.** $a = -2$

domain = $\{0, 1, 2, 3\}$;
range = $\{5, 4, 2\}$; yes

17. $2x + y = 3$ **19.** $2x + y = 4$ **21.** 265 girls **23.** $y_1 = 4\frac{1}{2}$ **25.** I is $\frac{3}{8}$ as large.

Pages 408–410   Chapter Review   1. zero

3.

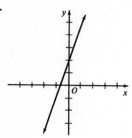

5. fourth   **7–9.**

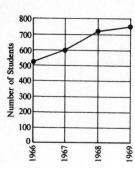

11. one   **13.** no   **15.** root
17. graph   **19.** one

21.

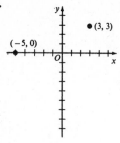

Ex. 41

23. positive; negative   **25.** no; zero   **27.** $y = -2x + 5$ **29.** $5x - y = 2$ **31.** $2x + y = 5$ **33.** $3x -$
$y = 0$ **35.** $\dfrac{y}{x}$ **37.** k **39.** $x; y; w; z$ **41.** (See above)   **43.** (0, 3)   **45.** $\dfrac{y_2}{y_1}$ **47.** $r_2 = 72$ **49.** $m = 240$

Page 413   Extra for Experts   Exercises

1.

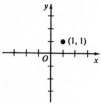

3. not possible **5.**

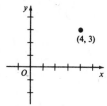

7. eight $3\frac{1}{2}$ yd. pieces; six $4\frac{1}{2}$ yd. pieces
9. $x = 41$ **11.** 9 dimes, 1 nickel,
5 pennies

Chapter 11.   Systems of Open Sentences in Two Variables

Pages 418–419   Written Exercises

A 1. $\{(1, 1)\}$;

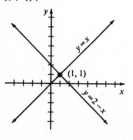

3. $\{(2, 1)\}$;

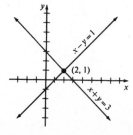

5. $\{(-2, 2)\}$;

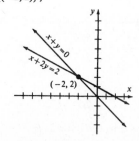

7. ∅;

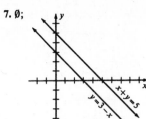

9. $\{(-2, 0)\}$

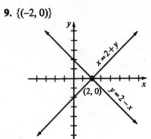

11. $\{(-1, -1)\}$;

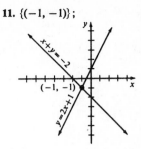

B 13. $\{(5.7, 0.7)\}$;

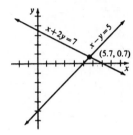

15. $\{(-3.6, 1.8)\}$;

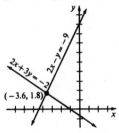

17. $\{(1, 1)\}$;

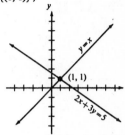

C 19. 25;

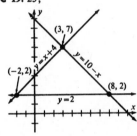

Pages 420–421   Written Exercises   A 1. $\{(8, -1)\}$ **3.** $\{(5, -3)\}$
5. $\{(8, 2)\}$ **7.** $\{(7, -2)\}$ **9.** $\{(-3, 2)\}$ **11.** $\{(-2, -1)\}$
13. $\{(0, -3)\}$ **15.** $\{(10, 2)\}$ **17.** $\{(5, -2)\}$ **B 19.** $\{(6, 2)\}$
21. $\{(3, 1)\}$ **23.** $\{(45, 29)\}$ **25.** $\{(6, 8)\}$

Pages 422–423   Problems   A 1. 200 ft.; 150 ft.   **3.** 10, 7   **5.** 225
points; 200 points   **7.** 3 large boxes; 2 small boxes   **9.** hamburgers, 45¢; hot dogs, 20¢   **B 11.** 6 nickels; 9 dimes

Pages 424–425   Written Exercises   A 1. $\{(4, -1)\}$
3. $\{(3, 4)\}$ **5.** $\{(1, -1)\}$ **7.** $\{(-3, 2)\}$ **9.** $\{(2, 3)\}$
11. $\{(3, -2)\}$ **B 13.** $\{(\frac{1}{3}, \frac{1}{2})\}$ **15.** $\{(-5, 3)\}$
17. $\{(3, 5)\}$

Pages 425–426   Problems   A 1. $140   **3.** 15 yr.
5. 150 ft.   **7.** potato chips, 59¢; pretzels, 39¢   **9.** stock
A, $2000; stock B, $3000

Page 426   Written Exercises   A 1. $\{(1, 2)\}$ **3.** $\{(-3,$
$-2)\}$ **5.** $\{(1, 1)\}$ **7.** $\{(5, -1)\}$ **9.** $\{(1, 0)\}$
11. $\{(3, 1)\}$ **B 13.** $\{(6, 4)\}$ **15.** $\{(5, 2)\}$ **17.** $\{(5, 2)\}$

Page 427   Problems   A 1. 6, 9   **3.** Lynn, 5 blocks;
Janet, 3 blocks   **5.** 7 men   **B 7.** $\frac{7}{12}, \frac{1}{3}$ **9.** $2000 in
special account; $500 in regular account

Page 427   Extra Problem

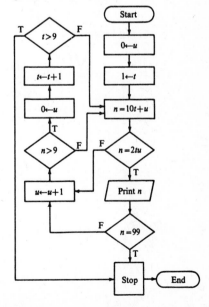

Pages 429–430   Problems   A 1. 38   **3.** 39   **5.** 39   **7.** 52
9. 79¢   **B 11.** 632   **13.** 49   **C 15.** 0.36   **17.** 0.25

Pages 430–431   Problems   A 1. 15 m.p.h.   **3.** 5 m.p.h.   **5.** $1\frac{3}{4}$
m.p.h.   **B 7.** 3 m.p.h.; $2\frac{2}{3}$ m.p.h.   **9.** approx. 144 m.p.h.; 29
m.p.h.   **11.** 8 m.p.h.; 2 m.p.h.

Pages 432–433   Problems   A 1. 2 yr.   **3.** 9 yr.   **5.** Ann, 12
yr.; Judy, 16 yr.   **B 7.** 18 yr.   **9.** $m = \frac{3}{2}l$ **C 11.** Mary, 16 yr.;
Jane, 12 yr.

Page 434   Problems   A 1. $\frac{3}{7}$ **3.** $\frac{7}{8}$ **5.** $\frac{12}{18}$ **B 7.** $\frac{18}{81}$ **9.** $\frac{37}{73}$
C 11. $\{\frac{21}{12}, \frac{42}{24}, \frac{63}{36}, \frac{84}{48}\}$

Page 431   Extra Problem

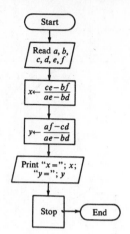

Page 437   Written Exercises

A 1.

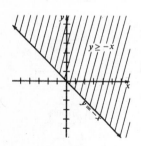

3.

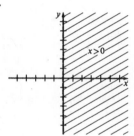

5.

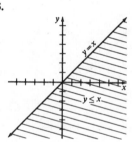

7.

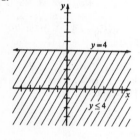

9.

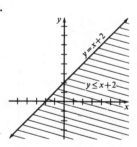

11.

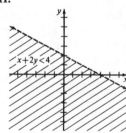

B 13.

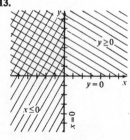

15.

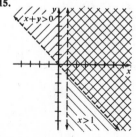

17.

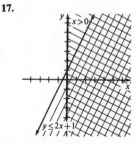

C 19.   **21.**   **23.**

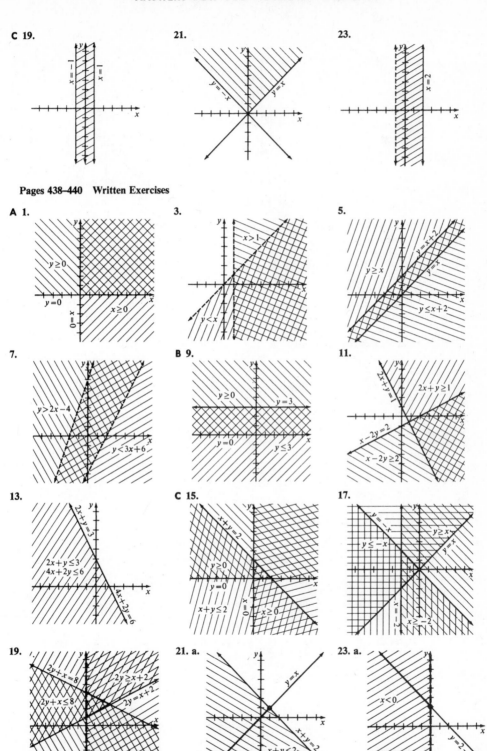

Pages 438–440   Written Exercises

A 1.   **3.**   **5.**

7.   **B 9.**   **11.**

13.   **C 15.**   **17.**

19.   **21. a.**   **23. a.**

b. $\{y = x; \, x \le 1; \, y \le 1\}$ **b.** $\{y = 2 - x; \, x < 0; \, y > 2\}$

Page 441   **Chapter Test**

1.

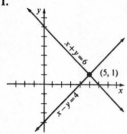

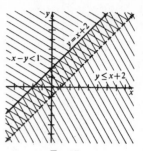

Ex. 15   Ex. 17

3. $\{(-1, 5)\}$ **5.** 23 lb.; 19 lb.   **7.** $\{(2, 1)\}$ **9.** $\{(2, -2)\}$ **11.** 24   **13.** Maria, 28 yr.; Carl, 12 yr.
15. (See above)   **17.** (See above)

Pages 442–444   **Chapter Review**   **1.** both   **3.** dependent; infinite   **5.** Any point on the line except (2, 4);
answers will vary.   **7.** $\{(2, 1)\}$ **9.** $\{(3, 2)\}$ **11.** $a = b + 3; a + b = 49$ **13.** 32 ft., 78 ft.
15. $\{(2, -2)\}$ **17.** $\{(5, -5)\}$ **19.** $\{(-2, -3)\}$ **21.** 95   **23.** $s - r; s + r$ **25.** plane, 150 m.p.h.;
wind, 30 m.p.h.   **27.** Mrs. Thomas, 35 yr.; daughter, 14   **29.** $\frac{18}{14}$ **31.** below   **33.** (See below)
35. Answers will vary, for example $(-3, 10)$.

Pages 448–449   **Extra for Experts**   **Exercises**

1.

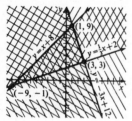

3. $(4, 2)$

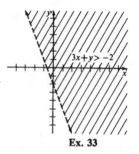

Ex. 33

Chapter 12.   Rational and Irrational Numbers

Pages 456–457   **Written Exercises**   **A 1.** >   **3.** >   **5.** <   **7.** <   **9.** $\{-\frac{3}{4}, \frac{5}{9}, \frac{2}{3}\}$ **11.** $\{-2.1, -2.0, -\frac{4}{3}\}$
13. $\{\frac{1}{4}, \frac{4}{15}, \frac{7}{24}, \frac{5}{16}\}$ **15.** $\frac{19}{30}$ **17.** $-\frac{11}{200}$ **19.** $4\frac{31}{48}$ **B 21.** $\frac{15}{16}$ **27. a.** F   **b.** T   **c.** T   **d.** F

Page 460   **Written Exercises**   **A 1.** 0.14   **3.** 0.09375   **5.** $-0.\overline{81}$ **7.** $-0.\overline{428571}$ **9.** 2.05   **11.** -0.1875
13. $\frac{33}{100}$ **15.** $\frac{107}{900}$ **17.** $\frac{7}{33}$ **19.** $-3\frac{148}{999}$ **B 21.** $0.00\overline{18}$; e.g., 0.1818   **23.** $0.0\overline{8}$; e.g. 0.88   **25.** 0.001;
e.g., 0.1255   **C 27.** $\{0.\overline{142857}, 0.\overline{285714}, 0.\overline{428571}, 0.\overline{571428}, 0.\overline{714285}, 0.\overline{857142}\}$ **29.** $\{0.\overline{09}, 0.\overline{18}, 0.\overline{27}, 0.\overline{36},$
$0.\overline{45}, 0.\overline{54}, 0.\overline{63}, 0.\overline{72}, 0.\overline{81}, 0.\overline{90}\}$

Pages 463–464   **Written Exercises**   **A 1.** 15   **3.** 26   **5.** -36 **7.** $-\frac{16}{7}$ **9.** $\pm\frac{1}{16}$ **11.** $\pm\frac{5}{22}$ **13.** $\{4, -4\}$
15. $\{\frac{2}{3}, -\frac{2}{3}\}$ **17.** $\{4, -4\}$ **B 19.** 5   **21.** 31   **23.** 4   **C 25.** $\{-3\}$

Page 468   **Written Exercises**   **A 1.** 1.7   **3.** 3.6   **5.** 43   **7.** -17.6 **9.** 168   **11.** 1.73   **13.** 6.38
15. -16.53 **17.** 13.78   **B 19.** $\{29, -29\}$ **21.** $\{2.4, -2.4\}$ **23.** $\{11.0, -11.0\}$ **25.** 6.4   **C 27.** $\{2.9, -2.9\}$
29. $\{1.8, -1.8\}$

Page 469   **Problems**   **1.** 8.2 in.   **3.** 4.9 cm.   **5.** 1.3 m.   **7.** 26.4 m.; 6.6 m.

Page 471   **Written Exercises**   **A 1.** yes   **3.** yes   **5.** 10 ft.   **7.** $12\frac{1}{2}$ yd.   **9.** 12 mi.

Pages 471–472   **Problems**   **A 1.** 8 ft.   **3.** 58.31 ft.   **5.** 8 in.; 15 in.; 17 in.   **B 7.** 16 cm.; 30 cm.
C 9. 9.56 ft.

Page 474 Written Exercises **A 1.** 30 **3.** 10 **5.** $2\sqrt{105}$ **7.** 1 **9.** $\dfrac{\sqrt{5}}{2}$ **11.** 3 **13.** $4\sqrt{3}$ **15.** $5\sqrt{6}$

17. $18\sqrt{2}$ **19.** 4 **21.** $4\sqrt{2}$ **23.** 1 **25.** $10\sqrt{6}$ **27.** $\dfrac{4\sqrt{6}}{5}$ **29.** $\dfrac{\sqrt{5}}{3}$ **31.** $3a\sqrt{6}$ **B 33.** $-8x^2y$

35. $a + 2\sqrt{a}$ **37.** -48 **39.** $14x\sqrt{2}$ **41.** $18x^3$ **43.** $12\sqrt{3} + 3\sqrt{6}$ **45.** $-\sqrt{21}$ **47.** $-\frac{2}{3}\sqrt{30}$
49. $2 + 3\sqrt{2}$ **51.** $2 - \sqrt{2}$ **53.** $5x + 1$

Pages 474–475 Problems **B 1.** 0.9; 4.3 **3.** 6.9 in.; 5.2 in. **5.** 9.0 sq. in. **C 7.** 3.7 ft. **9.** no;
diagonal = 8.5 in.; diameter = 8.3 in. **11.** 0.9 ft.

Page 477 Written Exercises **A 1.** $4\sqrt{3}$ **3.** $\sqrt{7}$ **5.** $5\sqrt{2}$ **7.** 0 **9.** $\frac{4}{3}\sqrt{3}$ **11.** $8\sqrt{6}$ **13.** $\frac{8}{5}\sqrt{10}$
15. $4\sqrt{2}$ **B 17.** $-\sqrt{2}$ **19.** $2\sqrt{10}$ **21.** $15\sqrt{5}$ **C 23.** $6\sqrt{2y}$ **25.** $\frac{5}{12}x$ **27.** $\{\frac{5}{2}\}$ **29.** $\{25\}$

Pages 478–479 Written Exercises **A 1.** 7 **3.** 3 **5.** $13 - 5\sqrt{5}$ **7.** $30 + 10\sqrt{5}$ **9.** $21 - 12\sqrt{3}$

11. $15 + 30\sqrt{2}$ **B 13.** $28 - \sqrt{10}$ **15.** $-2 + 4\sqrt{3}$ **17.** $\sqrt{2} - 1$ **19.** $-3 - 2\sqrt{3}$ **21.** $-\dfrac{5 + 3\sqrt{3}}{2}$

23. $\dfrac{10\sqrt{7} - 15}{19}$ **25.** $3 - 4\sqrt{2}$ **27.** 0 **C 31.** $a - b^2$ **33.** $6a^2b + 5ac\sqrt{b} - 4c^2$

Page 481 Written Exercises **A 1.** $\{12\}$ **3.** $\{\frac{1}{28}\}$ **5.** $\{1\}$ **7.** $\{\frac{121}{9}\}$ **9.** $\{3\}$ **11.** $\{14\}$ **13.** $\{2\}$
15. $\emptyset$ **17.** $\{\frac{2}{3}\}$ **19.** $\{48\}$ **B 21.** $\{37\}$ **23.** $\{18\}$ **25.** $\{4, -4\}$ **27.** $m = \dfrac{2E}{V^2}$ **29.** $\{\frac{1}{2}\}$ **31.** $\{0\}$
C 33. $\{5\}$ **35.** $\{0\}$ **37.** $\{4\}$ **39.** $\emptyset$

Pages 481–482 Problems **A 1.** 121 **3.** 315 **5.** $38\frac{1}{2}$ sq. in. **7.** 8 **B 9.** \$2023 **11.** 85.8° **13.** $w =$
$6(5t)^2 = 600$ (lb.) **15.** 52

Page 484 Chapter Test **1.** $\frac{7}{25}, \frac{4}{23}, \frac{3}{20}$ **3.** $\frac{47}{48}$ **5.** 0.075 **7.** $-0.\overline{45}$ **9.** $\frac{2}{11}$ **11.** $3\frac{13}{99}$ **13.** 40 **15.** $\{50, -50\}$
17. 1.78 **19.** 12 **21.** 66 **23.** 120 **25.** $-2\sqrt{7}$ **27.** $13\sqrt{2}$ **29.** $-1 - \sqrt{3}$ **31.** $\dfrac{-3 - \sqrt{5}}{2}$ **33.** $\{9\}$

Pages 486–487 Chapter Review **1.** rational; irrational **3.** $\frac{37}{112}$ **5.** $1.\overline{142857}$ **7.** 0.71875 **9.** $\frac{8}{33}$
11. $\frac{26}{111}$ **13.** $\sqrt{7}; -\sqrt{7}$ **15.** $\frac{9}{5}$ **17.** -14 **19.** $\{3, -3\}$ **21.** $\{-6, 2\}$ **23.** 5.29 **25.** 0.85 **27.** Pythagorean
29. 40 ft. **31.** yes **33.** 75 **35.** 7 **37.** $2\sqrt{30} + 18$ **39.** conjugates **41.** $3\sqrt{3}$ **43.** $\dfrac{\sqrt{3}}{3}$ **45.** $4\sqrt{3}$
47. $12 + \sqrt{5} + 2\sqrt{10}$ **49.** $67 + 12\sqrt{7}$ **51.** $-4 - 8\sqrt{3}$ **53.** $\{12\}$ **55.** $\{9\}$

Page 489 Extra for Experts Exercises **1.** 17 **3.** 13 **5.** 13

Page 489 Extra Problem

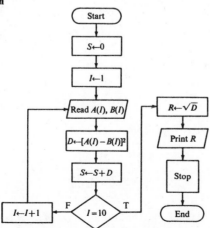

Pages 492–493 **Cumulative Review 1–12** **1.** 2 **3.** 0 **5.** $R = \{21, 5, 13\}$ **7.** $3y^2 - 4y - 1$ **9.** $3z^3 -$
$2z^2 + z$ **11.** $\dfrac{3x + 2}{5}$ **13.** $\dfrac{yz}{2}$ **15.** $a(2a - 1)$ **17.** $\{-4\}$ **19.** $\{7\}$ **21.** $\{7, -2\}$

23.

25. 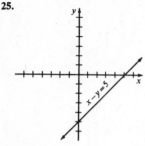 **27.** 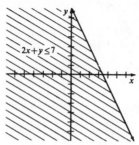 **29.**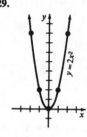

31. $\{(4, -5)\}$ **33.** $8n$ **35.** $4z^2$ **37.** 11 A.M. **39.** 13, 14 **41.** $1\frac{7}{8}$ days

---

Chapter 13. Quadratic Equations and Inequalities

Pages 496–497 **Written Exercises** **A 1.** $\{11, -11\}$ **3.** $\{\frac{9}{2}, -\frac{9}{2}\}$ **5.** $\{2\sqrt{3}, -2\sqrt{3}\}$ **7.** $\{\frac{1}{5}, -\frac{1}{5}\}$
9. $\{\frac{1}{12}, -\frac{1}{12}\}$ **11.** $\{18, -18\}$ **13.** $\{1, -5\}$ **15.** $\{6, -4\}$ **17.** $\{0, -6\}$ **19.** $\{1, -\frac{1}{3}\}$ **21.** $\{2, -4\}$
23. $\{7, 3\}$ **B 25.** $\{4 + \sqrt{3}, 4 - \sqrt{3}\}$ **27.** $\{-5 + \sqrt{7}, -5 - \sqrt{7}\}$ **29.** $\left\{\dfrac{-1 + \sqrt{2}}{2}, \dfrac{-1 - \sqrt{2}}{2}\right\}$
31. $\{0, 1, -1\}$ **33.** $\{0, -3, 3\}$ **35.** $\{\sqrt{5}, 0, -\sqrt{5}\}$ **C 37.** $\{\sqrt{5}\}$ **39.** $\{-\sqrt{6}\}$

Pages 498–499 **Written Exercises** **A 1.** yes **3.** yes **5.** yes **7.** yes **9.** yes **11.** no **B 13.** $x^2 -$
$4x + 3 = 0$ **15.** $x^2 + x - 6 = 0$ **17.** $x^2 - 5x = 0$ **19.** $x^2 - 6 = 0$ **21.** $x^2 - 2x\sqrt{11} + 11 = 0$
23. $x^2 - 4x + 1 = 0$

Pages 501–502 **Written Exercises** **A 1.** $\{4, -6\}$ **3.** $\{4 + 2\sqrt{5}, 8.5; 4 - 2\sqrt{5}, -0.5\}$ **5.** $\{-1 + \sqrt{2}, 0.4;$

$-1 - \sqrt{2}, -2.4\}$ **7.** $\{5.0\}$ **9.** $\left\{\dfrac{1 + \sqrt{13}}{2}, 2.3; \dfrac{1 - \sqrt{13}}{2}, -1.3\right\}$ **11.** $\left\{\dfrac{3 + \sqrt{19}}{2}, 3.7; \dfrac{3 - \sqrt{19}}{2}, -0.7\right\}$

13. $\left\{\dfrac{1 + \sqrt{17}}{4}, 1.3; \dfrac{1 - \sqrt{17}}{4}, -0.8\right\}$ **15.** $\left\{\dfrac{-1 + \sqrt{13}}{6}, 0.4; \dfrac{-1 - \sqrt{13}}{6}, -0.8\right\}$ **B 17.** $\left\{\dfrac{2 + \sqrt{13}}{3}, \right.$

$1.9; \dfrac{2 - \sqrt{13}}{3}, -0.5\}$ **19.** $\left\{\dfrac{-1 + \sqrt{7}}{6}, 0.3; \dfrac{-1 - \sqrt{7}}{6}, -0.6\right\}$ **21.** $\left\{\dfrac{1 + \sqrt{6}}{5}, 0.7; \dfrac{1 - \sqrt{6}}{5}, -0.3\right\}$

23. $\{-1 + \sqrt{2}, 0.4; -1 - \sqrt{2}, -2.4\}$ **C 25.** $x = 1 \pm \sqrt{1 - c}$ **27.** $x = \dfrac{-b \pm \sqrt{b^2 - 4c}}{2}$

Pages 502–503 **Problems** **A 1.** 9 in.; 11 in. **3.** 11 in.; 14 in. **5.** 5 in.; 12 in. **7.** 80 members
9. Marla, 5 mi.; Kay, 12 mi.

Page 505 **Written Exercises** **A 1.** $\{5, 4\}$ **3.** $\{-5 + 3\sqrt{3}, 0.2; -5 - 3\sqrt{3}, -10.2\}$
5. $\left\{\dfrac{-2 + \sqrt{2}}{2}, -0.3; \dfrac{-2 - \sqrt{2}}{2}, -1.7\right\}$ **7.** $\{1 + \sqrt{6}, 3.4; 1 - \sqrt{6}, -1.4\}$ **9.** $\left\{\dfrac{2 + \sqrt{10}}{3}, 1.7; \dfrac{2 - \sqrt{10}}{3}, \right.$

$-0.4\}$ **11.** $\left\{\dfrac{-1 + \sqrt{11}}{5}, 0.5; \dfrac{-1 - \sqrt{11}}{5}, -0.9\right\}$ **13.** $\{0, 1\}$ **B 15.** $(x - 1 - \sqrt{2})(x - 1 + \sqrt{2})$

17. $(s - 3 - \sqrt{10})(s - 3 + \sqrt{10})$ **19.** $x = \dfrac{-2 \pm \sqrt{-28}}{2}$ **21.** $z = \dfrac{-5 \pm \sqrt{-11}}{2}$

Pages 506–507 **Problems** **A 1.** living room, 14 ft. by 21 ft.; kitchen, 14 ft. by 14 ft. **3.** approx. 21.8 in.
by 21.8 in. **5.** 9 in.; 12 in.; 15 in. **7.** 500 m.p.h. **9.** 20 **B 11.** 15 m.p.h. **13.** 9 days

Page 507   Extra Problems

1.

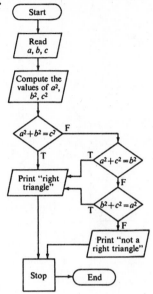

Page 509   Written Exercises

A   1. a. Two different real roots

b.

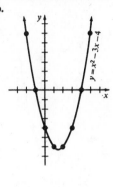

3. a. No real roots

b.

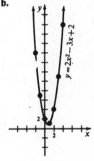

5. a. Two different real roots

b.

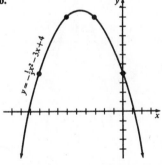

7. a. No real roots

b.

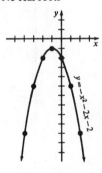

9. a. No real roots

b.

B 11. $(x - 4)(x - 1)$ **13.** $(-3x + 2)(x - 1)$ **15.** Not factorable over $\mathcal{R}$ **17.** $\frac{1}{6}y(1 + 2y)(1 - 3y)$

Page 510   Problems   A 1. 0.6 sec.; 3.4 sec.; 4 sec. after object is thrown   **3.** 12   **5.** 10 in.   **7.** 2.2
B 9. −6; 18

Page 513   Written Exercises

A   1. −1 < x < 4

3. $t < -3$ or $t > -2$

5. −1 < x < 2

7. $-\frac{1}{2} < y < 2$

9. 0 ≤ a ≤ 4

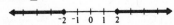

11. $n \leq -2$ or $n \geq 2$

B 13. $t > 1$ or $t < 1$

15. $\{-4\}$

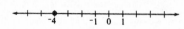

17. $y > 0$ or $y < 0$

C 19. $x \geq 0$ or $x \leq -\frac{1}{2}$

21. $x \geq 7$ or $x \leq -4$

Page 515   Written Exercises

A 1.

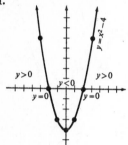

3.

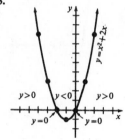

5.

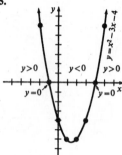

7.

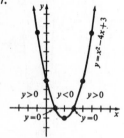

9.

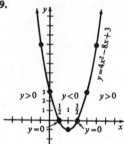

11.

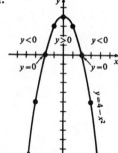

B 13.

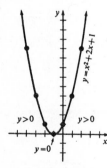

15.

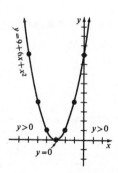

C 17. $x \geq 4$ or $x \leq -1$

Page 518   Chapter Test   1. $\{5, -5\}$ **3.** $\{\frac{8}{5}, 0\}$ **5.** yes   **7.** 0.01; $(x - 0.1)^2 = 0$ **9.** $\{-3 + \sqrt{5},$
-0.8; $-3 - \sqrt{5}, -5.2\}$ **11.** $\{-3 + \sqrt{2}, -1.6$; $-3 - \sqrt{2}, -4.4\}$ **13.** Two different real roots

15. $-2 \leq s \leq 1$

Pages 518–520 Chapter Review 1. $x^2 + 2x - 3 = 0$ **3.** $\{6, -6\}$ **5.** $-b; c$ **7.** no **9.** $49; (t - 7)^2$
11. $\{-3, 2\}$ **13.** $\left\{\dfrac{5 + \sqrt{13}}{2}, 4.3; \dfrac{5 - \sqrt{13}}{2}, 0.7\right\}$ **15.** 14 ft.; 16 ft. **17.** standard **19.** $\left\{\dfrac{-2 + \sqrt{2}}{2},\right.$
$\left. -0.3; \dfrac{-2 - \sqrt{2}}{2}, -1.7\right\}$ **21.** $\left\{\dfrac{7 + \sqrt{85}}{6}, 2.7; \dfrac{7 - \sqrt{85}}{6}, -0.4\right\}$ **23.** 17.8 in. **25.** x-intercepts
27. Two different real roots **29.** Two different real roots **31.** $>; <$
33. $y > 4$ or $y < 1$ **35.** $-\frac{5}{2} \le x \le 3$

37. $<$ **39.** 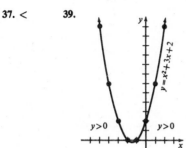 **41.**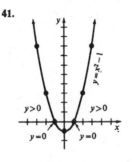

Chapter 14. Geometry and Trigonometry

Pages 526–527 Written Exercises A 1. Axiom II **3.** Axiom VII **5.** Axiom V **7.** E **9.** $E, F,$ or B
11. 9 **13.** 12 **15.** 13 **17.** 4

19.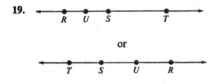

21.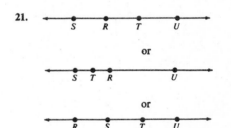

Page 529 Written Exercises A 1. $\angle CPE$ **3.** $\angle APB; \angle BPA$ **5.** yes **7.** yes **9.** yes

11. point; **13.** ray;

15. line; **17.** 2 rays;

Page 533 Written Exercises A 1. not right **3.** right **5.** not right **7.** $AC = BC = 2\sqrt{2}$ **9.** $90°$
11. $40 + 50 + 60 \ne 180; 60 + 70 + 80 \ne 180$

Page 537 Written Exercises A 1. $\frac{5}{3}$ **3.** $-\frac{2}{5}$ **5.** $\frac{3}{10}$ **7.** 0 **9.** $\dfrac{b}{a}$ **11.** true **13.** true **15.** false

Pages 542–543 Written Exercises A 1. $\frac{3}{5}$ **3.** $\frac{3}{5}$ **5.** 1 **7.** $\dfrac{\sqrt{21}}{5}$ **9.** $\frac{1}{2}$ **11.** $\dfrac{\sqrt{2}}{2}$
13. $\dfrac{\sqrt{3}}{2}$ **15.** $\dfrac{\sqrt{3}}{3}$ **17.** $\sqrt{3}$ **19.** 1 **B 21.** $\frac{4}{5}$ **C 23.** $\frac{1}{3}$

Pages 544–545 Written Exercises A 1. a. 0.1736 **b.** 0.9848 **c.** 0.1763 **3. a.** 0.3584 **b.** 0.9336 **c.** 0.3839
5. a. 0.6947 **b.** 0.7193 **c.** 0.9657 **7. a.** 0.8660 **b.** 0.5000 **c.** 1.7321 **9. a.** 0.9925 **b.** 0.1219 **c.** 8.1443
11. 22° **13.** 57° **15.** 3° **17.** 37° **19.** 52.6 **21.** 0.7 **23.** 58.9

Pages 548–551   Problems   A 1. 8 ft.   3. 43 ft.   5. 254 ft.   7. 28 ft.   9. 14,826 ft.   11. 477.4 ft.
13. 35,667 ft.   15. 42,705 ft.   17. 21°   19. 72°   21. 47°   **B** 23. 126°

Page 552   Written Exercises   A 1. 28°   3. 5.6 in.   5. $5\frac{5}{8}$ cm.   7. $\frac{3}{4}$ 9. $\frac{4}{5}$

Pages 554–555   Problems   A 1. 42 ft.   3. $1\frac{1}{8}$ ft.   5. 45 ft.   **B** 7. $14\frac{2}{3}$ ft.

Pages 558–559   Written Exercises   A 1. no   3. yes   5. yes   7. yes   9. $\overrightarrow{BC}$ 11. $\overrightarrow{AD}$ 13. $\overrightarrow{AF}$
15. $\overrightarrow{ED}$ 17. $\overrightarrow{ED}$

19. 100 lb. at an angle of 53°
from the horizontal;

21. 130 m.p.h. on a
heading of 293°;

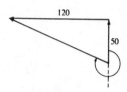

Pages 559–560   Problems   A 1. 128 lb. at an angle of 30° from the horizontal   3. 26 ft. per min. at an angle
of 67° from the horizontal   5. 50.2 m.p.h. on a heading of 355°

Pages 561–562   Problems   A 1. 17.7 lb.   3. 19.1 lb.   5. 23.2 lb.   **B** 7. 3111 lb.

Pages 563–564   Chapter Test   1. A 3. ray   5. obtuse   7. $\frac{4}{5}; \frac{3}{5}$ 9. 21°   11. 50 ft.   13. 19.5 lb.

Pages 564–565   Chapter Review   1. plane   3. AC 5. segment   7. ray   9. 90; 180   11. 180   13. $\frac{3}{8}$
15. $-1, 1$ 17. 0.6691   19. 35.5 ft.   21. in proportion   23. 250° at an angle of 53° from the horizontal

Page 568   Extra for Experts   Exercises   1. a. $8i$ **b.** $3i\sqrt{3}$ **c.** $\frac{2}{5}i$ **d.** $0.5i$ **3. a.** $3 + 8i$; $3 + 6i$; $3i - 7$;
$-3i + 7$ **b.** 16; $14 + 2i$; $16 - 14i$; $7 + 8i$ **c.** $1 - 3i$; $-1 + i$; $-2 - i$; $\frac{2}{5} - \frac{1}{5}i$ **d.** $-3 + 3i$; $3 - i$; $-2 - 3i$;
$\frac{2}{13} - \frac{3}{13}i$ **e.** $16 + 3i$; $2 - 9i$; $81 + 33i$; $\frac{9}{17} - \frac{15}{17}i$ **f.** $3 - 4i$; $-9 - 6i$; $-13 - 33i$; $-\frac{23}{37} - \frac{27}{37}i$
5. a. $\{5i, -5i\}$ **b.** $\{5i\sqrt{3}, -5i\sqrt{3}\}$ **c.** $\{1 + i, 1 - i\}$ **d.** $\{2 + 3i, 2 - 3i\}$ **e.** $\{3 + 5i, 3 - 5i\}$
f. $\{-3 + 5i, -3 - 5i\}$

Comprehensive Review and Tests

A. Properties of Numbers: Structure   1. Distrib. ax.   3. Definition of subt.   5. Mult. prop. of equality
7. Distrib. ax.   9. Add. prop. of equality   11. Order prop. of nos.   13. Defn. of subset   15. Defn. of multiple
17. Add. prop. of eq.   19. T   21. T   23. F   25. D   27. A

B. Fundamental Operations   1. -9 3. $5x^2 - 11x + 2$ 5. $(3a + c)^4$ 7. $y^2 - 3y + 9$
9. $3t^2 + 22t + 64 + \dfrac{185}{t - 3}$ 11. $-15x - 17$ 13. $\dfrac{c + 3}{c}$ 15. $\dfrac{y - 1}{y + 1}$ 17. $\dfrac{(3x - 1)(4c - 1)}{c(4c + 1)}$
19. $(3y + 1)(3y - 1)$ 21. $(a - 3)(a + 2)$ 23. $p(1 + rt)$ 25. $(x + 0.3)(x - 0.3)$ 27. $2(x^3 + 3)(x^3 - 3)$
29. $13r(1 - 2r - 5r^2)$ 31. 1   33. $\dfrac{2x + y}{12z}$ 35. $-\dfrac{x^2 - 5}{x^2 - 4}$ 37. $\dfrac{d(3d + 1)(3d - 1)}{45(d + 1)}$

C. Radicals   1. $4\sqrt{2}$ 3. $\sqrt{2}$ 5. b^2 7. $6\sqrt{x^2 + y^2}$ 9. $\dfrac{\sqrt{6}}{4}$ 11. $\dfrac{\sqrt{3} + 2}{3}$ 13. $\dfrac{\sqrt{3} + 1}{2}$
15. $2\sqrt{2} - 8$ 17. $8\sqrt{3} - 3 - 18\sqrt{2}$ 19. $\frac{1}{3} - 9\sqrt{2}$ 21. $4 - 2\sqrt{2}$ 23. 11   25. 3.9   27. 8.4

D. Equations   1. $\{-5\}$ 3. $\{-\frac{17}{10}\}$ 5. $\{3\}$ 7. $\{-1\}$ 9. $\{7\}$ 11. $\{-14\}$
13. $\left\{\dfrac{-3 + \sqrt{2}}{2}, \dfrac{-3 - \sqrt{2}}{2}\right\}$ 15. $\{0\}$ 17. $\{\sqrt{a - 1}, -\sqrt{a - 1}\}$ 19. $\{(1, 1)\}$ 21. $\{(28, 5)\}$

23. 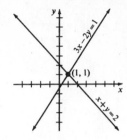 25.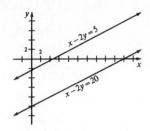

27. $(0, 0)$ 29. -2 31. $2x + y = -3$ 33. $3x - 4y = -20$ 35. $x + y = -6$

E. Functions; Variation 1. 2; 4   3. $\dfrac{V}{lw}$ 5. $\sqrt{\dfrac{A}{\pi}}$ 7. $y = x - 3$ 9. $y = 3x + 2$ 11. $2h(l + w) -$

$d(c + a)$ 13. 112 15. $\dfrac{x_1}{x_2} = \dfrac{y_1}{y_2}$ 17. $\dfrac{a_1}{a_2} = \dfrac{b_1 c_2}{b_2 c_1}$ 19. $\dfrac{x_1}{y_1} = \dfrac{x_2}{y_2}$ 21. $d = kt$ or $\dfrac{d}{t} = k$ 23. $Id^2 = k$

25. -2 27. $\frac{1}{3}$ 29. $\left(\dfrac{3h - 12}{h}\right)$ girls

F. Inequalities

1. $y < -6\frac{1}{2}$    7.

3. $y > 1$ or $y < -4$

5. $-2 < y < 8$

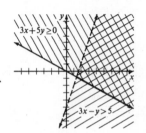

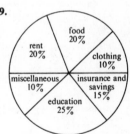

G. Problems 1. 84   3. 576 sq. ft.   5. \$3750 at 6%; \$1250 at 4%   7. $7\frac{1}{5}$ hr.   9.
11. approx. 175.5 lb.   13. 48 mi.   15. 12 ft.; 2 ft.   17. 30 lb. of \$1.00 per
lb. coffee; 10 lb. of \$1.40 per lb. coffee   19. Karen, 17 yr.; Linda, 13 yr.
21. 5 m.p.h.   23. 6 points   25. 58°; 32°   27. 9 cm.; 10 cm.; 11 cm.   29. 7 P.M.
31. 40 seats   33. 20%   35. 48   37. approx. 33.3 g.   39. 25°   41. 32.1
43. 3   45. 81°   47. 345.3 ft.   49. 38.3 lb.

towards castleton
left 75 or 71
    down to L shoreland
right across street
from shell

    late   right into
        Castleton apts
        2nd street on
        left 7